THE OLD TESTAMENT
IN THE
GOSPEL PASSION NARRATIVES

DOUGLAS J. MOO

THE OLD TESTAMENT IN THE GOSPEL PASSION NARRATIVES

DOUGLAS J. MOO

WIPF & STOCK · Eugene, Oregon

Wipf and Stock Publishers
199 W 8th Ave, Suite 3
Eugene, OR 97401

The Old Testament in the Gospel Passion Narratives
By Moo, Douglas J
Copyright©1983 by Moo, Douglas J
ISBN 13: 978-1-55635-757-2
ISBN 10: 1-55635-757-5
Publication date 12/5/2007
Previously published by The Almond Press, 1983

TABLE OF CONTENTS

ABBREVIATIONS ix

INTRODUCTION 1

CHAPTER I. THE HERMENEUTICS OF LATE JUDAISM 5

   Introduction; Methodology 5
   Literary Framework 9
   Appropriation Techniques 25
   Hermeneutical Axioms 56
   Conclusions 75

CHAPTER II. THE USE OF THE ISAIANIC SERVANT SONGS
IN THE GOSPEL PASSION TEXTS 79

   The Old Testament Background 79
   The Passion Predictions (Son of Man) 86
   Mark 1:11/Matthew 3:17/Luke 3:22 (Isaiah 42:1) 112
   Mark 10:45/Matthew 20:28 (Isaiah 53:10-12) 122
   Mark 14:24/Matthew 26:28/Luke 22:20 (Isaiah 53:12) 127
   Luke 22:37 (Isaiah 53:12) 132
   Mark 14:65/Matthew 26:67-8; John 18:22-3;
   Mark 15:19/Matthew 27:30; John 19:1,3 (Isaiah 50:6) 139
   Matthew 27:57 (Isaiah 53:9) 144
   Mark 2:19-20/Matthew 9:15/Luke 5:34-35 (Isaiah 53:8) 145
   John 19:30 (Isaiah 53:12) 146
   John 10:11,15,17 (Isaiah 53) 146
   Mark 14:61/Matthew 26:63; Luke 23:9; Mark 15:5/
   Matthew 27:14; Matthew 27:12; John 19:9 (Isaiah 53:7) 148
   Luke 23:34a (Isaiah 53:12) 151
   Matthew 27:38/Mark 15:27/Luke 23:33; John 19:18 (Isaiah 53:12) . 154
   Titles of Jesus 155
   Mark 14:8 (Isaiah 53:9) 159
   Luke 22:21-38 (Isaiah 53, passim) 159
   Miscellaneous Details 161
   Conclusions 162

CHAPTER III. THE USE OF ZECHARIAH 9-14
IN THE GOSPEL PASSION TEXTS 173

   The Old Testament Background 173
   Matthew 21:4-5/John 12:14-15 (Zechariah 9:9) 178
   Matthew 26:31/Mark 14:27 (Zechariah 13:7) 182
   Matthew 26:15 (Zechariah 11:12) 187
   Matthew 27:3-10 (Zechariah 11:13; Jeremiah 19:1-13) 189
   John 19:37 (Zechariah 12:10) 210

Matthew 26:32/Mark 14:28 (Zechariah 13:8-9) 215
John 19:34 (Zechariah 12-14) 217
Luke 23:27 (Zechariah 12:10-14) 221
Conclusions 221

CHAPTER IV. THE USE OF THE LAMENT PSALMS
IN THE GOSPEL PASSION TEXTS 225

The Old Testament Background 225
John 2:17 (Psalm 69:9) 233
Matthew 26:3-4a (Psalm 31:13) 234
Mark 14:18/John 13:18 (Mark 14:20/Matthew 26:23/
Luke 22:21) (Psalm 41:9) 235
Mark 14:34/Matthew 26:38; John 12:27 (Psalms 42:5,11;
43:5; 42:6; 6:3; Jonah 4:9) 240
John 15:25 (Psalms 69:4; 35:19) 243
John 17:12 (Psalm 41:9) 244
The Gethsemane Scene (Psalm 31:23, et al.) 245
John 18:6 (Psalms 27:2; 35:4; 56:9) 246
Mark 14:57-58 (Psalms 35:11; 27:12) 247
Matthew 27:34 (Psalm 69:21) 249
Matthew 27:35a/Mark 15:24/Luke 23:34b/John 19:24
(Psalm 22:18) 252
The Mockery of Christ 257
Matthew 27:46/Mark 15:34 (Psalm 22:1) 264
John 19:28 (Psalm 69:21) 275
Matthew 27:48/Mark 15:35-36/John 19:28-29;
Luke 23:36 (Psalm 69:21) 278
Luke 23:46 (Psalm 31:5) 280
Matthew 27:55a/Mark 15:40a/Luke 23:49
(Psalms 38:11; 88:8) 282
John 20:25; Luke 24:39 (Psalm 22:16) 283
Conclusions 285

CHAPTER V. THE USE OF OLD TESTAMENT SACRIFICIAL IMAGERY
IN THE GOSPEL PASSION TEXTS 301

Introduction 301
The Last Supper 301
Paschal Imagery 311
The "Sacrifice" of Isaac (Genesis 22; the Akedah) 325
Conclusions 328

CHAPTER VI. THE USE OF MISCELLANEOUS OLD TESTAMENT PASSAGES
IN THE GOSPEL PASSION TEXTS 331

Passion Predictions 331
Results of Jesus' Death 337
Two Figures 346
Miscellaneous Parallels 348

CHAPTER VII. CONCLUSIONS 351

  The Literary Framework 363
  Appropriation Techniques 374
  Hermeneutical Axioms 381
  A Comparison with Jewish Approaches to Scripture 388
  The Function of the Old Testament in the Passion Texts 392

BIBLIOGRAPHY 398

  Texts and Translations 398
  Reference Works 400
  Commentaries 402
  Monographs and Articles 409
  Unpublished Material 453

LIST OF TABLES

Table 1. References to the Servant Songs
          in the Gospel Passion Texts 163-64

Table 2. References to Zechariah 9-14
          in the Gospel Passion Texts 222

Table 3. References to the Lament Psalms
          in the Gospel Passion Texts 285-86

Table 4. Summary of Old Testament Passages Used
          in the Gospel Passion Texts 352-56

PREFACE

The work published in these pages is my doctoral dissertation, submitted to St. Mary's College, University of St. Andrews, in April 1979. I have foregone any substantive editing, since no major work directly relating to the topic has appeared since 1979. Only minor changes, involving punctuation, grammar, incorrect references and the form in which rabbinic literature is cited, have been made.

Instrumental in the production of this thesis were my mentors at St. Andrews, (former) Principal Matthew Black and Professor R. McL. Wilson. I would like to thank them for their assistance and careful editorial scrutiny. Administration and colleagues at Trinity Evangelical Divinity School have helped in innumerable ways. On a more personal level, my wife's and my families have been most supportive; special thanks are due to my father, Mr. John E. Moo, and my brother-in-law and his wife, Mr. and Mrs. Roger Larson. Finally, and most of all, I would thank my wife Jenny, and my five children for their patience, support and hard work (my wife typed this manuscript). To them this book is dedicated.

Douglas J. Moo
Palm Sunday, 1983

ABBREVIATIONS

AB	Anchor Bible
AJSL	American Journal of Semitic Languages and Literature
ALUOS	Annual of Leeds University Oriental Society
AnBib	Analecta Biblica
APOT	R.H. Charles (ed.), Apocrypha and Pseudepigrapha of the Old Testament
ATANT	Abhandlungen zur Theologie des Alten und Neuen Testaments
ATD	Das Alte Testament Deutsch
ATR	Anglican Theological Review
BA	Biblical Achaeologist
BAG	W. Bauer, W.F. Arndt, F.W. Gingrich, Greek-English Lexicon of the New Testament
BASOR	Bulletin of the American Schools of Oriental Research
BBB	Bonner biblische Beiträge
BDB	F. Brown, S.R. Driver and C.A. Briggs, Hebrew and English Lexicon of the Old Testament
BETL	Bibliotheca ephemeridum theologicarum lovaniensium
BEvT	Beiträge zur evangelischen Theologie
BFCT	Beiträge zur Förderung christlicher Theologie
BHT	Beiträge zur historischen Theologie
Bib	Biblica
BibOr	Biblica et orientalia
BJRL	Bulletin of the John Rylands University Library of Manchester
BKAT	Biblischer Kommentar: Alten Testament
BNTC	Black's New Testament Commentaries
BTB	Biblical Theology Bulletin
BWANT	Beiträge zur Wissenschaft vom Alten und Neuen Testament
BZ	Biblische Zeitschrift
BZAW	Beihefte zur ZAW
BZNW	Beihefte zur ZNW
CBQ	Catholic Biblical Quarterly
CGTC	Cambridge Greek Testament Commentary
CNT	Commentaire du Nouveau Testament
ConB	Coniectanea Biblica
ConNT	Coniectanea neotestamentica
CTM	Concordia Theological Monthly
DBSup	Dictionnaire de la Bible, Supplément
DJD	Discoveries in the Judean Desert
EBib	Etudes bibliques
EstBib	Estudios biblicos
ETL	Ephemerides theologicae lovanienses
EvQ	Evangelical Quarterly
EvT	Evangelische Theologie
ExpTim	Expository Times

FRLANT	Forschungen zur Religion und Literatur des Alten und Neuen Testaments
FZB	Forschung zum Bibel
GKC	Gesenius' Hebrew Grammar, ed. E. Kautzsch, trans. & ed., A.E. Cowley
HAT	Handbuch zum Alten Testament
HDR	Harvard Dissertations in Religion
HKAT	Handkommentar zum Alten Testament
HKNT	Handkommentar zum Neuen Testament
HNT	Handbuch zum Neuen Testament
HTKNT	Herders theologischer Kommentar zum Neuen Testament
HTR	Harvard Theological Review
HTS	Harvard Theological Studies
HUCA	Hebrew Union College Annual
IB	Interpreter's Bible
ICC	International Critical Commentary
IDB	G.A. Buttrick, ed., Interpreter's Dictionary of the Bible
IEJ	Israel Exploration Journal
Int	Interpretation
JA	Journal Asiatique
JAAR	Journal of the American Academy of Religion
JBL	Journal of Biblical Literature
JE	The Jewish Encyclopedia
JETS	Journal of the Evangelical Theological Society
JJS	Journal of Jewish Studies
JQR	Jewish Quarterly Review
JR	Journal of Religion
JSJ	Journal for the Study of Judaism
JSS	Journal of Semitic Studies
JTS	Journal of Theological Studies
KAT	Kommentar zum A.T.
LSJ	Liddell-Scott-Jones, Greek-English Lexicon
MeyerK	H.A.W. Meyer, Kritisch-exegetischer Kommentar über das Neue Testament
M-M	Moulton, J.H., Milligan, G. The Vocabulary of the Greek New Testament
MNTC	Moffatt NT Commentary
NICNT	New International Commentary on the New Testament
NIDNTT	Colin Brown, ed., New International Dictionary of New Testament Theology
NovT	Novum Testamentum
NovTSup	Novum Testamentum, Supplements
NRT	La nouvelle revue théologique
NTAbh	Neutestamentliche Abhandlungen
NTD	Das Neue Testament Deutsch
NTS	New Testament Studies
OTS	Oudtestamentische Studien

PEQ	Palestine Exploration Quarterly
PNTC	Pelican New Testament Commentaries
RB	Revue Biblique
RevQ	Revue de Qumran
RGG	Religion in Geschichte und Gegenwart
RHR	Revue de l'histoire des religions
RNT	Regensburger New Testament
RSPT	Revue des sciences philosophiques et théologiques
RSR	Revue de Science religieuse
SANT	Studien zum Alten und Neuen Testament
SB	Sources Bibliques
SBB	Stuttgarter biblische Beiträge
SBL	Society of Biblical Literature
SBLDS	Society of Biblical Literature Dissertation Series
SBS	Stuttgarter Bibelstudien
SBT	Studies in Biblical Theology
SE	Studia Evangelica
SEÅ	Svensk Exegetisk årsbok
Sem	Semitica
SJ:FWJ	Studia Judaica: Forschungen zur Wissenschaft des Judentums
SJT	Scottish Journal of Theology
SNT	Studien zum Neuen Testament
SNTSMS	Society for New Testament Studies Monograph Series
SPB	Studia Postbiblica
ST	Studia Theologica
STDJ	Studies on the Texts of the Desert of Judah
Str-B	H. Strack and P. Billerbeck, Kommentar zum Neuen Testament
SUNT	Studien zur Umwelt des Neuen Testaments
SVTP	Studia in Veteris Testamenti Pseudepigrapha
TB	Torch Bible
TB	Tyndale Bulletin
TDNT	G. Kittel and G. Friedrich, eds. Theological Dictionary of the New Testament
THKNT	Theologische Handkommentar zum Neuen Testament
TLZ	Theologische Literaturzeitung
TNTC	Tyndale New Testament Commentaries
TOTC	Tyndale Old Testament Commentaries
TR	Theologische Rundschau
TS	Theological Studies
TSK	Theologisches Studien und Kritiken
TU	Texte und Untersuchungen
TWNT	G. Kittel and G. Friedrich, eds. Theologisches Wörterbuch zum Neuen Testament
VT	Vetus Testamentum
VTSup	Vetus Testamentum, Supplements
WC	Westminster Commentaries
WMANT	Wissenschaftliche Monographien zum Alten und Neuen Testament
WUNT	Wissenschaftliche Untersuchungen zum Neuen Testament
ZAW	Zeitschrift für die alttestamentliche Wissenschaft
ZNW	Zeitschrift für die neutestamentliche Wissenschaft
ZTK	Zeitschrift für Theologie und Kirche

INTRODUCTION

Although the manner in which the OT is used in the New has been a popular field of inquiry since the earliest Christian centuries, it is especially in recent decades that a strong preoccupation with the subject has been manifest.[1] This renewed interest in an ancient problem owes much of its impetus to the discovery of the Dead Sea Scrolls, which have given scholars a revealing look at the way in which the OT was used by a Palestinian Jewish sect at about the time of Christ. Recent contributions to this topic have focused on the use of the OT in the New generally,[2] on a particular author's use of the OT,[3] or on the way in which a limited OT passage, or series

---

[1] D. Moody Smith ("The Use of the Old Testament in the New," The Use of the Old Testament in the New and Other Essays (Studies in honor of William Franklin Stinespring), ed. by James M. Efird (Durham, N.C.: Duke University Press, 1972), 3-65) provides a useful survey of recent study.

[2] E.g., Leonhard Goppelt, Typos. Die typologische Deutung des Alten Testaments im Neuen (Gütersloh: Bertelsmann, 1939); J. W. Doeve, Jewish Hermeneutics in the Synoptic Gospels and Acts (Assen: van Gorcum, 1954); James Barr, Old and New in Interpretation (London: SCM, 1966); Richard N. Longenecker, Biblical Exegesis in the Apostolic Period (Grand Rapids: Eerdmans, 1975).

[3] E. Earle Ellis, Paul's Use of the Old Testament (Edinburgh: Oliver & Boyd, 1957); Edwin D. Freed, Old Testament Quotations in the Gospel of John, NovTSup, XI (Leiden: Brill, 1965); Alfred Suhl, Die Funktion der alttestamentlichen Zitate und Anspielungen im Markusevangelium (Gütersloh: Mohn, 1965); Robert Horton Gundry, The Use of the Old Testament in St. Matthew's Gospel, NovTSup, XVIII (Leiden: Brill, 1967); Friedrich Schröger, Der Verfasser des Hebräerbriefes als Schriftausleger, Biblische Untersuchungen, IV (Regensburg: Pustet, 1968); Martin Rese, Alttestamentliche Motive in der Christologie des Lukas, SNT, I (Gütersloh: Mohn, 1969); W. Rothfuchs, Die Erfüllungszitate des Matthäus-Evangeliums: eine biblische-theologische Untersuchung, BWANT, V:8 (Stuttgart: Kohlhammer, 1969); R. S. McConnell, Law and Prophecy in Matthew's Gospel. The Authority and Use of the Old Testament in the Gospel of St. Matthew (Basel: Reinhardt, 1969); R. T. France, Jesus and the Old Testament (London:

of related passages, is employed throughout the NT.[1] Of special significance, both in terms of the general discussion and as factors influencing the genesis and development of the present study, are C. H. Dodd's *According to the Scriptures*, Krister Stendahl's *The School of St. Matthew*, and Barnabas Lindars' *New Testament Apologetic*.[2]

Dodd surveyed the OT passages employed in the NT and concluded that certain limited texts acted as the basic "quarries" from which quotations and allusions were drawn. Furthermore, Dodd claimed, references to these passages demonstrate a surprising coherence and respect for the original context. Writing shortly after the discovery of the DSS, Stendahl argued that the phenomena presented in Matthew's OT quotations are best explained by supposing that a "school" of OT students, similar to that which apparently was at work at Qumran, was responsible for the "formula" quotations. Many points of contact between Qumran exegetical practices and the situation presupposed in Matthew's quotations were isolated. Lindars focused especially on the purpose for which the OT was appropriated and sought to trace the development through which the use of specific passages had gone. Generally, the Resurrection was seen as the starting point for the use of most passages, a process of "reading them back" into the ministry of Jesus ensuing, whose purpose was essentially apologetic. Each of these studies raised issues which

---

Tyndale, 1971); Günter Reim, *Studien zum alttestamentlichen Hintergrund des Johannesevangeliums*, SNTSMS, XXII (Cambridge: University Press, 1974).

[1] H. W. Wolff, *Jesaja 53 im Urchristentum* (Berlin: Evangelische Verlag, 1942); D. M. Hay, *Glory at the Right Hand: Psalm 110 in Early Christianity* (New York: Abingdon, 1973).

[2] C. H. Dodd, *According the the Scriptures: The Substructure of New Testament Theology*, Fontana Books (London: Collins, 1952); Krister Stendahl, *The School of St. Matthew and its Use of the Old Testament* (Lund: Gleerup, 1954); Barnabas Lindars, *New Testament Apologetic: The Doctrinal Significance of the Old Testament Quotations* (London: SCM, 1961).

are of central importance in any attempt to understand the NT use of
the Old -- the question of exegetical procedure, its relationship with
contemporary Judaism and the process through which the OT was taken
up by the early church.

The approach utilized in this study does not fall into any
of the categories mentioned above, but takes its starting point from
a NT theme, the passion of Jesus. The advantage in employing this
approach is that a comprehensive view of the OT background for a
single subject can be attained, within which the diversity among
NT authors can also be clearly perceived. Since the topic of Jesus'
passion is far too broad for a survey of all the NT to be included,
the study has been limited to the four gospels. The inclusion of
John's Gospel is warranted inasmuch as the problems relating to
the relationship between the Fourth Gospel and the Synoptics are
not of crucial importance to the subject, while the very distinctiveness of John's presentation will allow a more accurate portrayal of
the situation.

Within the subject area chosen, particular emphasis will be
placed on the hermeneutical question. The subject of hermeneutics
has become one of the major theological issues of our era, and while
the discussion has focused on the problem from the standpoint of the
relevance and process of "contemporization" of the Scriptures for
modern man, the descriptive investigation of this process as observed
in the NT remains of central importance.[1] The passion texts of the

---

[1] In general, the plural "hermeneutics" is retained here because
it properly designates the "rules of exegesis," and, looked at in the
broad sense, as including theological perspective (for which, see
Richard E. Palmer, Hermeneutics: Interpretation Theory in Schleiermacher,
Dilthey, Heidegger and Gadamer (Evanston, Ill.: Northwestern University
Press, 1969), 36-37), this is the subject of our descriptive study.
The singular "hermeneutic" has come to denote the existentialist-
oriented approach to interpretation initiated by Ernst Fuchs and

gospels provide a most interesting "test-case" for such a descriptive study, inasmuch as the suffering of Jesus Messiah was at the same time the most important event proclaimed by the early church and the one which most clearly distinguished it from Judaism. The process whereby Scripture was appropriated for the task of proclaiming the significance of Jesus' passion and justifying it as a divinely-willed circumstance should prove illuminating. Therefore, while many other matters will require investigation, the hermeneutical question will be central.

The major part of this study, then, will be devoted to a study of the gospel passages in which an OT text is brought into relationship with Jesus' passion. (Included also will be texts which pertain to Judas and his betrayal since these are inseparably associated with the passion.) The NT material will be organized according to the OT background involved, as this will best allow for the discussion of hermeneutical approach. Before the NT is encountered, however, a major preliminary inquiry must be undertaken. The study of hermeneutical procedure in the NT inevitably involves a comparison with contemporary Jewish procedures. As a means of providing the basis for meaningful and accurate comparisons, a critical survey of these Jewish hermeneutical procedures is required. It is to this topic that we turn in the first chapter.

Gerhard Ebeling (On the terminological distinction, see Paul J. Achtemeier (An Introduction to the New Hermeneutic (Philadelphia: Westminster, 1969), 8) and, from the standpoint of an adherent to the "new hermeneutic," James M. Robinson ("Hermeneutic since Barth," The New Hermeneutic, ed. by James M. Robinson and John B. Cobb, Jr., New Frontiers in Theology, II (New York: Harper, 1964), 9, n. 18)).

CHAPTER I

THE HERMENEUTICS OF LATE JUDAISM

Introduction; Methodology

The use of Scripture in late Judaism has been the subject of numerous recent studies, but it cannot be said that any measure of agreement has been attained with reference to the outstanding issues. Much of the responsibility for this lack of consensus must be attributed to the enormity and complexity of the material, but some avoidable confusion is introduced through methodological inadequacies. The customary approach to the subject (when more than one "community"[1] is studied) is to investigate the hermeneutics of the various groups in isolation, comparisons being made only at the conclusion of these separate investigations. This approach has definite advantages and it is possible to achieve accurate and worthwhile results within this framework. However, there are some equally obvious disadvantages to this method, particularly if a major purpose is the drawing of comparisons. In the first place, it is easy, having isolated the "essence" of a particular hermeneutic, to focus on this characteristic only, and on that basis to contrast all other approaches with it, with the consequence that minor, but significant similarities may be neglected.[2]

---

[1] We use "community" in this chapter to designate a religious group with a distinguishable theological position.

[2] The essence of a hermeneutical approach has been variously isolated in the literary genre (cf. Addison G. Wright, The Literary Genre Midrash (Staten Island, N.Y.: Alba House, 1968) (= CBQ, XXVIII (1966), 105-38; 417-457; Joseph A. Fitzmyer, "The Use of Explicit Old Testament Quotations in Qumran Literature and in the New Testament," NTS, VII (1961), 299 (this seems to be the reason for his hesitancy in

As a matter of fact, it will be seen below that such a methodology has created much confusion in the study of the relationship of pesher and midrash. In the second place, this type of approach, by concentrating on terminology peculiar to a particular community, can overlook similarities with other communities where the terminology is distinct. A final consideration has to do with the purpose of this chapter. It is not our intention to describe systems of hermeneutics, but to delineate the various alternatives available to the first-century Jewish interpreter at different points in the hermeneutical process. If it can be granted as a presupposition that the NT approach does not exactly duplicate any of its predeccesors, then the isolation of individual points of contact with various systems becomes important and is the most reliable means of achieving accurate results.

In light of these difficulties, and because our aim is to make comparisons, a different methodology will be followed in this chapter, one which takes a "horizontal" approach and uses as its organizing principle general aspects of hermeneutical procedure which are integral to any process of Scripture appropriation. By investigating the subject within such logically-derived categories, it should be possible to delineate and compare the approaches of different communities at specific

---

speaking of pesher in the NT)), exegetical conclusions (cf. Joseph Dawidowitsch Amussin, "Bemerkungen zu den Qumran-Kommentaren," Bibel und Qumran: Nachträge zur Erforschung der Beziehungen zwischen Bibel- und Qumranwissenschaft, ed. Siegfried Wagner (Berlin: Evangelische Haupt-Bibelgesellschaft, 1968), 13; Anthony Tyrrell Hanson, Studies in Paul's Technique and Theology (London: SPCK, 1974), 208), methods of exegesis (cf. William H. Brownlee, "Biblical Interpretation among the sectaries of the Dead Sea Scrolls," BA, XIV (1951), 54-76), and theological axioms (Richard N. Longenecker (Biblical Exegesis in the Apostolic Period (Grand Rapids: Eerdmans, 1975), 41-42) and E. Earle Ellis ("Midrash, Targum and New Testament Quotations," Neotestamentica et semitica, ed. E. E. Ellis and Max Wilcox (Edinburgh: T&T Clark, 1969), 62) mention both technique and theological perspective).

points and, in this manner, more clearly illuminate similarities and differences. There are, of course, disadvantages accruing to this approach as well. If the "vertical" approach too easily leads to generalizing and misleading contrasts, that suggested for use here can result in a failure to view hermeneutical systems wholistically and consequently overlook their distinguishing ethos (the whole is greater than the parts). The final section of the chapter, in which the systems are viewed in their entirety, should help overcome this drawback. Another obvious question arises in relation to the validity of the categories selected as the organizing principle. It will be necessary to say more about the identification and justification of these "levels."

At the heart of and indispensable to any appropriation of an ancient text is the process by which "meaning" (i.e., the results of exegesis) and "significance" (the application or extension of the meaning to the interpreter's own context) are related.[1] The interpreter must ask himself, "How can this text, with its inseparable historical, cultural and religious context, be made meaningful to me and my readers?" Answers to this question (which, of course, are not always consciously given) have been varied, ranging from the simplistic to the complex, the straightforward to the subtle. For the investigator seeking to describe the answers given to this question in the past, the most immediate and

---

[1] "'Meaning' is that which is represented by a text; it is what the signs represent. Significance, on the other hand, names a relationship between that meaning and a person, or a conception, or a situation, or indeed anything imaginable." (E. D. Hirsch, Jr., Validity in Interpretation (New Haven: Yale University Press, 1967), 8). See also Daniel Patte (Early Jewish Hermeneutic in Palestine, SBLDS, XXII (Missoula, Mont.: SBL, 1975), 5-6) and Geza Vermes ("Bible and Midrash: Early Old Testament Exegesis," The Cambridge History of the Bible, Vol. I: From the Beginnings to Jerome, ed. P. R. Ackroyd and C. F. Evans (Cambridge: University Press, 1970), 202) who distinguishes between "pure" and "applied" exegesis. "Exegesis" should be restricted to the process of determining meaning, apart from and prior to application. (R. T. France, Jesus and the Old Testament (London: Tyndale, 1971), 41).

obvious source of information is statements which express the beliefs about Scripture and about how the Scripture relates to a particular community. Some writings will, by their nature, not have such statements, but most will, or can be related to writings which do. This information, which we will call the hermeneutical axioms, represents one of the levels at which our study of hermeneutics will proceed. Another source of data, sometimes obvious, often not, is found in the techniques by which specific texts have been "contemporized" or "actualized." These techniques are governed by the hermeneutical axioms, but furnish indispensable data which must be used to illuminate further the nature of the hermeneutical system. This is the second level at which hermeneutical systems may be analyzed. The third comprises the significant, yet often neglected factor of literary framework. The genre in which an interpreter chooses to appropriate Scripture, as well as the methods by which he inserts Scripture into his narrative, are important considerations bearing upon the process of appropriation as a whole.

It is our contention that these three levels together constitute the basic aspects characteristic of any hermeneutical process and that everything significant about a scheme of Scripture appropriation can be related to one of these. These, then, will act as the methodological framework for the investigation into late Jewish hermeneutics. The levels will be discussed in inverse order to their introduction above, as such an order best allows for the development of the study.

Before launching into the topic of literary framework, it must be stressed that the following survey is just that and makes no pretense at being exhaustive or definitive. Limitations are necessary when confronted with such a complex field of study, and we have attempted to concentrate on literature of most relevance to the NT. Primary attention has been focused on the DSS, for which two justifications can be given. First, it would be a matter of general scholarly consensus that the

Qumran documents attest the single most important hermeneutical system for comparison with the NT. Second, many of the practices characteristic of Jewish hermeneutics as a whole can be observed in the scrolls, which make them representative sources. Many important hermeneutical procedures are, of course, not found in the DSS, and these gaps must be filled with reference to other sources.

Literary Framework

Genre

It must be asked whether, and to what extent, the study of genre, integral to general hermeneutical procedure,[1] has relevance to the descriptive study of hermeneutical systems. Inasmuch as a relationship between particular methods of quoting Scripture and the genre in which the references occur has been claimed to exist,[2] it appears that such an investigation could prove useful. The literature with which we are concerned will be grouped into categories which are purposefully general, in order to avoid a reductionistic approach that can be misleading as to the degree of commonality shared by different writings. This is not to say that very clear differences between works assigned to the same categories below do not exist, but that these differences are usually matters of substance rather than form. Indeed, only by first associating documents at this level can the real differences be accurately perceived. The possibly composite nature of many of the writings to be considered and the mixture of genres within a particular document complicate the study of genre,[3] but can be dealt with when the passage in question is the object of scrutiny.

---

[1] ". . . valid interpretation is always governed by a valid inference about genre." (Hirsch, Validity, 113). And note the recent interest in gospel genre (i.e., C. H. Talbert, What is a Gospel? Philadelphia: Westminster, 1977).

[2] Patte, Jewish Hermeneutic, 250-55, 278; Svend Holm-Nielsen, Hodayot. Psalms from Qumran, Acta Theologica Danica, II (Aarhus: Universitetsforlaget, 1960), 302-307.

[3] See the cautions expressed by R. LeDéaut in "Apropos a Definition

Translation-paraphrase

No attempt is made to distinguish these, since it is difficult to draw a clear demarcation line and the use of Scripture varies by degree, not kind. That the Targums and, to a lesser extent, the LXX[1] engage in tendentious interpretation of the texts which they translate is widely acknowledged.[2] The Targum functioned as a means by which the Scriptural text could be rendered meaningful for the Jews who gathered in the Synagogue for worship and edification. To this end, straightforward renderings are mixed with harmonistic modifications, expansionistic and homiletic paraphrases and glosses which often reflect lines of traditional interpretation extant elsewhere.[3] Geza Vermes,

---

of Midrash." (Int, XXV (1971), 270-71, 281-2 (ET of "A propos d'une définition du Midrash," Bib, L (1969), 395-413)).

[1] Renée Bloch, "Midrash," DBSup, V, col. 1278.

[2] John Bowker claims that the Targums " . . . make an attempt to represent the text verse by verse but at the same time they introduce into it extensive and often far-ranging interpretations." (The Targums and Rabbinic Literature: An Introduction to the Jewish Interpretation of Scripture (Cambridge: University Press, 1969), 9). On the methodology and presuppositions of Targumic exegesis, see Martin McNamara, Targum and Testament (Grand Rapids: Eerdmans, 1972), 69-75; Patte, Jewish Hermeneutic, 55-77; and especially, Geza Vermes, Scripture and Tradition in Judaism: Haggadic Studies, SPB, IV (Leiden: Brill, 1961), 127, 228-229, et al.
Since the recent discovery of some Palestinian Targum MSS, most are prepared to concede that the Targums contain some, perhaps much, pre-Christian material. (Cf. A. Diez Macho, "The Recently Discovered Palestinian Targum: Its Antiquity and Relationship to the Other Targums," VTSup, III (1959), 226-236; Paul E. Kahle, The Cairo Geniza (2nd ed.; Oxford: Blackwell, 1959), 208 (" . . . in the main material coming from pre-Christian time . . . "); Matthew Black, An Aramaic Approach to the Gospels and Acts (3rd ed.; Oxford: Clarendon, 1967), 20-22; Merrill P. Miller, "Targum, Midrash and the Use of the Old Testament in the New Testament," JSJ, II (1971), 36; Ernst Würthwein, Der Text des Alten Testaments: Ein Einführung in die Biblica Hebraiaca (4th ed.; Stuttgart: Württembergische Bibelanstalt, 1973), 84). Nevertheless, the cautionary remarks of Roger Le Déaut as to the difficulty of isolating pre-Christian traditions are well-taken ("The Current State of Targumic Studies," BTB, IV (1974), 22-24).

[3] Le Déaut, "Current State," 20; Patte, Jewish Hermeneutic, 63-64.

in his study of certain themes of early Jewish interpretation, concludes that the Targums contain some of the most ancient examples of this procedure.[1] Le Déaut, in agreement, says: " . . . the Targum represents the first link between Scripture and interpretation.. . ."[2] Within this genre, Scripture is not really "used," but is the fabric of the literary work itself -- a fabric, however, into which numerous threads have been introduced from other material.

Re-writings of Biblical Stories

Distinguished from the former genre by the extent to which the writer departs from the text (the Targums, for all their additions, remain closely tied to the text[3]), these writings utilize the Biblical characters, and usually the Biblical structure, in a "re-telling" of the Scriptural narratives with contemporary needs in mind. In two of the clearest examples of the genre, the Book of Jubilees[4] and the Genesis Apocryphon,[5] the patriarchal stories are modified to such an

---

[1] Scripture and Tradition, 127, 228-229.

[2] Roger Le Déaut, "Targumic Literature and New Testament Interpretation," BTB, IV (1974), 244.

[3] Bowker (Targums, 8) situates the Targums midway between the LXX and the retelling of Biblical stories.

[4] The difficulties of categorizing this work are evident from the descriptions in Charles' introduction: "triumphant manifesto of legalism;" "apocalyptic;" "the most advanced pre-Christian representative of the midrashic tendency." (APOT, II, 1). But Charles includes the book in his category "Primitive History Rewritten from the Standpoint of the Law." Patte treats Jubilees as an apocalyptic work (Jewish Hermeneutic, 159-167).

[5] For the view that the Genesis Apocryphon is neither a Targum or a midrash, see Joseph A. Fitzmyer, The Genesis Apocryphon of Qumran Cave I, BibOr, XVIII (Rome: Pontifical Biblical Institute, 1966), 6-9, and the literature cited there. For the contrary opinion, reference may be made to Matthew Black, The Scrolls and Christian Origins. Studies in the Jewish Background of the New Testament (New York: Nelson, 1961), 193-198. E. E. Ellis terms the Genesis Apocryphon an "implicit midrash" ("Midrash," 62) and Vermes, the "most ancient midrash of all." (Scripture and Tradition, 124).

extent that the original narrative is virtually obliterated. Scripture is used as the starting point or "story line" of a more elaborate, homiletical and tendential exposition.

Testimonia

Their existence long posited by scholars seeking to explain certain phenomena observed in the NT quotations,[1] a pre-Christian list of OT "proof-texts" has now come to light at Qumran.[2] 4QTest is composed of rather literal quotations from five different Scriptural passages, all of which are of obvious importance to the community.[3] Beyond this, no certain conclusions about the role of this document in the Qumran appropriation of Scripture can be made, but it does re-open the possibility that such testimonia were employed by the early Christians.

Commentaries and Midrashim

These two are often not distinguished,[4] but there seems to be legitimacy in regarding them as independent genres. The commentaries,

---

[1] The classic treatment is that of Rendel Harris (Testimonies, with the assistance of Vacher Burch (2 vols.; Cambridge: University Press, 1916, 1920)).

[2] Joseph A. Fitzmyer, "'4 Q Testimonia' and the New Testament," TS, XVIII (1957), 513-37.

[3] Chaim Rabin (The Zadokite Documents (Oxford: Clarendon, 1954), ix) believes that the "Admonitions" portion of the Damascus Document is "a clever presentation of testimonies," but he is obviously working with a much broader definition of "testimonies" than is the case here.

[4] Brownlee, "Biblical Interpretation among the Sectaries of the Dead Sea Scrolls," BA, XIV (1951), 74. Wright, commenting on the literary phenomenon, says: " . . . the basic midrashic structure, common to all forms that can be labelled midrash down to the smallest independent unit, is merely that one begins with a text of Scripture and proceeds to comment on it in some way." ("Midrash," 133). Even when the text serves only "as a peg upon which to hang expositions of the most divergent sort" (Herman L. Strack, Introduction to the Talmud and Midrash (Philadelphia: Jewish Publication Society of America, 1931), 202), the formal features remain the same.

which include mainly the Qumran pesharim,[1] are distinguishable from the midrashim by the former's attempt to deal systematically with every item of the text quoted and to limit itself (ostensibly) to that text. As Elliger says of the author of IQpHab: "Zweifellos stützt sich der Verfasser stark auf den Wortlaut des Textes; er will wirklich einen Kommentar geben, der Wort für Wort und Satz für Satz der Verkündigung des propheten Habakuk gerecht wird."[2] The text of Scripture in the midrashim, on the other hand, often serves only as " . . . a kind of peg upon which to hang a discourse that soon went its own luxuriant way."[3] While the appropriateness of the designation "commentary" for the pesharim has been contested,[4] the term may be retained as long as it is emphasized that structure, rather than content, is being denoted.[5]

---

[1] We include 4QFlor as a commentary, though distinct in its interpretation of passages from both II Sam and Psalms (cf. William R. Lane, "A New Commentary Structure in 4 Q Florilegium," JBL, LXXVIII (1959), 343-346).

[2] Karl Elliger, Studien zum Habakuk-Kommentar vom Totem Meer, BHT, XV (Tübingen: Mohr, 1953), 149. Cf. also Millar Burrows, The Dead Sea Scrolls (New York: Viking, 1955), 211.

[3] G. D. Kilpatrick, The Origins of the Gospel According to Saint Matthew (Oxford: Clarendon, 1946), 61.

[4] E. V. Dietrich argues that the pesharim " . . . sind weder eigentliche Kommentare noch Midraschim, sondern sektiererische Gelegenheitsdeutungen ohne ersichtliche Methode." ("Schriftauslegung. II. Im Judentum," RGG, 3rd ed., V, col. 1517).

[5] As Silberman says: " . . . the commentator made the biblical text say what he wanted to, but he did so systematically." (Lou H. Silberman, "Unriddling the Riddle, A Study in the Structure and Language of the Habakkuk Pesher (1QpHab)," RevQ, III (1961-1962), 334).

14 The OT in the Gospel Passion Narratives

Compilations of Religious Laws

As a genre, the Mishnah is, of course, post-Christian, and it is doubtful whether any written examples of this type have their origins in the period with which we are concerned. However, such traditions undoubtedly existed at an early date in oral form (the "Traditions of the Elders") and must be reckoned with in our investigation. What sets the Mishnaic genre off from others is the continual appeal to traditional teachers for validation of the halakah. While Scripture is often appealed to,[1] there is a significant degree of independence from the OT.

Community Guides

Distinguished from the Mishnah by both a lack of appeal to tradition and intermixture with narrative and homily are the Qumran "rules" which embody the essential paranaesis of the sect.[2] Within

---

[1] V. Aptowitzer, Das Schriftwort in der Rabbinischen Literatur (New York: KTAV, 1970 (=1906-1908)).

[2] Although Rabin points out the "far-reaching similarity between the terminology of the legal chapters of CDC [sic] and Rabbinic literature." (Qumran Studies, Scripta Judaica, II (Oxford: University Press, 1957), 108).
The Damascus Document (CD) and the War Scroll (1QM), though distinct in some ways from 1QS, 1QSa and 1QSb, are regarded as belonging to this general class, the former because, although it opens with a brief historical recapitulation of the founding of the community, it seems to be oriented toward halakah. More justification will be required for placing 1QM in this category. The possibly composite nature of the document (most commentators suggest at least four major portions: I, II-IX, X-XIV, and XV-XIX (see, especially, J. van der Ploeg, Le Rouleau de la Guerre, STDJ, III (Leiden: Brill, 1959), 11-22; Philip R. Davies, 1QM, The War Scroll from Qumran: Its Structure and History, BibOr, XXXII (Rome: Biblical Institute Press, 1977), 20-21) Yigael Yadin, however, assumes unity of authorship (The Scroll of the War of the Sons of Light Against the Sons of Darkness, trans. Batya and Chaim Rabin (Oxford: Oxford University Press, 1962),6)) makes such a decision more difficult, but we have chosen to regard it as a "community rule" because its central aim appears to be instructional with respect to the eschatological climax rather than predictive or visionary. Note Yadin's comment: "The revelations and visions which are in apocalyptic literature ascribed to righteous men of the past and whose aim is to confirm the apocalyptic, deterministic doctrine, appear in this scroll solely as a background and starting point for

the genre, several different types of material can be found: recapitulations of OT history, legal stipulations, and exhortations. The OT is appealed to sporadically as an undergirding and reference point for the community's formulations.[1]

Didactic Writings and Wisdom literature

For the sake of convenience, these two genres may be introduced together.[2] Neither employs clear OT citations frequently, although allusions are found, particularly in the wisdom literature.[3] Reference to OT events and teachings are, however, more numerous, adduced for exemplary and hortatory purposes.

Liturgical writings

Scripture is woven into the fabric of works which stem from a setting of worship, whether individual or corporate. 1QH and Pss. Sol., the longest extant examples of this genre, contain not a single explicit OT quotation, but are thoroughly permeated with OT language.[4] The author has clearly spent long hours in meditation upon the OT, considering its significance for himself and his community, and the

---

explaining the course of the war and for determining the methods of administration and warfare." (Scroll, 15).
  Again, we disagree with Patte's apocalyptic classification (Jewish Hermeneutic, 135).

[1]CD has a far greater density of OT quotations that the others.

[2]IV Maccabees is the most obvious example of a didactic work, Ecclesiasticus and the Wisdom of Solomon of the wisdom literature.

[3]Commenting on Ben Sira, Box and Oesterley say: "He does not merely quote from the Old Testament, but he utilizes the words and teaching of the inspired writers as the authority for what he has to say, and then proceeds to set forth his own ideas upon a given subject." (APOT, I, 208).

[4]J. Carmignac, "Les citations de l'Ancien Testament, et spécialement des poèmes du Serviteur, dans les hymnes de Qumran," RevQ, VI (1960), 357-394. See the notes in Holm-Nielsen (Hodayot) and his conclusion (301-315).

results of this meditation are spontaneously expressed. This particular method of appropriating the OT ("anthological style") will come under our observation at a later point.

Apocalypses

Several literary and theological features set off the apocalypses from other genres: pseudonymity, visionary revelations expressed in cryptic and symbolic language, a pseudo-prophetic recasting of past history, and, of course, a concentration on the events surrounding the imminent eschaton.[1] Re-interpreted prophecy and the use of "unfulfilled" prophecies play a prominent role in the appropriation of Scripture. Explicit quotations, on the other hand, are rare.

Historical narratives

Complete examples of this genre (in which we include any writing whose central aim is to narrate contemporary events, whatever their historicity) from the last two pre-Christian centuries are found only in I, II and III Maccabees, Tobit, Judith, and the Letter of Aristeas. Only four explicit quotations of Scripture are found in these six books, none of which is used to interpret an historical incident.[2] The use of Scriptural language and references to OT passages occur with regularity, the Pentateuchal laws providing the main source in

---

[1] On the apocalyptic genre, see especially D. S. Russell, The Method and Message of Jewish Apocalyptic, 200 B.C.-A.D. 100 (London: SCM, 1964). As pre-Christian apocalypses, we would include I Enoch (except perhaps 37-71 (J. T. Milik, "Problèmes de la littérature Hénochique a la Lumière des Fragments Araméens de Qumrân," HTR, LXIV (1971), 333-78; J. C. Hindley, "Towards a Date for the Similitudes of Enoch: A Historical Approach," NTS, XIV (1968), 551-565)), Jubilees, Sybilline Oracles III, The Testaments of the Twelve Patriarchs (Christian interpolations not being ruled out (cf. M. de Jonge, Studies on the Testaments of the Twelve Patriarchs: Text and Interpretation, SVTP, III (Leiden: Brill, 1975), 143-146), Assumption of Moses, and the Life of Adam and Eve (on the dates, see Leonard Rost, Judaism outside the Hebrew Canon: An Introduction to the Documents, trans. by David E. Green (Nashville: Abingdon, 1976).

[2] I Macc. 7:17; II Macc. 7:6; Tobit 2:5; Aristeas 155.

Tobit and Judith, while the author of I Maccabees employs many portions, endeavoring through stereotyped language to identify the enemies of the Maccabees with the enemies of God's people.

The preceding categorization of literary genres is, perhaps, overly simplistic, but it fulfills the requirements of the present study, which is to provide a basis for the possible correlation of genre with the methods and purposes of Scripture appropriation. Conclusions on this subject are possible only after the types of citation procedure have been outlined.

Citation Procedures

The means by which individual OT references are linked to their literary contexts are multiple, but the following basic procedures are the most prevalent.

General linguistic influence

It is inevitable that men steeped in the OT and writing on religious topics should employ Scriptural language, without consciously thinking of, or intending to "evoke," a specific OT passage.[1] The difficulty in distinguishing, in particular instances, between the use of Scripture as a mere language and with intended referential value should not be underestimated, but a determination can usually be made through a study of the context and the author's usual style. While of no direct importance in assessing hermeneutical procedure (since the reference is, as it were, unintentional), these examples of

---

[1] Holm-Nielsen says, with respect to 1QH: "It may simply be a matter of the use of certain permanent phrases, stereotyped expressions, customary terminology, which may well have originated somewhere or other in the Old Testament, but which existed in the everyday language of the time." (Hodayot, 302). Cf. also Lars Hartman on the apocalypses (Prophecy Interpreted: The Formation of Some Jewish Apocalyptic Texts and of the Eschatological Discourse Mark 13 Par., ConB, NT Series I (Lund: Gleerup, 1966), 87).

linguistic influence are indicative of a writer's background and may represent the product of a prior process of Scriptural appropriation. That is, the original hermeneutical process by which the text was consciously applied to the community may have receded so far into the background that the original source of the language is forgotten or neglected.[1]

Explicit quotations

The most obvious references to Scripture are those which employ an "introductory forumula" to set them off from the context. Such introductions not only provide valuable data about the writer's attitude toward Scripture, but may also provide a clue to his understanding of the relationship between his community and Scripture. The introductory formulae employed by "normative" Judaism[2] and the Qumran sect are similar, with forms containing either כתוב or אמר making up the preponderance of examples.[3] The relative frequency of

---

[1] Numerous Scriptural references in 1QH are cited as examples of the end of such a process. (Patte, Jewish Hermeneutic, 268-69).

[2] By which, broadly speaking, Pharisaic Judaism is meant, without implying the existence of a set orthodoxy in this period.

[3] Bruce M. Metzger has analyzed the introductory formulae used in the Mishnah and found אמר used most frequently, כתוב often and דבר occassionally. ("The Formulas introducing quotations of Scripture in the NT and the Mishnah," JBL, LXX (1951), 298-300; cf. also Danby (Mishnah, xxiv). Joseph Bonsirven, studying the rabbinical literature generally, finds the same general situation (Exégèse rabbinique et Exégèse paulinienne, Bibliothèque de théologie Historique (Paris: Gabalda, 1939), 27-32)).
Fitzmyer ("Quotations," 300-301) has surveyed the Qumran evidence. The following tables, compiled independently of his article, represent only minor variations. (1QS, 1QSa, 1QSb, CD, 1QM, 4QFlor, 4QTest, 1QpHab, 4QpNah, and 11QMelch were examined.)

A. using a form of אמר (on this type, cf. Millar Burrows, "The meaning of ʾšr ʾmr in DSH," VT, II (1952), 255-260.)

      CD: 3:7, 3:21-4:2, 4:13-14, 4:20, 5:8-9, 6:8, 6:13, 7:8,
             7:14-15, 7:16, 8:9, 8:14, 9:2, 9:7-8, 9:9, 10:16-17,
             16:6-7, 16:10, 16:15, 19:12, 19:15, 19:27-28, 20:16

quotations with introductory formulae in the different Qumran scrolls furnishes an interesting statistic, and may be a significant factor in determining literary genre, composition techniques and the date of the respective scrolls.[1] With a look ahead to the NT, it might be mentioned that the use of a "fulfillment" word in non-Christian formulae is virtually non-existent.[2]

Implicit quotations

Relatively lengthy, word-for-word parallels to the OT which should be characterized as quotations, although a specific indication as to

---

    1QM: 10:1, 10:6

    4QFlor: 1:7

    11QMelch: 1:2, 3, 10, 11, 15, 18

  B. Using a form of גד

    1QM: 11:5-7

  C. Using a form of כתב

    1QS: 5:15, 5:17, 8:14

    CD: 1:13-14, 5:1-2, 7:6B, 7:11-12, 7:19, 9:5, 11:18, 11:20-21

    4QFlor: 1:2-3, 1:12, 1:15, 1:16

  D. Using both כתב and אחר

    11QMelch: 1:9, 19, 24

[1] The similarity in frequency of specific types between Qumran and the rabbinic material is clear (pace Chaim Rabin, Qumran Studies, Scripta Judaica, II (Oxford: Oxford University Press, 1957), 96). Fred L. Horton ("Formulas of Introduction in the Qumran Literature," RevQ, VII (1971), 505-514) attempts to trace the development of the formulas.

1QS - 3; CD - 31; 1QM - 3 (and all in the same portion of the scroll). The divergence between 1QS and CD is particularly remarkable.

[2] The piel of קים appears rarely in the Mishnah (Seqal. 6:6; b. Qam. 3:9), and only with reference to the fulfilling of specific legal stipulations (Metzger, "Formulas," 307). מלא is found 16 times in the scrolls, while קום occurs once, but neither are applied to the OT (cf. Fitzmyer, "Quotations," 303).

the Scriptural origin is omitted,[1] are found in both rabbinic and Qumran literature.[2] The fact that a source is being appealed to will usually be clear from the context.

Allusions

An extremely popular citation technique,[3] sometimes termed "anthological style,"[4] utilizes Scriptural words and phrases without introduction and without disrupting the flow of the narrative.[5] Whether such an occurrence of OT language is due to desire on the part of the writer to make reference to a particular passage or is simply a result of his acquaintance with OT phraseology and style is, as we have pointed out, sometimes difficult to determine. Appropriateness in the context, citation of the OT text elsewhere and the author's characteristic style must be taken into consideration. A conscious allusion may often function as a "pointer" to a significant OT passage and be the result of an underlying hermeneutical process: "Such a style anthologique involves an implicit exegesis and is usually due to thorough acquaintance with and a reverent meditation upon the Old Testament."[6] As an example, the description of the "seekers after smooth things" in CD 1:13-2:1 might be cited.

---

[1] Cf. especially on this class of quotations Robert Gordis, "Quotations as a Literary Usage in Biblical, Oriental and Rabbinic Literature," HUCA, XXII (1949), 157-219.

[2] E.g. 1QS 2:13-14; CD 4:21; 1QM 10:2b-6, 11:11-12; 4QFlor 1:10, 1:14, 1:18-19a. Fitzmyer ("Quotations," 304) calls these "virtual citations."

[3] 1QH and 1QM among the Qumran Scrolls are particularly fond of such a style. The author of 1QH favors Isaiah and the Psalms (Carmignac, "Citations," 391-392).

[4] "Style anthologique", following A. Robert ("Genres Litteraires," DBSup, V, col. 411).

[5] "Allusion" will be used exclusively in this study to denote this type of Scriptural use.

[6] Fitzmyer, "Quotations," 298. On the underlying exegetical

After an initial explicit quotation from Hos. 4:16, other
Scriptural passages furnish the language by which the misdeeds and
subsequent judgment of the sects' enemies are described: דרשו בחלקות
("[who] sought pleasant things") in v. 18 is taken from Is. 30:10;
במההתלות . . לפרצות("illusion [and spied out] breaches") in vv. 18b-
19a is from Is. 30:13 and ויגודו על נפש צדיק ("they threatened the
soul of the righteous") in v. 20 reproduces exactly Ps. 94:21a. It is
probable that these allusions are made with the context in mind, since
Ps. 94:21 is quoted in 4QPs[b] and a pesher on Is. 30:1-5, 15-18 is found
in 4QpIsa[c].

It is, of course, incumbent upon the scholar to demonstrate
the presence of such an "implicit exegesis" in particular passages,
but the undoubted frequency of such "contextual allusions" means
that the oft asserted atomistic character of Jewish exegesis requires
qualification, or at least delimitations.

Structural style

In the anthological style, the writer's own narrative purposes
structure the sequence and the OT allusions lend interpretative "color,"
but, at other times, a Scriptural passage furnishes the basic structure
around which a narrative is composed.[1] The "rewritings" of Scripture

---

process, see especially Patte, <u>Jewish Hermeneutic</u>, 252-261. He
notes differences in "density" of allusions in 1QH, and concludes that
more important doctrinal passages evidence the higher number.
On the "evocative" force of allusions, see J. A. E. van
Dodewaard, "La force evocatrice de la citation," <u>Bib</u>, XXXVI (1955), 484;
L. Hartman, "Scriptural Exegesis in the Gospel of St. Matthew and the
Problem of Communication," <u>L'Évangile selon Matthieu: Rédaction et
théologie</u>, ed. M. Didier (Gembloux: Duculot, 1972), 146-147.

[1]Patte, <u>Jewish Hermeneutic</u>, 206; Hartman, <u>Prophecy Interpreted</u>,
57-101.

are obvious examples of this procedure; the homiletical additions are inserted into the framework provided by the OT stories. In most cases, the Scriptural structure is not so obvious, but can be discerned in the background as a (conscious or unconscious) feature of an author's composition. Especially prevalent is the style in the apocalypses, where the vision of the eschatological dénouement often takes its essential outlines from one or more OT narratives.[1] The apocryphal book Tobit may represent a lengthy example of a structural style, since it is fairly obvious that the plot closely follows the outline of the Genesis patriarchal narratives.[2]

Conceptual influence

Many of the basic categories in which devout Jews thought can be traced to the influence of the OT revelation (e.g., the covenant concept). In addition to these general categories, there can sometimes be traced the influence of a more restricted concept, passage or figure on a writer's narrative. Differing from allusions for lack of a verbal reference and from the structural style by reason of the latter's impact being confined to organizational elements,[3] these restricted conceptual influences are important in revealing the interpretative framework in which a narrative is situated.

Summaries of OT history and teaching

Without quoting or alluding to a particular verse, a writer may explicitly appeal to OT incidents or teachings by way of illustration

---

[1] Hartman, Prophecy Interpreted, 185-199; citing Sybilline Oracles 3:8-91; I Enoch 90:13-19; 1:3-9; Assumption of Moses 10:1-10.

[2] D. C. Simpson, APOT, I, 192 (n. 7).

[3] Patte seems to lump these categories together, but it seems justified to separate them on the basis of whether structure (organization, flow of ideas, order), or concept predominates.

or validation. Frequently a series of OT events is so enumerated, as in CD 2:14-3:12, which documents the history of Israel's rebellion against God through the time of the Judges as a warning to those whom the author addresses;[1] the climax, of course, presents the men of the writer's own community as the "remnant," now enjoying God's covenant blessings (CD 3:13-19).[2]

Before investigating the relationship between citation procedure and literary genre, it should be emphasized that the categories just outlined are not always mutually exclusive. A combination of procedures is frequently in evidence, as when an explicit quotation is followed by a series of allusions which pick up verbal and thematic motifs from the quotation,[3] or when an anthological style is the visible evidence of an underlying structural style. Conceptual influence will, of course, be present most of the time.

On the basis of the preceding survey, some tentative conclusions with respect to the relationship of literary genre and citation procedure can be suggested. Some of the genres, by their very nature, determine the type of citation procedure which must be employed, as with translations-paraphrases, rewritings of Scripture, testimonia and commentaries. In the case of others, while a particular procedure is not made necessary, one is often more appropriate than others. Thus, the authors of the apocalypses, with their pseudonymous perspective, could hardly quote Scripture supposedly written long after their own deaths; a structural or anthological style is clearly called for.[4] However, some of the genres (community rules, didactic

---

[1] This portion of the summary reminds one inevitably of Stephen's speech recorded in Acts 7.

[2] Other examples, chosen at random: III Macc. 2:1-12; Judith 5:5-19.

[3] E.g., CD 4:13-20.

[4] Cf. Hartman, Prophecy Interpreted, 108.

and wisdom literature, historical narratives, liturgical writings) could theoretically use a variety of citation procedures and the choice of certain techniques may be related to the purpose of writing. Patte points to the evidence of the Qumran scrolls in this respect. Those with an apologetic or polemical orientation (e.g., CD) contain more explicit references, while those directed toward the community, where the fundamental assertions of the sect would already be accepted (e.g., 1QS, 1QH), are characterized by the indirect anthological style.[1]

These observations are grounded in the logic of the situation: if one grants that any conscious use of Scripture is intended to have communicative effect, then the writer will have to keep in mind his intended audience and introduce the degree of explicitness required. For the outsider, an explicit quotation, perhaps with introductory formula will be necessary, while a single "trigger" word may suffice for the faithful.

Another datum deserving comment is the general lack of OT influence in certain genres, most notably the historical. Very little direct or indirect use of Scripture occurs and a sense of relatedness to God's revelation is entirely lacking.

Finally, the fact that a significant degree of correlation between literary genre and certain citation techniques seems to exist suggests that the way in which Scripture is used is related to the genre in which the author perceives himself to be writing. This conclusion is of special significance in that it demonstrates that the question of genre must be taken into account as an important factor in situations where a particular use of Scripture is not clearly established.

---

[1] Jewish Hermeneutic, 242-278.

Appropriation Techniques

Theoretical Foundations; The Middoth

Common to any appropriation of Scripture is the need to "actualize"[1] the text so that the relevance of God's ancient Word to a new historical, cultural and community situation can be demonstrated. Without such an actualization, Scripture becomes a dead historical document and the community is left without authoritative direction. In cases where Scripture was exactly applicable to the circumstances, no "technique" of appropriation was required and the literal sense of the text could be directly taken over.[2] More often, however, an existing situation or legal pronouncement could not be illuminated or justified in such a straightforward manner, in which case some device by which the text and the interpreter's desired application could be correlated was required.[3] The actual form which these appropriation techniques took is a product of the Jewish doctrine of Scripture. While a section will later be devoted to this question as it relates to the specific communities, it is necessary, in order to understand the techniques, to indicate briefly some of the more important features of the Jewish attitude toward Scripture at this point.

Accepted, without question, by all Jews was the belief that God had inspired every word of the Scriptures.[4] Two consequences of

---

[1] We use "actualize" to indicate any contemporization of Scripture. Patte (Jewish Hermeneutic, 117-18) implies a narrower meaning, in which actualization is contrasted with legitimation.

[2] Termed by the later rabbis פשט. (Georg Aicher, Das Alte Testament in der Mishna, Biblische Studien, 11:4 (Freiburg: Herder, 1906), 106; Bonsirven, Exégèse, 42-68).

[3] Bonsirven, Exégèse, 116-117; cf. also J. W. Doeve, Jewish Hermeneutics in the Synoptic Gospels and Acts (Assen: van Gorcum, 1954), 52-55.

[4] On the doctrine of Scripture in Judaism, see J. Bonsirven, Le Judaïsme Palestinien au temps de Jésus-Christ, Vol. I. La Théologie

importance in understanding the appropriation techniques were drawn from this. First, Scripture is a unity. Since all of it is equally divine, it speaks with one voice; contradictions must be shown to be apparent rather than real,[1] and as the product of one divine mind, Scripture is its own interpreter.[2] Secondly, since every word, indeed every letter of the OT is inspired, each is important in its own right and can be used to uncover meaning: "Just as the rock is split into many splinters, so also may one Biblical verse convey many teachings."[3] Furthermore, Scripture represents the complete revelation of God to man. In m. 'Abot 5:22 it is said of Scripture: "Turn it, and turn it over again, for everything is in it, and contemplate it and wax grey and old over it, and stir not from it, for thou canst have no better rule than this."[4] As George Foot Moore says: "The conviction that everywhere in his revelation God is teaching religion and that the whole of religion is contained in this revelation is the first principle of Jewish hermeneutics."[5] This doctrine of Scripture leads directly and inevitably to the subject of our investigation:

Dogmatique (2nd ed.; Paris: Beauchesne, 1934), 247-303; Solomon Schechter, Aspects of Rabbinic Theology (New York: Schocken, 1961), 116-169; George Foot Moore, Judaism in the First Centuries of the Christian Era: The Age of the Tannaim (New York: Schocken, 1958), I, 235-249.

[1] Geza Vermes notes the easing of contradictions as one of the primary purposes of what he calls "pure exegesis." ("Bible and Midrash," 202). Cf. also Bonsirven, Exégèse, 252.

[2] The comparison of Scripture with Scripture is properly indicated by Doeve (Jewish Hermeneutics, 116) to be a determinative component of Jewish interpretation.

[3] R. Ishmael (A.D. 90-130) in b. Sanh. 34a. Cf. Richard N. Longenecker, Biblical Exegesis in the Apostolic Period (Grand Rapids: Eerdmans, 1975), 19.

[4] On this see, e.g., C. Montefiore and H. Loewe, eds., A Rabbinic Anthology (New York: Meridian, 1938), 142; Fritz Maas, "Von den Ursprüngen der rabbinischen Schriftauslegung," ZTK, LII (1955), 137.

[5] Moore, Judaism, I, 248.

. . . if one can say that it is a characteristic trait of the Jewish relgion at the beginning of our era to conceive itself as revealed religion, in which the source of revelation (or one of its sources) is Scripture, then it must be added that apposite explanation of Scripture is a characteristic trait immediately related therewith.[1]

The actual techniques by which an "apposite explanation" was carried out represents the subject which now engages our attention.

In exploring these techniques, it will be helpful to orient ourselves to the subject by looking first at the later explicit formulations of hermeneutical rules (the middoth). The first, and most famous, of the lists of middoth, embodying seven basic procedures, is that attributed to Hillel.[2] Three of the techniques have to do with logical processes: 1) Qal waḥomer ("lightness and heaviness") -- that which is true in one case is applicable to more important cases; 5) Kelal upherat upherat ukelal ("General and particular; particular and general") -- general principles are applicable to specific cases and vice versa; 7) Dabar halamed me'inyano -- a meaning determined from the context. The four other middoth of Hillel rely on verbal associations: 2) Gezerah Shawah -- on the basis of a verbal similarity between two texts, considerations having to do with one can be applied to the other; 3) Binyan ab mikathub 'ehad -- the principle of gezerah shawah employed with a number of texts; 4) Binyan ab mishene kethubim -- a further extension of gezerah shawah in which two initial texts provide the basis for the building up of a "family" of related passages; and 6) Kayoze bo bemaqom 'aher ("as it is found in another place") --

---

[1]Doeve, Jewish Hermeneutics, 55.

[2]Hillel's rules can be found in Aboth de R. Nathan 37, t. Sanh. 7. 11 , and the introduction to Sifra 3a. Cf. also Wilhelm Bacher, Die exegetische Terminologie der jüdischen Traditionsliteratur. (Leipzig: J. C. Hinrichs'sche Buchhandlung, 1899, 1905), I, 100-101; Georg Aicher, Das Alte Testament in der Mishna, Biblische Studien, 11:4 (Freiburg: Herder, 1906), 141-48; Strack, Introduction, 93-94; Bonsirven, Exégèse, 80-115. S. Zeitlin points out that Hillel should not be regarded as the initiator, but as the codifier of the middoth ("Hillel and the Hermeneutic Rules," JQR, LIV (1963), 161-73).

explanation by means of similar passages (the point of contact not necessarily verbal). Already in these middoth, there can be seen exemplified the two most characteristic hermeneutical techniques of Judaism: comparison and combination of texts, and an emphasis on single words in isolation.

In reaction to the exegetical innovations introduced by R. Akiba,[1] R. Ishmael b. Elisha is associated with the compilation of thirteen middoth which are closely related to those of Hillel. The only real addition is number thirteen, which provides for the clearing up of a contradiction between two passages by appeal to a third.[2] Culminating the promulgation of hermeneutical rules were the series of middoth attributed to R. Eliezer b. Jose ha-Galili (A.D. 130-160). His thirty-two axioms clearly presuppose the later more intense Tannaitic scribal activity and include several new techniques liable to abuse: paronomasia, gematria (using the numerical values of letters), notrikon (using single letters of words to stand for other words) and a justification for ignoring the chronological context of a passage.

These middoth, sometimes termed exegetical rules, are better called hermeneutical rules since their purpose is not so much to establish procedures by which meaning can be attained as to lay down guidelines for the appropriation of Scripture. One might also question the validity of characterizing these principles as "rules;" they seem rather to be codifications of contemporary practices, or perhaps even limitations imposed upon current practice. In the last analysis, the rabbinic methodology for actualizing Scripture defies codification, because it proceeds often by ad hoc, intuitive and almost instinctive approaches, developed in the exigencies of specific situations.[3] The

---

[1] Particularly in the time of Akiba did the need become pressing to justify existing oral tradition by means of the Scripture. The typical halakic approach embodied in the Mishnah was the response to this need. (Bowker, Targums, 54-55).

[2] Strack, Introduction, 95. [3] Cf. Doeve, Jewish Hermeneutics, 64.

procedures embodied in the <u>middoth</u> should, then, be regarded not as set and established techniques, but as indications of the type of approach which was popular. With this general picture in mind, we can now turn to the definitely pre-Christian sources.

In order to bring focus to this investigation, and in accordance with the general methodology already established, we will begin by suggesting some basic categories within which the various techniques can be examined. These categories can be derived from an understanding of the basic tension between the text and the situation (be it an event, law or tradition) to which the text is to be applied. Three basic procedures for the resolving of this tension exist: 1) the meaning of a text may be applied directly to the situation of the interpreter without recourse to a technique; 2) a dissimilarity between text and application can be overcome by a re-orientation of the text; or 3) the gap between text and the contemporary situation is bridged by a modification in the point of application. Some observations with respect to these categories are required.

In the first category are included not only cases in which the interpreter's application coheres with the original author's intention, but, generally, any appropriation that does not require a modification in either text or point of application. This is not to deny that such a distinction is not important, but to point out that, <u>at the level of technique</u>, the two are indistinguishable. Thus, to take an example, the identification made by the author of 1QpHab between Habakkuk's "Chaldeans" and his own "<u>Kittim</u>" (the Romans) almost certainly does not represent Habakkuk's intended reference, but it does proceed naturally from the text, <u>given that author's presuppositions about his own community and the nature of the prophecy</u>. He has not violated the general meaning established by Habakkuk (i.e., the "Chaldeans" as a godless oppressor of Israel), but he has changed the <u>dramatis personae</u>

and introduced new identifications. The transfer from meaning to significance is accomplished at this deeper level, legitimatizing the direct appropriation technique. An important observation might be made with respect to this situation: The ultimate validity of this kind of interpretation can be determined only by assessing the validity of the author's presuppositions, or, as we term them, the hermeneutical axioms.

Secondly, to state that a text was often modified to suit a desired application is not to imply that the interpreter involved did not therefore consider his "exegesis" to represent the actual meaning of the text. As Lauterbach puts it, the Tannaim believed " . . . their _derash_ was the actual sense of Scripture, and therefore _peshat_."[1] Nevertheless, from our perspective, a shift from the natural meaning has taken place and needs to be pointed to as such.[2]

Direct Appropriation

Examples of the direct appropriation of the meaning of particular Scriptural passages abound in all varieties of Jewish literature. OT

---

[1] J. Z. Lauterbach, "Peshat," _Jewish Encyclopedia_, IX, 653. Cf. also Bacher, _Terminologie_, I, 86; J. Weingreen, "The Rabbinic Approach to the Study of the Old Testament," BJRL, XXXIV (1951-1952), 167-168. The saying attributed to R. Judah is indicative of the rabbis' attitude toward the natural sense of Scripture: "If one translates a verse literally, he is a liar; if he adds thereto, he is a blasphemer and a libeller. Then what is meant by translation. Our (authorized) translation." (Kidd. 49a).

[2] The difficulty of labelling any interpretation as "correct" or not is obvious to anyone who has followed the twentieth-century hermeneutical debate. The problem of subjectivity in interpretation is real, (emphasized particularly by Hans Georg Gadamer, _Truth and Method_, trans. and ed. by Garrett Borden and John Cumming (from 2nd German ed.; New York: Seabury, 1975) but not finally insuperable (cf. Emilio Betti, _Allgemeine Auslegungslehre als Methodik der Geisteswissenschaften_ (Tübingen: Mohr, 1962); Hirsch, _Validity_, 135 and A. C. Thistleton, "The New Hermeneutic," _New Testament Interpretation: Essays on Principles and Methods_, ed. by I. Howard Marshall (Grand Rapids: Eerdmans, 1977), 326-327). As Hirsch says, "Validity requires a norm -- a meaning that is stable and determinate no matter how broad its range of implications and application. A stable and determinate meaning requires an author's determining will." (Hirsch, _Validity_, 126).

laws, admonitions and doctrines are taken up and applied directly to new communities and situations, a phenomenon unremarkable in terms of appropriation technique. Only one such technique does demand our attention: typology.[1] This appropriation technique sets in relationship a contemporary or future individual, set of circumstances or institution with a Biblical individual, situation or institution. Basic to the method is the conviction that " . . . the history of God's people and of his dealings with them is a single continuous process in which a uniform pattern may be discerned."[2] As God has acted in the past, so He may be expected to act in the future, only in an incomparably greater way.[3] Typology is fundamentally retrospective; there is no attempt to assert that the original text had any forward-looking element at all.[4] Typology is included in this discussion of direct techniques

---

[1] Derived from τύπος, "mark, example, pattern": On the etymology see: Goppelt, "τύπος . . . ," TDNT, VIII, 246-248; David L. Baker, "Typology and the Christian Use of the Old Testament," SJT, XXIX (1976), 144-146.

[2] G. W. H. Lampe, "Typological Exegesis," Theology, LVI (1953), 201; cf. also Francis Foulkes, The Acts of God: A Study of the Basis of Typology in the Old Testament (London: Tyndale, 1958), 20; K. J. Woolcombe, "The Biblical Origins and Patristic Development of Typology," Essays on Typology, ed. by G. W. H. Lampe and K. J. Woolcombe, SBT, XXII (London: SCM, 1957), 75; and especially Leonhard Goppelt, Typos: Die typologische Deutung des Alten Testaments im Neuen, BFCT, II, 43 (Darmstadt: Wissenschaftliche Buchgesellschaft, 1969), 18-19. Against Bultmann's attempt to tie typology to a cyclical view of history ("Ursprung und Sinn der Typologie als hermeneutischer Methode," TLZ, LXXV (1950), cc. 205-212) cf. Martin Rese, Alttestamentliche Motive in der Christologie des Lukas, SNT, I (Gütersloh: Mohn, 1969), 40.

[3] "Bei aller typologischen Wiederholung steht das Kommende im Gegensatz zum Alten. Es ist nicht eine reichere, vollkommende Form des Alten, auch keine neue Entwicklungsstufe . . . , sondern die eschatologische Erfüllung. Es besteht also weder das Verhältnis der Repetition noch das Komparitius, sondern das der einzigartigen endzeitlichen Vollendung." (Kurt Frör, Biblische Hermeneutik. Zur Schriftauslegung in Predigt und Unterricht (3rd ed.; Munich: Kaiser, 1967), 86-87; Foulkes, Acts of God, 23).

[4] Jean Daniélou, "The Fathers and the Scriptures," Theology, LVII (1954), 85; From Shadows to Reality: Studies in the Biblical Typology of the Fathers, trans. by Dom Wolstan Hibberd (London: Burns and Oates, 1960), 125; Baker, "Typology," 149; Foulkes, Acts of God, 39. However, Eichrodt refers to "divinely established pre-representations." ("Is Typological Exegesis an Appropriate Method?" trans. by James Barr,

because it utilizes the natural meaning of the text in its historical setting, unlike allegory: "Typologie sieht die Entsprechungen zwischen Personen und Ereignissen im Rahmen des Geschichtsablaufes, während Allegorese einen Tieferen Sinn in der Erzählung selbst zu finden sucht."[1] Typology is usually confined to eschatological passages, where God's culminatory redeeming activity is understood in terms of and (sometimes) patterned after His past acts of redemption.[2]

Although some apparently regard typology as a peculiarly Christian phenomenon,[3] the method seems to have been utilized by the Jews long before the time of Christ,[4] and occurs, though rarely, in the rabbinic literature.[5] In the light of what has been said, it is not surprising that typology is most prevalent in the apocalypses and at Qumran. A good example of the approach, adduced by Patte, is found in chapter five of the Book of Jubilees, in which the situation described in Genesis 6 is retold, but in such a way that it is obvious that this situation is being regarded as a pattern for the eschatological apostasy and judgment.[6]

There are many cases in which it seems likely that a typological identification lies at the foundation of a series of OT allusions. In

---

Essays on Old Testament Interpretation, ed. by C. Westermann (London: SCM, 1963), 226-227).

[1]H. Nakagawa, "Typologie II. Im NT," RGG, VI, 1095. The distinction is customary, although James Barr contests its validity. (Old and New in Interpretation: A Study of the Two Testaments (New York: Harper, 1966), 107).

[2]Leonhard Goppelt, "Apokalyptik und Typologie bei Paulus," TLZ, LXXXIX (1964), c. 334.

[3]Jean Daniélou, "La typologie d'Isaac dans le Christianisme primitif," Bib, XXVIII (1947), 368-369; Woolcombe, "Typology," 39.

[4]R. P. C. Hanson, Allegory and Event: A Study of the Sources and Significance of Origen's Interpretation of Scripture (London: SCM, 1959), 19.

[5]Goppelt, Typos, 34-46.

[6]Jewish Hermeneutic, 161-167.

Jubilees 23:23, the author portrays the eschatological conflict in terms borrowed from OT descriptions of God's punishing of Israel through the intermediary of Gentile nations. The scattered Scriptural allusions are associated through the typological identification of the coming judgment with God's past judgments.[1] In a similar fashion, the author of CD castigates the compromising Jews of his own day in terms drawn from OT prophetic denunciations of Israel (CD 5:11b-19),[2] implying an identification of the sect with Israel and its enemies with Israel's enemies. This citing of several thematically-associated texts is a favorite technique of the apocalyptists and the Qumran sectaries. While the associations are sometimes strained and arbitrary, predicated upon atomistic interpretation and word-plays, many such complexes are completely coherent (again, granting the hermeneutical presupposition). With respect to some pre-Christian apocalyptic texts, Lars Hartman makes this significant comment:

> This shows that the OT texts were not regarded here in so atomistic a fashion as is often assumed was the case in contemporary Judaism. A typical wording from a text draws with it its context, so that this context may form a spring-board or goal for a new association. In this connection, I may also point out that practically 100% of the OT passages to which allusion is made "fits," i.e., they have not been lifted out of their contexts and have not had their meanings radically altered.[3]

In many instances, then, typology can be seen to be a basic appropriation technique, leading to other appropriations which are related to, or derive from, this underlying identification.[4] It presupposes the identification between the interpreter's own community

---

[1] Hartman, *Prophecy Interpreted*, 80-81.

[2] Is. 50:11 is cited in 5:13, Is. 59:5 in 5:13b-14, Is. 27:11 in 5:16 and Dt. 32:28 in 5:17. Each of these OT contexts is concerned with judgments upon Israel for her rebelliousness.

[3] Hartman, *Prophecy Interpreted*, 126.

[4] Patte also points to several examples in the Dead Sea Scrolls and sees a typological identification as lying at the basis of many individual quotations and allusions (*Jewish Hermeneutic*, 291-293).

and the Israel of the OT, upon which basis an almost infinite variety of correspondences can be found. Herein may lie one of the sources for the complete confidence in ultimate victory so characteristic of the apocalyptists and the Qumran commentators: God's ways are unchanging and as He has preserved His people in the past, so will He again.

Reorientation of the Text

For the interpreter who wishes to discover meaning in a text beyond that of the natural sense, two paths are open: He can read new meaning into the existing, or standard words, or he can utilize different words. Both of these methods, which might be termed shift in meaning and modification of text, respectively, were employed by Jewish interpreters of Scripture. A related and very popular procedure, which was frequently the stimulus for or result of the reorienting of a text, was the combination of passages. This technique will be seen in operation along with the other two in the following summary. Particular attention is paid to the Qumran literature, since the rabbinic procedures are so well documented[1] and have, at any rate, been delineated in the discussion of the middoth above.

Shift in meaning

Included in this category is any technique which had as its purpose the uncovering of a meaning which did not correspond to the natural understanding of the passage in question, as best as that can be determined from the context. Recognizing the difficulty inherent in determining exactly what that meaning might be in given cases, we will confine our treatment here to instances in which there is an obvious departure from the natural sense.

---

[1] Cf. especially Aicher, Alte Testament, 73-104; Bonsirven, Exégèse, 131-144; Doeve, Jewish Hermeneutics, 71-90; I. L. Seeligmann, "Voraussetzungen der Midraschexegese," Congress Volume: Copenhagen, 1953, VTSup, I (Leiden: Brill, 1953), 154-167.

Shifts in meaning were accomplished at two levels, according to whether the interpreter sought to reorient the words themselves (the philological approach) or penetrate behind the words to find a deeper meaning (the allegorical approach).[1] In the first instance, phrases, words, even letters were interpreted out of context; unlikely etymologies were used; and a variety of word-plays, involving both the form and sound of words were resorted to. In the allegorical approach, words are regarded as symbols of spiritual realities, the parameters of possible interpretations being limited only by the interpreter's ingenuity. Since these two approaches are often conjoined, it will be easiest to investigate both at the same time.

The targums, representing perhaps the earliest form of Jewish Scripture interpretation, already evidence many of the techniques that would become so characteristic of the rabbinic approach to the OT. As would be expected of the genre, philologically based reinterpretations are frequent, while the influence of the combination of texts is especially obvious.[2] The apocalyptists are not as fond of these techniques. While shifts in meaning are found in the apocalyptic literature, they are not as frequent as in the Qumran or rabbinic literature. Lars Hartman has demonstrated the creative influence of the OT on many apocalyptic texts, but he finds little evidence of atomistic-type approaches to the Scripture.[3] Again, genre may have much to do with this factor; the seers allowed the natural sense of Scripture to structure and give content to their visions and were not as concerned with fitting Scripture into a contemporary situation.

---

[1] Bonsirven (Exégèse, 33) suggests this helpful division (he calls the second "parabolic").

[2] Hartman, Prophecy Interpreted, 138-139.

[3] Patte, Jewish Hermeneutic, 55-62.

The conclusion that the Qumran sectaries extensively employed many of the same philological techniques which were later summarized in the rabbinic middoth is inescapable.[1] A few examples must suffice by way of demonstrating this assertion.

In CD 11:18, which concludes a series of Sabbath restrictions, the offering of anything but the Sabbath burnt offering is prohibited on the grounds that "it is written [מלבד כי']כן כתוב 'Besides your Sabbaths.'" Apparently, the author of CD took מלבד ("besides") to mean "exclusively" and lifted the phrase out of its context (a concessionary parenthesis in a summary of festival sacrifices -- Lev. 23:37-38) as a restriction on Sabbath activity.[2]

CD 7:9-8:2 furnishes a complex example of allegory and combinations of texts based on word-plays. The ostensible starting point for the interpretation is the reference to a withdrawal to the north on the part of those "who held firm" (המחזיקים-- the Qumran community) in vv. 13b-14a. This leads the author to cite Amos 5:26-27, originally adduced, perhaps, because of the reference to Damascus (i.e., the "north"). The text itself, however is rearranged: והגלתי is moved up from v. 27 and סכות becomes its object; a change necessitated

---

[1]Brownlee's list of "hermeneutical presuppositions," derived from a study of 1QpHab, contains several practices identical to those found in the middoth: 2) the use of forced and abnormal constructions; 3) reading significance into textual and orthographic peculiarities; 5) using analogous circumstances to determine application; 7) attaching more than one meaning to a word; 11) dividing words up differently; 12) understanding words or parts of them, as abbreviations; 13) utilizing other Scriptural passages to illuminate a text. ("Biblical Interpretation," 60-61). Elliger's critique of some of these presuppositions is partially justified inasmuch as Brownlee finds perhaps more verbal play than is necessary (Habakuk-Kommentar, 159-162), but the main point is well-taken: the Qumran interpreter employed devices in applying Scripture that are exactly similar to those in "classical" Judaism. Cf. also Patte, Jewish Hermeneutic, 230.

[2]Cf. Theodore H. Gaster, The Dead Sea Scriptures in English Translation with Introduction and Notes (3rd ed.; Garden City, N.Y.: Doubleday, 1976), 112, n. 55; A. Dupont-Sommer, The Essene Writings from Qumran, trans. by G. Vermes (New York: World, 1961), 153, n. 6.

by the application the interpreter plans to make. סכות[1] is then allegorized in terms of the law and serves as the point of contact with the next quotation, Amos 9:11, where the word סוכת ("booth of") occurs. But Amos 9:11 predicts that this "booth of David" will be raised up, giving the interpreter the right (keeping in mind his allegorization of סכות) to identify Amos 9:11 as a prophecy of the proper establishment of the law through the Qumran community. Our interpreter next turns back to Amos 5:26-27, and identifies the "king" with the community, the "'Kiyyum' [כיון] of the images" with the faithfulness (כיון) of the images of God found in the prophets, and the "Star" (omitted in the quotation) with the "seeker of the law" (חרש התורה). The reference to the star leads the well-read interpreter to yet another OT text, Num. 24:17,[2] in which the words "journeyed out of Jacob" can be taken as an allusion to the withdrawal of the "seeker" to the land of Damascus.[3]

One's view of the origin of this involved interpretation depends on the decision rendered with respect to the meaning of the enigmatic "withdrawal to Damascus."[4] Three basic interpretations have been suggested, according to which the migration is understood respectively

---

[1] In the Amos passage, סכות is the name of an Assyrian god (C. von Orelli, The Twelve Minor Prophets, trans. by J. S. Banks (Minneapolis: Klock & Klock, 1977 (=1897)), 132).

[2] Num. 24:17 is one of the most frequently cited OT verses in the Scrolls (cf. also 4QTest, 1QM 11:5-7).

[3] On the passage, see Dupont-Sommer, Essene Writings, 134 nn.; Ottilie Johanna Renata Schwarz, Der erste Teil der Damaskusschrift und das Alte Testament (Lichtland: Diest, 1965), 40-42, 113-114.

[4] Another reference to an emigration to Damascus is found in CD 6:5; also in CD 6:19, 8:21, "those who entered the new covenant in the land of Damascus."

as: 1) a literal removal to the area of Damascus;[1] 2) the founding of the community in the domain of the Nabataeans, whose capital was Damascus;[2] or 3) a symbolic reference to the community's initial withdrawal into the wilderness.[3] If either of the first two options is taken, the historic circumstance of the community's exile near or in the land of Damascus presumably led the author of CD to the reference in Amos 5:26, from whence the remainder of the interpretation developed. On the other hand, if "Damascus" is only a symbol, the origin of the interpretation is more probably to be found in the prophecy of Amos itself (probably 9:11, quoted also in 4QFlor). In other words, one must ask here whether the Amos quotation(s) functions as the means of interpreting an actual circumstance in the life of the community or whether it has actually given rise to the whole tradition. The former alternative is perhaps more probable,[4] but we are interested, at this point, more in pointing to the hermeneutical importance of the question than in answering it.

Allegory, utilized in the preceding example, is found more extensively in the Qumran scrolls than in either contemporary or later Palestinian Jewish literature.[5] Prominent especially in the Damascus

---

[1] J. T. Milik, Ten Years of Discovery in the Wilderness of Judaea, trans. by J. Strugnell, SBT, XXVI (London: SCM, 1959), 90; C. T. Fritsch, "Herod the Great and the Qumran Community," JBL, LXXIV (1955), 173-81.

[2] R. North, "The Damascus of Qumran Geography," PEQ, LXXXVII (1955), 34-48.

[3] Gaster, Dead Sea Scrolls, 109, n. 22.

[4] "There must surely have been something to suggest the connection between Amos' prophecy of exile beyond Damascus and the community's life in the desert of Judah." (Millar Burrows, More Light on the Dead Sea Scrolls: New Scrolls and New Interpretations (New York: Viking, 1958), 220).

[5] Hanson characterizes allegory as: " . . . the interpretation of an object or person or a number of them as in reality meaning some object or person of a later time, with no attempt made to trace a relationship of 'similar situation' between them." (Allegory and

Document, Qumran allegory frequently has its starting point in an OT quotation, which provides the material for the detailed metaphors. A well-known example of this allegorical approach is found in CD 6:2b-11a, where the individual elements of Num. 21:18 ("the well which the princes dug, which the nobles of the people delved with a rod") are treated as symbols of the covenanters' situation ("the well" = the Law; "the princes" = the sectaries; "the rod" = "Seeker of the Law;" "the nobles" = the interpreters of the Law). As Betz says, "Die Aufgabe der Auslegung gleicht nun der Öffnung einer verschlüsselten Botschaft, und die Begriffe eines Schriftzitates werden als Metaphern betrachtet, die es in die theologische Sprache der Sekte zu übersetzen gilt."[1]

A final example, involving dual meaning, might be mentioned. In a passage condemning the enemies of the community, the author of CD quotes Deut 32:33, which reads "their wine is the poison of serpents, and the cruel venom [ראש] of asps." The comment on the text applies the latter phrase to "the chief [ראש] of the 'Yawan.'" In this case, the dual meaning of ראש has facilitated the desired application.[2] The

---

Event, 22; cf. also John Bright, The Authority of the Old Testament (London: SCM, 1967), 79-80, n. 52; Goppelt, Typos, 62; Longenecker, Biblical Exegesis, 49, n. 111).
Allegory was discouraged by the rabbis (perhaps because of Christian allegorizing -- Hanson, Allegory and Event, 35), but was almost certainly a pre-Christian Jewish development, not necessarily uninfluenced by Hellenistic allegorical interpretation (Hanson, 63-4). But the extensive Hellenistic influence on inter-testamental Judaism (cf. Martin Hengel, Judaism and Hellenism: Studies in their Encounter in Palestine during the early Hellenistic Period, trans. by John Bowden (2 vols., 2nd ed.; Philadelphia: Fortress, 1974)) renders such a conclusion problematic. Philo's allegorizing methodology is well-known, but the remarks of H. A. Wolfson are worth repeating: "To Philo, then, we may assume, no allegorical interpretation of a scriptural story, whether justified by him on the ground of some inherent difficulty of the text or not so justified by him, means the rejection of the story itself as a fact." (Philo: Foundations of Religious Philosophy in Judaism, Christianity and Islam (2 vols.; Cambridge: Harvard University Press, 1947-48), I, 126).

[1] Otto Betz, Offenbarung und Schriftforschung in der Qumransekte, WUNT, VI (Tübingen: Mohr, 1960), 176.

[2] Cf. Dupont-Sommer, 135, n. 3. The translation of Gaster (Dead Sea Scrolls) is followed. (CD 8:9-10).

task of judging how typical of the Qumran appropriation of Scripture such examples are is unavoidably subjective.¹ That such instances demonstrate the validity of our earlier assertion about the similarities between Qumran and the rabbis seems clear,² but it would seem that the techniques are less involved, and perhaps, less frequently resorted to in the Dead Sea Scrolls.³ This difference can plausibly be explained by the fact that we do not possess from Qumran as extensive an attempt to relate the Scriptures to every aspect of life as we have in, e.g., the Mishnah. That is, the difference was not necessarily the result of divergent presuppositions about Scripture, or a disagreement about the techniques appropriate in interpreting Scripture, but stems from the different purposes for which Scripture is appropriated.

Modification of the text

The utilization of unusual and often unnatural meanings was (and is!) the simplest and most popular method of giving a text a new orientation appropriate to the situational needs of the interpreter, but the opposite technique, changing the actual words of the text, is also well-attested. This method of appropriation, as defined here,

---

¹For numerous examples of the same type, see: P. Wernberg-Møller, "Some Reflections on the Biblical Material in the Manual of Discipline," ST, IX (1955), 52-63; Elieser Slomovic, "Toward an Understanding of the Exegesis in the Dead Sea Scrolls," RevQ, VII (1969), 6-15; Silberman, "Unriddling the Riddle," 335-44; Betz, Offenbarung, 155-176; Elliger, Habakuk-Kommentar, 142-146.

²Judah M. Rosenthal, "Biblical Exegesis of 4QpIs," JQR, LX (1969), 27-36; Fitzmyer, "Quotations," 299; Patte, Jewish Hermeneutic, 230; Geza Vermes, "Le 'Commentaire d'Habacuc' et le Nouveau Testament," Cahiers Sioniens, V (1951), 343.

³"In HK [1QpHab] ist die Methode der Auslegung grösser und grosszügiger, nicht so detailliert und ausgebildet wie bei den Rabbinen." (Elliger, Habakuk-Kommentar, 163).

The Hermeneutics of Late Judaism   41

involves the conscious modification of the text available to the interpreter, or the choosing of a particular reading from among known variants, in the interest of providing a point of contact with the interpreter's context. While genres such as Scriptural paraphrases and re-writings incontestably contain text modifications, the degree of modification and the lack of clear information as to the situation within which modification takes place render them inappropriate as subjects of this part of the investigation. Attention will be focused on documents which cite Scripture sporadically and in observable contexts so that the desired hermeneutical conclusions can be attained.

Even so, additional limitations must be imposed, and the Qumran materials have been singled out for specific study. These provide sources that can be regarded as representative of this technique and furnish the foundation for a consideration of the issues. While text modification is not unknown in the rabbis, it is not nearly as extensive as in the Scrolls.[1]

The following data have been collected from a study of 1QS, 1QS^a, 1QS^b, CD, 1QM, 4QTest, 4QFlor, and 11QMelch. Before proceeding, it should be noted that the study, at this point, is descriptive, listing deviations from the standard MT. To what extent such differences represent <u>actual deviations</u> (i.e., from the OT text as it was known at Qumran), will be the subject of a later portion of this chapter.

Before noting examples of divergence, the significant number -- 30% -- of cases in which the OT citation in the Scrolls is identical to the MT should not be overlooked.[2] A frequent minor text difference

---

[1]Bonsirven, Exégèse, 117-130.

[2]1QS 5:17, 8:14; CD 1:20, 3:7(?), 4:14, 5:2, 5:16, 6:3b-4a, 6:8, 7:19-21, 8:9b-10a, 9:2, 10:16b-17, 16:6b-7a, 19:1-2, 19:7-9, 19:22, 20:16, 20:21; 1QM 11:6, 11:11-12.

occurs in the number, person or tense of verbs.[1] On other occasions, a word, or words, are omitted,[2] added,[3] changed in order[4] and substituted for.[5] Many of these modifications seem to be accidental,[6] while others do not materially affect the sense of the passage quoted.[7] Contemporization is accomplished, but the actual meaning is retained. Others serve to make easier an application which, without the modification, would have been difficult, but possible.[8] Finally, some textual modifications seem to be wholly tendential; the appropriation is completely dependent upon, and possible only with the change.[9] It is helpful to summarize the effect of these textual modifications in two large categories: those that serve to make the text contemporary,

---

[1] 1QS 2:13; CD 4:12, 4:19, 5:17, 6:13, 7:11, 7:15, 8:3, 11:18, 16:10, 19:15-16; 1QM 10:2-3.

[2] CD 4:1, 6:13, 6:16, 7:11, 8:3, 8:12, 11:21, 14:21, 19:12; 1QM 10:3, 10:6-8a.

[3] 1QS 5:15; CD 1:13b-14a, 3:21-4:1.

[4] CD 5:14, 8:13, 1QM 10:3.

[5] CD 4:1, 4:20, 5:9, 5:13, 5:17, 6:17, 7:8, 8:12, 9:7b-8, 11:21, 16:15, 19:5.

[6] E.g., the six words omitted from the quotation of Ez. 44:15 in CD 4:1 (Dupont-Sommer, Essene Writings, 127, n. 1). Raphael Weiss points out several accidental changes in 4QpNah ("A Comparison between the Massoretic and the Qumran Texts of Nahum III, 1-11," RevQ, IV (1963-64), 433-39. Brownlee states: "One may often suspect textual alteration for the sake of interpretation but where the reading may be explained by a common type of scribal error or where it is to be found in agreement with the versions the charge of deliberate alteration is hazardous." (The Text of Habakkuk in the Ancient Commentary from Qumran (Philadelphia: SBL, 1959), 115).

[7] In CD 5:16-17, Is. 27:11c ("they are not a people with understanding") and Dt. 32:28 ("there is no understanding in them") are quoted together. In the Dt. quote, תבונה is replaced by בינה, almost certainly because the latter word occurs in Is. 27:11. Similarly, the substitution of רעי ("companion") for MT עמית ("neighbor") in CD 9:7b-8 (= Lev. 19:17) does not alter the sense.
There are also, of course, numerous incidents of orthographic differences and substitutes for יהוה.

[8] E.g. the replacement of בת ("daughter") with בן ("son") in the quotation of Num. 30:17 in CD 19:5.

[9] E.g., the insertion of ו before the second and third items of

without changing the basic meaning, and those which introduce a decided change into the meaning. In the former category would be cases of tense change to indicate fulfillment of a prophecy, a shift from third to second person to apply directly a text and the omission of irrelevant, or addition of explanatory material. The distinction between these categories is hermeneutically crucial, inasmuch as only the latter signifies a real shift in meaning. It is important to note that this survey discovered relatively few examples of the latter type.[1] A similar situation prevails in 1QpHab. While Brownlee finds some 50 variants from the MT,[2] most of them are minor, hardly affecting the meaning, while some of the differences may be accounted for by the existence of different OT texts available to the expositor.

This latter possibility leads us into a consideration of the influence of variant texts on the quotation of Scripture at Qumran. It was early claimed, notably by Brownlee, that the author of 1QpHab not only modified the text of Habakkuk, but did so, at times, on the basis of variant readings known to him.[3] Furthermore, he went on to assert, there are indications that the interpreter had occasionally

---

the series in CD 3:21-4:1 enables the interpreter to apply the words to three separate groups.

[1] It must be questioned whether it is justified to stress the "freedom" with which the OT is cited in 4QFlor (pace J. M. Allegro, "Fragments of a Qumran Scroll of Eschatological Midrashim," JBL, LXXVII (1958), 350). Of the 9 quotations, 5 are identical to MT (neglecting orthography), and only 1 (1:10) shows any marked divergence.

[2] Text of Habakkuk, 209-112.

[3] In The Dead Sea Scrolls of St. Mark's Monastery, Vol. I: The Isaiah Manuscript and the Habakkuk Commentary, ed. by Millar Burrows (New Haven, Conn.: Yale, 1950), xx, and "Biblical Interpretation," 61. Cf. also Krister Stendahl, The School of St. Matthew and its Use of the Old Testament (Philadelphia: Fortress, 1968), 185-190; C. Rabin, "The Dead Sea Scrolls and the History of the O.T. Text," JTS, n.s., VI (1955), 175-179; M. H. Gottstein, "Bible Quotations in the Sectarian Dead Sea Scrolls," VT, III (1953), 82.

quoted Habakkuk according to one text, while utilizing a variant reading in his commentary on the passage.[1] The latter assertion particularly has come under attack,[2] while there is little more agreement on the extent of text selection.[3] The disagreement admits of no easy resolution, since the precise textual situation to be presupposed for the Qumran writers cannot be discovered. While precision is impossible, the large amount of OT material available in the scrolls enables the drawing of a number of conclusions which are of great significance for this question of text modification. It will be advantageous, then, to insert a digression at this point, whose purpose will be to delineate the status of OT textual studies, especially in light of the Qumran evidence. This investigation is very important as a background against which to evaluate the text of the NT quotations as well.

While much is still unclear, and even the complexities of the evidence cannot be fully indicated here, several conclusions of importance for our study are matters of general agreement. First, there is conclusive evidence that a recension of at least several OT books, its text very close to that of the extant MT, was in existence by at least 150 B.C. W. F. Albright claims: "The greatest textual surprise of the Qumran finds has probably been the fact that most of

---

[1] St. Mark's Monastery, xx; and more recently in The Text of Habakkuk in the Ancient Commentary from Qumran (Philadelphia: SBL, 1959), 109-117. He is followed by Stendahl (School, 185-190).

[2] Bertil Gärtner, "The Habakkuk Commentary (DSH) and the Gospel of Matthew," ST, VIII (1955), 1-6; Elliger, Habakuk-Kommentar, 133, 159-162; Silberman, "Unriddling," 341, 361; Longenecker, Biblical Exegesis, 40; Herbert Braun, Qumran und das Neue Testament (Tübingen: Mohr, 1966), II, 307-308.

[3] E.g., Elliger, Habakuk-Kommentar, 133.

the scrolls and fragments present a consonantal text which is virtually indistinguishable from the text of corresponding passages in our Massoretic Bible."[1] Secondly, the discovery of readings previously considered peculiar to the LXX in Qumran Hebrew MSS strongly suggests that a Hebrew OT text tradition similar to, and probably the basis of, the LXX is to be posited.[2] Thirdly, the Samaritan Pentateuch probably represents a third recension of the Hebrew text, perhaps conforming to an ancient Palestinian text tradition.[3] Fourthly, and of especial significance for NT studies, evidence from a leather scroll of the Minor Prophets in Greek, deposited in a Judean cave at the time of the Bar Cochba revolt, indicates that a Jewish recension of the Greek Bible (or some parts of it), emended on the basis of the proto-MT, was in existence by the first Christian century. The recension was apparently used by both Aquila and Symmachus, has many agreements with the citations of Justin and with Codex Washingtoniensis(W), and has been identified by Barthélemy with the so called καιγε recension in other OT books.[4] Finally, the texts attested to by the

---

[1]"New Light on Early Recensions of the Hebrew Bible," BASOR, XL (1955), 28. 1QIsa^b and, to a lesser extent, 1QIsa^a stand very close to the MT (Bleddyn J. Roberts, "The Second Isaiah Scroll from Qumran (1QIs^b)," BJRL, XLII (1959-1960), 135-144), and most of the fragments from 4Q are proto-MT (Frank Moore Cross, "The Evolution of a Theory of Local Texts," Qumran and the History of the Biblical Text, ed. by Frank Moore Cross and Shemaryahu Talmon (Cambridge, Mass.: Harvard, 1975), 308).

[2]4QSam^a is especially important here. Cf. Albright, "New Light," 29; F. M. Cross, Jr., "The Contribution of the Qumran Discoveries for the Study of the Biblical Text," IEJ, XVI (1966), 81-95.

[3]Cross, "Evolution," 310.

[4]Cf. especially Dominique Barthélemy, Les Devanciers d'Aquila. Première Publication intégrale du Texte des Fragments du Dodécapropheton, VTSup, X (Leiden: Brill, 1963)(cf. 266-270); and, in addition: Frank Moore Cross, "The History of the Biblical Text in the Light of Discoveries in the Judean Desert," HTR, LVII (1964), 282-283; P. Katz, "Justin's Old Testament Quotations and the Greek Dodekapropheton Scroll," Studia Patristica, I (TU, LXIII) (Berlin: Akademie, 1957), 349-350; J. W. Wevers, "Septuaginta Forschungen seit 1954," TR, XXXIII (1968), 50; Otto Eissfeldt, The Old Testament: An Introduction,

Targums[1] (particularly the Palestinian Targum (Pal. Tg.) and Targum Jonathan (Tg. Ps.-J.)), as well as that of the Peshitta,[2] must be seriously considered as sources for pre-Christian readings. Some scholars, perhaps prematurely, are summarizing the situation in terms

---

trans. by P. R. Ackroyd (3rd ed.; New York: Harper, 1965), 708-709.
    Studies on this scroll have served to confirm Lagarde's Ur-LXX hypothesis as over against Kahle's "Greek Targum" theory. ("Unser Text sollte nun ein fur allemal Kahle's Theorie von den 'vielen Übersetzungen' begraben. Hier ist ein Text der offensichtlich jüdisch ist und der ebenso offensichtlich zeigt, dass er eine Revision des so-genannten 'christlichen' LXX-textes ist." (Wevers, "Septuaginta Forschungen," 67-68). See also B. J. Roberts, The Old Testament Text and Versions (Cardiff: University of Wales Press, 1951), 115; H. M. Orlinsky, "Qumran and the Present State of OT Text Studies: The Septuagint Text," JBL, LXXVIII (1959), 33; Patrick W. Skehan, "The Biblical Scrolls from Qumran and the Text of the Old Testament," History of the Biblical Text, 268-269 (=BA, XXVIII (1965)); Peter Walters, The Text of the Septuagint: Its Corruptions and their Emendation, ed. by D. W. Gooding (Cambridge: University Press, 1973), 272-273). For Kahle's theory, see especially The Cairo Geniza, 209-218; "Der gegenwärtige Stand der Erforschung der in Palastina neu gefundenen hebräischen Handschriften 27: Die im August 1952 entdeckte Lederrolle mit dem griechischen Text der kleinen Propheten und das Problem des Septuaginta," TLZ, LXXIX (1954), 81-94.

    [1]Roberts, Text, 210-211, 214-221; Würthwein, Text, 86-87; Stendahl, School, 167-168; Martin McNamara, The New Testament and the Palestinian Targum to the Pentateuch, AnBib, XXVII (Rome: Pontifical Biblical Institute, 1966), 257; Kahle, Geniza, 208; Macho, "Palestinian Targum," 226-236; Black, Aramaic Approach, 20-22; Bowker, Targums, 16-26. Although Robert P. Gordon finds contacts between the text of 1QpHab and the targum to be "rather insubstantial."("The Targum to the Minor Prophets and the Dead Sea Texts: Textual and Exegetical Notes," RevQ, VIII (1974), 425-29). The caution of Miller (on the Palestinian targums) is, however, justified: "In the present circumstance, one must continue to utilize a comparative historical approach to individual PT traditions in order to determine questions of date. The presence of a tradition in the PT is not of itself a guarantee of its relevance for the elucidation of the NT text." ("Targum," 36; cf. also Le Deaut, "Current State," 22-24).
    It is likewise important to keep in mind the fact stated by Bowker: " . . . there is no such thing as a single Aramaic translation: there was a continuous process of exegesis which produced traditions of interpretation in different areas of Judaism, and the synagogue targums undoubtedly reflected that process. There was, therefore, no such thing as the targum, only a Targum tradition, or perhaps more accurately Targum traditions." (Targums, 15).

    [2]The Peshitta is very uneven and its readings must always be cautiously evaluated. (Eissfeldt, Introduction, 700).

of three major Heb. recensions of the OT: the proto-MT, with its origins in a post-Exilic Babylonian editorial process; the Egyptian, ancestor of the LXX and other Greek versions related to it; and the Palestinian, preserved in a late form in the Samaritan Pentateuch.[1]

The consequences of these advances in the knowledge of the pre-Christian OT text for the investigation of OT quotations at Qumran and in the NT are not far to seek. The supposition advanced long ago by Swete that LXX^A was not a "Christianized" text, but represented a text type antedating the Christians, has been vindicated.[2] And, with respect to NT quotations, the fact that many "LXX" Hebrew readings are found in the DSS means that "The text tradition of the LXX must be taken seriously and the differences between it and the MT can no longer be written off merely as 'free' translations or as mistranslations."[3] Agreement with a peculiarly LXX reading can no longer be justification, without further evidence, for dependence on the Greek version. With respect to the Hebrew text, the MT can be looked upon with some confidence as a witness to at least one type of OT text extant in the Christian and immediately pre-Christian era.[4]

---

[1] Ralph W. Klein, Textual Criticism of the Old Testament: The Septuagint after Qumran (Philadelphia: Fortress, 1974), 69; Albright, "New Light," 27-33; McNamara, Targum and Testament, 24; Eissfeldt, Introduction, 684; and especially Cross, "Contribution," 280-82; "Evolution," 291-292. But see the cautionary remarks of Shemaryahu Talmon in "The Textual Study of the Bible -- A New Outlook," History of the Biblical Text, 325.

[2] Henry Barclay Swete, An Introduction to the Old Testament in Greek (Cambridge: University Press, 1900), 395. Cf. A. C. Sundberg, The Old Testament of the Early Church, HTS, XX (Cambridge, Mass.: Harvard University Press, 1964), 93; and see the earlier suggestion of Alexander Sperber (NT and LXX (New York: Jewish Publication Society, 1940 (=JBL, LIX, 193-293)), 202-205).

[3] Joseph A. Fitzmyer, "'4Q Testimonia' and the New Testament," TS, XVIII (1957), 535-536.

[4] Stendahl, School, 167.

Finally, recognizing the diversity of OT text traditions, one must be somewhat circumspect in suggesting the presence of ad hoc translations; the possibility that a textual variant unknown to us has been responsible for a seemingly unique reading must always be reckoned with. Admittedly, in cases where the unique reading precisely fits the application intended by the author, some degree of suspicion must accrue to the antiquity of the rendering. Even here, though, caution is required, for the application may have been suggested to the author only because of the appropriateness of the text, in the reading known to him.

That the several text traditions represented by the Qumran literature[1] have variously been drawn upon for Biblical quotations is antecedently probable and, indeed, is confirmed by the evidence. To cite one, admittedly limited statistic: of the four explicit quotations in 1QS, two agree with the MT against the LXX, Tg., and Pesh.,[2] while the other two agree with the LXX against the MT.[3] A similar situation has been shown to exist in 1QpHab.[4] Is it, however, probable that the author had before him two or more OT texts and chose to quote from

---

[1] Talmon says: "All the extant major versions of the Old Testament, as we know them today, are already represented in Qumran manuscripts . . . " ("Old Testament Text," 34).

[2] In 1QS 5:17, בחה, as in MT is read, against בכחה in Pesh. and Tgm.; LXX is lacking. The quotation of Is. 40:3 in 1QS 8:14 follows the MT in regarding במדבר and בערבה as parallel rather than combining them as in LXX (simply ἐν τῇ ἐρήμῳ), Tgm., Pesh. (cf. P. Wernberg-Møller, The Manual of Discipline: Translated and Annotated with an Introduction, STDJ, I (Grand Rapids: Eerdmans, 1957), 97, n. 65; 129, n. 45).

[3] The quotation of Dt. 29:18-19 in 1QS 2:13-14 manifests several differences from the MT, one at least agreeing with the LXX: the jussive 'ה' rather than MT perfect ה'ה' (LXX γένοιτο). In 1QS 5:15 (= Ex. 23:7) כל ("all") is added, as in LXX (παντὸς).

[4] Brownlee, Text of Habakkuk, 117-119.

one or the other, as his need dictated? This is the procedure attributed to the author of 1QpHab by Brownlee and Stendahl. As evidence, Brownlee adduces four passages in which he claims one reading is adopted in the text while the <u>pesher</u> on the quotation presupposes another attested by the MT. There are, however, good reasons for questioning the existence of such a procedure in each of these.

In 1QpHab 3:6b-14a, the verb יבאו is omitted in the citation of Hab. 1:8-9a, although the verb appears later in the <u>pesher</u> (v. 11).[1] But the omission is unsupported by any other textual tradition, seems rather insignificant and it is by no means probable that this very ordinary verb (which is not emphasized) owes its presence to the influence of the MT. The use of a dual reading in 4:9-11 has been contested on the grounds that the comment applies the word in question (ראש, found in MT, while רשע is quoted in 4:9) in a manner different from its function in the OT context.[2] However, the legitimacy of this objection is questionable in light of the frequent tendency in 1QpHab to apply the OT passage without regard for its actual contextual meaning. More damaging is the observation that the <u>lacunae</u> of the text render any interpretation uncertain.[3] The use of third person plural verbs in the interpretation of Hab. 1:14-16, in contrast to the singular verbs in the quotation, is surely a case of <u>constructio ad sensum</u> rather than deliberate text selection. The final passage put forward by Brownlee[4] (1QpHab 11:9-13; Hab. 2:16) is difficult to interpret, but it is not at all clear that when it is stated that the Wicked Priest "did not circumcise the foreskin of his heart" a paraphrase of the word ערל (MT; "to uncover one's

---

[1] Cf. also Stendahl, <u>School</u>, 186.

[2] Gärtner, "Habakkuk Commentary," 2-3.

[3] Silberman, "Unriddling," 341.

[4] Also Stendahl, <u>School</u>, 188-189.

nakedness," for which הרעל is substituted in the quotation) is present.[1] Beyond these specific examples, it must be said in general that the relative freedom with which the author of 1QpHab treats the OT text renders the hypothesis of such dual readings both improbable and unnecessary.[2]

As a conclusion on the question of text modification in OT citations at Qumran, then, it can be established that such changes were often introduced, although purely creative modification was not as extensive as some have implied.[3] The evidence for the practice of employing two known variants in the same context is, as we have suggested, inconclusive, although in the nature of the case the possibility cannot be definitely eliminated. On the other hand, it is clear that the sectaries sometimes selected the text of their OT quotations from among several traditions known to them, although even here one must reckon with the possibility that the text employed by a particular author was mixed, accounting thereby for the different text backgrounds of the quotations. At any rate, one conclusion is

---

[1] The difference here is probably due to an accidental metathesis of letters (Silberman, "Unriddling," 361).

[2] "The comment does not require the Massoretic text, for as is evident, the commentator has no hesitation about dealing freely with the biblical text." Silberman, "Unriddling," 361; Gärtner, "Habakkuk Commentary," 3-4; Elliger, Habakuk-Kommentar, 133.

[3] E.g., Elliger: "Der Schluss dürfte nicht zu umgehen sein, dass der Ausleger auf Genauigkeit des Zitats im modernen Sinn keinen Wert legt, sondern sich die Freiheit nimmt, das Zitat, sei es seiner eigenen Aussprache (X2) und Syntax (IX 7; Prosaisierung!) oder seinem eigenen Sprachgebrauch (III 10, VI 2) anzupassen, sei es den Bedürfnissen seiner Auslegung entsprechend umzugestalten (VII 3, XII 6/7), wobei gelegentlich die Grenze zwischen rein formaler und schon inhaltlichen Veränderung des Textes gestreift wird (VII 3)." (Habakuk-Kommentar, 132).
Against too great an emphasis on freedom in citation, Rabin justifiably points to the widespread agreement between Qumran citations and known textual traditions. ("The Dead Sea Scrolls and the History of the OT Text," JTS, n.s., VI (1955), 176-177).

certain: "... pesher interpretation has affected the form of the biblical text upon which it bases itself, however that text came about."[1]

Conclusions

Before leaving the general area of text reorientation, a final comment on the relationship between Qumran and the rabbis is called for. Many who understand pesher as a form of midrash base their argument on the undoubted similarities that exist at the level of actualization techniques,[2] while those who deny the appropriateness of the classification minimize the contacts with rabbinic procedures and emphasize the revelatory stance of Qumran interpretation of Scripture.[3] The latter aspect is important, as we will see, but it should not be allowed to obscure the essentially similar methodology for the appropriation of Scripture embodied in the rabbinic and Qumran literature. If midrash were to be defined solely in terms of actualization procedure, then pesher could legitimately be classified as a form of midrash.

Modification in the Point of Application

The reorientation of a passage implies that Scripture is being subordinated to some other element which furnishes the stimulus for such modification. That is, "Continuity is ... provided not by the original sense and context, but by the new historical context into which the biblical material is introduced and in terms of which

---

[1] Longenecker, Biblical Exegesis, 40.

[2] Brownlee, "Biblical Interpretation," 54-76; Stendahl, School, 190-193 (although he stresses, too, the "greater audacity" of Qumran interpretation (193)).

[3] Elliger, Habakuk-Kommentar, 159-164.
Slomovic clearly presents the alternatives mentioned above ("Exegesis in the Dead Sea Scrolls," 4-5).

it is explained."[1] This statement, made with reference to Qumran, applies equally to the procedure of the rabbis, only "tradition" must be substituted for "the new historical context." On the other hand, the influence often moved in the opposite direction: the text exercised a creative impact upon the point of application. In the case of theological formulations or ethical and practical stipulations, such is the situation which we might expect to be the case and is unremarkable. The Jews' beliefs and practices were derived from and regulated by Scripture. This context, whether it be tradition, a cultural or religious situation, or the interpreter's own bias, influences the appropriation process to varying degrees, sometimes merely bringing a particular focus to the formulation, at other times decisively re-directing the formulation. To be sure, the influence was hardly ever completely uni-directional, since the context of the exegete exercised an influence on both the questions asked of Scripture and the form of the answers attained. Quite different is the situation when it is suggested that the influence of Scripture has brought about a modification in the description of an existing situation. For convenience in discussing this situation, three general relationships can be posited: the Scripture can be used to interpret, modify or create narrative.

The first of these possibilities hardly requires comment: both the apocalyptists and the Dead Sea covenanters extensively employed Scripture as a means of interpreting current events. 1QpHab is filled with references to the sect's own history, seen in the light

---

[1] C. K. Barrett, "The Interpretation of the Old Testament in the New," Cambridge History of the Bible, I, 388-389; Elliger, Habakuk-Kommentar, 142 (". . . nicht der Zusammenhang des Textes, sondern der Zusammenhang der Auslegung, d. h. der eigenen Gedanken des Auslegens den Sinn des Textes bestimmt."); Hartman, Prophecy Interpreted, 138-139.

of Habakkuk's prophecy. Similarly, history on the grand scale is understood in the perspective of Scripture in the apocalypses. This application of the OT to past and contemporary history frequently necessitates a shift in the text itself (as we have seen in 1QpHab), but the events themselves are not reoriented, except insofar as the OT serves to cast the events in a certain light. Thus, the "seekers after smooth things," an historical group of people, probably the Pharisees, are portrayed in a certain way through the OT passages used to characterize them (with which characterization the Pharisees might not have agreed!).

On the other hand, some of the details of the practices attributed to this party by the Qumran interpreters may be exaggerated or misrepresented because of the desire to apply certain denunciatory OT texts to them. In this case, the actual events are modified by the Scripture. The line between this and the former procedure is a fine one, involving the difficulty of determining the appropriateness of some of the descriptions. Nevertheless, there is a clear theoretical distinction: in one case Scripture interprets an event which any objective observer would agree exists; in the other, details creep into the description whose historicity might be debatable, at best.

Finally, it must be asked whether the text exercised a creative impact on the events it was supposedly interpreting. In the case of certain genres, what passes for historical narration must certainly be viewed as such creative "historicizing;" the Targums, rewritings of Scripture and *midrashim* include many details which have no foundation in the Biblical narrative and whose historicity is questionable. While the stimulus for such additions came usually from the tradition rather than Scripture, Scripture did frequently act as the source for such developments, and some degree of creative influence from the

Scripture on the narratives in these genres cannot be denied.[1] The apocalyptists used the Scripture to interpret past history and to sketch the delineaments of the eschaton,[2] but do not seem to have created narrative on the basis of the OT.

At Qumran, there was a more concerted effort to understand contemporary history on the basis of the Scriptures; it was crucial for the community in this way to provide a validation for its existence and for the sentence of judgment passed on "apostate" Judaism. It is possible that such a desire led to the invention of "historical" events. Yet the evidence seems to point almost entirely in the other direction. The freedom with which the OT is quoted and the flexibility with which the context of these quotations is handled argue strongly that the influence has been from event to Scripture rather than vice versa. The passage, studied earlier, which mentions a "flight to Damascus" may be understood literally or symbolically,[3] but no one suggests that the community invented this as a stage in the history of the sect solely to fulfill Amos 5:26.[4]

It would be a lengthy and involved task to examine all the historical references found in the scrolls, but as a general observation, it can be said with some degree of confidence that the creative impact of the OT on these references is very slight. Of course, it is always necessary to determine whether a particular narrative is meant to be understood as narrative history or as symbolic. In the latter case, one must not speak of the creation of narrative.

---

[1] Cf. especially Vermes, Scripture and Tradition, passim.

[2] Russell, Method and Message, 184-185; Hartman, Prophecy Interpreted, 71-101; Patte, Jewish Hermeneutic, 184-199.

[3] Bleddyn J. Roberts, "Bible Exegesis and Fulfillment in Qumran," Words and Meanings: Essays Presented to David Winton Thomas, ed. by Peter R. Ackroyd and Barnabas Lindars (Cambridge: University Press, 1968), 199-201.

[4] See the survey of views in Burrows, More Light, 219-227.

Therefore, the observation that Jewish interpreters frequently created narrative under the influence of the OT text must be carefully qualified. Particularly important here is the consideration of genre. The writings mentioned which "create" narrative all belong to genres which are operating within what we might call a "closed system." That is, none of them is involved, at least directly, in the elucidation of contemporary events, but confine themselves to the interpretation and contemporization of Scriptural stories. Those historical and "quasi-historical" writings which originated in the immediate pre-Christian period hardly use Scripture at all, as we have seen, while certain Qumran scrolls, in which historical allusions are somewhat frequent, do not clearly evidence any OT-based creative historiography. It would seem, then, that the invention of details in past religious narratives of the OT ("sacred" history) under the influence of tradition and other Scripture is well-attested, but that the creation, under similar influence, of contemporary events portrayed as historical or believed to be factual, by the author is a much more poorly established phenomenon.

Conclusions

Some general remarks on the second level of our hermeneutical investigation, appropriation techniques, can be made before proceeding to the third, hermeneutical axioms. First, while the essential unity among Jewish interpreters at this level has been made clear, it would be a mistake to assume that the later rabbinic techniques are exactly representative of pre-Christian interpretational methodology, whether normative or sectarian. A chronological development can be traced from the relatively simple and straightforward to the more scholarly and ingenious.[1] Secondly, to reiterate what has already

---

[1] Note Vermes' comment: "The haggadic developments of Genesis

been stated, the sweeping generalization that Jewish interpretation is "atomistic" must be qualified. As Doeve says, "Sometimes it [Jewish exegesis] may mention a single word in order to recall a whole context, and sometimes it may employ a single word it happens to need, while totally ignoring the context."[1] The point, then, is not that Jewish exegesis is not often atomistic, but that it cannot simply be assumed in every case that it is. It is, furthermore, important to indicate what aspect of the appropriation process is being labelled as "atomistic" -- the deriving of meaning apart from context (the stage of exegesis), or the use of Scriptural language without the intention of evoking the wider context (the stage of application). Thirdly, one must be circumspect in speaking about the "freedom" with which the Biblical text is cited. While no one could deny the fact that various interpreters sometimes (even frequently, in certain cases) felt free to alter the text of a quotation to fit the intended application, it must not be forgotten that literal citations are not infrequent, that many changes are relatively minor and that the uncertainties about the exact OT text available to a given interpreter exclude too dogmatic a conclusion on this question.

Hermeneutical Axioms

The appropriation techniques just outlined and, to a lesser extent, the literary frameworks sketched earlier, cannot ultimately

---

Apocryphon are therefore organically bound to the biblical text. . . . His technique is simple and he exercises no scholarly learning; no exegetical virtuosity, no play on words." (Scripture and Tradition, 126). This remark cannot, of course, be taken as representative since it is made with reference to one particular writing, dissimilar in many respects from much of the relevant material. But the progression from simpler, text-oriented exegesis to freer and more ingenious interpretation may be historically justified (Vermes, Scripture and Tradition, 228-229; Danby, Mishnah, xxiv-xxv).

[1] Jewish Hermeneutics, 134.

be understood without a knowledge of the beliefs that gave rise to
them. Interpretational methodology owes its origin to, and is molded
by, the convictions held by a particular interpreter, or the community
of which he is a member.[1] These convictions include doctrines which
extend far beyond the realm of traditional "hermeneutics," and together
make up what might be termed the matrix of interpretation. In the
last analysis, this matrix involves the entire theological system,
but two general areas are particularly crucial for the hermeneutical
structure: the understanding of the nature of Scripture and the
community's own sense of self-identity.

These beliefs are, in turn, the product of the interplay
between the teaching of Scripture and the previously formulated
doctrines that give a particular community its distinctive identity.
The situation is circular, but it can generally be supposed that a
circumstance outside Scripture (a particular cultural and relgious
context, a visionary experience, an historical situation) leads to a
new viewpoint on Scripture and the way in which it can be applied.
As Sandmel puts it:

> . . . . an innovator had his idea or his prepossession to begin
> with, and thereafter justified it by recourse to Scripture. I
> am aware, of course, that those who pored over Scripture were
> prompted by Scripture to create their innovations. Yet proof-
> texting as such, the seeking of a Scriptural sanction for an
> innovation, would imply to my mind that first came the conclusion
> and then only thereafter the prooftext.[2]

---

[1]Longenecker, at the conclusion of his survey of Jewish exegesis, states: "Each of these, Pharisees, sectarians, and Philo alike, worked from distinctive doctrinal and ideological commitments, which produced distinctive features in their exegetical methodologies." (Biblical Exegesis, 50). And Holm-Nielsen claims that the authors' of 1QH use of Scripture is, ". . . dictated by their understanding of their own situation, their theology and their whole concept of life." (Hodayot, 307).
Patte addresses this level particularly in his Early Jewish Hermeneutic.

[2]Samuel Sandmel, The First Christian Century in Judaism and Christianity: Certainties and Uncertainties (New York: Oxford, 1969), 31.

At the root of a hermeneutical system, then, is a particular Weltanschauung which determines the way in which Scripture is understood and the self-understanding of the community involved. To put it another way, the community's self-understanding frames the questions which are asked of Scripture, while the view taken of Scripture determines the manner in which the answers are attained.[1] In the following pages an attempt will be made to outline the attitudes of the various communities on these two questions as a means of elucidating their particular matrix of interpretation. Because of the inseparable relationship between particular communities and their beliefs, it will be necessary to abandon the "horizontal" approach hitherto employed in favor of a procedure that focuses upon each community in turn. It should also be noted that the information on these questions must be gathered not only from explicit statements on these issues, but from the implicit evidence of the actual use of Scripture as well.

Classical Judaism

The centrality of Torah in post-exilic Jewish religion justifies a concentration on this factor as a focus for a discussion of the axioms determinative for the interpretation of Scripture in classical Judaism. Without entering into the debate over the date at which a canon was recognized, it can safely be asserted that Scripture, by the last pre-Christian century, was regarded as a closed continuum.[2]

---

[1] Of course, the process continues beyond this, as the scrutiny of Scripture molds the community's perception of itself.

[2] Cf. I Macc 4:46, where the opinion that prophecy had ceased from Israel is clearly presumed. Josephus (Contra. Ap. I, 8), is the first to express the later widely held opinion (cf. also IV Ez. 14:44-47, t. Yad. 2.13) that the time of Ezra (Josephus refers to Artaxerxes) represented the final period of prophetic inspiration. Pirke Abot 1:1 seems to assume a cessation of inspired writings. Cf. on this Moore, Judaism, I, 86-87; Russell, Apocalyptic, 77-82; Eissfeldt, Introduction, 564-568; Sundberg, Old Testament, 114-116; Doeve, Jewish Hermeneutics, 54-55.

What uncertainty existed pertained to the question as to which books "defiled the hands," not to whether new Scripture was still coming into existence. This meant that the continuity between the Israel of the Pentateuch, the prophets and the writings and the Judaism of the first century B.C. was perceived in a certain way: not as a prolongation of the experience of the revealing acts of God and their prophetic accompaniment, but as a new embodiment of the elect nation[1] which looked back to earlier revelation for evidence of its identity and direction for its life.[2] As corollaries of this, two other features can be singled out as characteristic of classical Judaism: a lack of interest in history as a revelatory stage[3] and a non-eschatological perception of itself.

Broadly speaking, the two occupations of classical Judaism with respect to the Scriptures, discovering its identity and directing its conduct, corresponded to two forms, haggadah and halakah and two Sitze im Leben, the synagogue and the school.[4] In the former instance, the OT narratives were contemporized through translations, paraphrases, homilies, sermons and liturgy. Halakhic approaches within this context are found, of course, but the emphasis was on the value of the OT for sustaining and confirming the self-perception of the community and

---

[1] Cf. Bonsirven (Judaïsme, I, 73) for the importance of election in Jewish theology.

[2] I am indebted to Patte (Jewish Hermeneutic, 122-125) for this two-fold perspective.

[3] "Rabbinic Judaism neglects history, for its concentration is on religion." (Sandmel, First Christian Century, 68; cf. Patte, Jewish Hermeneutic, 120; Doeve, Jewish Hermeneutics, 54). That such an attitude antedates A.D. 70 is clear from the failure to attach revelatory significance to historical events in pre-Christian Pharisaic writings (II Maccabees, Tobit, Judith, Pss. Sol.).

[4] See particularly Patte's perceptive treatment (Jewish Hermeneutic, 49-115).
We are using halakah in the wider sense to denote any predominantly juridical development, including those independent of and linked with Scripture. (For the distinction, see Moore, Judaism, I, 132).

exhorting the present embodiment of the elect to emulate the example of the old. As Sifre Deut. has it, "If you wish to know the creation of the world, learn Haggadah: for from it you will learn to know God and to cleave to his ways."[1] Within this approach, Scripture was considered to be "closed;" no new revelations of the nature, characteristics and destiny of the community were to be found.[2] This situation, in which the interpreter was forced to operate with a closed system of signs, made necessary great ingenuity in the combining and understanding of these signs in order to derive the required relevancy. It is, therefore, often the result that Scripture " . . . is very often little more than a stimulus for a composition which is developed in complete independence of it."[3]

In the school, on the other hand, the identity of the community was assumed, and attention was directed to the task of informing this community about how it might relate its identity to the practical situations of a life and culture very different from that of the patriarchs, David, or even Ezra.[4] An "openness" to the shifting cultural contexts existed, which led to the development of the oral torah (תורה שבעל פה). This was considered to be equal in

---

[1] Sifre Deut., #49 (Montefiore-Loewe, Rabbinic Anthology, 162). J. Theodor states as the purpose of Haggadah "to influence the mind of man and to induce him to lead a religious and moral life 'that he might walk in the ways of God.'" ("Midrash Haggadah," JE, VIII, 550). Sometimes haggadah is characterized as being all that is not halakah (cf. Bacher, Terminologie, I, 33-34).

[2] Patte, Jewish Hermeneutic, 122.

[3] R. Le Déaut, "Apropos a Definition of Midrash," Int, XXV (1971), 274.
  For an attempt to establish the history of some haggadic traditions, cf. especially Vermes, Scripture and Tradition, who utilizes the methodology laid down by R. Bloch ("Note méthodologique pour l'étude de la Littérature rabbinique," RSR, XLIII (1955), 194-227).

[4] Wilhelm Bousset (Die Religion des Judentums im Spāthellenistischen Zeitalter, ed. by Hugo Gressmann, HNT, XXI (3rd ed.; Tübingen: Mohr, 1926), 159) speaks of this as "Buch-frömmigheit."

antiquity[1] and authority[2] to the written. The precise evolutionary relationship between the two toroth is difficult to unravel, but it seems likely that the oral traditions arose both independently of, and in conjunction with, the Scriptures.[3] Particularly the tension between traditions seemingly unrelated to the OT and the desire to adduce Scripture as support for such traditions was exceedingly important in determining the delineaments of Pharisaic hermeneutics. A situation of mutual influence between tradition and Scripture developed: "Die Ueberlieferung will nur die Schrift auslegen, aber die Auslegung der Schrift geschieht nach der Ueberlieferung."[4] One can speak, therefore, of "retroactive justification"[5] and, as a consequence, writes Bonsirven:

> l'exégèse n'est pas entreprise, dans un esprit desintéressé, pour découvrir le sens d'un texte, mais pour démontrer une thèse déjà acquise; toutes les particules des livres sacrés ayant une valeur divine peuvent être exploitées de toutes les façons en vue d'y déceler les vérités divines qu'elles renferment.[6]

---

[1] The first verse of Pirke Aboth states: "Moses received Torah from Sinai and delivered it to Joshua, and Joshua to the Elders, and the Elders to the Prophets, and the Prophets delivered it to the men of the Great Synagogue." (Herford's translation. APOT, II). The "five pairs" of great teachers carried the tradition down to the Christian era (cf. m. Hag. 2:2).

[2] Occasionally one reads of "two toroth": Sifre Deut. #351 (on Dt. 33:10); Num. R. on 14:10. Cf. Bousset, Religion, 156-159; Moore, Judaism, I, 262.

[3] The well-known debate on the priority of mishnaic or midrashic halakah between Lauterbach and Zeitlin need not be gone into here (cf. Jacob Z. Lauterbach, "Midrash and Mishnah: A Study in the Early History of the Halakah," Rabbinic Essays (New York: KTAV, 1973 (= 1915-1916)), 164; Solomon Zeitlin, "The Halaka: Introduction to Tannaitic Jurisprudence," JQR, XXXIX (1948-1949), 17). Bacher states: "In der Schulsprache bezeichnete man mit הלכה die normirte religiöse Satzung, die geltende Vorschrift ohne Rücksicht auf ihre Herleitung aus der heiligen Schrift." (Terminologie, I, 42).

[4] Bousset, Religion, 156.

[5] S. Horovitz, "Midrash," JE, VIII, 548; Cf. Patte, Jewish Hermeneutic, 118 -- "legitimation by means of Scripture."

[6] Bonsirven, Exégèse, 116-117.

It would be misleading to characterize the interpretational methodology of classical Judaism as a whole in these terms, however. For one thing, the desire to correlate closely Scripture with tradition seems only to have arisen at the time of R. Akiba (although certain tendencies in that direction must certainly have existed before that time). For another, not all Scriptural interpretation was directed to this sort of "retroactive justification." But the principle underlying these techniques, that God's will for Israel can be discerned in a creative interpretation of tradition and Scripture, does seem to be characteristic of classical Judaism generally.[1] Israel's identity as the chosen people was known, although it had to be continually re-affirmed, but her calling, which was regarded as co-extensive with life, had to be worked out anew in each generation and cultural situation.[2]

In conclusion, then, we can summarize the hermeneutical axioms of classical Judaism as involving a particular understanding of <u>revelation</u> (closed with reference to the impact of history, open to the influence of changing cultural and religious norms), <u>vocation</u> (all of life must reflect Israel's status and be directed by God) and <u>Scripture</u> (all-sufficient as the guide for this vocation).

<u>Midrash</u>

This is the most natural point at which to consider the hermeneutical method designated by midrash. An attempt has been made

---

[1]Cf., on the synagogue cycle as evidence of early interpretation procedure, Jacob Mann, <u>The Bible as Read and Preached in the Old Synagogue: A Study in the Cycles of the Readings from Torah and Prophets, as well as from Psalms, and the Structure of the Midrashic Homilies</u>, The Library of Biblical Studies (New York: KTAV, 1971), cf. 10-13.

[2]The Sadducees operated with a different conception of revelation (closed) and vocation (pertaining only to the religious life). Cf. Patte, <u>Jewish Hermeneutic</u>, 125-126.

to avoid this word up till now because of the difficulties surrounding the precise connotation to be given the term. A. G. Wright complains:

> . . . the word midrash at present is an equivocal term and is being used to describe a mass of disparate material. Indeed, if some of the definitions are correct, large amounts, if not the whole of the Bible, would have to be called midrash. Hence, the word as used currently in biblical studies is approaching the point where it is no longer really meaningful.[1]

One can sympathize with such a complaint when current characterizations of midrash are encountered: "Le midrash est en effect tout un univers que l'on ne découvrira qu'en acceptant d'emblée sa complexité. Il envahit toute l'approche juive de la Bible qu'il pouvrait même désigner dans sons ensemble."[2] However, Wright's own suggestion, that "midrash" be confined to a designation of a literary genre, is hardly to be accepted, for it is clear that the term had a considerably broader meaning in the period with which we are concerned.[3] No unanimity exists on any other distinguishing characteristic, whether it be exegetical method,[4] the dynamic between text and interpreter,[5] the penetrating to a deeper sense,[6] or generally, an "attitude toward

---

[1] Addison G. Wright, "The Literary Genre Midrash," CBQ, XXVIII (1966), 108.

[2] R. Le Déaut, "Apropos d'une définition du Midrash," Bib, L (1969), 401-402. (ET in Int, XXV (1971), 259-283).

[3] Cf., e.g., Sirach 51:23, CD 20:6, 4QFlor 1:14 (Ellis, "Midrash," 62; Miller, "Targum," 43; Patte, Jewish Hermeneutic, 117, n. 1).
Wright claims that " . . . the basic midrashic structure, common to all forms that can be labelled midrash down to the smallest independent unit, is merely that one begins with a text of Scripture and proceeds to comment on it in some way." The broader sense of midrash as "free rabbinic interpretation" was first used by the Babylonian Amoraim. ("Literary Genre," 108, 119).

[4] Longenecker (Biblical Exegesis, 37) seems to imply this sort of characterization.

[5] Miller, "Targum," 44; Le Déaut, "Apropos," (ET, 282, n. 85).

[6] Horovitz ("Midrash," 548) says: " . . . 'midrash' designates an exegesis, which, going more deeply than the more literal sense, attempts to penetrate into the Spirit of the Scripture, to examine the text from all sides, and thereby to derive interpretations which are not immediately obvious." Cf. also Moore, Judaism, I, 72 (n. 21). This

Scripture."[1] A study of the root דרש reveals that the idea of a "recherche appliquée,"[2] especially an "inquiring of God"[3] is basic. A clear and consistent progression in the use of the term can be traced, marked by the change of object from אלהים or יהוה to the Law,[4] which came to be regarded as the embodiment of God's will, and hence that which must be "searched for" and "inquired after."[5] This particular transition is indicative of the shift from a cult-centered to a torah-centered religious outlook[6] and suggests that any description of midrash must at least include the element of a seeking out of the divine will.

That this searching out of the will of God always took its departure from the Scriptural text is questionable.[7] While an OT text is always involved, it is clearly often introduced only retrospectively.[8]

---

distinction is based especially on the Amoraitic distinction between דרש and פשט exegesis.

[1] Patte, <u>Jewish Hermeneutic</u>, 117, n. 1.

[2] Bloch, "Midrash," c. 1263.   [3] Patte, <u>Jewish Hermeneutic</u>, 124.

[4] דרש, found 161 times in the OT has most often God, or the Lord as its object; only once the "law" (Ez. 7:10). The substantive occurs only twice (II Chron. 13:22, 24:27), each time with reference to a source employed by the chronicler.

[5] דרש is used in the Dss over 40 times; 16 of those with reference to Scriptural interpretation. (Wright, "Midrash," 117, n. 54). מדרש denotes the community's judicial "inquiry" in 1QS 6:24, 8:26, and the study of the law in 1QS 8:15, CD 20:6 (<u>torah</u> is the object), 4QFlor 1:14. Sir 51:23 speaks of the בית המדרש, "house of learning."

[6] Cf. Solomon Zeitlin, "Midrash: A Historical Study," <u>JQR</u>, XLIV (1953), 21-36.

[7] <u>Pace</u> Bloch, "Midrash," c. 1265, followed by Vermes (<u>Scripture and Tradition</u>, 7) and Longenecker (<u>Biblical Exegesis</u>, 37), who, however, adds the important qualification "ostensible point of departure."

[8] Patte, <u>Jewish Hermeneutic</u>, 117-118. E. P. Sanders (<u>Paul and Palestinian Judaism: A Comparison of Patterns of Religion</u> (Philadelphia: Fortress, 1977), 27) points out that Bloch fails to distinguish carefully between <u>haggadah</u> and midrash and by concentrating too exclusively on the former distorts the picture slightly. Perhaps this is a case in point.

Intensive study and the actualization of Scripture for the contemporary situation are legitimate characterizations, but are not specific enough to be really useful.[1] A more valuable approach is to seek to characterize midrash (like Le Déaut, we refrain from attempting a definition[2]) in terms of the hermeneutical axioms just outlined. It is legitimate to confine the parameters of midrash to the matrix of rabbinic literature because it is only in these writings that the term occurs as a technical designation of Scriptural interpretation. While it would be an indefensible a priori to claim that midrashic procedure must thereby be found only in rabbinic literature, it would seem to be methodologically sound to seek for its normative traits within that corpus. It should be noted that this approach is consonant with the suggestions of Le Déaut and others, that midrash should be regarded as involving a general understanding of religion.

The axioms crucial for an understanding of the rabbinic approach to Scripture involve, as we have seen, a realization that God is no longer revealing Himself in history, that the Israelite must possess clear divine guidance for every aspect of his life and that Scripture provides the material for this guidance. Within this matrix, midrash can be understood as the process by which the divine will is sought and discovered within the compass of a "closed" system of signs. The Pharisaic Jew, as he sought God's guidance in particular situations, was hedged about by an established written revelation and a traditional body of teaching that could be added to only through an interaction between that revelation and tradition. This situation is, of course, particularly relevant to the producing of halakah, but is also

---

[1] The third and fourth characteristics of midrash given by Bloch ("Midrash," cc. 1265-1266).

[2] "Apropos," 401-402.

applicable to the haggadic approach, for here also, though greater freedom was allowed, Scripture and the tradition represented the foci with which the interpreter had to deal.

Thus, it is our contention that midrash should be characterized not according to its literary genre,[1] or in terms of its appropriation techniques, but in terms of the hermeneutical axioms which guide the approach.[2] It must be emphasized that such a conclusion is by no means definitive, nor is it meant to exclude the possibility of midrashic approaches in literature that is not generally characterized by the same hermeneutical axioms: but where it is claimed a midrash is present, such axioms must be shown to be involved at that point.

Apocalyptic

Just as the sages of classical Judaism traced the descent of the oral _torah_ back to the revelation at Mt. Sinai, so the apocalyptists believed themselves to be the possessors of a visionary revelation equally ancient and authoritative.[3] As IV Ezra 14:1-18 clearly indicates, this secret revelation has to do particularly with the course of history. The apocalyptists, viewing the past in terms of their own depressing situation, enunciated a clear philosophy of

---

[1]Wright distinguishes three types of midrashic literary structure: exegetical (brief comments on a text), homiletical (more extended discussion of texts), and narrative ("rewritten Bible"). ("Literary Genre," 124-128. He is followed by Hanson, Studies, 206).
See, on the distinction between homiletic and expositional midrashim, Joseph Heinemann, "Profile of a Midrash: The Act of Composition in Leviticus Rabba," JAAR, XXXIX (1971), 142-143.

[2]Patte, while not explicitly stating this as the definitive characteristic of midrash, stresses this aspect of midrash (Jewish Hermeneutic, 117-122).

[3]Bousset, Religion, 154; Russell Apocalyptic, 185. Russell cites the tradition in IV Ezra 14, which traces the "secrets" back to Moses (cf. the ancestry of the Pharisaic oral law!)(85-88). Likewise Patte points to the "heavenly tables" in Jub. 32:21-30, which are seen to contain the secrets of world history. (Jewish Hermeneutic, 150-51).

history. As Amos Wilder says, apocalyptic " . . . took history with
utter seriousness, confronting the seemingly total disaster of the
present and assigning meaning and hope to it in terms of the wider
cosmic drama."[1] Unlike classical Judaism, then, apocalyptic was
interested in history and it must be asked how this interest related
to revelation and Scripture interpretation.

While it has been claimed that the apocalyptists believed
God to be revealing Himself in "new Acts in the contemporary history,"[2]
von Rad seems to be correct when he states that the apocalyptic view
of history " . . . no longer knows anything of those acts of God on
which salvation was based and in the light of which previous accounts
of the nation's history had been concentrated."[3] The apocalyptists
are fond of recasting history in symbolic guise through a pseudonymous
"revelation" as a means of encouraging belief in the sovereign plan of
God, but they say very little about contemporary events and what is
said is almost entirely negative. As "crisis literature," apocalyptic
is very much the product of a specific historical context, but it
must be doubted whether the seers, any more than the rabbis, interpreted
that context by means of the Scripture or allowed the situation to
color their understanding of Scripture. The historical situation has
only negative value: " . . . the eschaton interrupts the history; it
is not something which the history prepares for, or in any way causes
to occur."[4] The fulfillment of the "unfulfilled prophecies," which

---

[1] Amos N. Wilder, "The Rhetoric of Ancient and Modern Apocalyptic," Int, XXV (1971), 443. Cf. also Russell, Apocalyptic, 205-234.

[2] Patte, Jewish Hermeneutic, 166; cf. also Russell, Apocalyptic, 205.

[3] Gerhard von Rad, Old Testament Theology, trans by D. M. G. Stalker (Edinburgh: Oliver and Boyd, 1965), II, 303-304.

[4] Stanley Brice Frost, "Apocalyptic and History," The Bible in Modern Scholarship: Papers Read at the 100th Meeting of the Society of Biblical Literature, December 28-30, 1964 (New York: Abingdon, 1965), 112.

plays such a vital role in the apocalyptic visions, comes not in the present, but in the ("wholly-other") future: God has acted, and will act, but is not now acting. The very nature of apocalyptic suggests that this would be the case. "No longer is God's deed bound up with his word as it is in ancient spoken prophecy; the context of revelation breaks free from what happens here and now and, as timeless event, has reference to the consummation of all things."[1]

This discussion provides the indispensable context for an assessment of the hermeneutical axioms of the apocalyptists. God's imminent eschatological intervention is structured by, and portrayed in terms of, the OT Scriptures, which are regarded as incomplete without the secret revelation vouchsafed to the visionaries. As Russell says, "The ancient prophecies were to be read in terms of 'the End' and were to be interpreted and reinterpreted so as to fit into the great final drama in which the triumph of God and of God's people would be made known over all the nations round about."[2] While ethical and practical exhortations linked to the Scriptures are by no means unheard of in the apocalyptic literature, there can be little doubt that the eschatological thrust is dominant. Detailed instructions about behavior in this life are immaterial when the time is so short;

---

[1] Russell, Apocalyptic, 185.
Paul D. Hanson, in an article tracing the growth of apocalyptic, says: "We have been describing prophetic eschatology as the prophet's vision of Yahweh's plans for his people which the prophet is commissioned to translate into the politico-historical events of his time. Prophetic eschatology is transferred into apocalyptic at the point where the task of translating the cosmic vision into the categories of mundane reality is abdicated." ("Old Testament Apocalyptic Reexamined," Int, XXV (1971), 469). Cf. also George Eldon Ladd: "the apocalyptists lost the reality of God's acting in present history." ("Apocalyptic and New Testament Theology," Reconciliation and Hope: New Testament Essays on Atonement and Eschatology presented to L. L. Morris on his 60th Birthday, ed. by Robert Banks (Grand Rapids: Eerdmans, 1974), 202).

[2] Apocalyptic, 183.

likewise, in contrast to the rabbis, the cultural history is completely eliminated as an influence on revelation. The manifold "vocation" as understood by the rabbis becomes reduced to the simple exhortation: hope and trust.

The matrix of apocalyptic interpretation is determined, then, largely by the concentrated purpose of the literature. Scripture, supplemented and interpreted by the esoteric revelation, furnishes a framework within which past history can be understood and the future consummation depicted. The stimulus for such interpretation comes from the contemporary situation, but is not strongly influenced by it. Rather the dominant influence on the way Scripture is approached stems from the consciousness of inspiration.

Qumran

The familiar passage of 1QpHab 7:1-8 may be chosen as the basis for our discussion of the hermeneutical axioms which governed Scriptural interpretation at Qumran:

> And God told Habakkuk to write the things that were to come upon the last generation, but the consummation of the period [גמר הקץ] he did not make known to him. And as for what it says, "that he may run who reads it" [Hab. 2:2], this means [פשרו] the teacher of righteousness, to whom God made known all the mysteries [רזי] of the words of his servants the prophets. "For still the vision is for an appointed time; it hastens to the period and does not lie" [Hab. 2:3]. This means [פשרו] that the last period extends over and above all that the prophets said; for the mysteries of God are marvelous.[1]

This text is appropriately oft-quoted as a <u>locus classicus</u> for an understanding of Biblical interpretation at Qumran, as it touches upon each of the beliefs involving the community and Scripture which are determinative for their approach.

---

[1] The translation is Burrows' (<u>Dead Sea Scrolls</u>).

The eschatological perspective, shared with the apocalyptists, is significant for much of the sectaries' life and many of their beliefs. So intense is the expectation in the culminatory intervention of God that the community, while maintaining the futurity of this event[1] yet views itself as already partaking in the eschatological reality. 1QSª begins: "And this is the order for the whole congregation of Israel at the end of days [באחרית הימים]" and there is frequent reference to "the last generation" and "the appointed time."

Since the Qumran community identified itself with God's eschatological covenant people, the words of the prophets may be applied to them in their situation, for the prophets spoke (often unconsciously) of the last days. Brownlee summarizes the sectaries' viewpoint: "Everything the ancient prophet wrote has a veiled, eschatological meaning."[2] Here lies the theoretical justification for the direct contemporizing of Scripture characteristic of the DSS. The prophets themselves were not privy to the meaning of what they wrote, as the passage quoted above makes clear. The text of Scripture does not, and never did, refer to the prophets' own day, but to this day in which its meaning is for the first time being clearly understood: " . . . This is the true and only meaning of Scripture."[3]

The discovery of the true meaning of the prophetic text is attributed to the Teacher of Righteousness, "to whom God made known

---

[1] E.g., 1QS 3:23; 1QSa 5:20-23. On the nearness of the end, cf. especially Heinz-Wolfgang Kuhn, Enderwartung und gegenwärtiges Heil: Untersuchungen zu den Gemeindeliedern von Qumran, SUNT, IV (Göttingen: Vandenhoeck & Ruprecht, 1966), esp. 176-188.

[2] Brownlee, "Biblical Interpretation," 60; cf. also Betz, Offenbarung, 80.

[3] Russell, Method and Message, 181; F. F. Bruce, Biblical Exegesis in the Qumran Texts (Grand Rapids: Eerdmans, 1960), 15-16; Eva Osswald, "Zur Hermeneutik des Habakuk-Kommentars," ZAW, LXVIII (1956), 250; Betz, Offenbarung, 75-76; Longenecker, Biblical Exegesis, 38-39.

all the mysteries of the words of his servants the prophets." Who this Teacher was, and what his relation was to the founding of the sect are questions too difficult and unrelated to our purposes to consider at this point, but it is important to investigate further the understanding of Scripture implied here. רז, "mystery," used in 1QpHab 7:5,8 to characterize Habakkuk's prophecy, occurs frequently in the scrolls with reference to the hidden plan of God, now revealed to the Teacher and his followers.[1] While רז is not used often in conjunction with Scripture, it would seem from 1QpHab 7:1-8, the evident intensity of Scriptural study and the nature of the commentaries that it was especially through an enlightened search of the Scriptures that the mystery was unravelled.[2] As R. E. Brown concludes in an article devoted to pre-Christian understandings of "mystery," " . . . in the mysteries of the special interpretation of the Torah, Qumran stands alone in the pre-Christian literature: this concept is part of the sectarian heritage."[3]

What form did this search of the Scriptures take? A well-known debate, involving the question as to whether pesher interpretation can be classified as a type of midrash, has been joined on just this point, some maintaining strongly the revelatory character of Qumran exegesis, in distinction to midrash,[4] others pointing to the

---

[1] Cf. 1QS 3:23, 9:18. Particularly frequent and important are the references to the רז in the Hymns, the most characteristic use being a confession of or thanksgiving for, in the first person sing., the fact that God had made his mysteries known (1:21, 2:13, 4:27, 5:25, 7:27, 12:13, 12:20, 13:2,3; 11:10 in the 3rd plural). Whether the speaker here is the Teacher of Righteousness or not is a debated question which can hardly be delved into here. Patte, Jewish Hermeneutic, 226; Betz, Offenbarung, 83.

[2] Betz, Offenbarung, 85-86; Bruce, Biblical Exegesis, 8.

[3] R. E. Brown, "The Pre-Christian Semitic Concept of 'Mystery,'" CBQ, XX (1958), 443.

[4] Pioneering this position was Elliger (Habakuk-Kommentar, 162-164).

similarities between Qumran and rabbinic appropriation techniques.[1] It is helpful to view this disagreement in terms of our three levels of Scriptural interpretation: should pesher be characterized according to its hermeneutical axioms, or techniques?[2] If the theoretical independence of these levels be allowed, it can be asserted that pesher is both revelatory (with respect to its basic axioms) and "scholarly" (with respect to its methods): a revelatory exegesis.[3] As for the latter, the presence in the scrolls of word-plays, tallying of passages, and other such techniques common to the rabbinic literature has already been demonstrated.[4] On the other hand, the revelatory character of Qumran exegesis has strong support in the texts and is widely acknowledged,[5] although the principle has

---

[1]Especially vocal has been Brownlee ("Biblical Interpretation," 74). Cf. also Stendahl, School, 184; Schwarz, Damaskusschrift, 107-110; A. R. C. Leaney, The Rule of Qumran and its Meaning: Introduction, Translation and Commentary (Philadelphia: Westminster, 1966), 73; Rabin, Qumran Studies, 99; McNamara, Palestinian Targum, 79-80; E. Earle Ellis, "How the New Testament uses the Old," New Testament Interpretation: Essays on Principles and Methods, ed. by I. Howard Marshall (Grand Rapids: Eerdmans, 1977), 206; J. van der Ploeg, "Bijbelverklariag te Qumrān," Mededelingen der koninklijke nederlandse Akademie van Wetenschappen, AFD Letterkunde, n.s., XXIII (1960), 207-229.

[2]Wright, true to his stress on literary genre, characterizes pesher as a midrash haggadah ("Midrash," 418-421).

[3]Cf. also Miller, "Targum," 52-53; Slomovic, "Exegesis," 5.

[4]Silberman claims: " . . . although the Habakkuk Pesher itself offers a theory of revelatory interpretation, in practice its interpretations are in large measure identified with literary devices used in many of the early midrashim where no such claim is made." ("Unriddling," 327).

[5]Note the frequent reference to "making known" the mystery and the cruciality of the evidence of the Teacher of Righteousness. As B. Rigaux says of pesher, "Il n'est pas une explication ni une explicitation du texte. Il contient une nouvelle révélation ajoutée au texte lui-même." ("Révélation des mystères et perfection a Qumran et dans le Nouveau Testament," NTS, IV (1957-1958), 247). Cf. Betz, Offenbarung, 81-82; Russell, Apocalyptic, 185; Geza Vermes, "The Qumran Interpretation of Scripture in its Historical Setting," ALUOS, VI (1966-1968), 91-92; Bruce, Biblical Exegesis, 8; Longenecker, Biblical Exegesis, 43; Osswald, "Hermeneutik," 248.

been improperly thrust forward in isolation by Elliger who has been justly criticized on this point.¹

If both the revelatory and the scholarly aspects of Qumran interpretation are recognized, it can be seen, in fact, that "Revelation occurred in an inspired search of Scripture."² "If pesher is the revelation of prophetic mysteries, these mysteries are exegetically discerned. They are the product of a meditative study on biblical texts."³ This point can be elucidated further by recognizing the significance of the term correlative to פשר, רז. "Pesher" is used repeatedly to introduce interpretations following the scriptural citations in the commentaries at Qumran and only rarely outside the commentaries.⁴ פשר occurs only once in the MT (Ecc. 8:1 -- apparently not with reference to dreams or Scripture), but its Aramaic equivalent, פשר is found 31 times in the book of Daniel, each time with reference to the interpretation of (prophetic) dreams. In addition, the interpretations of Joseph's dreams in Gen. 40 and 41 are characterized as פתר or פתרון, cognates to פשר.⁵ This linguistic background, along with the allegorical identifications of individual elements in the Qumran commentaries which are characteristic of the interpretation of dreams and visions, provides solid substantiation for the view that

---

¹Silberman, "Unriddling," 327; Longenecker, Biblical Exegesis, 43.

²Patte, Jewish Hermeneutic, 218.

³Miller, "Targum," 52-53. Betz says: "Die geoffenbarten und die durch das Studium gefundenen Dinge in der Tora sind demnach identisch." (Offenbarung, 44).

⁴CD 4:14, introducing a scriptural interpretation. It is legitimate, however, to use the word to characterize Qumran biblical interpretation in general (Schwarz, Damaskusschrift, 112).

⁵Isaac Rabinowitz, "'Pĕsher/Pittārōn': Its Biblical Meaning and Its Significance in the Qumran Literature," RevQ, VIII (1973), 220-226.

pesher is properly understood in terms of a "dream-interpretation" model: " . . . the biblically sanctioned term referring to dream interpretations and riddle solutions in Daniel was available to the Qumran writers as an introductory term for their unriddling words of the prophets which were, after all, reports of visions."[1]

To summarize: the Qumran sectaries regarded themselves as the eschatological community. The prophets, they believed, spoke of these last days, but in "mysteries," which could be understood only by those possessing the requisite divine insight. The interpretations of these mysteries, accomplished as they were through widely-used techniques, were considered to be new revelation.

If, finally, we return to the question as to the propriety of categorizing pesher as a type of midrash, it must first be emphasized that both similarities and differences exist. However, although pesher is much like midrash in many of its techniques, the dissimilarities greatly outweigh the points of contact. Unlike the midrashim, the pesharim are genuine commentaries, adhering closely to the text, even when it is treated in a cavalier manner. In terms of hermeneutical axioms, the differences are even more pronounced: the eschatological consciousness of the covenanters, the understanding of prophecy as "mysteries" whose interpretation requires a new revelation, and the

---

[1] Silberman, "Unriddling," 331; Asher Finkel, "The Pesher of Dreams and Scriptures," RevQ, IV (1963-1964), 368; Rabinowitz, "Pēsher," 230, Patte, Jewish Hermeneutic, 301-308.

Silberman also makes reference to the later rabbinic "petirah (פתרה) midrash" (e.g., Qohelet Rabbah 12:1), which "introduces the specific point of reference from which the entire verse is to be understood." (327-330). The technique in question, being late, is of doubtful value in shedding light on the Qumran pesher.

The few linguistic exceptions mentioned by Ellis ("Midrash," 16, n. 9) are hardly sufficient to overturn this general picture.

attempt to contemporize Scripture in relation to contemporary events sharply distinguish Qumran interpretation from midrash. In the words of Matthew Black, "midrash-pesher is a modern invention probably best forgotten."[1]

Conclusions

Studies of the use of the OT in the New have sometimes been remiss in characterizing adequately the Jewish hermeneutical background and in defining key terms. While the limitations in scope imposed by the nature of the research topic have obviated a definitive treatment of Jewish hermeneutics, the preceeding study should be adequate as a basis for an understanding of the approaches utilized in first century Palestinian Judaism, the drawing of comparisons between the NT and this background and the clear and consistent use of key terminology. Before moving on to do these things with respect to the Gospel passion texts, it will be advantageous to summarize some of the major conclusions and to draw implications of importance for the investigation.

The order in which the three basic levels have been studied corresponds generally to the order in which one would investigate the phenomena. It will be good, in summarizing, to reverse the sequence and approach the process from the standpoint of the interpreter himself. As a foundation for, and preliminary to, the actual interpretative process lie the hermeneutical axioms. These provide the "matrix of interpretation," community beliefs which bear most directly on the way in which Scripture is used. While certain beliefs,

---

[1]Matthew Black, "The Christological Use of the Old Testament in the New Testament," NTS, XVIII (1971-1972), 1. Also Cecil Roth, "The Subject Matter of Qumran Exegesis," VT, X (1960), 52; Holm-Nielsen, Hodayot, 305, n. 14; Rabinowitz, "Pesher," 231; Longenecker, Biblical Exegesis, 41; Vermes, "Commentaire," 344-345.

particularly about Scripture, are held in common by the various communities, there are, naturally, many differences on this and other questions which lead to characteristically different appropriation models. Two important terms, midrash and pesher, have been used to describe different approaches at this level and it is important to reiterate that in this study, they will be used primarily with reference to a general hermeneutical approach.

It is therefore legitimate to speak, in a given instance, of a "midrashic" approach, as long as it is kept in mind that general orientation, not technique, is thereby described.

Furthermore, it must be emphasized that the approaches designated by the terms midrash and pesher are both broader and more narrow than the use of Scripture within the communities whose matrices of interpretation provide the distinctive milieu for each. Thus, many instances of Scriptural appropriation in the DSS are not properly labelled pesher (e.g., allegory); only where the distinctive Qumran hermeneutical axioms are clearly implemented is it legitimate to speak of pesher. On the other hand, pesher approaches can exist outside the scrolls; again, if a matrix of interpretation similar to that found at Qumran is operative. One must, of course, be careful not to apply this criterion too rigidly, with the result that pesher approaches are defined out of existence. But, on the other hand, some criteria are essential if pesher (and midrash) is to connote anything meaningful.

The process through which the appropriation of scripture took place has been described in terms of three basic alternatives. The following outline summarizes the possibilities.

I. Direct Appropriation (X = X)
   A. Interpretative -- Scripture is applied directly to the interpreter's contemporary situation, without introducing alterations in either

B. Comparative (typology) -- a situation, person or institution is seen to reproduce a principle inherent in a Scriptural situation, person or institution

II. Re-orientation of the Text (X ← X)
   A. Shift in Meaning
      1. New or unusual meanings of a passage are adduced, often through the use of philological devices
      2. A secondary meaning, symbolized by the words, is utilized (allegory)
   B. Modification of the text
      1. Minor adaptions introduced to suit the context
      2. Use of variant readings
      3. Creation of new readings

III. Modification in the Point of Application (X → X)
   A. Interpretative Impact
      1. Characterizations of existing phenomena
      2. The use of Scriptural terms or passages with symbolic intent (i.e., the withdrawal to the Land of Damascus as symbolic of the community's exile (on one interpretation))
   B. Creative Impact
      1. The formulation of doctrinal, didactic, ethical, etc. statements on the basis of Scripture, as well as prophetic descriptions of future events
      2. The invention of events presented as, and/or understood by the interpreter, to be historical

Several comments about this scheme can be made by way of reiteration and amplification.

The term appropriation is being used to denote the process sometimes described with the two words, exegesis and application. To use the latter two terms would be to suggest that the process was carried out in these separate stages, which was normally not the case in the literature with which we are concerned. Of crucial significance to the process is whether Scripture is made conformable to the existing situation (II) or whether it, itself, molds the situation (III). (It is possible, of course, that a degree of each could be present in a given situation.) The factor which will usually determine which method is employed is the nature of the point of application: if it is fixed or well-established, the Scripture must be modified; if not, it can perhaps be altered by Scripture. Even in the situation in which the "purest" exegesis would be practiced, i.e., the formulation of doctrine, situational factors or a previously established tradition often mold the interpretation.

Since the appropriation technique lies at the heart of the hermeneutical process and is usually discernible through a study of the passage, it will be an important focus of the thesis. An attempt will be made to determine which aspect, Scripture or context, is altered and how frequently, and to compare these instances with the number of occasions when a direct appropriation process is in evidence. This data will provide important information with respect to the means of "legitimation" practiced by the NT Christians. Finally, it should be noted that typology and allegory are being used to indicate types of appropriation techniques.

The larger literary framework, genre, can be significant as a factor determining, or at least influencing, the kind of citation procedure and appropriation technique utilized. The relationship may be reversed as well; citation procedure may provide a clue to the genre and purpose of the composition as a whole. It will be necessary to pay attention to citation procedure in the NT material and to attempt the drawing of conclusions on that basis.

Finally, it is necessary once again to stress the importance of comparing hermeneutical approaches at every level and so carefully to indicate both the similarities and differences between systems. Only in this manner can the variegated phenomenon of the NT use of the OT be fully appreciated.

CHAPTER II

THE USE OF THE ISAIANIC SERVANT SONGS IN THE GOSPEL PASSION TEXTS

The Old Testament Background

The methodology employed in this chapter and the following four will be to examine first the OT passage involved, then to study, in general order from the more explicit to the more obscure, the references to that passage in the gospels, and finally to summarize and draw conclusions as to the significance of the passage for the passion and the fundamental hermeneutical situation. Within this framework, matters having to do with a specific text only will be discussed at that point, whereas more general issues, pertaining to the passage as a whole, will be left for the conclusions.

Since the pioneering study of Duhm, it has been customary to speak of four passages in Isaiah, related in theme and content, as the "Servant Songs": Is. 42:1-4; 49:1-6; 50:4-9 and 52:13-53:12.[1] However, objections have been raised against isolating these passages and, in practice, interpreting them apart from their context in Isaiah.[2] These protests are undoubtedly justified, but as long as it is not

---

[1] D. B. Duhm, Das Buch Jesaja, HKAT, III, 1 (Göttingen: Vandenhoeck & Ruprecht, 1892), 284-5.

[2] Charles Cutler Torrey, The Second Isaiah: A New Interpretation (Edinburgh: T & T Clark, 1928), 137-140; P.-E. Bonnard, Le Second Isaïe: Son Disciple et leurs éditeurs, EBib (Paris: J. Gabalda et Cie, 1972), 39; Eissfeldt, Introduction, 340; Morna D. Hooker, Jesus and the Servant: The Influence of the Servant Concept of Deutero-Isaiah in the New Testament (London: SPCK, 1959), 25-30.

attempted to understand the Servant apart from the total message of Isaiah, it is valid to continue speaking of four "Servant Songs" in which the nature and mission of this enigmatic figure are the central themes. Morna Hooker contests this, maintaining that the characterization "My Servant" does not represent "a concrete figure, for whom an identification must be sought, but the qualities of an already existing figure, the people who serve their God in obedience to his strange plan . . . ." Jesus could not have been identified with the Servant "for the simple reason that there was not, and never had been a 'servant figure' with whom to identify him."[1] However, the fact that many individuals in the OT were called "servants," to which she draws attention, is no justification for denying that the term could become so identified with a particular figure as to attain a quasi-titular status; the expectation of the Messiah or the Prophet in late Judaism may be cited as parallel developments. Furthermore, "Servant" seems to be used in a unique way in Isaiah, especially in chapters 50-53, where lengthy descriptions of this figure are introduced with the simple, independent designation "my servant," in contrast to the use of the term elsewhere in the OT, where the identity of the servant is clearly indicated in the context.[2] Clearly Isaiah employs the term as the appropriate description of a definite figure, about whom the court official of Candace, Queen of the Ethiopians could inquire (Acts 8:32-5). Whether the figure is Israel or not, it is clear that a special concept emerges which can be treated in isolation and which Jesus <u>could</u> have applied to Himself.[3]

---

[1] Hooker, Servant, 157.

[2] Cf. Walter Zimmerli and Joachim Jeremias, The Servant of God, trans. by Harold Knight, et al., SBT, XX (London: SCM, 1965), 28. Zimmerli speaks of "the striking element of objectification and concealment under the anonymous title."

[3] Hooker identifies the Son of Man with Israel in her work The

This raises the vexing problem of the identity of the Servant, a question that has stimulated an extraordinary amount of scholarly discussion.[1] While Is. 49:3 seems to settle the issue by identifying the servant with Israel, the servant is, in the same passage (49:5-6), depicted as carrying out a ministry to Israel, and the individualizing language of the fourth Song, in particular, renders any purely collective interpretation difficult. It will suffice to say that it seems necessary to attribute both collective and individual traits to Isaiah's picture of the Servant,[2] and that the fourth Servant Song, with its detailed and personalized imagery, must refer to an individual, who, whether based on a contemporary of the prophet or not, is expected in the future.[3] The basic purpose, unlike the person, of

---

Son of Man in Mark, but this does not hinder her from correlating Son of Man with Jesus.

[1] Summaries of the literature and views taken may be found in Christopher R. North, The Suffering Servant in Deutero-Isaiah: An Historical and Critical Study (London: Oxford University Press, 1948); H. H. Rowley, "The Servant of the Lord in the Light of Three Decades of Criticism," The Servant of the Lord and Other Essays on the Old Testament (2nd ed.; Oxford: Basil Blackwell, 1965), 3-51; Joseph Coppens, Le Messianisme et sa Relève prophétique. Les anticipations vétérotestamentaires. Leur accomplissement en Jésus, BETL, XXXVIII (Gembloux: Duculot, 1974), 68-73.

[2] Rowley, "Servant," 52-3; North, Suffering Servant, 214; Bonnard, Second Isaïe, 41; Claus Westermann, Isaiah 40-66: A Commentary, trans. by David M. G. Stalker (London: SCM Press, Ltd., 1969), 20; Oscar Cullmann, The Christology of the New Testament, trans by Shirley L. Guthrie and Charles A. M. Hall (London: SCM, 1959), 54-5. Although over 80 years old, Delitzsch's "pyramid" interpretation probably still captures the concept best: "The lowermost basis is the whole of Israel; the middle section, Israel not merely after the flesh, but after the Spirit; the summit is the person of the Mediator of salvation arising out of Israel." (Franz Delitzsch, Biblical Commentary on the Prophecies of Isaiah, Vol. II, trans. by J. S. Banks and James Kennedy (4th ed.; Edinburgh: T & T Clark, 1892), 165).

[3] After exhaustively surveying the various positions, North concludes: "We have, then, when we have done our best with the historical interpretations, to deal with a plus, a plus to any one of them singly, a plus to any selection of them, a plus even to all of them taken together. That plus is a unique individual who has not yet appeared." (Suffering Servant, 214). Cf. also Delitzsch, Isaiah, II, 279; T. K. Cheyne, The Prophecies of Isaiah, Vol. II (London: C. Kegan Paul, 1881), 196; Hans Walter Wolff, Jesaja 53 im Urchristentum (2nd ed.; Berlin: Evangelische Verlagsanstalt, 1950), 36-7; Westermann, Isaiah 40-66, 264;

82   The OT in the Gospel Passion Narratives

the servant is clearly indicated in the fourth Song: "Die grosse Bedeutung der Tat des 'Ebed liegt darin, dass er die Sünden der Vielen auf sich nahm (v. 12). . . . Dieser Gedanke des stellvertretenden Leidens steht im Mittelpunkt des ganzen Liedes."[1]

There can be little doubt that this fundamental characteristic of the Servant's work, a vicarious atonement of universal validity, was almost entirely neglected in the theology and Messianic expectation of late Judaism. This is contested by Jeremias, who has argued at length that the Fourth Servant Song was applied to a suffering Messiah probably in pre-Christian Palestinian Judaism. He claims that the Messianic interpretation is found in I Enoch and Sir 48, while the suffering Messiah is found in the translation of the Peshitta, Aquila, and the Targum, b. Sanh. 98b, Ruth R. 5 on 2:14, Midr. San 19:1 and later Rabbinic material and in Justin's Dialogue with Trypho.[2] This evidence is not, however, conclusive. As Jeremias admits, no traits of suffering are applied to the figure in I Enoch,[3] and it cannot be demonstrated that Christian influence has not been at work in the Peshitta. The Targum, while interpreting the Servant

---

Rowley, "Servant," 54-55; Zimmerli-Jeremias, Servant, 33.

[1] Eduard Lohse, Märtyrer und Gottesknecht. Untersuchungen zur urchristlichen Verkündigung vom Sühntod Jesu Christi, FRLANT, XLVI (2nd ed.; Göttingen: Vandenhoeck & Ruprecht, 1963), 97.

[2] Zimmerli-Jeremias, Servant, 59-79. Cf. W. D. Davies, Paul and Rabbinic Judaism (London: SPCK, 1948), 280-3, North, Suffering Servant, 11; Christian Maurer, "Knecht Gottes und Sohn Gottes im Passionsbericht des Markusevangeliums," ZTK, L (1953), 5-6 (hesitatingly). See also the literature cited in Rowley, "Suffering Servant," 67-87.

[3] Martin Rese, "Überprüfung einiger Thesen von Joachim Jeremias zum Thema des Gottesknechtes im Judentum," ZTK, LX (1963), 33; Matthew Black, "Servant of the Lord and Son of Man," SJT, VI (1953), 10; North, Suffering Servant, 8; Lohse, Märtyrer, 108; Wolff, Jesaja 53, 42.

messianically, transfers all references to suffering to others and there is no evidence that any other understanding was ever countenanced in the Targum.[1] The translation of Aquila and the Rabbinic references are mainly concerned with the "leprous" Messiah, as an interpretation of Is. 53:4-5. While Jeremias claims that such a doctrine could not have arisen <u>after</u> the Christian appropriation of Is. 53,[2] it is not implausible that the tradition was, in fact, a conscious reaction against the Christian interpretation, substituting a natural blemish in the character of Messiah for the Christian concept of penal substitution.

It has been urged that the Qumran sectaries understood themselves or their leader, the Teacher of Righteousness, to be fulfilling the role of the Servant.[3] Brownlee has cited the translation of Is. 52:14 in 1QIsa as evidence of the Messianic understanding of the Servant at Qumran: "I, by my anointing, have given him a countenance more than human."[4] This translation has not, however, gone unchallenged,[5]

---

[1] Paul Seidelin, "Das 'Ebed Jahwe und die Messiasgestalt im Jesajatargum," ZNW, XXXV (1936), 217; Rese, "Überprüfung," 37; Hooker, Servant, 57.

[2] Cf. also Robert A. Aytoun, "The Servant of the Lord in the Targum," JTS, XXIII (1922), 173-76.

[3] William H. Brownlee, "The Servant of the Lord in the Qumran Scrolls," BASOR, CXXXII (1953), 8-15; CXXXV (1954), 33-38; "Messianic Motifs of Qumran and the New Testament," NTS, III (1956-57), 18-20; Vermes, Scripture and Tradition, 56-66; Black, "Servant," 7-9; F. F. Bruce, "Qumran and Early Christianity," NTS, II (1955-56), 184-85; Bertil Gärtner, The Temple and the Community in Qumran and the New Testament: A Comparative Study in the Temple Symbolism of the Qumran Texts and the New Testament, SNTSMS, I (Cambridge: University Press, 1965), 123-126.

[4] William Hugh Brownlee, The Meaning of the Qumran Scrolls for the Bible with Special Attention to the Book of Isaiah, The James W. Richard Lectures in Christian Religion (New York: Oxford University Press, 1964), 204-215.

[5] Adam Simon van der Woude, Die Messianischen Vorstellungen der Gemeinde von Qumrân (Assen: van Gorcum, 1957), 166-167; Rowley, "Suffering Servant," 88-9.

and it is doubtful that the Servant was a Messianic figure at Qumran.[1] That individual traits of the servant have been applied to the Qumran community and its leader is undeniable, but it has not been convincingly demonstrated that the community or its leader was <u>identified</u> with the servant[2] or that the atoning function of the community was derived from, or connected with, the Servant's mission.[3] Among "mainstream Judaism," conceptions concerning the atoning value of a righteous man's death were arising as a response to the martyrdoms of Maccabean times, but these ideas developed independently of Is. 53.[4]

---

[1] Rowley, "Suffering Servant," 89-90.

[2] Van der Woude, <u>Messianischen Vorstellungen</u>, 165-9; J. Carmignac, "Citations," 383; Raymond E. Brown, "The Messianism of Qumran," <u>CBQ</u>, XIX (1957), 66-72; Burrows, <u>More Light</u>, 336. Passages adduced are 1QS 5:5ff, 8:3ff, 9:4, 1QH 3, 7:10, 7:26ff, 8:26ff. And note Carmignac's comments with respect to the allusions: "Le petit nombre de ces citations et, dans la plupart des cas, leur insignificance théologique donnent l'impression que ces 'Poèmes du Serviteur' n'ont pas spécialement marqué l'auteur des 'Hymnes.'" ("Citations," 383).

[3] Atonement does figure in the community's conception of its purposes but, " . . . it seems unlikely that the suffering which the community and its leaders had to undergo were regarded as atoning." (Gärtner, <u>Temple</u>, 126). Cf. also Lohse, <u>Märtyrer</u>, 219; Wiard Popkes, <u>Christus Traditus: Eine Untersuchung zum Begriff der Dahingabe im Neuen Testament</u>, ATANT, XLIV (Zürich/Stuttgart: Zwingli, 1967), 70-71; Braun, <u>Qumran</u>, II, 317; Jean Carmignac, "La théologie de la souffrance dans les Hymnes de Qumrân," <u>RevQ</u>, III (1961), 383: " . . . Dieu pardonne les péchés de ses élus, mais lorsque les modalités de ce pardon sont indiquées, il est mis en relation soit avec des rites liturgiques . . . , soit avec l'entrée dans la communauté . . . , mais jamais avec une veritable 'compensation' fournie par le pécheur ou par une autre personne." 1QS 8:3 is the passage that gives the strongest support for linking suffering with atonement at Qumran. In a passage describing the Council of 12 men and 3 priests, it is said that their duty is "to maintain loyalty in the land, with integrity of purpose and a broken spirit; to expiate wrongdoing as men who uphold the righteous cause or act justly and who endure the afflictions of the refiner's furnace . . . " (ולרצת עון עושׂי משפט וצרת מצרף . . .) and further in vv. 6ff they are called "true witnesses to judgment, and the chosen of grace to atone for the land" (עדי אמת למשפט ובחירי רצון לכפר בעד הארץ -- translations from Black, <u>The Scrolls</u>, 128). However, the cultic language that predominates in vv. 5-6 may suggest that this concept, as often, is the dominant impulse. (Cf. Pierre Benoit, "Qumrân et le Nouveau Testament," <u>NTS</u>, VII (1960-61), 283). It should be noted that the reference to suffering is separated from the reference to "atoning for the land" by several verses. Moreover, there is nothing in the context that is reminiscent of the servant.

[4] Lohse, <u>Märtyrer</u>, 64-110.

The evidence from late Judaism relating to the Servant presents, therefore, a contradictory picture: " . . . in dem gleichen Augenblick, da das Spätjudentum Züge des Knechtes aus Jes. 53 in sein Messiasbild einzeichnet, die Botschaft dieser grossen Prophetie von der Einzigartigkeit seines Leidens, von der Frucht seiner Stellvertretung und der Vollendung seines Sieges für die spätjüdische Gemeinde verlorenging."[1] While it seems that the Qumran community came closest to a true apprehension of the significance of the Servant's mission, even there it does not seem that the concept of a suffering which led to forgiveness of sins for others was linked with the servant conception. It would, of course, be presumptuous to deny the existence of any pre-Christian doctrine of a suffering Messiah based on, or influenced by, the Servant conception, but it must have been at best, "marginal and weak."[2] In relation to our present investigation, this means "dass darum von der Übertragung eines geläufigen Deutungsschemas auf Jesus schwerlich die Rede sein kann."[3]

---

[1]Wolff, Jesaja 53, 43.

[2]Cullmann, Christology, 60. For this view, see also Wilhelm Bousset, Kyrios Christos: A History of the Belief in Christ from the Beginnings of Christianity to Irenaeus, trans. by John E. Steely (Nashville: Abingdon, 1970), 56; Eduard Schweizer, Erniedrigung und Erhohung bei Jesus und Seinen Nachfolgern, ATANT, XXVIII (Zürich: Zwingli, 1962), 72; Werner Georg Kümmel, Promise and Fulfillment, trans. by Dorothea M. Barton, SBT, XXIII (London: SCM, 1957), 73; Richard N. Longenecker, The Christology of Early Jewish Christianity, SBT, n.s. XVII (London: SCM, 1970), 105; Reginald H. Fuller, The Foundations of New Testament Christology (London: Lutterworth, 1965), 46; Leonhard Goppelt, Theologie des Neuen Testaments Part I: Jesu Wirken in Seiner theologischen Bedeutung, ed. Jürgen Roloff (Gottingen: Vandenhoeck & Ruprecht, 1975), 238-39; George Eldon Ladd, A Theology of the New Testament (Grand Rapids: Eerdmans, 1974), 156; Frederick Houk Borsch, The Son of Man in Myth and History (London: SCM, 1967), 175; Rowley, "The Suffering Servant and the Davidic Messiah," Servant of the Lord; Hooker, Servant, 61.

[3]Jürgen Roloff, "Anfänge der Soteriologischen Deutung des Todes Jesu (Mk. x. 45 und Lk. xxii. 27)," NTS, XIX (1972-1973), 44; cf. also Ferdinand Hahn, The Titles of Jesus in Christology, trans. by Harold Knight and George Ogg (London: Lutterworth, 1969), 55.

As a result of this cursory survey, it may be concluded that, while individual traits of the Servant were applied to various figures (The Teacher of Righteousness, the Qumran community, the figure described in I Enoch and Test. Benj. 3:8), no concept of an "atoning Servant" lay at hand in the time of Christ. It must be asserted, however, that such a conception did exist in Isaiah itself, connected, in the case of the Fourth Servant Song at least, with an individual figure of the future. Both these facets of the issue must be borne in mind as we turn to investigate the evidence for the influence of the Servant conception on the gospel passion texts.

The Passion Predictions (Son of Man)

That Jesus believed Himself to be going to the cross in accordance with God's plan as revealed in the OT scriptures is a basic motif developed by each of the evangelists. This conviction is expressed primarily in quotations of or allusions to specific OT passages. In addition, on several occasions, Jesus expresses this fundamental belief in general terms, without, apparently, alluding to any particular scriptural context (Mk. 14:21 = Mt. 26:24 = Lk. 22:22; Mk. 14:49 = Mt. 26:56; Mt. 26:54). Are these examples to be seen as the earliest attempts to link Jesus' Passion to the OT, expressed as a postulate and prior to the adducing of specific "proof-texts"?[1] This seems unlikely, for two reasons. First, as Barrett says, " . . . if Jesus predicted his death (and there is no reason why he should not have done so), he also interpreted it."[2] Such an interpretation

---

[1] " . . . the witness of the scripture may have been spoken of before it was really adduced." (Martin Dibelius, From Tradition to Gospel, trans. by Bertram Lee Woolf (2nd ed.; London: Ivor Nicholson and Watson, 1934), 184). Cf. also Hahn, Titles of Jesus, 8-9 (who regards these announcements without scriptural allusion as more primitive).

[2] C. K. Barrett, Jesus and the Gospel Tradition (London: SPCK, 1967), 38. For the overwhelming evidence that Jesus predicted his own death, see especially Heinz Schürmann, "Wie hat Jesus seinen Tod

The Isaianic Servant Songs   87

implies the utilization of specific texts. Secondly, it is both historically and editorially more credible that the briefer, general sayings, found later in the gospels, presuppose the earlier, more specific ones, than vice versa.

It is presumably Mark who is responsible for the dramatic arrangement of the three parallel "passion predictions," which occur between the climactic Messianic confession of Peter and the final entry into Jerusalem.[1] These sayings, reproduced in essence by Matthew and Luke (Mk. 8:31 = Mt. 16:21 = Lk. 9:22; Mk. 9:31 = Mt. 17:22b-23 = Lk. 9:44b; Mk. 10:33-34 = Mt. 20:18-19 = Lk. 18:31b-33), along with two closely related logia, Mk. 9:12b and Lk. 17:25, have several recurring features in common: the Son of Man title; the element of necessity; and the use of the passive voice of παραδίδωμι to designate Jesus' betrayal.

That the OT provides an important foundation for these announcements is clear from the express allusion to scripture in Mk. 9:12b (γέγραπται), and Lk. 18:31b (τελεσθήσεται πάντα τὰ γεγραμμένα διὰ τῶν προφητῶν), as well as in Mk. 14:21 and 14:49. This conviction is strengthened by the recognition that δεῖ is probably to be understood as a reference to necessity <u>according to the scriptures</u>.[2] However, the determination of the specific OT

---

bestanden und verstanden?" Eine methodenkritische Besinnung," <u>Orientierung an Jesu: Zur Theologie der Synoptiker (Josef Schmid)</u>, ed. by Paul Hoffmann, with Norbert Brox and Wilhelm Pesch (Freiburg: Herder, 1973), 325-363.

[1] H. E. Tödt, <u>The Son of Man in the Synoptic Tradition</u>, trans. by Dorothea M. Barton (London: SCM, 1965), 145-148; Ralph P. Martin, <u>Mark: Evangelist and Theologian</u> (Exeter: Paternoster, 1972), 189-90.

[2] The connection between δεῖ and the Scriptures is not at all close in the NT. Only three times does it occur with specific reference to the accomplishment of prophecies, and in each case it is used in combination with another, more usual introductory word (Mt. 24:44, Lk. 22:37, Acts 1:16). Therefore it is not surprising that the reference to the OT, when δεῖ occurs by itself in the passion predictions,

passages thereby alluded to is a matter of considerable disagreement. It will be necessary to consider certain words and phrases from the sayings for evidence of influence from particular passages.

Perhaps the place to begin is with the most clear-cut allusions in the Passion sayings, the use of ἐμπτύω and μαστιγόω in Mk. 10:33-4 par. ἐμπτύω and its cognate noun occur only three times in the LXX and the verb is used in the NT only in predictions of, or descriptions of, Jesus' mockery.[1] One of the Septuagintal occurrences (in noun form) is Is. 50:6, a portion of the third "Servant Song."[2] That this text lies behind the occurrence of ἐμπτύω here is rendered likely by the use of μαστιγόω, which, like ἐμπτύω, is found in its cognate form in Is. 50:6 as well. While μαστιγόω alone would not

---

has been disputed.
    Ernst Lohmeyer (Das Evangelium des Markus, MeyerK, II (17th ed.; Göttingen: Vandenhoeck & Ruprecht, 1967), 166) has argued that the primitive passion Kerygma was founded on an apocalyptic eschatological "law of sufferings" which was intimately related to the Son of Man title itself: "Aus dem Gesetz Seines Wesens folgt das Gesetz Seines Leidens; und da dieses Gesetz von Gott her ist, leidet Er, weil er von Gottes Art ist, und ist Er von Gottes Art, weil er leidet." Erich Fascher seems to distinguish in a similar manner between apocalyptic and prophetic "necessity" ("Theologische Beobachtungen zu δεῖ," Neutestamentliche Studien für Rudolf Bultmann, BZNW, XXI (2nd ed.; Berlin: Alfred Töpelmann, 1957), 239-240). However, Tödt raises cogent objections to this interpretation (Son of Man, 188-191). He notes that the use of δεῖ to denote "apocalyptic eschatological regularity" is found only in Dan. 2:28 and that the general NT application of the word does not bear out Lohmeyer's thesis. The word δεῖ undergoes a transformation in the NT, in which the original impersonal and fatalistic connotations of the term are personalized under the conviction that necessity arises from the will of a personal God (Grundmann, "δεῖ, δέον, ἐστί," TDNT, III, 23). But the particular element which mediates this will to men must be determined in each respective context. Thus, the grounding of Jesus' sufferings in the OT revelation in formulations parallel to those with δεῖ, in addition to specific OT allusions in these sayings, is conclusive evidence that δεῖ implies a necessity based on OT prophecy. Bennett, indeed, seeks to reverse the tables by claiming that the meaning of γέγραπται should be supplied by δεῖ, but this attempt to define the specific term by reference to the general is methodologically objectionable ("'The Son of Man must . . . ,'" NovT, XVII (1975), 128).

    [1] Mk. 10:34 = Lk. 18:32; Mk. 14:65 = Mt. 26:67; Mk. 15:19 = Mt. 27:30.

    [2] Although the attribution of Is. 50:4-10 to the Servant Songs is disputed by Coppens (Messianisme, 49-51).

The Isaianic Servant Songs   89

unambiguously point to Is. 50:6,[1] the occurrence of the two together, in addition to the use of ἐμπτύω again, with other references to Is. 50:6, in Mk. 14:65, is conclusive evidence for the existence of an allusion. Thus, the most unambiguous OT allusions in the sayings establish a prima facie case for the influence of the Suffering Servant conception on the predictions of Jesus' passion. This evidence is not entirely free from doubt, however, since the allusions occur in a saying which may be an elaboration of a simpler, more basic, form.

There can be little doubt that ἀποδοκιμάζω, found in Mk. 8:31 = Lk. 9:22 and Lk. 17:25, is taken from the "rejected stone" testimonium of Ps. 118:22.[2] The word is employed nine times in the NT, five of them in direct connection with Ps. 118:22. The situation is more problematic with regard to the use of ἐξουδενέω in Mk. 9:12b. ἐξουδενέω is a legitimate translation of מאס in Ps. 118:22 (9t. in LXX), a translation attested, in fact, in the citation of Ps. 118:22 in Acts 4:11, so that the use of the word in Mk. 9:12b may be a variant

---

[1] μαστιγόω is not infrequent in the LXX (30tt.) and could be the Greek equivalent of the Latin penal term verberatio (BAG, 496).

[2] Georg Strecker, "Die Leidens- und Auferstehungs-voraussagen im Markusevangelium," ZTK, LXIV (1967), 26; Gerhard Delling, Der Kreuzestod Jesu in der urchristlichen Verkündigung (Göttingen: Vandenhoeck & Ruprecht, 1972), 60; Paul Hoffmann, "Mk 8, 31. Zur Herkunft und markinischen Rezeption einer alten Überlieferung," Orientierung an Jesu, 177-8; Hooker, Son of Man, 114; C. E. B. Cranfield, The Gospel According to Saint Mark, CGTC (Cambridge: University Press, 1959), 277-8; M.-J. Lagrange, Évangile Selon Saint Luc, EBib (6th ed.; Paris: J. Gabalda, 1941), 267. Objections to this derivation have been raised. Bennett ("'The Son of Man must . . . '") claims that מאס is frequently used of religious rejection (cf. 1QH 4:8) and need not indicate reliance on Ps. 118:22. Fuller (The Mission and Achievement of Jesus, SBT, XII (London: SCM, 1954), 56-57) asserts that ἀποδοκιμάζω is a "legitimate paraphrase" of Is. 53:3 בזה. Michaelis ("πάσχω," TDNT, V, 915) and A. R. C. Leaney (A Commentary on the Gospel According to St. Luke, BNTC (London: Adam & Charles Black, 1958), 165) refer to Is. 53 in general. However, בזה is never translated by ἀποδοκιμάζω in LXX, and the NT use of the word must be the decisive criterion.

of ἀποδοκιμάζω.[1] However, it is also urged that ἐξουδενέω refers to Is. 53:3, since בזה, used twice in the verse, often is translated by ἐξουδενέω, as it is in A, Σ and θ in Is. 53:3.[2] ἐξουδενέω in the Acts 4:11 citation may, then, be an importation from the Is. 53-influenced Passion Kerygma (cf. also Lk. 23:11).[3] A third alternative is Ps. 89:39, in which ἐξουδενέω (= מאס) is employed in a passage that expressly speaks of the rejection by Israel of its Messiah (משיחו; note also the reference to the spurning of "the covenant of thy servant" in v. 40).[4] The influence of Ps. 118:22 in similar sayings provides a solid basis for ascribing ἐξουδενέω to the same OT background. But, it must then be asked why a different word was substituted: Mark uses ἀποδοκιμάζω in both his references to Ps. 118:22 (Mk. 8:3; 12:10) and nowhere else employs ἐξουδενέω. While influence from Ps. 89:39 cannot be ruled out, the fact that this psalm is not used in the Passion Narrative or predictions of suffering is against the suggestion. There is little to be said for or against the derivation from Is. 53:3. Another line of investigation may contribute to the resolution of this ambiguity. The fact that Mk. 9:12b

---

[1] See especially, Tödt, Son of Man, 166-8; also Hahn, Titles of Jesus, 41 and Lloyd Gaston, No Stone on Another: Studies in the Significance of the Fall of Jerusalem in the Synoptic Gospels, NovTSup, XXIII (Leiden: E. J. Brill, 1970), 400.

[2] Zimmerli-Jeremias, Servant, 90; C. H. Dodd, According to the Scriptures: The Substructure of New Testament Theology, Fontana Books (London: Collins, 1952), 92; Barnabas Lindars, New Testament Apologetic: The Doctrinal Significance of the Old Testament Quotations (London: SCM, 1961), 81; Fuller, Mission and Achievement, 56; Michaelis, "πάσχω," 915, n. 79; France, Jesus, 126; Ezra P. Gould, A Critical and Exegetical Commentary on the Gospel According to St. Mark, ICC (Edinburgh: T & T Clark, 1896), 165; Cranfield, Mark, 298; Walter Grundmann, "Sohn Gottes," ZNW, XLVII (1956), 122.

[3] Lindars, Apologetic, 81.

[4] Rudolf Pesch, "Die Passion des Menschensohnes: Eine Studie zu den Menschenworten der vormarkinischen Passionsgeschichte," Jesus und der Menschensohn (für Anton Vögtle), ed. Rudolf Pesch and Rudolf Schnackenburg, in cooperation with Odilo Kaiser (Freiburg/Basel/Vienna: Herder, 1975), 174; cf. Dodd, According to the Scriptures, 97; Wolff, Jesaja 53, 67.

is introduced with an explicit scriptural reference (γέγραπται) indicates that the phrase πολλὰ παθεῖν, like ἐξουδενηθῇ, must have a basis in the OT. Ps. 34:20 (LXX πολλαὶ αἱ θλίψεις τῶν δικαίων) is sometimes cited as the appropriate parallel,[1] but it is doubtful that the necessity for Jesus' uniquely important sufferings would have been derived from a gnomic statement of this kind. If ἐξουδενηθῇ and πολλὰ παθεῖν are to be taken closely together, Is. 53:3 would be decisively favored, because the list of the servant's afflictions in vv. 3-7 may be admirably described as a "suffering many things," while nothing in the context of Ps. 118:22 could be so characterized.[2] However, it is not certain that both parts of the saying need be derived from the same OT passage (note especially that Lk. 17:25 has πολλὰ παθεῖν with ἀποδοκιμάσω) and it is perhaps more likely that πολλὰ παθεῖν is meant as a general reference to the various scriptural prefigurements of Jesus' sufferings: "Jesus ist nicht an einer 'Stelle' gelegen, sondern an der Schrift."[3] It cannot, therefore, be concluded with certainty what OT passage ἐξουδενέω has been derived from, but the balance of probabilities favors Is. 53:3.

---

[1] Pesch, "Passion des Menschensohnes," 168; cf. Hoffmann, "Mk 8, 31," 181; Tödt, Son of Man, 167; and Heinz Schürmann, Das Lukasevangelium, Vol. I: Kommentar zu Kap. 1, 1-9, 50, HTKNT, III (Freiburg/Basel/Vienna: Herder, 1969), 534.

[2] Fuller, Mission and Achievement, 56; Rudolf Otto, The Kingdom of God and the Son of Man, trans. by Floyd V. Filson and Bertram Lee Woolf (London: Lutterworth Press, 1938), 251. Michaelis ("πάσχω," 915) seeks to derive πολλὰ παθεῖν from Is. 53 linguistically. He notes that πάσχω in NT is sometimes translated by Syr. "saibar," "to bear, endure," which may be derived from Heb. סבל, used in Is. 53:4, 11. (See also Walter Grundmann, Das Evangelium nach Lukas, THKNT, III (2nd ed.; Berlin: Evangelische Verlagsanstalt, n.d.), 169; and William L. Lane, The Gospel According to Mark, NIC (Grand Rapids: Eerdmans, 1974), 30). The parallel is, however, improbable for saibar never translates πάσχω in the Passion sayings.

[3] Wolff, Jesaja 53, 68.

A recurring element in the Passion sayings is the use of παραδίδωμι in the passive (Mk. 9:31 par., 10:33-4 par., 14:21 par., 14:41 par., Mt. 26:2). A general term that has a variety of connotations in the NT, παραδίδωμι becomes "Mk.'s technical term for Jesus' passion"[1] and for the betrayal of Jesus by Judas (who is ὁ παραδιδούς : Mk. 14:42 par., 14:44 par., Mt. 26:25, Jn. 18:5). However, this application of the word by no means exhausts its connotations with respect to Jesus' passion, for behind Judas' action stands the initiative of God the Father, Who delivers His Son into the hands of men. We are, no doubt, to see this theological conception behind the passive use of παραδίδωμι in the Passion sayings.[2] While παραδίδωμι may simply be a reflection of contemporary secular use of the word,[3] the strong element of scriptural necessity that pervades the sayings raises the possibility that it is related to, or derived from, an OT passage.[4]

---

[1] Werner H. Kelber, "The Hour of the Son of Man and the Temptation of the Disciples (Mk. 14:32-42)," The Passion in Mark: Studies on Mark 14-16, ed. by Werner H. Kelber (Philadelphia: Fortress, 1976), 51.

[2] Cranfield, Mark, 306; Vincent Taylor, The Gospel According to St. Mark (2nd ed.; London: MacMillan, 1966), 403. The passive is the "reverential" passive, the subject being God (Tödt, Son of Man, 158; Zimmerli-Jeremias, Servant, 96; Hooker, Son of Man, 135; Roloff, "Anfänge," 40 n.; Fror, Biblische Hermeneutik, 341). W. Kramer (Christ, Lord, Son of God, SBT, L, trans. by Brian Hardy (London: SCM, 1966), 117) suggests that παραδίδωμι may have originally been related to Christ's coming into the world -- an interpretation that has close analogies to that advocated above.

[3] Norman Perrin, "The Use of (Para)didonai in connection with the Passion of Jesus in the New Testament," Der Ruf Jesu und die Antwort der Gemeinde (für Joachim Jeremias), ed. by Eduard Lohse, Christoph Burchard and Berndt Schaller (Göttingen: Vandenhoeck & Ruprecht, 1970), 204-210. This secular sense of παραδίδωμι, used especially in judicial contexts, is to be seen in the trial narratives (i.e. Mk. 15:1,15) where no theological or scriptural significance should be attached to the word (contra. Taylor, Mark, 578; Joseph Blinzler, Der Prozess Jesu (2nd ed.; Regensburg: Friedrich Pustest, 1955), 173).

[4] Popkes (Christus Traditus, 224) believes the Christological Dahingabe sayings were derived from a combination of influences from Jewish "righteous-sufferer-martyr" theology and apocalyptic traditions. (Pesch ("Passion des Menschensohnes," 176) and Georg Bertram (Die Leidensgeschichte Jesu und der Christuskult: Eine formgeschichtliche

This OT background has frequently been found in Is. 53. Jeremias notes that Rom. 4:25 ($παρεδόθη \ διὰ \ τὰ \ παραπτώματα \ ἡμῶν$) is a literal translation of the Tg. on Is. 53:5 (אֲנַחְנָא חָטֵינָא) and suggests that all the NT passive $παραδίδωμι$ sayings have been derived from this verse.[1] $παραδίδωμι$ figures prominently in the LXX of Is. 53, being used once in the active (v. 6) and twice in the passive (v. 12). It is possible that Paul alludes to the LXX of Is. 53:12 in Rom. 4:25 rather than the Tg. on 53:5, and Rom. 8:32 certainly alludes to Is. 53:6.[2] There is, therefore, some basis for relating the Christological "deliverance" sayings to the linguistic influence of the Fourth Servant Song, particularly the last phrase of v. 12: $διὰ \ τὰς \ ἁμαρτίας \ αὐτῶν \ παρεδόθη$.[3] This derivation has not, however, gone unchallenged. Tödt claims that $παραδίδωμι$, in view of its widespread use, is by itself insufficient to prove dependence on Is. 53:

> The term "to be delivered" provides conclusive evidence for the dependence of a synoptic text upon Isa. 53 only if this term is combined in the synoptic text with a phrase similar to one in Isa. 53.

Untersuchung, FRLANT, XV (Göttingen: Vandenhoeck & Ruprecht, 1922), 20) similarly stress the passio justi background.) However, as Popkes himself admits (p. 78), the characteristic formulation in the martyrologies stresses the active self-giving of the victim, rather than the surrendering up by God, prominent in the Passion sayings. The use of $παραδίδωμι$ in the righteous sufferer psalms is not amenable to this interpretation, since the word is generally used there in pleas from the psalmist(s) that God not betray them to their enemies. For another possible background, see Borsch (Son of Man, 289-91) who sees sacrificial connotations in the use of the word.

[1]Zimmerli-Jeremias, Servant, 96; Joachim Jeremias, New Testament Theology, Vol. I: The Proclamation of Jesus, trans. by John Bowden (London: SCM, 1971), 286, 296.

[2]C. E. B. Cranfield, A Critical and Exegetical Commentary on the Epistle to the Romans, ICC, n.s. (2 vols.; Edinburgh: T & T Clark, 1975-), 251. Note also I Cor. 11:23, Gal. 2:20, Eph. 5:2.

[3]Lindars, Apologetic, 80; Matthew Black, "Christological Use," 5; Walter Grundmann, Das Evangelium nach Markus, THKNT, II (2nd ed.; Berlin: Evangelische Verlagsanstalt, n.d.), 193.

He also asserts that, while παραδίδωμι alone can hardly be characterized as a "formula" (contra. Jeremias), the expression "to be delivered into the hands of . . . " becomes a "formula-like" saying, but this phrase does not occur in Is. 53.[1] Perrin, in a <u>traditionsgeschichtliche</u> investigation, isolates three stages in the use of παραδίδωμι, according to which the term is used first with a non-theological, descriptive force, then with an apologetic emphasis, finally with a soteriological thrust (Rom. 4:25, 8:32). The Passion predictions fit in the second category and therefore evidence a stage in the tradition before Is. 53 had been used to interpret Jesus' death.[2] However, Mk. 10:33-34 uses παραδίδωμι alongside language drawn from, if not Is. 53, the third Servant Song, and Perrin's suggested traditions-history, with its "pre-soteriological" stage, probably is not well-founded. As Black says:

> This is a distinction within the tradition which it is impossible to prove: a far higher degree of probability attaches to the opposite proposition that those prophecies were soteriological from the start whether they were actually uttered by Jesus or not.[3]

Furthermore, Perrin must suppose that Mk. 10:45 and Rom. 4:25 stem from a stage in the history of the tradition <u>later</u> than the passion predictions, but this is questionable in light of the greater Semitic flavor in these two sayings than in the passion predictions.[4]

---

[1]Tödt, Son of Man, 156-61. It should be noted that Fuller (Mission and Achievement, 58) does seek to relate "into the hands of . . . " to Is. 53:3, though his argument is hardly convincing.

[2]Perrin, "Use of (Para)didonai," 208; Cf. also Tödt, Son of Man, 161. The dependence of παραδίδωμι on Is. 53 is disputed by Hooker, Servant, 95; Alfred Suhl, Die Funktion der alttestamentlichen Zitate und Anspielungen im Markusevangelium (Gütersloh: Mohn, 1965), 126; Martin, Mark, 193-194; B. M. F. van Iersel, "Der Sohn" in den synoptischen Jesusworten, NovTSup, III (Leiden: E. J. Brill, 1961), 57, Roloff, "Anfänge," 42, n. 2.

[3]Matthew Black, "The 'Son of Man' Passion Sayings in the Gospel Tradition," ZNW, LX (1969), 4.

[4]On Mk. 10:45, cf., infra, 122-27.

To return to Tödt's objections: it is not legitimate to speak of "to be delivered into the hands of . . . " as a "formula-like" expression, when παραδίδωμι is found without the prepositional phrase in a majority of its occurrences in the Passion sayings (Mk. 10:33-34 par., Mt. 26:2, Mk. 14:21 par.), and the criterion for an OT allusion advocated in the quotation above is far too rigid.

Some difficulty remains, however, with the derivation of passive παραδίδωμι from Is. 53. The subject of the phrase which Jeremias adduces from the Targum to Is. 53:5 is "sanctuary," not the servant.[1] And the use of παραδίδωμι in the LXX does not correspond to the Hebrew Vorlage, rendering it difficult to attribute the expression to Jesus, which, on the basis of its ubiquity, seems necessary.[2] However, even if παραδίδωμι cannot be derived from Is. 53 linguistically, the influence of that prophecy on the concept evoked by that word can hardly be denied.

At this point, it is important to recall what was said earlier about the significance of παραδίδωμι in the Passion sayings. Not only the betrayal by Judas on the human plane, but, more importantly, the deliverance of the Son of Man to the maltreatment of sinful men by the initiative of God Himself is evoked by the term. If, however,

---

[1] והוא יבנ׳ בית מקדשא דאיתחל בחוב נא אתמסר בעויתנא.
It is possible, of course, that the early Christians would simply have "bracketed" the sanctuary phrase and related the verse to the servant (Jeremias, New Testament Theology, I, 296, n. 4, following Hagermann), but it cannot be proven that it was a later (post-Christian) insertion (Seidelin, "'Ebed Jahwe," 212).

[2] נתן, the Heb. word in v. 12, is not rendered elsewhere by παραδίδωμι, although it must be noted that נתן (14tt. in the MT) has here an unusual sense (cf. BDB, 788). παραδίδωμι renders פגע only in v. 6, v. 12 and Is. 47:3. Katz claims that, in the LXX translation of Is., παραδίδωμι was "one of its guess words applied wherever there was a blank in this translator's very imperfect Hebrew." ("Justin's Old Testament Quotations," 348). However, France's attempt to distinguish between παραδίδωμι in the Passion sayings as referring to betrayal and παραδίδωμι in Is. 53 as referring to death, fails to take into consideration the wider implications of παραδίδωμι, noted above (Jesus, 126).

this significant theological conception underlies the παραδίδωμι Passion sayings, which are explicitly based on the Scriptures, Isaiah 53 presents itself as the natural background for this idea. For here, as nowhere else in the OT, are the sufferings of the (Messianic) figure explicitly and consistently attributed to the activity of Yahweh: " . . . the Lord has caused the iniquity of us all to fall on him" (v. 6); " . . . the Lord was pleased to crush him . . . " (v. 10). It is instructive that Jesus chooses to express a very similar sentiment in words taken from Is. 53:12 in Lk. 22:37: "He will be reckoned [or God will cause him to be reckoned?] with the transgressors." In the passion sayings, Jesus chooses to express succinctly this concept, so basic to His mission, through the widely used Aram. מסר, which is used 4tt. in Is. 53. Not only is παραδίδωμι a natural equivalent for מסר,[1] but it can be supposed that the evangelists sought to preserve this reference to Is. 53 by using the Greek word found three times in the LXX of that chapter. The formulation with the passive and the ambiguity of the term lent itself admirably to Jesus' desire to veil His status, while at the same time being sufficiently clear so as to enable those "with ears to hear" to recognize the truth of the matter. Therefore, linguistically, the influence of Is. 53 comes indirectly through the Aramaic מסר, but the crucial correspondence exists in the conceptual similarity: It is Jesus' destiny, as the Servant's, to be given over to sinful man by God.[2]

---

[1] מסר is "ein volles Äquivalent zu paradidonai." (Popkes, Christus Traditus, 21). מסר is used only twice in Biblical Hebrew (Num. 31:5, 16) with uncertain meaning, but it became very popular in Rabbinic Hebrew (Cranfield, Mark, 306).

[2] It should be noted that these remarks apply only to the use of παραδίδωμι in Christological affirmations regarding Jesus' suffering. Thus, the word is used frequently in the Passion Narrative as a judicial term and cannot, in these contexts, be linked to Is. 53. It is probably true, therefore, that one cannot speak of a "παραδίδωμι formula" (Hahn, Christology, 59).

The specific OT passages which have influenced the Synoptic Passion sayings are, therefore, Is. 50:6 (μάστιγόω, ἐμπτύω), Is. 53(:12) (παραδίδωμι), and Ps. 118:22 (ἀποδοκιμάζω),[1] while a general reference to those scriptures understood to indicate the necessity of Messianic suffering is implied by πολλὰ παθεῖν.[2]

As far as the method of appropriation is concerned, it must be said that the allusions to Is. 50:6 are applied with the same reference as in the OT context, and the text (probably LXX) has not been modified. The use of παραδίδωμι, as we have argued, implies a broader, conceptual link, assisted, perhaps, through the Tg. מסר -- LXX παραδίδωμι linguistic contact. The ultimate legitimacy of the allusions depends upon the basic hermeneutical process whereby the Servant Songs were applied to Jesus. With this situation, it is necessary to turn to the Johannine passion predictions, which, like their synoptic counterparts, utilize (usually) the Son of Man title.

The Son of Man in John's Gospel possesses several features which are somewhat distinct in comparison with the synoptic portrayal, yet some significant affinities must not be overlooked, and it is probable that the Johannine Son of Man sayings are solidly founded upon earlier tradition.[3] As in the synoptic logia, Jesus links the

---

[1] A link between Ps. 118:22 and Is. 53 has been seen in Tg. Ps. 118:22-29, where טליא ("lamb," "son") occurs, and the description of the stone has certain similarities with the task of the servant. (Bertil Gärtner, "טליא als Messiasbezeichnung," SEÅ, XVIII-XIX (1953-1954), 100-104).

[2] An attempt is sometimes made to distinguish between Passion formulations without reference to the OT and those with such influence, the latter representing a secondary stage of the tradition which has taken over the motive of scriptural fulfillment from the Passion Narrative (cf. Hahn, Titles, 41-2). Against this it must be firmly asserted that the scriptural element is constitutive to these sayings. It is improbable that a traditionsgeschichtliche distinction among the sayings can be made. As Hahn admits: "In spite of the mixed forms and the somewhat more sharply devious later formulations they show an astonishing unity, a sign of the power exercised by the underlying Christological conception in the primitive church." (42).

[3] See especially Stephen S. Smalley, "The Johannine Son of Man

destiny of the Son of Man with a divinely imposed necessity (δεῖ).[1] For our purposes, two particular concepts, associated with these sayings, require investigation: "to be lifted up" (ὑψόω) and "to be glorified" (δοξάζω). As the latter concept is found in a wider sphere than Son of Man sayings only, these will engage our attention at the same time.

That both ὑψόω and δοξάζω can have reference to Jesus' death in John's Gospel is clear; the former always carries with it this connotation,[2] the latter on several occasions.[3] Not only does ὑψόω manifestly refer to Jesus' death, but it also indicates the particular manner of death, as the comparison with the serpent in 3:14 and the explicit interpretation in 12:33 demonstrate. But that ὑψόω signifies more than death by crucifixion seems equally clear;[4]

Sayings," NTS, XV (1968-9), 278-301. That "Son of Man" in John is simply a variant for "Son of God" cannot seriously be considered (contra. E. D. Freed, "The Son of Man in the Fourth Gospel," JBL, LXXXVI (1967), 402-9).

[1] Jn. 3:14, 12:34 (the crowd's interpretation of Jesus' words in v. 32).

[2] Jn. 3:14, 8:28, 12:32,34; each time "Son of Man" is used. That ὑψόω signifies death in these verses is made explicit in 12:33, a comment on Jesus' preceding statement about the "lifting up" of the Son of Man: τοῦτο δὲ ἔλεγεν σημαίνων ποίῳ θανάτῳ ἤμελλεν ἀποθνῄσκειν (on this passage, see especially C. H. Dodd, The Interpretation of the Fourth Gospel (Cambridge: University Press, 1965), 378-9). Schulz disputes the connection with Jesus' death in 3:14, but without adequate substantiation (Untersuchungen zur Menschensohn - Christologie im Johannesevangelium. Zugleich ein Beitrag zur Methodengeschichte der Auslegung des 4 Evangeliums (Göttingen: Vandenhoeck & Ruprecht, 1957), 107-8). Interestingly, ὕψωτε in 8:28 apparently implies that men do the "lifting up." In the context, this almost certainly means "bring to the gallows" (Georg Bertram, "ὕψος, . . . " TDNT, VIII, 610; more fully, Dodd, The Fourth Gospel, 376-7).

[3] Note especially 12:23ff, where the hour of the Son of Man's glorification is interpreted in terms of the seed that must die before it bears fruit. The connection of Jesus' δόξα with His death is almost certainly to be seen in 13:31, 7:39 and 12:16 as well.

[4] Contra. J. H. Bernard, A Critical and Exegetical Commentary on the Gospel According to St. John, ICC (2 vols.; Edinburgh: T & T Clark, 1928), I, 113.

the word is consistently applied elsewhere in the NT to the exaltation of Christ (cf. Acts 2:33; 5:31; Phil. 2:9 (ὑπερυψόω). Thus, as Dodd expresses it:

> The death of Christ by crucifixion, the only method of execution which (along with other modes of hanging) can appropriately be classified in the terms ὑψωθῆναι ἐκ τῆς γῆς, is a σημεῖον of the reality which is the exaltation and the glory of Christ.[1]

In the theology presented in the fourth gospel, the crucifixion is at the same moment the exaltation of Christ, a dual significance perfectly conveyed by the <u>double</u> <u>entendre</u> implied in ὑψόω. ὑψόω, by itself, would not have conveyed the sense of crucifixion and many scholars plausibly suggest that the two-fold connotation may have its source in a Hebrew or Aramaic word which meant both "crucify" and "exalt."[2] Unlike ὑψόω, δοξάζω does not connote death, but as Lindars puts it: ". . . the glory of Jesus as the Son of Man consists in his union with the Father, and the cross most fully reveals this because it is the ultimate expression of the union of His will with the Father."[3] The application of δοξάζω to Jesus' death is only

---

[1] Dodd, <u>The Fourth Gospel</u>, 379. "It is the upward swing of the great pendulum of the Incarnation corresponding to the descent of the Word which became flesh." (R. E. Brown, <u>The Gospel According to John</u>, AB, XXIX (2 vols.; London: Geoffrey Chapman, 1971), I, 146).

[2] Aram. קף can mean both "exalt" (cf. Targ. Job 13:11) and "impale" (cf. Ezra 6:11) and may lie behind ὑψόω in John's sayings (G. Kittel, "קףדזקּ= ὑψωθῆναι = gekreuzigt werden," <u>ZNW</u>, XXXV (1936), 282-5; Black, "Passion Sayings," 7; C. K. Barrett, <u>The Gospel According to St. John</u> (London: SPCK, 1955), 9; J. N. Sanders, <u>A Commentary on the Gospel According to St. John</u>, ed. and completed by B. A. Mastin, BNTC (London: Adam & Charles Black, 1968), 128; Barnabas Lindars, <u>The Gospel of John</u>, NCB (London: Oliphants, 1972), 157; Brown, <u>John</u>, I, 146). Dodd (<u>The Fourth Gospel</u>, 377-8) points out that in Gen. 40 (vv. 13, 16) "lift up the head" is a metaphor for both advancement to high office and decapitation and hanging, and that the Heb. word used here, נשא, is often translated by ὑψόω in LXX. This wordplay seems also to have been present in Greek circles, and Dodd conjectures that ὑψόω is used with reference to this popular background (cf. also Brown, <u>John</u>, I, 146).

It has even been suggested that John's Son of Man passion sayings, being more simple and based on a Semitic word-play, may be more ancient than the form of the sayings in the synoptic gospels (Black, "Passion Sayings," 7; Brown, <u>John</u>, I, 146).

[3] Barnabas Lindars, "The Son of Man in the Johannine Christology,"

derivative, therefore, dependent on the surrounding context, not inherent in the word.

The basis for this theologica crucis need not be found outside the mind of Jesus or the interpretation of the fourth evangelist, but it has persuasively been argued that the fourth servant song has contributed significantly to its development. Is. 52:13 (ἰδοὺ συνήσει ὁ παῖς μου καὶ ὑψωθήσεται καὶ δοξασθήσεται σφόδρα) furnishes a striking linguistic point of contact with the Johannine sayings: "Hier stehen die beiden joh. Leitbegriffe in gleicher Bedeutung nebeneinander."[1] In addition to this possible linguistic parallel, Blank points to a perhaps more significant conceptual similarity: ὑψόω in the NT always has reference to God's intervention to transform the circumstances of an individual from humiliation to glory and there is good reason for tracing this concept back to the influence of Is. 53.[2] If Jesus used the Aram. זקף, the allusion to Is. 52:13 would probably have been conveyed by the combination of the words "exalted" and "glorified."[3] The Greek text, as has been noted, reproduces two of the words in the LXX of Is. 52:13, but the meaning has been extended to include the idea of crucifixion, certainly not present in Is. 52:13.

Christ and Spirit in the New Testament: In honor of Charles Francis Digby Moule, ed. by Barnabas Lindars and Stephen S. Smalley (Cambridge: University Press, 1973), 48. See further on this: Kittel, "δοκέω, . . . " TDNT, II, 249; and especially Josef Blank, Krisis. Untersuchungen zur johanneischen Christologie und Eschatologie (Freiburg-im-Breisgau: Lambertus Verlag, 1964), 269, n. 12.

[1] R. Schnackenburg, "Der Menschensohn im Johannesevangelium," NTS, XI (1964-5), 130. Cf. also Dodd, Fourth Gospel, 247; Barrett, John, 179; Wolff, Jesaja 53, 85, n. 355; Smalley, "Son of Man," 291-2; Brown, John, I, 146; Reim, Hintergrund, 135; Blank, Krisis, 83; E. M. Sidebottom, "The Son of Man in the Fourth Gospel," ExpTim, LXVIII (1956-7), 235; Matthew Black, "From Schweitzer to Bultmann: The Modern Quest of the Historical Jesus," McCormick Quarterly, XX (1967), 280. On other suggested backgrounds and their unsuitability, see Blank, Krisis, 80-83.

[2] Blank, Krisis, 83.

[3] The MT has ירום ונשׂא וגבה מאד.

The Isaianic Servant Songs   101

It would be premature to claim that this discussion has satisfied the problems posed by the Passion sayings, for a most important element remains to be integrated: the Son of Man title. Hooker, disputing the influence of the Servant conception on these sayings, objects: " . . . he [Jesus] would hardly have appealed to his hearers concerning the things which are written of the Son of Man if he were referring primarily to passages which they connected with a totally different concept."[1] She asserts that the OT background for the sufferings of the Son of Man is to be found in Dan. 7, the only OT passage that is demonstrably linked to "Son of Man" in the NT. In Dan. 7, the identification of the Son of Man with the "saints of the most high," who suffer tribulation before attaining the kingdom, demonstrates that "the necessity for suffering and death is, contrary to expectation, integral to the concept of the Son of Man."[2] While this line of interpretation finds other advocates,[3] the attempt to transform the Son of Man into a suffering figure in Dan. 7 is not wholly successful. Though Israel is identified in some sense with the Son of Man (on the analogy of the beasts, it is probable that the Son of Man is a representative head, not merely a symbol[4]), the connection is

---

[1] Hooker, Servant, 96.   [2] Hooker, Son of Man, 142.

[3] Dodd, According to Scriptures, 117, n. 2; C. F. D. Moule, "From Defendant to Judge -- and Deliverer," The Phenomenon of the New Testament (London: SCM, 1967), 89; R. G. Hamerton-Kelly, Pre-existence, Wisdom and the Son of Man: A Study of the Idea of Pre-existence in the New Testament, SNTSMS, XXI (Cambridge: Cambridge University Press, 1973) 60. For the view that the Son of Man in Dan. 7 is a suffering figure, see Davies, Paul, 280 and Longenecker, Christology, 87. Black ("Servant of the Lord," 8, n. 1), Brownlee ("Servant," 8-15) and F. F. Bruce (This is That: The New Testament Development of Some Old Testament Themes (Exeter: Paternoster, 1968), 90-91) suggest that Daniel has been influenced by the Isaianic Suffering Servant conception (cf. "justification of many": Dan. 12:3 and Is. 53:11-12; Dan. 11:33 (מ שׂכי׳ל׃) and Is. 52:13 (ישׂכיל) (cf. also Wolff, Jesaja 53, 38, but, contra. C. K. Barrett, "The Background of Mark 10:45," New Testament Essays: Studies in Memory of Thomas Walter Manson, ed. by A. J. B. Higgins (Manchester: University Press, 1959), 2-3).

[4] Cullmann, Christology, 140; France, Jesus, 170-71; Barnabas

not made in <u>suffering</u>, but in glorification: "The saints suffered before the appearance of the Son of Man, for this is a figure for the saints only after they are invested with power."[1] The Son of Man is never associated with suffering in Jewish interpretations (although this could easily be accounted for),[2] and it is not, perhaps, by chance that Dan. 7 is explicitly alluded to only in Son of Man "coming" sayings.[3] Dan. 7 is, therefore, too fragile a foundation upon which to build the suffering Son of Man doctrine. The repeated emphasis on the "it is written" in these sayings " . . . demands something more than the possible implication that Daniel's 'one like a son of man' is a suffering figure."[4]

Other attempts have been made to explain the origin of the Son of Man Passion sayings by understanding suffering as an integral component of the "Son of Man" idea,[5] but the classic explanation for the sayings has been that they are the result of a fusion of the figure of the Son of Man with the Servant of the Lord: "Jesus' combination of <u>these</u> two titles was something completely new. 'Son of Man' represents the highest conceivable declaration of exaltation

---

Lindars, "Re-enter the Apocalyptic Son of Man," <u>NTS</u>, XXII (1975-76), 55; Cranfield, <u>Mark</u>, 274.

[1] Rowley, "The Suffering Servant and the Davidic Messiah," 64, n. 3; Jacques E. Menard, "<u>Pais Theou</u> as Messianic Title in the Book of Acts," <u>CBQ</u>, XIX (1957), 83-92.

[2] France, <u>Jesus</u>, 128.   [3] Cf. France, <u>Jesus</u>, 48.

[4] Bruce, <u>Old Testament Themes</u>, 98.

[5] Borsch (<u>Son of Man</u>) traces the figure back to near-Eastern King ideologies in which the royal figure symbolically "suffered and rose." Wilfred Stott ("'Son of Man' -- A Title of Abasement," <u>ExpTim</u>, LXXXIII (1972), 278-81) surveys the Biblical use of "Son of Man" and concludes it indicates "man in his frailty."

in Judaism; ebed Yahweh is the expression of deepest humiliation."[1] While the latter half of this contrast is not at present disputed, the former assertion is now widely questioned. A steadily growing consensus of scholarly opinion denies the titular significance of "Son of Man"[2] and asserts, as Lindars puts it, that "Son of Man" offered no "single, defined concept which could be taken over into early Christian thinking."[3] The apocalyptic-oriented interpretation of the Son of Man has been founded on the use of the phrase in

---

[1] Cullmann, Christology, 161. See also Vincent Taylor, The Names of Jesus (London: MacMillan and Co., Limited, 1953), 27-35; S. Mowinckel, He that Cometh, trans. by G. W. Anderson (Oxford: Basil Blackwell, 1959), 448ff; Fuller, Mission and Achievement, 155-59; Ladd, New Testament Theology, 158. Black ("Servant," 10-11) advances the hypothesis that the fusion took place through the figure of the Martyred Prophet, an expectation based on Dt. 18 and found at Qumran. This combination is sometimes claimed to be pre-Christian: D. S. Russell, The Method and Message of Jewish Apocalyptic 200 BC - AD 100 (London: SCM Press, Ltd., 1964), 337-8, 340; Gaston, No Stone on Another, 379-81; Zimmerli-Jeremias, Servant, 61; John Bowman, "The Background of the Term 'Son of Man,'" ExpTim, LIX (1947-8), 288 (possibly). Doeve (Jewish Hermeneutics, 146-8) conjectures that the fusion arose through a midrashic combination of Is. 53 and Dan. 7, stimulated by Is. 52:14: אדם בני. Bruce (Biblical Exegesis, 57-58) claims that the Qumran community understood itself both as Son of Man and Servant of the Lord. Hamerton-Kelly (Pre-existence, 98-160) posits the apparently Messianic title גבר in the scrolls (1QH 3:7-10; 1QS 4:18-23) as the background for Son of Man.

[2] Geza Vermes, "The Use of בר נש/בר אנש in Jewish Aramaic," Appendix E in An Aramaic Approach to the Gospels and Acts, by Matthew Black (3rd ed.; Oxford: Clarendon Press, 1967); Ragnar Leivestad, "Exit the Apocalyptic Son of Man," NTS, XVIII (1971-72), 244-64; J. Y. Campbell, "The Origin and Meaning of the Term Son of Man," JTS, XLVIII (1947), 145-55; C. Colpe, "ὁ υἱὸς τοῦ ἀνθρώπου," 429; William O. Walker, "The Origin of the Son of Man Concept as Applied to Jesus," JBL, XCI (1972), 485; G. N. Stanton, Jesus of Nazareth in New Testament Preaching, SNTSMS, XXVII (Cambridge: Cambridge University Press, 1974), 160-1; T. W. Manson, "The Son of Man in Daniel, Enoch and the Gospels," BJRL, XXXII (1949-50), 174-88; Gaston, No Stone on Another, 374; Eduard Schweizer, "The Son of Man," JBL, LXXIX (1960), 119-29; "Menschensohn und eschatologischer Mensch im Fruhjudentum," Jesus und der Menschensohn (fur Anton Vogtle), ed. by Rudolf Pesch and Rudolf Schnackenburg in cooperation with Odilo Kaiser (Freiburg/Basel/Vienna: Herder, 1975), 101-103; Norman Perrin, "The Son of Man in the Synoptic Tradition," A Modern Pilgrimage in New Testament Christology (Philadelphia: Fortress, 1974), 25-33; I. H. Marshall, "The Synoptic Son of Man Sayings in Recent Discussion," NTS, XII (1965-1966), 350-51.

[3] Lindars, "Re-enter," 60.

Dan. 7 and in the "Similitudes" of I Enoch (37-71), but serious doubt exists as to the pre-Christian provenance of the Similitudes,[1] and, in any case, "Son of Man" can hardly be called a title since it renders three different Ethiopic phrases and is regularly introduced with the demonstrative. As Black says,

> The view . . . that the early church took over its Son of Man conception from a form of apocalyptic Judaism which held a belief in a "pre-existent heavenly being" receives therefore only a very qualified support from the Ethiopic "Similitudes" -- and that would seem hitherto to have been the main prop of the theory.[2]

If a pre-Christian titular use of the expression is denied, Jesus' use of the designation must, therefore, be in accordance with contemporary Jewish usage, in which (א) בר נש was simply an indefinite pronoun.[3] Far from carrying definite apocalyptic or any other sort of overtones, asserts Schweizer, "Son of Man" is not an answer, but rather a question, asking the listener just who Jesus is."[4]

---

[1] For the literary argument (from the "silence" of Qumran), see especially, Milik, "Problèmes," 377; for the historical argument, Hindley, "Similitudes," 551-565.

[2] Matthew Black, "The Son of Man Problem in Recent Research and Debate," BJRL, XVL (1963), 312.

[3] Vermes ("בר נש") shows conclusively that בר נש is often used in the sense of "one," but he has not shown that the phrase is a circumlocution for "I." All his examples retain a general or gnomic aspect, although the speaker obviously has particular reference to himself. (Cf. also Jeremias, New Testament Theology, I, 261 and the critique of Vermes' Aramaic evidence by Joseph Fitzmyer (Review of An Aramaic Approach to the Gospels and Acts (3rd ed.), by Matthew Black in CBQ, XXX (1968), 424-428).

[4] Eduard Schweizer, Jesus, trans. by David E. Green, The New Testament Library (London: SCM Press, Ltd., 1971), 21. Schweizer thinks that the question was answered through the importation of the righteous sufferer "Erniedrigung und Erhöhung" theology. The term Son of Man was used by Jesus as a convenient vehicle "die Doppelheit seines Wirkens als Irdischer in Niedrigkeit und Leiden, als Erhöhter in Vollmacht und Herrlichkeit zu umschreiben." (Erniedrigung und Erhöhung, 14; "Der Menschensohn (Zur eschatologischen Erwartung Jesu)," Neotestamentica (Zürich/Stuttgart: Zwingli, 1963), 58-80; "The Son of Man," 122; "The Son of Man Again," NTS, IX (1962-3), 256-61.) For criticisms of Schweizer's position, see Philipp Vielhauer ("Jesus und der Menschensohn: Zur Diskussion mit Heinz Eduard Tödt und Eduard Schweizer," ZTK, LX (1963), 168) and Black ("Son of Man Problem," 310).

This understanding of the background of the term "Son of Man" and its implications for Jesus' application of the phrase to Himself is a salutary development in Son of Man research, but it is possible that the pendulum has swung back too far. Thus Hamerton-Kelly asserts: " . . . although the Son of Man was not a well-defined figure or 'concept' in Jewish apocalyptic, there was a relatively stable group of ideas associated with the term."[1] Lindars has drawn attention to these conceptions and emphasized that Jesus' use of the phrase must have carried suggestions of a "high claim."[2] Son of Man, while not a totally neutral concept, enabled Jesus to express his identity and claims in a circumlocutory fashion so that His refashioning of Messianic doctrine could be accomplished without being compromised by a theologically or politically "loaded" title from the beginning. It is in this sense that Son of Man can be integrated into the "Messianic secret":

> "Son of Man" was thus a perfect vehicle for expressing the divine self-consciousness of Jesus while at the same time preserving the secrecy of his self-revelation from those who had blinded their eyes and closed their ears.[3]

It becomes clear then why the Son of Man appears as Jesus' self-designation in the Passion sayings. In the midst of the variety of Messianic expectations current in first century Palestine, it was vital for Jesus to clarify His conception of Messiahship by introducing the most important, and unexpected aspect of His ministry: suffering and death.[4] This startling conception of His Messianic mission was

---

[1] Pre-existence, 41.

[2] Lindars, "Re-enter," 71-2. It is significant that the Rabbis always interpreted Dan. 7:13 messianically, in spite of the Christian appropriation of the passage. (Colpe, "ὁ υἱὸς τοῦ ἀνθρώπου," 430). Perhaps the fact that the Rabbis never use the title "Son of Man" (Geza Vermes, Jesus the Jew: A Historian's Reading of the Gospels (London: Collins, 1973), 172) was because of its strongly Christian associations (Cranfield, Mark, 273).

[3] Marshall, "Son of Man," 350-1; cf. also Cranfield, Mark, 275.

[4] Richardson expresses, perhaps too simply, this fact:

not achieved through a fusion of Messianic "titles" because neither "Son of Man" nor "Servant of the Lord" were Messianic titles. Jesus' understanding of His vocation did not arise from the study and correlation of OT passages, still less Messianic ideologies, but stemmed from the nature of the Person He was and His own consciousness of His Father's will. The point is put admirably by Smart:

> The continuity of Jesus with the Old Testament is not to be interpreted as though he consciously drew certain elements from the Old Testament and others from elsewhere to combine them into his own unique message and ministry. He did not take the Suffering Servant idea from Second Isaiah and the Son of Man idea from Daniel and Enoch and blend them together to form a new concept of Messiah. Rather, what he was in himself was primary.[1]

Messianic passages and conceptions that hitherto had lain unrelated to one another (as, e.g., in I Enoch) were brought together in a unique, because personal, unity in Jesus Christ. "It was written" that the Son of Man must suffer, not because Jesus was the Son of Man, but because the Son of Man was Jesus.

Before leaving these sayings, it is necessary to look briefly at the "general" sayings within the Passion Narrative. In the case of Mk. 14:21 par., this background is especially important. Jesus, having identified his betrayer as one of the twelve, concedes that

---

" . . . Jesus used the self designation 'Son of Man' to mean precisely, 'a Messiah who suffers according to the scriptures.'" (An Introduction to the Theology of the New Testament (New York: Harper, 1958), 134). Cf. also Wolff, Jesaja 53, 64.

[1] James D. Smart, History and Theology in Second Isaiah: A Commentary on Isaiah 35, 40-66 (Philadelphia: Westminster Press, 1965), 298. Cf. also Wolff (Jesaja 53, 63) and William Manson (Jesus the Messiah: The Synoptic Tradition of the Revelation of God in Christ with Special Reference to Form-criticism (London: Hodder and Stoughton, Limited, 1943), 101: "The occurrence together in the record of concepts like Christ, Son of God, and Son of Man are by no means necessarily indications of confusion of thought or conflation of divergent traditions. On the contrary it may be regarded as a point in favor of the tradition that it attributes to Jesus a great breadth and inclusiveness of outlook upon the religious history of his people in the past, and a rich appreciation of what prophets and righteous men in one way or another had felt as they projected their thoughts formed upon the symbol of the coming salvation."

his "departure" (ὑπάγει) is according to the scriptures (καθὼς γέγραπται), but that this will not lessen the guilt of "that man" δι' οὗ ὁ υἱὸς τοῦ ἀνθρώπου παραδίδοται. Here are found two elements, explicitly claimed to be in accordance with prophecy, that are recurring components of the Passion sayings: the Son of Man and passive παραδίδωμι. While Mark and Matthew display an almost word-for-word agreement,[1] Luke considerably shortens the saying, eliminating the second "Son of Man," changing ὑπάγει to the more prosaic πορεύεται and substituting for the scripture formula κατὰ τὸ ὡρισμένον. Montefiore conjectures that this substitution was made because Luke could find no specific scriptural passage as a background,[2] but this does not elsewhere bother Luke (e.g., 18:31).[3] ὁρίζω, a peculiarly Lukan term, is probably introduced to strengthen the idea that the terrible events now about to unfold are by "the predetermined (ὡρισμένῃ) plan and foreknowledge of God" (Acts 2:23).[4] The presence of παραδίδοται makes it probable that Is. 53 features as at least one component in the background of the saying.[5] It is, of

---

[1] Particularly striking is the fact that only in these two verses in the NT is an indicative (ἐγεννήθη) used in a "contrary to fact" protasis (James Hope Moulton, Prolegomena, Vol. I of A Grammar of New Testament Greek by James Hope Moulton (4 vols.; Edinburgh: T & T Clark, 1906-1976), 200; C. F. D. Moule, An Idiom-Book of New Testament Greek (Cambridge: University Press, 1953), 149) and with οὗ (BDF, 428).

[2] C. G. Montefiore, The Synoptic Gospels (2 vols., 2nd ed.; London: MacMillan, 1927), II, 594.

[3] Hooker, Servant, 190.

[4] Cf. Hans Conzelmann, The Theology of St. Luke, trans. by Geoffrey Buswell (London: Faber and Faber, 1961), 158; Heinz Schürmann, Einer quellenkritischen Untersuchung des lukanischen Abendmahlsberichtes Lk 22, 7-38, Vol. III: Jesu Abschiedsrede: Lk 22, 21-38, NTAbh, XX (Münster: Aschendorffsche, 1955), 4.

[5] Mauer, "Knecht Gottes," 9; Lindars, Apologetic, 81; Richardson, Theology, 135; Allan Menzies, The Earliest Gospel: A Historical Study of the Gospel According to Mark (London: MacMillan, 1901), 251; R. V. G. Tasker, The Gospel According to St. Matthew, TNTC (London: Tyndale, 1961), 245.

course, true that παραδίδοται is used here in a particular and restricted sense, referring to the act of betrayal itself, but that the basic significance of the term in its relationship to Is. 53 is retained is demonstrated by the fact that Judas remains only an instrument (δι' οὗ), albeit a responsible one, in God's deliverance of His servant. Other OT backgrounds for the saying have been suggested. Thus, the fact that an allusion to Ps. 41:9 is present in Mk. 14:18 raises the possibility that this psalm is the basis of Jesus' prediction.[1] It would be presumptuous to exclude a reference to this psalm, but it may be significant that Ps. 41 is applied only to the relation of the betrayer to Christ and not to the necessity for the betrayal itself, for which Ps. 41 is much less appropriate. J. Christensen argues that ὑπάγει with reference to suffering in Mark and Matthew must be interpreted in the light of the more widespread use of the term in John to refer to Jesus' path to glory. The background of Mk. 14:21 must therefore be a passage which is capable of giving rise to both these conceptions, a background which Christensen finds in Ez. 12:8-16.[2] However, the use of ὑπάγει may be explained simply as an attempt to avoid repeating παραδίδοται,[3] and, as Higgins points out, " . . . the influence of the prophet/son of man in Ezekiel on the gospel tradition is very questionable."[4] The conception of the

---

[1] A. E. J. Rawlinson, St. Mark, WC (London: Methuen, 1925), 202; France, Jesus, 57; Burton Scott Easton, The Gospel According to St. Luke (Edinburgh: T & T Clark, 1926), 322. Pesch ("Passion des Menschensohnes," 182) refers also to Ps. 55:14, Jer. 20:10, 1QH 5:23f as evidence for the influence of the righteous sufferer theme. (Cf. also Julius Schniewind, Das Evangelium nach Markus, NTD, II (6th ed.; Göttingen: Vandenhoeck & Ruprecht, 1952), 189).

[2] Jens Christensen, "Le Fils de l'homme s'en va, ainsi qu'il est écrit de lui," ST, X (1956), 28-35.

[3] Lindars, Apologetic, 81. ὑπάγω here appears to be an Aramaism (Black, Aramaic Approach, 302).

[4] A. J. B. Higgins, Jesus and the Son of Man (London: Lutterworth Press, 1964), 50-51, n. 3. Easton (Luke, 322) and Otto (Kingdom of God, 271) mention Obadiah 7, presumably referring to the phrase "[those who eat]

Suffering Servant, which was in Jesus' mind at this time, as Mk. 14:24 shows, must therefore be understood as the primary background for the saying in Mk. 14:21 par., although, once again a general reference to other Scriptures foretelling Jesus' suffering should not be excluded.

Two other sayings in the Passion Narrative, while not explicitly referring to Scripture, should undoubtedly be classed with Mk. 14:21, since both refer to the Son of Man's paradosis: Mt. 26:2, Mk. 14:41= Mt. 26:45. The latter saying immediately precedes the arrest scene itself, indicating the further "Konkretisierung" of the theological conception of Jesus' deliverance. When Jesus' seizure is a fait accompli, he again links this event with the Scriptures, introducing this time the concept of fulfillment (ἵνα ¹ πληρωθῶσιν αἱ γραφαί) (Mk. 14:49 = Mt. 26:56).

The scriptural necessity for Jesus' arrest is particularly emphasized by Matthew, who interpolates a section into the Markan material just before this, in which Jesus refuses angelic help, asking "How then shall the scriptures be fulfilled that it must (δεῖ) be so?" (Mt. 26:54). The plural γραφαί, used in each of these verses, clearly indicates that more than one OT passage is in mind, and it would not be amiss to understand these sayings as comprehensively encompassing the Scriptures which prophesy the betrayal (Is. 53 and Zech. 13:7 (cf. Mk. 14:27 = Mt. 26:31))² and those many passages which find their fulfillment in the course of Jesus' Passion as well.

---

your bread will set an ambush for you." The resemblance is surely purely incidental.

¹ ἵνα may be imperatival (C. J. Cadoux, "The Imperatival Use of ἵνα in the New Testament," JTS, XLII (1941), 168), but more likely is used elliptically (supply γένοιτο) (Cranfield, Mark, 437).

²The influence of Zech. 13:7 on the saying is clear from the sequel to Mk. 14:49; καὶ ἀφέντες αὐτὸν ἔφυγον πάντες (cf. Mk. 14:27 πάντες σκανδαλισθήσεσθε. . . τὰ πρόβατα διασκορπισθήσονται (Zech. 13:7b). It has been asserted that the manner of Jesus' arrest (ὡς ἐπὶ λῃστήν) is the focal point for the scriptural allusion in Mk. 14:49 par., so that the specific reference is to Is. 53:12 (cf.

It is frequently asserted that the Passion sayings are all vaticinia ex eventu. However, it is certain that Jesus foresaw his own death,[1] and it seems perverse to deny that He would have warned his disciples and instructed them in its significance. It is unnecessary, and perhaps fruitless, to become involved in an attempt to assess the authenticity of the details in all the sayings and our remarks will be confined to those specific OT elements which have been isolated. Some Semitic linguistic features provide conclusive evidence that several of the sayings must be Palestinian in origin.[2] The general character of these predictions, the relative sparseness of OT citations, and the lack of explicit soteriological emphasis, give reason to question the extent to which they have been influenced by the post-Easter community.[3] παραδίδωμι, being very widespread, must certainly be attributed to the bedrock of the tradition.[4] Even the more specific details, influenced by Is. 50:6, which are supplied in the third prediction, cannot be rejected out of hand, for it seems very difficult

---

Lk. 22:37) (Mauer, "Knecht Gottes," 8; Pierre Benoit, The Passion and Resurrection of Jesus Christ, trans. by B. Weatherhead (New York: Herder & Herder and London: Darton, Longman & Todd, 1969), 38; Erich Klostermann, Das Markusevangelium, HNT, III (4th ed.; Tübingen: Mohr, 1950), 153; Manfred Karnetzki, "Die alttestamentlichen Zitate in der synoptischen Tradition," (unpublished Ph.D. dissertation, University of Tübingen, 1955), 6). While the arrest may no doubt be a part of the fulfillment of Jesus' being numbered as a transgressor, the pl. γραφαί and the general interpretation of Lk. 22:37 which has been advocated, argue for a broader reference.

[1]See especially Schürmann, "Wie hat Jesus seinen Tod bestanden und verstanden?"

[2]Black, Aramaic Approach, 86; "Passion Sayings," 2-7; Jeremias, New Testament Theology, I, 282; D. Meyer, "ΠΟΛΛΑ ΠΑΘΕΙΝ," ZNW, LV (1964), 132.

[3]Borsch, Son of Man, 334-40; Pierre Benoit, "Jésus et le Serviteur de Dieu," Jésus aux origines de la christologie, ed. by J. Dupont (Gembloux: Leuven University Press, 1975), 127; Étienne Trocmé, The Formation of the Gospel According to Mark, trans. by Pamela Gaughan (London: SPCK, 1975), 228-9.

[4]Schweizer, "Der Menschensohn," 70.

to understand why these comparatively minor details should have been imported into the saying.[1] It is unnecessary to trace all the sayings back to a single prediction, perhaps uttered on one occasion; in the course of a three-year ministry, Jesus must surely have instructed his disciples in this most crucial aspect of His earthly work more than once and with varying degrees of detail. What may, therefore, safely be concluded is that the basic conception of the necessity to suffer and the importance of Scripture (Is. 53 in particular, but other passages as well) in mediating this necessity are authentic representations of Jesus' own teaching.

The investigation of the synoptic Passion sayings has demonstrated that the Servant Songs of Isaiah have played an important, even primary role, in their formulation. It is necessary, however, in conclusion, to inject a note of caution. The influence of the Servant Songs of Isaiah on the conception and formulation of the Passion sayings is extensive and undeniable. A false perspective would be attained, however, if it were not recognized that other OT passages were certainly very influential in the formulation of these sayings. Certainly Ps. 118:22 and probably many other OT passages are meant to be referred to in the "it is written."[2] Wolff stresses the necessity to strike this balance:

> Wir dürfen aus diesem Befund schliessen, dass er Jes. 53 nicht als einzig dastehend in der Schrift angesehen hat; in der gesamten Schrift wo immer von Leiden und Verachtung die Rede war, erkannte er Seinen Weg![3]

---

[1] A concealed bias against the possibility of predictive prophecy is often an important factor in denying authenticity, but as Marshall ("Son of Man," 329) notes: "It would be a notable lack of scholarly objectivity if an a priori denial of the possibility of prophecy was made a decisive argument against the authenticity of these sayings."

[2] Pesch ("Passion des Menschensohnes") therefore is correct in his assertion that Jewish righteous-sufferer theology, based largely on the Psalms, has played a role in Jesus' passion sayings, but he is not correct in ascribing to it the preeminent role.

[3] Wolff, *Jesaja 53*, 68.

112   The OT in the Gospel Passion Narratives

The Servant Songs provide much of the language in which Jesus announces his sufferings and must thereby be accorded primary place, but in the final analysis these predictions are based on the entirety of God's revelation[1] because they stem from One who recognized His destiny proclaimed in all the Scriptures: "These are my words which I spoke to you, while I was still with you, that everything written about me in the law of Moses and the prophets and the psalms must be fulfilled." (Lk. 24:44).

Mark 1:11 / Matthew 3:17 / Luke 3:22 (Isaiah 42:1)

The baptism of Jesus by John is an event whose interpretation is critically important in forming a proper estimate of Jesus' person and work. As such, the narrative has for long been a storm-center of controversy. A matter of particular debate, and that which interests us, is the question concerning the relationship of the baptism to the death of Jesus, the answer to which is bound up with the significance accorded to the OT allusions in the voice from Heaven.[2]

The most common view sees in these words a combination of references to Ps. 2:7 and Is. 42:1. Others seek to confine the background to one or the other, or perhaps to some other OT passage, particularly Gen. 22.[3] Especially popular of late has been the

---

[1] D. E. Nineham (The Gospel of St. Mark, PNTC (rev. ed.; London: Adam and Charles Black, 1968), 228) is too general in grounding the necessity for Jesus' suffering in the nature of a world opposed to God and the consequent inevitability of suffering by the righteous. This Socratic conception is inadequate to explain the necessity for the Messiah to suffer.

[2] It must at least be questioned whether it is legitimate to speak of a bath qol here (literally, "a daughter of the voice") since the bath qol was considered to be but an imperfect echo of the voice of the Lord (Grundmann, Markus, 32; Rudolf Pesch, Das Markusevangelium, HTKNT, II (2 vols.; Freiburg/Basel/Vienna: Herder, 1976), I, 92. On the bath qol, see Str-B, I, 125-34; Otto Betz, "φωνή . . . ," TDNT, IX, 298; C. K. Barrett, The Holy Spirit in the Gospel Tradition (London: SPCK, 1947), 39-40).

[3] For a defence of the primacy of the Gen. 22 background, see

attempt to limit the allusion to Is. 42:1, where the advent of the ebed Yahweh is announced. Comparison with Mt. 12:18 (= Is. 42:1), it is argued, suggests that the υἱός in the heavenly declaration has replaced an original παῖς, in which case "The voice from heaven comes to Jesus as a summons to accept the task of the one who is addressed in the same way at the beginning of the ebed Yahweh hymns in Isa. 42:1."[1] Further support for this view is found in the alleged allusion to Is. 53:11 in Mt. 3:15 (πληρῶσαι πᾶσαν δικαιοσύνην -- interpreted as "effect all righteousness"), which is attractive because it neatly solves the difficulty raised by Jesus' submission to a baptism of repentance.[2] Furthermore, attention is drawn to the "earliest interpretation" of the baptismal narrative, which seems to have its background in the Servant Songs (cf. Jn. 1:29 ὁ ἀμνὸς τοῦ θεοῦ -- Is. 53:7; Jn. 1:34 ἐκλεκτός (v. 1)[3] -- Is. 42:1)[4]

---

especially Ernest Best, The Temptation and the Passion: The Markan Soteriology, SNTSMS, II (Cambridge: University Press, 1965), 169-73. Bretscher ("Exodus 4:22-23 and the Voice from Heaven," JBL, LXXXVII (1968), 301-311) seeks to establish a case for Ex. 4:22: υἱός πρωτότοκός μου Ισραηλ. But the closest NT parallel, as he admits, is II Pet. 1:17, certainly late, and his attempt to explain the alteration from πρωτότοκος (בכור) to ἀγαπητός is unconvincing. (ἀγαπητός never translates בכור in the OT; even the DSS text he cites demonstrates that πρωτότοκος was retained even when the concept was that of "uniqueness").

[1]Cullmann, Christology, 66. Cf. also Ernst Lohmeyer, Das Evangelium des Matthäus, rev. by Werner Schmauch, MeyerK, I (4th ed.; Göttingen: Vandenhoeck & Ruprecht, 1967), 51; Jeremias, Theology, 54; Lindars, Apologetic, 140.

[2]G. W. H. Lampe, The Seal of the Spirit. A Study in the Doctrine of Baptism and Confirmation in the New Testament and the Fathers. (2nd ed.; London: SPCK, 1967), 37-38; Richardson, Theology, 180; France, Jesus, 124-125.

[3]ἐκλεκτός has early support, and the tendency may have been to assimilate to the other baptismal texts and to John's more customary usage (cf. Burnett Hillman Streeter, The Four Gospels: A Study of Origins (London: MacMillan, 1924), 143 and Lk. 9:35 ἐκλελεγμένος). However, the support for υἱός is also early and far more diverse and accords with Johannine usage.

[4]Oscar Cullmann, Baptism in the New Testament, trans. by J. K. S. Reid, SBT, I (London: SCM Press, 1950), 20-21; Jeremias, Theology, 53-54.

and to Jesus' use of the word βάπτισμα as a metaphorical reference to his death (Mk. 10:38, Lk. 12:49).[1]

While, as we shall see, a reference to Is. 42:1 is undoubtedly present, the attempt to confine the background to that context alone must be rejected. First, it is highly improbable that the baptismal voice ever contained παῖς. There are no NT examples in which υἱός has replaced an earlier παῖς [2] and the importance of the Son of God title in the following temptation narrative (in Matthew and Luke) renders it likely that the category of sonship has already been introduced in the stories of the baptism.[3] No doubt, even if υἱός is retained, no reference beyond Is. 42:1 need be present, but the evidence suggests that, in fact, Ps. 2:7 has influenced the saying. The words of the voice from Heaven undoubtedly remind one of that important Christian testimonium;[4] the difference in word order from the LXX is not decisive if, as seems probable, a Semitic background is assumed.[5] On the other hand, it is certainly unjustified to jettison the influence of Is. 42:1 altogether.[6] εὐδοκέω ἐν is a perfectly natural rendering of רצה and ἀγαπητός, although clearly adjectival,[7] may well be

---

[1] Cullmann, Christology, 67; Lampe, Seal, 39-40.

[2] A. Feuillet, "Le Baptême de Jésus," RB, LXXI (1964), 325; Evald Lövestam, Son and Saviour. A Study of Acts 13, 32-37. With an Appendix: "Son of God" in the Synoptic Gospels, trans. by Michael J. Petry, ConNT, XVIII (Lund-Copenhagen: G. W. K. Gleerup and Ejnar Munksgaard, 1961), 95; I. Howard Marshall, "Son of God or Servant of Yahweh? -- A Reconsideration of Mark I. 11," NTS, XV (1968-69), 328-30.

[3] C. E. B. Cranfield, "The Baptism of our Lord -- A Study of St. Mark 1:9-11," SJT, VIII (1955), 60; Gundry, Old Testament, 30.

[4] Cf. Dodd, According to the Scriptures, 31-32.

[5] With Gundry, Old Testament, 30, n. 2; Marshall, "Son of God," 332-33; contra Cranfield, "Baptism," 60.

[6] Pace Eduard Schweizer, "υἱός (N.T.)," TDNT, VIII, 368; Hooker, Servant, 68-73; Max-Alain Chevallier, L'esprit et le messie dans le bas-judaïsme et le Nouveau Testament (Paris: University of France, 1958), 59-67.

[7] Cf. G. D. Kilpatrick, "The Order of Some Noun and Adjective Phrases in the New Testament," NovT, V (1962), 112-13.

derived from בְּרִידִי.¹ Moreover, the descent of the Spirit upon Jesus offers an interesting parallel to Is. 42:1b, "I have put my spirit upon him."² While influence from Gen. 22 cannot be ruled out, there is little beyond ἀγαπητός that reminds one of that passage.³

Thus, the voice at Jesus' baptism confirms His unique filial relationship with the Father⁴ and, at the same time, indicates that

---

¹εὐδοκέω ἐν is, in fact, the standard translation of רָצָה in the OT (22 out of 40 occurrences of רָצָה), and the word is used by A, Σ, and Θ in Is. 42:1.
It should be noted that ἀγαπητός may be derived from Targ. Ps. 2:7 (רְחִימָא -- cf. Schweizer, "υἱός," 368; Lövestam, Son and Saviour, 96; Gundry, Old Testament, 30), but the parallel in Mt. 12:18 points to Is. 42:1. It is possible that Is. 44:2, a passage which may have been linked with 42:1, influenced the choice of ἀγαπητός in the NT texts (Barrett, Holy Spirit, 40-41; Lampe, Seal, 36-37).

²Feuillet, "Baptême," 324. But Is. 63 is the most pertinent direct reference (cf. LXX, v. 19: σχίσω and v. 14: κατέβη πνεῦμα παρὰ κυρίου (Ivor Buse, "The Markan Account of the Baptism of Jesus and Isaiah LXIII," JTS, n.s., VII (1956), 74-75).

³If Test. Levi 18:6 could be proven to be pre-Christian, it would provide an important background for the baptismal texts in terms of Gen. 22 (cf. Matthew Black, "The Messiah in the Testament of Levi xviii," ExpTim, LX (1949), 321-2).

⁴It is often suggested that Mk. 1:11 presents the moment of Messianic "adoption," along the lines of the "adoption formula" in Ps. 2:7 (e.g., Hans Conzelmann, An Outline of the Theology of the New Testament, trans. by John Bowden (London: SCM, 1969), 78). Barrett has drawn attention to several contexts in which anointing, sonship and endowment with the Spirit are closely linked (I En. 49:3, Pss. Sol. 17:42, Test. Levi 18:2-14, Test. Jud. 24:2f) and concludes: ". . . it appears that the Messiahship, since it underlies the office of Jesus as the Servant of the Lord, his status as Son of God and the descent upon him of the Spirit, is the key to the understanding of the baptism narrative." (Holy Spirit, 41-44). Both Lindars (Apologetic, 141-3) and Fuller (Christology, 169-70) claim that Ps. 2:7 could not have originally been used at the baptism, since it was a prooftext for Jesus' exaltation.
However, the attempt to reserve Son of God as a title for Jesus only in exaltation or to regard it as a consequence of Messianic status, fails to give due weight to the strongly attested evidence that sonship was a basic category in Jesus' consideration of himself and to the fact that Son of God does not seem to have been a Messianic title (4QFlor links "son" with the Davidic Messiah, but the title is not used; 1QSa 2:11ff is disputed. Cf. Lövestam, Son and Saviour, 89-90). As Marshall says: "The evidence strongly suggests that the fundamental point in Jesus' self-understanding was his filial relationship to God, and that it was from this basic conviction that he understood the tasks variously assigned to the Messiah, Son of Man and Servant of Yahweh, rather than that the basic datum was consciousness of being, the Messiah." (I. Howard Marshall, "The Divine Sonship of Jesus," Int, XXI (1967), 93. Cf. also Cranfield, "Baptism," 62 and Lane, Mark, 58).

this relationship must be further defined with reference to the figure of the ebed Yahweh. Whether the introduction of this figure carries with it a reference to suffering and death can be decided only after the sayings in which Jesus likens his death to a baptism have been considered.

In both Mk. 10:38 and Lk. 12:49-50, Jesus claims that he has a "baptism with which to be baptized" (cognate accusative) and links the metaphor with another, a cup to be drunk in Mark and a fire to kindle (active) in Luke. The Lucan logion occurs in the midst of a series of detached sayings, while that in Mark is Jesus' reply to the request of the sons of Zebedee that they be granted positions of honor in Jesus' Kingdom. The first step in determining the precise significance of the reference to baptism is to establish the meaning of the metaphors with which it is associated: the fire and the cup. The latter term is prominent also, of course, in the Gethsemane scene, where it has generally been understood to connote the judgmental wrath of God,[1] a meaning consistent with the OT use of the symbol.[2] It is urged against this interpretation that the use of the term in intertestamental literature, where "cup" often means no more than "the destiny which God decrees" is overlooked[3] and that this weakened

---

[1] C. E. B. Cranfield, "The Cup Metaphor in Mark xiv. 36 and parallels," ExpTim, LIX (1947-1948), 138; G. Delling, "βάπτισμα βαπτισθῆναι," NovT, II (1957), 95; L. Goppelt, "ποτήριον," TDNT, VI, 153; Best, Temptation, 153; Grundmann, Markus, 292-93; Ladd, Theology, 191; A. Feuillet, "La coupe et le baptême de la passion (Mc, x, 35-40; cf. Mt, xx, 20-23; Lc, xii, 50)," RB, LXXIV (1967), 372.

[2] Delling, "βάπτισμα," 93-95; Cranfield, "Cup Metaphor," 137-8; Goppelt, "ποτήριον," 149-50; J. W. Doeve, "Die Gefangennahme Jesu in Gethsemane. Eine traditionsgeschichtliche Untersuchung," SE, I (= TU, LXXIII) (1959), 464, n. 1; A. M. Hunter, The Work and Words of Jesus (London: SCM, 1950), 96.

[3] M. Black, "The Cup Metaphor in Mark xiv. 36," ExpTim, LIX (1947-48), 195; Anthony Tyrell Hanson, The Wrath of the Lamb (London: SPCK, 1957), 47-66. Agreeing with this, and stressing the martyrological associations are: Hans-Werner Surkau (Martyrien in jüdischer und frühchristlicher Zeit, FRLANT, XXXVI (Göttingen: Vandenhoeck & Ruprecht, 1938), 33, 84-85); Bertram (Leidensgeschichte, 44-45); Ludger Schenkel

sense must be accepted since it is said that the disciples share this cup (Mk. 10:39).[1] However, the most the intertestamental evidence shows is that "cup" did not always retain the sense of divine wrath, while 1QpHab 11:10-15, which interprets Habakkuk's "cup" as the "cup of wrath" (כוס חמה), proves that the OT image was still remembered. In Mk. 14:36, the retention of the wrath connotation better explains the terror with which Jesus confronted this destiny and is compatible with the cry of dereliction (Mk. 15:34).[2] These considerations support the understanding of "cup" in Mk. 10:38 as meaning a suffering which is brought on by God's judgmental wrath.

While some dissenting opinions are registered, the "fire" in Lk. 12:49 is almost certainly a reference to the eschatological judgment.[3] In light of the parallelism present in both verses, it is necessary to define the baptismal metaphor in such a way that its reference is closely associated with Jesus' experience of God's wrath and the inbreaking of the eschatological judgment. That this reference is to the death of Jesus can scarcely be doubted.

(Studien zur Passionsgeschichte des Markus: Tradition und Redaktion in Markus 14:1-42, FzB, IV (Würzburg: Echter Verlag Katholisches Bibelwerk, 1971), 502-503); and John Downing ("Jesus and Martyrdom," JTS, n.s., XIV (1963), 287-88).

[1]Gustav Stählin, "ὀργή, E. The Wrath of Man and the Wrath of God in the NT," TDNT, V, 437; Kümmel, Promise and Fulfillment, 69.

[2]Goppelt, "ποτήριον," 153; cf. Schniewind, Matthäus, 187. Lane suggests a background for Jesus' dread and decision to embrace God's will in two OT passages where the "cup" figures prominently -- Is. 51:17-23 and Jer. 49:12 (Mark, 517).

[3]On the figurative sense of πῦρ, Lang says: "The reference in the Synoptists is always to eschatological judgment." (πῦρ, . . .," TDNT, VI, 942 (cf. 942-44); also Delling, "βάπτισμα," 105-07; Fuller, Mission and Achievement, 62. Others suggest that the fire of Pentecost is the reference (J. A. T. Robinson, "The One Baptism as a Category of New Testament Soteriology," SJT, VI (1953), 260 (reprinted in Twelve New Testament Studies, SBT, n.s., XXXIV (London: SCM Press, 1962)); Feuillet, "Coupe," 369.

An obvious difficulty with this interpretation, already mentioned above, must be admitted: in what sense can the disciples be understood to share this uniquely eschatological judgment and death (cf. Mk. 10:39)? As a response to this, Feuillet has drawn attention to the frequency with which the disciples are challenged to imitate Jesus in ways that seem impossible: they are to take up their crosses (Mk. 8:34), serve as he serves (Mk. 10:40-45) and love as he loves (Jn. 13:34).[1] Highly relevant to the present discussion are Paul's statement in Col. 1:24 that he is completing "what is lacking in Christ's afflictions" and Peter's command in I Peter 4:13 to "rejoice in so far as you share Christ's sufferings." There seems, therefore, to be a fairly widespread conception that disciples of Christ are to imitate the example he has set (albeit in a qualitatively distinct fashion) and even to participate in his sufferings. While the answer to Jesus' question in Mk. 10:38 must obviously be "no" inasmuch as Jesus' death is unique in both its intensity and significance, there is a derivative sense in which James and John will indeed experience the eschatological tribulation associated with Jesus.

We are now able to return to the problem with which we are most concerned: what is the basis for Jesus' use of baptism to refer to His death? To this question two different answers are given: the baptism of Jesus itself and the OT imagery of engulfment in many waters.[2]

---

[1] Feuillet, "Coupe," 364-5.

[2] Some scholars (e.g., Rudolf Bultmann, *The History of the Synoptic Tradition*, trans. by John Marsh (Oxford: Basil Blackwell, 1963), 153) think primarily of martyrdom, but the phrase "baptism in blood" to denote a martyr's death is not found before Irenaeus (Albrecht Oepke, "$\beta\acute{\alpha}\pi\tau\omega$, . . . " *TDNT*, I, 538, n. 44). Braumann ("Leidenskelch und Todestaufe (Mc 10, 38f)," *ZNW*, LVI (1945), 178-83) thinks the original reference was to the Last Supper and Christian baptism.

The Isaianic Servant Songs   119

The latter interpretation has had a strong following in recent years.[1] It is argued that the incontestable OT background for the metaphors of cup and fire leads one to expect a similar OT basis for the baptismal symbolism. In the OT, envelopment in calamities is often pictured as a flood of water, or submersion in many waters.[2] The technical, Christian sense of "baptism" should not be read back into this saying of Jesus; he employs βαπτίσομαι in its attested pre-Christian sense to evoke this OT imagery for disaster.[3] No reference, therefore, need be present either to John's or Christian baptism. While this line of reasoning has much to be said for it, one incontrovertible fact stands in its way: the use in both Mark and Luke of βάπτισμα, a word which elsewhere always refers to either John's baptism or Christian baptism.[4] In the minds of the evangelists, this could only connote baptism in the NT sense and it would require more evidence than is available to demonstrate that their interpretation of Jesus' words is incorrect.[5] If, therefore, Jesus speaks of his

---

[1]See especially Delling, "βάπτισμα,"; and G. R. Beasley-Murray, Baptism in the New Testament (London: MacMillan, 1963), 73-77. (For an excellent defense: J. H. Bernard, "A Study of St. Mark X. 38, 39," JTS, XXVIII (1927), 266-7). Best (Temptation, 153-55) thinks the original reference was to this OT metaphor, but that Mark has discerned in it the conception of baptism.

[2]Cf. Pss. 18:4f, 69:14, 88:6f, 69:3, Job 9:31(A) and especially Ps. 11:6 (fire and cup), Is. 30:27-28 (fire and flood) and Is. 21:4 LXX (ἡ ἀνομία με βαπτίσει).

[3]Cf. M-M, 102.

[4]M-M, 103. It is important to note that βαπτίσεσθαι (only 4t in LXX) is never used in the OT for the metaphor of being overwhelmed in disaster. Indeed, Oepke ("βάπτω," 536) claims that the meanings "to sink, to perish" are quite absent from Heb. and Aram. טבע, and hence from βαπτίζειν in Jewish Greek. Cf. also J. Ysebart, Greek Baptismal Terminology: Its Origin and Early Development, Graecitas Christianorum Primaeva, I (Nijmegen: Dekker & van de Vegt, 1962), 43-44.

[5]Contra. Best, Temptation, 153-55.

passion with a reference to the rite of baptism, the next step is to enquire as to the special significance thereby accorded to both Jesus' baptism and his death.[1] At the very least, the metaphor demonstrates that there was something about Jesus' baptism that allowed for an association with his death. Can more be said? Feuillet argues that, since the cup denotes God's wrath against human sin, and Jesus was sinless, the baptismal symbolism may accord to Jesus' death a representative significance, an interpretation that is rooted in Jesus' baptism, a time at which Jesus identifies himself with sinful men for their redemption as the ebed Yahweh.[2] This line of interpretation, which is essentially Cullmann's as well, has inadequate bases. The cup metaphor may imply the concept of representation or substitution, but there is no need to carry this implication over to the figure of baptism. That Jesus' submission to a baptism which was characterized above all by repentance implies an identification with sinful mankind is clear, but, as Beasley-Murray points out, this involves nothing more than solidarity.[3] Other scholars, while not insisting on the representative significance, believe that Jesus' words give us solid grounds for viewing the baptism almost solely as a prefigurement of, or initiation into, the sufferings of the ebed Yahweh: "The baptism is the anticipation of the Cross, in which Jesus in Jordan foresuffered all, and as such it gives to the Cross and all that lies between the

---

[1] E. F. Scott (The Kingdom and the Messiah (Edinburgh: T & T Clark, 1911), 229), followed by W. F. Flemington (The New Testament Doctrine of Baptism (London: SPCK, 1964), 32) suggests that the application of the metaphor to Jesus' death means that the death is viewed as a transition to renewed activity. However, it is doubtful whether the baptismal metaphor actually influences the significance of the death.

[2] "Coupe," 360-383. Cf. also Lane, Mark, 380-81.

[3] Baptism, 57-58. Cf. also the criticism of Cullmann by R. E. O. White, The Biblical Doctrine of Initiation (London: Hodder and Stoughton, 1960), 100-106.

two events its own character of a baptism."[1] However, it is perhaps unjustified to focus so exclusively upon suffering as the sole category in terms of which the baptism is interpreted. The placement of the narrative within the tradition, the emphasis upon "unique sonship" and the descent of the Holy Spirit suggest that the baptism is the inauguration of the earthly ministry of the obedient Son, a ministry which culminates in suffering and death, but which involves much more as well.[2]

To summarize: the allusion to Is. 42:1 in the voice from Heaven at the conclusion of Jesus' baptism, taken in conjunction with the application of $\beta\acute{\alpha}\pi\tau\iota\sigma\mu\alpha$ to Jesus' death, clearly indicates that Jesus' destiny involves death as the ebed Yahweh. While the element of vicariousness may be deduced from the nature of the baptism itself, this is certainly not explicated, and it would be better, perhaps, to speak of nothing more than solidarity at this point. Two further conclusions can be drawn from our investigation of this text. If the saying can be shown to belong to this stage in the gospel narrative, it provides conclusive evidence that Jesus knew his destiny to involve suffering and death at the very beginning of the ministry. And, secondly, a connection is established between Jesus' death and a portion of the Servant Songs that does not mention the humility of

---

[1] Robinson, "The One Baptism," 261 (he stresses the present tenses in Mk. 10:38, but they are probably "futuristic" presents). Cf. also, for this approach, Lampe, Seal, 39-40; Fuller, Mission and Achievement, 61-62.
    In another article, Robinson seeks to establish a connection between the Qumran belief that their mission was one of atonement (cf. 1QS 8:3f) and John's baptism as a preparation for this redemptive work. Jesus' baptism would then be a time of identification with this movement and, to be sure, in terms of the Isaianic servant. ("The Baptism of John and the Qumran Community, Testing a Hypothesis," HTR, L (1957), 185-8). However, there is little evidence that the Qumran covenanters associated baptism with their mission of atonement.

[2] Beasley-Murray, Baptism, 55-67.

the Servant, a conclusion that has obvious relevance to the question as to whether the Servant texts were exegeted contextually or atomistically in the early church.

Mark 10:45 / Matthew 20:28 (Isaiah 53:10-12)

It has been traditionally assumed that Jesus' words about service in Mk. 10:45 (= Mt. 20:28) have as their background Is. 53, but this assumption has been strongly challenged by C. K. Barrett and others, so it will be necessary to devote some space to a consideration of the evidence.

Barrett's argument falls into two stages: the language of the saying and its conceptual background. Linguistically, he claims, no direct relationship between Mk. 10:45 and Is. 53 can be sustained. עבד is never translated by the root διακ-, δοῦναι τὴν ψυχήν does not point unambiguously to the fourth Servant Song, λύτρον is an impossible substitute for אשם (Is. 53:10), ἀντί occurs in Is. 53, but "not significantly," and πολλῶν is too common a term for any dependence to be suggested. Conceptually, Barrett poses as an alternative background the theology of atoning suffering which had developed as a response to the Maccabaean martyrdoms.[1]

While possessing some merit, the linguistic arguments are not convincing. With regard to the suggested dependence of διακονέω on

---

[1] Barrett, "Mark 10:45," 1-18. Cf. also Hooker, Servant, 74-79; Suhl, Alttestamentlichen Zitate, 119; Hartwig Thyen, Studien zur Sündenvergebung im Neuen Testament und seinen alttestamentlichen und jüdischen Voraussetzungen, FRLANT, XCVI (Göttingen: Vandenhoeck & Ruprecht, 1970), 157-60; Sam K. Williams, Jesus' Death as Saving Event: The Background and Origin of a Concept, HDR, II (Missoula, Mont.: Scholar's Press, 1975), 211-213; Whiteley, "Salvation," 121-22; F. C. Grant, "Biblical Theology and the Synoptic Problem," Current Issues in New Testament Interpretation. Essays in Honor of Otto A. Piper, ed. by William Klassen and Graydon F. Snyder (New York: Harper & Brothers, 1962), 81-2; Best, Temptation, 14-43; Alan Hugh McNeile, The Gospel According to St. Matthew (London: MacMillan, 1928), 291 (the last two scholars allow some influence from Is. 53, however).

עבד, the point is well-taken: that word alone cannot be taken to point to the עבד יהוה.¹ Again, the Semitic δοῦναι τὴν ψυχήν need not be dependent on Is. 53:10, but in this case there is a sound basis for the correspondence. "His soul" is repeated three times in Is. 53:10-12 and the Greek of Mk. 10:45 is a fairly literal rendering of אם־תשים נפשו (v. 10).² Dispute rages over the precise connotation of λύτρον in the NT. Deissmann pointed to the use of the word with reference to manumitting slaves,³ and many scholars feel that the concept of purchase price (i.e., "ransom") is always implied.⁴ However, Hill has sought to cast doubt on this conclusion by investigating the occurrences of λύτρον in the LXX. While admitting that the λυτ- word group basically refers to the payment of a price as a means of release, he argues that, especially when the subject is God, λυτ - comes to have the more general meaning "deliver" without any stress on the means of deliverance. In Mk. 10:45, therefore, λύτρον signifies " . . . not a price paid, but a representative action accepted as having

---

¹France, Jesus, 118, pace Jeremias, "Das Lösegeld für Viele (Mk. 10:45)," Abba (Göttingen: Vandenhoeck & Ruprecht, 1966) (reprinted from Judaica, III (1947-8), 249-64), 227. It should be noted, however, that the evidence is slight (διάκονος is used only 7t in the LXX, διακονέω never) and it is not impossible that δουλεύω and διακονέω could be considered equivalent.

²δίδοναι = שים 26t in OT (although admittedly out of over 1600 occurrences). δίδοναι is frequently used with reference to the death of martyrs among the Jews and soldiers among the Greeks (Friedrich Büchsel, "δίδωμι, . . . ," TDNT, II, 166).

³Adolf Deissmann, Light from the Ancient East. The New Testament Illustrated by Recently Discovered Texts of the Graeco-Roman World, trans. by Lionel R. M. Strachan (new, rev. ed.; New York: George H. Doran, 1927), 327: " . . . when anybody heard the Greek word λύτρον, 'ransom,' in the first century, it was natural for him to think of the purchase-money for manumitting slaves."

⁴Leon Morris, The Apostolic Preaching of the Cross (Grand Rapids: Eerdmans, 1955), 9-26; M. J. Lagrange, Évangile selon Saint Marc, EBib (6th ed.; Paris: Gabalda, 1942), 282: " . . . le λύτρον, dans les LXX, est toujours un prix qu'on fournit pour donner satisfaction a celui qui a droit d'exiger autre chose . . . ." And note Cranfield's comments with respect to Pauline usage (Romans, I, 206-207).

atoning value."[1] The specific point of dispute is thus whether λυτ- continues to carry connotations of payment when the transaction is not mentioned. Even if this were so, the relevance to Mk. 10:45 may be questioned, since the concept of substitution, clearly implied with ἀντί,[2] suggests that, in fact, a transaction is in view. It is therefore probable that λύτρον retains here its basic meaning, in both Jewish and secular Greek, of a price paid for release.[3]

This excursus has been a necessary preliminary to consideration of the possible equivalence of λύτρον with אשם. On the one hand, it is true that the LXX never employs λύτρον as a rendering for אשם and it is claimed that this is not by accident: " . . . λύτρον, as we have seen was the redemption of a person or thing by a purchase; the אשם was the repayment of something wrongfully withheld, together with a guilt-offering by means of expiation: the one is a business transaction, the other involves a sacrifice for sins."[4] But it is doubtful if this rigid demarcation in meaning can be sustained:

---

[1] David Hill, Greek Words and Hebrew Meanings: Studies in the Semantics of Soteriological Terms, SNTSMS, V (Cambridge: University Press, 1967), 58-80 (quote, 80).

[2] See below on ἀντί. Even if the meaning of ἀντί is weakened here, the concept of substitution seems clearly to be implied (Friedrich Büchsel, "λύτρον," TDNT, IV 343).

[3] Hill claims, with regard to λυτρόω, that " . . . the other Greek words which are used to translate גאל and פדה contain no suggestion of the ransom idea, but express simply the action of Yahweh in rescuing or releasing men. This suggests that this aspect of the meaning of λυτρόω is dominant when that verb is used to translate the same Hebrew words and to describe the action of Yahweh." (Greek Words, 62-3). But, as Feuillet points out, what is noteworthy is that λυτρόω translates כפר, פדה and גאל only when these words occur in contexts which presuppose a "ransom" ("Le logion sur la rançon," RSPT, LI (1967), 384). Furthermore, the evidence with respect to λύτρον is far more clear-cut than is the case for the verbal form. Procksch suggests that the Hebrew כפר lies behind Mk. 10:45, and when λύτρον renders this word " . . . it always denotes a vicarious gift whose value covers a fault, so that the debt is not just cancelled." ("λύω," TDNT, IV, 329. Cf. also Morris, Apostolic Preaching, 20).

[4] Hooker, Servant, 77.

Kellermann notes that "The greatest diversity of meaning appears in the noun 'asham" and suggests that it means in Lev. 5, a "compensatory payment."[1] While אשם generally has clear sacrificial overtones not usually present in λύτρον, the concept of payment is integral to both. It is probably legitimate, therefore, to regard λύτρον as a free translation, or, perhaps better, interpretation of אשם in Is. 53:10.[2]

The substitutionary concept implied by ἀντί [3] accords well with the sin-bearing function of the Servant described in Is. 53 and πολλοί, the "many" is certainly a prominent feature of that chapter.[4]

Concluding this survey of the linguistic evidence, it must be admitted that, in the terms proposed by Barrett and Hooker, the argument for the dependence of Mk. 10:45 on Is. 53 falls short of proof. But the criteria proposed by these scholars for the determination of allusions to the OT are indefensible[5] and, in the present instance, the atomistic approach overlooks the very impressive cumulative evidence for the presence of an allusion to Is. 53:10-12.

---

[1] D. Kellermann, "אשם," TDOT, I, 430, 433.

[2] Jeremias, "Lösegeld," 227; Popkes, Christus Traditus, 221; France, Jesus, 120; Hahn, Titles, 57; Fuller, Mission and Achievement, 37; Cranfield, Mark, 342. Hill (Greek Words, 79), Feuillet ("Rançon," 388) and Wolff (Jesaja 53, 61-2) prefer to consider λύτρον a term which sums up the meaning of the work of the Servant.

[3] There is little to suggest that ἀντί ever has a weakened sense of "on behalf of." Mt. 17:27 is the verse generally appealed to to prove the contrary, but once it is recognized that the half-shekel tax was originally a redemption tax, the usual meaning of ἀντί can be retained here (R. E. Davies, "Christ in our Place -- The Contribution of the Prepositions," TB, XXI (1970), 74-81; Nigel Turner, Grammatical Insights into the New Testament (Edinburgh: T & T Clark, 1965), 173). Turner says: "The sole significance of the preposition in each New Testament context is that of substitution and exchange." (193). Cf. also Harris, "Prepositions and Theology in the Greek New Testament," 1171-1215.

[4] The use of רבים in the DSS to refer to the community raises the possibility that the "elect" are intended by the phrase (On Qumran, cf. Ralph Marcus, "'Mebaqqer' and 'Rabbim' in the Manual of Discipline vi, 11-13," JBL, LXXV (1956), 298-302).

[5] Cf., infra, 165-67.

The background for the theology implied in Mk. 10:45 must, therefore, be found primarily in the description of the mission of the suffering Servant, and there can be little doubt that the general tenor of the ransom saying agrees perfectly with the concepts expressed in Is. 53: "Die besondere Bedeutung der universalen Wirkung des Todes Jesu in Verbindung mit dem Gedanken von der stellvertretenden Sühne verweist unmissverständlich auf Jes. 53."[1] The vast majority of scholars, from varied theological positions, continue to advocate a reference to Is. 53 in Mk. 10:45.[2] The textual basis of the reference is certainly Semitic, probably the MT.[3]

The authenticity of v. 45 (sometimes only 45b) is often called into question, for the following reasons: 1) the context of vv. 40-45 involves the disciples' imitation of Jesus and they clearly cannot surrender their lives as "ransoms for many";[4] 2) the phraseology of the saying betrays the influence of the Hellenistic church;[5] 3) the Servant conception was not employed by Jesus;[6] 4) likewise, Jesus never elsewhere refers to the saving significance of his death;[7] and 5) Lk. 22:27 preserves the authentic logion.[8] None of these objections

---

[1] Karl Kertlege, "Der dienende Menschensohn (Mk 10, 45)," Jesus und der Menschensohn, 231.

[2] Since Barrett's article: Tödt, Son of Man, 205; Schweizer, Jesus, 93; Higgins, Son of Man, 46; France, Jesus, 118-20; Roloff, "Anfänge," 52.

[3] Lane (Mark, 384) suggests that the text of Is. 53:12 in 1QIsa may have influenced the form of the saying.

[4] Hastings Rashdall, The Idea of Atonement in Christian Theology, The Bampton Lectures, 1915 (London: MacMillan, 1920), 51; Tödt, Son of Man, 207; Popkes, Christus Traditus, 169-70; Kertlege, "Der dienende Menschensohn," 227-28.

[5] Bultmann, Synoptic Tradition, 144.

[6] Eduard Schweizer, Das Evangelium nach Markus, NTD, I (Göttingen: Vandenhoeck & Ruprecht, 1968), 219.

[7] Schweizer, Jesus, 93, n. 6.

[8] Bousset, Kyrios Christos, 39; Rashdall, Atonement, 50.

is especially convincing. The ransom saying is neither something which the disciples are to imitate, nor a μετάβασις εἰς ἄλλο γένος, but functions as a "topical illustration" of the behavior which Jesus has just commanded.[1] The addition is a perfectly natural one and has many parallels (cf. Phil. 2:5ff!) and the degree of scepticism with which it is regarded is hardly warranted. There is nothing especially late or "hellenistic" or Pauline about the saying[2] and to say that Jesus could not have uttered these words because he did not think of himself as the Servant or dwell on the soteriological meaning of his death is *petitio principi*. Finally, Lk. 22:27 is probably either later[3] or independent of Mk. 10:45.[4]

Mark 14:24 / Matthew 26:28 / Luke 22:20 (Isaiah 53:12)

As it will be our task to demonstrate, several OT passages have influenced the eucharistic words of Jesus. Our concern at this point is with suggested allusions to the fourth Servant Song. As preliminary to this discussion, the textual problem in Lk. 22:15-20 must be dealt with.

Verses 19b-20 in this passage were omitted by Westcott and Hort as a "Western non-interpolation," the cumbersome term coined by them to describe the rare occasions when (according to them) the Western text preserved a shorter, and presumably earlier, reading than the other MSS traditions (and expecially ℵ and B). Although considerable

---

[1] France, *Jesus*, 117.

[2] λύτρον is not Pauline. Even Tödt (*Son of Man*, 210) and Hahn (*Titles*, 57) admit that the saying has its roots in the primitive Palestinian church. For some pertinent remarks on the validity of the Palestinian-Hellenistic dichotomy in Christology, see I. Howard Marshall, "Palestinian and Hellenistic Christianity: Some Critical Comments," *NTS*, XIX (1972-3), 271-87.

[3] Büchsel, "λύτρον," 341-2.

[4] Schürmann, *Jesu Abschiedsrede*, 92.

doubt now exists as to the validity of this judgment regarding "non-Western interpolations,"[1] a great number of scholars continue to regard vv. 19b-20 as secondary. There is good reason for this judgment, for it conforms to two cardinal principles in textual criticism -- that the shorter reading is to be preferred and that the more difficult reading is to be preferred. Further basis for the secondary character of vv. 19b-20 is found in the non-Lukan style of the passage,[2] the contrast between the sacrificial emphasis in the passage and Luke's general reticence to speak of the sacrificial nature of Christ's death,[3] the lack of reference to the eucharistic words in Acts,[4] and the cup-bread order of I Cor. 10:16 and the Didache which corresponds to Lk. 22:15-19a. The presence of the longer reading in the great majority of witnesses is explained as an early addition from I Cor. 11:23-25, made in order to restore the customary liturgical practice of the early church.

The longer reading, in addition to its strong external support, has several points in its favor. It is possible to turn on its head the argument concerning the difficulty of the text; the presence of two cups seems just as difficult as the reversed order. The circulation of two independent accounts of the Last Supper in the early church seems improbable.[5] The other arguments are not unanswerable:

---

[1] Kurt Aland, "Neue Testamentliche Papyri II," NTS, XII (1966), 193-210; Klyne Snodgrass, "'Western Non-Interpolations,'" JBL, XCI (1972), 269-279; Joachim Jeremias, The Eucharistic Words of Jesus, trans. by Norman Perrin (London: SCM, 1966), 148-152.

[2] G. D. Kilpatrick, "Luke xxii. 19b-20," JTS, XLVII (1946), 51; Henry Chadwick, "The Shorter Text of Luke xxii. 15-20," HTR, L (1957), 252.

[3] Montefiore, Synoptic Gospels, II, 589; Martin Rese, "Zur Problematik von Kurz- und Langtext in Luk. XXII. 17ff," NTS, XXII (1975), 27.

[4] Rese, "Problematik," 30.

[5] Lietzmann notwithstanding. Cf. A. J. B. Higgins, "H. Lietzmann's 'Mass and Lord's Supper' (Messe und Herrenmahl)," ExpTim, LXV (1954), 333-336.

the non-Lukan style of vv. 19b-20 may be due to its liturgical origin; Acts 20:28 demonstrates Luke's familiarity with the sacrificial interpretation of Jesus' death; Luke has no real occasion to give the eucharistic words in Acts; I Cor. 10:16 cannot be viewed as a liturgical practice and the Didache's order is perhaps influenced by the practice in the Jewish Kiddush meal.[1] The similarity of the cup words in Luke and I Cor. may be due to Luke's acquaintance with the liturgy of the Pauline churches.[2] Furthermore, several items in Luke's narrative seem to presuppose the longer reading.[3] The major difficulty facing advocates of the longer reading is the necessity to explain the origin of the shorter reading. Jeremias considers the deletion to have arisen through a desire to preserve the "arcanum," the secrecy of the rite,[4] but this hypothesis has been properly criticized.[5] If Luke has combined two versions of the Last Supper, scribes familiar with the shorter version may have excised vv. 19b-20,[6] but it is difficult to envision such an omission occurring in the face of the otherwise unanimous Last Supper tradition. The traditional explanation remains the most satisfactory: the longer text has been

---

[1] Pierre Benoit, "Le Récit de la Cène dans Lc. XXII 15-20," RB, XLVIII (1939), 366.

[2] Heinz Schürmann, Einer quellenkritischen Untersuchung des lukanischen Abendmahlsberichtes, Lk, 22, 7-38, Vol. II: Der Einsetzungsbericht. Lk 22, 19-20, NA, XX (Münster: Aschendorffsche, 1955), 80, 131.

[3] Cf., especially "to you" (22:21); "covenant" (v. 29). Ellis, Luke, 254.

[4] Eucharistic Words, 156-159.

[5] The disciplina arcani was mainly a later development, at a very preliminary stage even in the time of Origen and Tertullian (J. N. D. Kelly, Early Christian Creeds (3rd ed.; London: Longman Group Limited, 1972), 170). See also: Benoit, "Récit," 368-9; Chadwick, "Shorter Text," 233-5; Rese, "Problematik," 21.

[6] A. J. B. Higgins, The Lord's Supper in the New Testament, SBT, VI (London: SCM, 1952), 40.

shortened by a scribe who found the mention of two cups difficult; in the process, v. 19b has been omitted as well.[1]

In view of the difficulties, neither position warrants unequivocal support. On the whole, it seems easier to suppose that an early scribe has eliminated the reference to the second cup than to suppose that vv. 19b-20 have been interpolated.[2] The originality of the longer text will therefore be presumed in the following investigation but with the implied qualification that the text is not absolutely free from question.

Allusions to Is. 53 have been noted in ἐκχυννόμενον (v. 10 or 12), and in the phrase ὑπὲρ (περὶ) πολλῶν (ὑμῶν). Since the existence of these allusions to Is. 53 has been challenged, it is essential to look closely at the evidence. ἐκχύννω does not appear in the LXX of Is. 53. The term is used frequently in sacrificial passages ("pouring out" the libation) and when linked with αἷμα takes on the meaning "shed blood," i.e., to kill by violence.[3] Hence, its function in the cup-word may be to draw attention to the sacrificial nature of Jesus' death[4] or to indicate the violent death which awaited

---

[1] Bruce M. Metzger (A Textual Commentary on the Greek New Testament (New York, et al.: United Bible Societies, 1971), 174-6) mentions the possibility that scribal misunderstanding is responsible for the omission.
Schürmann notes that by 2nd c. the church had separated the "community meal" from the eucharist, earlier celebrated together. The long text of Luke depicts both together (2 cups), but offense was taken at this in 2nd c. Verse 19b was taken out as well because its omission corresponded with liturgical practice of the church in which the omission was made. ("Lk 22, 19b-20 als ursprüngliche Textüberlieferung," Bib, XXXII (1951), 364-92, 522-41).

[2] Metzger, Textual Commentary, 174-176; E. Earle Ellis, The Gospel of Luke, NCB (London: Thomas Nelson and Sons, Ltd., 1966), 254; Eduard Schweizer, "Das Herrenmahl im Neuen Testament," TLZ, LXXIX (1954), 578; C. S. C. Williams, Alterations to the Text of the Synoptic Gospels and Acts (Oxford: Basil Blackwell, 1951), 48-49.

[3] Johannes Behm, "ἐκχύνω, ἐκχύννω," TDNT, II, 467.

[4] Tödt, Son of Man, 204-205.

him.[1] However, ἐκχυννόμενον is a literal translation of Heb. הערה (Is. 53:12)[2] and in conjunction with πολλῶν (πολλοί twice in Is. 53:12) is best understood as a conscious allusion to this OT verse. While the same idea of surrendering the soul to death for others is present in Is. 53:10 as well,[3] the verbal similarity to Is. 53:12 suggests that the latter passage is the source of the allusion. Sacrificial connotations need not be eliminated, for ὑπέρ may well be an attempt to introduce sacrificial significance into the death of the Servant in Is. 53.

πολλοί is regularly used in the inclusive sense in the NT, corresponding to Heb. רבים and Aram. סגיאין which are used in this way because these Semitic languages have no word for "all," in the sense of the "sum."[4] This fairly common use of the word has led some scholars to suggest that its presence in the cup-word need not represent an allusion to Is. 53 at all.[5] However, πολλοί in the inclusive sense is not all that common and a thread which runs throughout Is. 53.[6] When taken with the concept of vicarious suffering (ὑπέρ), which represents the essential thrust of Is. 53, the phrase must be seen as an attempt by Jesus to evoke the picture of the

---

[1]Hooker, Servant, 82; France, Jesus, 122; Ferdinand Hahn, "Die alttestamentlichen Motive in der urchristlichen Abendmahlsüberlieferung," EvT, XXVII (1967), 363.

[2]BDB lists several verses, including Is. 53:12, where the meaning of הערה is "poured out," i.e., in death (788). Cf. Gundry, Old Testament, 58.

[3]Is. 53:10 is regarded as the verse alluded to by Schürmann (Einsetzungsbericht, 20-21, 117), Hahn ("Alttestamentlichen Motive," 358-359), and W. F. Albright and C. S. Mann (Matthew, AB, XXVI (Garden City, N.Y.: Doubleday, 1971), 322-323).

[4]Joachim Jeremias, "πολλοί," TDNT, VI, 536-537.

[5]Hooker, Servant, 82; Suhl, Alttestamentlichen Zitate, 116; Best, Temptation, 146.

[6]Joachim Jeremias, Review of M. Hooker's Jesus and the Servant, JTS, n.s., XI (1960), 143; Jeremias-Zimmerli, Servant, 95. They speak of πολλοί as a "veritable keyword" in Is. 53.

suffering servant as a model for His own destiny. Again, while the individual components of the expression would not certainly need to be dependent on Is. 53, the phrase taken as a whole demonstrates undeniable verbal and conceptual affinities to Is. 53:12.[1]

Matthew's substitution of περί for Mark's ὑπέρ seems strange at first sight, unless he has chosen περί for its sacrificial connotations.[2] On the other hand, περί and ὑπέρ are often used interchangeably in the NT.[3]

The textual basis for the allusion to Is. 53:12 (ἐκχυννόμενον) is probably the MT and it is probable that the phrase ὑπέρ πολλῶν is taken from the Heb. as well (ὑπέρ is not used in the LXX of Is. 53). The application of the allusion does not effect an alteration in the meaning of the phrase.

Luke 22:37 (Isaiah 53:12)

The "Abschiedsrede" which Luke appends to his Last Supper narrative are climaxed with Jesus' warning concerning the new situation of hostility which the disciples will face from that time forward (ἀλλὰ νῦν). These hostile circumstances, explicitly contrasted with the peaceful nature of the missions of the twelve and seventy, are due, claims Jesus, to the fact that he, in fulfillment of the prophetic word, is about to be reckoned as a transgressor. Emphasis is placed on this quotation by the long and impressive introductory formula.

---

[1] It is probable that Mk. 10:45 is an allusion to Is. 53:10 or 12 and its similarity to Mk. 14:24 would be further evidence for an allusion in the cup-word (Tödt, Son of Man, 204-207).

[2] LXX translates חטאת "sin-offering" by περὶ ἁμαρτίας (McNeile, Matthew, 382).

[3] περί for ὑπέρ in I Cor. 1:13, I Pet. 3:18, Mk. 1:44, Lk. 5:14, Acts 26:1, Gal. 1:4, Eph. 6:18-19, Heb. 5:1, 3 (BDF, 121; Moule, Idiom Book, 63; Senior, Passion Narrative, 81).

Only here in the NT are three verbs used in the introduction to a citation, two of which, δεῖ and τελέω, are never employed elsewhere in connection with an explicit OT quotation.¹ δεῖ conveys a sense of divine necessity and τελέω the climactic character of the scriptural fulfillment.² Another unique feature of the introduction is the note of personal destiny conveyed by the phrase ἐν ἐμοί. When, finally, the concluding phrase of v. 38, which repeats the note of finality (τέλος ἔχειν)³ and the sense of personal involvement (τὸ περὶ ἐμοῦ), is added to the ledger, the balance compels a recognition of the deep significance which Jesus attached to the fulfillment of the prophecy.⁴

That the text of the quotation is related to the LXX in the use of ἐλογίσθη is clear, for this word is not the usual rendering

---

¹As pointed out earlier, δεῖ is infrequently used with reference to the accomplishment of the OT prophecies.

²τελέω properly signifies "bring to an end, complete" (BAG, 818) and this meaning is reflected in NT usage, where the verb refers to the completion of Scripture generally (Lk. 18:31, Acts 13:29), the accomplishment of Jesus' mission (Lk. 12:50, Jn. 19:28, 30) and to the culmination of God's guidance of history (Revelation, 8t.).

³τέλος ἔχειν is used by Josephus of the completion of prophecies (BAG, 819), and in secular Greek of the fulfillment of oracles and predictions (Alfred Plummer, A Critical and Exegetical Commentary on the Gospel According to St. Luke, ICC (Edinburgh: T & T Clark, 1896), 506).

⁴The singular τό most naturally refers to the OT citation (against Grundmann, Lukas, 409). Bartsch argues that the introductory formula shows clear signs of belonging to Luke's redaction ("Jesu Schwertwort," 196-98; cf. also Schürmann, Abschiedsrede, 124). While Bartsch is correct in pointing to Luke's fondness for δεῖ , the word is firmly imbedded in the pre-lukan tradition (Mk. 8:31). Luke's emphasis on the word need not be in conflict with Jesus' own use of the concept if the three occurrences of δεῖ in Luke 24 can be traced to Jesus' post-Resurrection ministry. (It is, of course, true that δεῖ has no equivalent in Aramaic, but the important point is to establish identity in meaning between Jesus and Luke). τελέω is strongly attested on Jesus' lips in Lk. 12:50. The singular use of ἐν ἐμοί in the introductory phrase is most easily understood as a reproduction of Jesus' own words (against Bartsch, II Cor. 1:20 is not strictly parallel, for specific OT passages are not involved). Therefore, while Lukan influence on the vocabulary cannot be ruled out, the unique features of the phrase, along with demonstrably dominical vocabulary are good reasons to trace the introduction back to Jesus.

of מנה and normally translates חשב in the LXX.¹ Similarly, dependence on the LXX should probably be recognized in ἄνομος, since it translates פשע only four times in the LXX (3t. in Is.), and is infrequent in the NT, especially in the general sense "one who is unrighteous."² However, while the quotation cannot, therefore, be derived from the Hebrew alone,³ μετά and the lack of the article are indications that the citation is not uninfluenced by the MT.⁴ These deviations from the LXX have been attributed to a variant Greek textual tradition, of the type seen in the background of the quotation in Mk. 14:27,⁵ but the evidence of Justin alone (Apol. I, 30, 2) is insufficient to establish the existence of this reading in a pre-Christian Greek recension. The text of the quotation is therefore a mixed one. It is not impossible that the text has been cited freely, perhaps from memory, since the brevity of the quotation and the relative insignificance of the variations make it doubtful that a conscious process of text selection has been undertaken.

Jesus' command to take up the sword, in contrast to his instructions for the provisions to be taken on the disciples' mission during the ministry, is a metaphorical indication of the new situation

---

¹Only in five cases does λογίζομαι translate a Heb. word other than חשב and is used for מנה only in II Chron. 5:6 and Is. 53:12. (H. W. Heidland, "λογίζομαι, λογισμός," TDNT, IV, 284; Traugott Holtz, Untersuchungen über die alttestamentlichen Zitate bei Lukas, TU, CIV (Berlin: Akademie Verlag, 1968), 42). The Septuagintal background to the use of the word λογίζομαι is pointed out by BDF par. 145 (2).

²The only other use of the word in this sense by Luke is in Acts 2:23. ἄνομος with the meaning "unrighteous" arises from the basic meaning of the word, "acting as if there were no law." "In this case ἄνομος can easily take on the more general sense of 'unrighteous,' with no strict reference to a specific law." (W. Gutbrod, "ἄνομος," TDNT, IV, 1086).

³Against Wolff (Jesaja 53, 57) and Grundmann (Lukas, 409).

⁴Zimmerli-Jeremias, Servant, 90; pace Higgins, Son of Man, 31.

⁵Heidland, "λογίζομαι," 287; Bartsch, "Schwertwort," 195; Benoit, "Serviteur," 129.

of hostility which the disciples will confront because of Jesus' being reckoned as a transgressor.¹ The citation from Is. 53:12 therefore represents the basis (γάρ) for the warning Jesus gives, a pattern of warning-scriptural foundation similar to that found elsewhere (cf. Mk. 14:27). Attempts have been made to link the prophecy with a specific event in the passion narrative,² particularly Jesus' crucifixion between two other criminals.³ Rese feels that Luke indicates this

---

¹Vincent Taylor, Jesus and His Sacrifice (London: MacMillan, 1937), 192; Plummer, Luke, 506; John Martin Creed, The Gospel According to St. Luke (London: MacMillan, 1930), 270; Bruce, Old Testament Themes, 95; William Manson, The Gospel of Luke, MNTC (London: Hodder and Stoughton, 1936), 247; Leon Morris, The Gospel According to St. Luke, TNTC (London: Inter-Varsity Press, 1974), 310.

²Several scholars have suggested a connection with the sword-play at the arrest: Alfred Loisy, L'Évangile selon Luc (Paris: Émile Nourry, 1924), 523; Jack Finegan, Die Überlieferung der Leidens- und Auferstehungsgeschichte Jesu, BZNW, XV (Giessen: Töpelmann, 1934), 16; Dibelius, From Tradition to Gospel, 200-201; Leaney, Luke, 271; Paul S. Minear, "A Note on Luke 22:36," NovT, VII (1964-65), 128-134; S. G. Wilson, "Lukan Eschatology," NTS, XV (1969-70), 335. (The last two authors go so far as to identify the ἄνομοι in the quotation with the disobedient disciple who uses the sword.) There is much against this interpretation: the only verbal link is μάχαιρα; two swords are mentioned in 22:38, one only in the arrest; Jesus would be pictured as having deliberately misled the disciples (Bartsch, "Schwertwort," 194); and the description of Jesus as λῃστής at the time of the arrest would be unusual (one would have expected ἄνομος)(Rese, Alttestamentliche Motive, 159; Schürmann, Abschiedsrede, 131).

³The following scholars believe that the two passages are related: Eduard Lohse, History of the Suffering and Death of Jesus Christ, trans. by Martin O. Dietrich (Philadelphia: Fortress Press, 1967), 96; Alan Hugh McNeile, "Our Lord's Use of the Old Testament," Cambridge Biblical Essays, ed. by Henry Barclay Swete (London: MacMillan, 1909), 240; John Pobee, "The Cry of the Centurion -- A Cry of Defeat," The Trial of Jesus, ed. by E. Bammel, SBT, n.s., XIII (London: SCM, 1970), 93; Karnetzki, "Die alttestamentlichen Zitate," 6; Eta Linnemann, Studien zur Passionsgeschichte, FRLANT, CII (Göttingen: Vandenhoeck & Ruprecht, 1970), 192; Bartsch, "Schwertwort," 194-195; "Historische Erwägungen zur Leidensgeschichte," EvT, XXII (1962), 453; Lonsdale Ragg, St. Luke, WC (London: Methuen, 1922), 298; Grundmann, Lukas, 432; Floyd V. Filson, A Commentary on the Gospel According to St. Matthew, BNTC (London: Adam & Charles Black, 1960), 295; Morris, Luke, 329; David M. Stanley, "The Theme of the Servant of Yahweh in Primitive Christian Soteriology and its Transposition by St. Paul," CBQ, XVI (1954), 402; Hermann Strathmann, Das Evangelium nach Johannes, NTD, IV (Göttingen: Vandenhoeck & Ruprecht, 1954), 249; R. V. G. Tasker, The Gospel According to St. John, TNTC (London: Inter-Varsity Press, 1960), 210; Lagrange, Marc, 429; G. W. H. Lampe, "Luke," Peake's Commentary on the Bible, ed. by Matthew Black and H. H. Rowley (rev. ed.; London, et al.: Nelson, 1962), 841; Karl Heinrich Rengstorf, Das Evangelium nach Lukas, NTD, III (6th ed.; Göttingen: Vandenhoeck & Ruprecht, 1952), 269.

connection by several redactional changes. Mt./Mk.'s λησταί, which carries political overtones,[1] has been changed to κακοῦργοι, a word more in harmony with the meaning of Is. 53:12. ἕτερος in 23:32 should be interpreted in the strict sense, "another of the same kind" which more closely identifies Jesus with the criminals than is true in the other gospels. Although Luke and John seem to be following a common tradition in this narrative, John fails to specifically identify the two as "evil-doers." The continuation of the story of the criminals in Lk. 23:39-43 provides further evidence for Luke's close identification of Jesus with the criminals; κρέμασθαι, used of the criminals in v. 39, elsewhere describes Jesus' death (Acts 5:30, 10:39) and v. 40 clearly indicates that Jesus is placed under the same judgment as the two others.[2] Bartsch notes that only Luke uses the word ἄνομος, which had come to signify "criminal" or "heathen" in contemporary Judaism and that even the two swords of Lk. 22:38 find their counterparts in the two criminals.[3] Despite these arguments and the extensive support for the connection of Lk. 22:37 and 23:33, it is improbable that Luke intends to connect the two passages. Rese seems to be involved in a contradiction when he seeks to establish Luke's particular redactional perspective on the basis of his changes from both Mt./Mk. and John in the same narrative. The various arguments used to demonstrate Luke's identification of Jesus with the criminals are not especially convincing.[4] However, the really decisive objection to this interpretation

---

[1] Josephus uses λῃστής of the Zealots (K. H. Rengstorf, "λῃστής," TDNT, IV, 158).

[2] Rese, Alttestamentliche Motive, 156-158.

[3] "Schwertwort," 194-195. Bartsch believes that Luke has transformed a saying which originally applied to the expectation of the eschatological conflict.

[4] κρέμασθαι is a natural word in the circumstances, and hardly lends emphasis to Jesus' identification with the criminals; ἕτερος is often used interchangeably with ἄλλος in NT Greek (Nigel Turner, Syntax, Vol. III of A Grammar of New Testament Greek, by J. H. Moulton

is the fact that Luke does not characterize the criminals in 23:33 as ἄνομοι, which is inexplicable if he intended to identify Jesus' crucifixion between the criminals as the fulfillment of the prophecy in Lk. 22:37 (especially since he has used a different word than is found in the other gospels).

The fulfillment of Jesus' prophecy should be seen as the events of the passion as a whole, which picture the sinless Messiah rejected, mocked and crucified by his own people -- in a phrase, "treated as a transgressor."[1] This understanding of the ἄνομος of Is. 53:12 is in keeping with the interpretation of the passage defended above, since the treatment of Jesus at the hands of the Jewish authorities is a shattering indication of what his followers have to expect. It is undeniable that the prophecy does not explicitly include a reference to sacrificial or substitutionary suffering,[2] but the concept of undeserved suffering obviously present could easily be understood to imply the further corollary of a suffering *for* others.[3]

The broad reference of the quotation advocated here corresponds closely to the meaning of Is. 53:12 in its own context. As Westermann

---

(Edinburgh: T & T Clark, 1963), 197); BDF suggests it is pleonastic here (160); ἄνομος proves nothing since it is taken from the quotation.

[1]Both Heb. נמנה and Greek λογίσθημαι convey the sense of "being treated as" or "classed with" (BAG, 477). This general application of the prophecy to the Passion Narrative as a whole is upheld by Taylor (Jesus and His Sacrifice, 187), Lohse (Märtyrer, 116, n. 2), Gerhard Schneider (Die Passion Jesu nach den drei älteren Evangelien (Munich: Kösel, 1973), 168), and William J. Larkin ("Luke's Use of the Old Testament as a Key to his Soteriology," JETS, XX (1977), 332-33).
 Rese notes that the two quotations from Isaiah on the lips of Jesus in Luke's gospel summarize the mission of Christ: Is. 61:1-2 in Lk. 4:18-19 and Is. 53:12 in Lk. 22:37. (Alttestamentliche Motive, 207).

[2]Hooker, Servant, 86; Lohse, Märtyrer, 116, n. 2; Rese, Alttestamentliche Motive, 158; Gerhard Delling, Der Kreuzestod Jesu in der urchristlichen Verkündigung (Göttingen: Vandenhoeck & Ruprecht, 1972), 80.

[3]Morris, Luke, 310; France, Jesus, 115.

notes, the hiphil of pāga⁽ ("intercede") signifies that " . . . with his [servant's] life, his suffering and his death, he took their place and underwent their punishment in their stead."[1] While the text of the quotation is mixed, it retains the meaning of the Heb. original. In other words, the appropriation technique utilized here may be classified as a direct one -- as has been the case with almost all the allusions and quotations studied thus far. This would suggest that the evangelists' use of the Servant imagery is based on an underlying identification that legitimizes the direct appropriation of "Servant" language to apply to Jesus.

While the authenticity of the saying has been questioned,[2] it seems probable that the quotation goes back to Jesus in view of the mixed text form,[3] the "hard-saying" concerning the sword,[4] a possible Semitic word-play,[5] the close connection of the quotation with the argument of the narrative,[6] and the fact that Luke does not seem to be interested in the Servant conception.[7]

---

[1] Westermann, Isaiah 40-66, 269.

[2] Hooker, Servant, 86; Lindars, Apologetic, 85; Higgins, Son of Man, 31; Leaney, Luke, 271; Hermann Patsch, Abendmahl und historischer Jesus (Stuttgart: Calwer, 1972), 162; Montefiore, Synoptic Gospels, II, 604; Grundmann, Lukas, 409.

[3] Zimmerli-Jeremias, Servant, 91; France, Jesus, 115; Wolff, Jesaja 53, 57.

[4] Benoit, "Serviteur," 129; France, Jesus, 115; Taylor, Jesus and His Sacrifice, 194.

[5] Black, Aramaic Approach, 179.

[6] Zimmerli-Jeremias, Servant, 105. Cf. also Coppens, Messianisme, 209. The quotation in Lk. 22:37 is recognized as pre-Lukan by Schürmann, Abschiedsrede, 134-140; Bartsch, "Schwertwort," 195 and Hahn, Titles of Jesus, 154.

[7] I. Howard Marshall, The Gospel of Luke, New International Greek Testament Commentary (Grand Rapids: Eerdmans, 1978), 825.

The Isaianic Servant Songs   139

Mark 14:65 / Matthew 26:67-8; John 18:22-3;
Mark 15:19 / Matthew 27:30; John 19:1,3 (Isaiah 50:6)

The Old Testament element in the descriptions of the mockery of Jesus is most conveniently examined in one section because of the great deal of similarity among the narratives. Is. 50:6 figures prominently in these passages. Suggested contacts between this verse and the gospel narratives are:

   ῥάπισμα -- Mk. 14:65 / Matthew 26:67 (-ίζω); Jn. 18:22; 19:3
   ἐμπτύω -- Mk. 14:65 / Mt. 26:67; Mk. 15:19 / Mt. 27:30
   μαστιγόω -- Jn. 19:1

The occurrence of both ῥάπισμα (-ίζω) and ἐμπτύω in Mk. 14:65 / Mt. 26:67 cannot be by chance. ῥάπισμα occurs only in Is. 50:6 in the LXX and only in contexts related to the mockery of Christ in the NT, while the verb ῥαπίζω is found only three times in the LXX and in Mt. 5:39 and 26:67 in the NT. A similar situation with respect to ἐμπτύω has already been noted.[1] On the other hand, πρόσωπον in Matthew and Mark and εἰς after ἐμπτύω in Matthew cannot be regarded as significant parallels to Is. 50:6, since the words occur in different contexts.[2] In the light of these word statistics, ἐμπτύω in Mk. 15:19 / Mt. 27:30 and ῥάπισμα in Jn. 18:22 and 19:3 must be taken from this OT-influenced mockery motif as well.

The situation is more ambiguous with respect to the use of μαστιγόω in Jn. 19:3. We have advocated a reference to Is. 50:6 in the use of this word in the passion predictions, but it occurred there with another word from Is. 50:6. Since it is the Greek equivalent for

---

[1] Cf., supra, 88-89. This linguistic evidence seems conclusive, although Hooker (Servant, 90-91) and Suhl (Alttestamentlichen Zitate, 58) entertain doubts.

[2] Against Gundry, Old Testament, 61 and McNeile, Matthew, 403.

140   The OT in the Gospel Passion Narratives

verberatio, the term designating the Roman custom of scourging a condemned prisoner,[1] it must be questioned whether it has any allusion to Is. 50:6.[2]

The textual background for the allusions to Is. 50:6 seems clearly to be Septuagintal. While μάστιγας and ἐμπτυσμάτων faithfully represent the Heb. Vorlage, εἰς ῥάπισμα ("blow, slap;" Pesh. ܠܐܦܐ ("blow, slap [on the cheek]")) does not correspond to the MT לֹמֹרְטִים ("to the pluckers;" Targ., idem.).[3] It is probable, therefore, that all the references to Is. 50:6 were drawn from the LXX of Is. 50:6.

While going beyond the limits of the present section, it will be convenient to deal with several other suggested OT reminiscences in Mk. 14:65 / Mt. 26:67-8. In I Kings 22:24, Zedekiah "strikes Micaiah on the cheek" (LXX ἐπάταξεν . . . ἐπὶ τὴν σιαγόνα) and rebukes him for his temerity for castigating the king's lot of "court

---

[1] BAG, 496.

[2] Jn. 19:3 is said to have an allusion to Is. 50:6 by Brown, John, II, 874; Anton Dauer, Die Passionsgeschichte im Johannesevangelium: Eine traditionsgeschichtliche und theologische Untersuchung zu Joh 18, 1-19, 30, SANT, XXX (Munich: Kösel, 1972), 126; Rudolf Schnackenburg, Das Johannesevangelium, HTKNT, IV (3 vols.; Freiburg: Herder, 1965-1975), III, 292; C. H. Dodd, Historical Tradition in the Fourth Gospel (Cambridge: University Press, 1963), 311; Reim, Hintergrund, 163.

[3] Gundry, Old Testament, 61. Elsewhere, Gundry has argued that the reading of LXX and Pesh. is an independent translation of a Heb. text closely resembling that found in 1QIs^a, למכלם, which has been understood in the sense of Arab. matala, "to beat, strike." However, as Gundry admits, matala does not ordinarily have this meaning. ("LMTLYM: 1Q Isaiah a 50,6 & Mk 14,65," RevQ, II (1960), 559-69). A more satisfactory derivation of the reading is to regard ῥάπισμα as a LXX translator's attempt to render the difficult Heb. "to the pluckers." Realizing that some sort of blow must be meant, he is stimulated by ·לט in the same phrase to translate with ῥάπισμα, since the latter word was frequently used with σιαγόνα in a stock phrase (BAG, 741-2; in LXX, Hos. 11:4 -- with nothing corresponding in MT!). Peshitta, as often, is influenced by the LXX.

prophets."[1] Three considerations tell against the influence of this OT passage on the scene of mockery: the verb is a different one; cheeks are not mentioned in the gospels; and Micaiah is chastised for prophesying, not taunted to do more. There is perhaps more justification for proposing Mic. 4:14 (LXX; MT 5:1) as a background to Mk. 14:65 / Mt. 26:67-8, since Mic. 5:2 (MT) is cited as a Messianic prophecy in Mt. 2:6.[2] However, a reference to LXX of Mic. 4:14, as is supposed, is difficult in view of the recipient of the slaps, τὰς φυλάς ("judge" in MT). Once again, cheeks are mentioned in the OT passage and not in the Gospels, and καλάμῳ is found in Mk. 15:19, rather than ῥάβδῳ which is used in Mic. 4:14.[3] Montefiore believes that the reference to the veiling of Jesus' face arose from a mistranslation of Is. 53:3 ונסתר פנים ממנו (LXX ὅτι ἀπέστραπται τὸ πρόσωπον αὐτοῦ).[4] The mistranslation does not, however, seem likely and Is. 53 does not otherwise figure in the descriptions of Jesus' mockery. It is even less likely that the veiling was included as a reference to 1QIs^a 50:6 למכלים, understood as the Hiph. ptcp. of סלל, "to cover, roof."[5] סלל is not a word that

---

[1] Montefiore, Synoptic Gospels, I, 366; A. Loisy, L'Évangile selon Marc (Paris: Émile Nourry, 1912), 437; H. J. Holtzmann, Der Synoptiker, HKNT, I (3rd ed.; Tübingen and Leipzig: Mohr, 1901), 178; S. D. F. Salmond, St. Mark, The Century Bible (Edinburgh: T. C. and E. C. Jack, n.d.), 339.

[2] Montefiore, Synoptic Gospels, I, 366; A. Schlatter, Der Evangelist Matthaus (Stuttgart: Calwer, 1957), 762 (as possible); Holtzmann, Die Synoptiker, 178.

[3] Pierre Benoit, "Les outrages à Jésus Prophète (Mc. xiv 65 par.)," Neotestamentica et Patristica, 96. (Loisy, Marc, 437 has linked Mic. 4:14 to Mk. 15:19).

[4] Synoptic Gospels, 366. Others who mention Is. 53:3 are Loisy, Marc, 437; Holtzmann, Die Synoptiker, 178; Hugh Anderson, The Gospel of Mark, NCB (London: Oliphants, 1976), 332; Schneider, Passion, 64.

[5] Gundry, "LMTLYM," 565-6.

would naturally spring to the mind of a reader, being rare (once in MT), and the hypothesis is based on the view that Mk. 14:65 / Mt. 26: 67-8 is dependent on the type of text preserved in 1QIs^a, which, as we have seen, is unlikely.[1]

The Judaism of Jesus' day expected Messiah to have prophetic ability, and although the textual situation is uncertain,[2] there can be no doubt that Mk. 14:65 / Mt. 26:67-8 describes a mockery of Jesus as a Messianic pretender,[3] a mockery which arises directly

---

[1] Hardly worth mentioning is the suggested parallel in Ez. 12:6, where the prophet is commanded to "cover his face" (G. Minette de Tillesse, Le Secret Messianique dans L'Évangile de Marc (Paris: Éditions du Cerf, 1968), 379).

[2] If the weakly attested question τίς ἐστιν ὁ παίσας ... is omitted in Mk. 14:65 as an assimilation, the veiling of Jesus' face seems to be without purpose. On the other hand, Matthew's inclusion of the question without the veiling seems equally incongruous. The easiest solution is to cut the knot and regard both the veiling in Mk. (omitted by D a f Syr^S, an omission the conflated texts in θ 700 565 Pesh Arm Geo seem to support) and the question in Mt. as assimilations to Lk. 22:64. While advocated by Streeter (Four Gospels, 325-6 -- followed by G. B. Caird, The Gospel of St. Luke, PNTC (London: Adam & Charles Black, 1963), 245 and Donald P. Senior, The Passion Narrative According to Matthew: A Redactional Study, BETL, XXXIX (Leuven: Leuven University Press, 1975), 189), the lack of textual support for the omission in Mt. is a decisive objection. Greater support is found for the spuriousness of the veiling in Mark (Taylor, Mark, 571; Anderson, Mark, 332; David R. Catchpole, The Trial of Jesus: A Study in the Gospels and Jewish Historiography from 1770 to the Present Day, SPB, XVIII (Leiden: Brill, 1971), 175; Gundry, "LMTLYM," 563-4; Benoit, "Outrages," 38; G. D. Kilpatrick, "Western Text and Original Text in the Gospels and Acts," JTS, XLIV (1943), 30; C. H. Turner, "Western Readings in the Second Half of St. Mark's Gospel," JTS, XXIX (1928), 10-11). While the scholarly support for this omission commands respect, and it represents the brevior lectio and gives a better sense, it must be rejected as too easy and without sufficient MSS support. Therefore, the veiling in Mk. and the question in Mt. must be retained and the interpreter will have to make the best of these texts. There are two likely possibilities: Mark's veiling may have nothing to do with the command to prophesy (note its separation from the command) and is to be explained as an isolated mockery, involving a popular contemporary game (David L. Miller, "EMΠAIZEIN: Playing the Mock Game (Luke 22:63-64)," JBL, XC (1971), 309-13). Matthew, then, sees the command to prophesy as a taunting request for Jesus to name his tormentors (M.-J. Lagrange, Évangile selon Saint Matthieu, EBib (5th ed.; Paris: Gabalda, 1941), 509). However, in view of Luke's probably independent tradition, it seems better to regard Mt. and Mk. as complementary, each assuming a component which is retained in the other (Tasker, Matthew, 257).

[3] David Hill, The Gospel of Matthew, NCB (London: Oliphants, 1972), 347; Benoit, Passion, 92. It is more problematic whether the mockery

from Jesus' claim in 14:62. While the mockery after the Sanhedrin hearing fits naturally into that context, such is the case as well with regard to the mockery following the Roman trial, for in this scene Jesus is mocked as a kingly pretender. Isaiah 50:6 is admirably suited as the background for these mockeries, since it seems that a public chastisement is envisaged there.[1]

The question as to the historicity of the mockery, in light of the OT allusions, must be faced as well. Is this a case of a "modification in the point of application"; an incident or details created on the basis of the OT prophecy? While this has been affirmed,[2] there are reasons for rejecting this interpretation. First, the mockery is not unnatural in its context -- the "scourging" of a convicted criminal was a well-known custom.[3] Second, the OT element is not so prominent as to provide a powerful enough motive for the creation. Third, the OT prophecy used is taken over only in part, and those parts are slightly altered. Is this likely had the incident been created on the basis of the prophecy? It is far more likely that the Scripture was brought in to describe what was known to have taken place.

While John diverges a great deal from the synoptics in the trial narratives, it seems that Jn. 19:1-3 should be identified with the mockery recorded in Mark 15:15ff (the mockery of Jesus as political usurper being a common denominator), and that of Jn. 18:22-3 with the

---

should be understood in the light of the expectation of the Mosaic eschatological prophet (Longenecker, Christology, 35).

[1] Christopher R. North, The Second Isaiah (Oxford: Clarendon Press, 1964), 203. North's comment on this verse is worth repeating: " . . . a startling anticipation of the maltreatment of Christ on the morning of the crucifixion."

[2] Paul Winter, On the Trial of Jesus, SJ:FWJ, I (Berlin: de Gruyter, 1961), 104-105.

[3] Lohmeyer, Markus, 340; Schniewind, Markus, 197.

Jewish tauntings. In any case, it is difficult to believe that John is dependent on the synoptics, but the shared Is. 50:6-influenced mockery motif suggests the use of a familiar tradition that linked this verse with the mockery of Christ.[1]

Matthew 27:57 (Isaiah 53:9)

Matthew characterizes Joseph of Arimathea as a "rich man," ἄνθρωπος πλούσιος, in contrast to Mark's εὐσχήμων βουλευτής, a change perhaps influenced by Is. 53:9: "They made his grave with the wicked and with a rich man in his death . . . ."[2] Although the meaning of being placed "with a rich man in his death" is debated, it is possible that Matthew has associated the concept with Jesus' burial in a grave owned by the well-to-do Joseph. Emendation of the Hebrew text has frequently been advocated in order to achieve synonymous parallelism,[3] but the structure of the verse could be construed as an antithesis; while the servant's grave was intended to be with the

---

[1] Dodd, Historical Tradition, 40.

[2] W. Boyd Barrick, "The Rich Man from Arimathea (Matt 27:57-60) and 1QIsa^a," JBL, XCVI (1977), 235; Filson, Matthew, 298; Friedrich Karl Feigel, Der Einfluss des Weissagungsbeweises und anderer Motive auf die Leidensgeschichte: Ein Beitrag zur Evangelien Kritik (Tübingen: Mohr, 1910), 47; J. C. Fenton, The Gospel of St. Matthew, PNTC (Harmondsworth: Penguin Books, 1963), 447; Gundry, Old Testament, 146; Karnetzki, "Die alttestamentlichen Zitate," 6; E. C. Hengstenberg, Commentary on the Gospel of St. John (3 vols.; Edinburgh: T & T Clark, 1865), III, 931. Mentioned as possible by Philip A. Micklem, St. Matthew, WC (London: Methuen, 1917), 276; Julian Morgenstern, Some Significant Antecedents of Christianity, SPB, X (Leiden: Brill, 1966), 56; Erich Klostermann, Das Matthäusevangelium, HNT, IV (2nd ed.; Tübingen: Mohr, 1927), 226; Holtzmann, Die Synoptiker, 295; Eduard Schweizer, The Good News According to Matthew, trans. by David E. Green (London: SPCK, 1975), 518.

[3] G. W. Wade, The Book of the Prophet Isaiah, WC (London: Methuen, 1911), 342; Torrey, The Second Isaiah, 420; C. R. North, Isaiah 40-55, TB (London: SCM, 1952), 137; John L. McKenzie, Second Isaiah, AB, XX (Garden City, New York: Doubleday, 1968), 130. 1QIsa supports MT -- עשׁיר׃

wicked, it turned out to be with the rich.[1] It is probable, if Matthew is referring to Is. 53:9, that he is dependent on the MT (LXX has the plural πλουσίους).[2]

Mark 2:19-20 / Matthew 9:15 / Luke 5:34-35 (Isaiah 53:8)

When questioned about the fact that, in contrast to the Pharisees and the disciples of John, his disciples were not fasting, Jesus employs the metaphor of the wedding feast to justify his and his disciples' practice: it is not possible for the wedding guests to fast while the bridegroom is with them and their joy is full. But, Jesus goes on, the time will come when the bridegroom will be taken away (ἀπαρθῇ), and fasting will be appropriate then.[3] That this saying represents the first hint of the passion on Jesus' lips seems clear (if the Markan arrangement at this point reflects the actual chronology), but conclusions any more explicit have little substantiation. ἀπαίρω does not, of itself, connote *violent* death[4]

___

[1] Delitzsch, Isaiah, 301; J. A. Alexander, The Prophecies of Isaiah (Glasgow: William Collins, n.d.), 793.

[2] Gundry, Old Testament, 146. Barrick suggests dependence on 1QIsa^a ("Rich Man," 236-39), but his argument is not convincing.

[3] On this passage, see C. H. Dodd, The Parables of the Kingdom (London: Nisbet, 1935); Joachim Jeremias, The Parables of Jesus, trans. based on that of S. H. Hooke (2nd ed.; New York: Charles Scribner's Sons, 1963), 52; Georg Braumann, "'An jenem Tag' (Mk. 2,20)," NovT, VI (1963), 264-7; Alistair Kee, "The Question about Fasting," NovT, XI (1969), 161-73. The "bridegroom" is probably not a Messianic title (Jewish evidence is lacking), but simply part of the imagery of the illustration (Joachim Jeremias, "νύμφη, νυμφίος," TDNT, IV, 1101-2). The attempt to relegate v. 20 to a secondary status because of the alleged allegory (Dodd, Jeremias) overlooks the essential unity of vv. 19-20 (Kee, 166-67) and presupposes a rigid exclusion of allegory from Jesus' sayings which cannot be maintained (Cranfield, Mark, 109; Taylor, Mark, 212). On the question of allegory in the sayings of Jesus, see especially Raymond E. Brown, "Parable and Allegory Reconsidered," NovT, V (1962), 37-45; Snodgrass, "Stone Testimonia," 114-28.

[4] LSJ give no example of this meaning for ἀπαίρω ; the word in the LXX means simply "remove, set out, take away"; any connotation of violence must be gleaned from the context.

nor does the word allude clearly to Is. 53:8.[1] It is, therefore, unlikely that there is a reference here to the Suffering Servant.

John 19:30 (Isaiah 53:12)

A reference to Is. 53:12 is said to be present in John's description of Jesus' death: παρέδωκεν τὸ πνεῦμα .[2] However, the LXX uses the passive παρεδόθη and ψυχή as opposed to the active voice and πνεῦμα in John, and the Hebrew הֶעֱרָה, though active, means "pour out," not "hand over, deliver, commit." So, while an allusion to Is. 53:12 is not impossible, the wording of the phrase itself betrays no influence from this verse.

John 10:11,15,17 (Isaiah 53)

Suggestions as to the background for the Shepherd analogy in John 10 are many and varied,[3] but, for our purposes, the larger discussion can be by-passed in order to concentrate on the statement that the Good Shepherd "lays down his life for his sheep" (τὴν ψυχὴν αὐτοῦ τίθησιν (v.l. δίδωσιν) ὑπὲρ τῶν προβάτων). It is interesting that even J. D. M. Derrett, who discovers a multitude of

---

[1] ἀπαίρω is used only in the three synoptic parallel passages here in the NT, but over 100t. in the LXX, where it never translates any of the Hebrew verbs in Is. 53:8. αἴρω is used twice in Is. 53:8, but in each case the Hebrew word translated is never elsewhere rendered by αἴρω . Suggesting the allusion to Is. 53:8 are: Lagrange, Marc, 48; Taylor, Mark, 211; A. Feuillet, "La controverse sur le jeûne (Mc 2, 18-20; Mt 9, 14-15; Lc 5, 33-35)," NRT, XC (1968), 255; Cranfield, Mark, 110; Grundmann, Markus, 66; Martin, Mark, 186; Hill, Matthew, 176-7; Schürmann, Lukas, I, 296.

[2] Brown, John, II, 910; Bernard, John, II, 641; Lindars, Apologetic, 80, n. 4 (as possible).

[3] See A. J. Simonis, Die Hirtenrede im Johannes-Evangelium: Versuch einer Analyse von Johannes 10, 1-18 nach Entstehung, Hintergrund und Inhalt, AnBib, XXIX (Rome: Pontifical Biblical Institute, 1967), 319-29. Ez. 34 is perhaps the most important background passage (Dodd, The Fourth Gospel, 358-60).

OT passages behind Jn. 10, fails to link this concept with a scriptural background.[1] Yet, two OT passages in particular would seem to afford excellent material for comparison. The first is Is. 53, which, while not comparing Jesus to a shepherd, does mention "sheep" as those who partake of the benefits won by the servant's sacrifice (v. 6) and provides the background for Mk. 10:45 and 14:24, which exhibit significant points of contact with Jn. 10:11 ("giving" or "laying down" the soul; $\overset{\text{'}}{\upsilon}\pi\overset{\text{'}}{\epsilon}\rho$).[2] The second text should not be overlooked as often as it is, for Zech. 13:7 not only specifically mentions the death of a shepherd who "stands near" to Yahweh, but is quoted by Jesus as well, with reference to his death (Mk. 14:27 = Mt. 26:31).[3] It would be consonant with the character of the fourth gospel to suggest that both passages have influenced Jesus' words about the Good Shepherd's supreme task.[4]

---

[1] J. D. M. Derrett, "The Good Shepherd: St. John's Use of Jewish Halakah and Haggadah," ST, XXVII (1973), 25-50.

[2] Lindars, John, 361. Simonis (Hirtenrede, 267-9) discusses the question of influence from Is. 53, and comes to no definite conclusion, although he clearly allows the possibility.
That $\tau\iota\theta\eta\mu\iota\ \tau\dot{\eta}\nu\ \psi\upsilon\chi\dot{\eta}\nu$ here means "to die" and not simply "to risk one's life" (Rudolf Bultmann, The Gospel of John: A Commentary, trans. by G. R. Beasley-Murray (Oxford: Basil Blackwell, 1971), 370, n. 5) is shown by the sacrificial connotations implied by $\upsilon\pi\epsilon\rho$ (Sanders-Mastin, John, 251). Simonis believes the concept in Jn. 10:11 lies at some point between these extremes: a moment by moment self-surrender is connoted (Hirtenrede, 266-7).

[3] See especially Schnackenburg, Johannes, II, 371, who notes the parallel between Jn. 10:12 ($\sigma\kappa o\rho\pi\iota\zeta\omega$), Jn. 16:32 ($\delta\iota\alpha\sigma\kappa o\rho\pi\iota\zeta\omega$) and Zech. 13:7 ($\delta\iota\alpha\sigma\kappa o\rho\pi\iota\zeta\omega$). Simonis (Hirtenrede, 272-3) objects, noting that the shepherd is passively "smitten" in Zech., but actively surrenders his soul in Jn. 10. However, a less direct dependence, such as we suggest, by-passes this difficulty.

[4] That death is the ultimate purpose of the shepherd and the basis for his "goodness" is not at all inconsistent with the passage, as Schnackenburg remarks: " . . . das Hirtenbilde von Joh 10, 11-15 (bzw. 18) nicht zum 'pastoralen' Typ, bei dem es um die leitende Funktion des Hirten geht, sondern zum 'soteriologischen' Typ, bei dem der Hirt zum Retter der Schafe wird." (Johannes, II, 371).

Mark 14:61 / Matthew 26:63; Luke 23:9;
Mark 15:5 / Matthew 27:14; Matthew 27:12; John 19:9
(Isaiah 53:7)

Jesus' refusal to defend himself in the face of his accusers is repeatedly mentioned in the course of the Jewish hearings and Roman trial.[1] It is generally believed that this motif is to be related to the description of the Servant in Is. 53:7: "He was oppressed and he was afflicted, yet he did not open his mouth [פיו יפתח ולא; LXX: οὐκ ἀνοίγει τὸ στόμα]; Like a lamb that led led to slaughter, and like a sheep that is silent [נאלמה; LXX: ἄφωνος] before its shearers, he did not open his mouth [as before]." The correspondence does not depend on linguistic similarity (the evangelists use σιωπω, οὐκ ἀπεκρίναντο (ἀπεκρίθη) οὐδέν (οὐδὲ ἓν ῥῆμα), ἀπόκρισιν οὐκ ἔδωκεν), but on the parallel emphasis on an analagous theme. The passive endurance of affliction is obviously the point of interest in Is. 53:7, and a similar preoccupation is clearly visible in the trial narratives; not only does it feature in all the recorded hearings, as well as being mentioned, at one point or another, in all four accounts, but the motif is also mentioned twice in Mk. 14:61 and in Mt. 27:12-14.[2]

However, objections to this suggested allusion have been raised,[3] most notably by M. Hooker. She begins by observing that

---

[1] Schniewind (Matthäus, 263) wishes to include Mt. 26:50-4 as well, but the concept is hardly present there.

[2] The emphasis in both instances is not on absolute dumbness, but on submissiveness (cf. Martin, Mark, 179).
Further evidence for the influence of the Servant conception with relation to Jesus' silence would exist if Mk. 15:5 (ὥστε θαυμάζειν τὸν Πιλᾶτον) were influenced by Is. 52:15 LXX (οὕτως θαυμάσονται ἔθνη πολλὰ ἐπ' αὐτῷ -- MT differs). The parallel is suggested by Lohmeyer-Schmauch (Matthäus, 382); Schweizer (Matthew, 507); Cranfield (Mark, 449) and Senior (Passion Narrative, 234 (?)). While influence from Is. 52:15 cannot be excluded, the parallel is not particularly close, and the wonder of the ἔθνη is not stimulated by the Servant's submissiveness.

[3] Wolff (Jesaja 53, 75-6) points out that the evangelists do

the silence motif forms a definite pattern, which is consistent and understandable as an authentic feature of Jesus' behavior during the judicial proceedings -- while Jesus unhesitatingly replies to direct and authorized queries regarding his status, he refuses to answer the false accusations of the Jews. This being so, it is not necessary to trace the silence motif to the influence of Is. 53:7. In any case, had an allusion been intended, it would have been made more explicit. Having dismissed the case which attributes this feature to the influence of Is. 53:7 on the evangelists, she considers the possibility that the trait was understood by Jesus to be a correspondence to the Servant's behavior, but objects:

> . . . there is no indication that Jesus was consciously acting in accordance with that picture, or that he understood his sufferings to be fulfilling the same purpose as those of the Servant.[1]

With respect to this interpretation, the isolation of a "silence pattern" within the trials is a very significant insight and effectively rebuts those who maintain that the silence of Jesus is a prophetically-based insertion into the tradition.[2] However, the

---

not use language from Is. 53:7 and believes, had this verse influenced the Passion, that an allusion to it would have been present in Mk. 14:49. However, a verbal relationship is not necessary for a relationship to exist and there seems to be no reason why Is. 53:7 should have played a part in Mk. 14:49, for Jesus is under no specific accusation there.

Ps. 38:13-14 is sometimes advocated as an alternative source for the silence motif (Schneider, Passion, 62; K.Weidel, "Studien über den Einfluss des Weissagungsbeweises auf die evangelische Geschichte," TSK, LXXXV (1912), 229; Detlev Dormeyer, Die Passion Jesu als Verhaltensmodell: Literarische und theologische Analyse der Traditions- und Redaktionsgeschichte der Markuspassion, NTAbh, n.s., XI (Münster: Aschendorff, 1974), 177), but the context of the psalm seems to imply an actual physical dumbness and the prominent confessions of sin (vv. 4-5, 18) render the context less appropriate than Is. 53, where an innocent sufferer is obviously presented.

[1]Hooker, Servant, 88-89 (89).

[2]Such as Ernst Haenchen, Der Weg Jesu: Eine Erklärung des Markus- Evangeliums und der kanonischen Parallelen (Berlin: Töpelmann, 1966), 514. For the "silence pattern," cf. also Filson, Matthew, 289.

case for denying a relationship between Is. 53:7 and Jesus' silence is not convincing. First, the evangelists do hint at this relationship by their emphasis on the feature; especially significant is the repetition of the detail in Mk. 14:61 and Mt. 27:12-14, which can be explained by supposing that it was the evangelists' desire to evoke the picture of the Servant's submissiveness. Secondly, the employment of this passage from the Servant Songs in this context would be particularly appropriate, since it is not impossible that Is. 53:7 itself depicts a trial scene.[1] Thirdly, and most importantly, the evidence for denying a relationship between Is. 53:7 and Jesus' own conception of his silence is not convincing. M. Hooker fails to find evidence that Jesus was "consciously acting" in accordance with the picture of the Servant, but this objection depends on a mechanical conception of Jesus' relationship to the OT. The correspondence between OT prophecy and details of Jesus' ministry and behavior need not be the result of a _conscious_ imitation of these features on Jesus' part, but may be based on a deeper unity between "prophecy and fulfillment." Jesus was no doubt _aware_ of these correlations, but it is illegitimate to demand evidence that, in every case, he consciously molded his behavior in imitation of the prophetic picture. Moreover, to deny a correspondence with Is. 53:7 on the grounds that the allusion gives no evidence of Jesus' awareness that he was "fulfilling the same purpose as that of the Servant," is to apply an unjustified criterion. Surely, every allusion to an OT passage does not have to include clear-cut evidence of the appropriation of the central message of the context to which the verse belongs.

It may, therefore, be the case that the evangelists _record_ the silence of Jesus at particular intervals in the judicial procedures because, in fact, it happened that way, but that they _stress_ the fact

---

[1] So Westermann, _Isaiah 40-66_, 257.

because it was recognized as a fulfillment of Is. 53:7. That this understanding of the matter is true to Jesus' own belief is probable, for as Gerhardsson puts it, "Le silence de Jésus exprime sa soumission digne, maîtrisée, volontaire, sous l'humiliation que le Père céleste lui impose";[1] and these same features are those emphasized in Is. 53.

Luke 23:34a (Isaiah 53:12)

Many scholars feel that Jesus' prayer from the Cross for his executioners is to be understood in relation to Is. 53:12, where it is written that the Servant "made intercession for the transgressors." (ולפשעים הפגיע); LXX: καὶ διὰ τὰς ἁμαρτίας αὐτῶν παρεδόθη).[2] In fact, it has been suggested that a scribe, desiring to adduce a fulfillment of Is. 53:12, has inserted the prayer with no dominical basis.[3] This contention cannot be examined without investigating the textual problem which this passage presents. The witnesses for the omission of the prayer are early and diverse (p75, B, D, et al.) and as Creed says " . . . the omission of a prayer so sublime and so Christ-like seems less probable than its insertion."[4] Harnack has attempted to account for its omission by suggesting that an early

---

[1] Birger Gerhardsson, "Jésus livré et abandonné d'après la Passion selon Matthieu," trans. by L.-M. Dewailly, RB, LXXVI (1969), 218.

[2] Henry Alford, The Greek Testament (4 vols; London: Rivingstons, 1865-76), I, 653; Gustav Dalman, Jesus-Jeshua: Studies in the Gospels, trans. by Paul R. Levertoff (London: Society for Promoting Christian Knowledge), 197; Plummer, Luke, 532; Taylor, Jesus and His Sacrifice, 194; Zimmerli-Jeremias, Servant, 100; Wolff, Jesaja 53, 76-7; Lohse, Märtyrer, 130; J. Wilkinson, "The Seven Words from the Cross," SJT, XVII (1964), 70; I. H. Marshall, Luke: Historian and Theologian (Exeter: Paternoster, 1970), 172.

[3] Feigel, Einfluss, 108; Montefiore, Synoptic Gospels, I, 1080.

[4] Luke, 286.

scribe had scruples about transmitting a prayer of Jesus, which, as the events of A.D. 70 seemed to demonstrate, went unanswered,[1] but this reconstruction does not appear to be plausible.[2] Nevertheless, the primitiveness of the passage is demonstrated by its strong attestation (ℵ, A, f[13], most of the early Fathers) and Stephen's dying words seem to presuppose Jesus' prayer as a model.[3] Furthermore, as Metzger says, the text "bears self-evident tokens of its dominical origin."[4] It seems best to conclude that, while not perhaps in its original position,[5] the prayer is dominical in origin[6] and cannot, therefore, be a later addition, inserted as an attempt to place a fulfillment of Is. 53:12 on Jesus' lips.

If the prayer is an authentic saying of Jesus, is there evidence at hand that Jesus or the evangelists considered it to be related to Is. 53:12? The fact that Luke records Jesus' quotation of Is. 53:12 (Lk. 22:37) and the possibility that Lk. 23:34b may also be an allusion to Is. 53:12 (see below) may be taken as indications that

---

[1] Adolf von Harnack, "Probleme im Texte der Leidensgeschichte Jesu," Studien zur Geschichte des Neuen Testaments und der alten Kirche, Vol. I: Zur Neutestamentlichen Textkritik (Berlin and Leipzig: de Gruyter, 1931), 94ff; cf. also Streeter, Four Gospels, 138; Caird, Luke, 251. Leaney (Luke, 284) conjectures that the prayer was excised by a Gentile scribe who refused to believe that Jesus forgave the Jews.

[2] Metzger, Textual Commentary, 180.

[3] Harnack, "Probleme im Texte," 95; Lohse, Märtyrer, 129; Rengstorf, Lukas, 268; Ellis, Luke, 267. Another early Christian parallel to this passage is James' dying prayer (Eusebius, H. E. II, 23, 16. Cf. Jeremias, New Testament Theology, 299, n. 2).

[4] Metzger, Textual Commentary, 180.

[5] The fact that Tatian placed the prayer after Lk. 23:46 may testify to the uncertainty of its position in the MSS tradition (Williams, Alterations, 8).

[6] In addition to those already noted, supporters of the dominical origin of the text are Joachim Jeremias, "Das Gebetsleben Jesu," ZNW, XXV (1926), 138; Ethelbert Stauffer, Jesus and His Story, trans. by Richard and Clara Winston (New York: Alfred A. Knopf, 1960), 137; D. Daube, "For they know not what they do: Luke 23:34," SP, IV (TU, LXXVIII) (Berlin: Akadamie Verlag, 1961), 59; Grundmann, Lukas, 433; Bernard, John, II, 634.

such a parallel is intended.[1] Jeremias notes that the אשם, mentioned in Is. 53:11, is a sacrifice for sins committed unwittingly, so that the context is a particularly appropriate source for Jesus' sentiments. He also interprets the prayer in light of the Jewish custom by which a dying man expressed an "atoning vow" that his death might atone for all his sins;[2] Jesus, characteristically, and through his mediatorial powers as Suffering Servant, extends the prayer to others:

> Jesus geht in den Tod mit dem Bewusstsein, als Schuldopfer für die Vielen zu sterben, und durch sein Gebet, in dem er seine Henker als aus Unwissenheit sündigend bezeichnet bezieht er sie ein in den Kreis derer, denen die Sühnkraft seines Todes gelten soll.[3]

While these arguments are impressive, certain other factors urge caution. The passage gives no indication that Jesus or the evangelists linked this prayer with his coming death in the sense that it would provide the basis for the forgiveness.[4] Moreover, "making intercession" (פגע) in Is. 53:12 does not mean that the Servant engaged in prayer for "the many," but "that with his life, his suffering and his death, he took their place and underwent their punishment in their stead."[5] It cannot be denied that Jesus may have extended the meaning of the passage to include the concept of intercessory prayer, but this should not be too readily assumed without clear evidence.

---

[1]The mixed textual background of Lk. 22:37 is sufficient refutation of the objection that Is. 53:12 could not be referred to in Lk. 23:34a because the allusion would depend on the MT, rather than LXX, which Luke habitually uses. (As argued by Schneider (Passion, 113) and Olof Linton ("Le 'parallelismus membrorum' dans le Nouveau Testament: Simple Remarques," Mélanges Bibliques en hommage R. P. Béda Rigaux, ed. by Albert Descamps and André de Halleux (Gembloux: Duculot, 1970), 494)).

[2]Zimmerli-Jeremias, Servant, 100; Cf. also Lohse, Märtyrer, 130.

[3]Jeremias, "Gebetsleben," 139.

[4]Lohse, Märtyrer, 130.

[5]Westermann, Isaiah 40-66, 269; cf. also North, Isaiah 40-55, 141. The Hiphil of פגע is consistently used in this way in Isaiah 40-60 (cf. also Is. 53:6, 59:16).

Therefore, while influence from Is. 53:12 on Lk. 23:34a cannot be definitely excluded, it does not seem likely that any relationship between the two exists.

Matthew 27:38 / Mark 15:27 / Luke 23:33; John 19:18 (Isaiah 53:12)

The detail, mentioned by all four evangelists, that Jesus was executed between two criminals, has lent itself to a number of symbolical and typological interpretations. Thus, it is suggested that this circumstance is recorded as a way of emphasizing Jesus' Kingship,[1] or of hinting at Jesus' status as the antitype of Moses, who, according to Ex. 17:12, stood with outstretched arms between Aaron and Hur in order to insure Israel's victory over Amalek,[2] or of alluding to Ps. 22:16 "a company of evildoers encircle me."[3] By far the most popular interpretation is that which regards Jesus' position between the two others as a fulfillment of Is. 53:12 "and he was numbered with the transgressors,"[4] a tradition of interpretation that stretches as far back as the time of the anonymous scribe who

---

[1] Brooke Foss Westcott, The Gospel According to St. John (2 vols.; London: James Clarke, 1958 (=1881)), II, 274; Dauer, Passionsgeschichte, 274.

[2] T. F. Glasson, Moses in the Fourth Gospel, SBT, XL (London: SCM, 1963), 41-43, referring particularly to John. He notes the verbal similarity between Jn. 19:18 (ἐντεῦθεν καὶ ἐντεῦθεν) and Ex. 17:12 LXX (ἐντεῦθεν εἷς καὶ ἐντεῦθεν εἷς), but the phrase is not uncommon.

[3] Brown, John, II, 906. But the stress in the psalm is on antagonists, not fellow sufferers.

[4] In addition to those already mentioned with reference to Lk. 22:37, the following may be mentioned: Delitzsch, Isaiah, II, 312; Finegan, Überlieferung, 75; I. D. Karabidopoulos, "[To Pathos tou doulou tou theou epi tou staurou kata tēn diēgēsin tou evangelistou Louka](23; 33-49)," DBM, I (1972), 210; Eric Franklin, Christ the Lord: A Study in the Purpose and Theology of Luke-Acts (London: SPCK, 1975), 91-2; Maurer, "Knecht Gottes," 8; Leaney, Luke, 284; Fenton, Matthew, 441; Loisy, Marc, 461-2 (?); Brown, John, II, 906 (?).

inserted an explicit quotation of this verse in Mk. 15:28.[1] Certain objections to this interpretation have already been raised with regard to the scope of Jesus' application of this prophecy to himself in Lk. 22:37. Of decisive importance, it will be recalled, was the fact that Luke, although he uses a different word to describe the criminals than does Mark, does not employ the word found in Lk. 22:37. If Luke, who alone records the quotation from Is. 53:12, in no manner indicates a relationship between Jesus' prophecy and the position of his Cross, it is improbable that the other evangelists related the detail to Is. 53:12. In fact, John, by describing those executed with Jesus simply as ἄλλους, seems to indicate that he, at least, was unaware of the correlation.[2] We have suggested that Jesus' application of Is. 53:12 to himself is to be understood as a prediction of the Passion events in general which may be summarily characterized as "being numbered with the transgressors." This treatment is, of course, literally exemplified in his crucifixion and, in this sense, Jesus' execution between two others may be regarded as a stage in the process of the fulfillment of this prophecy. But it is illegitimate to consider it <u>the</u> event to which Is. 53:12 refers.[3]

Titles of Jesus

ὁ ἐκλεκτός

According to Lk. 23:35, the Jewish leaders, in their mocking challenge of Jesus to save himself from the cross, address him as ὁ ἐκλεκτός, a title apparently equivalent to ὁ χριστὸς τοῦ θεοῦ. Jeremias claims that the use of the title cannot be attributed to

---

[1]Mk. 15:28 is weakly attested and suspect by reason of harmonization with Lk. 22:37.

[2]Lindars, John, 575.

[3]Hooker, Servant, 92; Benoit, Passion, 172.

Christian influence, since it is found elsewhere in the NT only in Jn. 1:34 (but note the textual problem) and never in the Apostolic fathers. Rather, the Jews' employment of the title is to be ascribed to the influence of I Enoch, where ὁ ἐκλεκτός "appears as a pre-Christian Jewish messianic predicate derived from Isa. 42:1."[1] It is possible that the title was current as a Messianic designation,[2] although the uncertainty over the date of the Similitudes must lend caution, but it is most improbable that the title had any direct connection with the figure of the Servant in I Enoch, and still less in the Judaism of Jesus' day. It may be that "the chosen one" was simply an appropriately paradoxical ascription employed in deriding one who was seemingly now abandoned by the Father with Whom he had claimed to have such an intimate relationship (and cf. Ps. 22:8b -- "let him [the Lord] rescue him, if he delights in him.").

ὁ υἱός

Jeremias, discussing the title παῖς θεοῦ given to Jesus in the early Church, which he believes is a reference to the Suffering Servant, offers the suggestion that "there arises above all the question whether the παῖς θεοῦ predication (along with scriptural texts like Ps. 2:7; II Sam. 7:14) does not play an essential part in the emergence of the messianic title ὁ υἱὸς τοῦ θεοῦ which was unknown to late Judaism."[3] This possibility, which stems from the dual meaning of

---

[1] Zimmerli-Jeremias, Servant, 62 (n. 260). The reading ὁ ἐκλελεγμένος in Lk. 9:35 should be noted as well. Influence from the Servant conception on the title is also advocated by Karabidopoulos, "Pathos," 210; Marshall, Luke: Historian, 113; and Grundmann, Lukas, 433. Leaney (Luke, 284, cf. 168) interprets the significance of the title here in connection with ὁ ἐκλελεγμένος in 9:35, which, he claims, presents Jesus as the new Moses (with reference to Ps. 106:23). However, Morris (Luke, 173) claims that, in the context, the title "emphatically differentiates him [Jesus] from Moses and Elijah."

[2] Braun, Qumran, II, 72-73.

[3] Zimmerli-Jeremias, Servant, 83, n. 354.

παῖς ("child/servant"), has been seized upon by Maurer as a means of explaining the lack of the "Servant" title in Mark's Passion Narrative which, according to him, is thoroughly saturated with Servant allusions. He notes the variation between υἱός and παῖς in Wisdom of Solomon 2:13-18, which is obviously dependent on the Servant Songs of Isaiah in the LXX translation,[1] and concludes that the Greek-speaking church may well have employed υἱός (in place of παῖς) to mean "Servant" as a reference to the Isaianic figure. Thus, when the High Priest asks Jesus if he is ὁ υἱὸς τοῦ εὐλογητοῦ, "mit dem Gottes<u>sohn</u> der Gottes<u>knecht</u> gemeint ist!"[2] However, passing over for the moment Maurer's belief in the thoroughgoing influence of the Servant conception on Mark's Passion Narrative,[3] there are serious difficulties with his reconstruction. The New Testament gives no instance in which παῖς is replaced by υἱός,[4] or of any case in which παῖς means "child."[5] Even in Mt. 12:18, a quotation of Is. 42:1ff which deviates from LXX,

---

[1]For the influence of LXX Is. 53 on Wisdom 2, see M.-J. Suggs, "Wisdom 2:10-5; a Homily Based on the Fourth Servant Song," JBL, LXXVI (1957), 26-33.

[2]Maurer, "Knecht Gottes," 24-28. Cf. also de Tillesse (Le Secret Messianique, 362): "Le titre de Fils connote donc de façon très dense les deux aspects inséperables de la mission de Jésus: Mission divine, que Jésus accomplit dans l'obéissance jusqu'à la mort." Cullmann (Christology, 284) likewise believes that the conception of Sonship in the Gospels carries with it the idea of Suffering Servant, although he bases this opinion on the alleged coalition of the concepts in the Heavenly voice at Jesus' baptism. Grundmann ("Sohn Gottes," 125) notes that the High Priest was called "Son of God" in late Judaism, that the High Priest is identified with the Servant in 1QIsa 52:14 and suggests that " . . . Gottesknecht und messianischer Hohenpriester, und damit Gottesknecht und Gottessohn, sind hier schon eine wenn auch nur gering bezeugte, aber doch mit grosser Wahrscheinlichkeit festzustellende Verbindung eingegangen." Grundmann places the emphasis on Jesus' own consciousness of God as Father in the origin of the "Son of God" title, however (133).

[3]Best (Temptation and Passion, 151) claims that Mark has simply taken over the Servant conception without emphasizing it. Cf. also Suhl, Funktion, 59-60.

[4]Schweizer, "υἱός," TDNT, VIII, 368, n. 237; Feuillet, "Baptême," 325.

[5]Marshall, "Son of God," 331-2; Lindars, Apologetic, 140.

$παῖς$, not $υἱός$, is used.[1] Moreover, it is unlikely that the High Priest would have asked Jesus if he was the Servant[2] or that, if the Greek Church had added the title, they would have used the Jewish periphrasis "Blessed." It is not improbable, in view of the Qumran evidence, that "Son of God" was a recognized Messianic title in first century Palestine, but, however this may be, it cannot be considered a substitute for "Servant."

$δίκαιος$

Another Passion Narrative description of Jesus, said to be influenced by the Servant Songs, is $δίκαιος$, used by the Roman centurion in his confession after Jesus' death (Lk. 23:47): $ὄντως\ ὁ\ ἄνθρωπος\ οὗτος\ δίκαιος\ ἦν$. Franklin, noting that Luke consistently uses $δίκαιος$ of a God-ward relationship, insists that more than simple moral innocence is indicated by these words.[3] He believes that the frequent occurrence of $δίκαιος$ as a title for Jesus in Acts is a reflection of the "righteous one" of Is. 53:11, as it may be in I Enoch.[4] Acts 3:13-14, where $δίκαιος$ is used as parallel to $παῖς$, is appealed to specifically by Franklin. However, it may be significant that $δίκαιος$ is not used in Is. 53:11 LXX. While Franklin is justified in his protest against understanding $δίκαιος$ simply as connoting moral uprightness,[5] the case for dependence on Is. 53:11 is not a strong one.

---

[1] Feuillet, "Baptême," 325.

[2] Marshall, "Son of God," 332; Blinzler, Prozess, 76, n. 30.

[3] Franklin, Christ the Lord, 62-3.

[4] Cf. also Zimmerli-Jeremias, Servant, 91; cf. Black, "Servant," 10.

[5] As Plummer (Luke, 539) paraphrases the centurion: "'He was a good man, and quite right in calling God His Father.'" Cf. also Morris, Luke, 330.

Mark 14:8 (Isaiah 53:9)

Jeremias, noting that the bodies of executed criminals were not normally embalmed (anointed), suggests that Jesus interprets the woman's action as an anticipatory anointing for burial (Mk. 14:8) because he is conscious that his destiny will be that of the Suffering Servant's, whose "grave was with the wicked" (Is. 53:9).[1] However, Jesus' conviction that he must suffer was, as we have seen, understood in relation to a broad scriptural background, and his words to the woman presuppose no more than this basic awareness. Is. 53:9 is not, moreover, clearly anticipatory of an ignoble burial; Matthew (27:57) uses the verse as a commentary on Jesus' burial in the tomb of a rich man. A more basic criticism of Jeremias' argument is that it understands more in Jesus' saying than is really there. The woman's act of love was obviously unsolicited and Jesus seizes the opportunity to predict his imminent suffering. His interpretation does not necessarily imply that he would not be anointed after his death, only that the woman has "anticipated" ($\pi\rho o \acute{\epsilon} \lambda a \beta \epsilon \nu$) the normal time of anointing, whether it occurs or not. It is therefore improbable that Jesus' saying specifically presupposes the application of Is. 53:9 to his burial.

Luke 22:21-38 (Isaiah 53, passim)

Otto suggests a rearrangement of Lk. 22:15-30 around the theme of "Covenant" with the resulting order vv. 17 - 18 - 19a - 29 - 30. Assuming that the covenant theme is derived from the Servant Songs,

---

[1] Zimmerli-Jeremias, Servant, 100, 104-5; cf. Martin, Mark, 202.
On the antiquity of the tradition and its place in the original passion narrative, see Rudolf Pesch, "Die Salbung Jesu in Bethanien (Mk, 14, 3-9): Eine Studie zur Passionsgeschichte," Orientierung an Jesu, 268-280.

he regards Jesus' promise of the Kingdom to the disciples in v. 29 as a reference to Is. 53:12b: "with many he will divide his spoil."[1] Ellis alludes to this same parallel in his treatment of Lk. 22:21-38 (in the traditional order and including vv. 19a-20), but only as one element of a Suffering Servant motif which he understands as underlying Jesus' words to the disciples. Thus, the passage begins (v. 20) and ends (v. 37) with clear citations of Is. 53:12. Jesus, as the serving Lord, is the example for his disciples to emulate (v. 27); it is through this service that the kingdom is attained (vv. 28-30); and the prediction of Peter's apostasy typifies the rejection "by all" that is Jesus' fate as the Suffering Servant (cf. Is. 53:3).[2] To this may be added the probable influence of Is. 53 on the Passion prediction in v. 22 (note παραδίδωμι).

It must be admitted that not all these suggestions are of equal value. The parallel between Jesus' words in vv. 28-30 and Is. 53:12 is not convincing, since, as we will see, the "covenant" concept in the Last Supper is influenced by Ex. 24:8 and Jer. 31:31-4 and plays, at best, a subsidiary role in the Servant Songs. Nor does the warning to Peter appear to be related to Is. 53:3. Having said this, it cannot be denied that, in specific instances, and in its general theme, there is much in Lk. 22:21-38 that is reminiscent of the Fourth Servant Song. The preoccupation with his imminent sufferings, the concept of betrayal as ordained of God (passive παραδίδωμι) and Jesus' characterization of himself as he who serves (which is surely to be understood in relation to Lk. 22:20), when taken into conjunction with the explicit citation of Is. 53:12 in vv. 20 and 37, provide sufficient basis for believing that the picture

---

[1]Otto, Kingdom, 268-291. [2]Ellis, Luke, 251.

of the Suffering Servant was uppermost in Jesus' mind as he spoke
to the disciples.

Miscellaneous Details

Lohmeyer, taking as his starting point the explicit allusion
to Is. 50:6 in Mk. 14:65, attributes several of the elements in the
Sanhedrin hearing to the influence of the Servant conception. He
notes that the passage alluded to in v. 65 clearly implies a judicial
setting and has probably contributed to the depiction of the dualistic
contrast between the "world," (represented by the Sanhedrinists
and the false witnesses) and God (represented by the innocent sufferer,
Jesus):

> Dann handelt es sich also zunächst nicht um eine richterliche
> Verhandlung, der jüdischen Rechtspraxis gemäss oder auch zuwider,
> sondern um eine Verhandlung, in der notwendig das Synedrium
> Richter und Gegner gegen den erkorenen Gesandten und Knecht
> Gottes ist.[1]

If, however, a background for this contrast is to be sought, it is more
probably to be found in the righteous-sufferer psalms, which perhaps
contribute linguistically to the description of the false witnesses.
Moreover, if the scene presented in Mk. 14:53-65 is understood as a
hearing rather than a formal trial, many of the difficulties in
relation to Jewish judicial procedure disappear and the narrative
can be accorded a firm historical basis.

Other parallels between depictions of Jesus' passion and the
Servant Songs which have been suggested are: the Barabbas scene and
Is. 53:8, which speaks of the Servant being treated harshly by his

---

[1]Lohmeyer, Markus, 330-1 (331); cf. John R. Donahue, Are You
the Christ? The Trial Narrative in the Gospel of Mark, SBLDS, X
(Missoula, Mont.: SBL, 1973), 99-100, who believes Mark has historicized
a catena of OT citations.

generation;[1] the Jews' mockery of Jesus on the Cross and the contrast inherent in Is. 53:4: "he has borne our griefs . . . but we esteemed him stricken, smitten by God . . . ";[2] the criminal's testimony to Jesus' innocence (Lk. 23:41) and Is. 53:9 "although he had done no voilence"; Jesus' promise to the repentant thief (Lk. 23:43) and Is. 53:12 "dividing the spoil."[3] Only the second of these suggestions is convincing. The Jews' mockery of Jesus on the Cross expresses as a central motif the insinuation that Jesus could be suffering so only if he were under the displeasure and judgment of God; a theme prominent, as well, in the righteous sufferer psalms which are used in narrating the mockery. The irony in the fact that such an insinuation is made at the very time when, as the early Church recognized, Jesus was bearing the sin of the world, exactly reproduces the situation envisaged in Is. 53:4. Although there are no explicit indications, the parallel was probably recognized by the evangelists and perhaps was a contributory factor in their preservation of this element in the mockery narratives.

Conclusions

It will be convenient to summarize the results of this portion of the investigation in a table, indicating the places in which a reference to the Servant Songs occurs, the citation technique employed[4] and whether the saying is the evangelist's or is attributed to Jesus (a * noting the latter).

---

[1] Ernst Lohmeyer, Gottesknecht und Davidssohn (2nd ed.; Göttingen: Vandenhoeck & Ruprecht, 1953), 31-2; cf. also Maurer ("Knecht Gottes," 16) who sees Jesus' substitution for Barabbas in the light of the Servant's substitutionary death.

[2] William Manson, The Gospel of Luke, MNTC (London: Hodder and Stoughton, 1930), 259.

[3] Karabidopoulos, "Pathos," 210.

[4] EQ = explicit quotation (with introduction); Q = quotation; All = allusion; Con = conceptual influence.

TABLE 1

REFERENCES TO THE SERVANT SONGS
IN THE GOSPEL PASSION TEXTS

Isaiah	Matthew	Mark	Luke	John	Citation Technique
42:1	3:17	1:11	3:22	-	All
50:6	20:19	10:34	18:32-33	-	*All
	26:67	14:65	-	18:22	All
	27:30	15:19	-	19:1,3	All
52:13	-	-	-	3:14;8:28;12:32	*All
53 (παραδίδωμι)	17:22	9:31	9:44	-	*All
	20:18	10:33	18:32	-	*All
	26:24	14:21	22:22	-	*All
	26:45	14:41	-	-	*All
53	-	-	22:21-38	-	*Con
53	-	-	-	10:11,15,17	*Con
53:3	-	9:12b	-	-	*All
53:4	27:39-43	15:29-32	23:35-37	-	Con
53:7	26:63	14:61	-	-	Con
	27:14	15:5	-	19:9	
	27:12	-	-	-	
	-	-	23:9	-	

TABLE 1 -- Continued

Isaiah	Matthew	Mark	Luke	John	Citation Technique
53:9	27:57	-	-	-	All
53:10-12	20:28	10:45	-	-	*All
53:12c	26:28	14:24	22:20	-	*All
53:12d	-	-	22:37	-	*EQ

The evidence of the gospels has persuaded most scholars that the conception of the Suffering Servant played a major role in Jesus' own estimation of his person and work.[1] Nevertheless, the situation is not altogether without complication, inasmuch as only a single explicit quotation of Is. 53 is found on Jesus' lips (and this in only one gospel). In light of this, there are many who either minimize the influence of Is. 53 on the gospel tradition in general, claiming that the number of allusions has been greatly exaggerated, or deny the importance of the Servant conception for Jesus, relegating

---

[1] John W. Bowman (The Intention of Jesus (London: SCM, 1944), 134) calls it the "central motive governing all his thought and activity," while Cullmann (Christology, 80) claims that " . . . the concept ebed Yahweh characterizes the person and work of the historical Jesus in a way which completely corresponds to the New Testament witness to Christ." Cf. also Otto, Kingdom, 248; W. Manson, Jesus the Messiah, 111; North, Suffering Servant, 25; Higgins, Son of Man, 197; Vincent Taylor, The Person of Christ in New Testament Teaching (London: MacMillan, 1958), 164; Maurer, "Knecht Gottes," 11-19; Stanley, "Servant," 410; Cecil John Cadoux, The Historic Mission of Jesus: A Constructive Re-examination of the Eschatological Teaching in the Synoptic Gospels (London: Lutterworth Press, 1941), 261-4; Goppelt, Theologie, 246-7; Hunter, Work and Words, 96; Lohse, Märtyrer, 145, 222-3; H. Wheeler Robinson, The Cross in the Old Testament (London: SCM, 1955), 100-103; Coppens, Messianisme, 212; Charles C. Torrey, "The Influence of Second Isaiah in the Gospels and Acts," JBL, XLVIII (1929), 24-6; Fuller, Mission and Achievement, 86; France, Jesus, 110-32; Benoit, "Serviteur," 132-9; Zimmerli-Jeremias, Servant, 106.

the influence of Isaiah 53 to a late stage in the tradition.¹ Very often these two approaches are combined, but it will be easier to evaluate them separately. The former approach, exemplified particularly well in Morna Hooker's Jesus and the Servant will be studied first.

As Hooker correctly emphasizes, presuppositions and methodology are crucially important in the study of the influence of the Servant-concept on Jesus and the early Church; and her criticism of those scholars who "quote numerous references and rely on the number as sufficient support to their claim" is at least partially justified.² In contrast to this, Hooker seeks to examine closely each alleged allusion, in which process the following criterion is utilized:

> To claim that there is a verbal similarity between a New Testament passage and an Old Testament one cannot be taken as conclusive evidence of direct influence unless it can be shown that the language and ideas found in the New Testament reference have come from, and could only come from, that particular Old Testament passage. (author's italics).³

A second crucial basis upon which the claims of individual passages to rest upon the Servant conception must be judged is the presence or absence of the characteristic feature of the Servant's mission: vicarious suffering. As Hahn, whose methodology with regard to the Servant Christology closely resembles Hooker's, puts it:

---

¹" . . . the tradition of Jesus' sayings reveals no trace of a consciousness on his part of being the Servant of God of Is. 53." -- Rudolf Bultmann, Theology of the New Testament, Vol. I, trans. by Kendrick Grobel (London: SCM, 1952), 31. Cf. also F. J. Foakes Jackson and Kirsopp Lake, Prolegomena: The Jewish, Gentile and Christian Backgrounds, Vol. I of The Beginnings of Christianity, Part I, ed. by Jackson and Lake (5 vols.; London: MacMillan, 1920-33), I, 381-90; Clarence Tucker Craig, "The Identification of Jesus with the Suffering Servant," JR, XXIV (1944), 240-5; Moule, "From Defendant to Judge," 96-97; Schweizer, Erniedrigung, 72; van Iersel, "Sohn," 60-65; Fuller, Christology, 118-19; Beare, Earliest Records, 229; Hooker, Servant; Hahn, Christology, 54-63; Patsch, Abendmahl, 162-3; Whitely, "Salvation," 122-3.

²Servant, 20.

³Ibid., 62.

> Since in the frequently atomistic exegesis of that time references to items of a text do not in any way involve a taking over of the basic ideas of the text concerned, all citations from and allusions to Isa. 53 which do not expressly contain the motif of vicarious atonement must be excluded.[1]

This methodology is the determinative influence on Hooker's study and it is precisely at this fundamental point that some sharp criticisms must be made. To demand, before influence from an OT passage on a NT one can be admitted, that the language or ideas in question could only have come from that particular background is to lay down an unrealistic and illegitimate criterion. The rigid application of this standard would lead to complete agnosticism in the area of backgrounds research, for it could always be claimed that concepts or language under consideration were original creations of the writer or movement. Each suggested allusion must be weighed on its merits, and different scholars will weigh differently the balance of probabilities in specific cases, but the utilization of a criterion such as proposed by Hooker et al. determines the conclusions of a study before it has begun. Moreover, her method leads to an unjustifiable isolation of phrases and words. In some cases, doubt may accrue to the provenance of a particular word or phrase, but the recognition that other elements in the context are closely paralleled in the context of the background passage may be a decisive factor and should not be neglected. The second touchstone which is utilized by Hooker (and Hahn) is similarly objectionable. Whether the application to Jesus of language and concepts drawn from the Servant Songs establishes an identification between the Servant's mission of vicarious atonement and Jesus', can only be concluded on the basis of all the evidence -- it should not be introduced as a preliminary requirement for the identification of particular allusions.[2] The justification for doing

---

[1] Hahn, Titles of Jesus, 54; Hooker, Servant, 63.

[2] Zimmerli-Jeremias, Servant, 88; Longenecker. Christology, 106.

so is the "atomistic" exegesis which is claimed to be dominant in late-Jewish Biblical interpretation, but, significantly, neither Hooker nor Hahn offer any documentation for the extensive employment of this practice, either in Jewish literature or, more importantly, in the NT.[1] And, in fact, as has been demonstrated in Chapter I, it is quite misleading to characterize all Jewish exegesis as "atomistic."[2] The fact that others have come to a diametrically opposite conclusion should at least give one pause: "Der Schriftgebrauch Jesu ist hinsichtlich Jes. 53 nicht zerpflückend, sondern zusammenfassend."[3]

Finally, Hooker must be criticized for failing to take into consideration the broad correlation that exists between the mission and accomplishment of Jesus as it is outlined in the New Testament and the work of the Servant as Isaiah describes him. The scrutiny of the NT scholar should not be so fixed on the details of the New Testament Christological canvas that the impact of the whole picture is overlooked. As Westermann properly emphasizes, Is. 53 depicts a life-span and

> . . . there is a point for point correspondence with the Church's confession as it is given in the Apostle's Creed -- born, suffered, died, and was buried. This similarity of structure (the Creed, too, is the confession of men who had been given salvation) is far more important than quotations from Isa. 52f. here and there in the New Testament.[4]

---

[1]Hooker refers only to Cadbury's article in Beginnings, V, 369-70. She mentions Dodd's thesis, but says: "unless we find any evidence to support Dodd's claim, however, either in a unified interpretation by the Jews of the whole Isaianic Servant concept, or in the New Testament passages themselves, we must assume that he has failed to prove his case, and that the 'atomistic' interpretation is therefore the correct one." (22-3). However, Dodd's thesis does not require a "unified interpretation," but the frequent use of limited OT passages. By a "unified interpretation," Hooker seems to mean a consistent reference to vicarious atonement, which is not a legitimate criterion for the determination of allusions.

[2]Cf., supra, 33, 56.

[3]Wolff, Jesaja 53, 70.

[4]Westermann, Isaiah 40-66, 257. Cf. Smart, Deutero-Isaiah, 297; Bruce, Old Testament Themes, 30.

But, was this pattern recognized by Jesus? The influence of Isaiah 53 is often relegated to a later stage in the history of the tradition, Jesus himself, it is argued, not having a "doctrine of the atonement." Something has already been said with regard to this view in connection with the Son of Man passion sayings[1] and the several clear citations of Isaiah 53 which can plausibly be attributed to Jesus speak against it,[2] but some other points need to be raised.

First, it is unlikely that the "point for point correspondence" between Jesus' career and the description of the Servant in Isaiah could have been overlooked by Jesus. It would indeed be strange if the death of Jesus, which very early was understood as "for" others (e.g. Rom. 4:25, I Cor. 15:3) had not been interpreted at a similarly early stage in relation to the figure of the Servant, who embodies the principle of atoning suffering as does no other figure in the OT. And it seems logical to trace such a revolutionary and far-reaching interpretation back to the mind of Jesus.[3]

Second, that Jesus does not explicitly quote from the Servant Songs more frequently is not a decisive point against attributing this understanding to Jesus. Part of the difficulty lies in an over-emphasis on the significance of Isaiah 53 for Jesus' ministry, which is characteristic of some presentations. To be sure, if Isaiah 53 was the guiding principle in Jesus' ministry, a greater reliance on this chapter in Jesus' teachings might be expected. But the figure of the Servant, while an important OT source for the interpretation of Jesus'

---

[1] Cf., supra, 94.

[2] I.e., Mk. 10:45//; 14:24//; Lk. 22:37.

[3] ". . . collective wholes do not create great revolutionary ideas, but rather great revolutionary ideas create new groupings with a new milieu." (Otto, Kingdom, 246-7). Cf. also Taylor, Person of Christ, 164.

ministry (perhaps even the most important source) was not the only one and certainly should not be elevated to a position of Jesus' "alter ego." Furthermore, the many allusions to these chapters should not be ignored and are perhaps more important than quotations, since the use of such casual references presupposes an acquaintance with the passage alluded to on the part of both writer and readers. As has been indicated in Chapter I, the allusive use of OT passages is sometimes an indication of the familiarity of the context to the writer and readers. The conformity to Isaiah 53 in Jesus' actions is more decisive than his actual use of the chapter in teaching: " . . . Jesus was conscious during his earthly life of being called first of all to live, not to teach the work of atonement."[1]

Third, the evidence of the actual citation of the Servant Songs in the gospels is clearly anomalous if the influence of the Servant is to be relegated to a later stage of the tradition. For the fact is that the evangelists themselves betray very little dependence on the Servant concept in narrating the passion of Christ. The few allusions and conceptual influences are related to matters which are embedded in the tradition and to which they do little to call attention. If, however, the Servant concept belonged to a later, soteriological stage of the tradition, it would be expected that allusions and quotations would be fairly evenly divided between sayings of Jesus and narratives and editorial comments on his death.[2] In fact, the large preponderance of references to Is. 53 which are attributed to Jesus presents a strong argument for the position that this represents the actual facts of the situation.

---

[1]Cullmann, Christology, 61; cf. Wolff, Jesaja 53, 70; Bowman, Intention, 130, Moule, "From Defendant to Judge," 98-9 (although he denies the influence of Is. 53).

[2]It is interesting that neither of the two explicit quotations from the Servant Songs in Matthew's special material refer to Jesus' passion (Mt. 8:17 (Is. 53:4); Mt. 12:18-21 (Is. 42:1-4)).

Why is it, however, that the Servant conception seems to play so small a role in the evangelists' narration of the passion events? As Taylor remarks, " . . . after the earliest period of Apostolic Christianity, the Servant Christology is the echo of a distant voice which reverberates from time to time in the later decades."[1] This indeed seems to be the case (the citation in I Peter may reflect Peter's preoccupation with the Servant conception, as seen in the earlier chapters of Acts[2]), but it goes no further in explaining <u>why</u> the Servant concept lost its popularity. It has been suggested that the popular religious feeling of the day regarded it as too great a scandal,[3] that the Servant concept had "not penetrated the early Church's consciousness to any considerable degree,"[4] that the evangelists' contemporaries would not have understood the concept,[5] or that the emphasis on Jesus' present position as κύριος overshadowed all else in the primitive community.[6]

While it is possible that all of these elements have been involved, none, nor all together, suffices as a final explanation. Perhaps two other observations are helpful. First, it should not be overlooked that the evangelists do, in fact, include a soteriology, based on Isaiah 53, through their preservation of Jesus' own teachings and actions. Second, the nature of the gospels makes it probable that the explicit doctrine of the efficacy of Christ's death is presumed.

---

[1]Vincent Taylor, "The Origin of the Markan Passion Sayings," NTS, I (1954-5), 163.

[2]Cullmann, Christology, 74-5.

[3]Longenecker, Christology, 108.

[4]Moule, "From Defendant to Judge," 96.

[5]Wolff, Jesaja 53, 78-9.

[6]Cullmann, Christology, 81; Franklin, Christ the Lord, 66 (with respect to Luke only).

The evangelists, addressing those who already know this basic Christian truth, are content to narrate the passion events without introducing, to any great extent, an explanation of the meaning of these events.

Jesus and the evangelists appealed to Is. 53 in order to give OT evidence that he must suffer, but it seems very likely that there was another deeper reason in addition: Isaiah 53, like no other OT text, portrays vicarious, redemptive suffering, and portrays it as the very will of God. As Lohse says, "Wie Gott den Knecht leiden liess und zum Tode auslieferte, so gab er Christus dahin, damit er in den Tode gehen sollte für unsere Sünden."[1] The παραδίδωμι sayings express the great divine "handing-over"; Mk. 10:45 and 14:24 clearly indicate the redemptive value of the "handing-over," while Lk. 22:37, if not clearly stating it, implies the concept.[2]

John, as might be expected, makes the least use of the Servant conception, although it will be argued below that the description of the work of the Lamb of God in 1:29,36 is influenced by Is. 53:7. This reference, however, taken with the allusion to the Good Shepherd who "lays down his life for the sheep" demonstrates that John has not entirely abandonned the traditional Isaiah 53-influenced vicarious atonement soteriology. The synoptists make approximately equal use of the Servant Songs, Luke's fewer allusions being balanced by his explicit quotation, which serves almost as a programmatic passion text.

Finally, it is necessary to investigate the basic hermeneutical scheme whereby the Servant Songs were appropriated and to seek for the central purpose in the application of the passages to Jesus and his work. Given the identification of Jesus with the figure described

---

[1] Lohse, Märtyrer, 146.

[2] Taylor, Jesus and His Sacrifice, 194; France, Jesus, 115-116; Morris, Luke, 310; Wolff, Jesaja 53, 70-71.

by Isaiah, the references are appropriated very directly. There seems to be no case in which the meaning or text of the OT passage is modified illegitimately to suit an application; nor are there cases in which actions are attributed to Jesus solely on the basis of the Isaiah prophecies.

The only explicit indication as to the general hermeneutical framework is given in Lk. 22:37, where a quotation of Is. 53:12 is introduced with (among others) the word $\tau\epsilon\lambda\epsilon\omega$, and is followed by the statement, "for the [statement] concerning me has an end" $[\tau\epsilon\lambda o s\ \epsilon\chi\epsilon\iota]$. As was noted at that point, these words point to the coming to completion of an oracle. Since the Servant Songs are embedded in a prophecy, it is natural that they should be understood in this way. Therefore, it can be asserted that Jesus and the evangelists regarded the Servant Songs as prophecies, whose completion came in the work of Jesus, in his life and passion. The more specific concept "fulfillment" is utilized in several of the general passion sayings, and it is probable that the relationship between Jesus and the Servant prophecies can be understood in this way. More will be said on this concept and its importance for the passion texts in the concluding chapter.

CHAPTER III

THE USE OF ZECHARIAH 9-14
IN THE GOSPEL PASSION TEXTS

The Old Testament Background

The importance of Zechariah 9-14 as a background for the death of Christ may be gauged from the fact that four explicit quotations (not including parallel passages) from these chapters occur in the passion texts (four times the number than in the case of Isaiah 53!). In sketching the significance of these chapters in their original setting, our attention can be focused on those texts which are prominent in the gospels. Each of the four passages in question -- 9:9-10, 11:12-13, 12:10, 13:7 -- features an individual whose description is applied to Jesus in the NT. These individuals are so characterized by Zechariah that it seems legitimate to regard them as different descriptions of a single figure. "My (i.e., God's) Shepherd" in 13:7 is probably to be compared with the prophet's assumption of the role of shepherd in 11:4-15;[1] in both passages

---

[1] Ernst Sellin, Das Zwölfprophetenbuch, KAT, XII (2 vols., 3rd ed.; Leipzig: A. Deichertsche, 1930), II, 567-8. CD 19:7-9 provides further evidence for this correlation for language from both Zech. 13:7 and 11:11 is there combined (Jan de Waard, A Comparative Study of the Old Testament Text in the Dead Sea Scrolls and in the New Testament, STDJ, IV (Leiden: Brill, 1965), 40). Several scholars seek to identify the shepherd in 13:7 with the evil shepherd of 11:15-17 (Karl Marti, Das Dodekapropheten (Tübingen: J. C. B. Mohr, 1902), 442; D. W. Nowack, Die kleinen Propheten, HKAT, III:4 (Göttingen: Vandenhoeck & Ruprecht, 1897), 374; H. G. Mitchell, John Merlin Smith and Julius A. Brewer, A Critical and Exegetical Commentary on Haggai, Zechariah, Malachi and Jonah, ICC (Edinburgh: T & T Clark, 1912), 316; Théophane Chary, Aggée, Zacharie, Malachie, SB (Paris: Gabalda, 1969), 184), but this is unlikely in view of the exalted status accorded him and the close connection with the figure in 12:10. The abrupt transition from

Yahweh is closely identified with the individual represented.[1] A similar intimate relationship to Yahweh characterizes the pierced one of 12:10, and the fact that both this figure and the shepherd of 13:7 are conceived of as suffering is persuasive evidence for their identification.[2] Furthermore, it is suggested that the "covenant . . . with all the peoples" in 11:10 is to be identified with the "peace" established between King and nation in 9:10.[3] More important than these detailed parallels are the broad correspondences that bind these conceptions together. The theme of humility and/or rejection, and the emphasis on a divinely ordained leadership are prominent in the characterization of all four figures.

Lamarche has drawn attention to the significant parallels which exist among these individuals and advocates a chiastic structure for Zech. 9-14 that succeeds admirably in relating to one another the diverse elements of the prophecy.[4] This interpretation accounts for

---

the evil shepherd of 11:15-17 to Yahweh's shepherd of 13:7 is paralleled by the frequent prophetic contrast between the present evil shepherds of Israel and God's future Messianic Shepherd (cf. Jer. 23:1-5; Ez. 34). Karl Elliger (Das Buch der zwölf kleinen Propheten, ATD, XXV (2 vols., 2nd ed.; Göttingen: Vandenhoeck & Ruprecht, 1951), II, 165) and Benedikt Otzen (Studien über Deuterosacharja, Acta Theologica Danica, VI (Copenhagen: Prostant and Munksgaard, 1964), 192-3), while denying any connection between 13:7 and 11:4-14, emphasize that the shepherd in 13:7 cannot be a wicked leader.

[1]The prophet's rejection in v. 13 is equated with Yahweh's. Cf. Chary, Zacharie, 190; C. F. Keil, The Twelve Minor Prophets, trans. by James Martin, Biblical Commentary on the Old Testament, by C. F. Keil and F. Delitzsch (Edinburgh: T & T Clark, 1868), II, 358.

[2]P. R. Ackroyd, "Zechariah," Peake's Commentary, 654-5; M.-J. Lagrange, "Notes sur les prophéties messianiques des derniers prophètes," RB, III (1906), 75; France, Jesus, 108; Paul Lamarche, Zacharie IX-XIV; Structure littéraire et messianisme, EBib (Paris: Gabalda, 1961), 109; Bruce, Old Testament Themes, 113; Jeremias, "ποιμήν . . . ," TDNT, VI, 488.

[3]Lamarche, Zacharie IX-XIV, 110.

[4]He finds that four basic concepts predominate, one of which is the figure of the "Shepherd-King." These themes fall into a double chiastic structure, the inner one (10:3b-13:1) utilizing only two of them, while the outer portions (9:1-10:3a and 13:2-14:21) employ all four (Zacharie IX-XIV, 105-115).

the abruptness with which the figures in 12:10 and 13:7 are introduced: "Le titre de pasteur en 11, 4ss, l'identification en 12,10 entre Yahweh et son représentant, les expressions de 13,7 'pasteur de Yahweh, l'homme qui lui est proche' ne font que rappeler et prolonger la présentation au roi de 9,9: 'Voici que ton roi vient à toi.'"[1] If this interpretation is accepted, there is every reason to believe that Zechariah regarded this composite figure as Messianic. Zech. 9:9-10 is unquestionably Messianic[2] and the "pierced one" of 12:10 is probably to be identified with the Messiah,[3] as is done in the Jewish interpretation of the verse.[4] This helps explain the difficult conception that God is pierced: " . . . it is not difficult to think of Yahweh as pierced in the person of His anointed representative."[5] In 13:7, the phrase גבר עמיתי, used elsewhere only in Lev. 6:2 and 18:20 where it means "near neighbor," implies that the shepherd is God's equal,[6] or, at least, His accredited vice-regent, and, especially

---

[1]Lamarche, Zacharie IX-XIV, 110. The "Shepherd" in 13:7 is usually understood as the King (Targ. translates שלטונא, "ruler" -- Vermes, Scripture and Tradition, 58. Cf. also Otzen Deuterosacharja, 193; Bruce, Old Testament Themes, 102).

[2]Mitchell, Zechariah, 275-6; Joyce G. Baldwin, Haggai, Zechariah, Malachi, TOTC (London: Tyndale, 1972), 143. France speaks of an "apparently unanimous application to Messiah in the earliest [rabbinic] sources." (Jesus, 188).

[3]Keil, Minor Prophets, 388; Chary, Zacharie, 206; Brownlee, "Servant of the Lord I," 13; Lamarche, Zacharie IX-XIV, 85. Elliger (Dodekapropheten, II, 161) thinks of a Messianic forerunner.

[4]Zech. 12:10 is one of the oldest OT verses linked with the Jewish "suffering" Messiah b. Joseph, regarded as the precursor of the Messiah ben David (b. Sukk. 52a; cf. Str-B, II, 292-99). Whether the Messiah b. Joseph figure is a pre-Christian (Charles C. Torrey, "The Messiah Son of Ephraim," JBL, LXVI (1947), 253-77) or post-Christian (Vermes, Jesus the Jew, 140) development, the exegesis is a significant indication of the current interpretation of Zech. 12:10. It is most unlikely that the doctrine has influenced Zechariah (pace G. H. Dix, "The Messiah ben Joseph," JTS, XXVII (1926), 138-39).

[5]Bruce, Old Testament Themes, 112.

[6]Baldwin, Zechariah, 198.

if royal ideas are present, must be intended by Zechariah to denote the Messiah:

> The description of the shepherd as "the man who stands next to me" -- an associate of God, a suitable term for a royal figure -- perhaps suggests a disaster to some messianic personage (should we compare 12:10?), so that the picture is one of messianic woes ushering in the final age.[1]

It is admittedly more difficult to fit the rejected shepherd of 11:4-14 into a messianic mold,[2] but the close relationship of the shepherd to Yahweh and his role as ideal ruler who makes a covenant with "all the peoples" may suggest such an interpretation. At any rate, the eschatological drama depicted in which the figure of the Shepherd-King is a prominent participant, along with the indications given above, amply warrant attributing Messianic status to Zechariah's figure.[3]

---

[1] Ackroyd, "Zechariah," 654-5; Cf. also Keil, Minor Prophets, II, 396-7; Elliger, Dodekapropheten, II, 165; France, Jesus, 108; Lamarche, Zacharie IX-XIV, 92.
The allusion to Zech. 13:7 in CD 19:5-9 demonstrates that the shepherd was understood as an eschatological figure, but whether as the Teacher of Righteousness (Rabin, Zadokite Documents, 31, n.; van der Woude, Messianischen Vorstellungen, 38-39, 61-44; Longenecker, Christology, 49), the leader of the sect's enemies (Bruce, Biblical Exegesis, 34; Betz, Offenbarung, 178-79), or the hellenizing aristocracy of Jerusalem (Rabinowitz, "Reconsideration," 27-28) is unclear. But, if a hiatus is understood in line 7 (as probably should be), a reference to the Teacher of Righteousness is most probable (France, Jesus, 176-77).

[2] Lamarche (Zacharie IX-XIV, 69) claims that Zechariah's imagery is taken from the messianic shepherd imagery in Ez. 34, 37 and Jer. 22-23. (Cf. also Ina Willi-Plein, Prophetie am Ende: Untersuchungen zu Sacharja 9-14, BBB, XLII (Cologne: Peter Haastein, 1974), 80).

[3] It is possible that Zechariah was indebted to the earlier Messianic Shepherd prophecies of Ez. 34-36 and Jer. 23-25 in these chapters. (M. Delcor ("Un Problème de critique textuelle et d'exégèse: Zach, XII,10: Et aspicient ad me quem confixerunt," RB, LVIII (1951), 190-94) notes that Ez. 36:23 speaks of the name of Yahweh being מחלל among the nations. While חלל means "profane" in the Piel, it can mean "pierce" in Qal and Delcor suggests that Zech. 12:10 has been influenced by Ez. 36:16-28 and perhaps Jer. 51:4 (חלל) as well. (cf. also Lamarche, Zacharie IX-XIV, 85). Elliger (Dodekapropheten, II, 165) suggests that Ez. 38 may have influenced Zech. 13:7-10).
A greater number of scholars feel that Zechariah is dependent to some extent on the Servant prophecies of Isaiah for his conception of the suffering Messiah. Mitchell (Zechariah, 273) links the description of the humble king in 9:9 as "just" with Is. 56:8 and 53:11ff and Brownlee

This is not to deny that Zechariah's visions may relate to a contemporary of the prophet, for the leader of the community may have served as the focus for Zechariah's Messianic expectations.[1]

The characterization of the Messiah by the rubric "Shepherd" is by no means a development original to Zechariah. Yahweh Himself is frequently called a Shepherd and Israel His flock in the OT (cf. Pss. 23; 78:52; 80:1; 75:7), and this is a title which is bestowed on the Davidic Messiah in later portions of the OT (Ps. 78:70-2; Jer. 23:4; Ez. 34:23; Mic. 2:3-5). That this hope remained a living one in Judaism is demonstrated by II Esdras 2:34, Pss. Sol. 17:40 and CD 13:9 and 19:5-9 (?).[2] This not only lends further support to the Messianic application of Zech. 13:7 (and possibly 11:4-14), but suggests also that Zechariah's prophecy of the smitten

---

("Servant of the Lord I," 13, n. 20) notes the use of the verb "smite" in Zech. 13:7 and Is. 53:4. Is. 53:4, like Zech. 12:10, speaks of "piercing" (although different verbs are used). It may be added that 1QIs^a 53:10 reads יחללהו for MT החלי (Joseph A. Rosenbloom, The Dead Sea Isaiah Scroll: A Literary Analysis (Grand Rapids, Mich.: Eerdmans, 1970), 61). Lamarche, while objecting to Brownlee's suggestion because the verb is a common one, posits a thorough-going conceptual dependence of Zech. on Isaiah's Servant prophecies. Like the Servant (Is. 42:1ff), the Shepherd-King is first presented to the people (Zech. 9:9-10), then he is rejected (Zech. 11:4-14, cf. Is. 49:4) and finally killed (Zech. 12:10, 13:7 -- Is. 53). Other parallel themes exist, too numerous to mention here (Lamarche, Zacharie IX-XIV, 138-147; Servant influence on Zech. is also seen by Bruce, Old Testament Themes, 103; Baldwin, Zechariah, 198; Wolff, Jesaja 53, 40). However, no literary contacts exist and many of the suggested parallels are not convincing or are matters of common ideas. That Zechariah presents a picture very similar to the Servant in many respects is undeniable, but the similarities should rather be ascribed to a common understanding of God's purposes and the nature of the Messiah.

[1]Lamarche (Zacharie IX-XIV, 148-56), who dates the prophecies 500-480 B.C., points to the speculation concerning Zerubbabel (cf. Hagg. 2:20-23).

[2]David E. Aune, "The Problem of the Messianic Secret," NovT, XI (1969), 27; Richardson, Theology, 392; Jeremias, "ποιμήν," 487-88. Shepherd was also widely used as a title for the Jewish leader, whether good or bad. The Messiah-Shepherd is frequently contrasted with the evil shepherds. It seems inexplicable that Zech. 9-14 should be ignored in treatments of the royal shepherd imagery in the OT, but note J. G. S. S. Thomson, "The Shepherd-Ruler Concept in the OT and its Application in the NT," SJT, VIII (1955), 406-18.

Shepherd represents an important culmination of the OT Messianic Shepherd imagery: " . . . at the end of the OT shepherd sayings there stands an intimation of the shepherd who suffers death according to God's will and who thereby brings about the decisive turn."[1]

Matthew 21:4-5 / John 12:14-15 (Zechariah 9:9)

The singular circumstances of Jesus' final, dramatic entry into Jerusalem are claimed by Matthew and John to be a fulfillment of Zech. 9:9. While the quotation does not allude directly to Jesus' sufferings or death, the emphasis on humility, as well as the affinities of Zech. 9:9 with other important "passion prophecies" in Zech. 9-14, render necessary its consideration.

It is usually assumed that Matthew's quotation has a mixed textual background, the LXX being followed in the first part and the MT in the second (with possible influence from the Targ., Pesh., and A).[2] There can be little doubt that the MT is the basis for the latter part of the verse ($\dot{\epsilon}\pi\grave{\iota}$ $\ddot{o}\nu o \nu$ . . .), with a possible dependence on a text like that preserved in the Tg. and Pesh. (singular $\dot{\upsilon}\pi o \zeta \upsilon \gamma \acute{\iota}o \nu$).[3]

---

[1] Jeremias, "$\pi o \iota \mu \acute{\eta} \nu$," 488.

[2] Gundry, Old Testament, 149; Stendahl, School, 119-20; Lindars, Apologetic, 114.

[3] MT has plural אתנות; Targ. אתן; Pesh. ܐܬܢܐ.
The three animal names certainly provide grounds for confusion, but the Greek word selected by Matthew in each case is the proper equivalent for the Hebrew:

$\ddot{o}\nu o \varsigma$, "donkey, ass" usually translates חמור ("(he) ass") (74t.)

$\pi\hat{\omega}\lambda o \varsigma$, "foal, any young animal" is used only 7t. in the LXX, but represents עיר (male ass (young and vigorous)) five of those times

$\dot{\upsilon}\pi o \zeta \upsilon \gamma \acute{\iota}o \nu$, a word whose meaning is fairly broad (any beast of burden), translates חמור all but once.

The most pressing question has been raised with regard to $\pi\hat{\omega}\lambda o \varsigma$. The great lexicographer, Walter Bauer, surveyed the occurrences of the word in Greek literature and concluded that $\pi\hat{\omega}\lambda o \varsigma$, when used independently, must mean "horse" (as in Mk. 11:2 and Lk. 19:30). Matthew

However, it is possible that the former part of the quotation is dependent on the MT as well. While Matthew's rendering does agree verbatim with the LXX, the words he employs are in each case the natural equivalents of the respective Hebrew words.[1] The introduction to the quotation, as is generally acknowledged, stems from Is. 62:11.[2]

John's quotation is an abbreviated one, possessing no clear affinities with any single OT text. In place of the three-fold description of the animal in both MT and Mt., John substitutes a legitimate paraphrase, πῶλον ὄνου. καθήμενος has no basis in any known text of Zech. 9:9.[3] It cannot be decided with any degree of certainty whether the quotation is a free adaption of Mt. 21:5[4] or a paraphrastic rendering (perhaps from memory?) of the MT or LXX,[5]

---

and John therefore change the description under influence from the Zechariah prophecy. ("The 'Colt' of Palm Sunday (Der Palmesel)," trans. by F. W. Gingrich, JBL, LXXII (1953), 220-29). But this conclusion has been decisively refuted by Michel ("Eine philologische Frage zur Einzugsgeschichte," NTS, VI (1959-60), 81-82; cf. also "πῶλος," TDNT, VI, 960) who notes that πῶλος is the natural equivalent of עיר and that the meaning of πῶλος in Palestinian usage is basically "ass, donkey." In addition, with respect to the narratives in Mark and Luke, it should be pointed out that if, as seems likely, these accounts have already been influenced by Zech. 9:9, πῶλος must mean "ass, donkey" (cf. Heinz-Wolfgang Kuhn, "Das Reittier Jesu in der Einzugsgeschichte des Markusevangeliums," ZNW, L (1959), 83-91; Michel, "Einzugsgeschichte," 82).

[1] ἐπιβαίνω is the standard LXX translation of רכב, and πραΰς renders both עני (9t.) and ענו (4t.). In any case, it is difficult to distinguish between these two words; BDB suggest that ענו may simply be a variant of עני (776).

[2] George M. Soares Prabhu (The Formula Quotations in the Infancy Narrative of Matthew: An Enquiry into the Tradition History of Mt. 1-2, AnBib, LXIII (Rome: Biblical Institute Press, 1976), 54, n. 41) notes that the opening words of Zech. 9:9 ("rejoice . . . ") would be inappropriate to describe Jesus' confrontation with his doom.

[3] Edwin D. Freed, Old Testament Quotations in the Gospel of John, NovTSup, XI (Leiden: Brill, 1965), 78, points out that καθήμαι = רכב only It. in LXX.

[4] Freed, Old Testament, 80.

[5] Brown, John, I, 460-61; Dodd, According to the Scriptures, 48-49.

but John's substitution of μὴ φοβοῦ (which may be a stereotyped expression rather than an allusion to a particular OT verse[1]) for Matthew's εἴπατε points to the latter.

The manner in which each evangelist links Zech. 9:9 to the context is indicative of their respective approaches to the concept of fulfillment. While John abbreviates both the citation and the narrative in order to concentrate attention on a single theological point, the royal dignity of Jesus, Matthew elaborates, mentioning two animals and quotes literally the Hebrew of Zech. 9:9 in order to point to the detailed fulfillment of the prophecy. Indeed, the desire on Matthew's part to draw a comparison between the two animals of the narrative and the double mention of an animal in Zech. 9:9 has been disputed,[2] but it seems an incredible coincidence that the only evangelist who refers to two animals should also be the only one who quotes Zech. 9:9 in such a text so as to create the possibility of a description of two animals. If we therefore grant a correspondence, it remains to determine the direction in which influence has proceeded. It has been suggested that Matthew introduces into the narrative a second animal on the basis of the text,[3] but it is unlikely that the

---

[1] Bent Noack, Zur johanneischen Tradition. Beiträge zur Kritik an der literarkritischen Analyse des vierten Evangeliums (Copenhagen: Rosenkilde OG Bagger, 1954), 75; Leon Morris, The Gospel According to John, NIC (London: Marshall, Morgan & Scott, 1971), 586, n. 46. Barrett (John, 348) suggests that μὴ φοβοῦ is John's citation of the beginning of Zech. 9:9 from memory, with possible influence from other OT passages. Most frequently mentioned are Zeph. 3:16 (Freed, Old Testament, 78; Brown, John, I, 458; Schnackenburg, Johannes, II, 472; Lindars, Apologetic, 113) or Is. 40:9 or 35:4 (Stendahl, School, 119-20).

[2] Gundry, Old Testament, 198-9; Roman Bartnicki, "Das Zitat von Zach IX, 9-10 und die Tiere im Bericht von Matthäus über den Einzug Jesu in Jerusalem (Mt XXI, 1-11)," NovT, XVIII (1976), 166. Gundry argues that Matthew quotes the Zech. text in this form in order to emphasize the youthfulness of the animal upon which Jesus rode. But his argument is vitiated by the fact that Matthew fails at any place to make explicit that Jesus rode upon the young animal (In contrast to the ὄνος).

[3] McNeile, Matthew, 296; Schniewind, Matthäus, 212; Michel, "πῶλος," 960.

text, in the form of a parallelismus membrorum, would ever have suggested such a possibility to a literate Jew.[1] A more satisfactory explanation is to view the actual circumstances of the Entry as the formative influence. On this understanding, Matthew is led to view Zech. 9:9 in a new way by the procession of events at the Entry and he cites the prophecy in a text which, at least, allows a reference to the animals.[2] This interpretation of the Hebrew would lead to the logical conclusion that both animals were ridden, but this is a step which Matthew does not take; the antecedent of αὐτῶν in v. 7 must be ἱμάτια.[3]

John states explicitly (v. 16) that the disciples did not link the prophecy with the event at that time, but only after Jesus had been glorified. As Lindars remarks, it was a matter of "a lack of scriptural understanding." The relevance of Zech. 9:9 to the entry became clear to the disciples only in the light of the Resurrection.[4] That the entry was Messianic from the beginning is possible;[5] and Messianic not only because of the approaching kingdom,

---

[1] As Stendahl points out, it would be counter-productive to his Jewish apologetic for Matthew to introduce a tradition of two animals when the rabbis' messianic interpretation of Zech. 9:9 (and the related Gen. 49:11) consistently refers to only one animal (School, 200).

[2] Stendahl, School, 119; Lindars, Apologetic, 114. It seems improbable that the presence of two animals was inferred from the inexperience of the colt, as Lindars suggests.

[3] As Plummer says, " . . . the Evangelist credits his readers with common sense." (An Exegetical Commentary on the Gospel According to St. Matthew (London: Robert Scott, 1909), 286).

[4] Apologetic, 112-13.

[5] Even Mark's narrative is not independent of Zech. 9:9. As Kuhn points out, the three basic emphases in the prophecy are likewise emphasized in Mark: the entrance, the Messianic animal and the rejoicing of the people ("Das Reittier Jesu," 90). Contra. Sherman E. Johnson, A Commentary on the Gospel According to St. Mark, BNTC (London: Adam & Charles Black, 1960), 185; Bauer, "Colt," 220. Lindars points to Luke's ἐπεριβασαν (19:35) in place of Mark's ἐκάθισεν as evidence of his dependence on Zech. 9:9 (Apologetic, 114).

but more importantly because of the coming of the King.[1] However, the Kingship of Jesus is placed in a certain light by the focus of the prophecy itself and by the position of the text at the head of the "passion commentary" in Zech. 9-14. The King comes, but as the Prince of Peace.[2] If, as John seems to imply, the crowds were already coming to meet Jesus when he selected the animal which was to bear him into the city, the choice may have been a deliberate attempt to modify the politico-nationalistic greeting suggested by the peoples' palm-fronds.[3]

Matthew 26:31 / Mark 14:27 (Zechariah 13:7)

At the beginning of the account of the agony, betrayal and arrest in Matthew and Mark stands Jesus' programmatic prediction: πάντες σκανδαλισθήσεσθε (Mk. 14:27). This solemn declaration is followed immediately with a quotation from Zech. 13:7 giving the

---

[1] Lindars (Apologetic, 112) suggests that the thrust of the original demonstration was not directed toward the person of Jesus but to the imminence of the Kingdom. However, his avowal that even the narrative of Mark has Zech. 9:9 in the background would indicate that the King himself, as in the prophecy, is the focal point.
  Zech. 9:9 was consistently interpreted Messianically by the rabbis, often in terms of the Son of David (Str-B, I, 842-4). The animal figured prominently in these interpretations: "Die rabbinischen Beispiele lassen deutlich erkennen, dass man auf Grund von Sach 9,9 den Esel als das Tier des Messias schlechthin verstanden hat (und zwar schon in der tannaitischen Zeit)." (Kuhn, "Das Reittier Jesu," 89). The reaction of the crowds in hailing Jesus as the Son of David (Mt. 21:9; Mk. 11:10) is therefore perfectly natural.
  It is possible that Gen. 49:11 forms a secondary background for the pericope. The verse speaks of τὸν πῶλον and τὸν πῶλον τῆς ὄνου αὐτοῦ, and was understood Messianically in rabbinic interpretation, often in conjunction with Zech. 9:9 (e.g., Gen. R. 98; cf. Kuhn, "Das Reittier Jesu," 88-89; Str-B, I, 843).

[2] ". . . the acted parable said what kind of leader he was and on what basis he offered himself to his people." (Filson, Matthew, 220).
  It is interesting to note that at Mari, an "ass's colt" referred to a "purebred," which qualified the animal to be a royal mount (Baldwin, Zechariah, 166).

[3] Brown, John, I, 461-2.

basis (γάρ) for Jesus' prediction. A similar saying is imbedded in the Johannine farewell discourses (16:32) and it is possible that Zech. 13:7 is alluded to there as well.[1] However, the only verbal connection is in σκορπισθῆτε which, while a possible equivalent of Heb. פוצ (3t. in LXX), is not the form found in Matthew, Mark, or in any LXX MS. Furthermore, σκορπίζω is employed in the Good Shepherd discourse (Jn. 10:12) and may owe its recurrence in Jn. 16:32 to the shepherd imagery of the fourth evangelist. The simple introductory phrase in Matthew and Mark (ὅτι) γέγραπται (γάρ) seems to be characteristic of Jesus' use of Scripture.[2]

Tracing the textual background of this quotation is a difficult undertaking. While obviously independent of the "received" LXX text, the variant readings διασκορπισθήσονται in LXX[A] and [Q] and τῆς ποίμνης in LXX[A] raise the possibility that the evangelists are employing a Greek text of this type. It is improbable that these readings are due to assimilation to the NT in view of the significant correspondences to the text type represented by these uncials in the pre-Christian Qumran materials. The presence of such readings in the DSS has led to a general acceptance of the hypothesis that a pre-Christian Palestinian Jewish Greek recension existed, sporadically attested in LXX[A,Q] and in the quotations of Justin Martyr from the Minor Prophets.[3] Assimilation to NT in this case is further unlikely

---

[1] Dodd, Historical Tradition, 58; Lindars, John, 514; Brown, John, II, 727.

[2] The use of γέγραπται with only one or two connecting particles to introduce scriptural quotations is confined to words of Jesus in all four gospels (the only exception being Mt. 4:6 = Lk. 4:10, where the devil's phrase may be a mocking imitation of Jesus'). Latter usage (e.g., Paul) does not conform to this distinction, but the pattern in the gospels is striking, and renders untenable the opinion that γέγραπται γάρ is redactional here (contra Senior, Passion Narrative, 91).

[3] Cf., supra, 44-48.

since neither LXX^A nor Q read πατάξω with Matthew and Mark.^{1} The isolation of a pre-Christian Greek recension of this type does not necessarily solve the problem of textual dependence, however, since LXX^Q accurately translates MT,^{2} and Mark's form of the quotation could be based on either. The use of διασκορπίζω is not conclusive evidence for dependence on the Greek, as the word occurs nine times in the NT (although only here in Mark) and is common in the LXX. Mark's word order varies from that of LXX^Q, but this could be due to stylistic considerations. Therefore, it cannot be definitely established whether the citation in Mark is based on the MT or on a LXX^Q-type Greek text;^{3} at any rate, the quotation is closer to the MT than to the standard LXX text.

The first singular indicative πατάξω, common to both Matthew and Mark, represents the only deviation from any known OT <u>Vorlage</u>.^{4} While a theological motivation has been adduced as the basis for the change from the imperative,^{5} it is more likely that the indicative is simply a modification made necessary by the omission of a definite subject in the abbreviation of the OT passage.^{6}

---

^{1}Gundry, <u>Old Testament</u>, 26; Stendahl, <u>School</u>, 81-82; de Waard, <u>A Comparative Study</u>, 38.

^{2}The plural τὰ πρόβατα is a natural rendering of the collective צאן (Stendahl, <u>School</u>, 81).

^{3}A. B. Bruce (<u>The Synoptic Gospels</u>, Vol. I of <u>The Expositor's Greek Testament</u>, ed. by W. Robertson Nicoll (5 vols.; London: Hodder and Stoughton, 1897), 313), Plummer (<u>Matthew</u>, 367) and J. Jeremias ("ποιμήν," 492) believe that the quotation rests on the Hebrew.

^{4}Older OT commentators suggested the emendation אָכֶּה in Zech. 13:7 (e.g., Nowack, <u>Die Kleinen Propheten</u>, 374), but the reading הך in CD 19:8 confirms the MT (de Waard, <u>Comparative Study</u>, 39; Rabin, <u>Zadokite Documents</u>, 30). No evidence exists for Plummer's hypothesis that the phrase may have been a proverb which circulated with both the indicative and imperative (A. Plummer, <u>The Gospel According to St. Mark</u>, Cambridge Greek Testament (Cambridge: University Press, 1926), 324).

^{5}To emphasize the initiative of God in the events of the betrayal and arrest -- Stendahl, <u>School</u>, 82; Grundmann, <u>Markus</u>, 288. Cf. also Menzies, <u>The Earliest Gospel</u>, 255.

^{6}Gould, <u>Mark</u>, 267; France, <u>Jesus</u>, 107-108; Cranfield, <u>Mark</u>,

The unique reading πατάξω in Matthew and Mark is conclusive evidence that the two forms of the citation are closely related, Matthew probably being dependent on Mark, although common use of the same tradition cannot be ruled out. In view of this, Matthew's deviations from Mark in the inverted word order and the addition of τῆς ποίμνης require explanation. While the changes may simply be stylistic,[1] the close agreement thereby attained with LXX[A] suggests that the text of the citation in Matthew has been influenced by that text type.[2] The form of the citation in Mark is therefore dependent on the MT or LXX[Q] while that in Matthew is closely related to LXX[A].

As noted above, the quotation from Zech. 13:7 functions as the scriptural basis for the prediction of the disciples' imminent σκάνδαλον. That the flight of the disciples at the arrest of Jesus is the fulfillment of the prediction seems to be confirmed by the

---

428. (The subject in Zech. 13:7 is no doubt God, even though רועי is feminine (GKC, par. 144a)). Gundry (Old Testament, 27) suggests that the following ἐπάξω in Zech 13:7 may have facilitated the change. The fact that Justin employs the testimonium with the imperative shows that the future indicative is not essential to the functioning of the text (de Waard, Comparative Study, 40-41). The latter observation also makes Harris' attempt to explain the reading as due to the presence of the quotation in a book of Testimonies difficult (Harris, Testimonies, I, 68).

[1] Gundry, Old Testament, 26; Stendahl, School, 81. Stendahl explains the addition of τῆς ποίμνης as due to a desire to emphasize the breaking up of a unit, but it is doubtful whether such emphasis is really gained by the addition (cf. Senior, Passion Narrative, 93). Gundry sees the addition as indicating a "Targumic love of expansion" which has used Ez. 34:21, but ποίμνιον is the word there.

[2] Wilhelm Rothfuchs, Die Erfüllungszitate des Matthäus-Evangeliums; eine biblisch-theologische Untersuchung, BWANT, V;8 (Stuttgart: Kohlammer, 1969), 83; Lindars, Apologetic, 130; W. C. Allen, A Critical and Exegetical Commentary on the Gospel According to St. Matthew, ICC (Edinburgh: T & T Clark, 1907), 277. Gundry argues that LXX[A] has been assimilated to the gospels in the reading τῆς ποίμνης because the addition is not found in LXX[Q] (26). However, τῆς ποίμνης is attested by Justin (Dial., 53), an important witness in view of the connection between many of his Minor Prophet quotations and the DSS Dodekapropheton scroll, and indirectly by the Peshitta: ܕܥܢܐ.

repetition of πάντες in Mk. 14:50, by the appropriateness of the "scattering" imagery in Zech. 13:7 as a reference to the dispersal of the disciples, and by the fact that Luke, who does not record the flight, also omits the prediction.[1] At the same time, a broader reference to the passion events as a whole is probably implied; the arrest is the first stage in the "smiting of the Shepherd." There is much to be said for the view that Jesus' prediction and the accompanying OT citation function as a kind of superscription to the narratives of the arrest (smiting the shepherd) and the disciples' flight (the scattering of the sheep).

The appropriation of the OT text is accomplished fairly directly. The text is modified, but the changes are slight and do not affect the meaning of the passage. Neither, we would argue, is the meaning of the text misapplied; there are good reasons, brought out above, to regard the figure in Zech. 13:7 as Messianic, or at least as an individual close to God and in His favor. On the other hand, it is most unlikely that the narrative of the arrest and the scattering of the disciples has been modified in any way under the influence of the OT text. While the quotation was no doubt valuable as a means of explaining the desertion of Jesus' followers at the time of the arrest, there is no need to assume therefore that the

---

[1] Linnemann (Passionsgeschichte, 84-93) attempts to demonstrate that the prediction refers to a falling away in faith, of which Peter's denial is a "Konkretisierung." The flight of the disciples would seem to presuppose a failure of faith, as does, of course, Peter's denial, but the primary reference of the prediction, for the reasons given above, must be to the physical flight.

Günter Klein ("Die Verleugnung des Petrus: Eine traditions-geschichtliche Untersuchung," ZTK, LVIII (1961), 297) claims that the prediction of Jesus is, in fact, in conflict with the fact that Peter follows Jesus "ins Zentrum der Gegner." But the prediction and its fulfillment do not preclude a hesitant return on Peter's part (Mk. 14:54 -- Peter followed ἀπὸ μακρόθεν!) and eventual denial.

citation must be a vaticinium ex eventu.¹ The imagery of the shepherd and the sheep, so often used by Jesus, the lack of conformity to the standard LXX text and the appropriateness of the quotation in the context, constitute a firm basis for the authenticity of the saying.²

No direct relationship between John 16:32 on the one hand and Matthew and Mark on the other, can be observed. If John does allude to Zech. 13:7, the allusion is independent of the synoptic quotation, as the vocabulary proves.³ Luke records neither the flight of the disciples nor the prediction.

Matthew 26:15 (Zechariah 11:12)

The narrative of the payment of the betrayal money to Judas in Matthew is certainly "colored" by language from Zech. 11:12. This is indicated by the parallel use of $\ddot{\iota}\sigma\tau\eta\mu\iota$ in the sense of "to weigh out"⁴ (only here in the NT) and by the connection between

---

¹Against Lohmeyer, Markus, 311; B. Harvie Branscomb, The Gospel of Mark, MNTC (London: Hodder and Stoughton, 1937), 265; Menzies, Earliest Gospel, 255. The authenticity is also called into doubt by Loisy (Marc, 408), Hans Conzelmann ("History and Theology in the Passion Narratives of the Synoptic Gospels," Int, XXIV (1970), 189), Best (Temptation, 158) and Montefiore (Synoptic Gospels, II, 340).

²Taylor, Sacrifice, 146-147; Maurice Goguel, The Life of Jesus, trans. by Olive Wyon (London: George Allen & Unwin, 1933), 484; France, Jesus, 107; Lagrange, Marc, 383; F. F. Bruce, "The Book of Zechariah and the Passion Narrative," BJRL, XLIII (1960-1961), 343; Longenecker, Christology, 49; Jeremias, New Testament Theology, I, 297-298. In view of the close relationship of the two concepts in Jesus' teaching and ministry, it is illegitimate to drive a wedge between the pastoral and redemptive application of the shepherd imagery (against Lindars, Apologetic, 177-178; Wilfred Tooley, "The Shepherd and Sheep Imagery in the Teaching of Jesus," NovT, VII (1964-1965), 18).

³Dodd, Historical Tradition, 58; Lindars, John, 514.

⁴$\ddot{\iota}\sigma\tau\eta\mu\iota$ is frequently used in LXX with the meaning "weigh out (money)" (=Heb. שׁקל). (Stendahl, School, 124; Gundry, Old Testament, 143). $\ddot{\iota}\sigma\tau\eta\mu\iota$ here must refer to the actual payment of the money, not a promise to reward Judas' treachery after the fact (contra Schlatter, Matthäus, 738). Mt. 27:3 indicates that Judas has already received the money and Matthew's use of the verb is almost surely conditioned by the Septuagintal meaning. (Pierre Benoit, "The Death

Zech. 11:13 and Judas' death in Mt. 27:3-10. Matthew's ἀργύρια probably reflects the plural in Zech. 11:12 while his shift from the LXX word ἀργυροῦς to ἀργύριον reflects the normal NT usage and is perhaps dependent on Mk. 14:11.[1] ἀργύρια does not, therefore, necessarily indicate independence from the LXX.[2]

The sum of the wages of the rejected shepherd in Zech. 11 is no doubt ironic (RSV, "the lordly price")[3] and is perhaps based on the pentateuchal legislation which fixes the compensation price for an accidentally slain slave at 30 shekels (Ex. 21:32). It is improbable that the latter passage has any direct bearing on Matthew's allusion.

The narrative allusion in Mt. 26:15 is undoubtedly introduced with a glance ahead to Mt. 27:3-10, which is strongly influenced by Zech. 11.[4] Matthew's concern with Judas' history is one example of the early church's desire to account for the seemingly inexplicable treachery of a close follower of Jesus. OT Scriptures are frequently employed to explain Judas' behavior: even his treachery is a part of God's plan which is finding its culmination in Christ.[5] This concern on the part of the early church to explain Judas' actions has led to serious doubts with regard to the historical reliability of these

---

of Judas," Jesus and the Gospel, trans. by Benet Weatherhead (2 vols.; London: Darton, Longman & Todd, 1973), I, 197, n. 4. Cf. also Haenchen, Weg Jesu, 474; Charles C. Torrey, "The Foundry of the Second Temple at Jerusalem," JBL, LV (1936), 249.

[1] D. Senior, "The Passion Narrative in the Gospel of Matthew," L'Evangile selon Matthieu, 353, n. 31. Matthew is the only NT writer who uses ἀργύρια (plural); it may be a Semitism (X. Léon-Dufour, "Mt et Mc dans le Récit de la Passion," Bib, XL (1959), 688. Cr. Turner, Syntax, 27.

[2] Against Gundry, Old Testament, 144.

[3] Mitchell, Zechariah, 309.

[4] Klostermann, Matthäusevangelium, 209; Lindars, Apologetic, 116.

[5] Cf. Acts 1:18-19; Mk. 14:21 par.; Jn. 17:12; 13:18. Another development with regard to Judas emphasizes Jesus' foreknowledge of the betrayal; Jn. 6:64-70, 13:18.

details in the gospels which link Judas with the OT. Indeed it has been alleged that the incident in Mt. 26:14-15 has been invented to point to the fulfillment of Zech. 11:12.[1] However, Mark's version of this incident, without scriptural allusions, obviates a thoroughgoing scepticism with regard to the narrative. With regard to details, ἵστημι, used in the anachronistic sense "weighed out," is no objection to the historicity of the incident;[2] Matthew must be accorded the literary license to describe reality with vivid, if out-of-date, metaphors. It is more difficult to know whether the number thirty has been taken from the Zechariah passage as a figure symbolic of low esteem or is a genuine historical reminiscence. More will be said on this in the following section.

Matthew 27:3-10 (Zechariah 11:13; Jeremiah 19:1-13)

The narrative of Judas' death, peculiar to the first gospel, is climaxed by the last (and perhaps the most problematical) of Matthew's Reflexionszitate. In addition to the formal quotation, OT elements seem to be woven into the fabric of the pericope. Lohmeyer expresses a widespread opinion when he says: "Es gibt wenig evangelische Erzählungen, welche so bis in jede Einzelheit von alttestamentlichen Wort und Geist durchdrungen sind wie diese."[3] Since most of these OT reminiscences are related to the formula quotation, they are most profitably studied in that context, but a suggested parallel, independent of the quotation, may be dealt with first. It is alleged that Mt. 27:5 has been influenced by the account

---

[1] E.g., Montefiore (Synoptic Gospels, II, 329) calls this narrative "one of the clearest examples of history made up from bits of Old Testament prophecy."

[2] Montefiore, Synoptic Gospels, II, 329.

[3] Lohmeyer-Schmauch, Matthäus, 375.

of the suicide of Ahithophel in II Sam. 17:23: "Ahithophel the treacherous friend of David and Judas, the treacherous friend of the Son of David, meet a similar end . . . ."[1] Adding credence to the suggested allusion are the far-reaching parallels between the descriptions of Ahithophel and Judas which have been discerned by some.[2] The use of ἀπάγχομαι in Mt. 27:5 is an important link to II Sam. 17:23, since the word is rare in the LXX (four times; three of them in Tob. 3:10) and appears only here in the NT. ἀπελθών in Matthew and ἀπῆλθεν in II Samuel may provide a further verbal connection. However, ἀπάγχομαι is frequently used in secular Greek to denote suicide by hanging[3] and the rarity of the word in Biblical Greek is probably simply due to the infrequency of the action itself.[4] A certain similarity in circumstances is obvious, but the differences should not be overlooked: Ahithophel, confident that he is right, commits suicide because his counsel was spurned, while Judas' suicide is a result of sorrow for his part in a successful endeavor.[5] In view of these mitigating factors, the presence of an allusion cannot be confirmed.

---

[1]McNeile, Matthew, 407. The parallel is noted by H. A. W. Meyer, The Gospel of St. Matthew, trans. by William P. Dickson and William Stewart, Pt. I, Vol. I of Critical and Exegetical Commentary on the New Testament (Edinburgh: T & T Clark, 1879), 248; Holtzmann, Die Synoptiker, 293; M. Plath, "Warum hat die urchristliche Gemeinde auf die Überlieferung der Judaserzählungen Wert gelegt?" ZNW, XVII (1916), 188; Micklem, Matthew, 264; Kirsopp Lake, "The Death of Judas," Beginnings of Christianity, Pt. I, Vol. V, 29; Lohmeyer-Schmauch, Matthäus, 375; Goppelt, Typos, 120; A. W. Argyle, The Gospel According to Matthew, The Cambridge Bible Commentary (Cambridge: University Press, 1963), 210; Benoit, "Death," 194-5; Senior, Passion Narrative, 384.

[2]Cf., e.g., Bertil Gärtner, Iscariot, trans. by Victor I. Gruhm; Facet Books: Biblical Series, XXIX (Philadelphia: Fortress, 1971), 30-39.

[3]See the references in BAG, 78.

[4]Benoit, "Death," 195; Senior, Passion Narrative, 384.

[5]W. C. van Unnik, "The Death of Judas in St. Matthew's Gospel," ATR, supp. ser., III (1974), 50-51; Lohmeyer-Schmauch, Matthäus, 375.

In any event, it is unnecessary to regard the mode of Judas' death as an interpolation from the OT, since hanging was a popular method of suicide in the ancient world.[1]

Lindars characterizes Mt. 27:3-10 as "the most elaborate product of the Church's midrash pesher in the New Testament,"[2] and whether one agrees with the terminology or not, it cannot be denied that the quotation and its context are more closely intertwined than in any other NT passage. The unravelling of the disparate threads which have gone into the completed narrative is best begun with the quotation itself. The formula introducing the citation is similar to those found at nine other places in the first gospel, which has led to the description of these quotations as "Reflexionszitate."[3] In keeping with the special problems encountered in this group of quotations, the precise passages alluded to in Mt. 27:9-10 are not immediately obvious. The text is drawn mainly from Zech. 11:13, although several important elements find no counterpart in Zechariah. In view of the ascription of the citation to Jeremiah, these extraneous elements are best explained by supposing that a passage from that prophecy has influenced the quotation.[4] It will be necessary to test

---

[1]Benoit, "Death," 195: "Hanging was one of the most frequent modes of suicide, especially in antiquity. And was there a more natural Greek word to express it?"

[2]Apologetic, 116.

[3]See the studies of Stendahl (School), Rothfuchs (Erfüllungszitate), Gundry (Old Testament) and Prabhu (Formula Quotations).

[4]Proposed explanations which attempt to account for the ascription to Jeremiah apart from influence on the quotation are not convincing: (1) the variant readings Ζαχαριου (22 Syr hrg) or Ησαιου (21 θ 33 157) should be followed. (2) Since Jeremiah stands first of the prophets in several OT book lists (J. P. Audet, "A Hebrew-Aramaic List of Books of the Old Testament in Greek Transcription," JTS, n.s., I (1950), 136; Charles C. Torrey, "The Aramaic Period of the Nascent Christian Church," ZNW, XLIV (1952-53), 222), his name may be used here as a general reference to the prophetic corpus (Str-B, I, 1030; H. F. D. Sparks, "St. Matthew's References to Jeremiah," JTS, n.s., I (1950), 155; Edmund F. Sutcliffe, "Matthew 27,9," JTS, n.s., III (1952), 227). (3) An apocryphal book (which Jerome claims to have

this hypothesis by looking closely at the relationship between the quotation, the narrative and suggested background passages from Jeremiah. The complexity of the textual background and the freedom with which the texts are used warrant a phrase-by-phrase investigation of the citation.

καὶ ἔλαβον τὰ τριάκοντα ἀργύρια is a fairly straightforward rendition of the beginning of the second major clause in Zech. 11:13. As in 26:15, Matthew uses the word ἀργύριον, which may be a reflection of his Markan Vorlage (cf. Mk. 14:11).[1] ἔλαβον is probably to be understood as a third person ("impersonal") plural, as against the first person sing. of the LXX.[2] The modification should probably be attributed to the influence of the tradition, in which the priests "take" the money (v. 6 λαβόντες τὰ ἀργύρια). Since ἀργύρια is perhaps a reflection of Matthew's Markan source, no decision can be reached regarding the textual background of the phrase.

τὴν τιμὴν τοῦ τετιμημένου is closer to MT than to LXX, which deviates considerably from the Heb. The personalized τετιμημένου perhaps depends on a vocalization of הַיְקָר "the price" as הַיָּקָר "the

---

seen) contained the conflated citation under Jeremiah's name (Origen; Hieronymus; Lohmeyer-Schmauch, Matthäus, 378; Georg Strecker, Der Weg der Gerechtigkeit: Untersuchungen zur Theologie des Matthäus, FRLANT, LXXXII (Göttingen: Vandenhoeck & Ruprecht, 1962), 80-81; Senior, Passion Narrative, 372 (as possible)). (4) The quotation was found in the Testimony Book under Jeremiah's name (Harris, Testimonies, I, 59-60; J. A. Findlay, "The First Gospel and the Book of Testimonies," Amicitiae Corolla, ed. by H. G. Wood (London: University of London, 1933), 65). (5) The ascription is due to a slip of memory (Meyer, Matthew, 249; Finegan, Überlieferung, 26; McNeile, Matthew, 407; Stendahl, School, 123). (6) The last part of the book of Zechariah was traditionally ascribed to Jeremiah.

[1] See under Mt. 26:15; Senior, Passion Narrative, 354.

[2] Lohmeyer-Schmauch, Matthäus, 378; Stendahl, School, 125. Senior (Passion Narrative, 353) and Gundry (Old Testament, 126) are more hesitant, the latter pointing out that the influence of the LXX may have outweighed that of the context. While relative degree of influence is difficult to assess, the probable reading ἔδωκαν (see below) is good reason to understand ἔλαβον as 3rd pl. as well.

honored one" (cf. the Pesh.).[1] τιμή beautifully captures the irony inherent in יקר ("excellence"), while retaining the basic meaning of "price," since τιμή can convey either of these ideas.[2] The freedom with which Matthew treats his Zechariah source is already evident, in the transposition of the two clauses, καὶ ἔλαβον . . . and τὴν τιμήν .

ὃν ἐτιμήσαντο ἀπὸ υἱῶν Ἰσραήλ. The change of person in the verb is a necessary translation modification, since τιμάω is transitive, while יקר is intransitive, but the change undoubtedly commended itself to Matthew as more closely approximating to the tradition as well.[3] The phrase undoubtedly depends on MT since LXX has nothing comparable. ἀπό has a partitive sense, corresponding to the use of Heb. מן, to mean "some of."[4] Matthew substitutes υἱῶν Ἰσραήλ for the Hebrew pronominal suffix, a modification required because of the lack of an antecedent for the pronoun.[5] The reading ἔδωκαν is generally preferred to ἔδωκα, the following μοι and the OT verse providing strong temptation to assimilate to the first person.[6] On the other hand, the following α may have led

---

[1] Stendahl, School, 125; Gundry, Old Testament, 126; Senior, Passion Narrative, 355; Meyer, Matthew, 351; A. Baumstark, "Die Zitate des Mt.-Ev. aus dem Zwölfprophetenbuch," Bib, XXXVII (1956), 302.

[2] BAG, 825; Stendahl, School, 126; Gundry, Old Testament, 126; Senior, Passion Narrative, 354.

[3] Senior, Passion Narrative, 355.

[4] BDF, par. 164 (2) note the unclassical use of ἐκ and ἀπό in this way. Cf. GKC, par. 199w for the Hebrew construction. The partitive interpretation is defended by Stendahl (School, 126), Gundry (Old Testament, 126) and Senior (Passion Narrative, 355).

[5] Gundry (Old Testament, 127, n. 1) notes that the Targum often expands with the phrase "the sons of Israel." Senior (Passion Narrative, 355) believes the change from indefinite to definite is characteristic of Matthew's redaction.

[6] Lagrange, Matthieu, 513; Stendahl, School, 125; Senior, Passion Narrative, 356.

to the addition of the ν[1] and the narrative context would have exercised a powerful attraction to the third person plural.[2] On the whole, ἔδωκαν is the more difficult and should probably be preferred. The less forceful δίδωμι (contrast LXX ἐνέβαλον, MT שׁלך) is perhaps used because the context " . . . calls for a less forceful action on the part of the Jewish leaders."[3]

With the phrase εἰς τὸν ἀγρὸν τοῦ κεραμέως the major crux of the quotation is reached. No extant text or version gives any hint that a field is involved in the events narrated in Zechariah 11. While its presence in the quotation is no doubt due to the prominence of a field in the tradition associated with the death of Judas, the attribution of the citation to Jeremiah invites attempts to relate the mention of a field to a passage from that OT book. The passages usually suggested are Jeremiah 18 and 32.[4] The former passage features Jeremiah's visit to the house of the potter, while the purchase of a field figures prominently in the latter. ἀγγεῖον ὀστράκινον, "earthenware jar," in Jer. 32:14 is often cited as the point of contact between Jeremiah 32 on the one hand, and Jeremiah 18 and Zechariah 11 on the other.[5] Torrey conjectures that the Hanamel

---

[1]Metzger, Commentary, 67.

[2]McNeile, Matthew, 408; Gundry, Old Testament, 126. ἔδωκα is supported by Allen, Matthew, 288; Montefiore, Synoptic Gospels, II, 343.

[3]Senior, Passion Narrative, 355.

[4]Bruce, "Zechariah," 341; Torrey, "Foundry," 252; Stendahl, School, 122; Strecker, Weg, 77; R. S. McConnell, Law and Prophecy in Matthew's Gospel: The Authority and Use of the Old Testament in the Gospel of St. Matthew, Theologische Dissertationen, II (Basel: Friedrich Reinhardt, 1969), 132; Lindars, New Testament Apologetc, 120; Schniewind, Matthäus, 168; Tasker, Matthew, 258-9; Micklem, Matthew, 264; Schweizer, Matthew, 504; Allen, Matthew, 289; Sherman E. Johnson and George A. Buttrick, "The Gospel According to St. Matthew," Interpreter's Bible, Vol. VII, 593. Jeremiah 32 only is mentioned by Schlatter, Matthäus, 770; A. Descamps, "Rédaction et Christologie dans le recit matthéen de la Passion," L'Évangile selon Matthieu, 389; Haenchen, Weg Jesu, 516; Lohmeyer-Schmauch, Matthäus, 379.

[5]Lindars, Apologetic, 120; Stendahl, School. 122.

of Jeremiah 32 may also have been the potter of Jeremiah 18, but this is without evidence.[1] כסף and שקל are common roots and do not provide sufficient basis for the joining of Zech. 11:13 with Jer. 32:9.[2] Therefore, the only real parallels are found in the fact that a potter is featured in Jeremiah 18 and Zech. 11:13 and the purchase of a field in Jeremiah 32 and the Judas tradition. The links between Jeremiah 18, 32 and Zech. 11:13 are tenuous at best and it is difficult to reconstruct a process by which they would have been joined together. It is therefore necessary to ask if any other passage from the book of Jeremiah may provide a more relevant background for the narrative in Mt. 27:3-8.

One's attention is immediately drawn to Jer. 19:1-13. Two verbal links exist between Jeremiah 19 and Mt. 27:3-10: "innocent blood" דם נקי -- LXX: αἱμάτων ἀθῴων -- 19:4), "potter" (יצר)' -- LXX: πεπλασμένον -- vv. 1,11). Even more striking is the thematic parallel: Jeremiah prophesies that a locality associated with potters (v. 1) will be renamed with a phrase connoting violence (v. 6), and used as a burial place (v. 11), as a token of God's judgment upon Jerusalem (and in particular, upon the Jewish leaders (v. 1)).[3] While a field is not specifically mentioned in Jer. 19, the

---

[1]"Foundry," 252. Gundry (Old Testament, 124) points out that Hanamel, Jeremiah's cousin, was probably of a priestly family and hence almost certainly not a potter.

[2]Against Doeve, Hermeneutics, 185-6. Doeve characterizes Mt. 27: 3-10 as a haggadah and believes the starting point of the complex was the connection between Mt. 27:5 and Jer. 26:15 through the phrase "innocent blood." Once Jer. 26 was associated with Judas' death, the similar theme of judgment against Jerusalem would have led the Haggadist to Jer. 19 and 32, the entire Jeremiah tradition then being tied into Zech. 11:13 on the basis of the roots כסף and שקל, found in Jer. 32:9. The foundation of the whole argument is weak, however; innocent blood is a common expression that would not alone have provided a point of contact between Matthew and Jer. 26. The motivation for the joining together of Jer. 19, 26 and 32 is weak, as well; practically the entire book of Jeremiah is characterized by prophecies against Jerusalem.

[3]See Gundry (Old Testament, 124-5) and Senior (Passion Narrative, 360) for these specific points. Jeremiah 19 had earlier been considered

contextual similarity to Mt. 27:3-10, taken in conjunction with the verbal connection (especially the key-word "potter") is a solid basis for associating Jeremiah 19 with the quotation in Mt. 27:9-10. If, as seems likely, the parallel between the tradition of Zech. 11:13 and Jeremiah 19 was first discovered through the common mention of a "potter," the MT has surely been the basic text employed, since LXX paraphrases יֹצֵר in Jer. 19:1 and 11.

The last phrase of the quotation again has no counterpart in Zech. 11:13.[1] Basing himself on the belief that the reference to the field is from Jeremiah 32, Torrey feels that Jer. 32:6 and 8 has given rise to the reference to God's command.[2] Lindars proposes a more complex background. The words καθὰ συνέταξεν κύριος are found in Ex. 9:12, where they indicate the fulfillment of God's promise to Moses that, notwithstanding the plague of boils, Pharaoh would continue to harden his heart against the requests of the Israelites. This verse from Exodus is related to Zech. 11:13 through the mention of the furnace used for the production of the ashes which caused the boils, in Ex. 9:8 (cf. LXX Zech. 11:13: χωνευτήριον "foundry"). The "ingenious" exegete "expresses the idea of the divine command, suggested to him by Jer. 32 (39). 14, in the phrase found in the Exodus passage."[3] The LXX word for "furnace" in Ex. 9:8 is not the same one found in Zech., however, and the whole reconstruction is tenuous at best.

---

the background to this quotation by Alfred Edersheim (<u>The Life and Times of Jesus the Messiah</u> (2 vols.; London: Longman, Green and Co., 1883), II, 596).

[1] A few later LXX MSS have assimilated the phrase from Matthew.

[2] "Foundry," 252.

[3] <u>Apologetic</u>, 121; Schweizer, <u>Matthew</u>, 504. Schniewind (<u>Matthäus</u>, 268) mentions Ex. 9:12.

Zechariah 9-14   197

While dependence on Ex. 9:12, mediated through Jeremiah 32, does not seem sufficient to explain the phrase in Matthew, an element of truth in this reconstruction can be seen when it is recognized that the phrase καθὰ συνέταξεν κύριος in Ex. 9:12 is only one of a number of similar sayings in the OT.[1] It is probable that Matthew draws on this stereotyped expression as a paraphrase of the opening words of Zech. 11:13, "and the Lord said to me."[2] That the words must be an attempt to introduce Zech. 11:13a into the citation is demonstrated by the anomalous μοι. The verbal agreement between the phrase in Matthew and the LXX rendition of many of the "obedience formulas"[3] indicates that Matthew was aware of the expression in its Greek form.

The formula quotation is therefore built up from several OT elements: the foundation and essential structure is provided by the phrases drawn from Zech. 11:13, but the mention of the field provides an important "remodelling" of the quotation, based on the Judas tradition and with reference to Jeremiah 19, while the concluding phrase adds a "decorative motif," drawn from the traditional "obedience formula." Jeremiah is mentioned in the introductory formula because

---

[1] The genre to which these sayings belong has been studied by Pesch, who calls them "Ausführungsformel." He notes several instances of the obedience formula pattern in Matthew's gospel. (Rudolf Pesch, "Eine alttestamentliche Ausführungsformel im Matthäus-Evangelium: Redaktionsgeschichte und exegetische Beobachtungen," BZ, n.s., X (1966), 220-245).

[2] Senior, Passion Narrative, 361. Montefiore (Synoptic Gospels, II, 343), Lohmeyer-Schmauch (Matthäus, 379), Gundry (Old Testament, 127) and Stendahl (School, 123) think the phrase is an attempt to introduce the opening words of Zech. 11:13. Stendahl's tentative suggestion that Matthew's phrase is an interpretation of יְהוָה דְּבַר as יְהוָה בְּיַד cannot be maintained. As Gundry (127, n. 3) points out in reply to a similar theory of Baumstark's, בְּיַד is always used with an instrumental sense in association with the Word of God.

[3] καθὰ συνέταξεν κύριος in Ex. 36:8, 12, 14, 28, 33; 37:20; 39:10; 40:19; Lev. 14:23; Num. 8:3; 9:5; 15:23; 20:9, 27; 27:11; 31:31, 41. Matthew's dependence on this phrase is confirmed by the fact that καθὰ is used only here in the NT.

Jeremiah 19 was the least obvious reference, yet most important from the point of view of the application of the quotation.[1]

Before turning to the narrative, a significant aspect of the text-form of the quotation should be emphasized: its close dependence on the MT. Several of the phrases from Zech. 11:13 must depend on the MT, the influence of Jeremiah 19 is probably mediated through familiarity with the Heb., and no part of the quotation depends on the LXX against the MT. (The phrase καθὰ συνέταξέν μοι κύριος, while dependent on the Greek, is not an exception, since it is a stereotyped formula independent of any one OT passage.) It is not unlikely, therefore, that the MT is the sole Vorlage for the quotation.[2]

The exceptionally detailed correspondences between the narrative of Judas' death and the OT quotation raise important questions concerning the relation of the citation to the context. On the one hand, there can be little doubt that the tradition has exerted considerable influence on the quotation. The introduction of the "field" is, of course, the most notable example of this influence, but other minor deviations (the third person plural verbs, δίδωμι for שׁקל) are best attributed to the impact of the tradition as well. In terms of the phraseology introduced in Chapter I, a case of the re-orientation of the text is present. It will be necessary to explore the extent of this re-orientation at a later point. On the other hand, it must be asked whether the reverse process has taken place. Have elements from the OT passages crept into or influenced the narrative? Ultimately, the answer to this question depends largely on one's over-all understanding of the way in which the NT authors use the Old. But the important role which Mt. 27:3-10 must play in any such understanding makes imperative an attempt to determine the extent to which OT elements have affected the recounting of Judas' end.

---

[1] Gundry, Old Testament, 125. [2] Allen, Matthew, 288.

The "thirty pieces of silver" in v. 3 is an allusive reference
to Zech. 11:13. That the idea of betrayal money is not taken from the
OT is certain since Mark records the transaction without alluding to
Zech. 11:13. It cannot be finally determined whether the exact sum
is an accommodation to the prophecy or an element in the tradition
which helped direct Matthew's attention to Zech. 11.[1] The latter
alternative should not, however, be ruled out as summarily as it often
is.

αἷμα ἀθῷον forms the first link in the chain of "blood"
references which serve as an important literary motif in the story
(price of blood -- v. 6, field of blood -- v. 8).[2] The phrase finds
an echo in the Trial before Pilate as well; the Roman governor
washes his hands and declares ἀθῷός εἰμι ἀπὸ τοῦ αἵματος τούτου
(Mt. 27:24). What Pilate refuses by washing his hands, the Jews take
on themselves in the thirty pieces of silver.[3] αἷμα ἀθῷον is,
therefore, suspect as a subsequent addition to the tradition, perhaps
based on the OT (Jer. 6:15 or 19:4, especially).[4] However, "to shed
innocent blood" is a standard OT expression for a particularly heinous
crime[5] and is not, therefore, unnatural on Judas' lips.[6] If Matthew

---

[1]Strecker (Weg, 77-9), who believes that Matthew has taken the story from oral tradition and added the quotation himself (cf. also Kilpatrick, Origins, 81), regards the "thirty pieces of silver" as one of the rare Matthean additions to the tradition.

[2]Lohmeyer-Schmauch, Matthäus, 375; Senior, Passion Narrative, 386-7.

[3]Lohmeyer-Schmauch, Matthäus, 376.

[4]Doeve, Hermeneutics, 185.

[5]Lohmeyer-Schmauch, Matthäus, 375.

[6]Van Unnik ("Death," 53-55) cites Dt. 27:25 ("Cursed be whoever takes gifts (bribes) to take the life of innocent blood") and conjectures that Judas, in light of this verse, takes his own life to remove the curse. While the parallel is striking, it is doubtful that Judas would have acted so drastically on the basis of this verse alone.

himself is responsible for the expression, he has probably been influenced by general usage rather than by a particular OT passage.

The action of Judas described in v. 4, ῥίψας τὰ ἀργύρια εἰς τὸν ναόν, echoes the command in Zech. 11:13 to throw the silver pieces into the יהוה בית (οἶκον κυρίου). While the verb is ἐνέβαλον in LXX, ῥίπτω is used in A' and ξ, so it is thought possible that Matthew has added this detail to the tradition on the basis of the OT text:

> It is underlined>known</u>, as in the Acts version, that Judas died suddenly and that the money was used to buy land, but it is <u>assumed</u> that the money was first thrown into the house of the Lord, because the prophecy says so.[1]

However, this interpretation is open to several criticisms. It is, perhaps, unlikely that Matthew would have presented Judas as throwing the coins into the <u>sanctuary</u> (ναός)[2] had he been creating the tradition. If the priests' role in the transaction is historical, their involvement must have been precipitated by an action similar to that described in v. 4. Furthermore, Judas' gesture may be understood as a Jewish legal custom, apparently valid in the time of Jesus, according to which a seller who wished to revoke a deal, but having been refused by the buyer, could deposit the money involved in the transaction in the Temple, and so effect a revocation. While the Mishnah rule in question refers to the purchase of houses, Jeremias believes that the

---

[1] Lindars, Apologetic, 118; Senior, Passion Narrative, 382. Stendahl (School, 126) believes that Matthew adds the detail to utilize an element from Zech. 11:13 that had been "left hanging" after his changes to the text. The freedom with which Matthew uses the OT text indicates that the retention of this phrase in the prophecy would have been no difficult matter. Lohmeyer-Schmauch (Matthäus, 376) argue that Judas could not have thrown the coins into the Temple because the Sanhedrin was not there, but at the Roman trial (cf. Mt. 27:1-2). But it is obvious that Matthew has added the Judas pericope to the Marcan framework at a break in the material so that the position of the narrative does not necessarily represent a chronological indication.

[2] While there is some dissent (Michel, "ναός," TDNT, 884-5), Matthew at least seems to distinguish ναός, the sanctuary, from ἱερόν, the temple precincts. (Compare 23:16,17,21,35 with 4:5, 21:12,14,15, 24:1, 26:55).

provision could have formed the background to Judas' action.[1] One further point might be raised with regard to the appropriation of the prophecy as a whole by Matthew. It is sometimes overlooked that the specific context of Zech. 11:13 is not as congenial to the function of the text as a prophecy of Judas' dealings with the Jewish leaders as it might be. For the "I" of Zech. 11:13 is unambiguously identified as the prophet himself, in the role of Yahweh's appointed good shepherd (i.e., ruler), which role seems to be understood as a prefigurement of Christ's as the rejected shepherd par excellence. Matthew seems to be at pains to interpret Zech. 11:13 so as to avoid the manifest absurdity of identifying Judas with the rejected shepherd while, at the same time, appropriating the passage as a prophecy of the history of the betrayal money. This he can do only by substituting circumlocutory constructions for the first person verbs of the OT passage. We have seen that, in fact, this is exactly what is done: "they" (the priests) rather than the rejected shepherd himself, as the prophecy strictly requires, take the silver coins and give them to the potter. The importance of this insight for the specific question before us is obvious: the necessity to avoid directly ascribing to Judas any of the actions of the rejected shepherd in Zechariah renders it unlikely that Matthew would introduce an action on Judas' part ("throwing the coins into the temple") that does just that. It cannot, therefore, be maintained that the reference to Judas' throwing the coins into the temple in v. 4 has been introduced on the basis of the OT quotation.[2]

---

[1] Joachim Jeremias, <u>Jerusalem in the Time of Jesus</u>, trans. by F. H. and C. H. Cave (3rd ed.; London: SCM, 1969), 139.

[2] Allen (<u>Matthew</u>, 288) thinks the detail was a known fact and has facilitated Matthew's use of the Zech. 11:13 text.

While v. 5 is said to represent an attempt to introduce an element from Zech. 11:13 into the narrative which was omitted from the quotation, it is argued that εἰς τὸν κορβανᾶν in v. 6 is a doublet of εἰς ... κεραμέως in the citation. Some scholars feel the dual understanding of the phrase from Zech. 11:13 is based on a variant reading of אוצר "treasury" for יוצר "potter."[1] While no Heb. MS reads אוצר, the Pesh. ܠܓܙܐ seems to presume such a reading, which, in view of the verbal similarity, could easily have been subsequently altered to יוצר.[2] However, the translation of the Pesh. is too slight a support for the suggested emendation and יוצר must surely be retained as the <u>lectio difficilior</u>.[3] Even if such a reading were known to the interpreter, the evidence for the use of variant readings in this way is slight.[4] If εἰς τὸν κορβανᾶν cannot rest on a variant reading, it is nevertheless possible that the phrase is evidence of Matthew's understanding of Zech. 11:13 in a dual sense, an interpretation facilitated by the word-play יוצר -- אוצר,[5] perhaps in combination with the belief that the יוצר in Zech. 11:13 was a

---

[1] As Bruce (<u>Old Testament Themes</u> 110) paraphrases the priests' thinking: "'How shall we fulfill the scripture? Shall we give it to the ʿōsar or to the yosar? We cannot give it to theʿōsar because it is blood money; let us give it to the yōsar.'" See also Allen, <u>Matthew</u>, 288; Montefiore, <u>Synoptic Gospels</u>, II, 342; McNeile, <u>Matthew</u>, 408; Benoit, "Death," 198; Kilpatrick, <u>Origins</u>, 45; Johnson-Buttrick, "Matthew," 593.

[2] T. Jansma, <u>Inquiry into the Hebrew Text and the Ancient Versions of Zechariah 9-14</u>, Oudtestamentische Studien, VII (Leiden: E. J. Brill, 1950), 35; Sidney Jellicoe, <u>The Septuagint and Modern Study</u> (Oxford: Clarendon Press, 1968), 320.

[3] Willi-Plein, <u>Prophetie am Ende</u>, 22. It is improbable that אוצר was changed to יוצר because a scribe felt the sum was too paltry to be placed in the treasury (contra. McNeile, <u>Matthew</u>, 408; Micklem, <u>Matthew</u>, 265).

[4] Cf., <u>supra</u>, 48-50.

[5] Stendahl, <u>School</u>, 124-5; Lindars, <u>Apologetic</u>, 118 (who does not dismiss the possibility that Matthew knew of a variant reading); Senior, <u>Passion Narrative</u>, 357-8.

minor temple official connected with the treasury.¹ The latter possibility is not, however, likely,² so the brunt of the argument must rest on the presumption that Matthew was aware of, and utilized the word play יֹצֵר -- אוֹצָר in the writing of Mt. 27:3-10. Several indications speak against this. To begin with, there is some doubt that κορβανᾶς in v. 6 actually means "treasury." This meaning for the word is very poorly attested, a single passage in Josephus (Bell. II, 175) being the only alleged example besides Mt. 27:6.³ Moreover, Gärtner has argued that the meaning of the word in Josephus is "sacred gifts," a definition more in accord with the meaning of the root קרבן

---

¹Stendahl, School. 125. This understanding of יֹצֵר in Zech. 11:13 is based on Torrey's thesis, according to which the "potter" was identified as an official, whose job it was to melt down and mold (hence יֹצֵר, in the sense of "moulder") the large amounts of metal that poured into the temple coffers. The readings of LXX (χωνευτήριον-- "foundry;" cf. also O' and ƛ'), A' (πλάστην -- "moulder") and Targum (אמרכלא -- a minor temple official) are adduced as support for this understanding of יֹצֵר. Torrey regards the Pesh. reading as an interpretative conjecture and denies any double understanding of יֹצֵר in Matthew (Torrey, "Foundry").
Torrey's theory has been accepted by Elliger (Kleinen Propheten, II, 154), Lamarche (Zacharie IX-XIV, 65, n. 1), Benoit ("Death," 198), Bruce ("Zechariah," 341) and M. D. Goulder (Midrash and Lection in Matthew, The Speaker's Lectures in Biblical Studies, 1969-71 (London: SPCK, 1974), 127).

²No historical or archaeological evidence supports the thesis. The readings in the versions are not persuasive evidence since θ and A are no doubt dependent on LXX, which in turn seems to offer a conjectural emendation, according to which it was understood that the thirty pieces of silver were tested for their genuineness (cf. δόκιμον) in a furnace. The Targum completely transforms the meaning of the verse, referring to pious Israelites whose deeds are written down and deposited in the temple (Str-B, I, 1030). Linguistic evidence is against Torrey, since יֹצֵר always refers to a worker in clay in the OT and גֹהוֹרָה is used to designate a founder or moulder. Finally, the context seems to demand an ignominous destination for the "Lordly price" with which Zechariah was paid off, while Torrey's hypothesis would obscure this basic concept in the passage. (Cf. Gundry, Old Testament, 123).

³... ἱερὸν θησαυρόν, καλεῖται δὲ κορβανᾶς, εἰς καταγωγὴν ὑδάτων ἐξαναλίσκων. BAG, 445; Karl Heinrich Rengstorf, "κορβᾶν, κορβανᾶς," TDNT, 861. κορβανᾶς is not found in LXX, DSS or the rabbinic literature (Str-B, I, 1028), although it has apparently been discovered in a pre-A.D. 70 Aramaic inscription, but with uncertain meaning (Albright-Mann, Matthew, 341).

elsewhere and appropriate in the context.¹ κορβανᾶν in Mt. 27:6 could, therefore, denote not the treasury, but sacred gifts which were deposited in the temple, to which the silver thrown by Judas could not be added because of the profane purpose for which it had been used.² Even if κορβανᾶς is understood as the treasury, a serious objection can be raised against the supposed double fulfillment of יצר': the priests' decision <u>not</u> to put the money into the treasury contradicts the explicit statement in Zech. 11:13 that the money was to be thrown אל־היוצר.³ This objection cannot be dismissed as demanding "too rigid an application of the quotation to the circumstances of the context" or as failing to reckon with the "more indirect applications of the quotation."⁴ An indirect application is one thing, but the deliberate introduction of an element, based on a variant interpretation, which expressly contradicts the command of the prophecy is quite another. Such a use of the OT passage would defeat the purpose for which Matthew applies it. There are, then, good reasons for questioning the interpretation according to which εἰς τὸν κορβανᾶν is regarded as an OT-based addition to the narrative.

---

¹Gärtner, "Habbakuk Commentary," 18-19. On the meaning of קרבן, see Rengstorf, "κορβάν," 860-66. The context in Josephus is concerned with Pilate's expropriation of the Jewish funds for the purpose of constructing an aqueduct. קרבנא is used meaning "gift" in b.Hul. 8a and perhaps also in b.Zebah 116b and Tg. Hos. 12:2 (Rengstorf, "κορβάν," 861, n. 4).

²This meaning is suggested as possible by M. Kohler in The Jewish Encyclopedia I, 436 (mentioned by Rengstorf, "κορβάν," 861).

³Gundry, Old Testament, 123.

⁴Senior, Passion Narrative, 357-8, n. 34.

⁵The presence of קרבנא in the Aram. inscription mentioned above may be indicative of the fact that the word was current for a short time in the first century before falling into disuse.

Verse 7 introduces an important link between the narrative and the mixed quotation of vv. 9-10 -- ἀγρὸς τοῦ κεραμέως. The fact that a field was in some manner involved in the tradition associated with Judas' death is generally accepted in view of the prominence of a field in the seemingly independent, Semitic-colored account in Acts 1:16ff. and the unexpected addition of "field" to the quotation in Matthew. However, it is generally believed that the "Field of Blood" mentioned in v. 8 is the historic kernel of the legend, while the connection with "potter" and the change of name has been invented in order to bring the money into contact with a "potter," as Zech. 11:13 indicates.[1] There is some basis, however, for thinking that a potter's field was a part of the original tradition. Benoit, alluding to Jeremiah 19, points out that the traditional site for "Hakeldama" was an area which was a source of clay for the potters of Jerusalem and which, in view of its evil reputation, was a natural location for the burial of strangers.[2] The priests' purchase of the field for this purpose is in accord with rabbinic custom.[3]

Several striking parallels between Jeremiah 19 and the narrative in Mt. 27:3-10 have been pointed out in connection with the mention of a field in the quotation of vv. 9-10, which were

---

[1] Strecker (Weg, 80) speaks of Mt. 27:3-10 as an aetiological legend on the name "field of blood." While this is an extreme view (cf. criticisms by Senior, Passion Narrative, 395-6), the belief that the "Field of Blood" lies at the heart of the tradition is held by Lindars, Apologetic, 122; Schweizer, Matthew, 504; Klostermann, Matthäusevangelium, 217; Senior, Passion Narrative, 387-8. It is often thought that the area was a cemetery, known as the "Field of Blood" before the events of Judas' death were associated with it (McNeile, Matthew, 408; Stendahl, School, 196; Lindars, Apologetic, 122; Klostermann, Matthäusevangelium, 127), but Benoit ("Death," 205-6) characterizes this as a "gratuitous assumption" in view of the lack of mention of the name outside the NT.

[2] Benoit, "Death," 200-202.

[3] Jeremias, Jerusalem, 140. Allen (Matthew, 289) feels the name change was due to influence from Jer. 19:11.

felt to be sufficient to demonstrate that Jeremiah 19 was in mind when the quotation was formulated. While it could be argued that the association of "field" and "potter" was derived from that, it is difficult on that basis to understand why Matthew would have employed Jeremiah 19 in the first place. The priests' purchase of an area, formerly associated with potters, is, as Benoit and Jeremias have shown, historically unobjectionable and provides the significant parallel to both Zech. 11:13 and the tradition which must have existed to direct Matthew's attention to Jeremiah 19.[1]

As a result of an examination of the specific points of contact between the formula quotation and the tradition of Judas' death, it can justifiably be claimed that the influence of the OT on the narrative has been slight.[2] Several general considerations

---

[1] The "potter's field" is regarded as a traditional element by Stendahl, School, 197; Montefiore, Synoptic Gospels, II, 343; Allen, Matthew, 288; Lagrange, Matthieu, 517.

[2] The preceding analysis has dealt with the narrative on the assumption that the OT background and the tradition were first brought together by Matthew himself in a single literary stage. It is felt, however, that the arguments presented are equally applicable to any hypothetical pre-literary stage of interaction between OT and tradition. Kilpatrick (Origins, 81), Strecker (Weg, 82) and Lindars (Apologetic, 118-22) believe that Zech. 11:13 (and possibly Jer. 32 as well) has influenced the tradition of Judas' death before the present narrative and quotation were brought together in Mt. 27. Lindars' is an especially detailed reconstruction, in which four stages are motivated by different hermeneutical principles. An adequate treatment of the theory would require an extensive excursus, but a few specific criticisms of this approach must suffice, in lieu of a more extensive investigation. Lindars suggests that the first stage of the pesher (based on an abbreviated Heb. version of Zech. 11:13 and directed toward the necessity to explain why Jesus was sold for money) and the second (using a Greek translation independent of the LXX and concerned with linking details in Judas' fate with the OT) were developed independently of the "field of blood" tradition, which was only introduced at the third stage (employing the Heb., conflating Jer. 32 with Zechariah and adding a comment on the text (καὶ δίδωμι...) which Matthew has incorporated into the citation, while the phrase replaced (καὶ ἔρριψα αὐτὰ εἰς τὸν ναὸν εἰς τὸν κορβανᾶν) has found its way into the narrative). However, it is almost certain that "field of blood" lies at the bottom of the tradition (cf. Acts 1) and it is difficult to understand how two stages of the narrative could have developed without reference to it. The evidence adduced for

serve to confirm this conclusion. The fact that Acts 1 presents an account of Judas' end that is, on the surface, at variance with Matthew 27, is evidence for the antiquity of and early belief in the reliability of the latter narrative.[1] Several points in the pericope are not in complete harmony with the OT prophecies cited, which suggests a restraint on the part of the transmitter of the tradition. Furthermore, the unique nature of the mixed quotation in vv. 9-10 constitutes a persuasive argument for the belief that, in this case, the tradition has had a creative effect on the OT text quotation, rather than vice versa:

> . . . the tradition recorded by Matthew in his gospel cannot be explained by reference to the biblical texts alone, since on the contrary, it governs the disconcerting use made of them . . . .[2]

In view of these considerations, therefore, the most reasonable explanation of the composition of Mt. 27:3-10 is that Matthew was dealing with a tradition that came to him substantially in the form in which we now have it in 27:3-8 and that he has been the first to connect the tradition with the OT passages.[3] It is probable that

---

the different versions and languages used is insufficient. $\acute{\rho}\iota\pi\tau\omega$ and $\acute{\epsilon}\nu\acute{\epsilon}\beta\alpha\lambda o\nu$ are too common to be the basis for positing the use of a Palestinian Greek version and the LXX, respectively. In fact, as we have noted above, the citation and the narrative give no indication that the exegete was aware of the LXX version of Zech. 11:13. The development Lindars proposes reduces Matthew to the level of an incompetent editor who leaves the attribution of the quotation to Jeremiah untouched, even though he is not interested in the element introduced from Jeremiah. In the last analysis, the major criticism of the reconstruction is that it is unnecessary: simpler and more satisfactory reconstructions of the exegetical background to Mt. 27: 3-10 are available.

[1]For the difficulties these narratives were felt to be in the early church, see, Lake, "The Death of Judas," Beginnings, Vol. V.

[2]Benoit, "Death," 206; cf. also Bruce, "Zechariah," 324; Lagrange, Matthieu, 517.

[3]It is not impossible that Matthew has written the tradition himself from facts available to him through association with former priests who had joined the church. (Senior (Passion Narrative, 395-6)

Jesus' betrayal for a sum of money first led Matthew to Zech. 11:13, where the singular mention of a "potter" reminded him that the site of the "Field of Blood," purchased with Judas' ill-gotten wages, was traditionally associated with the activity of potters. This, in turn, leads Matthew to the passage of Scripture which is concerned with this very area, Jeremiah 19. Finding several verbal and conceptual affinities to the Judas tradition, Matthew collates Jeremiah 19 and Zechariah 11:13, thereby indicating, at the same time, the fulfillment of the prophecy regarding the wages of the rejected shepherd and that concerned with the destiny of the Valley of Topheth.[1]

Presupposing this exegetical work is the identification of Jesus as the rejected shepherd of Zech. 11:4-14. Indeed, the correlation of the destiny of Jesus, the God-appointed leader of Israel, with the similar fate of Zechariah seems to be the primary motivation for the narrative and quotation.[2] Thus, stress is placed on the fact that the money was the price at which the "precious one" was valued by the Jewish leaders. This purpose is evident in Matthew's modifications of the quotation, which, as we have seen, serve to involve Judas and the priests in the action narrated in the text without destroying the identification of Jesus with the Shepherd.

---

concludes by ascribing the tradition and the quotation to Matthew.) If such information were unavailable to the compiler of the tradition in Acts 1, many of the discrepancies would be accounted for.

[1] Gundry, Old Testament, 125.

[2] Lohmeyer-Schmauch (Matthäus, 380), Lagrange (Matthieu, 517) and Bruce ("Zechariah," 346) stress the fundamental importance of the Shepherd motif in Mt. 27:3-10. Other motives are undoubtedly present, but are subordinate to this concept: Apologetic (Lindars, Apologetic, 116-17); desire to indicate fulfillment of prophecy (Senior, Passion Narrative, 316-7 (he lists this as the most important motive)); an indication of the guilt of the Jewish leaders (Strecker, Weg, 81-2; McConnell, Law and Prophecy, 133); moral (the futility of ill-gotten gains -- Descamps, "Rédaction et Christologie," 389).

Thus, the wages given to the prophet in Zech. 11:12 are given
to Judas in Matthew, the actions performed by the prophet in Zech.
11:13 are transferred to the priests, and the money goes not to a
potter directly but for the purchase of a "potter's field." While
these changes are major enough, it is important to note that there
is no departure from the basic thrust of Zechariah's prophecy. While
Judas is the direct recipient of the "wages" in Matthew, Jesus is
the one being evaluated at this level -- just as the prophet's
worth is evaluated in Zechariah 11. The verb changes serve to
describe the actions from the recipients' point of view, and the
addition of "the field" extends the idea of the money being given to
the potter. Nevertheless, it is obvious that the Mt. 27:9-10
quotation evidences a modification of text as an appropriation
technique. Another important technique, for which we have seen
ample precedent in Jewish literature, is the combination of passages,
based on the use of the same words or phrases.

In light of this, Matthew's procedure in this pericope can be
termed midrash, if this term is confined to the level of appropriation
technique. It is our contention, however, that this characterization
is too narrow and that midrash must be understood in terms of the
hermeneutical axioms which direct the method.[1] If this be accepted,
the situation is more problematic. On the one hand, a characteristic
of midrash is that it generally occurs within a "closed system," and
the interaction between text and tradition in Mt. 27:3-10 may
represent a similar situation. On the other hand, the element of
direct "fulfillment" in Matthew is in contrast to the lack of direct
historical correspondences in the midrashic approach. Therefore, it
is legitimate to speak of a midrashic _method_ here, but not of a

---

[1]Cf., _supra_, 62-66.

midrashic <u>perspective</u>. Furthermore, it is generally true of midrash that the OT text acts as the point of departure, while it is our contention that the circumstances have clearly guided the process in Mt. 27:3-10.[1]

Affinities with the pesher approach certainly exist as well: the attempt to utilize every element in the text; the identification of historical individuals and situations with individuals and situations described in the prophecy; the change in text form to accommodate the application of the prophecy. Again, as far as technique is concerned, the appropriation of Zech. 11:12-13 and Jeremiah 19 by Matthew is quite similar to pesher techniques. Nevertheless, the concept of fulfillment, unknown at Qumran, may suggest that, as in the case with midrash, the underlying perspective is fundamentally distinct.

John 19:37 (Zechariah 12:10)

This is the second of the explicit quotations introduced by John at the conclusion of his crucifixion narrative. The textual history of this verse is very complex, but it is certain that John is independent of the LXX, which apparently read רקדו "they danced (in triumph)," i.e., "they insulted" for דקרו "they pierced" (perhaps to avoid the anthropomorphism).[2] It is probable that John

---

[1] The same point is made by R. E. Brown in his discussion of midrash in the Infancy Narratives: "The birth stories were composed, not to make the OT Scriptures more intelligible but to make Jesus more intelligible." Consequently, he concludes that the Infancy Narratives are <u>not</u> midrashim, although midrashic <u>techniques</u> are employed. (<u>The Birth of the Messiah: A Commentary on the Infancy Narratives in Matthew and Luke</u> (Garden City, N.Y.: Doubleday, 1977), 560-61. Cf. also Davies, <u>Sermon on the Mount</u>, 208-209).

[2] Deissmann thinks that an original Heb. דקרו was changed to דקרו under the influence of Jewish Messianic theory. (<u>Die Septuaginta-Papyri und andere altchristliche Texte der Heidelberger Papyrus-Sammlung</u> (Heidelberg: Carl Winter, 1905), 66-68). However, it is to be doubted that Jewish Messianic theories of a suffering Messiah were influential enough to bring about such a change.

employs a tradition shared with Θ in ἐξεκέντησαν,¹ which is not improbable if an Ephesian origin for both John and "Ur-Theodotion" is granted.² The agreement of the Peshitta with John is probably due to assimilation to the NT.³ John diverges from the LXX, MT and Θ in reading εἰς ὅν rather than the first singular,⁴ a modification made necessary because of the divine revelatory "I" in the prophecy. (Note also, significantly, the change to the third person in Zech. 12:10 MT.) The use of Zech. 12:10 in Rev. 1:7 and Mt. 24:30 is reason to believe that the verse was a recognized <u>testimonium</u> in the early church.⁵ This testimony almost certainly circulated in a fixed textual form, for all three quotations agree in reading ὄψονται (-εται) against LXX ἐπιβλέψονται,⁶ while ἐξεκέντησαν and the

---

¹Swete, <u>Old Testament in Greek</u>, 398; Jellicoe, <u>Septuagint and Modern Study</u>, 87; Kahle, <u>Cairo Geniza</u>, 258; Stendahl, <u>School</u>, 179. Rahlfs has contested the alleged relationship between John and Theodotion, claiming that ἐξεκεντοῦν is a natural rendering of דקרו, on which both John and Theodotion depend. ("Über Theodotion-Lesarten im Neuen Testament und Aquila-Lesarten bei Justin," <u>ZNW</u>, XX (1921), 182-199. C. F. Burney (<u>The Aramaic Origin of the Fourth Gospel</u> (Oxford: Clarendon Press, 1922), 123) and Schlier ("ἐκκεντέω" <u>TDNT</u>, II, 447) agree with Rahlfs).

²Swete, <u>Old Testament in Greek</u>, 398.

³Roberts, <u>Old Testament Text</u>, 222. He conjectures that the Peshitta has undergone a Christian editing.

⁴The theological difficulty brought up by אל־ in Zech. 12:10 has given rise to a number of conjectural emendations, among which is one that is close to John's text, אל־אשר "upon whom" (GKC, 44b, n. 1). However, the MT reading should probably be retained as <u>lectio difficilior</u> (Otzen, <u>Studien über Deuterosacharja</u>, 264; Chary, <u>Zacharie</u>, 201-202; Baldwin, <u>Zechariah</u>, 191; Willi-Plein, <u>Prophetie am Ende</u>, 25; Lamarche, <u>Zacharie IX-XIV</u>, 82). For a summary of conjectures, see Magne Saebø, <u>Sacharja 9-14</u>, WMANT, XXXIV (Amsterdam: Neukirchener Verlag, 1969), 97-100.

⁵Lindars, <u>Apologetic</u>, 123-124; Norman Perrin, "Mark xiv. 62: The End Product of a Christian Pesher Tradition?" <u>NTS</u>, XII (1965-66), 153.

⁶Perrin ("Mark xiv. 62," 153) believes that the choice of ὄψονται in the testimony is partly motivated by the resultant word-play with κόψονται (cf. Rev. 1:7 and Mt. 24:30), a procedure similar to that employed by the Qumran sect in their <u>pesharim</u>.

third person object are found in both Jn. 19:37 and Rev. 1:7. John, therefore, utilizes a Christian exegetical tradition in which Zech. 12:10, in the Hebrew, was applied to Christ's death.

The immediate context of Zech. 12:10 refers to a "spirit of compassion and supplication" which God will pour out upon the house of David and Jerusalem "so that, when they look on me whom they have pierced, they shall mourn for him, as one mourns for an only child [LXX ἀγαπητόν] and weep bitterly over him, as one weeps for a first-born [LXX πρωτοτόκῳ]." Piercing is often used as a figure of speech for death in the OT and the mourning following the piercing in this passage confirms the fact that a death is represented.[1] The one pierced has been identified with an historical individual;[2] an unknown martyr;[3] God ("pierce" interpreted psychologically = mock);[4] or the king (in the humiliation rites).[5] However, piercing is never used in the sense of mock in the OT and the other hypotheses fail to do complete justice to אלי, "to me." The pierced one must be identified as a representative of God, whose sufferings and death can be spoken of as God's.[6] That this representative is the Messiah (described here with a possible allusion to Is. 53[7]) is probable.[8]

---

[1] Mitchell, Zechariah, 330; Lindars, Apologetic, 125.

[2] Onias III: Marti, Dodekapropheten, 447.

[3] Mitchell, Zechariah, 331.

[4] Eduard König, Die messianischen Weissagungen des alten Testaments (Stuttgart: Chr. Belsen A. G., 1925), 228-229.

[5] Otzen, Studien, 174.

[6] Lamarche, Zacharie IX-XIV, 83.

[7] Bruce (Old Testament Themes, 112) favorably mentions P. Lamarche's suggestion that the two figures are related. See also F.-M. Braun, Jean le Théologien (3 vols.; Paris: Gabalda, 1959-1972), II, 455-456.

[8] Cf., supra, 175-77.

The reference to the "beloved" (ἀγαπητός) and "first-born" (πρωτότοκος) would further identify the passage as Messianic to the early church.

In the context of Jn. 19:31-7, the quotation of Zech. 12:10 must be intimately linked with the piercing of Jesus' side in Jn. 19:34 (the quotation in v. 36 is introduced with a reference back to that (ταῦτα), and the citation in v. 37 is closely connected to this (καὶ πάλιν ἑτέρα ἡ γραφή)). However, the metaphorical meaning of "pierce" as equivalent to death was surely known to John, and the use of the <u>testimonium</u> elsewhere in the NT clearly applies "piercing" to Jesus' death, so it is not unwarranted to suppose that John uses Zech. 12:10 with a <u>double entendre</u>: immediately and literally of the piercing of Jesus' side and indirectly and metaphorically of Jesus' death.

Who are those who will "see" Jesus pierced and when will it take place? The third person plural is without immediate antecedent, and it seems most probable that the subjects are to be understood as people in general.[1] While the vision of the crucified Christ has been associated with the Resurrection,[2] it is more likely that the reference is to either the <u>Parousia</u>[3] or the spiritual vision of Christ by which men are saved and judged.[4] For the former is the use of Zech. 12:10 in <u>Parousia</u> contexts elsewhere (Mt. 24:30; Rev. 1:7), and the element of triumph implied by the placement of the text here: "'seeing' must

---

[1] Lindars, <u>John</u>, 591.

[2] E. Flessermann von-Leer, "Die Interpretation der Passionsgeschichte vom AT aus," <u>Zur Bedeutung des Todes Jesu</u>, ed. by Fritz Viering (Gütersloh: Mohn, 1967), 94.

[3] C. F. D. Moule, "The Influence of Circumstances on the Use of Christological Terms," <u>JTS</u>, n.s., X (1959), 258, n. 3.

[4] Brown, <u>John</u>, II, 955; Schnackenburg, <u>Johannes</u>, III, 344. Reference is made to Jn. 3:14-15 -- "And just as Moses lifted up the serpent in the desert, so must the Son of Man be lifted up, that everyone who believes may have eternal life in him."

mean seeing him vindicated and seeing themselves consequently in the wrong."[1] On the other hand, Jn. 19:37 could be regarded as the culmination of the Johannine theme of the centrality of the uplifted Christ for the world's judgment (cf. esp. 3:14, 8:28). Perhaps the latter interpretation, expressed in Dauer's words, has most to commend it:

> . . . der am Kreuz Erhöhte und Durchbohrte wird von Gott zum Zeichen gesetzt, zu dem alle von nun an aufschauen werden und müssen; zum rettenden Zeichen, das Heil und Leben bringt, für alle Glaubenden -- zum Zeichen des Gerichtes und des ewigen Todes für alle, die ihm den Glauben verweigern.[2]

It is unlikely that John has created the narrative of the piercing of Jesus' side in order to picture a fulfillment of Zech. 12:10:[3] the flow of blood and water, described in v. 34, is the real highlight of the passage, and is probably regarded as historical by John in view of the solemn witness statement in v. 35.[4] Furthermore, the word used to describe the puncture of Jesus' side in v. 34 is distinct from the word found in the quotation. If, then, there is little evidence for a modification in the point of application, there is little for a re-orientation of the text either. Granted the identification of Jesus with the figure of Zech. 12:10 (which seems legitimate, granted the probable Messianic meaning of the verse), the meaning of the text is quite naturally utilized. The use of a text from an eschatological passage is in keeping with John's emphasis on "realized eschatology."

---

[1] Moule, "Influence," 258, n. 3.

[2] Passionsgeschichte, 277.

[3] Pace Haim Cohn, The Trial and Death of Jesus (London: Weidenfeld and Nicolson, 1967), 234; Feigel, Einfluss, 39; Alfred Loisy, Le Quatrième Évangile (2nd ed.; Paris: Émile Nourry, 1921), 495.

[4] Barrett, John, 462; Dodd, Interpretation, 429; Brown, John, II, 948.

Matthew 26:32 / Mark 14:28 (Zechariah 13:8-9)

In Mk. 14:27 (= Mt. 26:31), Jesus quotes Zech. 13:7 as a substantiation of his prediction that all the disciples would fall away and it has been suggested that the context of the Zechariah prophecy has exerted further influence on this passage. The reference to the Mount of Olives in 14:26 is compared with Zech. 14:4 ("And in that day His feet will stand on the Mount of Olives . . . ")[1] and Jesus' reassuring announcement that after the Resurrection "I will go before you into Galilee" in v. 28 is said to carry on the Shepherd imagery ($\pi\rho o \acute{a} \gamma \omega$)[2] and to correspond to the deliverance promised in Zech. 13:8-9.[3] Wilcox, in an investigation of this passage as it relates to Peter's Denial, concludes that the quotation from Zech. 13:7, which, he claims does not fit well into the context, is in reality an "aside," serving as a pointer to the OT context which is important in Mk. 14:26-52 (perhaps -72). Jesus' saying in 14:30 is the starting point for the tradition about the time of testing foreshadowed in Zech. 13:7-14:4, which is interpreted generally through the "all" of Zech. 13:7, then particularly with reference to Peter (14:54, 66-72).[4] However, several criticisms may be leveled

---

[1] Albright-Mann, Matthew, 326; Max Wilcox, "The Denial-Sequence in Mark xiv. 26-31, 66-72," NTS, XVII (1970-71), 430; Evans, "'I will go before you into Galilee,'" JTS, n.s., V (1954), 7; Fenton, Matthew, 419; Brown, John, II, 807. Kirsopp Lake ("The Ascension," Beginnings of Christianity, V, 22) notes the importance of the Mount of Olives in Rabbinic Messianic expectation. Wilcox also suggests that Zech. 14:4 (τὸ ὄρος τῶν ἐλαιῶν τὸ κατέναντι Ἰερουσαλήμ) is deliberately employed in Mk. 13:3 (ὄρος τῶν ἐλαιῶν κατέναντι τοῦ ἱεροῦ) (431, n. 1; cf. also Albright-Mann, Matthew, 326).

[2] Gould, Mark, 267; Joachim Jeremias, The Central Message of the New Testament (London: SCM, 1965), 47-8.

[3] Alford, Greek Testament, I, 269; Best, Temptation, 158; Evans, "I will go before you," 9; Jeremias, "ποιμήν," 493.

[4] Wilcox, "Denial Sequence," 431-436.

at this reconstruction. Insufficient basis exists for separating 14:27b from its context;[1] the appeal to Scripture as a foundation for the prediction in v. 27a is perfectly understandable and accords with Jesus' habitual use of the Shepherd imagery.[2] The context of Zech. 13:7-14:4 is not entirely appropriate for the way in which Wilcox claims it is used; 14:4 can not easily be construed with 13:7-9 in view of the clear shift in subject matter at 14:1 and the emphatic distinction in vv. 7-9 between a third of the flock who are refined and come to call on God's name and the remainder who perish does not closely represent the situation in Mk. 14:32ff at all.[3] For these reasons, the utilization of Zech. 13:7-14:4 to the extent which Wilcox envisions cannot be maintained.

The situation with regard to Mk. 14:28 is more problematic. προάγω can mean "lead" in a sense appropriate to the image of a shepherd, but it is probable that the meaning here is "to go before" in a temporal sense, the more common connotation of the word in the gospels and the sense the word must have in Mk. 16:7, clearly related to 14:28.[4] Even so, there is something to be said for the view which relates v. 28 to Zech. 13:8-9. This verse is generally regarded as secondary because it seems to interrupt the flow of the passage,[5] but

---

[1] Against Wilcox (and others): The quote is entirely applicable to Peter (cf. v. 29), who fled at the time of the arrest (14:50) and followed Jesus only "at a distance" (ἀπὸ μακρόθεν -- 14:54); it is eminently suited to Jesus' prediction in v. 27a by giving the reason, along with scriptural support, for the disciples' failure; that Peter bypasses the quotation is not surprising: "it would be natural for him to be too taken up with the implied slur on his loyalty to pay much attention to anything else." (Cranfield, Mark, 429). Linnemann correctly rejects Suhl's objections (Alttestamentlichen Zitate, 62-3) because he assumes that the pericope is concerned mainly with Peter's denial (Passionsgeschichte, 89).

[2] Taylor, Mark, 548; France, Jesus, 107, n. 87.

[3] Lohmeyer-Schmauch (Matthäus, 358) note this difficulty.

[4] Taylor, Mark, 549; Cranfield, Mark, 429; Tooley, "Shepherd and Sheep Image," 18; cf. BAG, 709.

[5] "V. 28 ist also ein versprengtes Herrenwort, von Mk. nicht

it is possible to correlate it closely with v. 27 if the parallel structure of the two verses is recognized. Thus, Jesus' death as the event which leads to the scattering of the disciples is contrasted with his Resurrection as the event which enables the scattered flock to be reconstituted.[1] The latter thought is clearly implied in προάγω, which points to Jesus' restoration as leader (i.e., Shepherd!) and to the fact that the disciples would be reunited with him.[2] If this interpretation is accepted, Jesus may well have had in mind Zech. 13:7-9, which presents a similar movement from the scattering of the flock to its reconstitution.

John 19:34 (Zechariah 12-14)

The context of Zech. 12-14 has been suggested as a background which may contribute toward elucidating the significance accorded by John to the flow of blood and water from Jesus' side following the lance thrust of the Roman soldier (Jn. 19:34). Since Zech. 12:10 is quoted in Jn. 19:37 with reference to the immediately preceding events

---

sehr passend hier eingesetzt, um 16:7 vorzubereiten." (Lohmeyer, Markus, 311). It is omitted in the Fayyum fragment in the Rainer papyri (I, 53ff.).

[1] 14:28, along with 16:7, is often interpreted as a prediction of the παρουσία (cf. especially Ernst Lohmeyer, Galiläa und Jerusalem, FRLANT, XXXIV (Göttingen: Vandenhoeck & Ruprecht, 1936), 11-12; Robert Henry Lightfoot, Locality and Doctrine in the Gospels (London: Hodder and Stoughton, 1938), 52-77; Willi Marxsen, Der Evangelist Markus: Studien zur Redaktionsgeschichte des Evangeliums, FRLANT, XLIX (2nd ed.; Göttingen: Vandenhoeck & Ruprecht, 1959), 59-60), but the arguments of Stein for a Resurrection interpretation seem convincing (Robert H. Stein, "A Short Note on Mark XIV. 8 and XVI. 7," NTS, XX (1974), 445-52; cf. also Taylor, Mark, 549; Cranfield, Mark, 429; Best, Temptation, 174-6). Evans ("'I will go before you,'" 11-15) believes that Galilee represents the promise of the Gentile mission (similarly, though with modifications, T. A. Burkill, Mysterious Revelation: An Examination of the Philosophy of St. Mark's Gospel (Ithaca, N.Y.: Cornell University Press, 1963), 255, n. 5).

[2] Galilee may represent for the disciples that area in which the success of the gospel was most fully demonstrated. Is this the kernel of truth in Marxsen's theory of the theological importance of Galilee (cf. Der Evangelist Markus, 59-60 and the critique of Burkill, Mysterious Revelation, 252-57)?

($ \tau\alpha \hat{v} \tau\alpha $ -- v. 36), $ \alpha \hat{\iota} \mu\alpha $ may signify the death of the "pierced one," while $ \H{v}\delta\omega\rho $, closely related to the Spirit in John's theology, may correspond to the outpouring of the "Spirit of Grace," to be understood in the light of 13:1 ("a fountain will be opened . . . for sin and for impurity") and 14:8 ("living waters shall flow out of Jerusalem").[1] If this is so, John's purpose in so forcefully testifying to the significance of the flow of blood and water (which he undoubtedly regarded as historical[2]) is not sacramental[3] or apologetic[4] but

---

[1] J. Terrence Forestall, The Word of the Cross: Salvation as Revelation in the Fourth Gospel, AnBib, LVII (Rome: Biblical Institute, 1974), 89-90; Brown, John, II, 955; Lindars, John, 591 (Zech. 13:1); Braun, Jean le Théologien, III, 168; Edwyn Clement Hoskyns, The Fourth Gospel, ed. by F. N. Davey (2 vols.; London: Faber and Faber, 1940), II, 635 (Zech. 12:10).

[2] Barrett, John, 462; Brown, John, II, 948; Dodd, Interpretation, 429.

[3] The majority of patristic scholars (cf. Westcott, John, 328-33); Bultmann, John, 678; Macgregor, John, 350; Richardson, Theology, 203. The sacramental reference is seen as secondary by Wilhelm Thüsing, Die Erhöhung und Verherrlichung Jesu im Johannesevangelium, NTAbh, XXI (Münster: Aschendorff, 1960), 173; Brown, John, II, 952 (at most, probable).

[4] To emphasize the reality of Christ's death in opposition to docetic tendencies: Bernard, John, II, 647; R. H. Strachan, The Fourth Gospel: Its Significance and Environment (3rd ed.; London: Student Christian Movement, 1941), 332; Beasley-Murray, Baptism, 224-26. F. C. Burkitt (The Gospel History and Its Transmission (Edinburgh: T & T Clark, 1906), 233-4), noting that I Jn. 5:6-8 represents the three essential parts of man, water, spirit and blood, suggests that John presents Jesus as having given up the spirit in 19:30 and the water and blood in 19:34. Schnackenburg (Johannes, III, 339), while demurring at any anti-Gnostic motives, claims the incident means simply that Jesus' death has come to pass. Another interpretation is to link Jn. 19:34 with the tradition, found in Shemmoth R. 122a and Tg. Yer. Num. 20:11, that when Moses struck the rock in the wilderness, it gushed first blood, then water (Glasson, Moses, 52; M. E. Boismard, review of The Gospel According to St. John, by C. K. Barrett, RB, LXIII (1956), 271). Loisy (Quatrième Évangile, 492) follows an ancient Roman tradition in seeing a reference to the birth of the Church.

J. Massingberd Ford ("'Mingled Blood' from the Side of Christ (Joh. XIX. 34)," NTS, XV (1968-9), 337-8) suggests that John emphasizes the immediate flow of blood and water because this was required of sacrificial victims. In this way, the notice can be linked with the Paschal Lamb (cf. 19:36).

soteriological and Christological: " . . . from the Crucified there proceed those living streams by which men are quickened and the Church lives."[1] The Spirit, with the cleansing of sin that the Spirit brings, is given as the direct consequence of Jesus' atoning death.[2] This interpretation has the advantage of adhering closely to Jesus' teaching elsewhere in John regarding the "living water" that springs up in the believer, yielding eternal life (4:14), and the "rivers of water" which are identified with the Spirit, given only after Jesus' death (7:37-9; cf. 3:5). John may, in fact, regard the incident in 19:34 as a proleptic "fulfillment" of Jesus' words in 7:37-8.[3] These words are, of course, uttered on the last day of the Feast of Tabernacles, a festival at which Zechariah figured

---

[1] Barrett, John, 436. Cf. Morris, John, 820; Thüsing, Erhöhung, 167; Tasker, John, 213-14.

[2] Lindars (John, 587) is probably correct in ascribing to "blood" the concept of atonement (perhaps to be connected with the Paschal Lamb reference (Jn. 19:36, cf. 1:29)). John 6, the only other place in John's Gospel where "blood" is used as a symbol, obviously has this connotation. See also I John 1:7 "the blood of Jesus His Son cleanses us from all sin."
It has been suggested that Ez. 47:1 (water flowing out of the Temple) may provide a further symbolism for John: "When the sacrifice had been accepted by the shedding of blood, water (representing the Spirit) came forth from that New Temple which was the Body of Christ . . . " (Xavier Léon-Dufour, The Gospels and the Jesus of History, trans. and ed. by John McHugh (London: Collins, and New York: Desclee, 1968), 90; cf. Brown, John, II, 955). The interpretation of G. D. Bampfylde ("Old Testament Quotations and Imagery in the Gospel According to St. John" (unpublished M.A. dissertation, University of Hull, 1967), 402), who identifies blood with the atonement and water with cleansing is essentially that advocated above. Note also: Dodd (Interpretation, 428) -- water = spirit, blood = ἀληθὴς πόσις (Jn. 6:55); Sanders-Mastin (John, 411-12) -- blood = eucharist, water = spirit.

[3] Brown, John, II, 949-50. Lindars (John, 587) claims that no connection between 7:37-9 and 19:34 exists, because the rivers of water flow out of the believer's belly (κοιλία) in Jesus' words, and because 20:22 must represent the fulfillment of the giving of this water (-- Spirit). Even if "his belly" does not refer to Jesus (Barrett(John, 271), noting the Rabbinic tradition which characterized Jerusalem as the navel of the earth, suggests that John may have replaced a Person with the location), water-Spirit is obviously regarded by John as proceeding from Jesus into the believer. True, 20:22 is the point at which Jesus' promise of the Spirit became reality, but there can be no objection to viewing 19:34 as a preliminary symbol of that reality.

prominently,[1] lending further support to the connection of Zechariah with the water symbolism in the fourth gospel. This symbolism is, in fact, rooted in Zechariah 12-14 itself, where the "living waters" of 14:8 are probably to be understood in the light of the "fountain . . . for sin and impurity" (13:1) and the "Spirit of grace" (12:10). The interpretation of these elements as diverse symbols of the same concept corresponds to the recapitulative structure of these chapters.

Therefore, when John cites Zech. 12:10 as being fulfilled, he refers not only to the literal piercing of Jesus' side, but also to his death (αἷμα -- v. 34b), the reality conveyed by the metaphor in Zech. 12:10, and, with a view to the context of Zechariah 12-14, to the immediate consequences of that death, symbolically represented, in both Zechariah and in John, by water. This final, climactic σημεῖον represents a theological structure that rests upon a foundation far more extensive than Zech. 12-14 alone, but this OT context must certainly be regarded as one of its building blocks.

As John has repeatedly emphasized, Jesus' "lifting up" is the culmination of his life and work, and it is only as a result of this exaltation that eternal life through Jesus' sacrifice (Jn. 3:16) and the comfort and cleansing power of the Holy Spirit (14-16) are secured.

---

[1] I. Abrahams, Studies in Pharisaism and the Gospels, first series (Cambridge: University Press, 1917), 11-12; H. St. John Thackeray, The Septuagint and Jewish Worship. A Study in Origins, The Schweich Lectures, 1920 (London: Oxford University Press, for the British Academy, 1921), 65-66.

The γραφή to which Jesus refers in 7:38 is difficult to determine, but it is difficult to deny that Zech. 14:8 was not at least one of them (as the two last-named scholars think). Reim (Hintergrund, 56-88), taking the scriptural reference with ὁ πιστεύων εἰς ἐμέ, believes Is. 28:16 is referred to. But Barrett is probably justified in claiming that John represents Jesus here, as elsewhere, as using the OT by "elucidating its sense rather than quoting." ("The Old Testament in the Fourth Gospel," JTS, XLVIII (1947), 156).

It is significant therefore that when this glorification is
accomplished there flows at once from the side of the Crucified
what can be symbolically regarded as redeeming blood and
invigorating water. In the language of theology both justification
and sanctification are direct results of the crucifixion of
Jesus.[1]

Luke 23:27 (Zechariah 12:10-14)

Luke alone records the tradition that "a great multitude of people and of women," weeping and lamenting, followed Jesus on the Via Dolorosa (Lk. 23:27) and it has been supposed that the mention of this incident is intended as a reference to the mourning which follows upon the death of the "one pierced" in Zech. 12:10-14.[2] It is improbable that Luke has simply invented the detail to indicate a fulfillment of Zech. 12:10-14, since one would have expected him, in that case, to have placed the weeping after the crucifixion (= the piercing).[3] While Zech. 12:10 is appropriated as a testimonium to Christ's death in the NT, Luke evinces no knowledge of it, and this renders very unlikely the hypothesis that he has utilized this context in Lk. 23:27.

Conclusions

The results of our investigation of the influence of Zechariah 9-14 on the Passion texts may be summarized as follows.[4]

---

[1] Tasker, John, 213-14.

[2] Weidel ("Studien," 246-247), Loisy (Luc, 554), Montefiore (Synoptic Gospels, I, 1078), S. MacLean Gilmour ("The Gospel According to St. Luke," IB, VIII, 404) and Wolfgang Schenk (Der Passionsbericht nach Markus: Untersuchungen zur Überlieferungsgeschichte der Passionstradition (Gütersloh: Mohn, 1974), 90) suggest that Luke has invented the incident on the basis of Zech. 12. Others think Zech. 12:10-14 is referred to: Holtzmann, Synoptiker, 418; Plummer, Luke, 528; Easton, Luke, 347; Creed, Luke, 285; Lampe, "Luke," 341.

[3] Lagrange, Luc, 585. Leaney (Luke, 287) does, in fact, suggest that the lamenting in Lk. 23:48 has been invented by Luke on the basis of Zech. 12:10-14.

[4] A broader relationship between Zechariah 9-14 and the Passion

TABLE 2

REFERENCES TO ZECHARIAH 9-14 IN THE GOSPEL PASSION TEXTS

Zechariah	Matthew	Mark	Luke	John	Citation Technique
9:9	21:4-5	-	-	12:14-15	EQ
	-	11:7	19:35	-	All
11:12	26:15	-	-	-	All
11:12-13	27:9-10	-	-	-	EQ
12:10	-	-	-	19:37	EQ
13:7	26:31	14:27	-	-	*EQ
	-	-	-	16:32 (?)	*All
13:8-9	26:32	14:28	-	-	*Con
13:1, 14:8	-	-	-	19:34	Con
11:12, 12:10, 13:7	-	-	-	10:11,15,17?[a]	*Con

[a]Cf., supra, 146-47.

The use of these chapters of Zechariah presents a striking contrast to the situation with respect to the Suffering Servant. Whereas the Servant Songs are referred to mainly through allusions, each of the major verses in Zechariah 9-14 is explicitly quoted. And whereas the use of the Servant conception is confined mainly to sayings of Jesus, the evangelists seem to be more enamored of the Zechariah texts than does Jesus. Luke betrays no interest in the passage, retaining a single allusion found in his tradition; Mark preserves Jesus' quotation of 13:7, and two allusions; but Matthew and John, in distinctive ways, contribute to the tradition. Matthew, the only evangelist to make use of Zech. 11:12-13, finds the prophecy particularly useful for its applicability to the history of Judas, the betrayer. It is likely that he was drawn to this text by the recognition of the source of Jesus' quotation in 26:31 and by the similarities between the fate of Judas (and his "blood-money") and the prophecy. John emphasizes the royal theme in his quotation of Zech. 9:9 and introduces the theme of Jesus as the giver of life and the focus for the "$\kappa\rho\iota\sigma\iota s$" in 19:34 and 37.

The fact that a preponderance of explicit quotations occurs with Zechariah 9-14 suggests that this passage was not widely recognized

---

events is seen by some. Evans ("'I will go before you,'" 8), after noting these parallels and others, concludes: "If this is so, Mark will have intended the events in this week in Jerusalem to be understood as the judgment and redemption of the last days, the punishment of Israel, the purification of Jerusalem, and the establishment of a true temple not made with hands, by attachment to which the Gentiles will be brought to worship the one God, and his dominion will be extended to the ends of the earth . . . . ." This, however, is an extreme view, and while Jesus' death no doubt constitutes the decisive event of the eschatological day of salvation and judgment which Zechariah visualizes, the ramifications and culmination of that event await a final inbreaking of God.

Note Aune's interesting attempt to relate significant aspects of Jesus' ministry to the eschatological program outlined in Zech. 13. He specifically mentions: cleansing for sin (Jesus' forgiving sin); removal of idols; unclean spirits taken away (Jesus' exorcisms); shepherd struck and sheep scattered; judgment following the shepherd's death. ("Messianic Secret," 24).

as a background for the Passion and therefore required specific citation. C. F. D. Moule, in a perceptive article, has argued that the "Shepherd" Christological concept fell into disuse in the early church because the title was appropriate as a description of past (the death) and future (judgment) events, but not as a means of bringing out Christ's present relationship to the church.[1]

In discussing the techniques used to appropriate the descriptions of the figure(s) in Zechariah 9-14, it was noted that these are basically of the direct type, the notable exception being Mt. 27:9-10, in which case the history has fairly clearly effected a shift of meaning in the text, as well as a combination with another. By and large, however, the use of Zechariah 9-14 in the gospel passion texts demonstrates a high degree of respect for the OT context:

> If Jesus was the first to speak of His passion in terms of Zechariah ix-xiv, the Evangelists follow His example not only in finding other foreshadowings of His passion there, but in finding them in a manner that does not do violence to the original sense and context. These chapters provide a pattern of revelation and response which the Evangelists recognize as recurring in the story of Jesus.[2]

It can be assumed that Jesus and the evangelists, like their contemporaries,[3] understood these texts to be prophetic of the eschatological time. In quoting Zech. 13:7, Jesus clearly implies that the situation described by the prophet is about to become reality in his life and the life of the disciples, and the evangelists make clear their rectilinear understanding of these texts by introducing their quotations with $\pi\lambda\eta\rho\acute{o}\omega$ (Mt. 21:5; Mt. 27:9-10; (probably) Jn. 19:37).

---

[1] "Christological Terms," 258.

[2] Bruce, "Zechariah and the Passion Narrative," 352.

[3] Cf. the excellent survey in France, Jesus, 175-79, 183-84, 188-200.

CHAPTER IV

THE USE OF THE LAMENT PSALMS
IN THE GOSPEL PASSION TEXTS

The Old Testament Background

The psalms of the Righteous Sufferer correspond to the genre "lament of the individual" in Gunkel's form-critical classification, a category which has been retained by most scholars.[1] This genre, characterized by Gunkel as "der eigentliche Grundstock des Psalters,"[2] depicts the response of pious Israelites to adversity and persecution. The determination of the identity of the respective psalmists or of the Sitz im Leben which gave rise to these laments is unnecessary for the purposes of this study; it is sufficient to note that in Jesus' day, these psalms were regarded as having been composed by specific individuals (usually David) and, often, in particular situations.[3]

---

[1]Hermann Gunkel, Die Psalmen, Gottinger Handkommentar zum Alten Testament, II, 2 (Göttingen: Vandenhoeck & Ruprecht, 1926), ix. D. J. A. Clines ("Psalms Research Since 1955: II. The Literary Genres," TB, XX (1969), 105-25) provides a useful survey of the general subject and indicates the consensus of opinion regarding the validity of Gunkel's categories, although a shift of emphasis away from "Gattungsforschung" has occurred.

[2]Einleitung in die Psalmen, ed. and comp. by Joachim Begrich (2nd ed.; Göttingen: Vandenhoeck & Ruprecht, 1966), 173.

[3]Gunkel suggested that the cult was the focus for much of Hebrew psalmody, a suggestion that Mowinckel took up and extended to include virtually all the Psalms. The "I" in the psalms was simply the type of the "Pious One." (Signumd Mowinckel, Psalmenstudien (2 vols.; Amsterdam: P. Schippers, 1966), I, 137). The utilization by Mowinckel of Babylonian cultic ceremonies (such as the divine enthronement festival) to provide parallels for what was assumed to have been the Sitz im Leben for many of the psalms served as the impetus for the British "myth-and-ritual" school, which fit Israel's cult into a Near-Eastern worship pattern. (Cf. Myth and Ritual: Essays on the Myth and

What is of more significance for the study of the passion texts is the theme which these psalms have in common. The psalmist movingly depicts

---

Ritual of the Hebrews in Relation to the Culture Pattern of the Ancient East, ed. by S. H. Hooke (Oxford and London: Oxford University Press, 1933) and Myth, Ritual and Kingship: Essays on the Theory and Practice of Kingship in the Ancient Near East and Israel, ed. by S. H. Hooke (Oxford: Clarendon Press, 1958)). The symbolic annual "dying and rising" of the deified king provides the worship situation for the psalms of lament. (J. H. Eaton, Psalms, TB (London: SCM, 1967), 20). However, this general method of interpretation has come in for serious criticism. It is difficult, if not impossible, to force the diversity of Near-Eastern religions into a common Near-Eastern worship pattern. (Martin Noth, "God, Man and Nation," The Laws of the Pentateuch and Other Essays, trans. by D. R. Ap-Thomas (Edinburgh and London: Oliver Boyd, 1966), 149; Claus Westermann, The Praise of God in the Psalms, trans. by Keith R. Crim (London: Epworth Press, 1965), 21). That Israel's king was ever recognized as divine is highly doubtful and there is no explicit Biblical evidence for the existence of the divine enthronement festival in Israel (Noth, "God, Man and Nation," 165ff; Roland de Vaux, Ancient Israel: Its Life and Institutions, trans. by John McHugh (London: Darton, Longman & Todd, 1961), 111-112; E. J. Kissane, The Book of Psalms (Dublin: Browne and Nolan, Limited, 1964), xxii). Finally, this approach to the Psalms may be subjected to a fundamental criticism regarding methodology, as C. R. North implies when he upbraids Mowinckel for "working inwards from the wide circle of a primitive and general Semitic 'Unwelt," instead of outwards from the centre of the prophetic consciousness." ("The Religious Aspects of Hebrew Kingship," ZAW, L (1932), 35). As Gunkel says, Mowinckel's methodology leads to a situation "in dem alles möglich und nichts mehr wirklich gesichert ist." (Einleitung, 101).

If the extreme form of the cultic interpretation of the Psalms has serious drawbacks, some question must exist as to the general validity of the cultic approach. There can be no doubt that the Psalms were of importance in Israel's worship, but it is not impossible that the general direction may have been more often from the individual to the cult, rather than the reverse. Thus, a renewed emphasis on the role of the individual in the composition of the Psalms has been characteristic of the work of Westermann (Praise of God; cf. also G. Dahl, "The Messianic Expectation in the Psalter," JBL, LXII (1938), 1-12; Kissane, Psalms, xxi; Derek Kidner, Psalms, TOTC (2 vols.; London: Inter-Varsity Press, 1973-5), I, 16-17). The value assigned to the psalm titles is of significance in this respect. While it has become popular to translate the לדוד in 73 of the psalm titles "for David," i.e., "for [the use of] the Davidic King" (A. F. Kirkpatrick, The Book of Psalms (Cambridge University Press, 1902), xxxvii; H. Cazelles, "La question du 'lamed auctoris,'" RB, LVI (1949), 93-101; Hans Joachim Kraus, Psalmen, BKAT, XV (2 vols.; Vluyn: Neukirchener Verlag, 1959-60), LIX; Eaton, Psalms, 15), the earliest traditions (the titles themselves, NT, Qumran, Rabbis) understand it as referring to authorship (W. E. Barnes, The Psalms, WC (London: Methuen & Co., Ltd., 1931), xxiv. For the antiquity of the titles is the fact that the LXX translators did not understand them (Kidner, Psalms, I, 33). B. S. Childs ("Psalm Titles and Midrashic Exegesis," JSS, XVI (1971), 137-50) argues that the titles preserve early Midrashic interpretations). The association of David with the composition of the Psalter is becoming more widely accepted his distress, which often seems to be compounded by mockery and persecution,[1] laments his fate and calls out to God in his need for deliverance and vindication. While the poet sometimes confesses his sin, the stress is definitely on the righteousness of the one oppressed[2] and his consequent incomprehension at God's apparent indifference. A characteristic of some of the psalms is a sudden shift from lamentation to praise, a feature that has suggested to some the intervention at that point in the worshipper's prayer of a Heilsorakel, a gracious response from God, mediated perhaps through the priest. It is questionable, however, whether such a hypothesis is warranted in light of Westermann's observation that petition and praise are the two fundamental ways in which man talks with God.[3] The latter explanation is supported by psalms (e.g., 31) in which lamentation and praise alternate throughout, demonstrating that a psalmist could naturally shift from one to the other without external stimulus. A more adequate understanding of these psalms may be attained through a closer look at one of them. Psalm 22, because of its importance as a quarry for passion references, has been chosen for this purpose.

(Anderson, Psalms, 44; Kissane, Psalms, xxx; Barnes, Psalms, xxiv; Arthur Weiser, The Psalms (London: SCM, 1962), 23-4; Kirkpatrick, Psalms, xli; Kidner, Psalms, I, 33-34).

[1]The "enemies" of the psalmist in the Righteous Sufferer psalms were identified by Mowinckel with sorcerers, whose evil spells caused the poet's distress (Psalmenstudien, I, 77-124). However, most of his evidence is taken from Babylonian sources and the identification is not well-grounded in the Biblical evidence. On the supposition that the King is the sufferer, Birkeland (Die Feinde des Individuums in der Israelitischen Psalmenliteratur: Ein Beitrag zur Kenntnis der semitischen Literatur- und Religionsgeschichte (Oslo: Grøndahl & Sons, 1933)) equates the enemies with foreign nations, at war with Israel. The language of the psalms, however, indicates that the enemies are the psalmist's own countrymen and it seems best to keep the identification general and regard them as the ungodly among the Israelites (Gunkel-Begrich, Einleitung, 209, Kraus, Psalmen, I, 42).

[2]Popkes (Christus Traditus, 75) properly speaks of a "relative righteousness" in this respect.

[3]Praise of God, 64-65. Rudolf Kilian points out that there is no evidence for such a "salvation oracle" outside these psalms ("Ps. 22 und das priesterliche Heilsorakel," BZ, n.s., XII (1968), 172-85).

The psalm divides naturally into two parts: vv. 1-21, in which the psalmist intersperses his lament (1-2, 6-8, 13-18) with avowals of his trust in God and pleas for deliverance (3-5, 9-12, 19-21), and vv. 22-31, which depict the poet's thanksgiving for God's gracious vindication of his cause (22-26) and his conviction that this vindication has universal implications (vv. 27-31). While some scholars view the psalm as two originally separate units on the basis of the abrupt transition from lament to praise in vv. 21-22,[1] most concede that the psalm is a coherent entity. As is the case in many of the individual laments, it is difficult to identify precisely the cause of the psalmist's distress. A serious illness, looked upon by the psalmist's enemies as a mark of God's disfavor (cf. vv. 6-8), is the most popular suggestion.[2] Others think of a psychological disorder,[3] or political persecution.[4] It has been conjectured that the lament was composed for the use of the king at the annual humiliation rites.[5] Most interesting is the hypothesis that a scene of execution is depicted,[6] perhaps even a crucifixion.[7] In despair at attempting to fit the

---

[1] B. Duhm, Die Psalmen, Kurzer Hand-Commentar zum Alten Testament (Freiburg: Mohn, 1899), 66; Hans Schmidt, Die Psalmen, HAT, XV (Tübingen: Mohr, 1934), 36.

[2] Gunkel, Psalmen, 90; Schmidt, Psalmen, 36; Mowinckel, Psalmenstudien, I, 74 (brought about by the "magicians"); Anderson, Psalms, 185; Otto Eissfeldt, "'Mein Gott' im Alten Testament," ZAW, LXI (1945-46), 13.

[3] Weiser, Psalms, 220.

[4] W. O. E. Oesterley, The Psalms (2 vols.; London: Society for Promoting Christian Literature, 1939), I, 176; Duhm, Psalmen, 72.

[5] Eaton, Psalms, 72; Aage Bentzen, King and Messiah, ed. by G. W. Anderson (Oxford: Basil Blackwell, 1970), 29.

[6] Kidner, Psalms, I, 105.

[7] Rudolf Kittel, Die Psalmen, KAT, XIII (5th and 6th eds.; Leipzig: A. Deichertsche, 1929), 87; Goppelt, Typos, 125. This hypothesis seems to demand a Persian date for the psalm, since crucifixion was probably unknown in Israel before then (David Smith, "Crucifixion," A Dictionary of Christ and the Gospels, ed. by James Hastings (2 vols.; Edinburgh: T & T Clark, 1906-08), I, 397; Blinzler, Prozess, 177).

diverse imagery into a single situation, some scholars believe that the psalm is a picture of the ideal righteous sufferer.[1] The stereotyped language used to denote the suffering of the psalmist renders a decision difficult, since it is hard to know how much of the description is directly related to his present adversity. Perhaps the psalm is best understood as the anguished outburst of an individual[2] who is undergoing persecution and adversity for his advocacy of God's cause, the depths of which distress lead him to picture himself as being executed by his enemies. This Sitz im Leben accounts for the fact that the psalmist's humiliation is public (vv. 6-8), that he is mocked for his claim to be one in favor with God (v. 8), and that several elements (dividing of clothes -- v. 18; encircled by his enemies -- v. 16) are best explained as descriptions of an execution. The psalmist's physical and mental sufferings, as well as the sense of God's abandonment, are easily explained as the consequences of his despair and dread in this situation.

How, then, is the thanksgiving of vv. 22-31 to be explained? Either we are to suppose that the psalmist's despair has given way naturally to a renewed trust and confidence in God or a certain amount of time has elapsed in which the poet has experienced a gracious response

---

[1] J. J. Stewart Perowne, The Book of Psalms (2 vols.; London: Bell and Daldy, 1870), I, 227; C. A. Briggs, A Critical and Exegetical Commentary on the Book of Psalms, ICC (2 vols.; Edinburgh: T & T Clark, 1906), I, 190; L. Ruppert, Jesus als der leidende Gerechte? Der Weg Jesu im Lichte eines alt- und zwischentestamentlichen Motivs, SBS, LIX (Stuttgart: Katholisches Bibelwerk, 1972), 31.

[2] The "I" of this psalm cannot be collective (i.e., Israel), as v. 24 demonstrates (Gunkel, Psalmen, 94). As Kittel (Psalmen, 86) says: "Hier redet die Sprache des Herzens zu uns, nicht die Strenge der Logik noch auch ein hergebrachtes Schema." (Contra N. H. Ridderbos ("The Psalms: Style, Figures and Structure (Certain Considerations, with Special Reference to Pss. xxii, xxv and xlv)," Studies in Psalms, OTS, XIII (Leiden: E. J. Brill, 1963), 53-57), who sees a definite forensic structure in Psalm 22).

from God to his need. Whichever is the case, it seems that the author understands his deliverance to have far-reaching significance; apparently as a result of the psalmist's vindication, even the dead praise Yahweh (v. 29). This expression and others similarly universal in scope in vv. 25-31 may be hyperbole, but the possibility that God's vindication of the sufferer has eschatological consequences must be reckoned with.[1] If so, those who ascribe the psalm to the Davidic King may be correct, since only one who had been closely involved in God's promise could attach such a universal significance to his own salvation.[2]

Verses from Psalm 22 are referred to in the Qumran hymns, but, significantly, neither passages reflecting physical suffering nor those used in the NT are employed.[3] Psalm 22 was not interpreted messianically until the tenth century A.D. and was applied variously to David, Esther or Israel.[4]

This brief exposition of Psalm 22 may serve as an illustration of the Gattung under discussion. Other "Righteous Sufferer" psalms, while obviously different in many respects, are very similar in structure

---

[1] Hartmut Gese ("Ps. 22 und das Neue Testament: Der älteste Bericht vom Todes Jesus und die Entstehung des Herrenmahles," ZTK, LXV (1968), 13) believes that the psalmist's deliverance is seen collectively as Yahweh's saving acts for Israel and asserts: "In Ps. 22 kommt also eine bestimmte apokalyptische Theologie zu Worte, die in der an einem Einzelnen sich vollziehenden Errettung aus der Todesnot die Einbruchsstelle der βασιλεία τοῦ θεοῦ sieht . . . ."

[2] Eaton, Psalms, 72; Barnes, Psalms, I, 206. It is not, therefore, impossible that the title preserves authentic tradition in ascribing the psalm to David himself (Delitzsch, Psalms, I, 372; Kidner, Psalms, 105).

[3] Ps. 22:10 -- 1QH 3:9-10; 22:14 -- 1QH 15:10-11; 22:25 -- 1QH 7:4, 2:28; 22:22 -- 1QH 5:10-11; 22:23-4 -- 1QH 12:3; 22:25 -- 1QH 9:10 (Carmignac, "Citations," 357ff; de Waard, Comparative Study, 62). Holm-Nielsen (Hodayot, 308-09) notes the popularity of the "suffering righteous" psalms in 1QH.

[4] Str-B, I, 574; W. G. Braude, ed., The Midrash on Psalms, Yale Judaica Series, XII (2 vols.; New Haven: Yale University Press, 1959), I, xi, 302ff.

and theme to Psalm 22.[1] The "relative righteousness" of the sufferer and his identification with God's purposes, the intermingling of lament and thanksgiving, and the varied nature of the suffering depicted (physical distress, public mockery and humiliation and mental and spiritual anguish) feature in all of them. The over-all impression one receives is that these psalms were composed by pious men whose advocacy of God's cause had led to rejection and suffering; in poetry, they reflect their lack of understanding and continued trust in Yahweh: "Israel's hardest burden was probably that God had hidden himself so completely from the despairing man who had trusted in his mercy."[2] Underlying the Righteous Sufferer concept is the problem of theodicy, a problem treated *in extenso* in Job, but only hinted at and given no final answer in the psalms. While the depths of emotion expressed in these psalms demand that they be related to a specific individual in a specific situation, it does seem that the use of stereotyped figures of speech and the repetition of common themes is leading to the idealization of a "Righteous Sufferer" par excellence.[3]

It is now necessary to ask whether the particular imagery and concepts reflected in the lament psalms are taken up and applied elsewhere. Within the Old Testament, two passages are sometimes

---

[1] Psalm 69, also important in the Passion Narrative, differs from 22 in stressing the sinfulness of the poet (v. 5) and in including a diatribe against the psalmist's enemies (vv. 22-28). As in Psalm 22, the eschatological significance of the psalmist's deliverance is stressed. Eaton (Psalms, 178) says: "The psalm has told of suffering borne for God's sake, and of judgment, and of salvation that goes from Zion to the ends of the world."
The note of thanksgiving dominates that of lament in Psalm 31, and no universal significance is accorded to the psalmist's salvation. This feature is lacking in Psalm 41 as well, which seems to stress physical illness to a greater degree than other laments. However, the emphasis in the psalm is upon suffering which is occasioned by the hatred of enemies and desertion of friends.

[2] Von Rad, Theology, II, 377.

[3] Flesseman-van Leer, "Interpretation der Passionsgeschichte," 94.

associated with the psalms of lamentation: Isaiah 53 and Zechariah 9-14.[1] In Zechariah 9-14, however, the passages concerned (9:9, 12:10-12, 13:7) do not, like the psalms, convey a personal sense of affliction and lamentation, but briefly refer to the humility and death of one closely identified with God. No real linguistic parallels exist and the concentration in Zechariah 9-14 on the death of the individual described is in contrast to the prolonged period of suffering and eventual deliverance of the righteous sufferer in the psalms. The Servant in Isaiah 53 presents a closer parallel and some language from the passage is reminiscent of the psalms of lament,[2] but the description of the Servant, if indebted to the psalms, goes considerably beyond them in its comprehensiveness[3] and in the positive value attributed to suffering.[4]

The righteous-sufferer psalms are referred to more often in the passion texts than any other portion of the OT. The quick succession of allusions, particularly in the crucifixion narratives, is best handled through an approach that is organized according to the general order of the gospels.[5]

---

[1] H. E. W. Turner (Jesus: Master and Lord (London: A. R. Mowbray, 1953), 206) remarks that Pss. 22, 69 and Zech. 9 "might almost be called the 'Fellow Travellers' of the Servant Songs." Borsch (Son of Man, 126-30) links the three passages together through the sufferings of the ideal royal figure. Cf. also Edwyn Hoskyns and Noel Davey, The Riddle of the New Testament (London: Faber & Faber, 1931), 83 (with regard to Ps. 22 and Is. 53).

[2] Westermann, Isaiah 40-66, 262.

[3] Ibid., 261.

[4] Mowinckel, He that Cometh, 235. Borsch (Son of Man, 129) believes, however, that Isaiah has simply made explicit what is already implicit in the psalms.

[5] For convenience, the versification of the English translations of the Psalms has been followed, except where noted.

John 2:17 (Psalm 69:9)

John has transposed the setting of Jesus' Temple-cleansing from the passion (Mk. 11:15ff) to the beginning of the ministry[1] and introduces several motifs not found in the synoptists' portrayal of the incident, including the citation of Ps. 69:9. The first half of this verse, John informs us, was called to the disciples' minds as they witnessed Jesus' expulsion of the merchants.[2] The explicit quotation (ὅτι γεγραμμένον) follows the LXX, the only variation being the shift in tense from aorist to future,[3] a modification dictated by the purpose to which John puts the text: Jesus' death as a consequence of his active expression of zeal for his Father's house is likened to the persecution of David, which is traced to a similar concern for the Temple.[4] For John, therefore, the quotation

---

[1] Although it is not impossible that the Cleansing of the Temple was performed on two occasions (Cf. Morris, John, 189-91), it is more likely that John has transposed it to the beginning of his gospel for theological and structural reasons.

[2] The parallel with other occasions when the disciples "remember" the applicability of an OT passage to an action of Jesus' (2:22; 12:16) may suggest that the disciples' realization of the relationship between the cleansing and Ps. 69:9 dawned on them only after the "glorification" of Jesus (a meaning the present text would bear, if v. 17 were understood as a parenthesis). However, no explicit time indication is given here, and the more natural sense would indicate that the memory was contemporaneous with the event.

[3] A few, mainly "Western" MSS read the aorist in Jn. 2:17, and some LXX MSS have the future in Ps. 69:9 (68:10). But accommodation has taken place in both cases (Barrett, John, 165; Freed, Old Testament, 10).

[4] That καταφάγεταί has reference to Jesus' death rather than to the intensity of his zeal, is shown by the change in tense, the natural meaning of κατεσθίω, the consistent application of Psalm 69 to the passion of Jesus in the NT and the background in the psalm (see below) (Brown, John, I, 124; Lindars, John, 140; Reim, Hintergrund, 10; Sanders-Mastin, John, 117. Pace Westcott, John, 42; Bernard, John, I, 92; Barrett, John, 165; Freed, Old Testament 9; Morris, John, 196).
Concerning Ps. 69:9, Stumpff says: "The zeal here is a passionate, consuming zeal focused on God, or rather on doing His will

functions as a programmatic statement indicating a basic cause of the Jews' rejection of Jesus (hence, perhaps, justifying the displacement of the narrative). It also justifies Jesus' action as one in line with the highest expression of OT godly zeal and attributes to this zeal a measure of responsibility for his death. The phrase is applied with the same basic sense as it had in the context of the psalm.

Matthew 26:3-4a (Psalm 31:13)

The Passion Narrative in Matthew is introduced with the transitional phrase characteristic of the first gospel (καὶ ἐγένετο ὅτε ἐτέλεσεν ὁ 'Ιησοῦς πάντας τοὺς λόγους τούτους (26:1)), and immediately the stage is set by Jesus' prediction of his imminent "paradosis" (v. 2). This prediction is followed by the first step toward the fulfillment of Jesus' prophecy: the decision of the Jewish elders to seize Jesus "by stealth" (δόλῳ) and kill him. The description of the gathering of the Jewish leaders in Mt. 26:3-4a is said to allude to Ps. 31:13.[1] Psalm 31, the lament of a righteous sufferer, is of a genre employed extensively in the Passion Narrative and is the source of Jesus' last words from the Cross as recorded in Lk. 23:46. The use of either συνάγω or βουλεύομαι alone would not

---

and the maintaining of His honor in face of the ungodly acts of men and nations." ("קנאה," TDNT, II, 878). Similarly, most commentators imply that the reference of אכלתני is to the intensity of the zeal (קנאה). But it seems more likely, in view of the parallelism in the verse and the general meaning of אכל that the reference is to a calamity which results from the zeal (cf. Anderson, Psalms, I, 502). אכל and κατεσθίω often mean, in a figurative sense, "devour," i.e., "destroy, slay."

[1]Gundry, Use of the Old Testament, 56; Dibelius, From Tradition to Gospel, 187; Lindars, Apologetic, 94; R. H. Lightfoot, History and Interpretation in the Gospels, The Bampton Lectures, 1934 (London: Hodder and Stoughton, 1935), 162; A. Rose, "L'influence des psaumes sur les annonces et les récits de la Passion et de la Résurrection dans les Évangiles," Le Psautier: Ses Origines, Ses problèmes littéraires, Son influence, ed. by R. de Langhe (Leuven: Publications Universitaires, 1962), 333; Senior, Passion Narrative, 24.

indicate influence from Ps. 31:13, but the combination of the two verbs is sufficiently striking to show that an allusion is probably intended. Matthew may have dropped the prefix ἐπί with συνάγω as extraneous in his context (note the following ἐπί in LXX) and added σύν to βουλεύομαι under parallel influence from συνάγω.[1] Psalm 31:13 speaks of the whispering (דבר) of many who scheme together (LXX ἐπισυναχθῆναι) to take away the life of the righteous sufferer and forms a fitting context for Matthew's application of the verse. It is probable that Matthew has been drawn to this context by the recognition of the source of the cry from the Cross in Luke. Lindars' contention that the employment of this psalm "reflects the growing bitterness of the Church at the persecution which it has received"[2] goes beyond the evidence and is unlikely in view of Lk. 23:46, where no such bitterness is reflected. An allusion to Ps. 2:2 LXX is not likely, since συνάγω is so widespread.[3]

John uses συνάγω in a similar context (11:47), but the word is not unusual and dependence on Psalm 31 or Mt. 26:3-4a is unlikely.

Mark 14:18 / John 13:18
(Mark 14:20 / Matthew 26:23 / Luke 22:21)
(Psalm 41:9)

John has an explicit quotation of Psalm 41:9; Mark 14:18 is generally regarded as an allusion to the same verse; and a few scholars feel that Mk. 14:20 par. contains a reminiscence as well.[4] In Jn. 13:18,

---

[1] Gundry, Old Testament, 56. Senior (Passion Narrative, 24) believes σύν here is a reflection of Matthew's customary συνβουλεύομαι.

[2] Lindars, Apologetic, 94.

[3] Against J. C. Fenton, The Gospel of St. Matthew, PNTC (Harmondsworth: Penquin Books, 1963), 410; H. Benedict Green, The Gospel According to Matthew, The New Clarendon Bible (Oxford: University Press, 1975), 209.

[4] Lindars, John, 454; Weidel, "Studien," 178; McNeile, Matthew, 380.

Ps. 41:9 is cited as explanatory of the fact that Jesus has chosen (ἐξελεξάμην) his betrayer as a disciple. The quotation is introduced with the formula ἵνα ἡ γραφὴ πληρωθῇ, used elsewhere only by John (17:12 and 19:24).[1] While ἵνα has been understood as "imperatival ἵνα,"[2] it is better to translate in the usual way and interpret the construction as elliptical: "on the contrary (ἀλλ᾽) this happened in order that."[3] ἀλλ᾽ does not, therefore, indicate that Judas is an exception to those whom Jesus has chosen, but that the choice has, in fact, been made in order to fulfill the Scriptures (cf. Jn. 6:64, 71).[4]

John's quotation shows divergences from both LXX and MT: τρώγων for LXX ἐσθίων,[5] sing. ἄρτον[6] with MT (לחמי) against LXX ἄρτους; ἐπῆρεν in place of the literalistic rendering of הגדיל in the LXX (ἐμεγάλυνεν);[7] τὴν πτέρναν (πτέρνα in A' and Ϛ) for LXX

---

[1]Freed, Old Testament, 89.

[2]Turner, Syntax, 95; Moule, Idiom Book, 145.

[3]BDF, 223; A. R. George, "The Imperatival Use of ἵνα in the New Testament," JTS, XLV (1944), 58; Bultmann, John, 478; Morris, John, 622; Bernard, John, II, 467.

[4]Barrett, John, 370; Brown, John, II, 553.

[5]τρώγω is typically Johannine. It is found outside of John only in Mt. 24:38 (in the NT). Whether John introduces the word here under influence from the "bread of life" discourse (τρώγω 4t. in 6:54-9 -- Peder Borgen, Bread from Heaven: An Exegetical Study of the Concept of Manna in the Gospel of John and in the Writings of Philo, NovTSup, X (Leiden: Brill, 1965), 93; Max Wilcox, "The Composition of John 13:21-30," Neotestamentica et Semitica, 145) or whether the choice simply reflects the general tendency to replace ἐσθίω with τρώγω is difficult to say.

[6]Symmachus, Tertullian and Psalterium of Hieronymus also read the singular (de Waard, Comparative Study, 66).

[7]ἐπαίρω never translates גדל in LXX (Freed, Old Testament, 91). John's ἐπῆρεν may be an attempt to make the expression more understandable to Greek readers (Schnackenburg, Johannesevangelium, III, 30). Because גדל in the hiphil never means "lift up," Caird conjectures that the LXX translator took עקב as an abstract noun, meaning "going-behind-the-back" ("Towards a Lexicon of the Septuagint, II," JTS, n.s., XX (1969), 32).

πτερνισμόν;[1] αὐτοῦ against both LXX and MT. A further variation from both LXX and MT would be present if μετ' ἐμοῦ were the original reading. This text has strong support (P66, ℵ, A, D) but is suspect because of possible assimilation to Mk. 14:18. However, the other reading, μου, may similarly be suspect as having been conformed to LXX or MT and it is not certain that John is dependent on Mark at this point.[2] The reading of 1QH 5:23-4, which has an allusion to Ps. 41:9, raises an interesting possibility, for the placement of עלי before האכל in that text could lead to the translation "all who eat bread with me."[3] Though hypothetical, it is nevertheless possible that John is dependent on a similar reading and translates the phrase accordingly. At any rate, John's text clearly indicates independence from the LXX, and may be an independent translation of the MT,[4] perhaps in a form akin to that cited in 1QH 5:23-24.[5]

It is more difficult to decide if ὁ ἐσθίων μετ' ἐμοῦ in Mk. 14:18b is an allusion to Ps. 41:9. Mark does not use the participle of ἐσθίω in a substantive sense elsewhere, but its presence here may be due to ἐσθιόντων in the immediate context (14:18 and 22).

---

[1] πτέρνα is the only word used for "heel" in the NT and is more frequent in LXX (11t.) than πτερνισμός (2t.).

[2] Dodd (Historical Tradition, 37), Brown (John, II 571) and de Waard (Comparative Study, 65) argue for Johannine independence. See also Reim, Hintergrund, 48; Wilcox, "Composition," 156.

[3] de Waard, Comparative Study, 67. According to BDB (752), עלי can mean both "against" and "together with." μετ' ἐμοῦ is read by two 4th c. LXX MSS, 2013 and 2050.

[4] Noack (Johanneischen Tradition, 78) says: " . . . wahrscheinlich gehörte das Zitat schon der aramäischen Überlieferung der Urgemeinde an und ist ohne Benutzung irgendeiner Übersetzung des Alten Testaments in die griechische Übersetzung übergegangen." Cf. also Bernard, John, II, 467; Schnackenburg, Johannesevangelium, III, 30; Morris, John, 722; Reim, Hintergrund, 40; M.-J. Lagrange, Evangile selon saint Jean, EBib (6th ed.; Paris: Gabalda, 1936), 357.

[5] The third person plural verbs in 1QH 5:23-24 militate against dependence on that text-type alone.

Direct literary borrowing from John is improbable, but it is possible that both Mark and John are dependent on an early church tradition in which Ps. 41 was applied to Judas. Mk. 14:21 indicates that Mark was aware of an OT background for the betrayal.[1] Matthew's failure to reproduce the phrase is not a decisive objection to the presence of an allusion in Mark;[2] the words in Mk. 14:18 do not correspond to either LXX or MT and Matthew may have failed to notice the allusion.[3] While the evidence is not conclusive, it seems justified to regard Mk. 14:18 as an allusion to Ps. 41:9, in the form of a text similar to that found in Jn. 13:18.[4]

The characterization of the betrayer in Mk. 14:20// reproduces the phrase μετ' ἐμοῦ but a verbal allusion to Ps. 41:9 in this context is unlikely[5] because the key word ἐσθίω is omitted.

Verbal allusions to Ps. 41:9 occur only in Jn. 13:18 and Mk. 14:18 in the NT.[6] Like Psalm 31, Psalm 41 is a lament of the righteous sufferer. Among the sufferings inflicted on the psalmist, the most painful is the treachery of a "bosom friend" (RSV = אִישׁ שְׁלוֹמִי) who has "magnified" his heel against the sufferer. To "lift the heel" may be a gesture of contempt;[7] certainly rejection and betrayal are

---

[1] Brown, John, II, 571. [2] Taylor, Mark, 540.

[3] Lindars, Apologetic, 58-9.

[4] The lack of the allusion in Matthew is no reason to suppose that the phrase is a later addition in Mark (McNeile, Matthew, 380; Cranfield, Mark, 423). If Matthew failed to notice the OT allusion, he has undoubtedly omitted the phrase as superflous (Lindars, Apologetic, 98-9; Suhl, Alttestamentlichen Zitate, 51; Frederick W. Danker, "The Literary Unity of Mark 14:1-25," JBL, LXXXV (1966), 470).

[5] Pace McNeile, Matthew, 380; Leaney, Luke, 269; Lindars, John, 454.

[6] Several general fulfillment texts may include a reference to Ps. 41: Mk. 14:21 par., Jn. 17:12, Acts 1:16.

[7] G. H. C. Macgregor, The Gospel of John, MNTC (London: Hodder and Stoughton, 1928), 278; E. F. F. Bishop, "'He that eateth bread with me hath lifted up his heel against me' -- Jn. xiii. 18 (Ps. xli. 9),"

connoted by the figure of speech. Psalm 41 was applied to Ahithophel's relations with David by the Jews.[1] What makes the psalm so appropriate with respect to Judas' behavior is the emphasis on the breaking of table fellowship, which was regarded as a time of particular trust and intimacy in the ancient world. Thus, Jesus' words during the Last Supper are not intended to identify the betrayer, but to point out the heinous crime about to be committed by a trusted associate.[2]

The text of the quotation does not reproduce any known version, and has almost certainly undergone adaption to suit it to its context. If μετ' ἐμοῦ is read, this would represent the major change, but even this does not significantly alter the meaning of the original. That is, the textual changes made serve to adapt the text to the context without modifying the meaning. While it has been maintained that the narrative of the interaction between Jesus and Judas at the Last Supper was a fabrication, inserted to lessen the offence of the betrayal,[3] it is most unlikely that the betrayal was invented to present the fulfillment of Psalm 41:9. In this case, it is reasonably clear that the psalm has been used to illuminate an established tradition.[4] In light of the appropriateness of the application, then, the appropriation technique here can be seen to be the direct type.

The relationship between Mark and John in their use of Ps. 41:9 is instructive: each (probably) reads μετ' ἐμοῦ, but the contexts

---

ExpTim, LXX (1959), 331-3. Anderson (Psalms, 325) mentions other possible interpretations.

[1] Str-B, II, 558. And cf. especially Gärtner, Iscariot, 9-12.

[2] The τρύβλιον was a common bowl, so all would have been dipping in it. Even Mt. 26:25 was perhaps a whispered conversation (McNeile, Matthew, 380; Lindars, John, 354; Bultmann, John, 478).

[3] Bultmann, Synoptic Tradition, 281; Weidel, "Studien," 178.

[4] For a criticism of Bultmann's interpretation, see Suhl, (Alttestamentlichen Zitate, 51) and Schenke (Studien zur Passionsgeschichte, 211-12).

are quite dissimilar. Both evangelists probably rely on a tradition which employed Psalm 41 in connection with Judas. Matthew's failure to note the allusion in Mk. 14:18 renders Johannine dependence on Mark improbable.[1]

Mark 14:34 / Matthew 26:38; John 12:27
(Psalms 42:5,11; 43:5; 42:6; 6:3; Jonah 4:9)

Jesus' expression of deep sorrow as he prays in the Garden of Gethsemane is couched in language reminiscent of the "refrain" from Psalms 42 and 43 (which are closely related, if not an original unity[2]). περίλυπος, "afflicted beyond measure," "deeply sorrowful," is found only eight times in the LXX, never in Philo, Josephus or the papyri and occurs only twice in the NT,[3] so its presence here, along with ψυχή, confirms the allusion.[4] A reminiscence of Jonah 4:9 is sometimes noted in the expression ἕως θανάτου.[5] Gundry suggests that the point of contact was in the root λυπ-.[6] However, the phrase ἕως θανάτου occurs twelve times in the LXX, several times in a context very similar to that in the gospels.[7] The frequency of the

---

[1] Pace Freed, Old Testament, 92.

[2] Virtually all the commentaries.

[3] Rudolf Bultmann, "περίλυπος," TDNT, IV, 323; Gundry, Old Testament, 59.

[4] Pace Linnemann, Studien, 30.

[5] E.g., by J. Héring ("Zwei exegetische Probleme in der Perikope von Jesu im Gethsemane (Markus XIV 32-42; Matthäus XXVI 36-46: Lukas XXII 40-46)," Neotestamentica et Patristica: Eine Freundesgabe Herrn Professor Dr. Oscar Cullmann zu seinem 60. Geburtstag überreicht NovTSup, VI (Leiden: Brill, 1962), 67); Rawlinson (Mark, 211); Klostermann (Markusevangelium, 150); A. W. F. Blunt (The Gospel According to Saint Mark (Oxford: Clarendon Press, 1929), 253); Cranfield (Mark, 429); Gundry (Old Testament, 59).

[6] Old Testament, 59.

[7] Cf. Sir 37:2 λύπη ἔνι ἕως θανάτου; Sir 51:6 ἤγγισεν ἕως θανάτου ἡ ψυχή μου.

expression gives reason to believe that, rather than being dependent on Jonah 4:9, ἕως θανάτου is a reflection of the OT-tinged language which Jesus used.

Although John does not record the agony in Gethsemane, Jn. 12:27 is a saying of Jesus very close in sentiment to Mk. 14:34 = Mt. 26:38. The close similarity in language between Jn. 12:27 and Ps. 42:6,[1] taken in conjunction with the use of the same psalm in the synoptic saying, leads to the presumption that an allusion is intended.[2] However, Ps. 6:3 is in exact verbal agreement with Ps. 42:6 and σῶσόν με in 6:4 finds an echo in Jesus' words, so dependence on that verse is equally probable.[3] Therefore, while these psalm verses undoubtedly constitute the source of the expression in both Mk. 14:34 = Mt. 26:38 and Jn. 12:27, it is probably not due to an intentional allusion to any one verse, but to familiarity with the language of the Psalter on the part of Jesus. (If, as seems likely, Jesus spoke these words in Aramaic (Ἀββά -- v. 36), the evangelists may have recognized his dependence on the passages from the Psalms and used the equivalent Greek words). At any rate, it is probably a question here not of a direct allusion, but of a general stylistic borrowing.

Both the allusions must be dependent on the LXX; ταράσσω translates נפשׁ (Pss. 6:3; 42:5,6,11; 43:5) only two times in the LXX

---

[1] ταράσσω with ψυχή only three times in the LXX.

[2] Thüsing, Erhöhung, 79; Dodd, Scriptures, 100; Barrett, John, 354; John Marsh, Saint John, PNTC (Harmondsworth: Penguin Books, 1968), 466. Dodd (Historical Tradition, 37) notes a further use of Ps. 42:6 in Jn. 13:21, but the only point of contact is in the verb and the replacement of ψυχή by πνεῦμα renders the allusion improbable.

[3] Lindars, Apologetic, 99, n. 2. Both psalm verses are mentioned by Sanders-Mastin (John, 294), Westcott (John, II, 124) and Bernard (John, II, 436).

and περίλυπος only once. This is borne out by the unusual NT use of ψυχή to refer to the seat of the emotions.[1]

Whatever the background of Jn. 12:27, it is clearly independent of the synoptics, although both allusions may be dependent on a tradition that transmitted Jesus' words in language derived from the Psalms.[2]

The depths of sorrow (ἕως θανάτου -- " a sorrow that well-nigh kills"[3]) expressed here in very strong language (ἐκθαμβεῖσθαι) reveals the extent of the dread which Jesus experienced as he contemplated the destiny which lay before him -- an extremity of emotion best explained as resulting from the recognition that more than physical death awaited him, but the bearing of human sin as well.[4] In this situation it is appropriate that Jesus turns to the language of the unknown psalmist, even as a Qumran Covenanter did before him (cf. Ps. 42:5a in 1QH 8:32).[5]

---

[1] H. B. Swete (The Gospel According to St. Mark (London: MacMillan, 1898), 343) claims that Mk. 14:34 / Mt. 26:38 and John 12:27 represent the only NT examples of ψυχή with this meaning.

[2] Dodd, Historical Tradition, 38; Lindars, John, 430-431; Barrett, John, 354; Marsh, John, 466; against Goguel, Life, 494 and James D. G. Dunn, Jesus and the Spirit: A Study of the Religious and Charismatic Experience of Jesus and the First Christians as Reflected in the New Testament (London: SCM, 1975), 18.

[3] So Swete (Mark, 342), followed by Rawlinson (Mark, 211), Taylor (Mark, 553) and Grundmann (Markus, 292). This meaning is preferable to understanding "to be so full of sorrow I would rather be dead" (as Bultmann ("περίλυπος," 323) paraphrases; cf. also Klostermann, Markusevangelium, 150).

[4] Cranfield, Mark, 433; Taylor, Mark, 552.

[5] Johannes Beutler ("Psalm 42/43 im Johannesevangelium," NTS, XXV (1978), 33-35) suggests several other points of contact with Pss. 42-43: Mk. 14:35 and Ps. 42:9 LXX; the apparent indifference of God and Ps. 42:10 and the description of the enemy in Mk. 14:42 and Ps. 43:1. None of the parallels seems to have been in the minds of the evangelists.

John 15:25 (Psalms 69:4; 35:19)

In John 15:18ff, Jesus warns the disciples of the hatred which they soon will be encountering and associates their rejection with the similar treatment he has received. It is clear that it is the Jews to whom reference is made (cf. v. 25 -- "their law") when he condemns those who have persisted in unbelief, even after witnessing the mighty works he has done. But, continues Jesus, strange as it may seem,[1] this reaction to his ministry is not without its prophetic anticipation, for it has happened "in order that" (ἵνα [2]) the word of "their law" might be fulfilled (πληρωθῇ). The quotation that follows most closely resembles Ps. 69:4 or 35:19 (cf. also Ps. 119:161)[3] which are identical (in all versions) with respect to the words under consideration. Of the two, Ps. 69:4 is the more likely candidate by virtue of the frequent citations of the psalm with respect to Jesus' passion (cf. Jn. 2:17 and 19:28-29). The text of the LXX is probably utilized, although one cannot be dogmatic because the quotation consists of two words only which are accurate substitutes for the respective Hebrew words. The alteration of the OT participial construction has almost certainly been done in order to suit the quotation to the context.[4]

---

[1] Bultmann notes that ἀλλά contrasts the unexpressed thought which links v. 24 to 25 and paraphrases: "such a reaction is indeed inconceivable, but . . . " (John, 551, n. 6).

[2] The construction is elliptical (BDF, 448 (7)). Freed (Old Testament, 94) notes that ὁ λόγος = ἡ γραφή in an OT quote only here and in Jn. 12:38.

[3] A similar phrase occurs in Ps. Sol. 7:1 with a finite verb (οἳ ἐμίσησαν ἡμᾶς δωρεάν) but it is improbable that John would have referred to this book as part of νόμος αὐτῶν.

[4] Noack (Johanneischen Tradition, 75) suggests that the change may go back to a stage of tradition before the evangelist, but there is little to substantiate this.

The phrase taken from the psalm stresses the baselessness for the enmity which David experienced and is, therefore, admirably suited for the application which Jesus gives it.[1] The addition of the modifier αὐτῶν strengthens the statement by pointing out that ". . . the Jews, who hate Jesus, are convicted out of their own law."[2]

John 17:12 (Psalm 41:9)

In the "high-priestly prayer" Jesus expresses satisfaction that none of those whom he has guarded has perished (ἀπώλετο) except the "son of destruction" (ἀπωλείας), but notes that even this exception has its purpose in the fulfillment of Scripture (ἡ γραφή). If the fulfillment clause has reference to Judas as the exception, the OT verse (γραφή points to a single passage) in Jesus' mind is probably Ps. 41:9, which is applied to Judas in a similar manner in Jn. 13:18.[3] Less likely is the suggestion that the designation itself is the point of reference, with perhaps Prov. 24:22a or Is. 54:7 as the source.[4] It may very well be that the characterization was one which was current in apocalyptic circles,[5] although in light of the

---

[1] Both δωρεάν and חנם mean, in this context, "without cause" (cf. BDF, 336; Str-B, II, 565 (on Aram.) מגן לקבל), Bultmann, John, 551, n.8).

[2] Barrett, John, 402. Cf. also Hoskyns-Davey, John, 481; Reim, Hintergrund, 43.

[3] Bernard, John, II, 571; Westcott, John, 274; Lightfoot, John, 301 (perhaps Ps. 109:8); Morris, John, 729; Lindars, John, 525; Reim, Hintergrund, 45-46; Schnackenburg, Johannes, III, 267.

[4] Freed (Old Testament, 97) notes that Prov. 24:22a is the only place in the LXX where υἱός and ἀπωλεία occur together. Is. 54:7 has τέκνα ἀπωλείας (cf. Christensen, "Le fils de l'homme," 29; Bultmann, John, 504).

[5] Gärtner (Iscariot, 28) points out that the phrase could be a rendering of Heb. אישׁ בליעל or Aram. בר בליעל and argues that John's use of the term may depend on the concept of Belial as a Satan figure in inter-testamental Judaism. Lindars likewise suggests a background in Jewish-Christian apocalyptic speculation (John, 526). R. E. Murphy

paranomasia ($\dot{a}\pi\dot{\omega}\lambda\epsilon\tau o$ - $\dot{a}\pi\omega\lambda\epsilon\acute{\iota}\alpha s$), Jesus may be using the term independently of any particular background.[1] The suggestion of Freed, that $\gamma\rho\alpha\phi\acute{\eta}$ refers to the word of Jesus in Jn. 6:70f is extremely improbable in view of the consistent meaning of $\gamma\rho\alpha\phi\acute{\eta}$ in the NT.[2]

However, it should be pointed out that there is nothing that requires the fulfillment clause to be taken with the reference to Judas; the exception clause may be a sort of parenthesis, the $\iota\nu\alpha$ then going back to the finite verb $\dot{a}\pi\dot{\omega}\lambda\epsilon\tau o$. If this were the case, the Scripture referred to would be one associated with the safe preservation of the eleven, rather than with the falling away of one.

The Gethsemane Scene (Psalm 31:21, et al.)

Dibelius, citing the lack of eye-witnesses, dismisses the Gethsemane tradition as a soteriologically-motivated invention which contrasts Jesus' "agonized resignation" to the will of God with the uncomprehending disciples' sleep. In seeking the material from which the scene was constructed, he observes that Heb. 5:7 preserves an apparently independent tradition that Jesus had suffered such a time of temptation and that Ps. 31:23 has influenced that verse. This leads him to suggest that the psalms of suffering, which feature cries of distress (22:24, 31:22, 69:3) and impassioned pleas for deliverance (22:20, 31:9, 10, 22; 69:1f), have formed the basis for this narrative:

("sahat in Qumran Literature," Bib, XXXIX (1958), 66, n. 4) posits a derivation from sht, used at Qumran in the sense of corruption caused by Gehenna.

[1] $\upsilon\iota\acute{o}s$ with the genitive is a Semitic construction which indicates quality (Turner, Syntax, 207-8). The expression, then, refers not to destiny, but to character (Albrecht Oepke, "$\dot{a}\pi\acute{o}\lambda\lambda\upsilon\mu\iota$, $\dot{a}\pi\omega\lambda\epsilon\acute{\iota}\alpha$, $\dot{A}\pi o\lambda\lambda\acute{\upsilon}\omega\nu$," TDNT, I 397; Morris, John, 728).

[2] Old Testament, 96-98.

> Vielmehr ist die Szene in die Leidensgeschichte eingegliedert
> worden, weil die Gemeinde von diesem Kampf Jesu klar überzeugt
> war. Sie besass diese Überzeugung, weil ein derartiger Kampf
> und ein derartiges Gebot zu den Leidensmotiven gehörte, die man
> den Psalmen entnommen hatte, um Jesu Leiden zu verstehen.[1]

Against Dibelius, it seems impossible not to admit a historical core in the Gethsemane tradition,[2] and his attempt to derive the scene from the lament psalms must be deemed a failure. Heb. 5:7 demonstrates only that scriptural study was continuing (if, indeed, an allusion to Ps. 31:23 is present) and does not offer material for comparison with the Gospels.[3] If the tradition had been derived from that psalm, it is difficult to understand why Jesus' prayers, the high point of the scene, do not explicitly allude to any of the psalms.[4] The prayer to God for deliverance from distress is a common feature of the lament psalms, but Jesus' prayers are essentially different, being petitions for salvation from a tribulation that is imminent.

John 18:6 (Psalms 27:2; 35:4; 56:9)

A possible OT background for John's description of the remarkable behavior of Jesus' arresters is found in the description of the "turning back" or the "stumbling and falling" of the enemies of

---

[1]Martin Dibelius, "Gethsemane," Botschaft und Geschichte: Gesammelte Aufsatze I: Zur Evangelienforschung (Tübingen: Mohr, 1953), 261-271 (271); From Tradition to Gospel, 211-212 (211). Cf. also T. A. Burkill, "St. Mark's Philosophy of the Passion," NovT, II (1958), 262; Nineham, Mark, 390; Pesch, "Passion des Menschensohnes," 184.

[2]Taylor, Mark, 551; Branscomb, Mark, 267; Dunn, Jesus and the Spirit, 18-19.

[3]Lietzmann, "Bemerkungen zum Prozess Jesu," 212.

[4]Lietzmann, "Prozess," 212; Dunn, Jesus and the Spirit, 19; R. S. Barbour, "Gethsemane in the Tradition of the Passion," NTS, XVI (1969-70), 235. Cf. also Linnemann, Passionsgeschichte, 30, n. 48; Boman, "Gebetskampf," 263.

the psalmist(s) (Pss. 27:2, 35:4 and 56:9).[1] Verbal parallels exist with ἔπεσαν (Heb. נפלו) in 27:2 and εἰς τὰ ὀπίσω (Heb. אחור) in 35:4 and 56:9. While Psalms 27 and 56 are not elsewhere quoted or alluded to in the NT, John explicitly cites Ps. 35:19 in Jn. 15:25, where the reference is also to the enemies of Jesus. Yet, the verbal similarity between Jn. 18:6 and Ps. 35:4 is not striking, since εἰς τὰ ὀπίσω occurs 28 times in the LXX (13t. in the Psalms) and 6 times in the NT (2t. in John), and none of the suggested backgrounds has the most unique feature of John's narrative, the falling to the ground (χαμαί). However, in view of the use of Psalm 35 elsewhere by John, the slight verbal echo and the similarity in contexts, the allusion must be regarded as possible, although not certain.

Mark 14:57-58 (Psalms 35:11; 27:12)

It is possible that another reference to the psalms just mentioned is to be seen in Mark's peculiar emphasis on the false witnesses during the Sanhedrin hearing.[2] Donahue notes that the two activities of the false witnesses in Mk. 14:57-8, rising up and bearing false witness, are also found in Pss. 35:11 and 27:12. The lack of verbal agreement between LXX and Mark shows that the MT is the basis for the allusion. The Hebrew of Ps. 27:12, he claims, is elsewhere translated ψευδομαρτυρεῖν (Ex. 20:16) and ψεύδης μάρτυς (Prov. 6:19, 19:5,9), and the two Greek words for "rise up" in the

---

[1] Ps. 27:1 -- Macgregor, John, 325; Ps. 35:4 -- E. W. Hengstenberg, Commentary on the Gospel of St. John (3 vols.; Edinburgh: T & T Clark, 1865), II, 344; Christoph Ernest Luthardt, St. John's Gospel, trans. by Caspar René Gregory (3 vols.; Edinburgh: T & T Clark, 1878), III, 226. Pss. 27:2 and 35:4 -- Dodd, Historical Tradition, 76-7; Dauer, Passionsgeschichte, 34; Ernst Haenchen, "History and Interpretation in the Johannine Passion Narrative," trans. by James P. Martin, Int, XXIV (1970), 201. Pss. 35:4 and 56:9 -- Barrett, John, 434.

[2] Montefiore, Synoptic Gospels, I, 354; Nineham, Mark, 406; Holtzmann, Die Synoptiker, 292; Weidel, "Studien," 224-225; Brown, John, II, 795; Goppelt, Typos, 121; Schenk, Passionsbericht, 232 (he also mentions Ps. 108:2ff).

respective psalm verses both represent קום.¹ Although ψευδομαρτυρεῖν is used for עד שקר in Ex. 20:16, the construction is
different from that of Ps. 27:12,² but it is not impossible that Mark
has changed the substantive of the psalm verse into a verb for
stylistic reasons. It is unlikely, however, that ψευδομαρτυρεῖν could
be used to translate Ps. 35:11 עד חמס ("witness of violence").³
Mark does emphasize the false witness theme through the repetition
of the phrase ἐψευδομαρτύρουν κατ' αὐτοῦ , but it is difficult
to determine whether this is done to indicate an allusion to Ps. 27:12
or for another reason. The linguistic evidence permits no firm
decision either way and the allusion must be regarded only as
possible.⁴

Other elements in the narrative of the Jewish trial which
may relate to the Righteous Sufferer psalms have been isolated. Mk. 14:55,
which notes the failure of the Jews to procure adequate witnesses for
Jesus' condemnation is compared with Ps. 35:4 (" . . . Let those be
turned back and humiliated who devise evil against me"),⁵ Jesus'
silence is linked to Ps. 37:14-16 and 38:9ff⁶ and general influence
from themes prominent in these psalms is asserted.⁷ With respect to

---

¹Donahue, Are You the Christ?, 74-76.

²ψευδομαρτυρεῖν in Ex. 20:16 is used as the direct object of
ענה: yielding an entirely different construction than the substantival
personal use in Ps. 27:12.

³Of the 59 occurrences of חמס in the MT, ψευδής is used in
the LXX only once (Am. 6:3). The consistent translation of חמס in the
Psalms is ἄδικος . חמס עד occurs two other places, each time
translated μάρτυς ἄδικος .

⁴Donald Juel (Messiah and Temple: The Trial of Jesus in the
Gospel of Mark, SBLDS, XXXI (Missoula, Mont.: Scholar's Press, 1977),
33) characterizes Donahue's argument for the allusion as "extremely tenuous."

⁵Donahue, Are You the Christ?, 75, n. 2.   ⁶Dormeyer, Passion, 177.

⁷Martin Dibelius, "Das historische Problem der Leidensgeschichte,"
ZNW, XXX (1931), 199 (referring particularly to Ps. 31:11,13 and 22);
Pesch, "Passion des Menschensohnes," 187.

Mk. 14:55, the only linguistic contact with Ps. 35:4 is in the very common, and naturally used, ζητέω and the conceptual parallel is not apposite at all, since the psalmist prays earnestly for deliverance from death, while Jesus is, of course, condemned to death by the Sanhedrin. It has been demonstrated that Jesus' silence is to be understood in the light of Is. 53:7, which provides a better comparison to Jesus' situation than do the psalms. General influence from a broad category of psalms on a particular passage is difficult to prove or disprove. The attempt of the enemies to do away with the psalmist(s) through duplicity and unjust accusations is a consistent theme in these psalms and may have been consciously utilized by the evangelists in portraying the hearing. However, very little attempt has been made to employ specific linguistic features from the psalms and the situation is a common and natural one; just because the "Righteous Sufferer" is such a broad and universal concept, it is difficult to determine whether conscious borrowing has taken place or whether the parallel is simply coincidental, arising from the inherent nature of the situation. In this particular case, there is no compelling reason to regard any detail, except possibly the false witnesses, as directly related to the psalms in question.

Matthew 27:34 (Psalm 69:21)

It is quite certain that Matthew's χολῆς ("gall") (Mark: ἐσμυρνισμένον οἶνον) is due to influence from Ps. 69:21.[1] χολή is used only here in the NT and is not frequent in the LXX (less than 20 occurrences).[2] It is possible that the similarity of the Hebrew

---

[1] Schweizer (Markus, 199) believes that Mark alludes to Ps. 69:21 as well. While possible, Mark does nothing to indicate the presence of such an allusion.

[2] That Matthew does not conform οἶνος to the ὄξος of Ps. 69:21 (as some later MSS do), or substitute βρῶμα does not preclude an allusion, but does imply historical veracity (Schlatter, Matthäus, 779-80).

word for myrrh (מור) and the Aramaic word for gall (מררא) has facilitated the change, although it is unlikely that this has given rise to the alteration.[1] The allusion is too brief to allow a decision regarding the textual background, since χολή correctly translates Hebrew ראש and the allusion should be limited to this word.

The significance of this offer of a drink is difficult to determine, since neither Matthew nor Mark indicate the purpose of the action. The reference to Ps. 69:21 in 1QH 4:11 is not helpful, for חמץ is spiritualized and used to describe heresy.[2] That the gesture, at least in Mark, was a compassionate one has been widely assumed. The existence of a Jewish custom, by which a condemned man was given a stupefying drink to ease the pain, lends support to this interpretation.[3] But frankincense was mixed with wine for this purpose, according to the Jewish custom, while it is not certain that gall would have a narcotic effect and myrrh almost surely would not.[4] Apart from the alleged Jewish custom, there is nothing in the passage that would indicate that a compassionate gesture is described, while Matthew's χολή would indicate quite the opposite. In fact, a

---

[1] Pace J. Döller, "Der Wein in Bibel und Talmud," Bib, IV (1923), 165; J. Wellhausen, Das Evangelium Matthaei (Berlin: Georg Reimer, 1904), 147; W. L. Knox, The Sources of the Synoptic Gospels, ed. by H. Chadwick (2 vols.; Cambridge: University Press, 1957), I, 69. That the myrrh - gall alteration arose through mistaking לבנה ("myrrh") for לענה ("wormwood") is similarly improbable (Edersheim, Life and Times, II, 588, n. 1).

[2] "Der wesentliche Unterschied im Inhalt der Zitierung liegt darin, dass die Qumrantexte, wie auch gelegentlich die Rabbinen, unter Essig übertragen die Häresie verstehen während die Evangelien Essig und Galle in wörtlichgegenständlichen Sinne Jesus dargereicht sein lassen." Braun, Qumran, II, 312.

[3] b. Sanh. 43a; Str-B, I, 1037. The custom was based on Prov. 31:6 (Dalman, Jesus-Jeshua, 193-194). Nineham (Mark, 423) even suspects Mk. 15:23 to be a "fulfillment" of Prov. 31:6-7.

[4] Wilhelm Michaelis, "σμύρνα, σμυρνίζω," TDNT, VII, 459; Wilkinson, "The Seven Words," 77, n. 1.

compassionate gesture is difficult to fit into the context of either gospel, for it leaves unexplained why Jesus should have had to taste the wine before he refused it. If the mixture was a narcotic (which, as we have seen, is unlikely), and Jesus wished to die with full consciousness (the usual explanation of the refusal), he would not have had to taste the mixture first. This is true as well if the gesture was obviously mocking from the outset. However, if an undrinkable mixture was offered to Jesus under the guise of the usual custom, it would explain the taste and subsequent refusal.[1] This is compatible with Mark's account, for although myrrh was sometimes mixed with wine to strengthen it,[2] the word σμύρνα is never used in the Bible with reference to a liquid,[3] but only with reference to perfume or incense. Myrrh naturally has a bitter taste[4] and Mark's reference to "myrrhed wine" (σμυρνίζω -- a Biblical hapax legomenon) might refer to a drink made unpalatable by the addition of too much myrrh. It is not unlikely, then, that Matthew and Mark are in agreement in describing an offer of a drink to Jesus at the beginning of the crucifixion which was intended as a mockery; Mark describes it by its contents, Matthew by its taste, with reference to Ps. 69:21.[5]

---

[1]Gundry, Old Testament, 202-203.

[2]Michaelis, "σμύρνα," 458; Döller, "Der Wein," 165.

[3]The only possible exception is Song of Songs 5:13, "His lips are lilies, distilling liquid myrrh." But the allusion is surely metaphorical.

[4]G. E. Post, "Myrrh," Hastings Dictionary of the Bible, ed. by James Hastings (5 vols.; Edinburgh: T & T Clark, 1898-1904), III, 464-65.

[5]Str-B (I, 1038) note that χολή (= מרה) often has the force of an adjective: "bitter" (Prov. 5:4; Lam 3:15). See also Swete, Mark, 358; Plummer, Matthew, 394-95; Lohmeyer-Schmauch, Matthäus, 389; Wilkinson, "Words," 77. This interpretation counters the objections to Matthew's use of the word as an unfounded OT importation (Albert Vis, The Messianic Psalm Quotations in the New Testament: A Critical Study of the Christian 'Testimonies' in the Old Testament (Amsterdam: von Soest, 1936), 53).

Ps. 69:21 is probably to be understood metaphorically, although some commentators have supposed that the custom of bringing "consolation-bread" to the bereaved (supposedly described in II Sam. 12:17 and Jer. 16:7) forms the basis for this description.[1] However, the psalm probably antedates the custom[2] and the psalmist is not strictly in a position of bereavement. The LXX correctly understands the ב before בְּרוּתִי as the <u>beth essentiae</u>, translating εἰς τὸ βρῶμα, "for my food" (not "in my food").[3] The NT follows this interpretation as well. Matthew understands the verse in its literal sense, probably because the event at the crucifixion corresponded so closely with the psalm verse. The mockery of God's righteous sufferer is the point of contact between the OT text and Matthew's application.

While Matthew is almost surely dependent on Mark in this narrative, only Matthew alludes to Ps. 69:21. The application of this verse to the events of the crucifixion had already been made, of course -- cf. Mk. 15:36.[4]

<u>Matthew 27:35a / Mark 15:24 /
Luke 23:34b / John 19:24</u>
(Psalm 22:18)

The dividing of Jesus' garments by the casting of lots is related in all four gospels, and is an obvious allusion to

---

[1] Gunkel, <u>Psalmen</u>, 296; Oesterley, <u>The Psalms</u>, II, 331.

[2] Recognized by Anderson, <u>Psalms</u>, 305. It does not appear that Oesterley's claim that בְּרוּתִי is a quasi-technical term for "consolation-bread" can be substantiated.

[3] Perowne, <u>Psalms</u>, I, 532; Delitzsch, <u>Psalms</u>, II, 324. M. Dahood (<u>Psalms</u>, AB, XVI, XVII, XVIIA (3 vols.; New York: Doubleday, 1965-70), II, 162), however, translates "in my food."

[4] Perhaps Matthew is looking ahead to the scene in which all four evangelists explicitly use Ps. 69:21 (Mt. 27:48/Mk. 15:36/Lk. 23:36/Jn. 19:28-29). It is possible that Matthew sees an allusion to the first part of the psalm verse here and to the second part in 27:48: Lindars, <u>Apologetic</u>, 101-02; Schweizer, <u>Markus</u>, 199; Tasker, <u>Matthew</u>, 264; Finegan, <u>Überlieferung</u>, 31.

Ps. 22:18.[1] The LXX accurately translates the MT, except in rendering the Hebrew imperfect by the aorist in both verbs. John's formula quotation exactly reproduces the LXX, while the synoptic evangelists diverge from the LXX somewhat. These divergences, however, are due to the allusive nature of the quotation and consideration of Greek style (the Hebrew parataxis is changed to a subordinating construction with the participle). διαμερίζομαι is used only in these verses in Matthew and Mark (Luke has the only other occurrences of the verb in the NT besides Jn. 19:24), which would perhaps favor dependence on the LXX here. Mark's present tense (διαμερίζονται) does not necessarily indicate dependence on the Hebrew, since the historical present is a feature of Mark's style, particularly in the crucifixion narrative. Similarly, Matthew's aorist, rather than an approximation to the LXX, may be simply a characteristic avoidance of the historic present.[2]

The clothes of the condemned criminal were the prerogative of the Roman soldiers, so the dividing of Jesus' clothes would be normal procedure,[3] and it is, therefore, not necessary to suppose that the incident was invented under the influence of Ps. 22:18.[4] It may be, however, that the detail was remembered and preserved because of the OT link.[5] The psalm verse occurs at the end of a long complaint by the sufferer. The poet is afflicted by some sort

---

[1] Freed is surely in error in supposing that John was the first to see an allusion to Ps. 22:18 in the incident (Old Testament, 99).

[2] Senior, Passion Narrative, 278.

[3] A. N. Sherwin-White, Roman Society and Roman Law in the New Testament, The Sarum Lectures, 1960-61 (Oxford: Clarendon Press, 1963), 46.

[4] Linnemann, Studien, 152; pace Bertram, Leidensgeschichte, 84; Cohn, Trial, 236.

[5] Linnemann, Studien, 152.

of physical distress, as well as by mockery from his opponents, who are probably to be regarded as the ungodly, in general. The widespread custom of dividing the condemned criminal's clothes would suggest the possibility that an execution scene is here envisaged and that the sufferer sees his enemies already distributing his clothes in anticipation of his death.[1]

John's explicit formula quotation, in contrast to the synoptists' narrative allusion, seems to represent a tendency in the development of the use of the OT.[2] The introductory formula used here is characteristic of John's gospel, being found also in 13:18 and 19:36, but nowhere else in the NT. Only Matthew and John (5 times) use πληρόω in quotation introductions. ἵνα seems to be employed in an unusual way, but one characteristic of the fourth gospel, in introducing a "main sentence expressing fitness or necessity."[3] It has generally been supposed that John's incident of the seamless tunic (unique to his gospel) owes its origin to a misunderstanding of the Hebrew poetic device, synonymous parallelism (cf. Mt. 21:5).[4] However, as Lindars properly points out: "John must not be held ignorant of the most constant characteristic of Hebrew poetry."[5] It is unlikely that John has simply invented the incident of the seamless tunic in order to point to an exact fulfillment of both parts of the

---

[1] Anderson, Psalms, 191.

[2] Karnetzki, "Alttestamentlichen Zitate," 6; J. R. Scheifler, "El Salmo 22 y la Crucifixión del Señor," EstBib, XXIV (1965), 25-26; Dauer, Passionsgeschichte, 185.

[3] Cadoux, "Imperatival Use," 169-70.

[4] So Loisy, Quatrième Évangile, 486; J. Wellhausen, Das Evangelium Johannes (Berlin: Georg Reimer, 1908), 87; Haenchen, Weg Jesu, 328; Barrett, John, 458; Freed, Old Testament, 99.

[5] Apologetic, 91. Although the Qumran sectaries occasionally ignored this poetic device (Elliger, Habakuk-Kommentar, 136, 139-40).

psalm verse.[1] If this were so, he certainly would have used
$ἱματισμός$ (as in the psalm verse) rather than $χιτών$,[2] and $ἔβαλον$
$κλῆρον$ rather than the unusual $λάχωμεν$.[3] John's interest in
symbolism has been held accountable for the origin of this incident,
the seamless tunic representing the robe of the High Priest[4] or the
unbroken unity of the church.[5] A reference to the robe of the High
Priest is unlikely because $χιτών$ (although used in Ex. 28:4,
Lev. 16:4 and by Josephus of the High Priest's robe) would not be the
normal word for the High Priest's robe.[6] In addition, John shows no

---

[1] Pace Martin Dibelius, "Die alttestamentlichen Motive in der Leidensgeschichte des Petrus- und des Johannes-Evangeliums," Abhandlungen zur semitischen Religionskunde und Sprachwissenschaft (für W. W. G. von Baudissin), ed. by W. Frankenberg and F. Küchler, BZAW, XXXIII (Giessen: Töpelmann, 1918), 134.

[2] Rothfuchs, Erfüllungszitate, 57; Brown, John, II, 920.

[3] Brown, John, II, 920.

[4] Josephus (Ant. III, 161) and other authorities indicate that the High Priest's robe was to be seamless (Str-B, II, 573). Macgregor, John, 346; Lindars, Apologetic, 91 -- but see his John, 578; Braun, Jean le Théologien, I, 101; Joachim Gnilka, "Die Erwartung des messianischen Hohenpriesters in den Schriften von Qumran und im Neuen Testament," RevQ, II (1959-60), 423.

[5] This interpretation of the seamless tunic was especially popular among the Fathers, first advocated, apparently, by Cyprian (Jaroslav Pelikan, The Christian Tradition: A History of the Development of Doctrine, Vol. I: The Emergence of the Catholic Tradition (100-600) (Chicago and London: University of Chicago Press, 1971), 159). Walter Bauer, "Johannes" in Die Evangelien, HNT, II (Tübingen: Mohr, 1912), 173; Barrett, John, 458; Loisy, Quatrième Evangile, 486. That the seamless tunic represents Moses' robe is hardly likely. (pace G. Klein, "Zur Erläuterung der Evangelien aus Talmud und Midrasch," ZNW, V (1904), 144-153). It is improbable that anything about Moses' robe would have led John to attribute symbolic significance to it. Philo speaks of the Word as the $δεσμός$ $τῶν$ $ἁπάντων$ (Fug., 110-12 -- Barrett, John, 457), but this idea is distant from John's.

[6] Winter, Trial, 19. $ἱμάτια$ is used in Mt. 26:65 (cf. Ps. 22:18). Schnackenburg points out the difficulty with regard to the robe mentioned in Josephus: " . . . aber es handelt sich um das langwallende Obergewand des Hohenpriesters, das mit einem goldgestickten Gürtel zusammengehalten wurde." (Johannes, III, 318). See further, Dauer, Passionsgeschichte, 188.

interest in a High Priest typology elsewhere.¹ That the unity of the church is represented by the seamless tunic is even less probable. While John is undoubtedly interested in the unity of believers (Jn. 17:11, 21-23), nothing would indicate that Jesus' χιτών is symbolic of the church.² If suggested symbolic interpretations are not convincing,³ the most reasonable alternative is to suppose that John is aware of the application of Ps. 22:18 in the crucifixion narrative and that he has access to a tradition which mentions a seamless tunic that was gambled for. Not unnaturally, he sees in this incident a fulfillment of the other half of the psalm verse and accordingly records it.⁴ Is this separation of the two parts of the verse "legitimate?" As far as vocabulary is concerned, ἱμάτια and ἱματισμός are virtually equivalent in usage,⁵ as are לבוש and בגד.⁶ The Targum affords some basis for a distinction, translating לבוש in the first stich and פתגא in the second,⁷ but in light of John's word for word quotation from the LXX, it cannot be established

---

¹Lagrange, Jean, 491; Lindars, John, 578, Schnackenburg, Johannes, III, 318.

²Barrett's comment that the tunic symbolizes "the death of Christ as bringing into one flock the scattered children of God (cf. 11:52)" is not strictly appropriate; the tunic, one piece at the start, is kept intact, not sewn together now (John, 468).

³Schnackenburg (Johannes, III, 318-19) thinks the divesting of the tunic is representative of Jesus' sacrificial self-surrender, while its intactness symbolizes God's preservation of and care over Christ.

⁴Lagrange, Jean, 491; Strachan, Fourth Gospel, 319; Westcott, John, II, 275; Brown, John, II, 920, who says: " . . . it seems more likely that the interpretation of the psalm is stretched to cover an incident that the evangelist found in his tradition rather than vice versa."

⁵Pace Alford, The Greek Testament, I, 893.

⁶Pace F. Godet, Commentary on the Gospel of St. John, trans. by S. Taylor and M. D. Cusin (3 vols.; Edinburgh: T & T Clark, 1877), III, 266.

⁷Brown, John, II, 920.

that he was aware of the targumic rendering (if, indeed, it existed in his day). The psalm verse itself allows the possibility of being understood as John does by the switching from plural to singular (which could be pressed as distinguishing outer clothes from inner[1]), but it seems evident that John would never have separated the two parts of the verse without the influence of the circumstances. This is, consequently, a case in which the text has been re-oriented by the situation.

Either two of the synoptic evangelists are dependent on a third, or all three draw from a testimonium, for they agree in combining the same parts of the psalm verse ($\delta\iota\alpha\mu\epsilon\rho\iota\zeta o\mu\alpha\iota$ - $\dot{\iota}\mu\acute{\alpha}\tau\iota\alpha$ - $\beta\acute{\alpha}\lambda\lambda\omega$ - $\kappa\lambda\tilde{\eta}\rho o\nu$). John may be making use of the synoptic account,[2] dependent on a tradition (which probably included the seamless robe incident),[3] or on his own eyewitness reminiscence.[4]

The Mockery of Christ

The mockery of Christ on the Cross is influenced by the OT to a greater extent perhaps than any other NT passage. This influence is mediated through "narrative allusions," that is, the mockeries are couched in language drawn from various OT passages. The theological, critical and literary problems related to this scene will be glanced at following a study of the individual allusions.

---

[1]Hoskyns-Davey, Fourth Gospel, II, 629.

[2]Freed, Old Testament Quotations, 99.

[3]Dauer (Passionsgeschichte, 182-85) claims, on the basis of a stylistic investigation, that the incident stems from John's tradition. Dodd, Historical Tradition, 40; Schnackenburg, Johannes, III, 318.

[4]Bernard, John, II, 629.

Matthew 27:39 / Mark 15:29a
(Psalm 22:7; Lamentations 2:15)

Two phrases of this taunt are almost surely derived from the OT. That people would be "passing by" the crucifixion site is to be expected, but the unusual construction οἱ (δὲ) παραπορευόμενοι (one would have expected τινες τῶν παρεστώτων) is probably due to influence from Lam. 2:15 (cf. also Ps. 22:7).[1] The evangelists were probably led to this passage because of its similarity in form[2] and content (mockery, "shaking heads," God as the One really mocked) to the primary OT background, Ps. 22:6-8. "Shaking the head" is a relatively common OT metaphor for mockery (see II Kings 19:21; Job 16:4; Sir 13:7; Ps. 109:25),[3] but in view of the frequent use of Psalm 22 in the Crucifixion Narrative the expression here is almost surely taken from Ps. 22:7. Matthew and Mark agree in the use of κινέω in participial form, whereas it appears as an aorist in both LXX Ps. 22:7 and Lam. 2:15. However, the evidence is too weak to permit any firm conclusions as to text background. Psalm 109:25 (where LXX employs σαλεύω for the same Hebrew verb as is used in 22:7 and Lam. 2:15) is probably not referred to.[4]

---

[1] Taylor, Mark, 591; Suhl, Funktion, 61; Gundry, Old Testament, 630; Swete, Mark, 451; Plummer, Matthew, 397; Allen, Matthew, 294; Grundmann, Markus, 513; McNeile, Matthew, 419. ἐβλασφήμουν may be a loose rendering of Hebrew ישׁרקו in Lam. 2:15, but is more likely not part of the allusion. Other suggested OT contexts have probably not been used: Is. 51:23 (Plummer, Matthew, 397; and Swete, Mark, 451); Jer. 19:8 (Schlatter, Matthäus, 781).

[2] Gunkel classifies Lamentations 3 as a "lament of the individual" and Lamentations 2 is similar, though with a collective reference to Jerusalem (Gunkel-Begrich, Einleitung, 172).

[3] Taylor, Mark, 591.

[4] Against Lindars, Apologetic, 110; Gundry, Old Testament, 63.

Luke 23:35a (Psalm 22:7)

Luke is likewise dependent on Ps. 22:7 in his description of the mockery, but he uses a different part of the verse. ἐκμυκτηρίζω is used only here and in Lk. 16:14 in the NT and appears only four times in the LXX. θεωρῶν would not, by itself, imply dependence on Ps. 22:7, but the proximity of ἐξεμυκτήρισαν makes it probable that both words are derived from the psalm verse.[1] The verbal similarity, especially in the rare ἐκμυκτηρίζω, argues for dependence on the LXX.[2]

Matthew 27:40 / Mark 15:29b-30 (Psalm 22:8)

Lohmeyer suggests that σῶσον σεαυτόν is dependent on Ps. 22:8,[3] but the person is changed significantly -- the psalm verse speaks of God delivering the sufferer, Matthew and Mark of a self-deliverance. The taunt is undoubtedly based on Jesus' popular reputation as a miracle-worker; what he has done for others, he is mockingly challenged to do for himself.

Matthew 27:42 / Mark 15:31 (Psalm 22:29)

Based on a different translation of the Hebrew of Ps. 22:29c ("and himself he did not save") and a transposition of the phrase to the "original Psalm" (i.e., vv. 1-21), Aytoun conjectures that this verse forms the background for the Jewish leaders' challenge.[4] However,

---

[1] Schenk, Passionsbericht, 99; Easton, Luke, 348; Loisy, Luc, 527; Plummer, Luke, 532; Leaney, Luke, 284.

[2] G. Bertram, "ἐκμυκτηρίζω," TDNT, IV, 798.

[3] Markus, 343.

[4] R. A. Aytoun, "'Himself He Cannot Save' (Ps. xxii. 29 & Mark xv. 31)," JTS, XXI (1921), 245-248.

even if Aytoun's hypothetical reconstruction were to be accepted (which is doubtful, since most scholars see the psalm as a unity), the reproach of the Jewish leaders cannot refer to the concept of a voluntary self-sacrifice, as Aytoun thinks. Their attempt to discredit Jesus with this statement is perfectly understandable without theological overtones, although the evangelists undoubtedly view it as "one of the supreme ironies of history."[1]

Matthew 27:43
(Psalm 22:8; Wisdom of Solomon 2:18)

In addition to the generally recognized dependence on Ps. 22:8 in Matthew's rendition of the Jewish leaders' taunt, πέποιθεν ἐπὶ τὸν θεόν, ῥυσάσθω νῦν εἰ θέλει αὐτόν, it is often suggested that Matthew is drawing on Wis 2:13-18 (esp. v. 18).[2] This passage is an important example of the "righteous sufferer" theme in inter-testamental Judaism and is sometimes put forward as a significant background for Jesus' Passion. Wisdom 2 has been influenced heavily by Psalm 22, however, and it is possible that Matthew and the writer of Wisdom have independently employed the expressions of mockery from that psalm. It is alleged that the presence of the "Son of God" title, found in Wisdom, but not in Psalm 22 is evidence for Matthew's

---

[1]Taylor, Mark, 572: the Jewish leaders probably mean to refer to Jesus' healing miracles (Cranfield, Mark, 456-7).

[2]Lagrange, Matthieu, 529; Stendahl, School, 141; Karnetzki, "Die alttestamentlichen Zitate," 20; Finegan, Überlieferung, 31; Klosterman, Matthäusevangelium, 223-224; Schenk, Passionsbericht, 70; Frederick W. Danker, "The Demonic Secret in Mark: A Reexamination of the Cry of Dereliction," ZNW, LXI (1970), 57; Senior, Passion Narrative, 288-9; Schweizer, Matthew, 513.
Wisdom of Solomon is probably pre-Christian. See Ernest G. Clarke, The Wisdom of Solomon, Cambridge Bible Commentary (Cambridge: University Press, 1973), 26 (mid 2nd or early 1st century B.C.); Charles Holmes, "The Wisdom of Solomon," APOT, I, 524 (30-50 B.C.); pace W. O. E. Oesterley, An Introduction to the Books of the Apocrypha (London: SPCK, 1935), 209 (A.D. 40).

dependence on the former,[1] but this is not conclusive since the mockery itself is obviously directed toward the very points which were brought out at the Sanhedrin hearing, where Jesus' confession of Sonship was prominent (Mt. 26:63-4). The parallels between Mt. 27:43 and Wisdom 2 should therefore probably be ascribed to common dependence on Ps. 22.[2]

The allusion to Ps. 22:8 shows divergences from both LXX and MT. On the one hand, Matthew's text is closer to LXX in rendering the first verb as an indicative rather than an imperative (with the Peshitta).[3] On the other hand, πέποιθεν is a better translation of Heb. גלל ("to roll" (i.e., upon God, "to trust")) than LXX ἤλπισεν. Matthew differs from both LXX and Hebrew in τὸν θεόν and the conditional εἰ.[4] It is most likely that Matthew is dependent on the proto-MT and is slightly adapting that text to suit his narrative: "In the psalm the statement is ironic. But in a passing allusion the larger context of the psalm could not be brought into view. Therefore Matthew has εἰ for ὅτι to avoid the possibility his readers

---

[1] Casimir Romaniuk, "Le Livre de la Sagesse dans le Nouveau Testament," NTS, XIV (1967-68), 499.

[2] Clarke, Wisdom of Solomon, 26: " . . . the similarities [to NT] are due to the same Old Testament passage serving as the basis of this book and the New Testament."

[3] The Peshitta may have been assimilated to Matthew; it agrees with Matthew against LXX in the rest of the verse (Stendahl, School, 141).

[4] כי can be understood as conditional (GKC, par. 159l), but it is unusual and doesn't fit the context of Ps. 22:8 (Gundry, Old Testament, 145). The LXX reading ἐθέλει in U may go back to εἰ θέλει as in Lucian, etc., for this codex frequently writes ε for ει (Alfred Rahlfs, "Der Text des Septuagint-Psalters," Septuaginta-Studien (2 vols.; Göttingen: Vandenhoeck & Ruprecht, 1907), II, 149). Rahlfs thinks this reading is due to assimilation to the NT, but this has been contested (Stendahl, School, 140; cf. P. L. Hedley, "The Göttingen Investigation and Edition of the Septuagint," HTR, XXVI (1933), 71: " . . . if a New Testament quotation varies markedly from all known LXX manuscripts, agreement in some trivial point is probably not due to New Testament influence, especially if the minute agreement occurs over a wide geographical field" -- he specifically refers to Mt. 27:43).

might miss the irony . . . ."[1] He may have read the Heb. as בָּֽא instead of אֵל, accounting for the indicative. Even if a pre-Christian LXX text read εἰ θέλει,[2] it is doubtful that Matthew utilizes it, since he follows the MT in the rest of the verse.[3]

Matthew 27:44 / Mark 15:32b
(Psalm 42:10, 69:9)

The use of ὀνειδίζω to describe the criminals' abuse of Jesus has been viewed as a possible allusion to Ps. 69:9 or 42:10.[4] Both of these psalms are sources of testimonia, but ὀνειδίζω is a common enough word and cannot be said to be dependent on either of these verses.[5]

The presence of several OT allusions in the mocking of Jesus has led to scepticism regarding the historical reliability of the tradition. Bultmann speaks of " . . . a legendary formulation on the basis of a prophetic proof"[6] and Nineham believes the narrative is an "ideal picture" drawn from OT Scripture and designed to fit the church's anti-Jewish polemic.[7] Other scholars feel that the mockery, while no doubt an actual occurrence, has been expanded by means of OT allusions.[8] However, it is probably incorrect to speak of

---

[1] Gundry, Old Testament, 145-6; cf. also Strecker, Weg, 28; Sherman E. Johnson, "The Biblical Quotations in Matthew," HTR, XXXVI (1943), 143; Schlatter, Matthäus, 781.

[2] See note 4 on preceding page.

[3] Matthew and LXX understand the subject of בוֹ חָפֵץ to be God, correctly bringing out the sarcasm: "'for God obviously takes a great pleasure in him, that's why he is in trouble!'" (Anderson, Psalms, 188).

[4] Ps. 69:9 -- Hill, Matthew, 354; Fenton, Matthew, 441; Ps. 42:10 -- Cranfield, Mark, 457.

[5] Suhl, Alttestamentlichen Zitate, 61.

[6] Synoptic Tradition, 273.   [7] Mark, 425.

[8] Schweizer, Markus, 201; Hill, Matthew, 353-4.

"expansions" here. The OT language certainly adds interpretative detail through the use of metaphors, but should not be understood as describing activity as such. For example, "shaking the head" is probably not intended as the recounting of an actual circumstance, but a Biblical metaphor chosen to characterize the mockery. In the case of Mt. 27:43, the decision is more difficult, but, again, it is probable that Matthew has sought to capture the thrust of the Jewish leaders' taunt in his own, OT-influenced language. The taunts are no more than what would be expected at the execution of one who was regarded as a deluded religious fanatic. Much of the mockery presupposes a knowledge of what had transpired at the Jewish hearing, which is certainly not unexpected, but lends authenticity to the mockings. That the chief priests and scribes should have been present is indeed unusual, but then Jesus' case was not a usual one. They undoubtedly wished to make certain that the dangerous blasphemer met his deserved end; perhaps their taunt that he should "save himself" was not entirely in jest.[1]

The relationship between the synoptics in the use of these OT passages is instructive. Matthew and Mark closely agree with the narrative allusion to Ps. 22:7b and Lam. 2:15, while Matthew alone records the challenge of the Jewish leaders in language tinged by Ps. 22:8. Luke, however, omits the reference to "shaking heads," but adds an allusion drawn from Ps. 22:7a. While the singular relationship could be explained on the basis of direct literary dependence,[2] it seems much more likely that Luke is following a distinct source which had been

---

[1] Lagrange, Marc, 430.

[2] I.e., Luke may have omitted the description of the bystanders as "shaking their heads" because his Gentile readers could not be expected to understand the Jewish custom (Scheifler, "El Salmo 22," 33; Schneider, Passsion, 121).

influenced by Ps. 22:7 <u>independently</u> of Mt./Mk.[1] The implications of these observations must be fully explored at a later point.

Matthew 27:46 / Mark 15:34
(Psalm 22:1)

Jesus' climactic word from the Cross in Matthew and Mark presents a number of controversial and important issues, ranging from the question of the original language of the cry to theological implications for Christology, the Atonement and the doctrine of the Trinity. Our concern is, of course, with the Old Testament element specifically, but each of these areas of controversy includes significant ramifications for our study. To turn the tables, conclusions as to the way in which the OT is "actualized" by Jesus play a weighty role in determining the theological meaning of the cry.

Before considering the text form and function of this quotation, it is necessary to establish the original form of the text. In the transliterated portion the difficulty of representing Semitic words in the Greek alphabet has led to a bewildering variety of variants. The somewhat precarious task of reconstructing the Semitic original from the Greek text combined with the theological difficulty some have felt over the traditional interpretation of the cry from the Cross, has opened the way for several conjectures which do not represent a quotation from Ps. 22:1,[2] but none of the proposed

---

[1] Karabidopoulos, "[To Pathos]," 197.

[2] (1) Jesus, in his dying moment, bequeaths his people to God: עַל יָדְךָ אַפְקִיד עַמִּי (אֱלָהִי) (or אֱלָהִי) אֲדֹנִי: "Into thy hands I commend my people, O my Lord." (F. W. Buckler, "Eli, Eli, Lama Sabachthani?" <u>AJSL</u>, LV (1938), 378-91). (2) Jesus said, "My God you are," an allusion to Ps. 22:11, but it was misunderstood as אֵלִי אָתָה, "Elijah, come" (accounting for Mk. 15:35). Mark was assimilated to Mt. 27:46 (Harold Sahlin, "Zum Verständnis von drei Stellen des Markusevangelium (Mc. 4:26-29; 7:18f; 15:34)," <u>Bib</u>, XXXIII (1952), 53-66; cf. also Thorlief Boman, "Das letzte Worte Jesu," <u>ST</u>, XVII (1963), 103-119). (3) The words of Jesus originally

emendations is satisfactory.¹ Before considering the known variants, one other relevant matter must be discussed.

Strongly influencing the textual decision is the viewpoint adopted regarding the language which Jesus habitually used. While recent archaeological discoveries have demonstrated that both Hebrew and Greek were more widely employed in first century Palestine than has sometimes been assumed,² Aramaic must still be accorded primary consideration in the investigation of Jesus' sayings.³ However, it

---

were 'שכחתני למה (Ps. 42:10: "Why have you forgotten me"), but through a copyist's error (שבע for שבק), Ps. 22:1 has been substituted (D. Sidersky, "Un passage Hébreu dans le Nouveau Testament," Journal Asiatique, III (1914), 232-233). (4) If Ϳαβαχθανι were the original reading, it may have represented 'זבחתני and Jesus could have said, "My God, my God, why have you sacrificed me?" (Sidersky, "La Parole suprême de Jesus," RHR, CIII (1931), 151-154).

¹(1) Buckler's suggestion rests on dubious Near Eastern parallels regarding the practice of "testamentary dispositions" in Jesus' time and is not sufficiently founded on the texts. (2) Sahlin's conjecture must be rejected because it depends on the assumption that Jesus' Hebrew cry would have been misunderstood, while recent evidence indicates that Hebrew was widely used in first century Palestine. (3) and (4) Sidersky's reconstructions are motivated by the desire to explain the unusual transliteration of ק by χ . (κ would normally be used). However, the following θ explains the variant, since κθ is a combination repugnant in Greek (Gustaf Dalman, Grammatik des jüdischen Palästinischer Aramaisch: nach den Idiomen des Palästinischen Talmud des Onkelostargum und Prophetentargum und der Jerusalemischen Targume: Aramäische Dialektproben (2 vols., 2nd ed.; Darmstadt: Wissenschaftliche Buchgesellschaft, 1960), II, 365; W. Brandt, Die Evangelische Geschichte und der Ursprung des Christentums (Leipzig: O. R. Reisland, 1893), 229).

²R. H. Gundry, "The Language Milieu of First Century Palestine: Its bearing on the Authenticity of the Gospel Tradition," JBL, LXXXIII (1964), 404-408; J. N. Sevenster, Do you know Greek? How much Greek could the first Jewish Christians have known? NovTSup, XIV (Leiden: E. J. Brill, 1968), cf. esp. 176-83; James Barr, "Which Language did Jesus Speak? -- Some Remarks of a Semitist," BJRL, LIII (1970), 9-29; J. A. Emerton, "The Problem of Vernacular Hebrew in the First Century A.D. and the Language of Jesus," JTS, n.s., XXIV (1973), 1-23; A. W. Argyle, "Greek among the Jews of Palestine in New Testament Times," NTS, XX (1974), 87-89; Pinchas Lapide,"Insights from Qumran into the Languages of Jesus," RevQ, VIII (1975), 483-501.

³Black, Aramaic Approach, 15-28; Joseph A. Fitzmyer, "The Languages of Palestine in the First Century A.D.," CBQ, XXXII (1970), 501-531.

has been argued that, in this supreme moment, Jesus would have reverted to the language of devotion, Hebrew,[1] so it seems best to begin the study with no a priori decision with regard to language employed.

Advocates of a cry from the Cross in Hebrew argue that the misunderstanding of Jesus' cry presupposes the Hebrew אֵלִי,[2] as does the reading of the Gospel of Peter (ἡ δύναμίς μου); חֵילִי "my power" having been confused with אֵלִי.[3] Either Matthew's ηλι preserves the original which has been "Aramaicized" by Mark;[4] the reading of D and its allies is the original in Mark;[5] or Matthew and Mark originally agreed in attesting a Hebrew cry, which was changed to Aramaic by scribes who knew that Aramaic was more widely used in first century

---

[1] Dalman, Jesus-Jeshua, 205; Lapide, "Insights," 496-97.

[2] C. H. Turner, "Marcan Usage: Notes, Critical and Exegetical on the Second Gospel," JTS, XXVI (1925), 154-155; J. Wellhausen, Das Evangelium Marci (Berlin: Georg Reimer, 1903), 140; Taylor, Mark, 593; Cranfield, Mark, 457; Grundmann, Markus, 315; Kilpatrick, Origins, 104; Joachim Gnilka, "Mein Gott, mein Gott, warum hast du mich verlassen? (Mc. 15:34 par.)," BZ, n.s., III (1959), 294-297.

[3] Swete, Mark, 363; Lindars, Apologetic, 89-90; Frank Zimmermann, "The Last Words of Jesus," JBL, LXVI (1947), 465-466. Zimmermann seems to say that Peter's Galilean dialect led to a confusion of the Hebrew gutturals א and ח, but it is highly unlikely that the Gospel of Peter has any relation to the apostle of that name.

[4] Taylor, Mark, 593; Theodor Zahn, Introduction to the New Testament, trans. by J. M. Trout, et al. (3 vols.; Edinburgh: T & T Clark, 1909), I, 15. Grundmann (Markus, 315) attributes an anti-docetic motive to Mark who seeks to avoid possible confusion between אֵלִי and חֵילִי. It is doubtful if this motive would have been in Mark's mind (so Linnemann, Studien, 149).

[5] C. H. Turner has been outspoken in his advocacy of the Western reading in Mark ("Western Readings," 12). While anticipating other criticisms of the originality of D and its allies in Mk. 15:34, it might be noted here that Turner's hypothesis that Matthew has exchanged Mark's Hebrew with Aramaic is a problematic procedure, considering that Matthew betrays no fondness for Aramaic, not taking over Mark's Aramaic phrases. To account for the variants, T. W. Manson ("The Old Testament in the Teaching of Jesus," BJRL, XXXIV (1952), 327) thinks that the original Hebrew cry circulated with an accompanying Aramaic translation. Mark chooses to keep the Aramaic, but the Hebrew continued to be transmitted, finding its way into D eventually.

Palestine.¹ However, external evidence, based on the great majority of witnesses, decidedly favors an Aramaic cry in both Matthew and Mark.² Even the well-attested ηλι of Matthew does not militate against an Aramaic original, for the Targum to Ps. 22:2 uses אלי and one can readily understand how the Hebrew name for God would have been preserved even among those who normally spoke Aramaic (much like Jehovah or Yahweh is used among English-speakers).³ The reading of Codex D and its allies is best explained as an assimilation to the Hebrew text of Psalm 22:1.⁴ The Gospel of Peter rendering does not necessarily presuppose the reading אלי, for "my power" could simply be an independently adduced periphrasis for God (cf. Mt. 26:64).

---

¹Menzies, Earliest Gospel, 280-281; J. Vernon Bartlett, St. Mark (London: Thomas Nelson and Sons, n.d.), 421; Brandt, Evangelische Geschichte, 231.

²Mark's ελωι (ελωει) is Aramaic אלהי (The ω is to be accounted for either through the influence of Hebrew אלוהים (Dalman, Grammatik, I, 156) or by the fact that Greek could sometimes use ω to represent the Aramaic ā (Williams, Alterations, 39); λεμα, λιμα and λειμα are derived from Aramaic למה; σαβαχθανι(ει), σαβακτανει, σιβακθανει, σαβακτανει and ζαφθανει go back to Aramaic שבקתני.

³Jeremias can say: "Thus the cry from the cross in Mt. 27:46 has been transmitted in toto in Aramaic." (New Testament Theology, 5). While the extant Targum of the Psalms cannot, of course, be dated this early, it preserves many ancient readings, of which אלי, presupposing a mixed linguistic situation, is probably one.
It is possible that ελωι is the original reading of Matthew as well as Mark. Although understandably suspect because of assimilation to Mark, the desire to provide a better linguistic basis for the Elijah misunderstanding, as well as possible familiarity with the Targumic rendering would have provided some motivation for changing an original ελωι to ηλι.

⁴Williams (Alterations, 38-39); Zahn (Introduction, 16). ζαφθανει in both Matthew and Mark represents the Hebrew עזבתני, the initial vowel having dropped out because of the final α in λεμα (Metzger, Textual Commentary, 119-120. Metzger notes that the initial vowel has been retained in a MS of the Old Latin (i*) and in an Old Slavonic lectionary). Other derivations of ζαφθανει have been proposed: from Syriac ܫܒܩܢ (Frederick Henry Chase, The Syro-Latin Text of the Gospels (London: MacMillan and Co., Limited, 1895), 107); from Hebrew זעו (Eb. Nestle, "Mark xv. 34," ExpTim, IX (1897-98), 521-2); from Hebrew שׁדף (Ed. König, "The Origin of ζαφθανει in Cod. D of Matt. xxvii. 46 and Mark xv. 34," ExpTim, XI (1899-1900), 237-38).

One further difficulty remains in the way of accepting an Aramaic original of Jesus' cry; the Elijah misunderstanding which follows immediately is said to depend on the Hebrew ηλι, not the Aramaic ελωι. While various solutions have been proposed to get around this difficulty,[1] the simplest and most satisfactory alternative is to assume that the circumstances were such that ελωι could as easily be misunderstood for Ἐλείας as ηλι.[2] The words of a dying man, even in a "great cry," are easily misapprehended, especially since the area was no doubt noisy and the onlookers might be expecting a cry to Elijah (according to Jewish tradition, the deliverer in time of need).[3]

We conclude, therefore, that the transliterated texts of both Mt. 27:46 and Mk. 15:34 represent an Aramaic cry and that this has every claim to reproduce closely Jesus' words.

---

[1] A. Guillaume, accepting an original אלי, adduces evidence from 1QIs[a] (45:33, 65:19,22) for the existence of an ancient Semitic first person singular suffix in -iya and theorizes that Jesus could have used this suffix from the Cross ("Eliya"), so explaining the confusion ("Mt. 27:46 in the Light of the Dead Sea Scrolls," PEQ, LXXXIII (1951), 78-80). (But note Braun's objections to Guillaume's hypothesis: -iya could simply be a plene reading, which was not pronounced (Qumran, I, 58)). Scheifler cuts the Gordian knot, holding that the Elijah incident should be taken with what follows, not with the great cry ("El Salmo 22," 53). Lagrange (Marc, 434) and A. B. Bruce ("Synoptic Gospels," 332) attribute the Elijah incident to the maliciousness of the mocking Jews, who deliberately misunderstood the cry. M. Rehm suggests that "Eli" might have existed as a shortened form of Elijah (as other Biblical names, especially when compounded with -el or -yah). But he admits that no evidence exists for the shortened form. ("Eli, Eli lama Sabacthani," BZ, n.s., II (1958), 275-278). Other conjectures are less probable: that the Jews regard Jesus as the messianic High Priest (analogy to Qumran), who is closely linked in legend with Elijah (Gerhard Friedrich, "Beobachtungen zur messianischen Hohepriestererwartung in den Synoptikern," ZTK, LIII (1956), 265-311 -- see criticism by Braun (Qumran, I, 59)); that the bystanders think Jesus calls on the sun (helion -- read in one OL MS), which has just become visible after the three hours of darkness (C. H. Turner, "The Gospel According to St. Mark," A New Commentary on Holy Scripture, ed. by C. Gore, et al. (London: SPCK, 1928), 118).

[2] Lagrange, Marc, 531; H. C. Read, "The Cry of Dereliction," ExpTim, LXVIII (1957), 260.

[3] J. Jeremias, "Ἐλείας," TDNT, II, 931 -- but Mark 15:35 is the oldest reference.

The Greek translation of the cry from the Cross presents a textual difficulty of its own. Several witnesses in Mk. 15:34 read ὠνείδισάς με "reproached me" for the more strongly attested ἐγκατέλιπές με ("abandoned me") and this reading has found support among some scholars. Burkitt, after discovering the reading <u>maledixis</u> in Codex Bobiensis (k) was inclined to favor the reading of D.[1] Harnack links ὠνείδισας with a tradition of the ὀνειδισμὸς τοῦ θεοῦ, common to Hebrews (11:26 and 13:13) and Mark. He suggests that Mark knew the meaning of Σαφθανει but deliberately chose to represent it by ὠνείδισας, thereby lessening the chance that someone might be offended by ἐγκατέλιπες; a method of translation common in the LXX and Targums. Mark's original reading is preserved in only a few Western texts because of assimilation to Matthew, LXX and MT in the rest of the manuscript tradition.[2] Consistent with his advocacy of the Western text in Mk. 15:34, C. H. Turner argues that no one could have invented the reading ὠνείδισάς με so that Mark's Western text must be original, the combined influence of Matthew and LXX being sufficient to change all other authorities to ἐγκατέλιπές με.[3] However, these arguments are not convincing. The ὀνειδισμός motif might well be considered a stimulus for the reading of the Western text.[4] Against Turner, a scribe was more likely to have changed ἐγκατέλιπες to ὠνείδισας than vice versa.[5] The origin of the

---

[1]F. C. Burkitt, "On St. Mark xv. 34 in Cod. Bobiensis," <u>JTS</u>, I (1900), 278-9.

[2]Harnack, "Probleme im Texte," I, 98-102.

[3]C. H. Turner, "St. Mark," 118.

[4]Gundry, <u>Old Testament</u>, 64-5.

[5]Metzger, <u>Textual Commentary</u>, 120; Taylor, <u>Mark</u>, 583; Williams, <u>Alterations</u>, 40. Harnack claims that, had a scribe changed ἐγκατέλιπες to ὠνείδισας in Mark, he would have done so in Matthew as well. But that does not necessarily follow. Different scribes might have been at work, or the reading of Matthew, more popular than Mark, was too well-known to be changed.

reading in D has been explained as due to OT influence[1] or a scribal mistranslation of ζαφθανει,[2] but the difficulty in the idea that God had forsaken His Son is sufficient cause for the textual corruption of D and allies.

The transliterations in both Matthew and Mark are verbally closer to the Targum or the Peshitta[3] than to the MT, but the meaning is the same. In both the Aramaic and the Greek of the gospels (which accurately translates the Aramaic), Matthew and Mark diverge from the LXX in leaving out πρόσχες μοι.[4] Matthew further differs from the LXX (and Mark) in the vocative θεέ (only here in the NT and rare in LXX),[5] but is closer to the LXX with ἱνατί than Mark with εἰς τί.[6] However, Matthew's ἱνατί may be simply a stylistic change and not an assimilation to the LXX.[7]

---

[1] Williams, Alterations, 40. But the OT verses (Ps. 78:12 (LXX) and 88:51f (LXX)) are not sufficiently obvious so as to have motivated a change in the text.

[2] Dalman (Words of Jesus, 43), followed by Lagrange (Marc, 433) and Swete (Mark, 593), supposes that a Syriac speaking scribe recognized in ζαφθανει the Syriac ܫܒܩܢ and translated with ὠνείδισας. Chase (Syro-Latin Text, 107) notes that ܒܙܚ translates ἐμβριμάομαι, ἐπιτιμάω and ἀνακτείν in the Gospels; words similar in meaning to ὀνειδίζω. But, as Chase himself mentions, ܒܙܚ is normally followed by ܒ and ܒܙܚ is nowhere used to translate ὀνειδίζω in the New Testament. (Cf. also Black's general criticisms of Chase's view that D represents a "Syriacized" text (Aramaic Approach, 32-3), although these criticisms may not be strictly applicable in a text such as Mk. 15:34, which preserves the Semitic transliteration (Stendahl, School, 85)).

[3] ܫܒܩܬܢܝ ܐܠܗܝ ܐܠܗܝ.

[4] πρόσχες μοι in LXX may have originated from understanding the second 'אל as "to me" (Gundry, Old Testament, 66).

[5] BDF (par. 147 (3)) note that the nominative is more frequently used for the vocative, even in the LXX.

[6] εἰς τί is "translation Greek" (Black, Aramaic Approach, 123) and properly denotes purpose ("in order to what") rather than cause (Turner, Syntax, 267).

[7] Lagrange, Matthieu, 530; Gundry, Old Testament 66. ἐγκατέλιπες in Matthew and Mark need not be dependent on Ps. 22:1 LXX, for ἐγκαταλίπω is a common LXX word (over 150t.) and is regularly used to translate עזב (129t.).

We conclude that Mt. 27:46 and Mk. 15:34 show dependence on a Semitic original (Targum, Peshitta, or MT), while diverging from the LXX, as would, of course, be expected. Matthew seems to be largely dependent on Mark in the transliteration, while each evangelist gives an ad hoc translation of the cry.

While Mk. 15:34 was accepted by Schmiedel as one of the "foundation pillars," a significant number of scholars have come to question the authenticity of this saying, suggesting that the early community attributed the words to Jesus as a "filling-out" of the wordless cry of Mark 15:37 / Mt. 27:50.[1] The supposition that the early church has put this psalm verse on the lips of Jesus presupposes an interpretation of the verse that would not have been offensive to the Christology of the primitive community (as the traditional understanding of some sort of abandonment presumably would have been). Both these questions are bound up with the meaning and purpose of the quotation of Ps. 22:1. A number of alternatives are possible. The most popular interpretation in recent decades maintains that Jesus either quoted all of Psalm 22 on the Cross, or that the first verse of the psalm acted as a "motto" which evoked all the psalm, including the concluding note of victory and eschatological salvation.[2] Rabbinic sources indicate

---

[1] Loisy, Marc, 467; Nineham, Mark, 428-29; Bultmann, Synoptic Tradition, 273; Klostermann, Markus, 165; Feigel, Der Einfluss, 66-67; Burkill, "Philosophy," 248; Linnemann, Studien, 151-53; Suhl, Alttestamentlichen Zitate, 52; Schweizer, Markus, 203; Johannes Schreiber, Theologie des Vertrauens: Eine redaktionsgeschichtliche Untersuchung des Markusevangeliums (Hamburg: Furche-Verlag, 1967), 26; Francis Wright Beare, The Earliest Records of Jesus (Oxford: Basil Blackwell, 1962), 239; Winter, Trial, 109-110; Schneider, Die Passion, 124; Bartsch, "Historische Erwägungen," 452; Schenk, Passionsbericht, 43. The last three scholars believe the mention of a "loud voice," an apocalyptic sign, was the historical kernel of the cry.

[2] Loren R. Fisher, "Betrayed by Friends: An Expository Study of Psalm 22," Int, XVIII (1964), 20-38; Lagrange, Matthieu, 520; Menzies, Earliest Gospel, 281; Bartlett, Mark, 426; Dalman, Jesus-Jeshua, 206; Lightfoot, History and Interpretation, 159; Fred Smith, "The

that the first verse of a psalm could be used as a title of the whole,[1] but all of these references occur in liturgical settings in which opening verses would easily become titles (as in our hymns). Furthermore, while OT quotations were often made with the context in mind, there is little evidence that a verse could point to its context, while its own meaning was ignored. The abandonment that is clearly enunciated in the first part of the psalm as well as the victorious conclusion must be connoted. As Bonnard says, " . . . Mat. ne cite pas certains passages précis de l'A.T. pour nous inviter à les édulcorer par leur contexte."[2] Therefore, if Jesus quotes Ps. 22:1 contextually, it is reasonable to expect that the first verse has direct reference to his present experience, and that the triumphant conclusion alludes to the circumstances of the Resurrection and its consequences.

In a variation of this general line of interpretation, H. Gese seeks to lay the foundation for the use of Psalm 22 in the primitive Christian eucharist celebration at which time the elements of lament and praise contained in the psalm were employed to evoke and illustrate the sufferings and Resurrection of Christ.[3] While

---

Strangest Word of Jesus," ExpTim, XLIV (1972), 260; Blinzler, Prozess, 188; Stauffer, Jesus, 140-141; Williams, Alterations, 40; Nineham, Mark, 428-29; Johnson, Mark, 256; Loisy, Marc, 467; Ruppert, Jesus als leidende Gerechte, 51.
   L. Paul Trudinger suggests several textual emendations and claims that the note of victory is found within the opening verses of the psalm ("'Eli, Eli, Lama Sabachthani?': A Cry of Dereliction? or Victory?" JETS, XVII (1974), 235-38).

[1]Fisher, "Betrayed," 23-25. [2]Matthieu, 402.

[3]Gese, "Ps. 22," 17. Gese's theory is based on an understanding of Psalm 22 that situates its origin in the life of the cult. The sudden transition from petition to praise (v. 21) is accounted for by supposing a Heilsorakel, a gracious response from God, has been granted to the despairing pray-er in the Temple which brings him to praise God exultantly in a Danklied, perhaps with others in a tôdâh or thanksgiving meal. (On the Heilsorakel, see especially Joachim Begrich, "Das priesterliche Heilsorakel," ZAW, LII (1934), 81-92).

Gese's theory does justice to the undoubtedly eschatological references in the concluding verses of the psalm, it must be challenged at two points. First, the Heilsorakel interpretation of Psalm 22, which is the basis for Gese's theory, is open to serious criticism.[1] Secondly, the gospels offer little evidence for the use of the Danklied part of Psalm 22, nor are there clear indications that Psalm 22 was linked with the eucharist in the early church.[2]

Another popular alternative is to understand the cry as the prayer of a pious man, dying with a familiar psalm verse on his lips.[3] Schweizer adduces Rabbinic evidence for the use of Ps. 22:1 as a prayer of Esther,[4] but the passage is late[5] and is not really apropos to the problem in the gospels, since the prayer is *attributed* to Esther only.[6] As Reumann says, "Actual evidence for such use of Psalm 22 in individual piety is surprisingly sparse . . . ."[7] The argument that the cry was put on the lips of Jesus in order to illustrate the continual fulfillment of Scripture right up to Jesus' death,[8] ignores the question, why *this* verse? As Vincent Taylor properly objects:

---

[1]Cf., *supra*, 27-30.

[2]John H. Reumann, "Psalm 22 at the Cross," Int, XXVIII (1974), 58.

[3]Schenk, Passionsbericht, 71; Schweizer, Markus, 213; W. Blight, "The Cry of Dereliction," ExpTim, LXVIII (1957), 285; Schmid, Mark, 295-96; Weiser, Psalms, 226.

[4]Midrash on Psalm 22; Markus, 203.

[5]Tenth century: cf. Braude, Midrash on Psalms; Str-B, I, 1040.

[6]Reumann, "Psalm 22," 56. [7]Ibid.

[8]" . . . any quotation from the Old Testament for them would have been more suitable in the representation of the dying Jesus than a cry without words." (Winter, Trial, 110). Cf. also Siegfried Schulz, Die Stunde der Botschaft: Einführung in die Theologie der vier Evangelien (2nd ed.; Hamburg and Zürich: Furche-Verlag and Zwingli Verlag, 1970), 137; Suhl, Alttestamentlichen Zitate, 52; Burkill, "Philosophy," 262; Dibelius, From Tradition to Gospel, 193-94 (as probable only).

. . . with the whole Psalm [we might add the whole OT] at their disposal, it is incredible that the primitive communities should have passed by its radiant affirmations and should have selected a verse which proved a rock of offence for later evangelists, copyists and writers.[1]

It is fair to conclude that only an interpretation which takes seriously the sense of abandonment, clearly conveyed by Ps. 22:1, does justice to the meaning of Jesus' cry.[2] The "abandonment" may have consisted only in a *feeling* of abandonment on Jesus' part; the intensity of his sufferings obscured, for a moment, Jesus' consciousness of the Father.[3] However, it seems difficult to understand how Jesus, who had lived in the closest possible fellowship with the Father, could have been unaware whether he had, in fact, been abandoned. The interpretation that does most justice to all the evidence is that which posits some element of genuine disruption in fellowship between Jesus and his Father. While this context does not provide a reason

---

[1] Taylor, Jesus and His Sacrifice, 158-59. If Luke is using Mark, his failure to include the cry might show that he took offence at it. (J. A. Bailey, The Traditions Common to the Gospels of Luke and John, NovTSup, VII (Leiden: Brill, 1963), 80.

[2] Other interpretations may be briefly mentioned: Birger Gerhardsson ("Jesus livré et abandonné," 206-27) attributes the cry to Jesus' testing as one of God's chosen souls (followed by Senior, Passion Narrative, 298). Danker, building on a theory that interprets Jesus' life as one of constant conflict with the demonic, views the cry as evidence of demonic possession ("Demonic"). O. Betz ("Jesu HeiligerKrieg," NovT, II (1957), 116-137) reads the Qumran conception of a "holy war" into Jesus' life. Jesus, like the Qumran community, considered it his task to force God's Kingdom into the world through persecution. Jesus' final cry expresses his disappointment that the Kingdom had not come. However, Jesus' ministry cannot be understood on the analogy of the Qumran sect "holy war." (Cf. Braun, Qumran, I, 59).

[3] The following scholars, while not all agreed in detail, are united in attributing a genuine feeling of distress to Jesus: J. Jeremias, "Gebetsleben," 139; W. J. Kenneally, "'Eli, Eli, Lamma Sabacthani?' (Mt. 27:46)," CBQ, VIII (1946), 128; McNeile, Matthew, 421; Bonnard, Matthieu, 406; Rawlinson, Mark, 236; W. F. Lofthouse, "The Cry of Dereliction," ExpTim, LIII (1942), 192; C. F. D. Moule, The Gospel According to Mark (Cambridge: University Press, 1965), 127; M. Goguel, La vie de Jésus (Paris: Payot, 1932), 525; Taylor, Mark, 594; Gould, Mark, 294; Green, Matthew, 223; Hunter, Work and Words, 120; Benoit, Passion, 194-5; Cadoux, The Historic Mission of Jesus, 259; Gerhardsson, "Jesus livré," 224; Senior, Passion Narrative, 298.

for this abandonment, a comparison with other Scriptures supplies this lack:

> The burden of the world's sin, his complete self-identification with sinners, involved not merely a felt, but a real, abandonment by His Father. It is in the cry of dereliction that the full horror of man's sin stands revealed. But the cry also marks the lowest depth of the hiddenness of the Son of God -- and so the triumphant τετέλεσται of Jn. xix. 30 is, paradoxically, its true interpretation. When this depth had been reached, the victory had been won.[1]

It is not intended that this interpretation should deny the intention of Jesus to evoke the message of all of Psalm 22, but it does insist that the application of the portion actually quoted not be ignored.

The meaning adopted here does not conflict with the meaning of Ps. 22:1 in its context, while the text of the verse has been transliterated (and translated) quite literally. The appropriation technique is, therefore, of the direct type.

John 19:28 (Psalm 69:21)

John introduces this quotation with one of the longest introductory formulas in the NT and the only one which uses the verb τελειόω. This unusual employment of τελειόω, "to bring to an end, to accomplish," which seems to point to more than the simple fulfillment of one OT verse, in addition to the fact that ἵνα clauses are generally subordinated to what precedes, has led some scholars to think that the clause with τελειόω should be construed with ἤδη πάντα τετέλεσται as a broad reference to the accomplishment of the Scriptures through Christ's death.[2] Bampfylde, understanding the

---

[1] Cranfield, Mark, 458-9. Cranfield goes on to stress the theological importance of the fact that the unity of the Trinity was nevertheless unbroken -- the mystery of the atonement. Others who emphasize a real abandonment are: Schlatter, Matthäus, 783; Argyle, Matthew, 215; Richardson, Introduction, 77; Kidner, Psalms, I, 106; Leon Morris, The Cross in the New Testament (Grand Rapids: Eerdmans, 1965), 48; Read, "Cry," 262; Wilkinson, "Last Words," 76; Martin, Mark, 120.

[2] Meyer, Matthew, 352-3; G. Bampfylde, "John xix. 28: A Case

clause structure in this way, supposes that the reference must, therefore, be to a passage which could not be fulfilled until πάντα τετέλεσται (which he interprets as pointing to the death of Jesus). A theme of Johannine theology is that the Spirit cannot be given until Christ has been "lifted up" (ὑψόω -- crucified and exalted) and Bampfylde believes that Jesus' words "I thirst" refer to a spiritual thirst for the Holy Spirit, the OT background being Zech. 14:8 "living waters shall flow out from Jerusalem."[1] Other scholars agree in interpreting the thirst of Jesus as spiritual thirst, supporting their argument by appealing to the Johannine connection between water and the Holy Spirit (Jn. 4, 7:37-39), but interpret Jesus' cry in the light of Ps. 42:2 or 63:2 ("My soul thirsts for God").[2] Beutler notes that διψᾶν in first person singular occurs only twice in LXX, once in Ps. 42:1 (LXX 43:2) and that Ps. 42/3 is a favorite Johannine source for testimonia.[3] Another suggested OT passage is Ps. 22:15: "My tongue cleaves to my jaws."[4]

Before dealing specifically with the problem of the OT reference, the structure of the introductory clause must be determined. The arguments adduced for the connection of ἵνα τελειωθῇ . . . with

---

for a Different Translation," NovT, XI (1969), 247-60; Beutler, "Psalm 42/3," 25.

[1] Bampfylde, "John xix. 28," 247-60.

[2] Tasker, John, 211; Hoskyns-Davey, John, II, 632; Spurrell, "'I Thirst,'" 16: "Now thirst is being suffered on the cross by the giver of living water himself, which in terms of the previous use of the word must mean that he feels himself cut off from the knowledge and the Spirit of God."

[3] Beutler, "Psalm 42/3," 54-56.

[4] Finegan, Überlieferung, 47; Feigel, Der Einfluss, 38; Wellhausen, Johannes, 251; Bousset, Kyrios Christos, 113; Vis, Psalm Quotations, 33.

the preceding clause are not compelling: ἵνα clauses can depend on a following verb,[1] and the construction accords with Johannine usage elsewhere. If the ἵνα clause is understood as an introductory formula, the likelihood is that a single OT passage stands behind Jesus' cry of thirst (γραφή normally denotes a single OT passage in the Fourth Gospel). The suggested OT background passages are not entirely compatible with John's Spirit-water theology, since the psalm verses speak of a thirst for God, while John identifies the Holy Spirit with water. Bampfylde's interpretation rests on the understanding of γραφή as a general scriptural reference, which we have contested, and needlessly imports a symbolic use of the OT into the passage. Ps. 22:15 could only be suggested because the psalm is extensively used in the crucifixion narrative, but the verbal dissimilarity is against the allusion. In view of the use of Ps. 69:21 in Jn. 19:29-30 (ὄξος), the employment of this verse in the crucifixion narrative by the synoptic evangelists, John's fondness for the psalm,[2] and the explicit reference to "thirst" (διψᾶν), Ps. 69:21 should be understood as the γραφή of Jn. 19:28.[3] The explicit quotation (contrast the allusive reference in the synoptics) seems to represent a Johannine tendency (cf. also Jn. 19:23-4),[4] and while the emphasis John accords to the cry could be explained as an anti-docetic polemic,[5] it is more likely that, in conjunction with the use of τελειόω and Jn. 19:30, the cry represents a climactic fulfillment," . . . not the isolated fulfilling of a particular trait

---

[1] Turner, Syntax, 344.

[2] See especially Reim, Hintergrund, 94-5.

[3] Reim, Hintergrund, 94; Barrett, John, 459; Dodd, Historical Tradition, 41; Lindars, Apologetic, 100; Schlatter, Johannes, 351; Thüsing, Erhöhung, 65; Schnackenburg, Johannes, III, 330.

[4] Barrett, John, 459.   [5] Macgregor, John, 348.

in the scriptural picture, but the perfect completion of the whole prophetic image."[1] This interpretation finds added support in the observation that Jn. 19:28 represents the last explicit example of Jesus' <u>active</u> fulfillment of the Scriptures in John's gospel. The Cross, for John, is the climax of God's revelation in history, the scene at once of Jesus' deepest debasement and highest exaltation and the culmination of the ministry of the incarnate Logos. Hence, John seizes on Jesus' cry διψω as representative of the last stage in his OT-illuminated path to glory: "So ist der Durst des Sterbenden und der Durstruf ein Zeichen dafür, da<u>ss</u> die Inkarnation, in die der Wille des Vaters den Sohn hineingegeben hat, bis zur letzten Konsequenz durchgetragen wird."[2]

The very allusive nature of the quotation renders unlikely any suggestion that Jn. 19:28 was created by John under the influence of Psalm 69. That Jesus had said "I thirst" on the Cross is not unlikely, in view of the terrible thirst generally experienced by those suffering crucifixion, though it is apparently John who recognizes a link to Ps. 69:21 and hence preserves the saying. The quotation is indirect as far as its relationship to Ps. 69:21 is concerned, but stays within the general sense of the verse. It introduces as actively fulfilled a stage prior to that which is the focus of the verse in the psalm, and is a typical Johannine addition.

Matthew 27:48 / Mark 15:35-36 /
John 19:28-29; Luke 23:36
(Psalm 69:21)

ὄξος, "vinegar," (Heb. חמץ) is used to characterize the beverage in all four gospels and certainly establishes dependence on

---

[1] Westcott, <u>John</u>, 277. See also Barrett, <u>John</u>, 459; Brown, <u>John</u>, II, 929; Reim, <u>Hintergrund</u>, 49; Lindars, <u>Apologetic</u>, 100.

[2] Thüsing, <u>Erhöhung</u>, 69.

Ps. 69:21 (ὄξος is used 4t. in LXX and only with reference to Ps. 69:21 in the NT). ἐπότισεν in Matthew and Mark may be taken from this verse as well, although it is used elsewhere in Mark (1t.) and Matthew (4t.), in the sense of "give to drink."

The brevity of the allusion, confined probably to the single word ὄξος, does not afford the evidence necessary to determine the textual background, since ὄξος is the natural equivalent of חמץ.

The motive for this offer of drink is difficult to determine, due to the complexity of the parallel passages. Most interpret the offer in Matthew and Mark as a mockery,[1] and Luke explicitly designates it as such, although it is uncertain whether his narrative is parallel to that in Mk. 15:35-6/Mt. 27:48 or in Mk. 15:23/Mt. 27:34. John gives no indication that mockery was involved in the offer of the drink.[2] It is often suggested that the drink was posca,[3] the sour wine favored by the ordinary Roman soldier, and if so, it is difficult to envision a gesture of cruelty here. On the other hand, posca was composed of wine diluted with vinegar, whereas none of the evangelists mentions the wine. Mockery is probably involved in the context, for the bystanders' reference to Elijah is surely meant in jest.[4] While certainty on this point is impossible, it is perhaps more likely that Matthew and Mark intend to describe an act of mockery, John one of compassion. If so, the synoptists have retained the basic meaning

---

[1] Schweizer, Markus, 205; Haenchen, Weg Jesu, 536; Gundry, Old Testament, 204; Alford, Greek New Testament, I, 294; Bruce, "Synoptic Gospels," 332; Klostermann, Markus, 166; Schmid, Mark, 296; Rawlinson, Mark, 237; Lohmeyer, Markus, 346; Meyer, Matthew, 274; Dormeyer, Passion Jesu, 203.

[2] Brown, John, II, 909.

[3] Cf., e.g., H. W. Heidland, "ὄξος," TDNT, V, 288.

[4] The tradition, especially in Mark, is confused, but the details need not be elaborated here. Cf. Taylor, Mark, 594-96.

of Ps. 69:21, while John has shifted this a bit by omitting the mockery context. It is possible that Matthew intends to present a fulfillment of both halves of Ps. 69:21: Mt. 27:34 ($\chi o\lambda\acute{\eta}s$) and 27:48 ($\emph{ὄξος}$).[1]

Luke 23:46 (Psalm 31:5)

The last word from the Cross, probably to be identified with the wordless cry in Mt. 27:50 and Mk. 15:37 (note $\phi\omega\nu\tilde{\eta}\ \mu\epsilon\gamma\acute{\alpha}\lambda\eta$), is a quotation of Ps. 31:5. The citation follows the LXX, except for the change of tense in the verb and the addition of $\pi\acute{\alpha}\tau\epsilon\rho$. The Hebrew imperfect (אפקיד) is the natural tense used to indicate an action in process of accomplishment[2] and can be represented by either Greek present or future. The quotation may, therefore, be dependent on the Hebrew, but influence from the LXX is almost certainly to be seen in the use of $\pi\alpha\rho\alpha\tau\acute{\iota}\theta\eta\mu\iota$ ($\pi\alpha\rho\alpha\tau\acute{\iota}\theta\eta\mu\iota$ is used only twice for פקד in the LXX).[3]

Psalm 31 is another individual lament,[4] though the strong note of thankfulness and praise has led some to categorize it as a thanksgiving.[5] Perhaps this is a case in which the psalm should not be forced into an artificial "form." Although a collective interpretation has been advocated,[6] we are surely to recognize the dilemma of an

---

[1] Brown, John, II, 927; Lindars, Apologetic, 101; Tasker, Matthew, 264.

[2] GKC, par. 107a.

[3] Holtz, Untersuchungen, 58, the variant $\pi\alpha\rho\alpha\theta\acute{\eta}\sigma o\mu\alpha\iota$ may be assimilation to the LXX.

[4] Gunkel, Psalmen, 121; Kraus, Psalmen, 247.

[5] Anderson (Psalms, 246) regards it as a thanksgiving of the individual and Weiser (Psalms, 275) speaks of both lament and thanksgiving.

[6] Eaton, Psalms, 93; Briggs, Psalms, I, 264.

individual, a "righteous sufferer," as the loose structure and emotional language would indicate. The theme of the psalm is similar to that of 22 and 69, but the deliverance and consequent thanksgiving play a more important role and seem to be presupposed throughout the psalm, rather than left as a climactic conclusion. Perhaps the poet wrestles in prayer, alternating between despair and petition on the one hand (vv. 1-2, 9-12), and confidence and praise on the other (vv. 3-8, 19-24). The precise nature of the sufferer's distress is unclear, other than the fact that persecution plays a role. Probably the advocacy of a godly, but unpopular cause lies at the root of his trouble. In the context of the psalm, v. 5 represents a committal of life for preservation, but the absolute trust which characterizes this attitude is the fundamental element, so that a transfer of context to the time of death is natural.¹ The psalm verse was used in later Judaism as an evening prayer,² and is eminently suited as the last words of the dying Saviour whose life, from beginning to end, was lived in a unique relationship to the Father.

It is sometimes asserted that this cry is Luke's own substitution for the "cry of dereliction" in Matthew and Mark.³ While there is much to be said for the view that Luke has chosen to record the quotation of Ps. 31:5 rather than Ps. 22:1 for his own purposes, there is no compelling reason to deny the authenticity of the saying. The use of vocative πάτερ (confined to Jesus' words in the NT), favors the authenticity of the saying.⁴

---

¹Kirkpatrick, Psalms, 157.

²Str-B, I, 269; Haenchen, Weg Jesu, 530; Stauffer, Jesus, 142; Jeremias, "Gebetsleben," 139-40.

³J. Wellhausen, Das Evangelium Lucae (Berlin: Georg Reimer, 1964), 134; Holtz, Untersuchungen, 58; W. Trilling, "Der Tod Jesu, Ende der alten Weltzeit," Christusverkündigung in den synoptischen Evangelien (Munich: Kösel, 1969), 196; Knox, Synoptic Gospels, II, 147; Dibelius, From Tradition to Gospel, 203, n. 4.

⁴Taylor, Jesus and His Sacrifice, 200. As Lindars (Apologetic,

Matthew 27:55a / Mark 15:40a / Luke 23:49
(Psalm 38:11, 88:8)

Many commentators think that Matthew and Mark are influenced in their description of the women "who looked on" by Ps. 38:11 LXX; ἀπὸ μακρόθεν,[1] and that Luke adds an expression taken from Ps. 88:8 (γνωστός).[2] It is difficult to decide if ἀπὸ μακρόθεν is a conscious allusion to Ps. 38:11 (note also the use of ἵστημι in Luke). The psalm is one of the "righteous sufferer" type which has played such a prominent part in the crucifixion narrative. The scene in the gospels is similar to the context in the psalm, in which friends of the sufferer stand "far away" because of his distress. On the other hand, Psalm 38 is never used elsewhere in the NT and ἀπὸ μακρόθεν is used by Mark five times (although one of those, Peter's following Jesus (14:54) may be an allusion to the psalm as well). The same difficulty confronts us in the case of γνωστοί in Lk. 23:49; Psalm 88 is another poem of the righteous sufferer, little used in the NT. However, in this case γνωστοί seems to be something of a "Lukanism;" only he uses it in the sense of "acquaintance" (Lk. 2:44) and 13 of the 16 occurrences of the word are in Luke-Acts. Luke's characterization

---

95) has pointed out, the address may be Luke's own imitation of Jesus' habitual prayer practice, but it must be asked why, in that case, it is not added more often.

[1] Lohmeyer, Markus, 348; Schenk, Passionsbericht, 61; Dodd, Historical Tradition, 126; Fenton, Matthew, 447.

[2] Martin Hengel, "Maria Magdalena und die Frauen als Zeugen," Abraham unser Vater: Juden und Christen im Gespräch über die Bibel (für Otto Michel), ed. by Otto Betz, Martin Hengel and Peter Schmidt (Leiden/Cologne: Brill, 1963), 244, n. 4; Dodd, Historical Tradition, 126; K. Weidel, "Studien," 194; Blinzler, Prozess, 184; Bailey, Traditions, 81; Karnetzki, "Die alttestamentlichen Zitate," 20; Haenchen, Weg Jesu, 537; Rengstorf, Lukas, 273; Creed, Luke, 288; Loisy, Luc, 361; Plummer, Luke, 540; Grundmann, Lukas, 136; Montefiore, The Synoptic Gospels, 1084; Rose, "L'Influence," 320; Trilling, "Der Tod Jesu," 197; Holtzman, Synoptiker, 420.

of the women as γνωστοί may, therefore, simply be a matter of stylistic preference rather than a reminiscence of Ps. 88:8. An allusion to Ps. 38:11 in all three synoptics is more probable. If so, all three evangelists are obviously closely related, although Luke's significant changes (especially the shift of the feminine in Matthew and Mark to the masculine) may indicate that he is not directly dependent on Mark.

John 20:25; Luke 24:39 (Psalm 22:16)

The fact that Jesus' hands (and feet?) were pierced at the time of his crucifixion, mentioned in Jn. 20:25 (27) and implied in Lk. 24:39, must be considered here in relation to Ps. 22:16c. This verse is a well-known crux for, while LXX reads "they pierced (ὤρυξαν) my hands and feet,"[1] MT has the nonsensical "as a lion my hands and feet."[2] A variety of conjectural attempts to restore the "original" Hebrew phrases have been put forward,[3] but the two oldest and best attested readings are those offered by the MT and LXX, respectively, and since the context seems to demand a third person verb, "they pierced" may be preferred.[4] Several scholars feel that

---

[1] Apparently reading כארו for MT'כארי.

[2] כארי. Σ agrees, reading ὡς λέων, not ὡς ζητοῦντες δῆσαι, the reading of the Syro-Hexapla, which was occasioned by an orthographic error. (Cf. Lindars, Apologetic, 92, n. 5; C. Taylor, ed., Hebrew-Greek Cairo Genizah Palimpsests from the Taylor-Schechter Collection (Cambridge: University Press, 1900), Col. IV).

[3] כארו "deformed" -- Duhm, Psalmen, 71; from verb כרה "bind together" -- Kraus, Psalmen, 170; אכרו "bind" -- Oesterley, Psalms, 181, Mowinckel, Psalmenstudien, I, 73-74; from כרו "to dig" -- Dahood, Psalms, I, 141; כיאר "as a Nile" -- J. Magne, "Le texte du psaume xxii et sa restitution sur deux colonnes," Sem, XI (1961), 36; "they bound" -- G. R. Driver, "Mistranslations," ExpTim, LVII (1945-46), 192; MT כאלי, translating "like a hearth" -- W. Emery Barnes, "Two Psalm Notes," JTS, XXXVII (1936), 386.

[4] Lindars, Apologetic, 92, n. 5. A verb is read by Peshitta (ܒܙܥܘ), Targum (נכתין), Vulgate (foderunt) and A' (ἐπέχυναν). (The Targum retains כאריא as well.)

the influence of this verse is responsible for Luke's clear implication that Jesus' feet as well as his hands were pierced, whereas John simply mentions his hands.[1] However, Lk. 24:39 does not explicitly state that Jesus' feet were pierced: it may be that his feet were not pierced, but simply bound, in which case they still would have shown signs of bruising and provided evidence for the corporeality of his body, or the feet may have been pierced and John's tradition simply did not record the fact. At any rate, it is remarkable that Luke, if he is dependent on Ps. 22:16c, does not explicitly refer to the piercing. It is improbable, therefore, that Ps. 22:16c has influenced the tradition. The lack of reference to this verse in the crucifixion narrative calls for comment, inasmuch as the phrase seems to be eminently appropriate in the situation and is found in a context which has served as the most important OT background for the crucifixion. This omission may evidence the integrity of the evangelists in declining to falsify the tradition that Jesus' feet (and hands) had been bound, not pierced,[2] or their reticence in employing a verse whose reading was uncertain.[3] Dibelius draws the implication of this respect for the tradition: "Hence we cannot always, nor at once, reach a verdict about the historicity of a motif by showing it had an Old Testament basis."[4]

---

[1] David Smith, "Crucifixion," 398; Weidel, "Studien," 250-51; Rawlinson, Mark, 233 (?); Rose, "L'influence," 332; J. W. Hewitt, "The Use of Nails in the Crucifixion," HTR, XXV (1932), 44. Scholars disagree as to whether nails were commonly employed in fixing the condemned man's feet to the cross; Hewitt ("Nails," 44) thinks not, Smith ("Crucifixion," 398) implies that it was optional, while Blinzler (Prozess, 190) feels it was normal.

[2] Dibelius, From Tradition to Gospel, 188-9.

[3] Scheifler, "El Salmo 22," 77.

[4] Dibelius, From Tradition to Gospel, 189.

Conclusions

As a basis for the drawing of conclusions, it will be useful, once again, to summarize the evidence of the use of the lament psalms in the form of a table.

TABLE 3

REFERENCES TO THE LAMENT PSALMS
IN THE GOSPEL PASSION TEXTS

Psalm Verse	Matthew	Mark	Luke	John	Citation Technique
6:3	-	-	-	12:27(?)	*Ling[a]
22:1	27:46	15:34	-	-	*Q
22:7a	-	-	23:35a	-	All
22:7b (Lam. 2:15)	27:39	15:29a	-	-	All
22:8	27:43	-	-	-	Q
22:18	27:35a	15:24	·23:34b	-	All
	-	-	-	19:24	EQ
27:2	-	-	-	18:6 (?)	All
27:12	-	14:57-58 (??)	-	-	All
31:5	-	-	23:46	-	*Q
31:13	26:3-4a	-	-	-	All
35:4	-	-	-	18:6 (?)	All

[a]"Ling" refers to "linguistic influence."

TABLE 3 -- Continued

Psalm Verse	Matthew	Mark	Luke	John	Citation Technique
35:11	-	14:57-58 (??)	-	-	All
35:19	-	-	-	15:25 (?)	*EQ
38:11	27:55a	15:40a	23:49	-	All
41:9	-	14:18	-	-	*All
	-	-	-	13:18	*EQ
42:5,11; 43:5; 42:6	26:38	14:34	-	12:27	*Ling
69:4	-	-	-	15:25	*EQ
69:9	-	-	-	2:17	EQ
69:21a	27:34	-	-	-	All
69:21b	27:48	15:35-36	23:36	19:28b-29	All
69:21	-	-	-	19:28a	*EQ

The use of the lament psalms presents a consistent and striking feature with respect to the citation techniques employed. All the synoptic references are introduced as allusions or implicit quotations, while five of John's eight references occur as explicit citations. The use of a form of πληρόω in three of these introductory formulae is a distinctive Johannine feature: no other NT author employs πληρόω to introduce a quotation from the Psalms. The distinction between John and the Synoptics is by no means confined to the use of the lament psalms; John has a general proclivity for quotations at the expense of allusions. As has been suggested before, the reason for this proclivity should be sought in John's purpose and audience. In light of the evident need to indicate explicitly the use of Scripture, his purpose might plausibly be supposed to be apologetic, or else it is the case that his audience could not be presumed to be familiar with the OT passages in question.

While the synoptic evangelists employ similar citation techniques, a clear distinction in emphasis between Matthew and Mark on the one hand, and Luke on the other, can be discovered by means of noting the particular verses utilized. Luke has fewer references (five) than the others, and omits those which most clearly portray the degradation and despair of the suffering Christ (e.g., Pss. 22:1, 7b, 8; 42:5). This phenomenon is in line with the often observed tendency in Luke to portray Jesus as the innocent "benefactor" in the passion events.

That the synoptists are content to draw upon the lament psalms solely by means of allusions and implicit quotations suggests that their accounts, while not without apologetic motive,[1] are written particularly for those within the community who would already have identified these psalms.[2]

In viewing the four accounts together, it is necessary to investigate and, if possible, reconstruct, the process through which the references to the lament psalms have been introduced into the accounts. It is unlikely that the entire set of references is

---

[1] Lindars, naturally, stresses the apologetic motive (Apologetic, 90).

[2] Schweizer, Jesus, 92.

a post-Easter attempt to portray Christ as the "suffering just one"[1] in light of the strong case for authenticity which can be made for the use of Ps. 22:1 by Jesus,[2] but it is frequently asserted that the psalms (22, especially), after being introduced, provided a source from which the early Christians invented certain details. Beare summarizes this process:

> In the earliest stage, particular details, in themselves of minor significance, were preserved in the tradition because men observed how closely they corresponded to passages of the Old Testament which spoke of the sufferings of the upright. In the later stage there is an increasing tendency to add fresh particulars, not because they are found in an existing tradition, but because they can readily be drawn from a passage which has already been interpreted as a prophetic vision of the crucifixion. Psalm 22 affords instances of both, and it is not always possible to determine whether a given detail belongs to the original tradition conveyed by witnesses of the crucifixion or is the product of reflection upon the psalm.[3]

In the present case, however, this progression is unlikely. Only two incidents, narrated as historical, are brought into contact with references to the lament psalms and both (the dividing of the clothes and the offer of a drink) are documented as customary accompaniments to an execution. Jesus' quotations of the psalms are altogether natural in their contexts and the remainder of the references are employed by the evangelists to interpret events which could not have been created solely on the basis of the OT verses in question.

It is most likely that the evangelists, recognizing the sources of several of Jesus' quotations, have turned to these psalms

---

[1] Pace, e.g., Vis, Psalm Quotations, 38-39.

[2] Cf., supra, 271-75.

[3] Beare, Earliest Records, 220, n. 1; Cf. also Lightfoot, History and Interpretation, 158-59; Flessermann von-Leer, "Passionsgeschichte," 92, n. 32.

for illumination of the passion events.[1] In so doing, some incidents were recognized to be directly related to certain verses in the psalms and it is probable that it is for this reason they are preserved in the tradition.[2] On the other hand, the language of the psalms served admirably as a means of lending interpretative "color" to the portrayal of other events. Hence, e.g., the Jews' mockery of Jesus is described with words from Psalm 22. In so doing, the evangelists succeed in casting Jesus into the role of the innocent sufferer of the psalms and his enemies into the role of the impious persecutors.

It is at this point that it is necessary to move a step further back and inquire about the basic approach taken by Jesus and the evangelists in their appropriation of the lament psalms. What was it that "legitimized" this transfer? A very popular alternative has been the hypothesis that a well-defined "righteous sufferer/martyr" concept existed in first century Palestinian Judaism and that this figure provides the bridge between the OT lament psalms and the application to Jesus.

The intertestamental period is the time in which it is asserted that the concept of the Righteous Sufferer was developed and became popular. Such a concept was a not unnatural feature in light of the difficulties which the Jews experienced in these years. Ruppert sketches the course of this development:

> Im Laufe etwa eines Jahrtausends israelitisch-jüdischer Religionsgeschichte ist aus dem von Israels Frommen in

---

[1] For this general view, see: Scheifler, "Salmo 22," 78-82; Lindars, John, 577; France, Jesus, 57; Weiser, Psalms, 226; John Bowman, The Gospel of Mark: The New Christian Jewish Passover Haggadah, SPB, VIII (Leiden: Brill, 1965), 8; Josef Schmid, The Gospel According to Mark, trans. and ed. by Kevin Condon, RNT (Regensburg: Pustet, 1968), 299; McNeile, Matthew, 421; Johnson, Mark, 254.

[2] Cf. Lindars, John, 577.

notvoller Situation immer wieder erfahrenen Skandalon der
passio justi (vgl. die Gebete der Angeklagten) über "Gesetzes" --
Frömmigkeit (Ps. 119; späte Weisheit) und die Armentheologie
der Septuaginta schliesslich in der späten Apokalyptik ein
"Dogma" vom Leiden des Gerechten (passio justi) beziehungsweise
vom Leiden der Gerechten (passio justorum) geworden.[1]

In the pagan-dominated environment of late Judaism, the pious Jew's obedience to and service of God became especially prominent and the "way of the righteous" was characterized above all by humility and the inevitability of suffering (Ecclus. 3:18, Prov. 29:23, especially Wisdom 2-5).[2] The description of this suffering took on certain stereotyped features: the innocence of the one being abused, his devotion to the Torah and his bravery in the face of persecution; his prayers for his tormentors, the converting power of his behavior and his complete trust in Yahweh. It is asserted that this concept was embodied in a popular literary form, the "martyrology" which lies behind several of the stories in II and IV Maccabees.[3] Of further relevance is the contention that positive value was beginning to be attributed to suffering borne in a Godly cause, perhaps as a response to the martyrdoms of Maccabean times (Pss. Sol. 10:2; II Macc. 7:37f; IV Macc. 1:11, 6:28f, 17:20ff; Test. Benj. 3:8; 1QSa 1:3, IQS 5:6, 8:3f, 9:4).[4] The atoning power of suffering was first considered valid for one's own sins, then was extended to one's family and even to all of Israel.[5]

---

[1]Ruppert, Jesus als der leidende Gerechte, 28. Popkes (Christus Traditus, 76-79) has distinguished between the theology of suffering which arose in circles that emphasized the sinfulness of men and suffering as chastisement (i.e., Rabbis), and that which arose in dualistic climates in which suffering was seen as the result of the opposition of the unrighteous (Qumran, Apocalyptic).

[2]Schweizer, Erniedrigung, 22-24.   [3]Surkau, Martyrien, 7-29.

[4]Lohse, Märtyrer, 70-86; Schweizer, Erniedrigung, 24-26; Downing, "Martyrdom," 280-84; Surkau, Martyrien, 58-65.

[5]Schweizer, Erniedrigung, 25.

As a second feature in the conception of the Righteous Sufferer, Schweizer has emphasized the exaltation which follows upon suffering. Numerous passages are adduced which describe the great reward awaiting the righteous. This exaltation, already secretly accomplished on earth, reaches culmination only in the world to come and sometimes takes the form of a bodily ascension, such as in I Macc. 2:58 (describing Elijah's "translation"), Jubilees 4:23, IV Ezra 14:9,49; I Enoch 71:14, 89:52, 90:31; et al. Wisdom 2-5 is an especially clear exposition of the "humiliation and exaltation" of the righteous. This conception of exaltation is essentially distinct from the ideas of glory associated with Messiah, "whose Lordship is merely to be revealed at the end of time," but can be integrated with Son of Man, whose career embodies both humiliation and exaltation.[1]

Thus, there is evidence that a fixed set of associations, comprising a suffering which was of atoning value and followed by a reward conceived of in terms of exaltation, was involved with the Righteous Sufferer conception in pre-Christian Judaism. This concept has been viewed as the most fundamental background for the understanding of Jesus' Passion, for, as Schweizer notes, in relation to Wisdom 2-5: "Der Weg des Gerechte, wie er hier geschildert wird, ist bis in allerlei Einzelheiten hinein der Weg wie ihn Jesus tatsächlich gegangen ist."[2] The frequent verbal citations from the lament psalms

---

[1] Schweizer, Erniedrigung, 26-31; Lordship and Discipleship, SBT, XXVIII (London: SCM, 1960), 26-31 (30). Schweizer's understanding of Son of Man in terms of the humiliation and exaltation schema has already been noted. Cf. also Ruppert's remarks (Jesus als der leidende Gerechte, 71): " . . . da Jesus um seinen Weg als leidender Gerechter wusste, konnte er sich seine Vollendung als Einsetzung zum eschatologischen Menschensohn (in der Weise des Henoch) gedacht haben."

[2] Erniedrigung, 33; "The Son of Man Again," 261; cf. also Ruppert, Jesus als der leidende Gerechte, 58-9; Downing, "Martyrdom," 286-92; Pesch, "Die Passion des Menschensohnes," 190-95 (he attributes the use of the conception to the early church, not to Jesus); Schulz, Die Stunde der Botschaft, 137-8. On the use of the Righteous

in the passion sayings may be taken as evidence for the importance of this conception. Many other suggested allusions to the righteous sufferer/martyr concept in general have been posited,[1] but these need not be investigated in detail, inasmuch as the probability of such references depends almost entirely on the validity of the broad concept.

In assessing the relevance of this reconstructed schema for the passion of Jesus, it is important to differentiate between three different presentations of the righteous sufferer/martyr concept. The first confines itself to pointing out the significance of the lament psalms in the descriptions of Jesus' passion. Inasmuch as references to these psalms are numerous and insofar as a number of characteristics recur in these psalms, it is certainly legitimate to speak of such a concept at this level. Secondly, there is the view that emphasizes the intertestamental development of the theme and attaches great importance to the martyrologies as a background for the passion. The third position goes further and attributes to the righteous sufferer concept the earliest development of the significance of Jesus' sufferings. The salvific interpretation associated with Isaiah 53 is a later development, it is asserted;[2] Jesus' sufferings were first attributed significance

---

Sufferer concept in the NT, see also Dodd, According to the Scriptures, 96-102 and Lindars, Apologetic, 88-110.

[1] Cf., especially Surkau, Martyrien, 84-103. Two specific suggestions might be mentioned. Several scholars (Bultmann, Synoptic Tradition, 282; Dibelius, From Tradition to Gospel, 201-02) believe that the textually uncertain narrative of the "bloody sweat," Lk. 22:43-44, is part of Luke's important "Ur-martyr" theology. However, other OT backgrounds are more likely involved (cf. William J. Larkin, "The Old Testament Background of Luke XXII. 43-44," NTS, XXV (1978-79), 250-54). Pesch discovers a series of allusions to the righteous sufferer psalms in the Son of Man sayings and proposes that the early church has added this motif to Jesus' original Son of Man tradition ("Passion des Menschensohnes," 168-95).

[2] Schweizer, Jesus, 92; Ruppert, Jesus als der leidende Gerechte, 58-59.

because they were eschatological, "a suffering that fulfills all previous suffering."[1] Furthermore, as we have seen, the exaltation of Jesus finds its first and most basic explanation in this concept as well. The righteous sufferer psalms stand at the fountainhead of this concept, since the movement from suffering to exaltation is a consistent feature of these psalms.[2]

With respect to the second form of the theory, it is important to maintain a distinction between the lament psalms of the OT which describe the Righteous Sufferer and the post-canonical development of concepts associated with the martyrs. Some motifs are common to both traditions, and the martyrologies are probably indebted to the psalms for many of their characteristic concepts, but a significant number of features appear in the martyr legends which are lacking in the psalms. Furthermore, precisely those features found only in the post-canonical development receive little or no emphasis in the evangelistic description of the passion, such as the courage of the sufferer (contrast Mk. 14:34-36, 15:34!), the stress on faithfulness to the Torah and the exemplary nature of the sufferings. No clear reference to any of the intertestamental traditions is to be found in the gospels; the parallels to these traditions which have been isolated are almost entirely ideas which are found in the psalms as well. It would be going too far to deny any influence of this late Jewish conception on the passion; especially Luke can be viewed in terms of this development. Yet, there is little to indicate a need to go beyond the psalms themselves for a background to the concepts emphasized in the passion accounts.

---

[1]Schweizer, Jesus, 92; Erniedrigung, 61-2. Williams finds the decisive background for the salvific understanding of Jesus' death in the Greek world, especially in IV Macc. (Jesus' Death, 230-33).

[2]Ruppert, Jesus als der leidende Gerechte, 51.

The attempt to interpret Jesus' Resurrection/exaltation as equivalent to the glorification of the Righteous Sufferer founders at several points. The concept of exaltation associated with the Jewish martyrologies was neither as uniform nor as peculiar to these legends as has been implied. As Perrin pertinently remarks: "True, ancient Judaism expected the suffering righteous to be rewarded -- after all they believed in God! -- but that the concept existed in quite the concrete form Schweizer must assume is questionable."[1] In other words, the fact of Jesus' exaltation need not be specifically related to any particular background, since such a reward had always been regarded in Judaism as the righteous man's lot. From the point of view of the NT material, no evidence exists for the interpretation of Jesus' Resurrection or exaltation in relation to the "Thanksgiving" portion of the lament psalms used to describe Jesus' suffering.[2] This lack is a serious objection to the attempt to apply the whole of these psalms to Jesus' career; in fact, the NT employs only the suffering aspects. Further, Schweizer is compelled to eliminate the Resurrection as the specific form which Jesus expected his exaltation to take since Resurrection is foreign to the Righteous Sufferer legends. It is scarcely legitimate to do this, however, and seems to be an attempt to suit the facts to a theory.[3]

Serious difficulties exist in the view that Jesus' death was originally understood solely in terms of the Righteous Sufferer/martyr concept. The suffering of the martyrs was a totally uninvited consequence of their obedience to the law and faithfulness to God,

---

[1] Norman Perrin, "The Son of Man in the Synoptic Tradition," Modern Pilgrimage, 68. Cf. also the criticism of Ruppert, Jesus als der leidende Gerechte, 31.

[2] In Heb. 2:12, Ps. 22:22 is applied to Christ, but with no reference to his exaltation.

[3] "This looks like viewing the thought of Jesus in the light of early beliefs about him." (Higgins, Son of Man, 206).

but the evangelists strongly emphasize that Jesus' sufferings were of the very essence of his purpose in life.[1] Important distinctions exist between the concept of atonement as it was understood in relation to the martyrs' deaths and in NT soteriology.[2] Thus, the atonement purchased by the martyrs' blood was not of final validity, their deaths were regarded as effecting a gracious response from God, rather than as a result of God's grace, and the law was always presumed as the means to salvation.[3] And note Schweizer's comment: Jesus died

> . . . in physical and spiritual anguish. This exceeds all the expectations of the Old Testament and Judaism concerning the suffering of the "Servant of God." Terrible accounts were written of the deaths of the Maccabean martyrs and later of the prophets, but the dying are depicted as more or less impervious to all torment, going to their deaths praising God and strengthened by Him. The prosaic account of Jesus' death is shocking; it will not fit the pattern of the righteous sufferer and the "Servant of God" as found in Judaism.[4]

Moreover, the atonement wrought by the martyrs was always confined to Israel, because the theory depended on the concept of corporate solidarity, but this is, of course, in direct contrast to Jesus' death, which the NT understands not as a sacrifice valid within corporate Israel but as the means by which a new community is brought into being.[5] Roloff's conclusion is justified:

> Der Versuch, die soteriologische Deutungslinie als direkte Weiterfuhrung allgemeiner jüdischer Sühntodvorstellungen zu

---

[1] W. Manson, *Jesus the Messiah*, 164: " . . . the acceptance by Jesus of death was the price not simply of his fidelity to truth but of his carrying through to the end his task of reconciling the many to God and his conviction of herein serving the will of the Father in Heaven." Cf. also Lohse, Märtyrer, 110; Mauer, "Knecht Gottes," 21-22.

[2] Roloff ("Anfänge," 47), citing E. K. Wengst ("Christologische Formeln und Leiden des Urchristentums," Dissertation, Bonn, 1967) even doubts that the concept of vicarious atonement existed in pre-Christian Palestinian Judaism.

[3] Lohse, Märtyrer, 110, 145, 115.

[4] Jesus, 18.

[5] Lohse, Märtyrer, 104; Roloff, "Anfänge," 48-50.

erklären, muss also fehlgehen, weil er gerade dem zentralen Motiv der christlichen soteriologischen Aussagen nicht gerecht zu werden vermag.¹

Finally, the attempt to interpret Jesus' Passion solely in terms of the humiliation and exaltation of the Righteous Sufferer is inadequate because it fails to account for the uniqueness of Christ's ἐφάπαξ death. The evangelists, convinced that Jesus' death was of eschatological significance and that it was the Messiah who had suffered and died on Calvary, were required to seek OT illumination for this event in areas beyond the general Righteous Sufferer/martyr conception.² That Jesus' own understanding was similarly more specific than this conception as well is to be concluded from his own teaching regarding the soteriological significance of his death and from his unique conception of his destiny.

> Jesus' fundamental understanding of his mission then went far beyond (although it may have included it as a secondary element) the thought of the humiliation and exaltation of the righteous in contemporary Judaism. It was conditioned by a much more profound consideration -- the consciousness of his sonship to the Father, Abba.³

What, then, is the place of the Righteous Sufferer concept in the passion sayings? On the one hand, it is beyond question that the lament portions of the Righteous Sufferer psalms occupy a position of some importance, since they provide the sources for several of Jesus' sayings and for the evangelists' narrations, especially in the Crucifixion pericope. On the other hand, the psalms were inadequate as a final assessment of Jesus' Passion because of the lack of explicit relationship between suffering and benefit for others; a situation not really rectified in the post-canonical development of the concept. That this limitation was widely recognized in the early Church is

---

¹Roloff, "Anfänge," 50. Cf. also Hans-Werner Bartsch, "Die Ideologiekritik des Evangeliums dargestellt an der Leidensgeschichte," EvT, XXXIV (1974), 182.

²Lohse, Märtyrer, 223.   ³Higgins, Son of Man, 208.

apparent in the paucity of references to these psalms in the letters of the NT, where the meaning of Jesus' death is the focal point. It seems to be the case, therefore, that the Righteous Sufferer psalms, particularly 22, 31, 41, and 69, were valued as startlingly appropriate prefigurements of the kind of treatment to which Jesus was subjected in the course of the Passion. The infidelity of a close friend, the devious machinations of enemies, public mockery, physical suffering, perhaps even imagery applicable to a scene of execution, a real sense of the withdrawal of God's presence, yet a trust in Him which remains unshaken despite all, are themes characteristic of these psalms which were eminently suited to the portrayal of the events at Golgotha.

If in first century Palestinian Judaism there did not exist a well-defined and highly developed righteous sufferer/martyr concept which could have served as a link between the lament psalms and the gospels, the question as to the hermeneutical presuppositions which validate the transfer of words from the psalmist(s) to Jesus remains open. The problem is a particularly acute one inasmuch as there is little (some would say nothing) in these psalms which implies a reference to anything outside the experience of the psalmists themselves. While some psalms, especially the "royal" ones (e.g., 2, 110), were interpreted Messianically in late Judaism, the psalms as a collection were distinguished from the prophets and there is little evidence that the lament psalms were understood as containing predictive elements.[1] The Qumran documents attest some references to these psalms, but solely in terms of the writers' identification with

---

[1] Although Hanson points out the "three fold" application (David, Israel, "world to come") accorded to many of the psalms by the rabbis (Studies in Paul's Technique, 170). Note also Acts 2:30, where Peter attributes prophetic status to David in the context of a quotation from Ps. 16 (Cf., especially, on this: Joseph A. Fitzmyer, "David, 'Being therefore a prophet . . . ' (Acts 2:30)," CBQ, XXXIV (1972), 332-39).

the plight of the poets and language from these psalms does not serve to describe the particular eschatological situation of the community.[1]

In light of this, while it is possible to think that the Christians came to view the lament psalms as messianic prophecies,[2] it is more probable that they viewed the relationship as typological.[3] This is suggested by the general interpretation of the Psalms in late Judaism, by the lack of explicit citations in the synoptics and by the concentration on narrative allusions which serve to compare Jesus' way with the way of the psalmist(s). Typology is characterized by a deep identification between situations, a relationship that can clearly be perceived in this case. As Schmidt asserts:

> Nicht in solchen zufälligen Einzelheiten liegt die wahre Gemeinsamkeit zwischen einem alttestamentlichen Wort wie diesem und seiner neutestamentlichen "Erfüllung," sondern vielmehr in der Ähnlichkeit der inneren Lage, des tiefsten Erlebens, aus dem dort und hier der Blick zu Gott erhoben wird.[4]

While there is much to be said for the view that Jesus and the evangelists appropriated the lament psalms on the basis of an underlying typological identification,[5] those who argue that the specificity of the NT appropriation is thereby illegitimately abandoned, have a point.[6] It is especially difficult to fit John's

---

[1] H. D. Lange, "The Relationship between Psalm 22 and the Passion Narrative," *CTM*, XLIII (1972), 613.

[2] Weiser, *Psalms*, 226; Dahl, "Messianic Expectation," 11.

[3] M.-J. Lagrange, "Notes sur le messianisme dans les psaumes," *RB*, II (1905), 53; Kenneally, "'Eli, Eli,'" 128; Lange, "Psalm 22," 620; von Rad, *Theology*, II, 377; France, *Jesus*, 57.

[4] *Psalmen*, 38.

[5] Note the similarities to the apocalyptic and Qumran identifications with OT Israel.

[6] As William J. Larkin stresses, a strict prophecy-fulfillment scheme for the interpretation of these psalms does not do justice to the OT text, while a thorough-going typology obviates the NT fulfillment concept ("Luke's Use of the Old Testament in Luke 22-23"

fulfillment quotations into a purely typological framework. And note should be taken of Peter's explicit statement in Acts 2:31 that David (in Psalm 16) "foresaw" ($\pi\rho o\ddot{\iota}\delta\acute{\omega}\nu$) the Messiah, as indicative of early Christian belief. Several features serve to resolve this difficulty. First, typology, as Goppelt has asserted, is not purely "cyclical," but is construed within an eschatological, forward-looking time line.[1] This allows even a passage without an ostensible prophetic function to take on eschatological significance, as the events through which Israel passes are regarded as typical of those which will characterize the last days. Secondly, it has been argued that the psalms themselves contain elements which imply an eschatological application.[2] Clearer in some than in others, a case can be made for viewing many of the psalms as possessing semi-predictive elements.

A third consideration involves the determination of the specific point of typological identification. It may be that this point of contact is to be found in the general situation of unjust sufferings, or in the figure of the "righteous sufferer" par excellence. Others have suggested a narrower focus, based on the interpretation of the psalms as having a relevance to the Israelite King.[3] But it is probable that the focus can be narrowed even further. It should not be overlooked that David was universally considered to be the author of the psalms in the time of Christ, and that all the lament psalms appropriated in the passion sayings have in their titles "A Psalm of David."[4] Further, the history of David's traitorous adviser, Ahithophel,

---

(unpublished Ph.D. dissertation, University of Durham, 1974), 516). Goppelt hesitates to call this typology for the same reason (Typos, 124). Note also Barrett, "Interpretation of the Old Testament," 410-11.

[1]Cf., supra, 31-2.   [2]Cf., supra, 230.

[3]Mowinkel, He that Cometh, 12; Bentzen, King and Messiah, 35-43.

[4]Pss. 42-43 are no real exceptions, since, as we have argued, they are not directly alluded to.

has perhaps influenced the Judas tradition.[1] Jesus was hailed as "Son of David" early in the Christological development[2] and Davidic motifs are found throughout the gospels.[3] For all these reasons it is probable that the typological point of identification in the lament psalms should be sought in the Christological identification of Jesus with his ancestor, the heir of the promises (II Sam. 7).[4] This, in turn, lends further plausibility to the possibility that the church would have viewed the lament psalms as, to some degree, anticipatory of the sufferings of Christ. David, the recipient of God's promise that his son would inherit an eternal throne, sometimes looks beyond his immediate circumstances to the promised Son.[5] It is the underlying typological identification of Jesus with David that legitimizes the transfer of language from the record of the Israelite King's experiences to the narratives of the sufferings of the "greater Son of David."

---

[1]Cf. on Mt. 27:5, supra, 190 and Gärtner, Iscariot, 30-35.

[2]Cf. Rom. 1:3. See Hahn, Christology, 252-53.

[3]Sherman E. Johnson ("The Davidic-Royal Motif in the Gospels," JBL, LXXXVII (1968), 136-50) provides a useful summary. Mark 12:35ff should not be construed as a rejection of the Son of David concept, but as a re-interpretation of it. (Wilhelm Michaelis, "Die Davidssohnschaft Jesu als historisches und kerygmatisches Problem," Der historische Jesus und der kerygmatische Christus: Beiträge zum Christusverständnis in Forschung und Verkundigung, ed. by Helmut Ristow and Karl Matthiae (2nd ed.; Berlin: Evangelische Verlagsanstalt, 1961), 327; Goppelt, Typos, 98-99).

[4]John R. Donahue, "Temple, Trial and Royal Christology (Mk. 14: 53-65)," The Passion in Mark: Studies in Mark 14-16, ed. by Werner H. Kelber (Philadelphia: Fortress, 1976), 75-77.

[5]That the promise given to David was a living tradition in Palestinian Judaism is evident from the quotation of II Sam. 7:11-14 in 4QFlor.

CHAPTER V

THE USE OF OLD TESTAMENT SACRIFICIAL IMAGERY IN THE GOSPEL PASSION TEXTS

Introduction

In the previous chapters the influence on the passion texts of three important figures, described in delimited portions of the OT, has been investigated. It is necessary in this chapter to evaluate the importance of another kind of OT background, having to do more with general OT influence than with specific passages -- the institution of the Israelite sacrificial system and the imagery associated with it. The Christian church, at a fairly early period, announced the abrogation of the sacrificial system because it had been fulfilled and consummated in Jesus' death and Resurrection. Can this viewpoint be observed in the passion tradition of the gospels? In attempting to answer this question, three areas of investigation present themselves: the Last Supper narratives, Paschal imagery, and the influence of the Isaac tradition.

The Last Supper

The study of sacrificial imagery in the Last Supper narratives can best begin with an investigation of Jesus' words of interpretation. A clear allusion to an OT text occurs in the word over the cup, in the phrase τὸ αἷμά μου τῆς διαθήκης (Mt./Mk.; Lk.: ἡ καινὴ διαθήκη ἐν τῷ αἵματί μου).

$\tilde{\alpha}\hat{\iota}\mu\alpha$ is found in the same phrase with $\delta\iota\alpha\theta\acute{\eta}\kappa\eta$ only in Ex. 24:8 and Zech. 9:11. Of these, the verbal similarity to the cup-word is closer in Ex. 24:8 and the context of the passage (the ratification of the covenant at Sinai) would naturally come to mind. The primacy of Zech. 9:11 as the source of the allusion has not, however, been without advocates.[1] The interpretation found in the Targum, which links the verse with the blood of the passover Lamb, provides a possible correlation with the Last Supper setting.[2] And Zech. 9:11 occurs in a context that has provided several OT references in the passion texts. Lindars argues that Ex. 24:8 cannot be alluded to because such a use of the OT would presuppose a typological exegesis that was not utilized at this early stage of the tradition.[3] This last argument, however, is difficult to accept in view of the widespread use of typology in Qumran and apocalyptic literature, and rests on a reconstruction of early church exegetical practices that is by no means certain.[4] The interesting connection between the blood of the covenant and the blood of the Passover Lamb is made elsewhere and this identification may provide a background for the cup-word without express dependence on Zech. 9:11.[5] Whether Heb. 9:20 is evidence of an independent application of Ex. 24:8 in the early church, or of dependence on the eucharistic word, that citation supports the Exodus 24 derivation.

If the narrative is interpreted as it stands, the connection of "blood" with "covenant" must therefore refer to Ex. 24:8. However,

---

[1] Lindars, Apologetic, 132-33; Goppelt, Typos, 136; Bowman, Gospel of Mark, 270-71.

[2] Dalman, Jesus-Jeshua, 167; Goppelt, Typos, 135.

[3] Apologetic, 133.

[4] France, Jesus, 66; Gundry, Old Testament, 57, n. 1.

[5] Mek. Ex. 12:6. Dalman, Jesus-Jeshua, 167.

attempts have been made to sever this connection and so re-interpret the OT background of the phrase. On the one hand, it is argued that the covenant reference must be original, the sacrificial language being a later interpolation,[1] on the other, that the concept of covenant is a later insertion into a purely sacrificial saying.[2] In the former case, the OT passage referred to would be Jeremiah 31:31ff, in the latter, the general sacrificial system of the Old Covenant, or the atoning death of the servant in Isaiah 53. A variation on the second of these alternatives is to ascribe the covenant language to the influence of the Servant Songs of Isaiah (cf. Is. 42:6, 49:8).[3] However, each of these alternatives lacks any foundation in the texts; in all four accounts, "covenant" and "blood" are closely linked. The covenant is a very subsidiary concept in the Servant Songs and does not appear in contexts which speak of the death of the servant.[4] While the addition of "new" in Lk. 22:20 is almost surely made with

---

[1] Fuller, Mission and Achievement, 73; Johannes Behm, "διαθήκη," TDNT, II, 133; Schürmann, Einsetzungsbericht, 97-99; Otto, Kingdom of God, 291. Arguments for a purely covenantal reference: the importance of the eschatological covenant in inter-testamental Judaism (Behm); the emphasis of the early church on eschatology as opposed to sacrificial concepts; and the "inhaltliche Anspielung" in Luke with regard to the covenant as an earlier citation technique than "der wörtliche Anklang" in Matthew and Mark (Schürmann). It should be noted that the importance of Jeremiah 31 at Qumran can be overdrawn. Betz (Offenbarung, 44-45) notes that the new covenant idea was popular, but downplayed at the same time because it tended to contradict their intense study of the Law.

[2] Lindars, Apologetic, 133; Nineham, Mark, 382-383; Goguel, Life of Jesus, 448; Lohse, Märtyrer, 124; Higgins, Last Supper, 33; Downing, "Jesus and Martyrdom," 286-7.

[3] Fuller, Mission and Achievement, 73; Filson, Matthew, 274; Richardson, Theology, 231; Dalman, Jesus-Jeshua, 169; Pierre Benoit, "The Holy Eucharist," Jesus and the Gospel, I, 103; Lohmeyer, Gottesknecht und Davidssohn, 59; Wolff, Jesaja 53, 65; Stanley, "The Theme of the Servant of Yahweh," 396-97. Most of these scholars would then recognize in "blood" a reference to the death of the servant.

[4] Hooker, Jesus and the Servant, 82.

reference to Jer. 31:31ff, this passage, too, lacks a reference to blood or death.¹ In light of these considerations, therefore, equal weight must be given to both elements in the phrase and the reference confined to Ex. 24:8.

The texts of Matthew and Mark differ from both the LXX and MT in adding μου and in substituting τοῦτο for the interjection (הנה - ἰδού). μου is a change which is essential to the application of the allusion, but the presence of the demonstrative in Targ. and Pesh. raises the possibility of dependence on that textual tradition (cf. Heb. 9:20 as well).² It is possible, however, that τοῦτο in the cup-word is due to assimilation to the form of the saying over the bread and, in any case, τοῦτο should probably not be considered as part of the allusion. τοῦτο in Heb. 9:20 may be present due to familiarity with the words of institution. The textual source of the allusion is impossible to determine, for LXX and MT agree. It is possible, however, that the Targ. has influenced the use of Ex. 24:8 because it has the significant addition "to make atonement."³ Although it had at one time been denied that the phrase τὸ αἷμά μου τῆς διαθήκης could represent a Semitic original,⁴ it has now been conclusively demonstrated that such a construction is possible in Semitic.⁵

---

¹Dormeyer, Passion Jesu, 104-05.

²Gundry, Old Testament, 57-58.

³Le Déaut, "Targumic Literature," 252; Goppelt, Typos, 134-35.

⁴W. Wrede, "Miscellen," ZNW, I (1900), 69-74; Jeremias in the second edition of Eucharistic Words.

⁵J. A. Emerton, "The Aramaic Underlying τὸ αἷμά μου τῆς διαθήκης in Mk XIV. 24," JTS, n.s., VI (1955), 234-240, "τὸ αἷμά μου τῆς διαθήκης : The Evidence of the Syriac Versions," JTS, n.s., XIII (1962), 111-117, "Mark XIV. 24 and the Targum to the Psalter," JTS, n.s., XV (1964), 58-59; Reinhard Deichgräber, "Die Gemeinderegel (1QS) X,4," RevQ, II (1960), 280; J.-E. David, "to haima mou tes diathekes, Mt. 26:28: Un faux problème," Bib, XLVIII (1967), 291-92; Le Déaut, "Targumic Literature," 251. Jeremias has

Luke's version of the cup word presents several differences from the form seen in Matthew and Mark. The awkward expression "my blood of the covenant" is eased by subordinating "my blood" to "covenant" in a prepositional phrase and τοῦτο τὸ ποτήριον is identified with the covenant, which is modified by καινή. By giving καινὴ διαθήκη the place of emphasis, this version seems to stress the New Covenant passage in Jer. 31:31ff at the expense of Ex. 24:8.[1] However, this should not be regarded as a basic modification of the word as recorded in Matthew/Mark, for Luke's differences may be motivated partly by stylistic considerations (τὸ αἷμά μου τῆς διαθήκης is difficult in Greek), perhaps through the intermediary of the Pauline liturgy. While the covenant in Matthew/Mark is not specifically identified as "new," it is idle to deny that the concept is implicitly present in Jesus' claim that a covenant in <u>his</u> blood is about to be ratified.[2] Therefore, while the allusion to Ex. 24:8 is not as conspicuous as in Matthew/Mark, this passage must nevertheless be the basis for the expression, since the idea of death ("blood") is absent from Jer. 31:31-4. The allusion is too brief to allow a determination to be made regarding the textual background.

---

withdrawn his objection in the third edition of <u>Eucharistic Words</u>, (195).

[1] Richardson, <u>Theology</u>, 371; Manson, <u>Luke</u>, 241; Schürmann, <u>Einsetzungsbericht</u>, 97; Lonsdale Ragg, <u>St. Luke</u>, WC (London: Methuen, 1922), 279; Grundmann, <u>Lukas</u>, 398; Hahn, "Alttestamentlichen Motive," 368. R. Newton Flew (<u>Jesus and His Church: A Study of the Idea of the Ecclesia in the New Testament</u> (London: Epworth, 1938), 99-106) particularly emphasizes the role of the new covenant prophecy in the Last Supper accounts.

[2] The following authors refer to Jeremiah 31 in regard to Matthew and Mark: Schniewind, <u>Matthäus</u>, 183; Davies, <u>Paul and Rabbinic Judaism</u>, 251; France, <u>Jesus</u>, 67; Schweizer, <u>Matthew</u>, 491.

Matthew alone adds the words εἰς ἄφεσιν ἁμαρτιῶν as a conclusion to the cup-word. The phrase may be reminiscent of Is. 53:12 ("he bore the sins of many")[1] or Jer. 31:34 ("for I will forgive their iniquity and remember their sins no more").[2] ἄφεσιν appears only here in Matthew (but, see Mk. 1:4), but neither OT verse employs it. Both of these OT passages have played a role in the narrative, Isaiah 53 being alluded to in all three synoptic accounts, and Jeremiah 31 in (at least) Luke. While the phrase need not be based on either OT passage, it is likely that the allusion to Jer. 31:31-4 implied in Mark would have led to the addition of the phrase which characterizes an important element in the New Covenant. Forgiveness is undoubtedly to be understood as a result of the Servant's bearing of sins, but is not as explicit as in Jeremiah 31.

The allusion to the covenant sacrifice through Ex. 24:8 raises the possibility that other sacrificial conceptions are to be found in the Last Supper narratives. Jeremias has argued particularly forcefully for a sacrificial interpretation of Jesus' words over the bread. Claiming that the terms bread/wine form a correlative pair, to be interpreted closely with one another, he believes that the Aramaic underlying σῶμα must have been בשרא, a word which, taken in conjunction with "blood," has clear sacrificial overtones.[3] This

---

[1] Dalman, Jesus-Jeshua, 172; McNeile, Matthew, 283; Lohmeyer-Schmauch, Matthäus, 357; Coppens, Messianisme, 211; Hooker, Servant, 82; Schürmann, Einsetzungsbericht, 6; Lohmeyer, Gottesknecht, 59.

[2] Finegan, Überlieferung, 10; Markus Barth, Was Christ's Death a Sacrifice? SJT Occasional Papers, IX (Edinburgh and London: Oliver and Boyd, 1961), 42; Gundry, Old Testament, 58; Schürmann, Einsetzungsbericht, 6; Fenton, Matthew, 418; Green, Matthew, 213; Tasker, Matthew, 246.

[3] Eucharistic Words, 198-201, 221-2. Cf. also Joseph Bonsirven, "Hoc est corpus meum: Recherches sur l'original araméen," Bib, XXIX (1948), 218-19; Taylor, Mark, 544; A. G. Hebert, The Throne of David: A Study of the Fulfillment of the Old Testament in Jesus Christ and His Church (London: Faber and Faber, 1941), 190.

interpretation may find support in the rendering of Jesus' saying over the bread in Luke (longer text) and Paul, which includes the concept "[given] for you" (ὑπέρ). However, it cannot be established with certainty that this phrase was originally associated with the bread-word, and Jeremias' attempt to trace σῶμα back to בשרא has been generally rejected, in favor of Dalman's suggestion, גלפא.[1] In conjunction with this, it is claimed that the close association of the bread and wine word is difficult to maintain in view of the fact that they must have been separated by a certain amount of time in the context of the meal.[2] In reply to this criticism, Jeremias has stressed the fact that these statements act as a summary for Jesus' certainly more extensive teaching in the course of the Passover Haggadah, and that they are obviously closely related in the existing traditions.[3] The interpretation of these two <u>sayings</u> as a pair is probably therefore justified, although Jeremias' attempt to associate so closely the two <u>words</u> σῶμα and αἷμα must be rejected.

On the other hand, if גלפא is accepted as the word underlying σῶμα, it is illegitimate simply to translate "myself;"[4] the consistent translation σῶμα clearly shows that Jesus refers to his <u>body</u>, in the corporeal sense.[5] This leaves open the possibility that Jesus may have intended to characterize his broken body as a sacrifice. The attractiveness of this interpretation is enhanced by

---

[1] Dalman, Jesus-Jeshua, 111-13; Karl Georg Kuhn, "Die Abendmahlsworte," TLZ, LXXV (1950), 406; Kummel, Promise and Fulfillment, 119; Cranfield, Mark, 426; Lohse, Märtyrer, 125.

[2] Kuhn, "Abendmahlsworte," 406.

[3] Eucharistic Words, 200; cf. Fuller, Mission and Achievement, 75; Benoit, "Serviteur," 131.

[4] As do Dalman, Jesus-Jeshua, 111-13; Johannes Betz," "Die Eucharistie als sakramentale Gegenwart des Heilsereignisses 'Jesu' nach dem ältesten Abendmahlsberichte," Geist und Leben, XXXIII (1960), 171; Haenchen, Weg Jesu, 485; Cranfield, Mark, 426; Anderson, Mark, 313; Roloff, "Anfänge," 63.

[5] Taylor, Mark, 544.

the recognition that representative significance was accorded to the Passover loaf, to which Jesus compares his body: as the pious Jew partook of the bread, he was to consider himself as though he personally had been delivered from Egypt (cf. Dt. 16:3). As the passover sacrifice was effective in achieving deliverance from Egypt, so Jesus' death will be effective in a new deliverance.[1] However, these arguments are not conclusive, especially if the shorter form of the saying in Mark and Matthew is considered closest to the original. An understanding of Jesus' words in terms of a sacrifice remains a very real possibility, but the strongest evidence for the presence of sacrificial concepts in the Last Supper lies elsewhere.

In contrast to the bread-word, Jesus' interpretation of the wine is generally accorded sacrificial significance. Several aspects of the saying point to this conclusion. First, Jesus' explicit connection of his blood with the blood of the sacrifice by which the Sinai covenant was ratified (Ex. 24:8) unmistakably points to the sacrificial character of his death.[2] Lohse, though he regards the covenant concept as secondary, points this out clearly: "In dem nun die Bundesschliessung in Jesu Tod begründet wird, muss dieser als das Opfer verstanden werden das den Bund in Kraft setzt."[3]

A second indication that the cup-word associates Jesus' death with a sacrifice may be observed in the use of the word "blood." Crucifixion was a relatively bloodless form of execution, and it is probable that the early description of Jesus' death with the term "blood of Christ" was due to the concept of sacrificial death which

---

[1] Martin, Mark, 199.

[2] McNeile, Matthew, 382; W. Manson, Jesus the Messiah, 145; Schmid, Mark, 258; Goppelt, Typos, 134-35.

[3] Lohse, Märtyrer, 126.

was associated with it.[1] The concept of the "pouring out" of blood is especially sacrificial in its connotations (cf. Lev. 1ff, 16).[2] While it is unwarranted to attach too much significance to a single phrase, the fact that Jesus spoke of his death as blood poured out fits in admirably with a sacrificial interpretation.

A third contributing factor to this sacrificial atmosphere may be present in the allusion to Is. 53:12. The characterization of the Servant in Isaiah 53 as a "guilt offering" (אשם -- v. 10) and as one who "poured out his soul" and "bore the sins of many" quite clearly indicates that his death was conceived of as sacrificial in nature.[3] While it may be that the Jews believed atonement could be wrought apart from sacrifice,[4] this was not normative and it is difficult to evade the clear cultic elements in Isaiah 53.[5] Jesus' comparison of his blood with the shed blood of the Servant therefore associates his death with the sacrificial death of the Servant. The fact that Matthew relates the significance of the poured out blood for "the many" with the preposition περί may be due to the association of the word with Septuagintal sacrificial language,[6] but this is not certain.

---

[1]Blood in the NT signifies not life, but death (Leon Morris, "The Biblical Use of the Term 'Blood,'" JTS, n.s., III (1952), 216-27; VI (1955), 77-82; Behm, "αἷμα," TDNT, I, 173-4), and particularly sacrificial death (cf. Davies, Paul, 234-6 (for Paul); Ladd, Theology, 426). Pace, e.g., L. Dewar, "The Biblical Use of the Term 'Blood,'" JTS, n.s., IV (1953), 204-08.

[2]M. Barth, Christ's Death, 42; Hebert, Throne of David, 188.

[3]M. Barth, Christ's Death, 9, n. 1; Ladd, Theology, 188-9. See especially BDB on אשם (80): "The Messianic servant offers himself as an אשם in compensation for the sins of the people, interposing for them as their substitute . . . ."

[4]Hahn, Titles of Jesus, 59; Kuhn, "Abendmahlsworte," 466.

[5]Pace Hahn, "Alttestamentlichen Motive," 360-1.

[6]περὶ ἁμαρτίας = חטאת, "sin offering." McNeile, Matthew, 382; Lohmeyer-Schmauch, Matthäus, 356-57.

Finally, the fact that Jesus identified himself with the broken bread and wine and then gave these elements to his disciples to eat and drink forcefully reminds one of the procedure prescribed for OT sacrificial meals (which would be self-evident if it were certain that Passover was regarded as a sacrificial meal in Jesus' day).[1]

Therefore, there can be little question that the words of institution, as they have been preserved in the gospel eucharistic accounts, explicitly associate Jesus' death with a sacrifice. As Aalen summarizes,

> Wenn Jesus dabei von seinem Tode spricht und in Zusammenhang damit von seinem Fleisch und seinem Blut und dazu noch vom Essen und Trinken, und wenn das alles im Rahmen einer Opfermahlzeit geschieht, dann liess das für die Jünger keine andere Sinngebung zu als die, dass er von seinem Tod als Opfertod und von einer Aneignung dieses Opfers durch ein Opfermahl sprach.[2]

Specifically, two types of sacrifice seem to be referred to in the Last Supper accounts: the covenant sacrifice and the expiatory sacrifice (comprising the אשם and the חטאת).[3] The latter is

---

[1] Aalen appeals to the Beraka of R. Aquiba in support of his contention that the Passover was regarded as a sacrificial meal before the destruction of the Temple. ("Abendmahl," 148).

[2] "Abendmahl," 148. Cf. also Bernard Cooke, "Synoptic Presentation of the Eucharist as Covenant Sacrifice," TS, XXI (1960), 27-38. The words of Richardson are worth repeating in this context: ". . . it cannot seriously be denied that the Fathers of the ancient Church understood the apostolic tradition of the Eucharist in this way [as a sacrifice]. The burden of proving that their unanimous interpretation of the scriptural evidence was wrong rests upon those who would deny any form of doctrine of Eucharistic sacrifice." (Theology, 380-1).

For further support of the sacrificial interpretation, he claims that the remembrance formula is characteristic of sacrificial contexts in OT (Theology, 369). Jeremias' interpretation of the remembrance formula in the Last Supper ("that God might remember me" -- Eucharistic Words, 237-55), is probably to be rejected (See especially Hans Kosmala ("Das tut zu meinem Gedächtnis," NovT, IV (1960), 81-94) and Douglas Jones ("ἀνάμνησις in the LXX and the Interpretation of I Cor. XI. 25," JTS, n.s., VI (1955), 183-91)).

[3] On the "expiatory" sacrifices, cf. de Vaux, Ancient Israel, 418-421; Walther Eichrodt, Theology of the Old Testament, trans. by J. A. Baker (2 vols.; 6th ed.; Philadelphia: Westminster, 1961-1967), I,

certainly not as prominent as the former, but the phrase εἰς ἄφεσιν ἁμαρτιῶν in Matthew is probably to be related to this type of sacrifice.[1] The expiatory sacrifices were, of course, repeatable and provided the means of restoring a relationship with Yahweh within the covenant which had been disturbed because of sin. In contrast, the covenant sacrifice (Ex. 24:8) is a unique and foundational event, implying perhaps the taking away of sin as a necessary prelude to a relationship between man and God, but emphasizing more strongly the establishment of fellowship. It has been pointed out that the narrative in Exodus 24 is the only sacrificial ritual recorded in the OT in which the blood was sprinkled on the people, signifying "eine direkte und reale Gemeinschaft mit dem bundesstiftenden Altargeschehen."[2] Furthermore, Jewish tradition ascribed atoning significance to this blood.[3] It is not, therefore, with an ordinary sacrifice that Jesus connects his death, but with a unique atoning sacrifice that emphasizes the intimate involvement of those who participate.

Paschal Imagery

It would not be surprising if Jesus and the evangelists appealed to the Passover traditions in their explication of Jesus' passion, inasmuch as this tradition was supremely influential in Jewish theology and often regarded as a prefigurement of the eschaton.

158-62. Of importance to our conclusions is de Vaux's comment (with reference to the חטאת): "The blood played a more important part in this sacrifice than in any other." (419).

[1] Stanislas Lyonnet and Léopold Sabourin, Sin, Redemption and Sacrifice: A Biblical and Patristic Study, AnBib, XLVIII (Rome: Biblical Institute Press, 1970), 181.

[2] Aalen, "Abendmahl," 149.

[3] Targ. Onkelos on Ex. 24:8; cf. Str-B, I, 991; Dalman, Jesus-Jeshua, 166, Nineham, Mark, 358; Goppelt, Typos, 135.

As Le Deaut says: "La Paque est apparue comme un centre d'attraction dans la pensee religieuse d'Israël: elle a attire a elle les thèmes des origines . . . et ceux de l'eschatologie messianique . . . ."[1] Since it is in John's Gospel that references to the Passover are most clearly found, it will be in order to begin with his material.

John 1:29 (36)

While the characterization of Jesus as the "Lamb of God" by John the Baptist may seem to offer conclusive evidence of a tradition in which Jesus is related to the Passover Lamb, the number of suggested derivations renders the conclusion uncertain. Four of the possibilities deserve mention: the Messianic horned ram of Jewish apocalyptic,[2] the paschal lamb,[3] the Servant of Isaiah, who suffers like a "lamb led to the slaughter" (53:7),[4] and the sacrifice of

---

[1] La nuit Pascale, 374. Cf. also Davies, Sermon on the Mount, 113-15.

[2] Especially Dodd, Interpretation, 233-36.

[3] Barrett, John, 147; Schweizer, Erniedrigung, 117; Lohse, Märtyrer, 144-45; Hooker, Servant, 104.

[4] "Who takes away the sin of the world" could then be derived from Is. 53:11-12. Reim, Hintergrund, 178-9; Taylor, Jesus and His Sacrifice, 227; Barth, Christ's Death, 39; Stanley, "Servant," 403. It is sometimes suggested that $\dot{\alpha}\mu\nu\dot{o}s$ may be a mistranslation of Aram. טליא, which can mean "lamb" or "servant." In that case, John the Baptist explicitly announced Jesus as the Servant. (C. J. Ball, "Had the Fourth Gospel an Aramaic Archetype," ExpTim, XXI (1909-10), 91-3; Burney, Aramaic Origins, 105-8; Zimmerli-Jeremias, Servant, 83-4; Wolff, Jesaja 53, 81-2; Cullmann, Christology, 71). Dodd (Interpretation, 235; cf. Hooker, Servant, 104) has contested this interpretation, questioning whether John the Baptist would have used טליא as equivalent to עבד and pointing out that $\dot{\alpha}\mu\nu\dot{o}s$ never translates טלה in the OT. Jeremias partially rebuts these objections ("Ἀμνὸς τοῦ θεοῦ -- παῖς θεοῦ," ZNW, XXXIV (1935), 115-23), but the general mistranslation process must still be treated with scepticism.
Gärtner suggests a link between טליא and עבד through Tg. Ps. 118:22-28, where, it is claimed, both are used interchangeably of the Messiah ("טליא als Messiasbezeichnung," 100-104).
It is most improbable that the Lamb of God and the "Word" of Jn. 1:1-18 are combined here through the double meaning of the root אמר. (pace Athanase Negoïtsa and Constantin Daniel, "L'Agneau de Dieu et le Verbe de Dieu (Ad. Jo. i.29 et. 36)," NovT, XIII (1971), 30-34).

Isaac.[1] Complicating the situation are the possible two levels of meaning present, John the Baptist perhaps intending one idea, John the Evangelist another. Thus, it is frequently suggested that John the Baptist referred only to the Servant, or the Messianic figure, while John the Evangelist has added paschal allusions.[2]

Of these alternatives, it is probable that the first and the fourth can be omitted from consideration. $\dot{α}μνός$ would not be the most likely term chosen to connote the Messianic tradition to which Dodd makes reference, nor is his suggestion able to account adequately for the qualifying phrase $\dot{o}$ $α\dot{ι}ρων$ $τ\dot{η}ν$ $\dot{α}μαρτίαν$ $τοῦ$ $κόσμου$.[3] Again, $\dot{α}μνός$ does not naturally allude to the Isaac tradition, which, in any case, is not well-attested in the NT.[4] A decision between the final two alternatives, the Paschal Lamb and the Servant, is difficult, but perhaps it need not be made. At least in the narrative as it stands, it is not unlikely that allusions to both figures are present.[5] This dual reference is in keeping with John's penchant for double meanings and is the easiest way of explaining both the title and the qualifying phrase.

To what extent these associations should be attributed to John the Baptist is another question. That the Baptist could have addressed a messianic figure in language influenced by the Servant Songs seems

---

[1] Vermes, Scripture and Tradition, 93-94; Le Déaut, "Targumic literature," 270-71; Glasson, Moses, 100.

[2] See, e.g., Feliks Gryglewicz, "Das Lamm Gottes," NTS, XIII (1966-67), 146.

[3] See C. K. Barrett, "The Lamb of God," NTS, I (1954-55), 210.

[4] Cf., infra, 325-28.

[5] J. K. Howard, "Passover and Eucharist in the Fourth Gospel," SJT, XX (1967), 332; Le Déaut, La nuit pascale, 330; Braun, Jean le Théologien, III, 86; Brown, John, II, 953; Schnackenburg, Johannes, I, 288.

clear in view of the evidence from Qumran;[1] the Paschal reference would seem more unusual, although it cannot be said to be impossible. In any case, the reference is a conceptual one, and, as such, the question of appropriation technique does not really enter into the discussion.

John 19:36
(Exodus 12:46 / Numbers 9:12 /
Exodus 12:10 LXX; Psalm 34:20)

John regards the fact that Jesus' legs were not broken, as were those of the two other criminals, as a fulfillment (ἵνα ἡ γραφὴ πληρωθῇ [2]) of Scripture, but which Scripture was meant is a matter of controversy. The Pentateuchal regulations concerning the Paschal Lamb found in Ex. 12:46 and Num. 9:12 (cf. also LXX Ex. 12:10) are usually considered to be the primary source of the quotation,[3] but a significant number of scholars feel that Ps. 34:20 is the major source,[4] while others suppose that a combination of the two forms the background.[5] The passive verb in John may be a reflection

---

[1] Robinson, "Baptism of John," 189; E. W. Burrows, "Did John the Baptist call Jesus 'the Lamb of God'?" ExpTim, LXXXV (1974), 245-59.

[2] This introductory phrase is used only by John in the NT; cf. also 13:18 and 19:24.

[3] Reim, Hintergrund, 52; Beasley-Murray, Baptism, 225; Bruce, Old Testament Themes, 110; Lyonnet-Sabourin, Sin, Redemption and Sacrifice, 262; Freed, Old Testament, 113; Delling, Der Kreuzestod Jesu, 101-102; Cullmann, Christology, 72; Gryglewicz, "Lamm Gottes," 144; Sperber, New Testament and Septuagint, 199; Alford, Greek Testament, I, 896; Godet, John, III, 278; Schenk, Passionsbericht, 137; Loisy, Quatrième Évangile, 494; Strachan, John, 323; Bernard, John, II, 651; Lagrange, Jean, 501; Barrett, John, 464.

[4] Dodd, Historical Tradition, 43; Haenchen, Weg Jesu, 543; C. C. Torrey, Our Translated Gospels (London: Hodder and Stoughton, n.d.), 47; Forestall, The Word of the Cross; 90; Fortna, Gospel of Signs, 131; Bernhard Weiss, Das Johannes-Evangelium (Göttingen: Vandenhoeck & Ruprecht, 1902), 513.

[5] Brown, John, II, 953; Hoskyns-Davey, John, II, 634-635; Stanley, "Servant," 404; Le Déaut, La nuit pascale, 330; Braun,

of the LXX of Ps. 34:20, but in all other respects John's quotation is closer to the Exodus or Numbers passages: singular ὀστοῦν, singular αὐτοῦ, and the word order. With the third person plural, John is closer to Num. 9:12 than to Ex. 12:46 (or LXX 12:10). Changes in person, however, are frequent in the application of OT texts to NT situations,[1] so that need not indicate that the Numbers passage is to be preferred over Ex. 12:46. While the reading of LXX^A, with the passive verb, must be suspected of assimilation to the NT, the change in the voice of the verb is not unusual in quotations and may have been introduced to emphasize the person of Christ. With respect to the context, the Pentateuch passages again are to be preferred. Dodd points out that the psalms of the righteous sufferer are frequently used in the Passion Narrative, while the Pentateuch is never employed, so that Ps. 34:20 should be regarded as the scriptural reference.[2] Yet, John indicates that Jesus was <u>dead</u> when his legs were spared mutilation, while the psalm speaks of the preservation of life.[3] Ex. 12:46 or Num. 9:12 should, therefore, be regarded as the passages to which John refers in 19:36, although secondary influence from Ps. 34:20 cannot be excluded.

Jean le Théologien, I, 20; Sanders-Mastin, John, 413; Lightfoot, John, 327. It is sometimes felt that the mixed citation is present because John has "adjusted" an original quotation of Ps. 34:20 to the Paschal Lamb contexts -- Meeks, The Prophet-King, 77, n. 2; Schnackenburg, Johannes, III, 342; Lindars, Apologetic, 96; Schweizer, Jesus, 10.

[1] As also at Qumran (cf., supra, 40-43).

[2] Historical Tradition, 93.

[3] H. A. W. Meyer, The Gospel of John, trans. by William P. Dickson and Frederick Crombie, CECNT (2 vols.; Edinburgh: T & T Clark, 1875), II, 362; Godet, John, III, 278. Dodd seeks to get over this difficulty by recourse to a rabbinic tradition that connects the intact bones of the sufferer with the preservation of the body for resurrection. However, the tradition is probably post-Christian and John utilizes this verse with reference to Jesus' death, not the Resurrection. (Rothfuchs, Erfüllungszitate, 162).

It is probable that the textual background is the MT: συντρίβω is the normal rendering of שבר and John's αὐτοῦ could be a free translation of בו whereas all three Pentateuch verses have ἀπ' αὐτοῦ.[1] While the textual changes are relatively minor, the application of the words undergoes a transformation. That which was a stipulation for the proper preparation of the Paschal sacrifice becomes an interpretative "testimony" on the course of events at the Crucifixion. At the same time, the essential meaning of the verse(s) is retained: the legs of the sacrificial victim whose death is to be efficacious, must not be broken.

The Crurifragium was a customary procedure in the crucifixion of criminals[2] and it is much more likely that John (especially in view of Jn. 19:35) depends on a genuine reminiscence in his use of the scriptural passage than that he invents the incident to suit the testimony;[3] had he wanted to picture Jesus as the Paschal Lamb, he could have invented a more direct and suitable circumstance.

John 19:29; 19:14

Two other details in John's passion narrative are said to reinforce the paschal imagery. John's curious reference to ὑσσώπῳ, "hyssop," in 19:29 (Matthew/Mark -- καλάμῳ) may be an attempt to evoke the picture of the passover ritual, in which hyssop was employed (Ex. 12:22).[4] The plant hyssop is said to be inappropriate for the

---

[1] Reim, Hintergrund, 52.   [2] Brown, John, III, 934.

[3] It is unnecessary to suppose that John assumed Jesus' legs were not broken because of the intactness of Jesus' Resurrection Body (against Lindars, Apologetic, 96).

[4] Lyonnet-Sabourin, Sin, Redemption and Sacrifice, 263; Barrett, John, 460; Loisy, Quatrième Évangile, 489; Sanders-Mastin, John, 409; Macgregor, John, 348; Lightfoot, John, 317; Lindars, Apologetic, 101; Brown, John, II, 930; Jeremias, Eucharistic Words, 82.

extension of a sponge to the mouth of Jesus, lending support to the belief that John's ὑσσώπῳ must be an unhistorical addition, motivated by the desire to equate Jesus' death with the sacrifice of the Paschal Lamb. While it has been proposed that ὑσσώπῳ is a textual corruption of ὑσσῷ, "spear,"[1] due to dittography, ὑσσῷ is found only in the 11th century cursive 476 and ὑσσώπῳ should be preferred as the lectio difficilior.[2] The existence of a Passover Lamb typology in John is disputed, but even should such a typology exist, the reference to hyssop seems too allusive to have evoked images of the Passover ritual. In the light of the uncertain identity of the plant in question,[3] we should not, too hastily, conclude that John's narrative has been influenced by the Exodus passage.

The second detail concerns the specific time reference in Jn. 19:14. The "sixth hour" (presumably noon[4]), was the time at which the slaughter of the paschal lambs was begun on the "day of preparation,"[5] and the addition of this detail (which ostensibly

---

[1] Bernard, John, II, 640; Dalman, Jesus-Jeshua, 208; Bultmann, John, 674; Hoskyns-Davey, John, II, 632; Fortna, The Gospel of Signs, 130; Dodd, Historical Tradition, 124.

[2] Lindars, Apologetic, 100. ὑσσῷ may have been substituted by a harmonizing scribe (Brown, John, II, 909). ὑσσῷ is also difficult because it translates Lat. pilium -- a lance used only by legionnaires who were not stationed in Palestine until A.D. 66 (Tasker, John, 216). However, John, writing in the late first or early second century, may not have known that.

[3] Hyssop has been identified with over eighteen different plants -- Wilkinson, "Words," 77. Cf. also Bernhard Weiss, Das Marcusevangelium und seine Synoptischen Parallelen (Berlin: Wilhelm Hertz, 1872), 509; G. E. Post, "Hyssop," A Dictionary of the Bible, ed. by J. Hastings (Edinburgh: T & T Clark, 1899), II, 442; Morris, John, 814.

[4] It is improbable that John followed the "Roman" reckoning, whereby the day began at midnight (pace Westcott, John, 282; cf. J. Edgar Bruns, "The Use of Time in the Fourth Gospel," NTS, XIII (1966-67), 285-90).

[5] Which in John, it is argued, refers to the "day before Passover." Cf., infra, 322, n. 1.

conflicts with Mk. 15:25[1]), is claimed to be part of John's attempt to portray Christ as the Passover Lamb.[2] While this interpretation is possible, it must remain hypothetical in view of the fact that John does not append the time notice to the crucifixion specifically, as one would expect had he the Paschal parallel in mind.

The Date of the Crucifixion

Just as the minor chronological discrepancy between Mark and John with respect to the time of the crucifixion has possible implications for the paschal imagery, so has the major difficulty with respect to the <u>date</u> of Jesus' crucifixion. The problem is important for its significance in establishing the general framework of the Last Supper meal and because it is claimed that John has altered the chronology in the interest of his Passover Lamb typology. The complexity of the issue and the immense literature which has grown up around the question necessitate a summary and generalizing treatment here.

The Synoptic evangelists depict the Last Supper as a Passover Meal. This is evident from explicit claims within the narrative[3] and can be observed in certain characteristics of the meal itself.[4] Nevertheless, the prevailing trend in modern scholarship is to deny

---

[1] The discrepancy could have arisen as a result of reading Γ (3) as Ϝ (6) (Barrett, <u>John</u>, 454).

[2] Cf., e.g., Barrett, <u>John</u>, 454; Brown, <u>John</u>, II, 895-96. Bonsirven ("Hora Talmudica: La notation chronologique de Jean 19,4 aurait- elle un sens symbolique?" <u>Bib</u>, XXXIII (1952), 515) suggests that the time notice serves to characterize Jesus as the Unleavened Bread, complementing the Paschal Lamb depiction.

[3] Mark 14:12, 13-17 and parallels; Luke 22:15, in which τοῦτο must refer to the passover lamb (C. K. Barrett, "Luke xxii. 15. To eat the Passover," <u>JTS</u>, n.s., IX (1958), 305-307).

[4] See especially Jeremias, <u>Eucharistic Words</u>, 41-62.

that the Last Supper was a Passover Meal. Certain features within the synoptic Passion tradition that appear to be incompatible with the chronology that fixes the Last Supper on the Passover are pointed out.[1] Corresponding with an enhanced respect for the historical trustworthiness of the Fourth Gospel, the previous consensus that John had changed the dating to suit his Passover Lamb typology has given way to a suspicion that the synoptic evangelists, or an early tradition, have added certain statements in order to establish the Paschal character of the Last Supper.[2] Attempts have been made to vindicate the accuracy of both chronologies by seeking to demonstrate that Passover was celebrated on two different days in the year of Jesus' death, either because of a disagreement between the Pharisees and the Sadducees over the legal stipulations involved[3] or, because

---

[1] Much of the activity which, according to the synoptics, takes place on Thursday evening-Friday seems to be in violation of the Sabbath laws in effect on Passover, and the eating of ἄρτος during the meal is in violation of the rule that unleavened bread was to be eaten at the Passover. Furthermore, it is maintained that the arrest of Jesus on Passover night would contradict the authorities' explicit intention not to arrest Jesus during the Feast, as seen in Mk. 14:2.

[2] John seems to situate the crucifixion on the day before the Passover: 13:1 "before the feast of the Passover" begins the section in which John's last meal is related; 18:28 -- the Jewish authorities refuse to enter the Praetorium so as to preserve their purity for the eating of the Passover; 19:14 and 31 -- Jesus is buried on the "Preparation of the Passover" and the day after the crucifixion and burial is a "High Sabbath."

[3] The name of Daniel Chwolson (Das letzte Passamahl Christi und der Tag seines Todes (Leipzig, 1892)) is associated with the theory that the Passover Lambs were slaughtered an evening early in the year under consideration in order to avoid contravening the Sabbath work ban, for Passover fell on the Sabbath that year. The Pharisees (and Jesus) ate the lamb immediately on Thursday night, while the Sadducees waited for the official time of celebration. This hypothesis lacks the necessary foundation, for, according to Philo, the lambs were slaughtered in the afternoon in the time of Jesus (A. J. B. Higgins, "The Origins of the Eucharist," NTS, I (1954-55), 201; George Ogg, "The Chronology of the Last Supper," Historicity and Chronology in the New Testament, ed. by D. E. Nineham, et al. (London: SPCK, 1965), 78; Str-B, II, 846-47).

Billerbeck (II, 847-852) has related the discrepancy to a disagreement between the Sadducees and Pharisees over the correct

John and the synoptic evangelists were employing conflicting calendrical systems.

The latter theory, in the form advocated most recently, suggests that Jesus celebrated the Passover on Tuesday evening, according to an old solar calendar, which seems to have been followed at Qumran.[1] That such a calendar did, in fact, exist seems to be established,[2] but its applicability to the Passion week is more problematic. The evidence for the chronology in early Christian sources is weak[3] and the theory is difficult to reconcile with some aspects of the gospel narratives.[4] Another option is to assume

---

day for the celebration of Pentecost. This feast was to be held fifty days after the day following Passover. The Sadducees (and especially a certain High Priestly family) felt that Pentecost should always fall on Sunday (cf. Lev. 23:11) and hence sought to place Passover on the Sabbath as often as possible. In the year of Jesus' death, the Sadducees fixed the first day of Nisan (the sighting of the new moon was the official indication of the beginning of the month and hence of Passover) so that Passover would fall on a Sabbath. The Pharisees suspected the Sadducees of tampering with the evidence and claimed that the Passover should be celebrated on Friday. Agreeing to disagree, the Sadducees allowed the Pharisees to observe the festival on Thursday night, while the Sadducees observed the "official" time. According to this reconstruction, then, Jesus celebrated the Passover as did the Pharisees on Thursday night, while John has followed the "official" Passover date. Little can be said to contradict this hypothesis, but it remains wholly conjectural and it must be doubted whether the Jews ever would have celebrated the Passover on two different days.

[1]See especially Annie Jaubert, The Date of the Last Supper, trans. by Isaac Rafferty (Staton Island, New York: Alba House, 1965), "Jésus et le calendrier de Qûmran," NTS, VII (1960), 1-30, "Le mercredi ou Jésus fut livré," NTS, XIV (1967-68), 145-64; Eugen Ruckstuhl, Chronology of the Last Days of Jesus, trans. by Victor J. Drapela (New York: Desclee Company, 1965); James A. Walther, "The Chronology of Passion Week," JBL, LXXVII (1958), 116-122.

[2]Milik, Ten Years of Discovery, 107; Black, The Scrolls and Christian Origins, 199.

[3]Jaubert's attempt to bolster her argument by appealing to the Didascalia and other early Christian literature for evidence of the "three day chronology" falls short of conviction because the sources in question are almost surely concerned with justifying a current fasting practice rather than historically-based. (J. Jeremias, Review of Le Date de la Cène, by A. Jaubert, JTS, n.s., X (1959), 133; Ogg, "Chronology," 83; R. E. Brown, "The Problem of Historicity in John," New Testament Essays (London-Dublin: Geoffrey Chapman, 1965), 165; Burkill, Mysterious Revelation, 165).

[4]All four evangelists intimate that the Last Supper was

that a dual celebration resulted from a difference between the Galileans (and Pharisees) and Judaeans (and Sadducees) over the fixing of the beginning of Nisan 14,[1] but the evidence for such a discrepancy is slight. And, with reference to every hypothesis that depends upon two separate observations of Passover, Segal rightly remarks, "It is highly improbable that two systems of dating the Passover would have been observed side by side at this period without leaving some trace in Jewish writings . . . ."[2] An attempt has been made to follow John's chronology while retaining the Paschal character of the Last Supper by supposing that Jesus celebrated the Passover one night early.[3] This hypothesis is impossible to reconcile with Mark 14:12 which explicitly mentions the slaughter of the Paschal lambs on the day that the Last Supper preparations were made.

If current harmonization attempts are not completely convincing, the decision between the Synoptic and Johannine chronologies must lie with the one that is able to account for more of the evidence. On this basis, the synoptic presentation is to be preferred. Alleged inconsistencies within the synoptic account can be shown to be without foundation[4] and it should be noted that all of the Johannine

---

celebrated the night before the crucifixion (Burkill, Mysterious Revelation, 265; Ogg, "Chronology," 82); the "three-day chronology" contradicts the impression that the Jewish authorities wanted to do away with Jesus quickly (Brown, "Historicity," 165); Jesus seems to follow the normal Jewish times of feast celebration during the rest of his ministry (Milik, Ten Years of Discovery, 113).

[1]Harold Hoehner, Chronological Aspects of the Life of Christ (Grand Rapids: Zondervan, 1977), 81-90; cf. also Morgenstern, Antecedents, 10.

[2]J. B. Segal, The Hebrew Passover from the Earliest Times to A.D. 70, London Oriental Series, XII (London: Oxford University Press, 1963), 243.

[3]Godet, Luke, III, 285; Sanders-Mastin, John, 303-304; Benoit, "The Date of the Last Supper," Jesus and the Gospel, I, 92; Theo. Preiss, "Was the Last Supper a Paschal Meal?" Life in Christ, trans. by Harold Knight, SBT, XIII (London: SCM, 1954), 83.

[4]The alleged violations of Sabbath rules are dealt with by

evidence can be reconciled with this chronology except for a single verse which remains problematic, 18:28.[1] On the other hand, attempts to substantiate the tradition that places Jesus' death on the afternoon before Passover must disregard the clear statements of the synoptics concerning the Paschal character of the Last Supper: "Any attempt to find in the Last Supper an occasion other than the Passover celebration must accommodate several very awkward realities."[2] Therefore, it seems best to follow the synoptic presentation and regard the Last Supper as a Passover Meal. However, even if this identification is rejected, Paschal significance cannot be excluded from a meal celebrated the night before the regular Passover.[3]

Jeremias (Eucharistic Words, 62-84), Barrett (John, 39-41) and Higgins (Lord's Supper, 17-20). ἄρτος can refer to unleavened bread (cf. Jeremias). The contradiction between Mk. 14:2 and the arrest of Jesus during the feast is removed once it is realized that Judas' offer to betray Jesus intervened and forced a change in plan (Barrett, John, 40). Furthermore, ἔλεγον in Mk. 14:2 may be an example of the third person impersonal (Turner, Syntax, 292), erasing the contradiction.

[1]Grammatically, πρὸ δὲ τῆς ἑορτῆς Πάσχα in Jn. 13:1 must go with the following εἰδώς, the time of the actual meal is not indicated. παρασκευή (τοῦ πάσχα) in Jn. 19:14 and 31 probably refers to the Friday of Passover week, as it consistently does in Jewish literature (Higgins, "Eucharist," 207; Morris, John, 776). The Sabbath is called "Great" (μεγάλη) not necessarily because the Passover coincides with it; it could be considered a high Sabbath because the offering of the Omer was made on it (Higgins, "Eucharist," 207). The identification of Jesus as the Passover Lamb does not have to depend on a chronological coincidence. With respect to 18:28, the customary explanation has been that "to eat the Passover" referred to general festival meals, which occurred throughout Passover week (most recently by Fritz Chenderlin, "Distributed Observance of the Passover -- A Hypothesis," Bib, LVI (1975), 369-93). Although the evidence is slim, this alternative represents the most likely of the harmonization attempts.

Barrett (John, 444; cf. also Brown, John, II, 846) claims that John's statement regarding the priests' hesitation in entering the Praetorium lest they be prevented from eating the Passover is "questionable" because the uncleanness contracted would not have resulted in their exclusion. But Morris (John, 763) has refuted this objection by pointing out that the uncleanness which attached to a Gentile home was traced to the custom of putting abortions down drains, which meant possible contact with a dead body. And this uncleanness lasted for seven days (Num. 19:11,14). Cf. also Schnackenburg, Johannes, III, 278.

[2]Albright-Mann, Matthew, 320.

[3]"It should also be emphasized, however, that the Last Supper

It is possible, therefore, that John's passion chronology reflects an attempt to present Jesus' death on the Cross as the sacrifice of the great Passover Lamb. Nevertheless, and making every allowance for the subtlety of John's theology, the indications that such was John's intention are very sparse and depend upon the drawing of implications rather than explicit statements. It may be that John's chronology was part of his inherited tradition and that his identification of Jesus with the Passover Lamb was stimulated by this.[1]

Jesus as the Passover Lamb in the Last Supper

A final attempt to discover Paschal allusions in the passion texts must now be dealt with. A startling aspect of the Last Supper, if it were a Passover meal, is the lack of reference to the most important element in that meal, the Passover Lamb itself. This omission may be explained by supposing that an implicit identification of Jesus with the Passover Lamb exists. Jeremias theorizes that Jesus had interpreted the Passover Lamb with reference to himself during the Passover Haggadah and that this identification underlies Jesus' words of interpretation. In effect, therefore, Jesus claims that "He is the eschatological paschal lamb,[2] representing the fulfillment of all that of which the Egyptian paschal lamb and all the subsequent

---

would still be surrounded by the atmosphere of the Passover even if it should have occurred on the evening before the Feast." (Jeremias, Eucharistic Words, 88). Scholars of differing viewpoints are in agreement on this point: P. Benoit, "The Holy Eucharist," 98-99; Ogg, "Chronology," 86; Richardson, Theology, 371; Taylor, Jesus and His Sacrifice, 116-17; Eduard Schweizer, "Abendmahl I. Im N.T.," RGG[3], I, col. 18.

[1]Note the objection of Dodd (Interpretation, 424) and Dauer (Passionsgeschichte, 133-42) that John's Passover Lamb typology is not pervasive enough to have attributed to it the impetus for the change.

[2]The eschatological Passover Lamb was expected to be a sacrifice of atonement unlike the yearly lamb offering (Jeremias, Eucharistic Words, 226; Lohse, Märtyrer, 128, n. 2).

sacrificial paschal lambs were the prototype."[1] It must be admitted that this line of interpretation is largely an argument from silence since no explicit connection between Jesus and the Passover Lamb is evident in any of the existing accounts.[2] And, as has become clear, there is almost nothing in the Synoptic gospels which demonstrates any understanding of Jesus in terms of the Paschal Lamb. Since the synoptic Last Supper accounts are obviously highly abbreviated, it must be questioned whether the omission of the Lamb is really significant.

Conclusions

References to Jesus as the Passover Lamb are certainly to be seen in Jn. 1:29 and 19:36, while allusions to the concept may be intended in John's chronology of the day of Jesus' death (the sixth hour on the preparation day for Passover). Whether the synoptic evangelists view Jesus in this way is more problematic. While allusions to the Exodus experience occur throughout the synoptics,[3] the Last Supper accounts are the only narratives where specific paschal associations are plausibly found.[4] While, as we have seen, the evidence for an implicit identification of Jesus with the Passover Lamb in these accounts falls short of proof, it would be shortsighted to overlook the obvious parallel between the (Christian) Last Supper and the Jewish Passover. As Stauffer states it:

---

[1] Jeremias, Eucharistic Words, 222-225 (223). Cf. also: Goppelt, Typos, 135-6; Albrecht Oepke, "Der Herrnspruch über die Kirche Mt 16, 17-19 in der neuesten Forschung," ST, XI (1948), 144; Richardson, Theology, 371; Martin, Mark, 199; Higgins, Last Supper, 50-51; Stauffer, Jesus, 117.

[2] Lohse, Märtyrer, 127-8; Williams, Jesus' Death, 210.

[3] Cf. especially with reference to the Passion, Lk. 9:31.

[4] David Daube (The New Testament and Rabbinic Judaism (London: Athlone, 1965), 177) finds others, but they are improbable at best.

On the eve of God's act of deliverance in Egypt Moses celebrated the passover with the people of Israel, and in saving remembrance of that saving act the people of the old covenant from that time on celebrated the passover. On the eve of the divine act of salvation on Golgotha Jesus celebrated the Last Supper with his disciples, and in saving remembrance of that saving act the Christian covenant community from henceforth celebrated the eucharist.[1]

The "Sacrifice" of Isaac (Genesis 22; the Akedah)

Several details in the gospels are claimed to imply a parallel between Jesus' fate and the Isaac tradition in Genesis 22. On the basis of the omission of the Simon of Cyrene tradition in the Fourth Gospel, several scholars feel that John is purposely drawing a parallel between Jesus and Isaac, who bore the wood for his own sacrifice (Genesis 22).[2] Another parallel between Jesus and Isaac is said to be present in Mt. 26:36 where Jesus' separation from the disciples for prayer in the face of his imminent sacrifice is reminiscent of the similar withdrawal of Abraham and Isaac (Gen. 22:5 -- cf. the rare use of αὐτοῦ to mean "here").[3] Best conjectures that Jesus' understanding of his destiny in the light of Isaac's may underlie Mk. 15:34 and 37; the first cry expressing his disappointment that a ram had not been substituted and the second his triumphant obedience.[4]

---

[1] Ethelbert Stauffer, New Testament Theology, trans. by John Marsh (London: SCM, 1955), 163; cf. also Goppelt, Typos, 136.

[2] Macgregor, John, 344; Tasker, John, 210. It is seen as possible by Dalman, Jesus-Jeshua, 190-2; Sanders-Mastin, John, 405; Lightfoot, John, 316. The parallel is noted as early as Tertullian (Adv. Iud. X and XIII). The reference to Jesus being bound in Jn. 18:12 is also sometimes cited (cf. Westcott, John, II, 272). For the patristic utilization of Isaac typology, see Daniélou, From Shadows to Reality, 115-30. Barrett (John, 465) cites the Midrash on Genesis which says "as one who bears the cross on the shoulder." But the subject is Abraham, not Isaac (Glasson, Moses, 98).

[3] McNeile, Matthew, 389; Goppelt, Typos, 121; Senior, Passion Narrative, 101-2; Best, Temptation and Passion, 172 (on Mk. 14:32ff); A. Feuillet, "Le Récit Lucanien de l'agonie de Gethsémani (Lc XXII. 39-46)," NTS, XXII (1976), 416.

[4] Best, Temptation and Passion, 101.

The appropriateness of these alleged parallels is considerably enhanced if the evangelists were aware of the midrashic tradition, based on Genesis 22, referred to as the "binding of Isaac" (the Akedah). The beginning of this tradition may be found in the Targum on Genesis 22, which modifies the story in significant ways to stress Isaac's conscious acceptance of his fate. To insure his perfect and unflinching obedience, he asks to be bound. A definite significance is accorded to the sacrifice; Abraham prays that Isaac's obedience might be remembered for the sake of his children. Vermes suggests that the tradition arose through reflection on the blood of the martyrs and was stimulated by a midrashic combination of Isaiah 53 and Genesis 22.[1] The tradition was further embellished by later Rabbis, who linked Isaac's binding with the sacrifice of the Passover Lamb and ascribed expiatory value to the binding.[2] Adducing references in Josephus, Pseudo-Philo and IV Maccabees, Vermes argues that the Akedah tradition was current in first century A.D.[3]

Two comments may be made on the relevance of this tradition for the NT. First, with respect to the Akedah tradition in general, Barrett remarks that none of the passages adduced " . . . has the effect of bringing into the time of Paul the developed conception of Isaac as an intercessor and of his sacrifice (or readiness for sacrifice) as a meritorious and atoning act."[4] And Sanders criticizes

---

[1] Vermes, Scripture and Tradition, 202-203. Le Déaut (La nuit pascale, 199-210) agrees that the parallels between Isaiah 53 and the Isaac tradition must have been noticed, but he admits that contact is difficult to prove (cf. also J. E. Wood, "Isaac Typology in the New Testament," NTS, XIV (1967-68), 584).

[2] Cf. Mekilta of R. Ishmael: "and when I see the blood, I shall pass over you -- I see the blood of the binding of Isaac."

[3] Scripture and Tradition, 197; cf. also Le Déaut, La nuit pascale, 131-200.

[4] From First Adam to Last, 28. Lohse (Märtyrer, 91) believes that the Rabbinic emphasis on the atoning power of Isaac's sacrifice grew out of a conscious anti-Christian polemic.

Vermes for giving a one-sided picture, claiming that the references to the binding of Isaac are given "a significance far out of proportion to what they actually had in Rabbinic literature."[1]

Secondly, the existence of such allusive references to the Isaac tradition presume the importance of Isaac as a prefigurement of Jesus in the NT generally. It has been urged that the Akedah was an important factor in the development of Paul's soteriology (cf. especially Rom. 8:32)[2] and may have influenced Acts 3:25-6.[3] Allusions to the Genesis 22 story have been noticed in the baptismal voice (Mk. 1:11 -- $\dot{\alpha}\gamma\alpha\pi\eta\tau\acute{o}s$; cf. Gen. 22:29 LXX),[4] and in the Lamb of God title (Jn. 1:29).[5] However, while influence from Genesis 22 on this title or on the baptismal bath qol cannot be excluded, it is, at best, secondary to other factors. And, doubt has been cast on the importance of the Akedah for Paul.[6] Moreover, it is improbable that the Akedah tradition would have been employed in early Christian soteriological thinking because Isaac was not, of course, actually sacrificed, while the Christians were concerned to emphasize that "without the shedding of blood there is no forgiveness of sins" (Heb. 9:22).[7]

---

[1] Paul, 28.

[2] Hans-Joachim Schoeps, Paulus: Die Theologie des Apostels im Lichte der jüdischen Religionsgeschichte (Tübingen: Mohr, 1959), 144-52; Vermes, Scripture and Tradition, 215; Nils Alstrup Dahl, "The Atonement -- An Adequate Reward for the Akedah? (Ro 8:32)," Neotestamentica et Semitica. Glasson (Moses, 98) notes the parallel use of $\phi\epsilon\acute{\iota}\delta o\mu\alpha\iota$ (cf. also E. Earle Ellis, Paul's Use of the Old Testament (Edinburgh: Oliver and Boyd, 1957), 130).

[3] Vermes, Scripture and Tradition, 215.

[4] Richardson, Theology, 227; Marshall, "Son of God or Servant," 334-5.

[5] Richardson, Theology, 227; Vermes, Scripture and Tradition, 225; Best, Temptation and Passion, 171; Braun, Jean le Théologien, II, 180; Brown, John, II, 917.

[6] C. K. Barrett, From First Adam to Last, 27-30.

[7] Wood, "Isaac Typology," 586. The Rabbis felt this difficulty, too, and suggested that Isaac bled while being bound (Vermes, Scripture and Tradition, 205-6).

Therefore, while it is perhaps going too far to call the hypothesis of an allusion to Isaac in Jn. 19:17 "a patristic fancy,"[1] it is highly doubtful whether any parallel was intended.[2] Other motives are sufficient to account for John's failure to mention Simon's role.[3] Similar doubts must exist as to the alleged contacts in the Gethsemane scene[4] and in Mk. 15:34 and 37; in the light of the total absence of any explicit utilization of the Isaac parallel, these allusions are unlikely.[5]

Conclusions

The evidence of the gospels permits the conclusion that the interpretation of Jesus' death in sacrificial terms was utilized at an early stage,[6] although the concept is not pervasive. The sacrifices

---

[1] Bernard, John, II, 590.

[2] Bultmann, John, 668; Lindars, John, 574; Schnackenburg, Johannes, III, 312; Dauer, Passionsgeschichte, 286.

[3] He may wish to counter the docetic suggestion, found at a later date in the writings of the Gnostic Basilides, that Simon had changed places with Jesus (Howard, "John," 917; Weidel, "Studien," 249; Rawlinson, Mark, 232). Haenchen (Weg Jesu, 525) suggests that John wishes to present Jesus as an example to Christians, who similarly must bear their crosses. More probably, John wished to stress Jesus' sovereign control of his own destiny (Barrett, John, 456; Brown, John, II, 917; Dauer, Passionsgeschichte, 169; Schnackenburg, Johannes, III, 712).

[4] R. S. Barbour, "Gethsemane in the Tradition of the Passion," NTS, XVI (1969-70), 245.

[5] David Lerch (Isaaks Opferung christlich gedeutet. Eine auslegungsgeschichtliche Untersuchung, BHT, XII (Tübingen: Mohr, 1950), 19-20) questions the influence of Isaac or Genesis 22 on the NT.

[6] If, as is virtually certain, Jesus anticipated his death; and if, as is very probable, he anticipated that his death would have salvific consequences (cf., supra, 168), it is almost inevitable that he would have utilized sacrificial concepts in describing this effect. Barth argues: " . . . it seems to be obvious that Paul was not the inventor of a sacrificial sin- or blood-theology. Rather, he continued and unfolded what he heard and found in the churches in and outside Jerusalem and Antioch. Neither can any other among the New Testament authors be credited or blamed for inventing that doctrine. It is spread so widely over the earliest and latest books of the New Testament -- whatever books may belong to those two groups -- that either an unknown

of expiation, outlined in the early chapters of Leviticus, provide an important general background for the understanding of Jesus' death, while the covenant sacrifice of Exodus 24 and the Paschal sacrifice are specific points of contact. All three of these sacrifices are referred to in the Last Supper accounts, providing a comprehensive picture of the sacrificial significance of Jesus' passion. As Goppelt summarizes:

> Jesu Blut, sein Sterben, bedeutet wie das Blut der Passahlämmer: Verschonung, Errettung und Erlösung von dem Tode, von der Knechtschaft, von dem Zorngericht Gottes. Zugleich aber bedeutet es, wie das Bundesblut am Sinai, Versöhnung mit Gott und Aufrichtung eines neuen Bundes, einer neuen Gottesordnung. Beides gehört hier wie damals untrennbar zusammen . . . .[1]

While it would not be far-fetched, in light of the pervasiveness of sacrificial concepts among Jews, to suppose that general sacrificial concepts are presupposed throughout the presentation of Jesus' passion in the synoptic gospels, this conception is not explicitly found outside the Last Supper narratives. John, on the other hand, betrays a more consistent interest in sacrificial concepts. The "Bread of Life" discourse in John 6 is pervaded with sacrificial conceptions, particularly in vv. 51-58. The background here cannot be narrowed to a specific sacrifice, although the probable eucharistic[2] reference,

---

creative genius, or a simultaneous flash of enlightenment coming to all early churches, or Jesus Himself must be considered its originator." (Jesus' Death, 4). While some validity attaches to Barth's observation, it must be said that, so pervasive was sacrificial thinking among Jews, the concept could have arisen almost spontaneously in many different areas.

[1]Typos, 136.

[2]Eucharistic allusions are denied by some (e.g., recently, James D. G. Dunn, "John VI - A Eucharistic Discourse?" NTS, XVII (1970-71), 328-38), but are probably present. With Borgen, however, it is inappropriate to focus exclusively on eucharistic ideas and to read sacramentalism into the discourse (Bread from Heaven, 189-90).

combined with the emphasis on "blood" may suggest the primacy of the Levitical expiatory sacrifices.[1] Elsewhere, it is the Paschal sacrifice[2] with which John is most concerned -- 1:29, 19:6 (??), 19:36.[3]

The use of general sacrificial terminology in the passion texts should probably be characterized as conceptual influence. The intention of Jesus and the evangelists seems not so much to be to present Jesus as a sacrificial victim (although that, of course, is implied) as to characterize his death as sacrificial in its nature and benefits. Similarly, it is unlikely that the covenant sacrifice should be characterized as a type of Jesus' sacrifice. Jesus offers his life as a sacrifice whose benefits will inaugurate a covenant; it is not the antitype of the first occasion, but a second like the first.

The parallel between Jesus and the Passover Lamb, on the other hand, is certainly be be seen as typological. All of the components that constitute such a relationship are present: the lack of a forward-looking element in the OT conception, the single point of identity, the qualitatively greater value of the antitype. Nevertheless, John can use πληρόω to introduce a quotation pertaining to the Paschal Lamb -- an indication not that the typological identification is in error, but that John's use of πληρόω must be defined in a sufficiently broad manner.

---

[1] As noted already, the חטאת is the sacrifice in which the "blood" of the victim receives most emphasis (supra, 311, n.).

[2] Evidence seems to be conclusive that the Paschal Lamb was regarded as a sacrifice (cf. Josephus, Ant., II: 14, 312 and Lyonnet-Sabourin, Sin, Redemption and Sacrifice, 171-2).

[3] Paschal allusions may be present in John 6 as well (cf. especially Bertil Gärtner, John 6 and the Jewish Passover, ConNT, XVII (Lund: Gleerup, 1959), also André Feuillet, "The Principal Themes in the Discourse on the Bread of Life," Johannine Studies, trans. by Thomas E. Crane (Staten Island, N.Y.: Alba House, 1965), 121).

CHAPTER VI

THE USE OF MISCELLANEOUS OLD TESTAMENT PASSAGES IN THE GOSPEL PASSION TEXTS

It is surprising how few OT passages of significance for the passion texts remain after the four major backgrounds treated in the previous chapters have been exhausted. Nevertheless, there are several miscellaneous texts which must come under consideration before the survey can be complete. The obviously diffuse combination of texts to be studied demands a slight modification in methodology: conclusions must be drawn as each background is explained, rendering superfluous any general conclusion.

Passion Predictions

John 3:14 (Numbers 21:8-9)

The comparison of the "lifting up" of the Son of Man with the serpent elevated by Moses in the wilderness has significant antecedents in intertestamental speculation. Wis. Sol. 16:6f characterizes the serpent as a "token of salvation" ($\sigma\acute{u}\mu\beta o\lambda o\nu$ $\sigma\omega\tau\eta\rho\acute{\iota}\alpha\varsigma$) and goes on to relate how "he who turned toward it was not saved by that which he saw, but by thee, the Saviour of all."[1] The targums (Neofiti I and Pseudo-Jon.) in Num. 21:9, speak of Moses

---

[1] Translation by Holmes in APOT, I, 561. Cf. also m. Roš. Haš. 3:8: "every time that Israel direct their gaze on high and make their heart subservient to their Father in Heaven, they are healed." (Str-B, II, 425-6).

placing the serpent on "an elevated place (אתר עלי)", an understanding better suited to the use made of the imagery in the Fourth Gospel than the more prosaic "put" of MT and LXX.[1] Targum Pseudo-Jon. even refers to the "name of the memra" in the context. When, in addition to this, it is noted that the LXX translated נס "standard, pole" with σημεῖον, it should occasion no surprise to find the serpent utilized as a type of Christ's exaltation in John's Gospel.[2]

The point of comparison in Jn. 3:14 is clearly the "lifting up"; this is the focus of attention. But it must not be overlooked that the "lifting up" is not significant so much for the nature of the execution (an analogy that obviously could not be pressed) as for the saving benefits which are mediated through, or as a result of, the action. The comparison thus accords a clear soteriological interpretation to the death of Christ, an interpretation that is extensively developed in the following verses of John 3. While speculation on the incident related in Numbers 21 may have stimulated the development of the "lifting up" theology in John's Gospel, it is unlikely that it has created it.

The appropriation technique utilized by Jesus[3] in drawing this comparison is clearly the direct-typological type. One central analogy, the dependence upon the One lifted up for deliverance, lies

---

[1] Cf. Brown, John, I, 133. M.-E. Boismard ("Les citations targumiques dans le quatrième Évangile," RB, LXVI (1959), 378) suggests that the targumic text is cited in Jn. 3:14.

[2] Reim demonstrates that John is not dependent on Wis. Sol. 16, but there can be little doubt that he was acquainted with the tradition (Hintergrund, 196-8). The serpent typology is also employed in Barnabas (12, 5-7) and Justin (Apol. 60; Dial. 91, 94, 112), indicating that the tradition may well be pre-Johannine (Schulz, Christologie, 109, n. 5).

[3] Jn. 3:14, in light of the reference to Son of Man, should be included in Jesus' discourse. While the ipsissima verba Christi are notoriously difficult to separate from the reflections of the evangelist in John's Gospel, the Son of Man title is good reason for regarding this saying as ipsissima vox.

at the heart of the relationship. The Numbers incident serves as an illustration of the incomparably greater deliverance to be found in the "lifted up" Son of Man. The typological relationship should be confined to the action and its results.

As Barrett correctly insists, for John, "the point of comparison is not the Serpent but the lifting up."[1] It is possible that the "looking," central in Numbers 21:4-9, is implied here in John as well.[2]

Matthew 12:40 (Jonah 1:17)

The only exception to Jesus' refusal to perform a sign is that made in Mt. 12:40 -- "just as 'Jonah was in the belly of the great fish for three days and three nights,' so will the Son of Man be in the heart of the earth for three days and three nights." The quotation is taken from Jon. 1:17 (2:1 in MT, LXX) and reproduces exactly the LXX, which, in turn, is a literal translation of the MT.[3]

The precise point of comparison involved in the reference to Jonah is a matter of dispute. It is frequently asserted that the *real* point of comparison is the preaching of repentance, as in Lk. 11:29-30, and in Mt. 12:39-41 as well, if v. 40 be regarded as the evangelist's secondary insertion. Matthew, it is claimed, has, in his typical fashion, added a comparison based on the similarity in detail.[4] Against this, however, Jeremias has shown that it was

---

[1] *John*, 178. Cf. also William Healey Cadman, *The Open Heaven: The Revelation of God in the Johannine Sayings of Jesus*, ed. by G. B. Caird (Oxford: Basil Blackwell, 1969), 31.

[2] Glasson, *Moses*, 34-35.

[3] Cf. Gundry, *Old Testament*, 136.

[4] R. B. Y. Scott, "The Sign of Jonah: An Interpretation," *Int*, XIX (1965), 18; Tödt, *Son of Man*, 212-13; Hamerton-Kelly, *Pre-existence*, 33-34; Rengstorf, "$\sigma\eta\mu\epsilon\tilde{\iota}ov$," *TDNT*, VII, 233. It is

Jonah's miraculous deliverance that received particular attention among Jewish interpreters[1] and the difficult time reference is a strong argument for the authenticity of the saying.[2] If v. 40 be considered part of the original discourse, then, the point of comparison would seem to be in "the authorization of the divine messenger by deliverance from death."[3] "Jesus' preaching, which his hearers are rejecting, will in due course be attested by a still greater deliverance; therefore their condemnation will be the greater (verse 41)."[4]

Once again, a characteristic typological relationship is to be seen in Jesus' use of the Jonah incident. A basic correspondence in God's activity, in this case the miraculous deliverance of God's messenger, lies at the basis of the analogy.[5]

---

most improbable that v. 40 was interpolated after the work of Matthew (pace Stendahl, School, 132-33; cf. R. A. Edwards, The Sign of Jonah in the Theology of the Evangelists and Q, SBT, n.s., XVIII (London: SCM, 1971), 97).

[1] "Ἰωνᾶς," 409. He further notes the difficulty of regarding preaching as a σημεῖον. But cf. Rengstorf, "σημεῖον," 233.

[2] Hill, Matthew, 220; France, Jesus, 80-82.

[3] Jeremias, "Ἰωνᾶς," 409. Ἰωνᾶς should be understood as the epexegetic genitive (cf. Rengstorf, "σημεῖον," 233). Edwards (Sign of Jonah, 96-98) advocates this basic interpretation, though not regarding v. 40 as authentic and emphasizing the return to life. Cf. also France, Jesus, 44-45. Hill, on the contrary, sees the sign as judgment and death (Matthew, 220), but this is difficult to fit into the context.

[4] France, Jesus, 44-45.

[5] A further point of contact may be found if καρδία in Matthew can be understood as Hades (McNeile, Matthew, 182), for Jon. 2:3 (MT) uses שׁאול for "belly." (J. A. Motyer, "Jonah," NIDNTT, II, 351).

Mark 12:10-11 / Matthew 21:42 / Luke 20:17
(Psalm 118:22)

The quotation of Ps. 118:22(-3) forms the "capstone" of Jesus' parable about the wicked husbandmen in all three synoptic gospels, and the evangelists agree in transmitting the citation in the LXX translation (the LXX slavishly reproduces the Hebrew). It is obvious that the quotation functions as a continuation and epilogue of the parable by predicting the transformed status of the "son," who is rejected and slain: the λίθος represents Jesus as the one whose humiliation is turned into exaltation[1] by the intervention of God Himself (cf. Mk. 12:11 - Mt. 21:42b).[2] That the reference is to Jesus' death seems clear. The Resurrection is probably the second focal point, although Jeremias understands the παρουσία as the point of exaltation.[3]

The psalm text was valued in the early church for its applicability to the circumstances of the Messiah's rejection by "the builders" (perhaps the religious leaders[4]). Not surprisingly, a polemical motive is often present (Acts 4:11, ὑμῶν τῶν οἰκοδόμων). Whether Ps. 118:22 was given a Messianic interpretation in pre-Christian times is difficult to determine. On the one hand, the earliest clear attestation for the Messianic application is in Rashi's comment on Micah 5:1,[5] but, on the other hand, the Targum may imply (or have at one time explicitly indicated) an identification of the stone

---

[1] κεφαλὴν γωνίας probably refers to the keystone of the arch, not the foundation stone (Joachim Jeremias, "λίθος, λίθινος," TDNT, IV, 174).

[2] The building metaphor may have particular reference to Jesus' position of supremacy in the new spiritual temple, the church (cf. I Pet. 2:7 and Jeremias, "λίθος," 273; Hill, Matthew, 301).

[3] "λίθος," 275.   [4] Cf. Str-B, I, 875f.

[5] Str-B, I, 875-6; Jeremias, "λίθος," 273.

with the Davidic Messiah.¹ It is safest to conclude that there is no evidence that v. 22 was applied to the Messiah before Christ, although the psalm itself seems to have been interpreted with reference to the coming age of salvation (cf. vv. 26-27).²

There is no compelling reason for doubting the authenticity of the quotation.³ The appropriateness of the passage must have been as obvious to Jesus as it was to the apostles,⁴ while the use of ἀνέγνωτε has a dominical flavor.⁵ It is characteristic of Jesus' teaching to conclude with a pointed scriptural reference. Jesus' utilization of the text has the purpose of stimulating repentance on the part of the Jewish leaders by identifying his rejection with the rejection of the stone subsequently vindicated by God's own hand.⁶ As Filson says, "an incipient theology of the cross emerges here."⁷

---

¹The Targum reads: "A youth was rejected by the builders; He was among the sons of Jesse and was entitled to be appointed king and ruler." Gärtner has argued that the rejection of the אבנא in the Targum has definite affinities with the servant in Is. 53 and that the "stone" concept may form part of this same complex of themes ("אבנא als Messiasbezeichnung," 100-5). But the links with the servant concept are tenuous at best. Snodgrass concedes that the reference in the Targum is to David, but suggests that the present text represents a re-interpretation stimulated by the Christian application of the verse ("Stone Testimonia," 84-86).

²Snodgrass, "Stone Testimonia," 86.

³The basis for such doubts often rests on an alleged agreement with allegory implied in the preceding parable (Dodd, Parables, 98-99; Jeremias, Parables, 74). But the point of view, introduced by Jülicher, which makes a rigid distinction between parable and allegory and jettisons the latter from the ipsissima verba Jesu is founded on a misconception of the relationship between the two and cannot be sustained (Brown, "Parable and Allegory," 37-8; Snodgrass, "Stone Testimonia," 114-28).

⁴Taylor (Mark, 477) plausibly suggests that the church's widespread use of the verse goes back to the memory of Jesus' own teaching.

⁵Ellis, "Midrash," 67.

⁶Cf. Cranfield, Mark, 366-7; Jeremias, "λίθος," 275.

⁷Matthew, 229.

It may be that the central point of the parable is to be found in the "rejected Son" concept, the transition to the "stone" quotation being eased by the word-play בן-אבן.[1] The relationship between the parable and the quotation suggests that the method of appropriation is neither midrashic nor of the pesher type. Characteristic of both these is the intimate relationship between OT text and context. In the present instance, the quotation is adduced as a scriptural demonstration for the transition from rejection to dominion, while the story has concentrated on the process of rejection.[2]

Whether Jesus, or the evangelists, viewed Ps. 118:22 as directly Messianic, or simply as a convenient description of the reversal of positions to come is difficult to decide with any certainty. However, Ps. 118:22 has, as we have seen, influenced the passion sayings,[3] and it may be that the verse was generally applied to Jesus and his ministry in the early church. This implies, although it does not require, that the psalm was read as, to some degree, prophetic.

Results of Jesus' Death

The effect of Jesus' death is described in a variety of ways by the evangelists, some of which descriptions may be influenced by OT passages.

---

[1] Black, "Christological Use," 12; cf. Snodgrass, "Stone Testimonia," 161-62.

[2] Indeed, many scholars regard the quotation as a secondary addition to the parable (cf., e.g., Jeremias, Parables, 31).

[3] Cf., supra, 89. It is unnecessary to suppose that Ps. 118:22 was introduced into the Son of Man passion sayings through Daniel 2. (pace Snodgrass, "Stone Testimonia," 195-96). The independent appropriation of Ps. 118:22, and subsequent allusive use of its language in the passion predictions account for the situation.

The Temple

As is the case with regard to the sacrificial system and the Passover, the significance of Jesus' death for the Temple is not clearly elucidated in the Passion Narrative. But at two points, brief and somewhat ambiguous references provide some basis for speculation. One is the rending of the temple veil (καταπέτασμα) which, according to the synoptic evangelists, occurred at approximately the time of Jesus' death. Whether the outer Temple curtain or the inner veil, secluding the Holy of Holies is meant and whether the sign signified the judgment of God on the old worship system[1] or the establishment of a new access to God (cf. Heb. 6:19-20)[2] have long been debated. A definitive answer to the former question seems impossible, but it is probable that the evangelists regard the sign as both a negative judgment on the old Temple cult and the indication of a new soteriological era, since the inauguration of a new means

---

[1] A tradition preserved in Rabbinic sources records a miraculous portent of the destruction of the Temple forty years before A.D. 70 (b. Yom. 39b; j. Yom. 43c; cf. Str-B, I, 1044-6). However, Josephus dates the portent in A.D. 66 (B.J., VI, 288-309; cf. Marshall, Commentary on Luke, 875). The relationship between this tradition and the rending of the veil at Jesus' death is uncertain.
This interpretation accords with the Messianic expectation of the destruction of the Temple (Wolfgang Trilling, Christusverkundigung in den synoptischen Evangelien: Beispiele gattungsgemässer Auslegung, Biblische Handbibliothek, IV (Munich: Kösel, 1969), 201; Juel, Messiah and Temple, 140-42; Donahue, Are You the Christ? 202-3; Lohmeyer, Markus, 347; Ferdinand Hahn, Mission in the New Testament, trans. by Frank Clarke, SBT, XLVIII (London: SCM, 1965), 117).

[2] Gösta Lindeskog ("The Veil of the Temple," Coniectanea Neotestamentica: in honour of Anton Fridrichsen (Lund/Copenhagen: C. W. K. Gleerup & Ejnar Munksgaard, 1947), 134-7) correctly relates the sign to the Hebrews tradition and finds a "cultic pattern" in which Jesus assumes the role of the High Priest, offering atonement. Linnemann (Passionsgeschichte, 159-63) believes that a new access to God is signified, but claims that the curtain had the function of veiling God's Majesty, so its rending indicates that "Im Kreuzestode Jesu wird Gottes Majestät offenbar." (163; cf. also Martin, Mark, 183).

of divine access necessarily renders obsolete the former, and an abolishing of the old implies the creation of a new.[1]

The second indication within the Passion Narrative concerning Jesus' relationship to the Temple is found in the spurious allegations made by the witnesses at the Sanhedrin hearing. This accusation, that Jesus had threatened to destroy and rebuild the Temple, is probably a garbled reference to an authentic saying of Jesus, since similar sayings are imbedded in the tradition elsewhere (Jn. 2:19, Mk. 13:2 par., Mk. 15:29), and it is improbable that such a saying would have been invented by the church.[2] The testimony of the witnesses was probably considered false because Jesus did not, in fact, claim that _he_ would destroy the Temple, but that it would be destroyed.[3] Jesus' basis for this belief, symbolically represented in the cleansing of the Temple,[4] was at least partly due to the expectation that the old Temple would be destroyed and a new one established in the Messianic age, an expectation based upon Zech. 6: 11-12 (perhaps II Sam. 7) and found in Targ. Is. 53:5, and I En. 90:20ff.[5] Noting Matthew's alterations of the Temple word as over

---

[1] Senior, Passion Narrative, 308-11; Burkill, Mysterious Revelation, 247; Ellis, Luke, 269.

[2] Kümmel, Promise and Fulfillment, 100; Lohmeyer, Markus, 327; Gärtner, Temple and Community, 111; Otto Betz, What do we know about Jesus, trans. by Margaret Kohl (Philadelphia: Westminster, 1968), 91.

[3] Gottlieb Schrenk, "$\iota\epsilon\rho\acute{o}s$ . . . ," TDNT, III, 244; Betz, Jesus, 91.

[4] Gärtner, Temple and Community, 106-7. Jesus' action should therefore not be viewed as a condemnation of sacrifice as such (contra. A. Caldecott, "The Significance of the 'Cleansing of the Temple,'" JTS, XXIV (1923), 382-86; see F. C. Burkitt, "The Cleansing of the Temple," JTS, XXV (1924), 386-90; Taylor, Jesus and His Sacrifice, 70-74).

[5] Str-B, I, 1003-4, Otto Betz, "Die Frage nach dem messianischen Bewusstsein Jesu," NovT, VI (1963), 35-6; Kümmel, Promise and Fulfillment, 101; Dormeyer, Passion, 160. On Targum Is. 53:5, see Seidelin, "Jesajatargum," 212-13. This expectation was almost certainly pre-Christian (contra. Donahue, Are You the Christ? 112); it seems

against Mark's (addition of τοῦ θεοῦ, elimination of the contrast χειροποίητον -- ἀχειροποίητον), Lindars suggests that Matthew has purposely molded his form of the saying with Zech. 6:11-12 in mind.[1] This could well be, for it seems certain that Zech. 6:11-12 was a primary source for Jesus' saying(s) regarding the Messianic Temple which he equates with his own body.[2] (The phrase "in three days," preserved in the false witnesses' accusation, links this saying closely with the tradition found in Jn. 2:19-22). This represents a spiritualizing of the Temple concept, as the old worship centered on a building is replaced by a new fellowship with God, centered on the Resurrected Christ.[3] At this point, the diverse strands in the consideration of Jesus' relationship to OT rituals and institutions become intertwined, for the new worshipping fellowship which replaces the Temple is brought into being through the sacrifice of Jesus. And both aspects are inherent in the σῶμα of Christ, as Moule indicates:

> Thus σῶμα has sacrificial associations on the one hand, and ecclesiological ones on the other; it combines sanctuary and sacrifice. The sacrificial surrender of the body of Christ

---

to be explicitly stated in the undoubtedly Messianic passage, Zech. 6:11-12 (Joyce G. Baldwin, "Semah as a Technical Term in the Prophets," VT, XIV (1964), 93-97). After an extensive survey, Juel concludes that there is clear evidence for a pre-Christian Jewish belief that Messiah would rebuild the Temple, but the existence of a tradition in which Messiah was to destroy the Temple is less certain (Messiah and Temple, 169-204).

[1] Apologetic, 68-71. He points to other parallels in Matthew's narrative to Zech. 6 and to a possible allusion to Zech. 14:21 in Jn. 2:16 for further support of this suggestion.

[2] France, Jesus, 99-100.

[3] Gärtner, Temple and Community, 11; Schrenk, "ἱερός . . . ," 244; France, Jesus, 100. A. Vanhoye suggests that the destruction of the Temple relates to Christ's sufferings while the rebuilding points to the Resurrection ("Structure et théologie des récits de la passion dans les évangiles synoptiques," NRT, LXXXIX (1967), 156).

(and of the bodies of believers in union with him) leads to
the building of a Body which is God's New Temple, In two
directions, sacrifice and sanctuary, the Mosaic literature
is superseded by its spiritual counterpart.[1]

The Passion Narrative preserves a hint of this theological complex by closely relating Jesus' death to the judgment on and transformation of Temple worship and by including an inaccurate quotation of Jesus' own teaching on this subject. While several OT and apocryphal passages testify to the expectation of an eschatological Temple, the expectation is founded on the Davidic promise in II Sam. 7, reappearing again in Zech. 6:11-12.[2] The narrative of the rending of the Temple veil carries on this conception, although no specific OT background can be found for this incident. In the Temple tradition, then, a Messianic prophecy is spiritualized; the meaning of the OT promises is re-oriented so as to apply the prophecy to the creation of a new community through the death and Resurrection of Christ. The point of continuity is the theme of worship.

The Coming of the Eschaton

In this section are included several incidents which may be compared with certain OT images associated, in a general way, with the eschatological day of judgment and redemption. The time of Jesus' death is particularly important with respect to these cosmic manifestations of God's activity. In addition to the rending of the Temple veil, the

---

[1]C. F. D. Moule, "Sanctuary and Sacrifice in the Church of the New Testament," JTS, n.s., I (1950), 31-2.

[2]Donahue, Are You the Christ? 77; Vanhoye, "Structure et théologie," 156; Juel, Messiah and Temple, 169-204; Betz, Jesus, 88-9. It has been suggested that Jeremiah's denunciation of the Temple in chapter 26 has influenced the tradition in Mk. 14:58 (Doeve, Jewish Hermeneutics, 182-3; cf. Martin, Mark, 180), but the passage is not Messianic and is not as appropriate for Jesus' application as Zech. 6.

darkness "over all the land," the Resurrection of saints in Jerusalem and Jesus' last, wordless cry are signs closely associated with Jesus' death whose conceptual bases require comment.

The three hour period of darkness while Jesus was dying on the Cross (Mk. 15:33 / Mt. 27:45 / Lk. 23:44-45a) has been interpreted in various ways. Some understand it as a natural phenomenon, perhaps a "black sirocco," a severe dust storm which is common to Palestine in early spring.[1] Even if this were so, it seems certain that the evangelists attributed particular significance to the incident. Thus, the darkness has been viewed as indicating: 1) the mourning of nature at the death of a great man;[2] 2) a general apocalyptic sign;[3] 3) demonic activity;[4] 4) the inauguration of a new era of Heilsgeschichte;[5] 5) the intervention of God;[6] 6) the wrath of God;[7] 7) the "Day of the Lord," combining judgment with deliverance;[8] 8) a parallel to the

---

[1] Lagrange, Marc, 432; Rengstorf, Lukas, 271; Swete, Mark, 362; Johnson, Mark, 255-56. For the nature of the sirocco, see George Adam Smith, The Historical Geography of the Holy Land, The Fontana Library, Theology and Philosophy (25th ed.; London: Collins, 1966), 65. Luke's τοῦ ἡλίου ἐκλιπόντος need not refer to an eclipse, impossible at the time of the Paschal full moon, but can simply mean "the sun failed" (Plummer, Luke, 537; Rengstorf, Lukas, 271; Lagrange, Luc, 592; Taylor, Mark, 593; Morris, Luke, 329-30). The variant ἐσκοτίσθη probably represents the attempt of a scribe to avoid the suggestion of an eclipse.

[2] Taylor (Mark, 593) and Haenchen (Weg Jesu, 523) refer to the tradition of a supernatural darkness at Caesar's death. Str-B, I, 1040-42 cite stories of supernatural signs at the deaths of great rabbis.

[3] Schreiber, Theologie des Vertrauens, 32-3; Popkes, Christus Traditus, 230-1, n. 654.

[4] Danker, "Demonic Secret," 51.   [5] Schenk, Passionsbericht, 42.

[6] Albright-Mann, Matthew 333; Grundmann, Markus, 315.

[7] Schmid, Mark, 295.

[8] Rawlinson, Mark, 235; McNeile, Matthew, 420-21; Hans Conzelmann, "σκότος . . . ," TDNT, VII, 439; Burkill, Mysterious Revelation, 245; Bonnard, Matthieu, 405; W. D. Davies, The Setting of the Sermon on the Mount (Cambridge: University Press, 1964), 84; Anderson, Mark, 345.

darkness of creation.¹ These options are not, of course, mutually exclusive, but the decision as to which most closely represents the evangelists' own thinking depends to some extent on the derivation of the concept. It has been suggested that the darkness over the land of Egypt (Ex. 10:22), associated with the Exodus is a fitting parallel for the darkness at Jesus' "exodus."² While this passage is similar to the gospels' narrative in stressing that the darkness was over all the land,³ the incident in Ex. 10:22 is not closely associated with the event of the Exodus as such and the purpose of the sign is different from that presumed in the gospels. It is more likely that the darkness is to be seen in relation to the frequent prophetic association of darkness with the time of the eschatological convulsions (cf. Joel 2:10, 31; Is. 13:10, 50:3; Jer. 13:16, 15:9; Am. 8:9). Particularly appropriate, as most scholars recognize, is the reference to a supernatural darkness at noon, predicted for "that day" in Am. 8:9, and associated with "mourning for an only Son" (8:10), destruction of the Temple (9:1) and the taking of the dead out of Sheol (9:1). Joel 3:15 (MT 4:15) is another passage with a similar context,⁴ and it is probably inadmissible to confine the OT background to any single passage; "darkness" as a phenomenon appropriate to the eschaton is the general background conception. The primary

---

¹Davies (Sermon, 84) mentions this as a possibility only.

²J.F.A.Sawyer, "Why is a Solar Eclipse Mentioned in the Passion Narrative (Luke xxiii, 44-5)?" JTS, n.s., XXIII (1974), 124-8; Albright-Mann, Matthew, 353; Taylor, Mark, 593; Montefiore, Synoptic Gospels, II, 383 (along with Jer. 15:9 and Am. 8:9).

³Fenton, Matthew, 442. Senior (Passion Narrative, 293) suggests that Matthew's πᾶς in place of Mark's ὅλος may be due to the influence of Ex. 10:22. It is not certain whether "all the land" includes only Palestine or has a wider reference.

⁴Cf. André Pelletier, "La tradition synoptique du 'voile déchiré' à la lumière des réalités archéologiques," RSR, XLVI (1958), 174.

significance of the darkness will then be that the death of Jesus constitutes a decisive event in the eschatological Day of the Lord, a turning point in which God intervenes for both judgment and salvation.

The darkness and rending of the Temple curtain are recorded in all three synoptic gospels, but Matthew alone mentions an earthquake and the raising of the bodies of saints who then appeared to many in the "Holy City" (Mt. 27:51b-53). While I Kings 19:11 is occasionally adduced as the specific reference with regard to the earthquake and splitting of rocks,[1] the two form a natural combination (cf. also Nah. 1:5-6) as an indication in nature of God's activity and it is undoubtedly in this general sense that Matthew regards the occurrence. A stronger case can be argued for the connection of the resurrection of the saints with a particular OT passage. H. Riesenfeld has sought to isolate a pre-Christian typological interpretation of Ezekiel 37 which included the expectation of a bodily resurrection at the beginning of the Age to Come.[2] In fact, it is suggested by Riesenfeld and Grassi that Ezekiel 37 was read in this sense during Passover.[3] Several verbal and conceptual parallels between Ezekiel 37 and Mt. 27:51b-53 may indicate that Matthew has utilized this Messianic eschatological tradition "to show that Jesus' resurrection opened up the long-awaited Messianic era whose great sign was to be the resurrection of a new Israel."[4] It is probable that a tradition associating

---

[1] McNeile, Matthew, 423; Fenton, Matthew, 444.

[2] H. Riesenfeld, The Resurrection in Ezekiel XXXVII and the Dura-Europos Paintings (Uppsala: A. B. Lundequistskan and Leipzig: Otto Harrassowitz, 1948), 34-5.

[3] b. Meg. 31a. Riesenfeld, Resurrection, 35; J. Grassi, "Ezekiel XXXVII, 1-14 and the New Testament," NTS, XI (1964-5), 162-3.

[4] Grassi, "Ezekiel XXXVII, 1-14," 164. Grassi adduces the σεισμος (37:7), opening of tombs (Ez. 37:12), Holy City (37:12a); while

a resurrection of the dead with the Messianic Age was current in first century Palestine, but the specific utilization of Ezekiel 37 at that time is more difficult to prove.[1] The similarities between Ezekiel 37 and Mt. 27:52-3 are not particularly close or striking and it seems probable that Ezekiel 37 has influenced Matthew only as one component in the tradition to which he refers. Whatever the basis for Matthew's account, therefore, it is improbable that he makes direct use of any OT passage.[2]

A final element in the narrative of Jesus' death that is claimed to represent an indication of the eschaton is the notice in Mark (15:37) and Matthew (27:50) that Jesus uttered a great cry ($\phi\omega\nu\eta$ $\mu\epsilon\gamma\alpha\lambda\eta$) immediately before giving up the spirit.[3] The concept of a great cry is one that is claimed to be prominent in apocalyptic schemes relating to the end of the world and it is suggested that the notice of Jesus' final cry has originated in this tradition.[4]

---

the themes of Resurrection, the return of a reunified people (37:12,14), and the purpose of the sign as a manifestation of God's power (37:6,14) are mentioned by Senior (Passion Narrative, 320). Cf. also Noth, "God, King and Nation," 153; Schenk, Passionsbericht, 95; Schweizer, Matthew, 515; Albright-Mann, Matthew, 350. Jean Daniélou (Études d'exégèse judéo-chrétienne, Théologie Historique, V (Paris: Beauchesne & Sons, 1966), 111-16) collects patristic references which he believes indicate the general use of Ez. 37 as a testimonium in the early church.

[1]Davies (Sermon, 85), refers to the tradition but does not mention Ez. 37. Cf. also Donald Senior, "The Death of Jesus and the Resurrection of the Holy Ones," CBQ, XXXVIII (1974), 312-29.

[2]Other suggested OT backgrounds (Am. 9:2 -- Davies, Sermon, 85; Is. 26:19, Dan. 12:2 (through the tradition preserved in Jn. 5:25-9) -- W. G. Essane, "Matthew xxvii. 51-54 and John v. 25-29," ExpTim, LXXVI (1964), 103) are less probable. Le Déaut (La nuit pascale, 206) mentions a Jewish tradition that associated the resurrection of the Patriarchs with the appearing of the suffering Messiah b. Ephraim, but the date of the tradition is uncertain.

[3]Matthew's expression ($\dot{\alpha}\phi\tilde{\eta}\kappa\epsilon\nu$ $\tau\grave{o}$ $\pi\nu\epsilon\tilde{\upsilon}\mu\alpha$) has been related to Gen. 35:18 LXX, but $\psi\upsilon\chi\acute{\eta}$ is used there and the parallel is almost certainly coincidental. (Cf. McNeile, Matthew, 423; Albright-Mann, Matthew, 350).

[4]Schreiber, Theologie des Vertrauens, 32-8; Bartsch, "Historische

However, the existence of such an apocalyptic complex of events associated with the eschaton is difficult to isolate for this period,[1] and the lack of this complex renders unfeasible the apocalyptic understanding of Jesus' cry. Others suggest a reference to Righteous Sufferer psalms which feature cries,[2] but this too, is unlikely.

Two Figures

The Mosaic Eschatological Prophet

The expectation of a Messianic prophet figure, derived from Deuteronomy 18, was an important aspect of Jewish eschatological expectation in first century Judaism, as the evidence of Qumran and the Samaritan sect demonstrates.[3] There is little doubt that the NT portrays Jesus in this role in several places, and a few allusions to this expectation may be present in the passion sayings. The Jews' mockery of Jesus as a prophet (Mk. 14:65 par.) may reflect the knowledge that Jesus claimed to be, or was hailed as, the "prophet like Moses."[4] Meeks suggests that the emphasis on "hearing Jesus'

Erwägungen," 452; Popkes, Christus Traditus, 231-2, n. 656; Schenk, Passionsbericht, 37-49. Both Schreiber and Schenk isolate an apocalyptic-influenced tradition that has been integrated with another tradition to form the existing crucifixion pericope. Prominent elements in the former tradition are the cosmic signs which are linked with Jesus' death.

[1]Linnemann (Passionsgeschichte, 163-8) properly objects to Schreiber's reconstruction of this apocalyptic complex because the references utilized are too scattered.

[2]Dibelius, "Historische Problem," 196 (Pss. 22:25 and 31:23); Nineham, Mark, 430 (Pss. 31:22 and 39:12); Senior, Passion Narrative, 304 (Ps. 22).

[3]Howard M. Teeple, The Mosaic Eschatological Prophet, JBL Monograph Series, X (Philadelphia: SBL, 1957), 30-56; J. Louis Martyn, History and Theology in the Fourth Gospel (New York and Evanston: Harper & Row, 1968), 96-99.

[4]Longenecker, Christology, 35. He conjectures that the mockers

voice" in Jn. 18:37 recalls the figure of the prophet, whose words are identified with God's and upon which divine judgment hangs.[1] On a more general level, Black points to certain traditions (especially at Qumran) that expected the coming prophet to suffer martyrdom, an expectation based partly on Isaiah 53. He conjectures that this tradition may have helped to bridge the gap between Son of Man and Suffering Servant: "Such a Jewish belief in a 'prophet like unto Moses' meeting a martyr's death in fulfillment of Isaiah's prophecies may at any rate partly account for the origins of the NT doctrine that the Son of Man must suffer."[2]

The belief that Jesus fulfilled the role of the eschatological prophet very possibly underlies the incident recorded in Mk. 14:65 and may be important for the understanding of Jesus' claim in Jn. 18:37, but the meagerness of the evidence suggests that this aspect of Jesus' Person and work was not very important in the narrating and understanding of Jesus' sufferings.[3] It is in relation to Jesus' teaching and the necessity to obey it that the correlations with the prophet are prominent (cf. Acts 3:22ff).

Joseph

It has been urged that Joseph of Arimathea, who requested permission from Pilate to bury Jesus, is to be compared with Joseph the Patriarch, who begged the permission of Pharaoh to bury the body of his father.[4] Reference to Joseph has also been posited in Jesus'

---

would then be indicating, in effect, that Jesus was not like Moses, but like the veiled Balaam (Num. 24:3).

[1]Meeks, Prophet-King, 67.   [2]Black, "Servant of the Lord," 3-11.
[3]Teeple, Prophet, 93.
[4]Richardson, Theology, 204.

words to the penitent thief (cf. Gen. 40:14), in Christ's crucifixion between two robbers[1] and in his betrayal for money.[2] In the light of the almost complete lack of references to the Joseph tradition in the NT, however, these allusive parallels can hardly be confirmed.

Miscellaneous Parallels

Matthew 26:4b (Exodus 21:14)

Gundry, following the suggestion of Lohmeyer-Schmauch, finds an allusion to Ex. 21:14 in the words ($\dot{\epsilon}\nu$) $\delta\delta\lambda\omega$ . . . $\dot{\alpha}\pi\omicron\kappa\tau\epsilon\acute{\iota}\nu\omega\sigma\iota\nu$ (LXX . . . $\dot{\alpha}\pi\omicron\kappa\tau\epsilon\tilde{\iota}\nu\alpha\iota$ . . . $\delta\delta\lambda\omega$).[3] While $\delta\delta\lambda\omicron\varsigma$ is used only here in Matthew, it is not unexpected in the context and $\dot{\alpha}\pi\omicron\kappa\tau\epsilon\acute{\iota}\nu\omega$ is the normal verb for "to kill." The verbal parallel is not, therefore, striking, and the context of the Exodus passage (punishments for Sabbath-breakers) is certainly not a likely quarry of <u>testimonia</u>. That Matthew uses the verse ironically as an example of the hypocrisy of the Jewish authorities[4] attributes greater subtlety to Matthew in his use of the OT than is warranted.

Luke 23:6-12; 23:35 (Psalm 2:2)

It is frequently asserted that the narration of the appearance of Jesus before Herod Antipas, which emphasizes the friendship between Pilate and Herod which grew out of this consultation, is to be seen

---

[1] Klein, "Zur Erläuterung der Evangelien," 147.

[2] With reference to the selling of Joseph into slavery, Gen. 37:26ff (Fenton, <u>Matthew</u>, 413).

[3] Gundry, <u>Old Testament</u>, 56; Lohmeyer-Schmauch, <u>Matthäus</u>, 348.

[4] "Das Synedrium selbst begeht also den Frevel, den das von ihm zu hütende Gesetz Gottes aufs strengste ahndet." (Lohmeyer-Schmauch, <u>Matthäus</u>, 348).

in the light of Ps. 2:2, "The Kings of the earth take their stand, And the rulers take counsel together Against the Lord and against His Anointed."[1] This verse is quoted in Acts 4:25-6, and the examples of Herod and Pilate are specifically referred to (v. 27). This quotation renders it certain that Luke must have regarded the scene before Herod as a correspondence to Ps. 2:2, but this need not indicate that Luke has invented the incident with this purpose in mind:[2] "It seems doubtful, however, if the interpretation itself would have arisen at all had there not been some foundation for it in a historical connection between Herod (as well as Pilate) and the death of Jesus . . . ."[3]

It has been suggested that a possible allusion to LXX Ps. 2:2 may be seen in Luke's characterization of the "high priests and scribes" with ἄρχοντες in 23:35.[4] While Luke knows of the Messianic application of this passage, ἄρχοντες is a normal word for "rulers" (seven times elsewhere in Luke) and is not, therefore, when used alone, a significant link to Ps. 2:2.

---

[1] Loisy, Quatrième Évangile, 547; Caird, Luke, 247; Hoskyns-Davey, John, II, 612; Dodd, Historical Tradition, 118; Browning, Luke, 162; Grundmann, Lukas, 425; Lampe, "Luke," 841. It is also suggested that the incident fulfills the requirement that two witnesses agree in a condemnation (Dt. 19:15) -- Leaney, Luke, 280; Grundmann, Lukas, 424; Ellis, Luke, 261.

[2] Pace Weidel, "Studien," 239; Martin Dibelius, "'Herodes und Pilatus,'" ZNW, XVI (1915), 122-6; Finegan, Überlieferung, 28; Montefiore, Synoptic Gospels, II, 619; Gilmour, "Luke," 398; William Riley Wilson, The Execution of Jesus: A Judicial, Literary and Historical Investigation (New York: Scribners, 1970), 134-38.

[3] Matthew Black, "The Arrest and Trial of Jesus and the Date of the Last Supper," New Testament Essays, 24; cf. also Harold W. Hoehner, Herod Antipas, SNTSMS, XVII (Cambridge: University Press, 1972), 228-30; Rengstorf, Lukas, 261-2; Benoit, Passion, 144-5; Schneider, Die Passion Jesu, 90.

[4] Schenk, Passionsbericht, 98; Finegan, Überlieferung, 32.

Mark 15:20b (Numbers 15:36)

Wolfgang Schenk considers the word ἐξάγουσιν in Mark to be an allusion to Numbers 15:36, citing the use of ἐξάγω (hapax legomenon in Mark, although cf. 8:23 v.l.) and the analogous situation.[1] However, ἐξάγω is a common enough word and it is unlikely that Mark would describe Jesus' journey to the cross in terms borrowed from the execution of one "who has sinned with a high hand." Schenk's hypothesis is based, in part, on a source analysis of the crucifixion narrative that emphasizes the OT elements as a criterion for differentiating between two traditions.

---

[1] Schenk, Passionsbericht, 25.

CHAPTER VII

CONCLUSIONS

The purpose of this chapter is to bring together the results attained in the study of the passion texts with a view toward determining the basic hermeneutical methods employed. The three levels utilized in the description of Jewish hermeneutics in Chapter I will constitute the basic framework for the summary. A subsidiary purpose will be to rectify the lack of attention hitherto given to the four separate narratives by summarizing distinguishing features in each evangelist's presentation.

As a means of collecting the material, it will be advantageous to employ a table, which will include every OT reference isolated in the course of the study, along with information pertaining to citation technique, the source of the reference and the text-form of the verbal citations.[1]

---

[1] The nomenclature employed to designate text-form is self-explanatory, except for the abbreviation "Sem.," which will be used to designate a text-form which is clearly Semitic, but which cannot be certainly delimited to any one Semitic language.

TABLE 4

SUMMARY OF OLD TESTAMENT PASSAGES USED
IN THE GOSPEL PASSION TEXTS

OT	Matthew	Mark	Luke	John	Citation Technique; Text-Form
Unspecified; General	26:24	14:21	22:22	-	*Direct
	26:56	14:49	-	-	*Direct
	26:54	-	-	-	*Direct
Isaiah					
42:1(Ps. 2:7)	3:17	1:11	3:22	-	All - Heb
	20:19	10:34	18:32-33	-	*All - LXX
50:6	26:67	14:65	-	18:22(?)	All - LXX
	27:30	15:19	-	19:1,3 (?)	All - LXX
52:13	-	-	-	3:14, 8:28, 12:32	*All - LXX[a]
	17:22	9:31	9:44	-	
53 ($\pi\alpha\rho\alpha\delta\iota\delta\omega\mu\iota$)	20:18	10:33	18:32	-	*Con - Sem (All - LXX)[b]
	26:24	14:21	22:22	-	
	26:45	14:41	-	-	
53	-	-	22:21-38	-	*Con
53	-	-	-	10:11,15, 17	*Con
53:3	-	9:12b(?)	-	-	*All - Sem
53:4	27:39-43 (?)	15:29-32 (?)	23:35-37 (?)	-	Con

TABLE 4 -- Continued

OT	Matthew	Mark	Luke	John	Citation Technique; Text-Form
	26:63	14:61	-	-	
53:7	27:14	15:5	-	19:9(?)	Con
	27:12	-	-	-	
	-	-	23:9	-	
53:7	-	-	-	1:29	Con
53:9	27:57	-	-	-	All - Heb
53:10-12	20:28	10:45	-	-	*All - Heb
53:12c	26:28	14:24	22:20	-	*All - Heb
53:12d	-	-	22:37	-	*EQ - Heb, LXX

Zechariah

OT	Matthew	Mark	Luke	John	Citation Technique; Text-Form
9:9	21:4-5	-	-	12:14-15	EQ; Mt. - Heb, LXX? Jn. - ?
	-	11:7	19:35	-	All - ?
11:12	26:15	-	-	-	All - LXX
11:12-13	27:9-10	-	-	-	EQ - Heb
12:10	-	-	-	19:37	EQ - Heb; θ (?)
13:7	26:31	14:27	-	-	*EQ; Mk. - Heb; LXX^Q Mt. - Heb; LXX^A
	-	-	-	16:32(?)	*All - ?
13:8-9	26:32	14:28	-	-	*Con
13:1, 14:8	-	-	-	19:34	Con
12:10, 13:7	-	-	-	10:11,15,17	*Con

TABLE 4 -- Continued

OT	Matthew	Mark	Luke	John	Citation Technique Text-Form
Psalms					
6:3	-	-	-	12:27(?)	*Ling
22:1	27:46	15:34	-	-	*Q - Sem(Tg;Pesh?)
22:7a	-	-	23:35a	-	All - LXX
22:7b	27:39	15:29a	-	-	All - ?
22:8	27:43	-	-	-	Q - Heb (?)
22:18	27:35a	15:24	23:34b	-	All - LXX (?)
	-	-	-	19:24	EQ - LXX
27:2	-	-	-	18:6(?)	All - LXX
27:12	-	14:57-58 (?)	-	-	All - Heb
31:5	-	-	23:46	-	*Q - LXX (?)
31:13	26:3-4a	-	-	-	All - LXX
35:4	-	-	-	18:6(?)	All - LXX
35:11	-	14:57-58 (?)	-	-	All - Heb
35:19	-	-	-	15:25(??)	(*EQ - ?)
38:11	27:55a	15:40a	23:49	-	All - LXX
41:9	-	14:18	-	-	*All - Heb, DSS (?)
	-	-	-	13:18	*EQ - Heb, DSS (?)
42:5,11;43:5	26:38	14:34	-	-	*Ling - LXX
42:6	-	-	-	12:27	*Ling - LXX
69:4	-	-	-	15:25	*EQ - ?
69:9	-	-	-	2:17	EQ - LXX
69:21a	27:34	-	-	-	All - ?

TABLE 4 -- Continued

OT	Matthew	Mark	Luke	John	Citation Technique Text-Form
69:21b	27:48	15:35-36	23:36	19:28b-29	All - ?
69:21	-	-	-	19:28a	(*)EQ - Con
Sacrificial Passages and Concepts					
Ex. 24:8	26:28	14:24	22:20	-	*All - Sem (Tg.?)
Levitical expiatory sacrifices	26:28	-	-	-	*Con
	-	-	-	6:51-58	*Con
	26:25-30 (?)	14:21-25 (?)	22:15-20 (?)	-	*Con
	-	-	-	1:29	Con
Paschal Lamb	-	-	-	19:6(?)	Con
	-	-	-	19:29(?)	Con
(Ex. 12:46; Num. 9:12)	-	-	-	19:36	EQ - Heb (?)
Miscellaneous Passages					
Num. 21:8-9	-	-	-	3:14	*Direct
Ps. 2:2	-	-	23:6-12 (?)	-	Con
	21:42	12:10-11	20:17	-	*EQ - LXX
Ps. 118:22	-	8:31	9:22	-	*All - LXX (?)
	-	-	17:25	-	*All - LXX (?)
Jer. 19	27:9-10	-	-	-	Con
Lam. 2:15	27:39	15:29a	-	-	All - ?

356   The OT in the Gospel Passion Narratives

TABLE 4 -- Continued

OT	Matthew	Mark	Luke	John	Citation Technique Text-Form
Ez. 37	27:51-53 (?)	-	-	-	Con
Amos 8:9, Joel 3:15, et al.	27:45	15:33	23:44-45a	-	Con
Jon. 1:17	12:40	-	-	-	*Direct

^aWhile the reference to Is. 52:13 in these verses seems to be related to the LXX in its present form, it is likely that the original concept was expressed through a single Aramaic word (cf., supra, 100).

^bIt will be recalled that an original appropriation of the "handing over" concept in Aramaic, followed by a verbal allusion to the LXX of Is. 53 was the process reconstructed.

Before beginning the first major section on literary framework, it will be appropriate to summarize the evidence of this table as it relates to the use of the OT passages generally and to the relationships among the four accounts in this area.

First, the investigation has confirmed the generally held opinion that the Servant Songs of Isaiah form the OT context most often utilized as a background to describe Jesus' passion and death. Not only are these passages cited more often than any other,[1] they are the most popular in each of the gospels as well. (The only possible exception to this situation is John, who evidences little interest in the Servant conception.[2]) The remaining OT backgrounds are used in

---

[1]Isaiah -- 47; Lament Psalms -- 30; Zechariah 9-14 -- 14; Sacrificial conceptions -- 7; Ps. 118:22 -- 6; Other -- 9. Even when allowances are made for the two references to Isaiah 53 which are found in a number of places, the preponderance remains.

[2]John adds two allusions and one conceptual reference, but each of these is paralleled in the synoptics, and some degree of

approximately the same proportion in the four narratives, the only exception being Luke's almost total lack of interest in Zechariah 9-14.[1]

Secondly, it is significant how few references are made to OT passages outside the four major background contexts which have been isolated; a situation even more remarkable when it is noted that the several citations of Ps. 118:22 could conceivably be considered as within the scope of the lament psalms.

Thirdly, the number of references attributed to Jesus, relative to the number found in the evangelists' own narrations, should be noted. Looking first at this proportion within the four accounts, it is interesting that only in Matthew are there more references of the evangelist's than are attributed to Jesus. Mark stands at the other extreme, with the proportionately greatest number of references on Jesus' lips.[2] If the same evidence is collated with respect to the different OT contexts, it is discovered that the Servant conception, sacrificial terminology and several miscellaneous passages (especially Ps. 118:22) are referred to more frequently by Jesus than by the evangelists, while the reverse is the case with respect to the use of Zechariah 9-14 and the Lament Psalms.

Fourthly, although perhaps obvious, it is to be noted that Jesus is presented as making clear reference to every important OT background utilized in the passion sayings.

---

doubt concerning the presence of a reference exists. Reim's conclusion (Hintergrund, 95) that John himself used only Psalm 69 in the LXX translation, is interesting, although surely an exaggeration.

[1] Luke's single allusion, in the Triumphal Entry narrative, is hardly emphatic.

[2] The statistics are these (Evangelist/Jesus): Matthew -- 20/15; John -- 11/11; Luke -- 10/12; Mark -- 12/16.

Before leaving the area of actual OT text usage, it is appropriate to analyze briefly the relationship between the OT element and the general presentation of the passion in each gospel.

Burkill's characterization of Mark's passion is generally accurate:

> . . . the story of the passion in the second gospel is primarily a description of the dark passage, so to speak, through which the Messiah must proceed before he can appear to the world with great power and glory.[1]

The general tendency of Mark to present Jesus as the suffering Son of God is reflected in the frequent explicit statements concerning the necessity of suffering.[2] Furthermore, although few explicit citations of the OT are found, the passion is filled with allusions, "demonstrating how deeply determination according to the Scriptures has entered into his view of the Passion."[3] Is it the case, however, that this simple determinism and a general correspondence between Jesus' passion and the OT is all that is intended by Mark? Suhl, who, like his mentor Willi Marxsen, views Mark's Gospel as written under an overwhelming sense of the nearness of the end, claims that this conviction led to a lack of interest in history and, consequently, to a lack of concern with Jesus' fulfillment of specific prophecies. As Suhl puts it:

> . . . die als Gotteshandeln geglaubten Ereignisse unter dem Postulat der Schriftgemässheit so erzahlt wurden, dass man sie, sofern man sich dessen bewusst bzw. passende Formulierungen fand, in alttestamentlichen Wendungen erzählte. Dabei ging es zunächst noch gar nicht um 'Weissagung und Erfüllung,' sondern um Auslegung des Jesusgeschehens mit Hilfe des AT: In dem man das Neue in den

---

[1] "St. Mark's Philosophy," 252.

[2] As Conzelmann says, "Jesus is led as King to the Cross. And the cross is the presentation of the nature of his rule." (Theology, 191).

[3] Best, Temptation and Passion, 43.

'Farben' des Alten erzählte, machte man deutlich, dass es auch im Neuen um dasselbe wie in Alten, nämlich um Gottes Heilshandeln ging.[1]

There are, however, several weaknesses in Suhl's understanding of Mark's relationship to the OT. His entire viewpoint is conditioned by Marxsen's questionable theory concerning the Sitz im Leben of Mark's Gospel.[2] Second, Suhl is unsuccessful in his attempt to explain away the admittedly few, but nevertheless clear, references to "fulfillment" (14:49, cf. 14:27).[3] Third, and perhaps most importantly, it is not legitimate to conclude from the allusive nature of the majority of OT references in Mark that he intends them to have a solely descriptive function. As Miller properly indicates,

> The presence of OT words and phrases in a Gospel tradition not only can function as an interpretation of the Scripture, but can serve as well to give significance and meaning to that tradition beyond an abstract assertion of correspondence with the will of God.[4]

Maurer stresses this same point when he speaks about the "de facto" use of the OT in Mark; " . . . welcher durch die blosse Erzählung von Tatsachen die Erfüllung der Schrift in der Person Jesu schildert."[5]

---

[1] Alttestamentlichen Zitate, 46-7; cf. also Alexander Sand, "'Wie geschrieben steht . . . ' -- zur Auslegung der jüdischen Schriften in den urchristlichen Gemeinden," Schriftauslegung: Hermeneutik des Neuen Testaments und im Neuen Testament, ed. by Joseph Ernst (Munich/Paderborn/Vienna: Ferdinand Schöningh, 1972), 342.

[2] D. Moody Smith, "The Use of the Old Testament in the New," The Use of the Old Testament in the New and Other Essays (Studies in honor of William Franklin Stinespring), ed. by James M. Efird (Durham, N.C.: Duke University Press, 1972), 42; Hugh Anderson, "The Old Testament in Mark's Gospel," The Use of the Old Testament in the New and Other Essays, 286.

[3] Anderson, "Old Testament," 286; Joachim Rohde, Rediscovering the Teaching of the Evangelists, trans. by Dorothea M. Barton (London: SCM, 1968), 141.

[4] "Midrash," 72. [5] "Knecht Gottes," 7; Rohde, Rediscovering, 141.

Mark concentrates on two particular scriptural portions in describing the passion of Jesus; the Servant Songs and the Psalms of Lament. The latter are used to depict Jesus' way as the way of his royal forebear, David, who suffered innocently on his road to exaltation. References to the Servant Songs, generally allusive and on the lips of Jesus, provide an implicit theory of atonement -- especially Jesus' words in Mk. 10:45 and 14:24 stand out as clear announcements of the significance of Calvary in Mark.[1]

Matthew is substantially faithful to his Marcan source,[2] and, in terms of OT references, departs from Mark only in his attempt to furnish scriptural enlightenment on the act of betrayal.

Luke, on the other hand, modifies rather clearly the picture of the passion in Matthew and Mark, lightening "the unrelieved gloom" of those accounts.[3] His use of the OT contributes to this tendency: a prayer of trust (Ps. 31:5) is substituted for a cry of despair (Ps. 22:1) and the OT-influenced mockery narrative is shortened. While Luke has fewer OT references than Matthew or Mark, it is not fair to conclude that he is uninterested in the OT.[4] OT references occur at decisive points in the narrative; particularly to be noted is the programmatic announcement in Lk. 22:37 which is peculiar to the third gospel. It is true, however, that fewer detailed correspondences are

---

[1] Pace Kee, "Function of Scriptural Quotations," 183; Reumann, Psalm 22," 52.

[2] Senior, Passion Narrative, 336.

[3] To use Creed's, perhaps exaggerated, characterization (Luke, 284).

[4] Pace Schulz, Mitte der Schrift, 135. See, on Luke's attitude toward the OT, especially Paul Schubert, "The Structure and Significance of Luke 24," Neutestamentliche Studien für Rudolf Bultmann, ed. by W. Eltester, BZNW, XXI (2nd ed.; Berlin: Töpelmann, 1957), 165-86. Note also Franklin, Christ the Lord, 70-73.

to be found in Luke's passion account, corresponding to his general tendency to concentrate on the larger themes pertaining to the Heilsgeschichte.[1] Finally, the frequently expressed opinion that Luke fails to accord to Jesus' death redemptive significance must be questioned -- Luke 22:37 comes very close to doing just this, while Lk. 22:20 (if the longer text is read) certainly does.[2]

John's passion narrative presents Jesus in the role of a royal personage, moving to the cross, itself a point of exaltation rather than humiliation, with dignity and sovereign control over the situation.[3] Several features of this presentation are related to the use of the OT. The cross in John is regarded not so much as something which is essential because Scripture predicts it (cf. the δεῖ of the synoptic predictions), as a fate willingly embraced by Jesus.[4] The use of the OT in John's passion sayings is oriented toward demonstrating the significance of Jesus' "lifting up" rather than toward proving that Jesus' sufferings were willed by God. Second, in keeping with this approach, John's use of the lament psalms presents a striking contrast to their role in the synoptics. Whereas the latter use these passages predominantly through narrative allusions to characterize specific incidents in Jesus' suffering, John has many more quotations of than allusions to these psalms and their purpose

---

[1] Schneider, Passion Jesu, 168.

[2] Richard Zehnle ("The Salvific Character of Jesus' Death in Lucan Soteriology," TS, XXX (1969), 420-44) concludes that Luke does intend to teach the salvific meaning of Jesus' death, although not as a "substitution."

[3] Bultmann, John, 632-33; Schnackenburg, Johannes, III, 246; Dauer, Passionsgeschichte, 200; Winter, Trial, 115. John's emphasis on this theme certainly does not justify regarding the passion narrative in John as a "postscript" (pace Ernst Käsemann, The Testament of Jesus, trans. by Gerhard Krodel (Philadelphia: Fortress, 1968), 7); indeed, this would be to miss the very point of the exaltation theology in John.

[4] Dauer, Passionsgeschichte, 40.

is directed toward providing a rationale for the suffering. Thirdly, however, the general Johannine presentation of the crucifixion as an exaltation should not be emphasized to the extent that the reality of Jesus' human sufferings in the narrative is overlooked. With the Psalm 69:9-influenced cry in 19:28 ("I thirst"), this aspect is prominently included.

Another aspect of John's use of the OT in the passion might be pointed out -- the concentration of quotations in the crucifixion pericope. Four of John's nineteen OT quotations occur in Jn. 19: 23-37.[1] Barrett claims these quotations are distinctive as compared with John's general method of appeal to the OT because they fail to evidence "the range and freedom of knowledge and selection" found elsewhere.[2] While this may be true of Jn. 19:24 (= Ps. 22:18), it is unjustified so to regard the other three. These, it can be argued, are featured in this narrative as climactic summaries of three important Johannine themes: the humanity and real suffering of Jesus (19:28); the sacrificial nature of Jesus' death as the Passover Lamb (19:36 = Ex. 12:46); and the Cross as that event to which all men must look for salvation and judgment (Jn. 19:37 = Zech. 12:10).

Finally, the charge that John has abandoned the common early Christian view of Jesus' death as an atonement for sins[3] must be examined. While it cannot be denied that John introduces a new perspective on Jesus' salvific work which emphasizes particularly the significance of the incarnation as a revelation of God, it is unjustified to claim that the redemptive value and sacrificial

---

[1] Cf. Schenk, Passionsbericht, 138, on this.

[2] Barrett, "The Old Testament in the Fourth Gospel," 155-168 (168). On John's use of the OT to evoke "les grandes traditions d'Israël," cf. also Braun, Jean le Théologien, I, 225-27, et passim; Amsler, L'Ancien Testament, 39-44.

[3] Bultmann, Theology, II, 52-55.

significance of Jesus' death have thereby been abandoned. The sacrificial nature of Jesus' death is clearly enunciated in Jn. 1:29, 6:51-8 and 19:36, and the "exaltation" to which Jesus looks forward cannot be separated from the crucifixion.[1] Furthermore, Jn. 19:34 and 37 testify to the fact that, for John, the life-giving Spirit and "the judgment of the world" came only after, and as a result of, the death of Christ.

The Literary Framework

The subjects to be investigated in this context include a summary of the citation procedures employed in the passion texts, and an examination of the text-form of the verbal citations.

Citation Procedures

Some negative conclusions with respect to the citation procedures isolated earlier in Jewish literature should be made first. It is not surprising, given the subject matter of this study, that no example of a summary of OT history and teaching was found. Of more significance is the fact that no clear instance of a structural style was discovered. In no case, that is, was it evident that the portrayal of the passion events owed its basic outline to a specific OT passage. Probably the narratives that come closest to this style are the crucifixion accounts in Matthew and Mark as related to Psalm 22. Even here, however, the order of allusions to the psalm does not correspond to the sequence in the psalm

---

[1] Pace Bultmann, Theology, II, 53. Bultmann seeks to evade the force of verses like these by suggesting "one may wonder whether in using certain expressions John was adapting himself to the common theology of the church." (53).

364   The OT in the Gospel Passion Narratives

and other OT contexts are used at the same time. It is, of course, true that the general picture of sufferings presented in several of the psalms and in Isaiah 53 is substantially reproduced in Jesus' passion. But the conception is too general to warrant the conclusion that the gospel passages were based on these OT backgrounds.

Examples of all other citation procedures are found in the passion texts. Especially noteworthy is the large number of conceptual references and allusions. These outnumber quotations by a ratio of over four-to-one. Again, it is instructive to summarize citation procedures with reference both to the respective evangelists and the OT backgrounds. John represents an exception to the general picture sketched above; of his nineteen passion references, eight take the form of an explicit quotation. Furthermore, at three points, allusions to particular OT passages in the synoptics are found as quotations in John.[1] Of the synoptists, Matthew has the highest percentage of quotations, while Luke and Mark do not have a single quotation in their own material. The most striking aspect of the relationship between citation procedure and the OT passages involved is the fact that only one quotation from the Servant Songs occurs in any of the passion texts. Zechariah 9-14, on the other hand, is referred to most often by means of an explicit quotation.

It is doubtful whether any significant implications can be drawn from the incidence of citation procedures. In principle, the choice of citation technique may be dictated by at least four different factors: the intended audience of the author (more explicit citations being required for those less well-acquainted with the OT); the purpose of the reference (apologetically-oriented ones

---

[1] Jn. 13:18 (Mk. 14:18); Jn. 19:24 (Mk. 15:24/Mt. 27:35a/Lk. 23:34b); Jn. 19:28 (Mk. 15:35-36/Mt. 27:48/Lk. 23:36(?)).

requiring greater elaboration);[1] the nature of the OT passage involved; and the general hermeneutical approach of the author. Which of these considerations prevail in any given situation is almost impossible to determine. In general, however, the greater preference for explicit references in Matthew and John, and the predominance of narrative allusions in reference to the lament psalms in the synoptics should be noted.

The Text-Form of Verbal Citations

The relatively small number of references in which a textual source can be determined with any degree of probability renders tentative any conclusions drawn from this material, but several interesting trends can be observed.

A rather clear distinction can be seen in the relationship between citation procedure and text-form: narrative allusions tend to be Septuagintal in form, whereas all other types display a greater reliance on Semitic text-types.[2] This would indicate that OT references which are intimately related to the narrative were either originally adduced in Greek or have been assimilated to the LXX in the course of transmission;[3] while those citations which are set off from the narrative have retained a Semitic cast.

---

[1] Cf. Patte's comments on the practice at Qumran, supra, 23-24.

[2] Of seventeen narrative allusions, nine are Septuagintal. Of the thirty other references where a textual background can be discovered, only nine are Septuagintal.

[3] Although Johnson's caution about the extent of assimilation is probably justified: "If its tradition [Matthew's quotes] had become extremely corrupt, it seems to me that Mt., being the favorite gospel, would have been forced into much more conformity to the LXX than the others; but this is not the case." ("Biblical Quotations," 153).

One aspect of this situation worthy of comment is that allusions attributed to Jesus have not undergone the same process of assimilation. These are strongly Semitic-oriented,[1] as are most of the quotations found on his lips as well.[2] Moreover, several of Jesus' citations seem to show influence from variant Palestinian Semitic text-types.[3] The evidence of the passion texts, then, serves to confirm the conclusion of T. W. Manson, respecting Jesus' use of the OT:

> . . . our consideration of the texts points to the conclusion that our Lord did make frequent appeal to the Old Testament in his teaching, and we have definite traces in the Gospels of the fact that he quoted it in the original Hebrew and/or in the Aramaic Targum.[4]

Those instances in which an OT citation on Jesus' lips is related to the LXX can be accounted for by: (1) assimilation to the LXX on the part of the evangelist(s);[5] (2) quotation in a Semitic text-type underlying the LXX;[6] or (3) original quotation in the Greek of the LXX. Furthermore, the possibility that quotation was made by memory, accounting for mixed citations and unique renderings, must be reckoned with,[7] although the principle must not be used as a panacea for the solving of all textual difficulties. At any rate,

---

[1] Ten (perhaps thirteen) of sixteen are related to a Semitic text-type.

[2] The exceptions are the word-for-word LXX quotations of Ps. 118:22 in Mk. 12:10/Mt. 21:42/Lk. 20:17, and the LXX influence on Lk. 22:37 and 23:46.

[3] Mk. 15:34/Mt. 27:46 -- Tg.; Mt. 26:31/Mk. 14:27 -- $LXX^{A\&Q}$; Mk. 14:24/Mt. 26:28/Lk. 22:20 -- Tg.; Jn. 13:18, Mk. 14:18 -- DSS.

[4] "Old Testament," 331. The study also serves to confirm the more general results of M. Black (Aramaic Approach, 271).

[5] B. M. Metzger, "Scriptural Quotations in Q Material," ExpTim, LXV (1963-64), 125; Manson, "Old Testament," 322.

[6] Longenecker, Biblical Exegesis, 64-66.

[7] Karnetzki, "Alttestamentlichen Zitate," 24.

it is important to point out that, given the fluid status of the OT text in Jesus' day, conformity to the LXX in Jesus' OT references is no argument against authenticity. As Metzger says, " . . . in the main it cannot be assumed that every discourse which, as reported to us, contains quotations from the Old Testament in the words of the LXX could not have previously existed in Aramaic."[1] On the other hand, the presence of a Semitic text-form remains a factor favoring the authenticity of the saying.[2]

If the text-form of the citations found in each gospel is examined, the generally accepted position that Luke was strongly influenced by the LXX[3] is borne out. Only he has more references based on the LXX than on a Semitic version, and significantly more at that.[4]

The slight number of explicit quotations in Mark's gospel which have been examined in this study precludes any judgment on the validity of the observation that Mark's "formal quotations are almost purely Septuagintal."[5] But, as far as all OT references are concerned, the present investigation has tended to confirm the conclusion of Manson that, especially in Jesus' words, there can be found no special tendency to follow the LXX.[6] While often noted,[7]

---

[1] "Scriptural Quotations," 125.

[2] Smith, "Old Testament in the New," 24; Gundry, "Language Milieu," 407-08.

[3] Holtz (Untersuchungen, 166) believes Luke used only the LXX.

[4] Of Luke's ten references in which a text-form can be discerned, three are Semitic, six are Septuagintal and one is mixed.

[5] The conclusion of Gundry (Old Testament Quotations, 9).

[6] "Old Testament," 314.

[7] W. C. Allen, "The Old Testament Quotations in St. Matthew and St. Mark. II. St. Matthew," ExpTim, XII (1900-01), 284; Kilpatrick, Origins, 56; Stendahl, School, 162.

our study has furnished no example in which Matthew has assimilated an OT reference to the text of the LXX; on the other hand, the unique text-form of Matthew's "formula quotations" is clearly evident in the two citations which have come under our purview.[1] Nothing significant can be concluded as to John's text preference, inasmuch as the number of OT references researched (five) is too small.[2]

It is appropriate to inquire briefly into possible explanations for the phenomenon of the text-form of the OT citations just summarized, beginning with the relationship among the extant accounts. As R. E. Brown observes,[3] the Passion Narrative, with a similar sequence in all four gospels, offers an ideal place for the study of their literary relationships. Although the remarks made here must necessarily be

---

[1] Both quotations studied (21:4-5; 27:9-10) featured a combination of two OT passages and disagreement with every known OT text. The distinctiveness of Matthew's "formula quotations" was a basic prop in the thesis of Stendahl, but this prop has been rendered rather weak by two criticisms. First, Gundry has concluded that Matthew's formula quotations are not really distinctive; indeed, he claims, outside of Mark's formal quotations, " . . . a mixed textual tradition is displayed elsewhere -- in all strata of the synoptic material and in all forms (narratives, didactic, apocalyptic, etc.)" (Gundry, Old Testament Quotations, 150). Second, even if such a distinct textual form should be proven for Matthew's quotations, the implications drawn by Stendahl are questionable. Cross says: "Stendahl wrote before the character of the Old Testament text at Qumran had become fully known, so that his work presumes a view of the Old Testament text which virtually identifies the text of the early Christian era with the single Massoretic tradition. In view of the relatively fluid state of the Old Testament in the earliest Christian period, his results must be qualified at a number of points." (Frank Moore Cross, Jr., The Ancient Library of Qumran and Modern Biblical Studies, The Haskell Lectures, 1956-1957 (London: Duckworth, 1958), 164, n. 39).

[2] For what it is worth, two quotations are clearly related to the LXX (2:17, 19:24), while two are equally clearly related to the MT (13:18, 19:37).

[3] John, II, 787.

limited to the evidence derived from the OT element, the quotations provide valuable data, inasmuch as one is dealing with a fixed point of comparison, whose origin lies outside the gospels.

While hardly in need of further corroboration, the close literary relationship between Matthew and Mark in the Passion Narrative is clearly confirmed by the phenomenon of the OT references. Mark has only two OT references not found in Matthew, and both are brief and implicit.[1] The text-form of the verbal citations which they have in common is always generally similar and at several points identical. Furthermore, the fact that Matthew has two explicit quotations and several allusions not in Mark, and that every one of these occurs in his own narrative, rather than the sayings of Jesus, argues strongly in favor of Mark as the earlier of the two.[2] The phenomenon of the OT references, then, would be in accordance with the conclusion that Matthew is dependent solely upon Mark in the Passion Narrative.[3]

Discussion of Luke's sources has, since Streeter, focused on the question of "proto-Luke," a source distinct from Mark which, it is claimed, formed the basic structure for Luke's work.[4] The OT element in Luke's passion account is certainly fundamentally different from that in Matthew and Mark. Of Luke's thirteen OT references in the

---

[1] Mk. 9:12b; 14:18.

[2] Pace Léon-Dufour, "Mt. et Mc. dans le récit de la Passion," 684-96.

[3] Cf. also Schneider, Passion Jesu, 32 and Senior, Passion Narrative, 353.

[4] See especially: Streeter, Four Gospels, 199-222; Friedrich Rehkopf, Die lukanische Sonderquelle, WUNT, V (Tübingen: Mohr, 1959); Vincent Taylor, The Passion Narrative of St. Luke: A Critical and Historical Investigation, ed. by Owen E. Evans, SNTSMS, XIX (Cambridge: University Press, 1972); Schürmann, Quellenkritischen Untersuchung, III, 138-40; Jeremias, Eucharistic Words, 96-100.

Passion Narrative proper (22-23), six are unique to his gospel and, while most of the common allusions are too brief to allow valid inferences, at least three show distinctive elements.[1] That Luke has used a source in addition to Mark would seem to be a legitimate conclusion,[2] but whether he used this source in preference to Mark is another question. This might, however, be the most natural explanation for the interesting use of Psalm 22:7 in the crucifixion pericopae -- in the same context, with reference to a similar action, Matthew and Mark use the second part of Ps. 22:7, Luke the first.

John's differences from all three synoptics in the matter of OT passion texts are even greater than Luke's independence from Matthew and Mark. John has only six OT references in common with any of the synoptic evangelists; one allusion (of one word) found in the triple tradition,[3] one explicit quotation in common with Matthew,[4] one quotation which is related to an allusion in Mark,[5] and one related to an allusion in the triple tradition,[6] and two conceptual references (which are somewhat questionable) in common with Matthew and Mark.[7] In only one case does the text-form of John's citations display any remarkable agreement with that found in the synoptic references.[8]

---

[1] Lk. 22:20 (Mt. 26:28/Mk. 14:24); Lk. 22:22 (Mt. 26:24/Mk. 14:21); Lk. 23:44-45a (Mt. 27:45/Mk. 15:33).

[2] Cf. P. Winter, "The Treatment of His Sources by the Third Evangelist in Luke XXI-XXIV," ST, VIII (1954), 171; Karabidopolous, "[To Pathos]," 194-97. Pace Creed (Luke, 284) and J. Schreiber (Theologie des Vertrauens, 57).

[3] Jn. 19:28b-29 (Mt. 27:48/Mk. 15:35-36/Lk. 23:36).

[4] Jn. 12:14-15 (Mt. 21:4-5).

[5] Jn. 13:18 (Mk. 14:18).

[6] Jn. 19:24 (Mt. 27:35a/Mk. 15:24/Lk. 23:34b).

[7] Jn. 18:22 (Mt. 26:67/Mk. 14:65); Jn. 19:1,3 (Mt. 27:30/Mk. 15:19).

[8] Jn. 13:18 (Mk. 14:18).

These considerations, while offering no decisive evidence, are in keeping with that viewpoint which sees in John a tradition independent of the canonical synoptic gospels.[1] On the other hand, it is overwhelmingly probable that John was acquainted with sources lying behind the synoptics. As Dauer says:

> Der joh. Bericht von der Kreuzigung und dem Tode Jesu setzt die Synoptiker voraus; denn nur so lassen sich die Gemeinsamkeiten und Ähnlichkeiten mit der redaktionnellen Änderung des Matthäus und Lukas verstehen.[2]

As a stage prior to the extant Passion Narratives, it is frequently asserted that there existed a primitive passion account, usually regarded as a brief, "historical kernel," which has been expanded.[3] While very limited, the phenomena of the OT references provide little support for the existence of such a pre-canonical passion account; the sources involved, in combination with the redactional work of each evangelist, adequately account for the literary relationships. It is significant that a number of recent scholars have disputed the existence of such a pre-canonical narrative.[4]

---

[1] See especially P. Gardner-Smith, St. John and the Synoptic Gospels (Cambridge: University Press, 1938), (56-72); Dodd, Historical Tradition (21-151; 423-32); Brown, John, II, 789-91; Dauer, Passionsgeschichte, 226; Reim, Hintergrund, 92. Ivor Buse ("St. John and the Marcan Passion Narrative," NTS, IV (1957-58); "St. John and the Passion Narratives of St. Matthew and St. Mark," NTS, VII (1960-61)) suggests that John has used the Marcan "B" source, isolated by Taylor.

[2] Passionsgeschichte, 226.

[3] The early form critics regarded the passion narrative as an exception to the rule that the synoptic tradition circulated as small independent units (Bultmann, Synoptic Tradition, 275-84; Dibelius, From Tradition to Gospel, 178-217). Others who advocate the existence of such a narrative: Goguel, Life, 463; Lightfoot, History and Interpretation 126-28; Schulz, Stunde der Botschaft, 116-17; Burkill, "St. Mark's Philosophy," 246; Trocmé, Formation, 59-62; Jeremias, Eucharistic Words, 94-96; Goppelt, Theologie, I, 273; Best, Temptation and Passion, 90-100; Cranfield, Mark, 412; Nineham, Mark, 365. Taylor (Mark, 653-64) sees two separate sources behind Mark's passion narrative: an "A" source, a "simple and straightforward" narrative; and a "B" tradition, composed of supplementary details derived from Peter.

[4] See especially the valuable survey of Gerhard Schneider ("Das

As a final aspect of our investigation into the text-form of the OT references related to the passion, the relevance of the "testimony book" hypothesis must be raised. This hypothesis, whose most noted advocate has been Rendel Harris, seeks to account for certain characteristics of OT quotations in the New by positing the existence of a "reference" document, composed of certain key propetic texts.[1] Generally rejected after Harris' work, the hypothesis has been revivified as a result of the discovery of testimonia documents at Qumran.[2]

As an explanation for the OT quotations studied in this investigation, the testimony book theory is unnecessary. The hypothesis itself rests on the presence of certain unique features found in OT quotations which are shared by different NT authors: (1) peculiar text-forms; (2) composite quotations; (3) "erroneous" ascriptions of authorship; (4) recurring editorial comments; and (5) a fixed polemical orientation.[3]

As far as the passion texts are concerned, quotations with unusual text forms are shared by more than one evangelist, but in each case the common features can be explained either by direct borrowing

---

Problem einer vorkanonischen Passionserzählung," BZ, n.s., XVI (1972), 222-44). Note also: Gottfried Schille, "Das Leiden des Herrn: Die evangelische Passionstradition und ihr 'Sitz im Leben,'" ZTK, LII (1955), 161-205; Linnemann, Studien, 55-59, 171-74; Erhardt Güttgemanns, Offene Fragen zur Formgeschichte des Evangeliums, BEvT, LIV (2nd ed.; Munich: Chr. Kaiser, 1971), 228; Howard Clark Kee, "The Function of Scriptural Quotations and Allusions in Mark 11-16," Jesus und Paulus, 175; Werner H. Kelber, "Conclusion: From Passion Narrative to Gospel," The Passion in Mark, 158.

[1]For a survey of the "testimony book" hypothesis, see Rese, Alttestamentliche Motive, 218-22.

[2]Cf., supra, 12. The relevance of 4QFlor and 4QTest for the kind of book suggested as a source for the NT quotations has been questioned by Braun (Jean le Théologien, I, 27).

[3]Harris, Testimonies, I, 8; cf. also Rese, Alttestamentliche Motive, 218-21.

or by common dependence on an aberrant OT text.¹ A similar situation pertains with respect to composite citations: those found in the passion texts are either peculiar to one gospel (Mt. 27:9-10), or are to be explained by direct literary relationship (Mk. 14:24//). Furthermore, it might be noted that the composite citation in Mt. 21:4-5 (Zech. 9:9, Is. 62:11) is found with a different component in Jn. 12:14-15 (Zech. 9:9, Zeph. 3:16(?)). While Harris and others have appealed to the reference to Jeremiah in the introduction to the quotation in Mt. 27:9-10 as evidence of conflation in the testimony book, we have argued that the reference is made purposefully by Matthew to indicate the importance of Jeremiah 19 in the text. No evidence of relevance to the latter two phenomena is found in the passion texts.

It must be concluded, then, that the evidence for a testimony book in the OT quotations in the passion texts of the gospels is virtually non-existent. Nothing in these texts would suggest the necessity for such a hypothesis. As Prigent puts it:

> . . . il devient évident que les évangélistes ont disposé de traditions scripturaires sur la passion, mais qu'ils ne les ont pas simplement copiées. Ils y ont choisi tantôt un élément, tantôt un autre . . . dans un ensemble qu'il faut donc supposer plus vaste.²

---

¹The fluid state of the OT text in this era only became clear after Harris' work.

²P. Prigent, "Les récits évangeliques de la passion et l'utilisation des 'Testimonia,'" RHR, CLXI (1962), 131. Others who question the existence of a testimony book per se are: Jean-Paul Audet, "L'hypothese des testimonia," RB, LXX (1963), 381-405; Rese, Alttestamentliche Motive, 222-23; Braun, Jean le Théologien, I, 27; W. G. Kummel, "Schriftauslegung. III. Im Urchristentum," RGG³, V, 1518-19; Gundry, Old Testament, 164-65.

Appropriation Techniques

It is our conclusion, founded on the cumulative results of a detailed study of each of the OT references applied to Jesus' passion in the gospels, that Jesus and the evangelists utilize, on the great majority of occasions, a direct appropriation technique. The use of this technique implies, of course, that the two other general appropriation techniques, re-orientation of the text and modification in the point of application, are not frequently resorted to. Without repeating evidence deduced from the study of individual texts, it will be appropriate to examine each of these techniques with reference to the passages as a group and taking into consideration the more general discussion pertaining to these areas.

Re-orientation of the Text

It will be recalled that two particular procedures were utilized by Jewish interpreters of Scripture in order to introduce a meaning *into* an OT text: modification of text and shift in meaning. The former procedure must further be subdivided into two categories, according to whether the modification is a minor one, introduced merely to adapt the OT verse to its new context without altering its meaning, or is substantial, affecting the actual sense of the verse. A number of occurrences of the first type of minor text modification have been found in the gospel passion texts,[1] but it is most significant that only one instance which might be placed in the second category has been discovered. This quotation, in Mt. 27:9-10, could not have been applied directly to the circumstances of Judas'

---

[1] E.g., Mt. 26:31; Mk. 14:18 / Jn. 13:18; Mt. 27:43; Jn. 19:36, 19:37; Jn. 2:17, 15:25.

death without the text changes that Matthew introduces.[1] In another way, Mt. 27:9-10 is unique among the texts studied inasmuch as only in this quotation are major textual changes introduced without support in an extant OT text tradition. It does not seem, therefore, with respect to the passion texts, that any case can be made for the suggestion that Jesus or the evangelists engaged in the wholesale adaptation of the OT text to suit their applications.[2] On the contrary, a high degree of correspondence with known text traditions is characteristic of the verbal OT references in every stratum of the tradition.

A procedure which might be considered an aspect of text modification is the combination of passages, a practice widely employed among Jewish exegetes. Several examples of this technique are found in the passion texts.[3]

The second major way in which OT passages could be given a new orientation was through a shift in meaning, usually involving a violation of the sense of the words in their context. It should be reiterated that such a disregard for context is frequently found in Jewish appropriations of Scripture, but that there are many instances in which such is not the case. A priori, then, even if a strict continuity between Judaism and Christianity is required on this question, either atomistic or contextual exegesis could be expected.

---

[1] Even here, it will be recalled, the basic thrust of Zechariah's prophecy was not altered. Cf., supra, 206-210.

[2] In agreement with the findings of Gundry (Old Testament, 173-74) on Matthew and Hanson (Paul's Technique, 146-47) on Paul. As far as the passion texts are concerned, then, Ellis' statement that the NT is more creative in text creativity than Qumran is not borne out ("Targum," 68, n. 38).

[3] The passion predictions utilize several OT passages; cf. also Mk. 1:11//; 14:24//; Mt. 21:4-5, 27:9-10; Jn. 12:14-15.

The question as to the degree of respect for the OT context on the part of NT authors in their appropriation of Scripture is one which is strongly debated, and it is crucial to describe exactly what is meant by "respect for context" before going further.

It is sometimes implied that included in this "context" should be matters pertaining to the original locus of the scriptural passages in question, such as the Sitz im Leben of the Psalms or the identity of the Servant in Isaiah.[1] However, it is probably illegitimate to introduce these kinds of considerations at this stage in the investigation, for they involve questions of reconstruction, not always clear from the texts themselves and generally matters of debate among contemporary scholars. While these questions are of significance as far as the legitimacy of the NT hermeneutic is concerned,[2] they do not properly apply to the use of individual verses and passages within this larger scheme. The question as to whether individual OT texts seem to be appropriated by NT authors with their immediate contexts in view can and should be separate from the question as to whether these contexts themselves have been properly understood.

If the issue is formulated in this way, it can unhesitatingly be asserted that Jesus and the evangelists have shown a remarkable faithfulness to the original context in their appropriation of OT

---

[1] As Sundberg implies ("On Testimonies," NovT, III (1959), 227-28). Likewise, Miller ("Targum," 66) wants to define "context" as the "whole of Scripture and contemporary needs." This, to be sure, is the "context" in one sense, but is not a substitute for the question raised here.

[2] Jesus and the evangelists emphatically declared that God's activity in Christ was foretold in certain Scriptures. And, as Barr perceptively observes, this concept "at once leads to questions of purpose and intention, and purpose and intention cannot be otherwise expressed than as the purpose and intention of the writers at the time of writing." (Old and New in Interpretation, 152).

verses to interpret the passion. Reference must be made to the detailed argumentation at each stage of the investigation for substantiation of this statement, but some additional comments are in order here. In only one instance does it appear clear that an OT passage has had its meaning altered in the process of appropriation -- Mt. 27:9-10, in which Zech. 11:12 is given a significance distinct from its context through combination with another OT passage (Jeremiah 19) and textual modifications. Two other verses (cf. Mt. 21:4-5; Jn. 19:24) are, perhaps, "over-interpreted" by means of an illegitimate separation of two parts of a verse in synonymous parallelism, and one, Ps. 69:21 in Jn. 19:28-29, has perhaps been applied in a way not congruent with the original context. In other cases, granted the underlying identifications involved, the application of individual verses is accomplished directly.

This situation is in essential contrast to the prevailing methods of appropriation in Judaism. No example of allegory, of complex word-plays, of the use of unusual or unheard of meanings for words, of combinations of passages based on a verbal resemblance only, of any of the similar procedures which proliferate in Jewish literature, are found in the passion texts. While contextual exegesis was by no means unheard of, the percentage of such instances was far smaller than is the case in the passion texts. As Schrenk says, " . . . there is a greater sense of the persons of the authors in early Christianity than in Judaism, and therefore a greater regard for the natural and historical mediation of the divine utterance."[1]

It may be pointed out that the results of this investigation serve to validate the thesis of C. H. Dodd as far as the gospel passion texts are concerned. His contention that the early church turned to

---

[1] "γράφω," TDNT, I, 575.

a specific, limited group of OT passages for the interpretation of the
Christ-event and that they used individual texts from these passages
in accordance with the larger context, is clearly borne out by the
passion texts.[1]

Modification in the Point of Application

Virtually every appropriation of Scripture involves a modification in the point of application to the extent that the circumstance
brought into contact with Scripture is interpreted in a particular
way by the OT language. However, the distinction which is basic for
this investigation is between those instances in which the OT merely
interprets that which is already in existence and those in which the
force of Scripture is to create something entirely new. The
former, descriptive use of Scripture, can be observed throughout the
passion texts, as for example, in the description of Jesus' mockery
by the Jews as he suffered on the cross, where language from the
lament psalms is employed for the purpose of characterizing the
Jewish leaders as enemies of the psalmist, and by implication, of God.
It is widely believed that the second type of situation is found
also -- that incidents recorded in the passion accounts of the gospels
owe their existence solely to an OT text whose "fulfillment" was

---

[1] For Dodd's argument, see According to the Scriptures, (especially 59-60). Others stressing the basic respect for the OT context in NT quotations are: Manson, "Old Testament," 331-32 (with respect to Jesus); Gundry, Old Testament, 208 (In Matthew); Bruce, Old Testament Themes, 108 (Zech. 9-14 in the passion); Hanson, Paul's Technique, 193-95 (for Paul). Sundberg's criticism of Dodd ("On Testimonies") is inappropriate because he bases his statistics on entire books, rather than passages (Prabhu, Infancy Narrative, 68). Likewise, the critique of Dodd by S. L. Edgar ("New Testament and Rabbinic Messianic Interpretation," NTS, V (1958-59), 47-54), is unjustified because he seems to assume rabbinic interpretation as an absolute norm.

thereby created, or that more moderately, details have crept into the accounts under the influence of OT passages previously adduced.[1] While certainty is, of course, impossible, no instance in which this is the most probable explanation has been discovered in the course of this investigation. Once again, the arguments advanced in the study of individual texts must suffice as documentation, but a few summary points, some of which have already been introduced, may be added here.

First, it is important methodologically to establish the point that it is illegitimate to be suspicious of the historicity of a given incident simply because it is related to an OT reference. As Cohn says, "Fulfillment of a scriptural prophecy by a particular event would not in itself render that event improbable."[2] Therefore, it is necessary to separate the question concerning the ultimate historicity of an incident from the question concerning the effect of the OT.[3]

Second, in those cases where a check can be made, no evidence of a tendency to "historicize" OT references can be discovered[4] -- as, for example, a comparison of Matthew with his basic source, Mark, demonstrates.

Third, it is crucial that the difference between OT references which are intended by the author to describe an actual occurrence and those which involve a metaphorical description be noted and taken into consideration. In the latter case, of course, the question as to

---

[1] For the more moderate opinion, see Lindars, John, 536; Borsch, Son of Man, 345-46.

[2] Cohn, Trial, 223. Pace Boussett, who argues from the number of OT correspondences in the passion narrative to the unhistoricity of the events (Kyrios Christos, 113-14).

[3] Catchpole, Trial, 269.   [4] Dunn, Unity and Diversity, 100.

historicity is irrelevant. Thus, for example, the statement in Matthew and Mark that the Jewish leaders "wagged their heads" at Jesus on the cross may be intended not so much to describe that action as such as to evoke the sense of mockery that the image conveys.

Fourth, the re-orientation of text that occurs in some cases (e.g., Mt. 27:9-10) suggests that, in general, the influence has proceeded from the history to the text rather than vice versa.[1] The relatively small number of OT passages utilized in the passion texts presumes a strict selectivity, conditioned by the circumstances of the passion events.[2]

Fifth, the theoretical foundation for the creation of narrative on the basis of OT texts is often located in the postulate that the NT authors felt compelled to demonstrate the fulfillment of every messianic prophecy in the life of Jesus. But there is little evidence that such a presupposition actually guided the evangelists' use of Scripture. It is McConnell's conclusion that "<u>O.T. prophecies were not regarded as authoritative in themselves</u> so that it was believed by the early Church that Jesus had to fulfill them. Rather <u>the prophecies which were important were determined by the life of Jesus</u>."[3]

Sixth, the cruciality of the historical facts of redemption proclaimed by the early church renders the fabrication of incidents on the basis of Scriptures unlikely. Such a process would defeat the purpose for which the OT is appropriated. As Dodd avers, " . . . the

---

[1] Blinzler, Prozess, 34.

[2] For this point as related to the use of the OT in the New in general, see: Bruce, Old Testament Themes, 113-14; Blinzler, Prozess, 34; J. J. O'Rourke, "The Fulfillment Texts in Matthew," CBQ, XXIV (1962), 402-03; Linnemann, Studien, 176; Léon-Dufour, Gospels, 204-05. Dodd says: "The facts themselves exerted pressure upon their understanding of prophecy and fulfillment, and dictated their selection of testimonies." (Historical Tradition, 49).

[3] McConnell, Law and Prophecy, 138.

important thing is the correspondence of prophecy with the facts. That Isaiah foretold such behaviour on the part of the Servant of the Lord is important just because Jesus did in fact so behave."[1] The charge that the early church was uninterested in historical details simply cannot be squared with the evidence presented in the NT.[2]

A final argument against the historicizing of OT references is the lack of precedent. While the Jews frequently elaborated their ancient religious sagas, there is little evidence for the fabrication of contemporary historical events among those groups such as the apocalyptists and the Qumran covenanters who were interested in contemporary history.[3]

Hermeneutical Axioms

To be able to say anthing meaningful about NT hermeneutical principles generally would require a lengthy treatment, indeed, so it will be necessary to confine our comments to issues which arise directly from the study of the passion texts. Specifically, it must be asked how Jesus and the evangelists "legitimized" the transfer of language from various OT passages to the circumstances of Jesus' passion.

Several important conclusions can be derived from the evidence of the appropriation techniques. The most significant relates to the centrality of the historical Christ-event as the decisive determinant of the use of Scripture in the passion texts. As Amsler notes, this factor sets apart the NT from late-Jewish hermeneutics generally:

---

[1] The Apostolic Preaching and its Developments (London: Hodder and Stoughton, 1936), 53.

[2] See, e.g., C. F. D. Moule, "The Intention of the Evangelists," New Testament Essays, 165-77.

[3] Cf., supra, 51-55.

> En reconnaissant à l'Ecriture le rôle d'un témoignage rendu d'avance à l'événement évangélique mais reconnaissable seulement apres coup, le NT opere, par rapport a l'hermeneutique du bas-judaïsme, une révolution copernicienne.
> A l'Ecriture, révélation absolue des exigences de Dieu envers son peuple, telle que la lisait le légalisme juif, le NT oppose l'Ecriture, témoignage de l'oeuvre historique et salutaire de Dieu en Jésus-Christ. A la Loi, il oppose l'Histoire . . . .[1]

The evangelists were convinced that the decisive eschatological irruption of God's rule had come in the ministry, and especially in the death and resurrection of Jesus. This conviction legitimized for them the general transfer of OT texts to the passion of Jesus.[2]

The respect for context characteristic of the appropriation of Scripture in the passion texts can be attributed to the general justification for the use of specific OT passages. It has been argued that the various detailed appropriations of a particular OT context are related to a single, underlying point of identification. What Goppelt claims for the use of the OT in the New in general can be substantiated in the case of the passion texts:

> Die zahlreichen Anspielungen und Hinweise des NT auf das AT sind nicht Stücke eines überhaltenen Schriftbeweises -- und damit exegetisch peinliche und unfruchtbare Stellen -- sondern bei aller zeitgebundenen Form Zeugen einer weiten und tiefen heilsgeschichtlichen Schau, welche das Wegen des in Christo erschienenen Heils erfüllt und vor Verfalschung schutzt.[3]

The identifications of Jesus with the Suffering Servant, the martyred Shepherd-King and the Davidic sufferer provide the basis for legitimation for the application of details from these scriptural

---

[1] Amsler, L'Ancien Testament, 97.

[2] "The New Testament literature itself was evoked by what its authors believed to be the supreme manifestation in history of the judgment and mercy of God, and the Old Testament manifestation and the New Testament manifestation interacted in mutual illumination." (Barrett, "Interpretation of the Old Testament," 403; Cf. also H. M. Shires, Finding the Old Testament in the New (Philadelphia: Westminster, 1974), 40; Bruce, Biblical Exegesis, 77; Smart, History and Theology, 299).

[3] Typos, 248-49.

portions to the passion of Jesus. This is not to imply that the NT authors proceeded in a scholarly or "systematic" manner; their exegesis was clearly "pneumatic."[1] But it should not be concluded that a lack of "objectivity" necessarily impairs correct interpretation. Indeed, the opposite may be the case, for, as Barrett says, the "community of theme" which links OT and New " . . . makes possible for the New Testament writers an understanding of the essential meaning of the Old Testament which it would be hard to parallel."[2]

For further evidence of the general hermeneutical outlook, the conceptions utilized in the introductions to quotations must be considered. The word used most frequently in the passion quotations is πληρόω, found in ten of the twenty-two introductions. It is probable that τελειόω and τελέω, each used in one, can be related to the same conception, while the other ten introductions provide no words which are significant for this investigation.[3] As a basis for further discussion, the distribution and use of πληρόω in the passion texts must be detailed. On this point, a clear distinction among the evangelists emerges: Mark preserves the word only once, on the lips of Jesus in a general fulfillment text (14:49); Luke has no example in the passion texts (although note τελέω in 22:37); while Matthew and John each use πληρόω four times. Further, it is to be noted that only John attributes to Jesus a use of πληρόω in the introduction to a specific quotation, and that only he uses πληρόω with reference to the Psalms and the Pentateuch.

---

[1]Goppelt, Typos, 244; Bright, Authority of the Old Testament, 91-92; Sand, "Wie geschrieben steht," 334; Gerhard von Rad, "Typological Interpretation of the Old Testament," trans. by James Luther Mays, Essays on Old Testament Interpretation, ed. by Claus Westermann (London: SCM, 1963), 21-22.

[2]"Interpretation of the Old Testament," 403.

[3]A form of γράφω occurs six times; ἀναγινώσκω twice; ὁρίζω and λέγω once each.

The background of πληρόω is almost certainly to be found in the word מלא, which denotes the "filling up" of an actual or metaphorical volume.[1] When πληρόω translates מלא in the LXX, the focus is usually upon the filling of a literal volume or the completion of a stated period of time.[2] The NT use of πληρόω demonstrates these same two uses, in addition to the use of πληρόω with reference to the OT. When used with reference to the Scriptures, or to God's plan, the word often has a broad sense, implying the fulfillment of " . . . not any single, limited promise, but all the promise and hope attaching to all that is epitomized in the Bible by God's covenant with his people."[3] This broad application of πληρόω is found in several passion texts, where the reference is to the fulfillment of the Scriptures in the passion of Jesus. However, the word is also used, as has been noted, with reference to the fulfillment of specific, limited predictions, a usage which C. F. D. Moule characterizes as an "abuse" of the basic meaning of the term.[4] It is doubtful, however, whether such a criticism is warranted.

The lack of background for the use of πληρόω in relation to the Scriptures means that the essential thrust of the term must be

---

[1] πληρόω translates מלא on the vast majority of its occurrences in the LXX and never represents קום (Robert Banks, Jesus and the Law in the Synoptic Tradition, SNTSMS, XXVIII (Cambridge: University Press, 1975), 208), although it is true that מלא and קום are sometimes interchanged in the targums (John P. Meier, Law and History in Matthew's Gospel: A Redactional Study of Mt. 5:17-18, AnBib, LXXI (Rome: Biblical Institute Press, 1976), 74).

[2] On the use of πληρόω in the LXX, see especially Albert Descamps, Les Justes et la Justice dans les évangiles et le christianisme primitif, Universitas Catholica Louvaniensis Dissertation Series (II), XVIII (Louvain: Publications Universitaires de Louvain and Gembloux: Duculot, 1950), 124-25.

[3] C. F. D. Moule, "Fulfillment Words in the New Testament: Use and Abuse," NTS, XIV (1967-68), 294. Cf. also Brevard S. Childs, "Prophecy and Fulfillment: A Study of Contemporary Hermeneutics," Int, XII (1958), 269; Descamps, Justes, 126-27; Schrenk, "γράφω," 759.

[4] "Fulfillment Words," 294-303.

defined according to NT usage. And the word is used in the NT more often with reference to specific prophecies than with general promises.[1] Furthermore, on the only two occasions in the LXX when πληρόω is used in conjunction with God's promises, the promises are in each case specific.[2]

Second, in light of the previous discussion, it can often be assumed that when πληρόω is used to introduce a quotation, the NT author has in mind the fulfillment of the larger context as well.[3] Thus, specific fulfillments of passages in Zech. 9-14 or the Psalms may be related to the general heilsgeschichtlich identification of Jesus with the figures in these passages.

Finally, with respect to πληρόω and its implications for the way in which the NT authors viewed the OT, it must be maintained that the term cannot be restricted to include only instances in which a genuine predictive element was understood to have been present in the text.[4] Thus, when John characterizes the fact that Jesus' bones were

---

[1] πληρόω is used in the NT of the accomplishment of specific prophecies in Matthew (10 times), John (5 times), Luke (once -- although it is possible that this usage (4:16) is related to the ministry of Jesus generally (Prabhu, Infancy Narrative, 46-47)), Acts (once) and James (once). In general scriptural references, πληρόω occurs six times in the gospels (only in Jesus' sayings) and twice in Acts. Paul speaks of the "fulfillment of the Law" (Rom. 8:4, 13:8, Gal. 5:14) and the fulfillment of time, probably related to this general concept is mentioned by Jesus in Mk. 1:15, Lk. 21:24 and Jn. 7:8.

[2] I Kings 2:27; II Chron. 36:21, 22. Gerhard Barth ("Matthew's Understanding of the Law," Tradition and Interpretation in Matthew, by Günther Bornkamm, Gerhard Barth and Heinz Joachim Held; trans. by Percy Scott (London: SCM, 1963), 68) says: "Where πληρόω refers to a spoken or written word it means to bring this word to realization by deed."

[3] As Banks point out with respect to Matthew, " . . . in some instances it is not a prediction as such to which he turns, but a statement occurring in a particular heilsgeschichtlich context which is related to its uniquely new counterpart in the new age that has dawned." (Jesus and the Law, 212, n. 1; cf. also Rothfuchs, Erfüllungszitate, 48; Goppelt, Typos, 248).

[4] The broader sense of fulfillment is particularly stressed by those who stress the Heilsgeschichte as the basic unifying theme of the

not broken on the cross as a "fulfillment" of Ex. 12:46, he need not be implying that the regulation concerning the Paschal Lamb was itself forward-looking; what he does infer is that, in some sense, that provision remained "empty" until it was "filled" (or, perhaps, brought to completion) in Jesus' death. On the other hand, while πληρόω may be applied to OT verses only retrospectively, it cannot be denied that many, perhaps a majority, of cases in which πληρόω introduces a quotation are meant by the NT author to connote an instance in which something which the OT author himself had foreseen had come to pass.[1] This is indicated by occasions on which Jesus makes reference to "that [which was written] about me" (Lk. 22:37, referring to Is. 53:12) and the general thrust of the NT appeal to the Jews by means of Scripture. Thus, it is necessary, if the NT evidence is not to be ignored, to retain the element of a genuine predictive function in the NT view of the Old. As Barr puts it,

> The character of the scene is not adequately described if we say that it is one in which a new saving event, or a representation of the older saving events, or a new turn of the Heilsgeschichte is looked for; it is rather, much more precisely one in which a Christ is expected, and in which the use of Old Testament passages is heavily biased in this direction.[2]

To summarize, then, the evidence of the passion texts suggests that two fundamental presuppositions dominated the approach to the OT: the new revelational basis in the life and teaching of Jesus and a view of Scripture which understood Jesus (and his passion) to have been

---

Testaments (Oscar Cullmann, Salvation in History, trans. by Sidney G. Sowers (London: SCM, 1967), 25; 132-33; Goppelt, Typos, 239-40; von Rad, "Typological Interpretation," 28-38; Alan Richardson, Christian Apologetics (London: SCM, 1947), 190-91).

[1] Hamerton-Kelly states: "If Christ is the fulfillment of Scripture he must have been present -- at least as an idea in the mind of God -- when the plan of salvation to which the scriptures bear witness was formulated." (Pre-existence, 77). It might be noted that Hanson feels that Paul believed that the OT authors "knew the significance of what they wrote." (Paul's Technique, 190-91).

[2] Old and New in Interpretation, 133.

foreseen and foreshadowed in many OT passages. Simply, the early Christians were convinced that the OT spoke of the promised one and that Jesus was that promised one.

It must, however, be reiterated that the applicability of Scripture to Jesus' passion did not proceed haphazardly, but within a clearly marked out framework, which utilized certain key identifications as the basis for a remarkably unified interpretation of the OT passages in question. That this essential framework has its origin in the teaching of Jesus as well as his life is suggested by a number of factors. The very distinctiveness of the NT appropriation of Scripture presupposes a mind of "genuinely creative power," and as C. H. Dodd concluded, "The Gospels offer us one. Are we compelled to reject it?"[1] The fact that Jesus is represented as clearly quoting from each major OT passage employed in the passion texts and that his citations demonstrate a clear orientation toward a Semitic text-form, in distinction to citations in other strata, may be taken as indicative of the actual origin of the development. Finally, the very selectivity and unanimity of interpretation suggests the influence of a single dominant mind at the very fountainhead of the tradition.[2]

---

[1] According to the Scriptures, 110. See also France, Jesus, 225.

[2] The tendency to regard Jesus' fulfillment of the OT in a mechanical way, as if Jesus set out deliberately to accomplish certain predictions must be resisted. (Hooker, Son of Man, 108). As Dunn says, "His own experience of God, of divine power and inspiration, made clear to him what parts of OT prophecy were applicable to and descriptive of his ministry, and what were not." (Jesus and the Spirit, 61). As Barr points out, too many "fulfillments" occur which are outside Jesus' power to accomplish for this to be a satisfactory explanation. (Old and New in Interpretation, 137-38).

A Comparison with Jewish Approaches to Scripture

Rather than attempting to compare Jewish approaches to OT interpretation with the approach reflected in the passion texts at each level of hermeneutical procedure, it will be expedient to explore this question as a whole in a separate section.

Similarities to the appropriation techniques utilized by both the rabbis and the Qumran sectarians (which were discovered to be fundamentally similar), are found throughout the passion texts. Certain recognized citation techniques are employed, texts are conflated, textual modifications are introduced and typology is resorted to as a means of contemporizing the ancient message of the Scriptures. However, while many similarities exist, the method of appropriation in the passion texts appears to be distinct, at least in degree, from that favored by Jewish interpreters. The great preponderance of cases in which a direct appropriation of the OT occurs in the passion texts stands in clear contrast to the far smaller percentage of such examples in the rabbinic and Qumran literature. The tendency, especially marked in the rabbinic literature, to introduce new meanings into texts by means of lexical legerdemain and to conflate texts on solely linguistic grounds is simply not present in the passion texts. It has been argued that such a process lies behind many extant _testimonia_ in the NT,[1] but there is virtually no evidence for such "implicit midrashes" in the passion texts.[2] And, in

---

[1] E.g., by Ellis ("Midrash," 62; "How the New Testament uses the Old," 202-08) and Hartman ("Scriptural Exegesis," 149). Miller ("Targum," 61) says: "It is insufficient to treat the presence of OT allusions and citations in a NT passage as isolated entities. One must ask concerning possible relationships between the citations and whether Jewish exegetical methods and traditions shed light on the passage as a whole."

[2] _Pace_ Kee, "Function," 181.

general, as Lindars claims, "The actual provable use of the Old Testament in the New Testament does not support such a hypothesis."[1]

The Qumran technique, involving fewer word-plays of the rabbinic sort, is closer to the NT method, but differs in the direction of influence and, as a result, the extent to which the details of the OT text are regarded as significant. The general movement in the Qumran literature, even outside the commentaries, is from text to explication, whereas the NT generally utilizes the OT text as the commentary on an existing circumstance. As Léon-Dufour says, the NT authors " . . . were concerned not with interpreting the OT, but with interpreting an <u>event</u> in terms of the OT."[2] While the tendency among the covenanters is to seek a contemporary identification for every detail of the OT texts cited (a tendency which leads directly to the frequent allegorizing in the scrolls), the NT authors are generally content to allow the text to make a single point and often leave details unexplained.[3] Furthermore, the degree of textual modification is significantly less in the passion texts than in the DSS (although, as has been argued, the extent of text modification at Qumran has been exaggerated).

In summary, while it is certainly not the case that the NT authors, any more than the rabbis or the Qumran scribes, were engaged in "exegesis" as we know it, in the sense that they were concerned

___

[1] "Place of the Old Testament," 64.

[2] <u>Gospels</u>, 215. See also: Barrett, "Interpretation of the Old Testament," 394; Gärtner, "Habakkuk Commentary," 12-14; Fitzmyer, "Quotations," 299; Betz, <u>Offenbarung</u>, 79; Hanson, <u>Paul's Technique</u>, 207; Davies, <u>Sermon</u>, 208-09.

[3] "While the Qumran commentator tries to find a contemporary application for each detail in the oracle, the Christian preacher is more concerned to emphasize the permanent principles which it emphasizes . . . ." (Bruce, <u>Biblical Exegesis</u>, 71; also A. T. Hanson, <u>Jesus Christ in the Old Testament</u> (London: SPCK, 1965), 6).

with explaining the meaning of the OT for itself, they were able to appropriate Scripture in such a way as to preserve more often the actual sense of the original.

As is the case with regard to appropriation procedures, both similarities and differences in the hermeneutical axioms observable in the passion texts and those favored by Jewish interpreters exist. With all Jews, Jesus and the evangelists regarded Scripture as a divinely-given unity which had relevance for their present situation. The NT writers shared with the Qumran sectarians a sense of eschatological completion and the desire to apply Scripture to contemporary history. Again, however, the differences outweigh the similarities and can be observed in three particular areas: the function of Scripture, the understanding of the OT and the revelational basis.

In "normative" Judaism, Scripture functioned as the authoritative source book for ethical conduct and the quarry for edifying religious narration. Nowhere is the sense of the fulfillment of God's scripturally-mediated plan in history, so characteristic of the passion texts, evident. The function of Scripture at Qumran is more analogous to the NT, inasmuch as the covenanters sought to bring the OT into contact with events in their own history, but even here there are few examples of the use of the OT to comment upon the narration of history.

The use of the OT in the passion texts, in addition to certain explicit statements elsewhere,[1] implies that Jesus and the evangelists regarded the Scripture as a direct witness to the passion event; a witness which was clear and (should be) understandable by all in the light of its fulfillment. This belief in the perspicuous witness of the OT to Christ is in contrast to the attitude toward Scripture

---

[1] E.g., Lk. 24:25. And note Hanson's comments on Paul (Paul's Technique, 190-91).

among the rabbis, where scholarly ingenuity is required to make the
sense plain and that which prevailed at Qumran, where a special revelation had to occur before the "mystery" of the Scripture could be
made known.[1] Unlike the Teacher of Righteousness, Jesus brought no
new meaning to the OT texts, but demonstrated, in his life and
teaching, the proper application (or signification) of the text.

Finally, and most importantly, the use of the OT in the
passion texts is entirely determined by the new revelatory foundation,
God's act in Christ. While both the rabbis and the DSS sectarians
were influenced in their interpretation of Scripture by factors
outside of the OT, neither questioned the fundamental authority of
the Torah. In Jesus, on the other hand, the early Christians found
an authority which stood over the Torah, sovereignly determining its
continuing relevancy and applicability.[2] The life and teaching of
Jesus constituted a personal, historical and immensely influential
focal point in the Christian interpretation of the OT, unlike anything
found in other communities. It was this focal point that gave to the
NT interpretation of Scripture a unified outlook[3] and which, being
past, enabled the NT writers to look back at the OT through what they
believed to be its basic referant.

It must be emphasized again that the comments made here
apply only to the situation as it seems to exist in the gospel passion
texts; other NT passages may exhibit features which lend more
credence to the belief that NT interpretation is essentially similar

---

[1] Elliger, Habakuk-Kommentar, 155-57.

[2] Ethelbert Stauffer, "Jesus und seine Bibel," Abraham unser Vater, 440-46; Barrett, "Interpretation of the Old Testament," 399; Davies, Sermon, 209; Braun, Qumran, II, 15-17.

[3] Davies characterizes the NT outlook as having a "more directly personal involvement with the meaning of Scripture than was the case with the rabbis." (Sermon, 420).

to that practiced by the rabbis and the Qumran authors.[1] As far as the passion texts are concerned, however, it is questionable whether it is accurate to speak of "midrash" or "pesher."[2] To be sure, there are similarities in both techniques of appropriation and in hermeneutical axioms, but the number of differences is greater and the differences involve matters of more decisive importance. As Fitzmyer says, with respect to Qumran and the NT,

> Both depend on the Old Testament, but both have certain presuppositions in the light of which they read the Old Testament. It is these presuppositions which distinguish the two groups despite the similarities in their exegetical procedures.[3]

Therefore, while one can discern midrashic or pesher-type techniques in some of the passion texts, the characterization of these instances by the terms midrash or pesher would be to describe, illegitimately, the whole according to one of its parts.

The Function of the Old Testament in the Passion Texts

As a final consideration, it will be appropriate to investigate briefly the role of the OT as it relates to Jesus' passion. A basic preliminary issue concerning the relevance of the OT for NT theology has been succinctly summarized in the recent interchange between Barnabas Lindars and Peder Borgen in New Testament Studies,[4]

---

[1] E.g., it seems that midrashic procedures can be discerned in polemical contexts in the gospels and Acts.

[2] For the contrary viewpoint, based on the whole, or various passages, of the NT, see especially: Doeve, Jewish Hermeneutics, 28-29; Le Déaut, "Apropos," 408-09; Miller, "Targum," 44; Roberts, "Bible Exegesis," 207; Longenecker, Biblical Exegesis, 68-70, 212-13; Stendahl, School, 195.

[3] "Quotations," 332. Note also Braun, Qumran, II, 308.

[4] "The Place of the Old Testament in the Formation of New Testament Theology: Prolegomena and Response," NTS, XXIII (1976-77), 59-75.

which can profitably serve as a point of departure for the present discussion. True to his earlier established position which stressed the apologetic purpose in the use of the OT in the New, Lindars argues that the OT is "primarily a mode of expression for early Christian thought" and its place in the function of NT theology is "that of a servant, ready to run to the aid of the gospel whenever it is required, bolstering up arguments, and filling out meaning through evocative allusions, but never acting as the master or leading the way, nor even guiding the process of thought behind the scenes."[1] In response to this position, Borgen points to the many OT concepts which were applied to Christ and seeks to demonstrate that "the scriptures to a large extent guided the process of thought, and created many of the theological issues which were taken up in the New Testament."[2]

As related to the passion texts, the following points can be made. First, it has been an important conclusion of this work that the actual history and teachings of Jesus were the guiding factor in the use of the OT -- to this extent, Lindars is justified. Secondly, however, it is a major step from the position that the OT is not, by itself, determinative for any Christian theological teaching, to the position that the OT has contributed nothing (or very little) to the theology of Jesus' sufferings. Such a position involves, as Borgen implies, a disregard for the OT as the crucial determinant in the way Jews thought. To be sure, the Christ-event gave to Christian Jews a new center and touchstone, but it could hardly eliminate ingrained habits of thought, nor -- and this is a crucial point -- was it meant to. It seems certain that the OT element was integral to the

---

[1] "Place of the Old Testament," 64, 66.

[2] Ibid., 70.

description of Jesus' passion from the beginning,[1] implying an interpretative function. As soon as the early Christians began to think and preach about the significance of Jesus' death, they must have utilized categories provided by the OT-sacrifices, the atoning death of the Servant, the innocent sufferer. And, against Lindars, these images cannot be regarded as mere "modes of expression," for they have, from the earliest strata of gospel tradition to the latest NT book, provided the essential categories in which Jesus' death was understood.

In the passion texts, furthermore, Lindars' argument breaks down at a crucial point. He claims that the NT authors employed "texts already current in contemporary messianic speculation,"[2] applying these to Christ for apologetic purposes. But, in one important case at least, such was not the procedure -- there is little evidence that the Suffering Servant conception of Isaiah 53 had been applied to the Messiah before the Christian appropriation. The use of the Servant figure can more plausibly be attributed to the need for an explanation of Messiah's death _within_ the early church; a position that may find substantiation in the preponderance of allusive references to these chapters. And, in general, it may be said that the apologetic motivation for OT references in the New has been overdrawn. OT references are too much a part of the very fabric of the NT and its theology to be considered secondary and superficial additions[3] -- particularly is this true of the passion texts.[4]

---

[1] Dibelius, "Alttestamentliche Motive," 126-27.

[2] Lindars, "Place of the Old Testament," 63.

[3] Traugott Holtz, "Zur Interpretation des Alten Testaments im Neuen Testament," TLZ, XLIX (1974), 25; Dodd, Historical Tradition, 31; Lampe, Essays on Typology, 24-25; Hamerton-Kelly, Pre-Existence, 91; Gundry, Old Testament, 160-62.

[4] Edward Lohse, "Die alttestamentlichen Bezüge im neutestamentlichen

Therefore, while it must be firmly maintained that the significance of Jesus' sufferings was not deduced solely on the authority of OT texts, it is unjustified to reject the role of the OT in the process of developing a soteriology. The belief that the same God who spoke in Jesus had also spoken in the OT was axiomatic for Jesus and the first Christians, and this conviction in the unity of God's revelation legitimized the OT as the most important[1] resource[2] in the task of explaining the meaning of Jesus' sufferings.

It is sometimes argued that the soteriological interpretation of Jesus' death was a later development in the history of the tradition -- that the earliest preaching simply postulated the necessity of suffering.[3]

Zeugnis vom Tode Jesu Christi," Die Einheit des Neuen Testaments: Exegetische Studien zur Theologie des Neuen Testaments (Göttingen: Vandenhoeck & Ruprecht, 1973), 123; Vermes, Scripture and Tradition, 221.

Hans Conzelmann ("History and Theology in the Passion Narratives of the Synoptic Gospels," trans. by Charles B. Cousar, Int, XXIV (1970), 185) questions the importance of the apologetic motif in general, noting how difficult the retention of the Gethsemane scene is for this interpretation and claiming that "the story of suffering is an indispensable ingredient of the gospel" as a correction to a christologia gloriae.

[1]Pace those who would discover the source for the idea of Jesus' atoning death elsewhere. Recently, for example, Williams has argued that, inasmuch as no concept of an individual's death as a means of salvation existed in pre-70 Judaism, the origin of the Christian soteriology is most likely to be found in the Greek-influenced conceptions of IV Maccabees (Jesus' Death, cf. especially 223-33). However, even Williams admits that Isaiah 53 is an exception to the lack of atoning conceptions in pre-70 Judaism, and he has not succeeded in eliminating references to this chapter from early Christian sources. Williams' study is further vitiated by the assumption that the early church must have been enslaved to previous ideas and possessed of no creative power.

[2]As H. M. Shires says, " . . . Scripture was a primary resource for N.T. authors, but it could not be a source." (Finding the Old Testament in the New, 39).

[3]Thyen, Studien zur Sündenvergebung, 153; Flessemann-van Leer, "Interpretation," 95; Hahn, Titles, 172-73; Suhl, Alttestamentlichen Zitate, 40-41; Amsler, L'Ancien Testament, 91-92.

As far as this study goes, several points tell against this. First, the belief in the significance of Jesus' sufferings was very early -- it can hardly have arisen only at the time of the Gentile mission,[1] as is shown by the clear Semitic flavor of those sayings most clearly expressing an atoning theology (e.g., Mk. 10:45, 14:24). Secondly, it seems inherently unlikely that either Jesus or the early church would have been content with an "unexplicated assertion that suffering is a necessary pre-condition for the coming of the Age of Deliverance."[2] It is hardly conceivable that the question as to why this was so would not have occurred, and been answered, as it later certainly was, by means of the clear theology of Isaiah 53. Furthermore, the passion predictions themselves betray the evidence of an already-formulated theology of sufferings (passive παραδίδωμι), so, if there was a period when no positive significance was attributed to Jesus' death, it "is a period to which we have no access."[3] Thirdly, it is significant that the largest number of allusions to the Scriptural passage with the most clearly enunciated atonement theology (Isaiah 53) are attributed to Jesus. Surely, if the atoning value of Jesus' sufferings was only a late development, the evangelists would have themselves utilized a number of clear quotations. In fact, all the evidence points to Isaiah 53 having been used extensively at an earlier, and almost ignored in the later, stages of development.

---

[1] Martin Hengel, "Christologie und neutestamentliche Chronologie: Zu einer Aporie in der Geschichte des Urchristentums," Neues Testament und Geschichte: Historisches Geschehen und Deutung im Neuen Testament (Oscar Cullmann zum 70 Geburtstag), ed. by Heinrich Baltensweiler and Bo Reicke (Zurich: Theologischer Verlag, 1972), 72.

[2] Kee, "Function," 174-75.

[3] Dodd, According to the Scriptures, 123.

"Christ died for our sins according to the Scriptures"
(I Cor. 15:3) was a fundamental assertion of the Christian church
from the beginning, rooted in Jesus' own understanding of the
significance of his passion and death. Furthermore, it was not only
the necessity, but the significance as well, that was derived from
the will of God revealed in the OT. In conclusion, it may be
appropriate to summarize briefly this significance as revealed in
the gospel passion texts.

Jesus' death was an eschatological occurrence. The extraordinary
signs accompanying the crucifixion and the use of language from the
"apocalyptic" chapters of Zechariah's prophecy (9-14) reveal this
most clearly. In the passion and death of Jesus, God was acting
decisively, mediating both salvation (Jn. 19:36) and judgment (Jn. 19:37).

Jesus' death was a sacrifice, the fulfillment of the Paschal
feast and its significance (Jn. 19:36) and the foundation for the
new covenant of God with His people (Mk. 14:24//).

Jesus died as the Davidic King (the lament psalms), persecuted
though innocent, abandoned by God though righteous (Mk. 15:34/),
committed to God despite all (Lk. 23:46).

Jesus' death was vicarious (Mk. 14:24) and substitutionary,
an ultimate giving of himself which secured the release of "the
many" (Mk. 10:45).

When all the texts have been considered, it is this -- "The
Son of Man came not to be served, but to serve and to give his life
a ransom for the many" (Mk. 10:45) -- which most succinctly summarizes
the death of Jesus -- voluntary, sacrificial, substitutionary. And
it should be remembered by all who claim to participate in the
benefits of that death that Jesus speaks these words as indicative of
the kind of service required of those who follow him.

BIBLIOGRAPHY
(Sources Cited)

Texts and Translations

Apocalypsis Henochi Graece. Edited by Matthew Black. Leiden: Brill, 1970.

The Apocrypha and Pseudepigraha of the Old Testament in English. Edited by R. H. Charles. 2 vols. Oxford: Clarendon Press, 1913.

The Babylonian Talmud. Translated under the editorship of I. Epstein. 34 vols. London: Soncino, 1948.

The Bible in Aramaic: Based on Old Manuscripts and Printed Texts. Edited by Alexander Sperber. 4 vols. Leiden: E. J. Brill, 1959-1968.

Biblica Hebraica. Edited by Rudolf Kittel, in cooperation with P. Kahle, 3rd ed. Revised by A. Alt and O. Eissfeld. Stuttgart: Württembergische Bibelanstalt, 1971.

Biblia Sacra Polyglotta. Edited by Brian Walton. 6 vols. London: Thomas Roycroft, 1657.

The Dead Sea Scriptures in English Translation with Introduction and Notes. Translated and edited by Theodore Gaster. 3rd ed; Garden City, N.Y.: Doubleday, 1976.

The Dead Sea Scrolls in English. Edited by Geza Vermes. 2nd ed. Harmondsworth: Penguin, 1975.

The Dead Sea Scrolls of St. Mark's Monastery. Vol. I: The Isaiah Manuscript and the Habakkuk Commentary; Vol. II: Plates and Transcription of the Manual of Discipline. Edited by M. Burrows, J. C. Trevor and W. H. Brownlee. New Haven: The American Schools of Oriental Research, 1950, 1951.

Discoveries in the Judean Desert of Jordan. Oxford: Clarendon Press.
    Vol. I: Qumran Cave I. Edited by D. Barthélemy and J. T. Milik. 1955.
    Vol. II: Les Grottes de Murabba'at. Edited by P. Benoit, J. T. Milik and R. de Vaux. 1961.
    Vol. III: Les 'Petites Grottes' de Qumran. Edited by M. Baillet, J. T. Milik and R. de Vaux. 1962.
    Vol. IV: The Psalms Scroll of Qumran Cave II. Edited by J. A. Sanders. 1965.
    Vol. V: Qumran Cave 4. Edited by John M. Allegro. 1968.

The Essene Writings from Qumran. Edited and translated by A. Dupont-Sommer; Translated by G. Vermes. New York: World, 1961.

Bibliography   399

Evangelion Da-Mepharresche. Edited by F. C. Burkitt. 2 vols.
    Cambridge: University Press, 1904.

The Greek New Testament. Edited by Kurt Aland, Matthew Black, Carlo
    M. Martini, Bruce M. Metzger and Allen Wikgren in cooperation
    with the Institute for New Testament Textual Research Münster/
    Westphalia. 3rd ed. London, et. al.: United Bible Societies
    1975.

Hebrew-Greek Cairo Genizah Palimpsests from the Taylor-Schechter
    Collection. Edited by C. Taylor. Cambridge: University
    Press, 1900.

Josephus. Edited and translated by H. St. J. Thackeray, et. al.
    9 vols. The Loeb Classical Library. London: William
    Heinemann, 1926-65.

The Manual of Discipline: Translated and Annotated with an Introduction.
    Edited by P. Wernberg-Møller STDJ I. Grand Rapids: Eerdmans, 1957.

The Midrash on Psalms. Edited by W. G. Braude. Yale Judaica Series,
    XIII. 2 vols. New Haven: Yale University Press, 1959.

Midrash Rabbah. Translated and edited by H. Freedman and Maurice Simon.
    10 vols. London: Soncino, 1939.

MiqraotGedolot. Jerusalem: 721 (J. E.).

The Mishnah. Edited by Herbert Danby. Oxford: Clarendon Press, 1933.

New Testament Apocrypha. Edited by E. Hennecke and W. Schneemelcher.
    Translated and edited by R. McL. Wilson. 2 vols. London:
    Lutterworth Press, 1963.

Novum Testamentum Graece. Edited by Eberhard Nestle. Revised by Erwin
    Nestle and Kurt Aland. 25th ed. London: United Bible Societies,
    1971.

Novum Testamentum Graece ad antiquissimus testes denuo recensuit apparatum
    criticum omni studio perfectum. Edited by Constantine Tischendorf.
    Lipsiae: Giesecke & Devrient, 1869-72.

The Old Syriac Gospels or Evangelion Da-Mepharresche. Edited by Agnes
    Lewis Smith. London: Williams and Norgate, 1910.

Origenis Hexaplorum quae supersunt. Edited by Frederick Field. 2 vols.
    Oxford: Clarendon Press, 1875.

The Second Book of Maccabees. Edited by Solomon Zeitlin, Dropsie College
    Edition, Jewish Apocryphal Literature. Translated by Sidney
    Tedesche, published for the Dropsie College for Hebrew and
    Cognate Learning by Harper & Brothers, New York, 1954.

Septuaginta: Id est Vetus Testamentum graece iuxta LXX interpretes.
    Edited by Alfred Rahlfs. 2 vols. Stuttgart: Württembergische
    Bibelanstalt, 1935.

Septuaginta: Vetus Testamentum Graecum auctoritate Societatis
    Litterarum Gottingensis editum. Göttingen: Vandenhoeck &
    Ruprecht.
    Vol. X: Psalmi cum Odis. Edited by A. Rahlfs. 1931.
    Vol. XIII: Duodecim Prophetae. Edited by Joseph Ziegler. 1943.
    Vol. XIV: Isaias. Edited by Joseph Ziegler. 1939.

Synopsis Quattuor Evangeliorum. Edited by Kurt Aland. Stuttgart:
    Württembergische Bibelanstalt, 1964.

Le Talmud de Jerusalem. Translated by Moise Schwab. 6 vols. Paris:
    G. -P. Maisonneure, 1960.

Le Targum de Job de la Grotte XI de Qumrân. Edited by J. van der Ploeg
    and A. S. van der Woude. Leiden: Brill, 1971.

Die Texte aus Qumran: Hebräisch und deutsch mit massoretischer
    Punktuation Übersetzung, Einfuhrung und Anmerkungen. Edited by
    Eduard Lohse. Munich: Kösel-verlag, 1964.

The Third and Fourth Books of Maccabees. Translated and edited by
    Moses Hadas. Dropsie College Edition, Jewish Apocryphal Literature.
    Published for the Dropsie College for Hebrew and Cognate Learning
    by Harper & Brothers, New York, 1953.

Vetus testamentum Syriace: Eos Tantum Librus sistens qui in Canone
    Hebraico Habentur, ordire vero, quoad fieri potuit, apud syrus
    usitato dispositos. Edited by S. Lee. London: Impensis
    Ejusdem Societatis, 1823.

The Zadokite Documents. Edited by Chaim Rabin. Oxford: Clarendon Press,
    1954.

Reference Works

Arndt, W. F., Gingrich, F. W. A Greek-English Lexicon of the New
    Testament and other Early Christian Literature (A translation
    and adaption of Walter Bauer's Griechisch-Deutsches Wörterbuch
    zu den Schriften des Neuen Testaments und der übrigen
    urchristlichen Literatur. (4th ed.)). Chicago: University of
    Chicago Press, 1957.

Blass, F. and Debrunner, A. A Greek Grammar of the New Testament and
    Other Early Christian Literature. Translated and revised by
    Robert W. Funk. Chicago: University of Chicago Press, 1961.

Brockelmann, Carolo. Lexicum Syriacum. 2nd ed. Halis Saxonum:
    Max Niemeyer, 1923.

Cowley, A. E. Gesenius' Hebrew Grammar. Revised and edited by E.
    Kautzsch. 2nd ed. Oxford: Clarendon Press, 1910.

Dalman, Gustaf. Grammatik des jüdischen Palästinischer Aramäisch: nach
    den Idiomen des Palästinischen Talmud des Onkelostargum und
    Prophetentargum und der Jerusalemischen Targume: Aramäische
    Dialektproben. 2nd ed. Darmstadt: Wissenschaftliche
    Buchgesellschaft, 1960.

Hasting's Dictionary of Christ and the Gospels. Edited by James Hastings
2 vols. Edinburgh: T & T Clark, 1908 -.

Hasting's Dictionary of the Bible. Edited by James Hastings. 5 vols.
Edinburgh: T & T Clark, 1898-1904.

Jastrow, Marcus. A Dictionary of the Targumim, the Talmud Babli and
Yerushalmi: and the Midrashic Literature. 2 vols. New York:
Pardes, 1950.

The Jewish Encyclopedia. Edited by Isidore Singer, et. al. 12 vols.
New York and London: Funk and Wagnalls, 1901-05.

Liddell, Henry George, and Scott, Robert. A Greek-English Lexicon.
Edited by Henry Stuart Jones with the assistance of Robert
McKenzie; with a Supplement (1968) edited by E. A. Barber,
with the assistance of P. Mans, M. Scheller and M. L. West.
9th ed. Oxford: Oxford University Press, 1940.

Liskowsky, Gerhard. Konkordanz zum hebräischen Alten Testament. Stuttgart:
Württembergische Bibelanstalt, 1958.

Morgenthaler, Robert. Statistische Synopse. Zürich/Stuttgart:
Gutthelf, 1971.

Moulton, James Hope. A Grammar of New Testament Greek. Edinburgh:
T & T Clark.
Vol. I: Prolegomena. By J. H. Moulton. 1906.
Vol. II: Accidence and Word Formation. By J. H. Moulton and
W. F. Howard. 1929.
Vol. III: Syntax. By Nigel Turner. 1963.
Vol. IV: Style. By Nigel Turner. 1976.

_____, and Milligan, George. The Vocabulary of the Greek New
Testament illustrated from the Papyri and other non-literary
Sources. Grand Rapids: Eerdmans, 1963.

Moulton, W. F. and Geden, A. S. A Concordance to the Greek Testament.
Edited by H. K. Moulton. 4th ed. Edinburgh: T & T Clark, 1963.

Moule, C. F. D. An Idiom-Book of New Testament Greek. Cambridge:
University Press, 1953.

New International Dictionary of New Testament Theology. Edited by
Colin Brown. 3 vols. Grand Rapids: Zondervan, 1975-1978.

Die Religion in Geschichte und Gegenwart. Handwörterbuch für Theologie
und Religionswissenschaft. Edited by Kurt Galling, et. al.
6 vols. 3rd ed. Tübingen: Mohr, 1957-62.

Robertson, A. T. A Grammar of the Greek New Testament in the Light of
Historical Research. London: Hodder and Stoughton, n.d.

Strack, Herman L. and Billerbeck, Paul. Kommentar zum Neuen Testament
aus Talmud und Midrasch. 5 vols. Munich: C. H. Beck'sche,
1926-61.

Supplément au Dictionnaire de La Bible. Edited by Henri Cazalles.
8 vols. Paris: Letouzey, 1928-.

Theological Dictionary of the New Testament. Edited by Gerhard Kittel and Gerhard Friedrich. Translated by Geoffrey W. Bromiley. 10 vols. Grand Rapids: Eerdmans, 1964-76.

Theological Dictionary of the Old Testament. Edited by G. Johannes Botterweck and Helmer Ringgren. Translated by John T. Willis. Grand Rapids: Eerdmans, 1974-.

Turner, Nigel. Grammatical Insights into the New Testament. Edinburgh: T & T Clark, 1965.

Vollständige Konkordanz zum griechischen Neuen Testament. Edited by Kurt Aland. 2 vols. Berlin: Walter de Gruyter, 1975-78.

Commentaries

Ackroyd P. R. "Zechariah." Peake's Commentary on the Bible. Edited by Matthew Black and H. H. Rowley. London: Thomas Nelson and Sons, 1962.

Albright, W. F. and Mann, C. S. Matthew. AB XXVI. Garden City, New York: Doubleday, 1971.

Alford, Henry. The Greek Testament. 4 vols. London: Rivingstons, 1865-76.

Allen, W. C. A Critical and Exegetical Commentary on the Gospel According to St. Matthew. ICC. Edinburgh: T & T Clark, 1907.

Anderson, A. A. The Book of Psalms. NCB. London: Oliphants, 1972.

Anderson, Hugh. The Gospel of Mark. NCB. London: Oliphants, 1976.

Argyle, A. W. The Gospel According to Matthew. The Cambridge Bible Commentary. Cambridge: University Press, 1963.

Baldwin, Joyce G. Haggai, Zechariah, Malachi. TOTC. London: Tyndale, 1972.

Barnes, W. E. The Psalms. WC. 3 vols. London: Methuen, 1931.

Barrett, C. K. The Gospel According to St. John: London: SPCK, 1955.

Bartlett, John R. The First and Second Books of the Maccabees. The Cambridge Bible Commentary. Cambridge: University Press, 1973.

Bartlett, J. Vernon. St. Mark. London: Thomas Nelson & Sons, n.d.

Bauer, Walter. "Johannes." Die Evangelien. HNT, II. Tübingen: Mohr, 1912.

Bernard, J. H. A Critical and Exegetical Commentary on the Gospel According to St. John. ICC. 2 vols. Edinburgh: T & T Clark, 1928.

Blunt, A. W. F., The Gospel According to Saint Mark. Oxford: Clarendon Press, 1929.

Bonnard, Pierre. L'Évangile selon Saint Matthieu. Commentaire du Nouveau Testament. Neuchâtel: Delachaux & Niestlé, 1963.

Bonnard, P. E. Le Second Isaïe. Son Disciple et leurs éditeurs Isaïe 40-66. E Bib. Paris: Gabalda, 1972.

Branscomb, B. Harvie. The Gospel of Mark. MNTC. London: Hodder and Stoughton, 1937.

Briggs, C. A. A Critical and Exegetical Commentary on the Book of Psalms. ICC. 2 vols. Edinburgh: T & T Clark, 1906.

Brown, R. E. The Gospel according to John. AB, XXIX. 2 vols. London: Geoffrey Chapman, 1971.

Bruce, A. B. The Synoptic Gospels, Vol. I of The Expositor's Greek Testament. Edited by W. Robertson Nicoll. 5 vols. 7th ed. London: Hodder and Stoughton, 1912.

Bultmann, Rudolf. The Gospel of John: A Commentary. Translated by G. R. Beasley-Murray. Oxford: Basil Blackwell, 1971.

Caird, G. B. The Gospel of St. Luke. PNTC. London: Adam and Charles Black, 1963.

Chary, Théophane. Aggée, Zacharie, Malachie. SB. Paris: Gabalda, 1969.

Cheyne, T. K. The Prophecies of Isaiah. 2 vols. London: C. Kegan Paul, 1881.

Childs, Brevard S. Exodus. London: SCM Press, 1974.

Clarke, Ernest G. The Wisdom of Solomon. Cambridge Bible Commentary. Cambridge: University Press, 1973.

Cranfield, C. E. B. A Critical and Exegetical Commentary on the Epistle to the Romans. ICC, n.s. 2 vols. Edinburgh: T & T Clark, 1975-.

Cranfield, C. E. B. The Gospel According to Saint Mark. Cambridge Greek Testament Commentary. Cambridge: University Press, 1959.

Creed, John Martin. The Gospel According to St. Luke. London: MacMillan, 1930.

Dahood, Mitchell. Psalms. AB, XVI, XVII, XVIIA. 3 vols. Garden City, N.Y.: Doubleday, 1965-70.

Delitzsch, Franz. Biblical Commentary on the Prophecies of Isaiah. Translated by J. S. Banks and James Kennedy. 2 vols. Biblical Commentary on the Old Testament, by Franz Delitzsch and C. F. Keil. 4th ed. Edinburgh: T & T Clark, 1892.

_____. Biblical Commentary on the Psalms. Translated by David Eaton. 3 vols. Biblical Commentary on the Old Testament, by Franz Delitzsch and C. F. Keil. London: Hodder and Stoughton, 1888-89.

Duhm, D. Bernh. Das Buch des Jesaja. HKAT, III, 1. Göttingen: Vandenhoeck & Ruprecht, 1892.

Duhm, D. B. Die Psalmen. Kurzer Hand-Commentar zum Alten Testament. Freiburg: Mohr, 1899.

Easton, Burton Scott. *The Gospel According to St. Luke*. Edinburgh: T & T Clark, 1926.

Eaton, J. H. *Psalms*. TB. London: SCM, 1967.

Elliger, Karl. *Das Buch der zwölf kleinen Propheten*. ATD XXV. 2 vols. 2nd ed. Göttingen: Vandenhoeck & Ruprecht, 1951.

Ellis, E. Earle. *The Gospel of Luke*. NCB. London: Nelson, 1966.

Fenton, J. C. *The Gospel of St. Matthew*. PNTC. Harmondsworth: Penguin Books, 1963.

Filson, Floyd V. *A Commentary on the Gospel According to St. Matthew*. BNTC. London: Adam & Charles Black, 1960.

Godet, F. *Commentary on the Gospel of St. John*. Translated by S. Taylor and M. D. Cusin. 3 vols. Edinburgh: T & T Clark, 1877.

──────. *A Commentary on the Gospel of St. Luke*. Translated by M. D. Cusin. 2 vols. 2nd ed. Edinburgh: T & T Clark, 1875.

Gould, Ezra P. *A Critical and Exegetical Commentary on the Gospel According to St. Mark*. ICC. Edinburgh: T & T Clark, 1896.

Green, H. Benedict. *The Gospel According to Matthew*. The New Clarendon Bible. Oxford: University Press, 1975.

Grundmann, Walter. *Das Evangelium nach Markus*. THKNT III. 2nd ed. Berlin: Evangelische Verlagsanstalt, n.d.

──────. *Das Evangelium nach Markus*. THKNT II. Berlin: Evangelische Verlagsanstalt, n.d.

──────. *Das Evangelium nach Matthäus*. THKNT, I. 3rd ed. Berlin: Evangelische Verlagsanstalt, 1972.

Gunkel, Herman. *Die Psalmen*. Göttinger Handkommentar zum Alten Testament, II: 2. 4th ed. Göttingen: Vandenhoeck & Ruprecht, 1926.

Haenchen, Ernst. *Der Weg Jesu: Eine Erklärung des Markus-Evangelium und der kanonischen Parallelen*. Berlin: Töpelmann, 1966.

Hengstenberg, E. W. *Commentary on the Psalms*. Translated by P. Fairbairn & J. Thomson. 3 vols. 3rd ed. Edinburgh: T & T Clark, 1851.

Hill, David. *The Gospel of Matthew*. NCB. London: Oliphants, 1972.

Holtzmann, H. J. *Der Synoptiker*. HKNT I. 3rd ed. Tübingen and Leipzig: Mohr, 1901.

Hoskyns, Edwyn Clement. *The Fourth Gospel*. Edited by F. N. Davey. 2 vols. London: Faber and Faber, 1940.

Johnson, Sherman E. *A Commentary on the Gospel According to St. Mark*. BNTC. London: Adam & Charles Black, 1960.

Keil, C. F. The Twelve Minor Prophets. Translated by James Martin. 2 vols. Biblical Commentary on the Old Testament by C. F. Keil and F. Delitzsch. Edinburgh: T & T Clark, 1868.

Kidner, Derek. Psalms. 2 vols. TOTC. London: InterVarsity Press, 1973, 1975.

Kirkpatrick, A. F. The Book of Psalms. Cambridge: University Press, 1902.

Kissane, Edward J. The Book of Psalms. Dublin: Browne and Nolan, 1964.

Kittel, D. Rudolf. Die Psalmen. KAT, XIII. 5th & 6th eds. Leipzig: A. Dieichertsche Verlagsbuchhandlung, D. Werner Schoel, 1929.

Klostermann, Erich. Das Markusevangelium. HNT, III. 4th ed. Tübingen: Mohr, 1950.

_____. Das Matthäusevangelium. HNT, IV. 2nd ed. Tübingen: Mohr, 1927.

Kraus, Hans-Joachim. Psalmen. BKAT, XV. 2 vols. Netherlands: Neukirchener, 1959-60.

Lagrange, M.-J. Évangile selon Saint Jean. EBib. 6th ed. Paris: Gabalda, 1936.

_____. Évangile selon Saint Luc. 6th ed. Paris: J. Gabalda, 1941.

_____. Évangile selon Saint Marc. EBib. 6th ed. Paris: Gabalda, 1942.

_____. Évangile selon Saint Matthieu. EBib. 5th ed. Paris: Gabalda, 1941.

Lake, Kirsopp and Cadbury, Henry J. English Translation and Commentary. Vol. IV of The Beginnings of Christianity. Edited by F. J. Foakes Jackson and Kirsopp Lake. London: MacMillan and Co., Limited, 1933.

Lampe, G. W. H. "Luke." Peake's Commentary on the Bible. Edited by Matthew Black and H. H. Rowley. Rev. ed. London, et al.: Nelson, 1962.

Lane, William L. The Gospel according to Mark. NIC. Grand Rapids: Eerdmans, 1974.

Leaney, A. R. C. A Commentary on the Gospel according to St. Luke. BNTC. London: Adam and Charles Black, 1958.

Lightfoot, R. H. St. John's Gospel: A Commentary. Edited by C. F. Evans. Oxford: University Press, 1956.

Lindars, Barnabas. The Gospel of John. NCB. London: Oliphants, 1972.

Lohmeyer, Ernst. Das Evangelium des Markus. MeyerK, II. 17th ed. Göttingen: Vandenhoeck & Ruprecht, 1967.

Lohmeyer, Ernst. Das Evangelium des Matthäus. Revised by Werner Schmauch MeyerK, I. 4th ed. Göttingen: Vandenhoeck & Ruprecht, 1967.

Loisy, Alfred. L'Évangile selon Luc. Paris: Émile Nourry, 1924.

_____. L'Évangile selon Marc. Paris: Émile Nourry, 1912.

_____. Le Quatrième Évangile. 2nd ed. Paris: Émile Nourry, 1921.

Luthardt, Christoph Ernst. St. John's Gospel. Translated by Caspar René Gregory. 3 vols. Edinburgh: T & T Clark, 1878.

Macgregor, G. H. C. The Gospel of John. MNTC. London: Hodder and Stoughton, 1928.

McKenzie, John L. Second Isaiah. AB, XX. Garden City, N.Y.: Doubleday, 1968.

McNeile, Alan Hugh. The Gospel According to St. Matthew. London: MacMillan, 1928.

Manson, William. The Gospel of Luke. MNTC. London: Hodder and Stoughton, 1930.

Marsh, John. Saint John. PNTC. Harmondsworth: Penguin Books, 1968.

Marshall, I. Howard. The Gospel of Luke: A Commentary on the Greek Text. New International Greek Testament Commentary. Grand Rapids: Eerdmans, 1978.

Marti, Karl. Das Dodekapropheten. Tübingen: Mohr, 1902.

Menzies, Allan. The Earliest Gospel. A Historical Study of the Gospel According to Mark. London: MacMillan, 1901.

Micklem, Philip A. St. Matthew. WC. London: Methuen, 1917.

Mitchell, H. G.; Smith, John Merlin; and Brewer, Julius A. A Critical and Exegetical Commentary on Haggai, Zechariah, Malachi and Jonah. ICC. Edinburgh: T & T Clark, 1912.

Montefiore, C. G. The Synoptic Gospels. 2 vols. 2nd ed. London: MacMillan, 1927.

Morris, Leon. The Gospel According to John. NIC. London: Marshall, Morgan & Scott, 1971.

_____. The Gospel According to St. Luke. TNTC. London: Inter-Varsity Press, 1974.

Nineham, D. E. The Gospel of St. Mark. PNTC. Rev. ed. London: Adam & Charles Black, 1968.

North, Christopher. Isaiah 40-55. TB. London: SCM, 1952.

_____. The Second Isaiah. Oxford: Clarendon Press, 1964.

Nowack, D. W. Die kleinen Propheten. HKAT, III: 4. Göttingen: Vandenhoeck & Ruprecht, 1897.

Oesterley, W. O. E. The Psalms. 2 vols. London: Society for Promoting Christian Literature, 1939.

Orelli, C. von. The Twelve Minor Prophets. Translated by J. S. Banks. Minneapolis: Klock & Klock, 1977 (=1897).

Perowne, J. J. Stewart. The Book of Psalms. 3 vols. London: Bell and Daldy, 1870.

Pesch, Rudolf. Das Markusevangelium. HTKNT, II. 2 vols. Freiburg/Basel/Vienna: Herder, 1976-.

Plummer, Alfred. A Critical and Exegetical Commentary on the Gospel According to St. Luke. ICC. Edinburgh: T & T Clark, 1896.

―――. An Exegetical Commentary on the Gospel According to St. Matthew. London: Robert Scott, 1909.

―――. The Gospel According to St. Mark. Cambridge Greek Testament. Cambridge: University Press, 1926.

Ragg, Lonsdale. St. Luke. WC. London: Methuen, 1922.

Rawlinson, A. E. J. St. Mark. WC. London: Methuen, 1925.

Rengstorf, Karl Heinrich. Das Evangelium nach Lukas. NTD, III. 6th ed. Göttingen: Vandenhoeck & Ruprecht, 1952.

Salmond, S. D. F. St. Mark. The Century Bible. Edinburgh: T.C. & E.C. Jack, n.d.

Sanders, J. N. A Commentary on the Gospel According to St. John. Edited and completed by B. A. Mastin. BNTC. London: Adam & Charles Black, 1968.

Schlatter, A. Der Evangelist Matthäus. Stuttgart: Calwer, 1957.

Schmid, Josef. The Gospel According to Mark. Translated and edited by Kevin Condon. RNT. Regensburg: Friedrich Pustet (Mercier Press), 1968.

Schmidt, Hans. Die Psalmen. HAT, XV. Tübingen: Mohr, 1934.

Schnackenburg, Rudolf. Das Johannesevangelium. HTKNT, 3 vols. Freiburg: Herder, 1965-1975.

Schniewind, Julius. Das Evangelium nach Markus. NTD, II. 6th ed. Göttingen: Vandenhoeck & Ruprecht, 1952.

―――. Das Evangelium nach Matthäus. NTD, I. 7th ed. Göttingen: Vandenhoeck & Ruprecht, 1954.

Schürmann, Heinz. Das Lukasevangelium. Vol. I: Kommentar zu Kap. 1, 1-9, 50. HTKNT, III. Freiburg/Basel/Vienna: Herder, 1969.

Schweizer, Eduard. Das Evangelium nach Markus. NTD, I. Göttingen: Vandenhoeck & Ruprecht, 1968.

Schweizer, Eduard. _The Good News According to Matthew._ Translated by David E. Green. London: SPCK, 1975.

Sellin, D. Ernst. _Das Zwölfprophetenbuch._ KAT, XII. 2 vols. 3rd ed. Leipzig: A. Deichertsche, 1930.

Strachan, R. H. _The Fourth Gospel: Its Significance and Environment._ 3rd ed. London: Student Christian Movement, 1941.

Strathmann, Herman. _Das Evangelium nach Johannes._ NTD, IV. Göttingen: Vandenhoeck & Ruprecht, 1954.

Swete, H. B. _The Gospel According to St. Mark._ London: MacMillan, 1898.

Tasker, R. V. G. _The Gospel According to St. John._ TNTC. London: InterVarsity, 1960.

Tasker, R. V. G. _The Gospel According to St. Matthew._ TNTC. London: Tyndale, 1961.

Taylor, Vincent. _The Gospel According to St. Mark._ 2nd ed. London: MacMillan, 1966.

Torrey, Charles Cutler. _The Second Isaiah: A New Interpretation._ Edinburgh: T & T Clark, 1928.

Turner, C. H. "The Gospel According to St. Mark." _A New Commentary on Holy Scripture._ Edited by C. Gore, et al. London: SPCK, 1928.

Wade, G. W. _The Book of the Prophet Isaiah._ WC. London: Methuen, 1911.

Weiser, Arthur. _The Psalms._ Translated by Herbert Hartwell. London: SCM, 1962.

Weiss, Bernhard. _Das Johannes-Evangelium._ Göttingen: Vandenhoeck & Ruprecht, 1902.

_____. _Das Marcusevangelium und seine Synoptischen Parallelen._ Berlin: Wilhelm Hertz, 1872.

Wellhausen, J. _Das Evangelium Johannis._ Berlin: Georg Reimer, 1908.

_____. _Das Evangelium Lucae._ Berlin: Georg Reimer, 1904.

_____. _Das Evangelium Marci._ Berlin: Georg Reimer, 1903.

_____. _Das Evangelium Matthaei._ Berlin: Georg Reimer, 1904.

Westcott, Brooke Foss. _The Gospel According to St. John._ 2 vols. London: James Clarke, 1958 (=1881).

Westermann, Claus. _Isaiah 40-66: A Commentary._ Translated by David M. G. Stalker. London: SCM, 1969.

Monographs & Articles

Aalen, Sverre. "Das Abendmahl als Opfermahl in Neuen Testament." NovT, VI (1963), 128-52.

Abrahams, I. Studies in Pharisaism and the Gospels. First series. Cambridge: University Press, 1917.

Aicher, Georg. Das Alte Testament in der Mishna. Biblische Studien XI, 4. Freiburg: Herder, 1906.

Aland, Kurt. "Neue Neutestamentliche Papyri II." NTS, XII (1965-66), 193-210.

Albright, W. F. "New Light on Early Recensions of the Hebrew Bible." BASOR, CXL (1955), 27-33.

Allegro, J. M. "Fragments of a Qumran Scroll of Eschatological Midrashim." JBL, LXXVII (1958), 350-54.

Allen, W. C. "The Old Testament Quotations in St. Matthew and St. Mark. II. St. Matthew." ExpTim, XII (1900-01), 281-85.

Amsler, Samuel. L'Ancien Testament dans l'église. Neuchatel: Delachoux & Niestlé, 1960.

Amussin, Joseph Dawidowitsch. "Bemerkungen zu den Qumran-Kommentaren." Bibel und Qumran. Beiträge zur Erforschung der Beziehungen zwischen Bibel-und Qumran wissenschaft. Edited by Siegfried Wagner. Berlin: Evangelische Haupt-Bibelgesellschaft, 1968.

Anderson, Hugh. "The Old Testament in Mark's Gospel." The Use of the Old Testament in the New and other Essays: Studies in Honor of William Franklin Stinespring. Edited by James M. Efird. Durham, N.C.: Duke University Press, 1972.

Aptowitzer, W. Das Schriftwort in der Rabbinischen Literatur. New York: KTAV, 1970 (=1906, 1908).

Argyle, A. W. "Greek among the Jews of Palestine in New Testament Times." NTS, XX (1974), 87-89.

Audet, J. P. "A Hebrew - Aramaic List of Books of the Old Testament in Greek Transcription." JTS, n.s. I (1950), 135-54.

_____. "L'hypothèse des testimonia." RB, LXX (1963), 381-405.

Aune, David E. "The Problem of the Messianic Secret." NovT, XI (1969), 1-31.

Aytoun, R. A. "'Himself He Cannot Save' (Ps. xxii 29 and Mark xv. 31)." JTS, XXI (1921), 245-48.

_____. "The Servant of the Lord in the Targum." JTS, XXIII (1922), 172-80.

Bacher, Wilhelm. Die exegetische Terminologie der jüdischen Traditions-literatur. 2 vols. Leipzig: J. C. Hinrichs'sche Buchhandlung, 1905.

Bacon, Benjamin W. Studies in Matthew. London: Constable & Company, 1930.

Bailey, J. A. The Traditions Common to the Gospels of Luke and John. NovTSup, VII. Leiden: Brill, 1963.

Baker, David L. "Typology and the Christian Use of the Old Testament." SJT, XXIX (1976), 137-57.

Baldwin, Joyce G. "Semah as a Technical Term in the Prophets." VT, XIV (1964), 93-97.

Ball, C. J. "Had the Fourth Gospel an Aramaic Archetype." ExpTim, XXI (1909-10), 91-93.

Bampfylde, G. "John XIX 28: A Case for a Different Translation." NovT, XI (1969), 247-60.

Banks, Robert. Jesus and the Law in the Synoptic Tradition. SNTSMS, XXVIII. Cambridge: University Press, 1975.

Barbour, R. S. "Gethsemane in the Tradition of the Passion." NTS, XVI (1969-70), 231-51.

Barnes, W. Emery. "Two Psalm Notes." JTS, XXXVII (1936), 385-87.

Barr, James. Old and New in Interpretation: A Study of the Two Testaments. New York: Harper & Row, 1966.

_____. "Which Language did Jesus Speak? - Some Remarks of a Semitist." BJRL, LIII (1970), 9-29.

Barrett, C. K. "The Background of Mark 10:45." New Testament Essays: Studies in Memory of Thomas Walter Manson. Edited by A.J.B. Higgins. Manchester: Manchester University Press, 1959.

_____. From First Adam to Last: A Study in Pauline Theology. London: Adam & Charles Black, 1962.

_____. The Holy Spirit in the Gospel Tradition. London: SPCK, 1947.

_____. "The Interpretation of the Old Testament in the New." The Cambridge History of the Bible. Vol. I: From the Beginnings to Jerome. Edited by P. R. Ackroyd & C. F. Evans. Cambridge: Cambridge University Press, 1970.

_____. Jesus and the Gospel Tradition. London: SPCK, 1967.

_____. "John and the Synoptic Gospels." ExpTim, LXXXV (1974), 228-33.

_____. "The Lamb of God." NTS, I (1954-55), 210-218.

_____. "Luke xxii. 15. To Eat the Passover." JTS, n.s. IX (1958), 305-07.

Barrett, C. K. "The Old Testament in the Fourth Gospel." JTS, XLVIII (1947), 155-169.

Barrick, W. Boyd. "The Rich Man from Arimathea (Matt. 27:57-60) and 1QIs.ᵃ" JBL, XLVI (1977), 235-39.

Barth, Gerhard. "Matthew's Understanding of the Law." Tradition and Interpretation in Matthew by Günther Bornkamm, Gerhard Barth and Heinz Joachim Held. Translated by Percy Scott. London: SCM, 1963.

Barth, Markus. Was Christ's Death a Sacrifice? SJT Occasional Papers, IX. Edinburgh and London: Oliver and Boyd, 1961.

Barthélemy, Dominique. Les devanciers d'Aquilas. Première Publication Intégrale du Texte des Fragments du Dodécaprophéton. VTSup, X. Leiden: Brill, 1963.

Bartnicki, Roman. "Das Zitat von Zach IX, 9-10 und die Tiere im Bericht von Matthäus über dem Einzug Jesu in Jerusalem (Mt. XXI, 1-11)." NovT, XVIII (1976), 161-66.

Bartsch, Hans-Werner. "Historische Erwägungen zur Leidensgeschichte." EvT, XXII (1962), 449-59.

_____. "Die Ideologiekritik des Evangeliums dargestellt an der Leidensgeschichte." EvT, XXXIV (1974), 176-95.

_____. "Jesu Schwertwort, Lukas xxii. 35-38: Überlieferungsgeschichtliche Studien." NTS, XX(1974), 190-203.

Bauer, Walter. "The 'colt' of Psalm Sunday (Der Palmesel)." Translated by F. W. Gingrich. JBL, LXXII (1953), 220-29.

Baumstark, A. "Die Zitate des Mt.-Ev. aus dem Zwölfprophetenbuch." Bib, XXXVII (1956), 296-313.

Beare, Francis Wright. The Earliest Records of Jesus. Oxford: Basil Blackwell, 1962.

Beasley-Murray, G.R. Baptism in the New Testament. London: MacMillan, 1963.

Behm, Johannes. "διατίθημι, διαθήκη." TDNT, II, 104-134.

_____. "ἐκχέω, ἐκχύν(ν)ω." TDNT, II, 467-9.

_____. "αἷμα, αἱματεκχυσία." TDNT, I, 172-77.

Bennett, W. J. Jr. "'The Son of Man must ...'." NovT, XVII (1975), 113-129.

Benoit, Pierre. "The Date of the Last Supper." Jesus and the Gospel. 2 vols. Translated by Benet Weatherhead. London: Darton, Longman & Todd, 1973.

_____. "The Death of Judas." Jesus and the Gospel. Translated by Benet Weatherhead. 2 vols. London: Darton, Longman & Todd, 1973.

Benoit, Pierre. "The Holy Eucharist." Jesus and the Gospel. 2 vols. Translated by Benet Weatherhead. London: Darton, Longman & Todd, 1973.

_____. "Jésus et le Serviteur de Dieu." Jésus aux origines de la christologie. Edited by J. Dupont. Gembloux: Leuven University Press, 1975.

_____. "Les outrages à Jésus Prophète (Mc XIV 65 par.)." Neotestamentica et Patristica. Eine Freundesgabe Herrn Professor Dr. Oscar Cullmann zu seinem 60. Geburtstag überreicht. NovTSup, VI. Leiden: Brill, 1962.

_____. The Passion and Resurrection of Jesus Christ. Translated by B. Weatherhead. New York: Herder & Herder; London: Darton, Longman & Todd, 1969.

_____. "Qumrân et le Nouveau Testament." NTS, VII (1960-61), 276-96.

_____. "Le Récit de la Cène dans Lc XXII, 15-30." RB, XLVIII (1939), 357-93.

Bentzen, Aage. King and Messiah. Edited by G. W. Anderson. Oxford: Basil Blackwell, 1970.

Berger, Klaus. Die Auferstehung des Propheten und die Erhöhung des Menschensohnes. Traditions-geschichtliche Untersuchungen zur Deutung des Geschickes Jesu in frühchristlichen Texten. SUNT, XIII. Göttingen: Vandenhoeck & Ruprecht, 1976.

Bernard, J. H. "A Study of St. Mark X. 38, 39." JTS, XXVIII (1927), 262-70.

Bertram, Georg. Die Leidensgeschichte Jesu und den Christuskult. Eine formgeschichtliche Untersuchung. FRLANT XV. Göttingen: Vandenhoeck & Ruprecht, 1922.

_____. "$ὕψος$, et al." TDNT, VIII, 602-20.

Best, Ernest. The Temptation and the Passion: The Markan Soteriology. SNTSMS, II. Cambridge: University Press, 1965.

Betz, Johannes, "Die Eucharistie als sakramentale Gegenwart des Heilsereignisses 'Jesus' nach dem ältesten Abendmahlsberichte." Geist und Leben, XXXIII (1960), 166-75.

Betz, Otto. "Die Frage nach dem messianischen Bewusstsein Jesu." NovT, VI (1963), 24-37.

_____. "Jesu Heiliger Krieg." NovT, II (1957), 116-137.

_____. Offenbarung und Schriftforschung in der Qumransekte. WUNT, VI. Tübingen: Mohr, 1960.

_____. "$φωνή$, et al." TDNT, IX, 278-309.

_____. What do we Know about Jesus? Translated by Margaret Kohl. Philadelphia: Westminster, 1968.

Beutler, Johannes. "Psalm 42/43 im Johannesevangelium." NTS, XXV (1978), 33-57.

Birkeland, Harris. Die Feinde des Individuums in der Israelitischen Psalmenliteratur: Ein Beitrag zur Kenntnis der semitischen Literatur und Religionsgeschichte. Oslo: Grøndahl & Sons, 1933.

Bishop, E. F. F. "'He that eateth bread with me hath lifted up his heel against me' - Jn. xiii. 18 (Ps. xli 9)." ExpTim, LXX (1959), 331-33.

Black, Matthew. An Aramaic Approach to the Gospels and Acts. 3rd ed. Oxford: Clarendon Press, 1967.

_____. "The Arrest & Trial of Jesus and the Date of the Last Supper." New Testament Essays: Studies in Memory of Thomas Walter Manson. Edited by A. J. B. Higgins. Manchester: Manchester University Press, 1959.

_____. "The Christological Use of the Old Testament in the New Testament." NTS, XVIII (1971-1972), 1-14.

_____. "The Cup Metaphor in Mark xiv. 36." ExpTim, LIX (1947-48), 195.

_____. "From Schweitzer to Bultmann: The Modern Quest of the Historical Jesus." McCormick Quarterly, XX (1967), 271-83.

_____. "The Messiah in the Testament of Lev. xviii." ExpTim, LX (1949), 321-22.

_____. "The Problem of the OT Quotes in the Gospels." Journal of the Manchester Egyptian & Oriental Society. XXIII, (1942).

_____. "The 'Parables' of Enoch (I En 37-71) and the 'Son of Man.'" ExpTim, LXXVIII (1976), 5-8.

_____. The Scrolls and Christian Origins. Studies in the Jewish Background of the New Testament. New York: Nelson, 1961.

_____. "Servant of the Lord and Son of Man." SJT, VI (1953), 1-11.

_____. "The 'Son of Man' Passion Sayings in the Gospel Tradition." ZNW, LX (1969), 1-8.

Blank, Josef. Krisis. Untersuchungen zur johanneischen Christologie und Eschatologie. Freiburg: Lamberton, 1964.

Blight, W. "The Cry of Dereliction." ExpTim, LXVIII (1957), 285.

Blinzler, Josef. Der Prozess Jesu. 2nd ed. Regensburg: Friedrich Pustet, 1955.

Bloch, Renée. "Midrash." DBSup, V. 1263-81.

_____. "Notes méthodologique pour l'étude de la Littérature rabbinique." RSR, XLIII (1955), 194-227.

Boismard, M.-E. "Les citations targumiques dans le quatrième Évangile." RB, LXVI (1959), 374-78.

_____. Review of The Gospel According to St. John, by C. K. Barrett. RB, LXIII (1956), 267-72.

Boman, Thorlief. "Der Gebetskampf Jesu." NTS, X (1963-64), 261-73.

_____. "Das letzte Wort Jesu." ST, XVII (1963), 103-19.

Bonsirven, Joseph. Exégèse rabbinique et Exégèse paulinienne. Bibliotheque de Theologie Historique. Paris: Beauchesne and Sons, 1939.

_____. "Hoc est corpus meum: Recherches sur l'original araméen." Bib, XXIX (1948), 205-19.

_____. "Hora Talmudica." La notation chronologique de Jean 19,4 aurait-elle un sens symbolique?" Bib, XXXIII (1952), 511-15.

_____. Le Judaïsme Palestinien au temps de Jésus-Christ. Vol. I: La Théologie Dogmatique. 2nd ed. Paris: Beauchesne, 1934.

Borgen, Peder. Bread from Heaven: An Exegetical Study of Manna in the Gospel of John and the Writings of Philo. NovTSup, X. Leiden: Brill, 1965.

_____. "John and the Synoptics in the Passion Narrative." NTS, V (1958-59), 246-59.

Borsch, Frederick Houk. The Son of Man in Myth and History. London: SCM, 1967.

Bousset, Wilhelm. Kyrios Christos: A History of the Belief in Christ from the Beginnings of Christianity to Irenaeus. Translated by John E. Steely. New York and Nashville: Abingdon, 1970.

_____. Die Religion des Judentums im späthellenistischen Zeitalter. Edited by Hugo Gressmann. HNT, XXI. 3rd ed. Tübingen: Mohr, 1926.

Bowker, J. W. The Targums and Rabbinic Literature: An Introduction to the Jewish Interpretation of Scripture. Cambridge: University Press, 1967.

Bowman, John. The Gospel of Mark: The New Christian Jewish Passover Haggadah. SPB, VIII. Leiden: E. J. Brill, 1965.

_____. The Intention of Jesus. London: SCM, 1945.

Brandt, W. Die Evangelische Geschichte und der Ursprung des Christentums. Leipzig: O. R. Reisland, 1893.

Braumann, Georg. "'An jenem Tag' (Mk. 2, 20)." NovT, VI (1963), 264-7.

_____. "Leidenskelch und Todestaufe (Mc. 10, 38f.)." ZNW, LVI (1965), 178-83.

Braun, F.-M. Jean le Théologien. 3 vols. Paris: Gabalda, 1959-72.

Braun, Herbert. "Das Alte Testament im Neuen Testament." ZTK, LIX (1962), 16-31.

_____. Qumran und das Neue Testament. 2 vols. Tübingen: Mohr, 1966.

_____. Spätjudische-häretischer und frühchristlicher Radikalismus: Jesus von Nazareth und die essenische Qumransekte. BHT, XXIV. 2 vols. 2nd ed. Tübingen: Mohr, 1969.

Bretscher, P. G. "Exodus 4:22-23 and the Voice from Heaven." JBL, LXXXVII (1968), 301-11.

Bright, John. The Authority of the Old Testament. London: SCM, 1967.

Brown, Raymond E. The Birth of the Messiah: A Commentary on the Infancy Narratives in Matthew and Luke. Garden City, N.Y.: Doubleday, 1977.

_____. "John and the Synoptic Gospels: A Comparison." New Testament Essays. London/Dublin: Geoffrey Chapman, 1965.

_____. "The Messianism of Qumrân." CBQ, XIX (1957), 53-82.

_____. "Parable and Allegory Reconsidered." NovT, V (1962), 37-45.

_____. "The Pre-Christian Semitic Concept of 'Mystery.'" CBQ, XX (1958), 417-443.

Brownlee, William H. "Biblical Interpretation among the Sectaries of the Dead Sea Scrolls." BA, XIV (1951), 54-76.

_____. The Meaning of the Qumran Scrolls for the Bible with special attention to the Book of Isaiah. The James W. Richard Lectures in Christian Religion. New York: Oxford University Press, 1964.

_____. "Messianic Motifs of Qumran and the New Testament." NTS, III (1956-1957), 12-30.

_____. "The Servant of the Lord in the Qumran Scrolls." BASOR, CXXXII (1953), 8-15; CXXXV (1954), 33-38.

_____. The Text of Habakkuk in the Ancient Commentary from Qumran. Philadelphia: Society of Biblical Literature, 1959.

Bruce, F. F. Biblical Exegesis in the Qumran Texts. Grand Rapids: Eerdmans, 1960.

_____. "The Book of Zechariah and the Passion Narrative." BJRL, XLII (1960-1961), 336-53.

_____. "Qumrân and Early Christianity." NTS, II (1955-1956), 176-190.

Bruce, F. F. This is That: The New Testament Development of Some Old Testament Themes. Exeter: Paternoster Press, 1968.

Bruns, J. Edgar. "The Use of Time in the Fourth Gospel." NTS, XIII (1966-67), 285-90.

Buckler, F. W. "Eli, Eli, Lama Sabachthani?" AJSL, LV (1938), 378-391.

Büschel, Friedrich. "δέδωμι." TDNT, II, 166-73.

Bultmann, Rudolf. The History of the Synoptic Tradition. Translated by John Marsh. Oxford: Basil Blackwell, 1963.

_____. "περίλυπος." TDNT, IV, 323.

_____. "Prophecy and Fulfillment." Translated by C. C. Greig. Essays on Old Testament Interpretation. Edited by Claus Westermann. (English translation edited by James Luther Mays). London: SCM, 1963.

_____. Theology of the New Testament. Translated by Kendrick Grobel. 2 vols. New York: Scribner's, 1951-1955.

_____. "Ursprung und Sinn der Typologie als hermeneutischer Methode." TLZ, LXXV (1950), 205-12.

Burkill, T. A. Mysterious Revelation: An Examination of the Philosophy of St. Mark's Gospel. Ithaca: N.Y.: Cornell University Press, 1963.

_____. "St. Mark's Philosophy of the Passion." NovT, II (1958), 245-71.

Burkitt, F. C. "The Cleansing of the Temple." JTS, XXV (1924), 386-90.

_____. The Gospel History and Its Transmission. Edinburgh: T & T Clark, 1906.

_____. "On St. Mark xv 34 in Cod. Bobiensis." JTS, I (1900), 278-79.

Burney, C. F. The Aramaic Origin of the Fourth Gospel. Oxford: Clarendon Press, 1922.

Burrows, E. W. "Did John the Baptist Call Jesus 'the Lamb of God'?" ExpTim, LXXXV (1974), 245-49.

Burrows, Millar. The Dead Sea Scrolls. New York: Viking, 1955.

_____. "The Meaning of 'šr 'mr in DSH." VT, II (1952), 255-60.

_____. More Light on the Dead Sea Scrolls: New Scrolls and New Interpretations. New York: Viking, 1958.

Buse, Ivor. "The Marcan Account of the Baptism of Jesus and Isaiah LXIII." JTS, n.s. VII (1956), 74-75.

_____. "St. John and the Marcan Passion Narrative." NTS, IV (1957-58), 215-19.

_____. "St. John and the Passion Narratives of St. Matthew and St. Luke." NTS, VII (1960-61), 65-76.

Cadbury, Henry, J. "The Titles of Jesus in Acts." The Beginnings of Christianity Vol. V: Additional Notes to the Commentary. Edited by Kirsopp Lake and Henry J. Cadbury. London: MacMillan, 1933.

Cadman, William Healey. The Open Heaven: The Revelation of God in the Johannine Sayings of Jesus. Edited by G. B. Caird. Oxford: Basil Blackwell, 1969.

Cadoux, Cecil John. The Historic Mission of Jesus: A Constructive Re-examination of the Eschatological Teaching in the Synoptic Gospels. London: Lutterworth Press, 1941.

_____. "The Imperatival Use of ἵνα in the New Testament." JTS, XLII (1941), 165-173.

Caird, G. B. "Towards a Lexicon of the Septuagint, II." JTS, n.s. XX (1969), 21-40.

Caldecott, A. "The Significance of the 'Cleansing of the Temple.'" JTS, XXIV (1923), 382-86.

Calvert, D. G. A. "An Examination of the Criteria for Distinguishing the Authentic Words of Jesus." NTS, XVIII (1971-72), 209-19.

Campbell, J. S. "The Origin and Meaning of the Term Son of Man." JTS, XLVIII (1947), 145-155.

Carmignac, Jean. "Les citations de l'Ancien Testament dans 'La guerre des fils de lumière contre les fils de ténèbres.'" RB, LXIII (1956) 234-60, 375-90.

_____. "Les citations de l'Ancien Testament, et spécialement des poèmes du serviteur, dans les Hymnes de Qumran." RevQ, VI, (1960), 357-394.

_____. "La théologie de la souffrance dans les Hymnes de Qumrān." RevQ, III (1961-62), 365-86.

Catchpole, David R. The Trial of Jesus: A Study in the Gospels and Jewish Historiography from 1770 to the Present Day. SPB, XVIII, Leiden: Brill, 1971.

Cazelles, H. "La question du 'lamed auctoris.'" RB, LVI (1949) 93-101

Cerfaux, Lucien. "L'exegese de l'Ancien Testament par le Nouveau Testament." Recueil Lucien Cerfaux: Études d'Exégèse et d'Histoire Religieuse (réunie à l'occasion de son soixante-dixième anniversaire), BETL, VI-VII. 2 vols. Gembloux: Duculot, 1954.

Chadwick, Henry. "The Shorter Text of Luke xxii. 15-20." HTR, L (1957), 249-58.

Chase, Frederic Henry. The Syro-Latin Text of the Gospels. London: MacMillan, 1895.

Chevallier, Max-Alain. L'esprit et le messie dans le bas-judaïsme et le Nouveau Testament. Paris: University of France: 1958.

Childs, Brevard S. "Prophecy and Fulfillment: A Study of Contemporary Hermeneutics." Int, XII (1958), 259-71.

―――――. "Psalm Titles and Midrashic Exegesis." JSS, XVI (1971), 137-50.

Christensen, Jens. "Le fils de l'homme s'en va, ainsi qu'il est écrit de lui." ST, X (1956), 28-39.

Clines, D. J. A. "Psalm Research Since 1955, I. Cult." TB, XVIII (1967), 103-126.

―――――. "Psalm Research Since 1955: II. The Literary Genres." TB, XX (1969), 105-125.

Cohn, Haim. The Trial and Death of Jesus. London: Weidenfeld and Nicolson, 1967.

Colpe, Carsten. " ὁ υἱὸς τοῦ ἀνθρώπου ." TDNT VIII, 400-477.

Conzelmann, Hans. "History and Theology in the Passion Narratives of the Synoptic Gospels." Translated by Charles B. Cousar. Int, XXIV (1970), 178-97.

―――――. An Outline of the Theology of the New Testament. Translated by John Bowden. London: SCM, 1969.

―――――. "σκότος, ..." TDNT, VII, 423-45.

―――――. The Theology of St. Luke. Translated by Geoffrey Buswell. London: Faber and Faber, 1961.

Cooke, Bernard. "Synoptic Presentation of the Eucharist as Covenant Sacrifice." TS, XXI (1960), 1-44.

Coppens, Joseph. Le Messianisme et sa Relève prophétique. Les anticipations vétérotestamentaires. Leur accomplissement en Jésus. BETL, XXXVIII. Gembloux: Duculot, 1974.

Craig, Clarence Tucker. "The Identification of Jesus with the Suffering Servant." JR, XXIV (1944), 240-5.

Cranfield, C. E. B. "The Baptism of our Lord - A Study of St. Mark 1:9-11." SJT, VIII (1955), 53-63.

―――――. "The Cup Metaphor in Mark XIV. 36 and Parallels." ExpTim, LIX (1947-48), 137-38.

Cross, Frank Moore, Jr. The Ancient Library of Qumrân and Modern Biblical Studies. The Haskell Lectures, 1956-57. London: Duckworth, 1958.

―――――. "The Contribution of the Qûmran Discoveries for the Study of the Biblical Text." IEJ, XVI (1966), 81-95.

―――――. "The Evaluation of a Theory of Local Texts." Qumran and the History of the Biblical Text. Edited by Frank Moore Cross and Shemaryahu Talmon. Cambridge, Mass.: Harvard University Press, 1975.

Cross, Frank Moore. "The History of the Biblical Text in the Light of Discoveries in the Judean Desert." HTR, LVII (1964), 281-99.

Cullmann, Oscar. Baptism in the New Testament. Translated by J. K. S. Reid. SBT, I. London: SCM, 1950.

_____. Christ and Time: The Primitive Christian Conception of Time and History. Translated by Floyd V. Filson. Rev. ed. London: SCM, 1962.

_____. The Christology of the New Testament. Translated by Shirley C. Guthrie and Charles A. M. Hall. London: SCM, 1959.

_____. Salvation in History. Translated by Sidney G. Sowers. London: SCM, 1967.

Dahl, George. "The Messianic Expectation in the Psalter." JBL, LVII (1938), 1-12.

Dahl, Nils Alstrup. "The Atonement - An Adequate Reward for the Akedah? (Ro. 8:32)." Neotestamentica et Semitica: Studies in Honour of Matthew Black. Edited by E. Earle Ellis and Max Wilcox: Edinburgh: T & T Clark, 1969.

_____. "Der gekreuzigte Messias." Der historische Jesus und der kerygmatische Christus: Beiträge zum Christusverständnis in Forschung und Verkündigung. Edited by Helmut Ristow and Karl Matthiae. 2nd ed. Berlin: Evangelische Verlagsanstalt, 1961.

_____. "Die Passionsgeschichte bei Matthäus." NTS, II (1955-56), 17-32.

Dalman, Gustav. Jesus-Jeshua: Studies in the Gospels. Translated by Paul R. Levertoft. London: Society for Promoting Christian Knowledge, 1929.

_____. The Words of Jesus. Translated by D. M. Kay. Edinburgh: T & T Clark, 1902.

Daniélou, Jean. Etudes d'exégèse judéo-chrétienne (Les testimonia). Théologique Historique, V. Paris: Beauchesne & Sons, 1966.

_____. "The Fathers and the Scriptures." Theology, LVII (1954), 83-89.

_____. From Shadows to Reality: Studies in the Biblical Typology of the Fathers. Translated by Dom Wolstan Hibberd. London: Burns & Oates, 1960.

_____. "La typologie d'Isaac dans le christianisme primitif." Bib, XXVIII (1947), 363-93.

Danker, Frederick W. "The Demonic Secret in Mark: A Reexamination of the Cry of Dereliction." ZNW, LXI (1970), 48-69.

_____. "The Literary Unity of Mark 14:1-25." JBL, LXXXV (1966), 467-72.

Daube, David. "For they know not what they do: Luke 23:34." SP, IV (= TU, LXXVIII). Berlin: Akadamie Verlag, 1961.

_____. The New Testament and Rabbinic Judaism. London: Athlone, 1965.

Dauer, Anton. Die Passionsgeschichte im Johannesevangelium: Eine traditionsgeschichtliche und theologische Untersuchung zu Joh 18, 1-19,30. SANT, XXX. Munich: Kösel, 1972.

David, J.-E. "To haima mou tes diathekes, Mt. 26:28: Un faux problème." Bib, XLVIII (1967), 291-92.

Davies, Philip R. IQM, the War Scroll from Qumran: Its Structure and History. BibOr XXXII. Rome: Biblical Institute Press, 1977.

Davies, R. E. "Christ in our Place - The Contribution of the Prepositions." (The Tyndale Biblical Theology Lecture, 1959). TB, XXI (1970), 71-91.

Davies, W. D. "Matthew 5:17, 18." Christian Origins and Judaism. Philadelphia: Westminster, 1962.

_____. Paul and Rabbinic Judaism. London: SPCK, 1948.

_____. The Setting of the Sermon on the Mount. Cambridge: University Press, 1964.

Deichgräber, Reinhard. "Die Gemeinderegel (IQS) X, 4." RevQ, II (1960), 279-80.

Deissmann, Adolf. Light From the Ancient East: The New Testament Illustrated by Recently Discovered Texts of the Graeco-Roman World. Translated by Lionel R. M. Strachan. New York: George H. Doran, 1927.

Deissmann, Adolf. Die Septuaginta-Papyri und andere altchristliche Texte der Heidelberger Papyrus-Sammlung. Heidelberg: Carl Winter, 1905.

Delcor, M. "Deux Passages Difficiles: Zach XII II et XI 13." VT, III (1953), 67-77.

Delcor, M. "Le Midrash d'Habacuc." RB, LVIII (1951), 521-48.

_____. "Un Problème de critique textuelle et d'exégèse: Zach, XII, 10: Et aspicient ad me quem confixerunt." RB, LVIII (1951), 189-99.

Delling, Gerhard. "Βάπτισμα βαπτισθῆναι." NovT. II (1957), 92-115.

_____. Der Kreuzestod Jesu in der urchristlichen Verkundigung. Göttingen: Vandenhoeck & Ruprecht, 1972.

Derrett, J. D. M. "The Good Shepherd: St. John's Use of Jewish Halakah and Haggadah." ST, XXVII (1973), 25-50.

Descamps, Albert. Les Justes et la Justice dans les évangiles et le christianisme primitif: hormis la doctrine proprement paulinienne. Universitas Catholica Louvaniensis Dissertation Series II, Vol. XLIII. Louvain: Publications Universitaires de Louvain & Gembloux: Duculot, 1950.

Descamps, A. "Rédaction et christologie dans le récit matthéen de la Passion." L'Évangile selon Matthieu: Rédaction et théologie. Edited by M. Didier. Gembloux: J. Duculot, 1972.

Dewar, L. "The Biblical Use of the Term 'Blood'." JTS, n.s. IV (1953), 204-08.

Dibelius, Martin. "Die alttestamentlichen Motive in der Leidensgeschichte des Petrus-und des Johannes-Evangeliums." Abhandlungen zur semitischen Religionskunde und Sprachwissenschaft (für W. W. G. von Baudissin). Edited by W. Frankenberg and F. Küchler. BZAW, XXXIII. Giessen: Töpelmann, 1918.

_____. From Tradition to Gospel. Translated by Bertram Lee Woolf. 2nd ed. London: Ivor Nicholson and Watson Limited, 1934.

_____. "Gethsemane." Botschaft und Geschichte: Gesammelte Aufsätze I: zur Evangelienforschung. Tübingen: Mohr, 1953.

_____. "'Herodes und Pilatus.'" ZNW, XVI (1915), 113-26.

_____. "Das historische Problem der Leidensgeschichte." ZNW, XXX (1931), 193-201.

Dietrich, E. L. "Schriftauslegung II. Im Judentum." RGG, V, 1515-17.

Dix, G. H. "The Messiah ben Joseph." JTS, XXVII (1926), 130-143.

Dodd, C. H. According to the Scriptures: The Substructure of New Testament Theology. Fontana Books. London: Collins, 1952.

_____. The Apostolic Preaching and its Developments. London: Hodder and Stoughton, 1936.

_____. Historical Tradition in the Fourth Gospel. Cambridge: University Press, 1963.

_____. The Interpretation of the Fourth Gospel. Cambridge: University Press, 1965.

_____. The Parables of the Kingdom. Rev. ed. New York: Charles Scribner's Sons, 1961.

Dodewaard, J. A. E. van. "La force évocatrice de la citation." Bib, XXXVI (1955), 482-91.

Döller, J. "Der Wein in Bibel und Talmud." Bib, IV (1923), 143-67; 267-99.

Doeve, J. W. "Die Gefangennahme Jesu in Gethsemane. Eine traditionsgeschichtliche Untersuchung." SE, I (1959) (= TU, LXXXIII), 458-80.

_____. Jewish Hermeneutics in the Synoptic Gospels and Acts. Assen: van Gorcum, 1954.

Donahue, John R. Are You the Christ? The Trial Narrative in the Gospel of Mark. SBLDS, X. Missoula, Mont.: SBL, 1973.

Donahue, John R. "Temple, Trial and Royal Christology. (Mark 14:53-65." The Passion in Mark: Studies in Mark 14-16. Edited by Werner H. Kelber. Philadelphia: Fortress, 1976.

Dormeyer, Detlev. Die Passion Jesu als Verhaltensmodell: Literarische und theologische Analyse der Traditions-und Redaktionsgeschichte der Markuspassion. NTAbh, n.s. XI. Münster: Aschendorff, 1974.

Downing, John. "Jesus and Martyrdom." JTS, n.s. XIV (1963), 279-93.

Driver, G. R. "Mistranslations." ExpTim, LVII (1945-46), 192-93.

Dunn, James D. G. Jesus and the Spirit: A Study of the Religious and Charismatic Experience of Jesus and the First Christians as Reflected in the New Testament. London: SCM, 1975.

_____. "John VI - A Eucharistic Discourse?" NTS, XVII (1970-71), 328-338.

_____. Unity and Diversity in the New Testament. London: SCM, 1977.

Edersheim, Alfred. The Life and Times of Jesus the Messiah. 2 vols. London: Longmann, Green and Co., 1883.

Edgar, S. L. "New Testament and Rabbinic Messianic Interpretation." NTS, V (1958-59), 47-54.

Edwards, R. A. The Sign of Jonah in the Theology of The Evangelists and Q. SBT, n.s. XVIII. London: SCM, 1971.

Eichrodt, Walter. "Is Typological Exegesis an Appropriate Method?" Translated by James Barr. Essays on Old Testament Interpretation. Edited by Claus Westermann. (English translation edited by James Luther Mays). London: SCM, 1963.

_____. Theology of the Old Testament. Translated by J. A. Baker. 2 vols. 6th ed. Philadelphia: Westminster, 1961, 1967.

Eissfeldt, Otto. "'Mein Gott' im Alten Testament." ZAW, LXI (1945-46), 3-16.

_____. The Old Testament: An Introduction. Translated by Peter R. Ackroyd. Oxford: Basil Blackwell, 1965.

_____. Ras Schamra und Sanchunjaton, Beiträge zur Religionsgeschichte des Altertums, IV. Halle: Max Niemeyer, 1939.

Elliger, Karl. Studien zum Habakuk-Kommentar vom Toten Meer. BHT, XV. Tübingen: Mohr, 1953.

Ellis, E. Earle. "How the New Testament Uses the Old." New Testament Interpretation: Essays on Principles and Methods. Edited by I. Howard Marshall. Grand Rapids: Eerdmans, 1977.

_____. "Midrash, Targum and New Testament Quotations." Neotestamentica et Semitica: Studies in Honour of Matthew Black. Edited by E. Earle Ellis and Max Wilcox. Edinburgh: T & T Clark, 1969.

Ellis, E. Earle. Paul's Use of the Old Testament. Edinburgh: Oliver and Boyd, 1957.

Emerton, J. A. "The Aramaic Underlying τὸ αἷμά μου τῆς διαθήκης in Mark xiv. 24." JTS, n.s. VI (1955), 238-40.

_____. "Mark xiv. 24 and the Targum to the Psalter." JTS, n.s. XV (1964) 58-59.

_____. "The Problem of Vernacular Hebrew in the First Century A.D. and the Language of Jesus," JTS, n.s. XXIV (1973), 1-23.

_____. " τὸ αἷμά μου τῆς διαθήκης : The Evidence of the Syriac Versions." JTS, n.s. XIII (1962), 111-17.

Essane, W. G. "Matthew xxvii. 51-54 and John v. 25-29." ExpTim, LXXVI (1964), 103.

Evans, C. F. "'I will go before you into Galilee.'" JTS, n.s. V (1954), 3-18.

Fascher, Erich. "Theologische Beobachtungen zu δεῖ ." Neutestamentliche Studien für Rudolf Bultmann. BZNW, XXI. 2nd ed. Berlin: Alfred Töpelmann, 1957.

Feigel, Friedrich Karl. Der Einfluss des Weissagungsbeweises und anderer Motive auf die Leidensgeschichte: Ein Beitrag zur Evangelien Kritik. Tübingen: Mohr, 1910.

Feuillet, A. "Le Baptême de Jésus." RB, LXXI (1964), 321-52.

_____. "La controverse sur le jeune (Mc 2, 18-20; Mt. 9, 14-15; Lk. 5, 33-35)." NRT, XL (1968), 113-36; 252-77.

_____. "La Coupe et le baptême de la Passion (Mc, X, 35-40; cf. Mt. xx, 20-28 Luc, XII, 50)." RB, LXXIV (1967) 356-91.

_____. "Le logion sur la rançon." RSPT, LI (1967), 365-402.

_____. "The Principal Themes in the Discourse on the Bread of Life." Johannine Studies. Translated by Thomas E. Crane. Staten Island, New York: Alba House, 1965.

_____. "Le Récit Lucanien de l'agonie de Gethsémani (Lc XXII. 39-46)." NTS, XXII (1976), 397-417.

Findlay, J. A. "The First Gospel and the Book of Testimonies." Amicitiae Corolla. Edited by H. G. Wood. London: University of London, 1933.

Finegan, Jack. Die Überlieferung der Leidens - und Auferstehungsgeschichte Jesu. BZNW, XV. Giessen: Töpelmann, 1934.

Finkel, Asher. "The Pesher of Dreams and Scriptures." RevQ, IV (1963-1964), 357-370.

Fisher, Loren R. "Betrayed by Friends: An Expository Study of Psalm 22." Int, XVIII (1964) 20-38.

Fitzmyer, Joseph A. "David 'being therefore a Prophet... (Acts 2:30)." CBQ, XXXIV (1972), 332-39.

_____. "'4Q Testimonia and the New Testament." TS, XVIII (1957), 513-37.

_____. The Genesis Apocryphon of Qumran Cave I. A Commentary. BibOr, XVIII. Rome: Pontifical Biblical Institute, 1956.

_____. "The Languages of Palestine in the First Century A.D." CBQ, XXXII (1970), 501-31.

_____. Review of An Aramaic Approach to the Gospels and Acts. (3rd ed.), by Matthew Black. CBQ, XXX (1968), 417-428.

_____. "The Use of Explicit Old Testament Quotations in Qumran Literature and in the New Testament." NTS, VII (1960-61), 297-333.

Flemington, W. F. The New Testament Doctrine of Baptism. London: SPCK, 1964.

Flesseman-van Leer, E. "Die Interpretation der Passionsgeschichte vom A T aus." Zur Bedeutung des Todes Jesu. Edited by Fritz Viering. Gütersloh: Mohn, 1967.

Flew, R. Newton. Jesus and His Church: A Study of the idea of the Ecclesia in the New Testament. London: The Epworth Press, 1938.

Ford, J. Massingberd. "'Mingled Blood' from the Side of Christ (John XIX. 34)." NTS, XV (1968-69), 337-38.

Forestall, J. Terrence. The Word of the Cross: Salvation as Revelation in the Fourth Gospel. AnBib, LVII. Rome: Biblical Institute, 1974.

Fortna, Robert T. The Gospel of Signs. A Reconstruction of the Narrative Source Underlying the Fourth Gospel. SNTSMS, XI. Cambridge: University Press, 1970.

Foulkes, Francis. The Acts of God: A Study of the Basis of Typology in the Old Testament. London: The Tyndale Press, 1958.

France, R. T. Jesus and the Old Testament. London: Tyndale, 1971.

Franklin, Eric. Christ the Lord: A Study in the Purpose and Theology of Luke-Acts. London: SPCK, 1975.

Freed, Edwin D. Old Testament Quotations in the Gospel of John. NovTSup, XI. Leiden: Brill, 1965.

_____. "The Son of Man in the Fourth Gospel." JBL, LXXXVI (1967), 402-9.

Friedrich, Gerhard. "Beobachtungen zur messianischen Hohepriestererwartung in den Synoptikern." ZTK, LIII (1956), 265-311.

Frör, Kurt. Biblische Hermeneutik. Zur Schriftauslegung in Predigt und Unterricht. 3rd ed.; Munich: Chr. Kaiser Verlag, 1967.

Frost, Stanley Brice. "Apocalyptic and History." The Bible in Modern Scholarship: Papers Read at the 100th Meeting of the Society of Biblical Literature. December 28-30, 1964. Edited by J. Philip Hyatt. New York: Abingdon, 1965.

Fuchs, Ernst. Hermeneutik. Bad Constadt: R. Müllerschön, 1963.

Fuller, Reginald H. The Foundations of New Testament Christology. London: Lutterworth Press, 1965.

_____. The Mission and Achievement of Jesus. SBT, XII. London: SCM, 1954.

Gadamer, Hans-Georg. Truth and Method. Translated by Garrett Borden and John Cumming. New York: Seabury, 1975.

Gärtner, Bertil. "The Habakkuk Commentary (DSH) and the Gospel of Matthew." ST, VIII (1955), 1-24.

_____. Iscariot. Translated by Victor I. Gruhm. Facet Books: Biblical Series, XXIX. Philadelphia: Fortress, 1971.

_____. John 6 and the Jewish Passover. ConNT, XVII. Lund: Gleerup, 1959.

_____. The Temple and the Community in Qumran and the New Testament: A Comparative Study in the Temple Symbolism of the Qumran Texts and the New Testament. SNTSMS, I. Cambridge: University Press, 1965.

_____. " אׁ'שׁו als Messiasbezeichnung." SEA, XVIII-XIX, (1953-54), 98-108.

Gardner-Smith, P. Saint John and the Synoptic Gospels. Cambridge: University Press, 1938.

Gaston, Lloyd. No Stone on Another: Studies in the Significance of the Fall of Jerusalem in the Synoptic Gospels. NTSup XXIII. Leiden: Brill, 1970.

George, A. R. "The Imperatival Use of $\ddot{\iota}\nu\alpha$ in the New Testament." JTS, XLV (1944), 56-60.

Gerhardsson, Birger. "Jésus livré et abandonné d'après la Passion selon Matthieu." Translated by L.-M. Dewailly. RB, LXXVI (1969), 206-27.

Gerhardsson, Birger. The Testing of God's Son (Matt. 4:1-11 and Par.): An Analysis of an Early Christian Midrash. ConB, N.T. series II. Translated by John Toy. Lund: C. W. K. Gleerup, 1966.

Gertner, M. "Midrashim in the New Testament." JSS, VII (1952), 267-92.

Gese, Hartmut. "Ps. 22 und das Neue Testament: Der älteste Bericht vom Todes Jesus und die Entstehung des Herrenmahles." ZTK, LXV (1968), 1-22.

Glasson, T. F. Moses in the Fourth Gospel. SBT, XL. London: SCM, 1963.

_____. "The Son of Man Imagery: Enoch XIV and Daniel VII." NTS, XXIII (1976-77), 82-90.

Gnilka, Joachim. "Die Erwartung des messianischen Hohenpriesters in den schriften von Qumran und im Neuen Testament." RevQ, II (1959-60), 395-426.

_____. "Mein Gott, mein Gott, warum hast du mich verlassen? (Mc. 15:34 par.)." BZ, n.s. III (1959), 294-97.

Goguel, Maurice. The Life of Jesus. Translated by Olive Wyon. London: George Allen & Unwin, 1933.

Goppelt, Leonhard. "Apokalyptik und Typologie bei Paulus." TLZ, LXXXIX (1964), 321-344.

_____. "ποτήριον..." TDNT, VI, 135-60.

_____. Theologie des Neuen Testaments. Part I: Jesu Wirken in seiner theologischen Bedeutung. Edited by Jürgen Roloff. Göttingen: Vandenhoeck & Ruprecht, 1975.

_____. Typos: Die typologische Deutung des Alten Testaments im Neuen. BFCT, XLIII. Darmstadt: Wissenschaftliche Buchgesellschaft, 1969.

Gordis, Robert. "Quotations as a Literary Usage in Biblical, Oriental and Rabbinic Lit." HUCA, XXII (1949), 157-219.

Gordon, Robert P. "The Targum to the Minor Prophets and the Dead Sea Texts: Textual and Exegetical Notes." RevQ, VIII (1974), 425-29.

Gottstein, M. H. "Bible Quotations in the Sectarian Dead Sea Scrolls." VT, III (1953), 79-82.

Goulder, M. D. Midrash and Lection in Matthew. The Speaker's Lectures in Biblical Studies, 1969-71. London: SPCK, 1974.

Grant, F. C. "Biblical Theology and the Synoptic Problem." Current Issues in New Testament Interpretation. Essays in Honor of Otto A. Piper. Edited by William Klassen and Graydon F. Snyder. New York: Harper, 1962.

Grassi, J. "Ezekiel XXXVII, 1-14 and the New Testament." NTS, XI (1964-65), 162-64.

Grech, Prosper. "The 'Testimonia' and Modern Hermeneutics." NTS, XIX (1972-73), 318-24.

Grundmann, Walter. " $\delta\epsilon\hat{\iota}$, $\delta\acute{\epsilon}ov$, $\dot{\epsilon}\sigma\tau\acute{\iota}$." TDNT, II, 21-25.

_____. "Sohn Gottes." ZNW, XLVII (1956), 113-133.

Gryglewicz, Feliks. "Das Lamm Gottes." NTS, XIII (1966-67), 133-146.

Guillaume, A. "Mt. 27:46 in the Light of the Dead Sea Scroll of Isaiah." PEQ, LXXXIII (1951), 78-80.

Gundry, Robert H. "The Language Milieu of First-Century Palestine: Its bearing on the Authenticity of the Gospel Tradition." JBL, LXXXIII (1964), 404-408.

_____. "LMTLYM: IQ Isaiah a 50,6 and Mk. 14:65." RevQ, II (1960) 559-67.

_____. The Use of the Old Testament in St. Matthew's Gospel. NovTSup, XVIII. Leiden: E. J. Brill, 1967.

Gunkel, Hermann. Einleitung in die Psalmen: Die Gattungen der religiösen Lyrik Israels. Edited and compiled by Joachim Begrich. 2nd ed. Göttingen: Vandenhoeck and Ruprecht, 1966.

Gutbrod, W. "$\overset{,,}{\alpha}\nu o\mu o s$." TDNT, IV, 1086-87.

Güttgemanns, Erhardt. Offene Fragen zur Formgeschichte des Evangeliums: Eine Methodologische Skizze der Grundlagenproblematik der Form- und Redaktionsgeschichte. BEvt, LIV. 2nd ed. Munich: Chr. Kaiser, 1971.

Haenchen, Ernest. "History and Interpretation in the Johannine Passion Narrative." Translated by James P. Martin. Int, XXIV (1970), 198-219.

Hahn, Ferdinand. "Die alttestamentlichen Motive in der urchristlichen Abendmahlsüberlieferung." EvT, XXVII (1967), 337-74.

_____. Mission in the New Testament. Translated by Frank Clarke. SBT, XLVII. London: SCM, 1965.

_____. The Titles of Jesus in Christology. Translated by Harold Knight and George Ogg. London: Lutterworth Press, 1969.

Hamerton-Kelly, R. G. "Attitudes to the Law in Matthew's Gospel: A Discussion of Matthew 5:18." Papers of the Chicago Society of Biblical Research, XVII (1972), 19-32.

_____. Pre-existence, Wisdom and the Son of Man: A Study of the Idea of Pre-existence in the New Testament. SNTSMS, XXI. Cambridge: University Press, 1973.

Hanson, Anthony Tyrrell. Jesus Christ in the Old Testament. London: SPCK, 1965.

_____. Studies in Paul's Technique and Theology. London: SPCK, 1974.

_____. The Wrath of the Lamb. London: SPCK, 1957.

Hanson, Paul D. "Old Testament Apocalyptic Reexamined." Int, XXV (1971), 454-479.

Hanson, R. P. C. Allegory and Event: A Study of the Sources and Significance of Origen's Interpretation of Scripture. London: SCM Press, Ltd., 1959.

Harnack, Adolf von. "Probleme im Texte der Leidensgeschichte Jesu." Studien zur Geschichte des Neuen Testaments und der alten Kirche. Vol I: Zur neutestamentlichen Textkritik. Berlin and Leipzig: Walter de Gruyter, 1901.

Harris, M. J. "Prepositions and Theology in the Greek New Testament." Appendix to Vol. III of NIDNTT, 1171-1215.

Harris, R. Testimonies. With the assistance of Vacher Burch. 2 vols. Cambridge: University Press, 1916, 1920.

Hartman, Lars. Prophecy Interpreted: The Formation of Some Jewish Apocalyptic Texts and of the Eschatological Discourse Mark 13 par. ConB, NT series I. Lund: G. W. K. Gleerup, 1966.

_____. "Scriptural Exegesis in the Gospel of St. Matthew and the Problem of Communication." L'Évangile sélon Matthieu. Rédaction et theologie. Edited by M. Didier. Gembloux: Duculot, 1972.

Hasenzahl, W. Die Gottverlassenheit des Christus nach dem Kreuzeswort bei Mt. und Mk. und das christologische Verständnis des griechischen Psalters. BFCT, XXXIX. Gütersloh: Mohn, 1937.

Hebert, A. G. The Throne of David: A Study of the Fulfillment of the Old Testament in Jesus Christ and His Church. London: Faber and Faber, 1941.

Hedley, P. L. "The Göttingen Investigation and Edition of the Septuagint." HTR, XXVI (1933), 57-52.

Heidland, H. W. " $\lambda o\gamma i \zeta o\mu a\iota, \lambda o\gamma \iota \sigma \mu o's$." TDNT, IV (1967) 284-92.

Heinemann, Joseph. "Profile of a Midrash: The Act of Composition in Leviticus Rabba." JAAR, XXXIX (1971), 141-150.

Hengel, Martin. "Christologie und neutestamentliche Chronologie: zu einer Aporie in der Geschichte des Urchristentums." Neues Testament und Geschichte: Historisches Geschehen und Deutung im Neuen Testament. (Oscar Cullmann zum 70. Geburtstag). Edited by Heinrich Baltensweiler and Bo Reicke. Zurich: Theologischer Verlag, 1972.

_____. Judaism and Hellenism: Studies in their Encounter in Palestine during the Early Hellenistic Period. 2nd ed. 2 vols. Translated by John Bowden. Philadelphia: Fortress Press, 1974.

_____. "Maria Magdalena und die Frauen als Zeugen." Abraham unser Vater: Judea und Christen im Gespräch über die Bibel (für Otto Michel). Edited by Otto Betz, Martin Hengel and Peter Schmidt. Leiden/Cologne: Brill, 1963.

Héring, J. "Zwei exegetische Probleme in der Perikope von Jesu in Gethsemane (Markus XIV 32-42; Matthäus XXVI 36-46: Lukas XXII 40-46)." Neotestamentica et Patristica. Eine Freundsgabe Herrn Professor Dr. Oscar Cullmann zu seinem 60. Geburtstag überreicht. NovTSup, VI. Leiden: Brill, 1962.

Hewitt, J. W. "The Use of Nails in the Crucifixion." HTR, XXV (1932), 29-45.

Higgins, A. J. B. "H. Lietzmann's 'Mass and Lord's Supper' (Messe und Herrenmahl)." ExpTim, LXV (1954), 333-36.

_____. Jesus and the Son of Man. London: Lutterworth Press, 1964.

_____. The Lord's Supper in the New Testament. SBT, VI. London: SCM, 1952.

_____. "The Origins of the Eucharist." NTS, I (1954-55), 200-09.

Hill, David. Greek Words and Hebrew Meanings: Studies in the Semantics of Soteriological Terms. SNTSMS, V. Cambridge: University Press, 1967.

Hindley, J. C. "Towards a Date for the Similitudes of Enoch: A Historical Approach." NTS, XIV (1968), 551-565.

Hoehner, Harold W. Chronological Aspects of the Life of Christ. Grand Rapids: Zondervan, 1977.

_____. Herod Antipas. SNTSMS, XVII. Cambridge: University Press, 1972.

Hoffmann, Paul. "Mk. 8, 31. Zur Herkunft und markinischen Rezeption einer alten Überlieferung." Orientierung an Jesus: Zur Theologie der Synoptiker. (für Josef Schmid) Edited by Paul Hoffman, Norbert Brox and Wilhelm Pesch. Freiburg/Basel/Vienna: 1973.

Holm-Nielsen, Svend. Hodayot. Psalms from Qumran. Acta Theologica Danica II. Aarhus: Universitetsforlaget I, 1960.

Holtz, Traugott. Untersuchungen über die alttestamentlichen Zitate bei Lukas. TU, CIV. Berlin: Akadamie, 1968.

_____. "Zur Interpretation des Alten Testaments im Neuen Testament." TLZ, XLIX (1974), 19-32.

Hooke, S. H., ed. Myth and Ritual: Essays on the Myth and Ritual of the Hebrews in relation to the Culture Pattern of the Ancient East. Oxford and London: Oxford University Press, 1933.

_____. Myth, Ritual and Kingship: Essays on the Theory and Practice of Kingship in the Ancient Near East and Israel. Oxford: Clarendon Press, 1958.

Hooker, Morna D. Jesus and the Servant: The Influence of the Servant Concept of Deutero-Isaiah in the New Testament. London: SPCK, 1959.

_____. The Son of Man in Mark. London: SPCK, 1967.

_____. "Christology and Methodology." NTS, XVII (1971), 480-87.

Horovitz, S. "Midrash." JE, VIII, 548-50.

Horton, Fred L. "Formulas of Introduction in the Qumran Literature." RevQ, VII (1971), 505-514.

Hoskyns, Edwyn and Davey, Noel. The Riddle of the New Testament. London: Faber & Faber, 1931.

Howard, J. K. "Passover and Eucharist in the Fourth Gospel." SJT, XX (1967), 329-37.

Howard, Virgil. "Did Jesus Speak about His own Death?" CBQ, XXXIX (1977), 515-27.

Hunter, A. M. The Work and Words of Jesus. London: SCM, 1950.

Iersel, B. M. F. van. 'Der Sohn' in den synoptischen Jesusworten. NovTSup, III. Leiden: Brill, 1961.

Jackson, F. J. Foakes and Lake, Kirsopp, eds. The Beginnings of Christianity, Part I: The Acts of the Apostles. 5 vols. London: MacMillan, 1910-1938.

Jansma, T. Inquiry into the Hebrew Text and the Ancient Versions of Zechariah 9-14. OTS, VII. Leiden: Brill, 1950.

Jaubert, A. "The Calendar of Qumran and the Passion Narrative in John." John and Qumran. Edited by James H. Charlesworth. London: Geoffrey Chapman, 1972.

_____. The Date of the Last Supper. Translated by Isaac Rafferty. Staten Island, N.Y.: Alba House, 1965.

_____. "Jésus et le Calendrier de Qûmran." NTS, VII (1960-61) 1-30.

_____. "Le mercredi où Jésus fut livré," NTS, XIV (1967-68), 145-64.

Jellicoe, Sidney. The Septuagint and Modern Study. Oxford: Clarendon Press, 1968.

Jeremias, Joachim. "ἀμνός . . ." TDNT, I, 338-41.

_____. "Ἀμνὸς τοῦ θεοῦ — παῖς θεοῦ," ZNW, XXXIV (1935), 115-123.

_____. The Central Message of the New Testament. London: SCM, 1965.

_____. "Ἰωνᾶς." TDNT, III, 406-10.

_____. The Eucharistic Words of Jesus. Translated by Norman Perrin. 3rd ed. London: SCM, 1966.

_____. "Das Gebetsleben Jesu." ZNW, XXV (1926) 123-140.

_____. "Ἡλ(ε)ίας." TDNT, II, 928-941.

_____. Jerusalem in the Time of Jesus. Translated by F. H. and C. H. Cave. 3rd ed. London: SCM, 1969.

_____. "λίθος, λίθινος." TDNT, IV, 268-80.

Jeremias, Joachim. "Das Lösegeld für Viele (Mk. 10, 45)." Abba: Studien zur neutestamentlichen Theologie und Zeitgeschichte. Göttingen: Vandenhoeck & Ruprecht, 1966.

_____. New Testament Theology. Vol. I: The Proclamation of Jesus. Translated by John Bowden. London: SCM, 1971.

_____. "νύμφη, νυμφίος." TDNT, IV, 1099-1106.

_____. The Parables of Jesus. Translation based on that of S. H. Hooke. 2nd rev. ed., New York: Scribner's, 1963.

_____. "ποιμήν, ἀρχιποίμην, ποιμαίνω." TDNT, VI, 485-502.

_____. Review of La Date de la Cène by A. Jaubert. JTS, n.s. X (1959), 131-33.

_____. "Die Salbungsgeschichte Mc 14, 3-9." ZNW, XXXV (1936), 75-82.

Johnson, A. R. "The Psalms." The Old Testament and Modern Study. Edited by H. H. Rowley. Oxford: Clarendon Press, 1951.

Johnson, Sherman E. "The Biblical Quotations in Matthew." HTR, XXXVI (1943), 135-53.

_____. "The Davidic-Royal Motifs in the Gospels." JBL, LXXXVII (1968), 136-50.

Jones, Douglas. "ἀνάμνησις in the LXX and the Interpretation of I Cor. XI. 25." JTS, n.s. VI (1955), 183-91.

Jonge, M. de. Studies on the Testaments of the Twelve Patriarchs. Text and Interpretation. SVTP III. Leiden: Brill, 1975.

Juel, Donald. Messiah and Temple: The Trial of Jesus in the Gospel of Mark. SBLDS XXXI. Missoula, Mont.: Scholars Press, 1977.

Kahle, Paul E. The Cairo Geniza. 2nd ed. Oxford: Basil Blackwell, 1959.

_____. "Der gegenwärtige Stand der Erforschung der in Palästina neu gefunden hebräischen Handschriften 27: Die im August, 1952 entdeckte Lederrolle mit dem griechischen Text der kleinen Propheten und das Problem des Septuaginta." TLZ, LXXIX (1954), 81-94.

Karabidopoulos, I. D. [To pathos tou doulou tou Theou epi tou staurou kata tēn diēgēsin tou evangelistou Louka (23:33-49)]" DBM, I (1972), 189-211.

Katz, P. "Justin's Old Testament Quotations and the Greek Dodekapropheton Scroll." Studia Patristica, I. TU, LXIII. Berlin: Akademie Verlag, 1957.

Kee, Alistair. "The Question about Fasting." NovT, XIX (1969), 161-73.

Kee, Howard Clark. Community of the New Age: Studies in Mark's Gospel. Philadelphia: Westminster, 1977.

Kee, Howard Clark. "The Function of Scriptural Quotations and Allusions in Mark 11-16." Jesus und Paulus (für Werner Georg Kümmel). Edited by E. Earle Ellis and Erich Grasser. Göttingen: Vandenhoeck & Ruprecht, 1975.

Kelber, Werner H. "The Hour of the Son of Man and the Temptation of the Disciples (Mk. 14:32-42)." The Passion in Mark: Studies on Mark 14-16. Edited by Werner H. Kelber. Philadelphia: Fortress Press, 1976.

_____. "Conclusion: From Passion Narrative to Gospel." The Passion in Mark: Studies on Mark 14-16. Edited by Werner H. Kelber. Philadelphia: Fortress Press, 1976.

Kellermann, D. " אשם ," TDOT, I, 429-37.

Kelly, J. N. D. Early Christian Creeds. 3rd ed. London: Longman Group, 1972.

Kenneally, William J. "'Eli, Eli, Lamma Sabachthani?' (Mt. 27:46)." CBQ, VIII (1946), 124-34.

Kertelge, Karl. "Der dienende Menschensohn (Mk. 10, 45)." Jesus und der Menschensohn. Edited by Rudolf Pesch and Rudolf Schnackenburg in cooperation with Odilo Kaiser. Freiburg/Basel/Vienna Herder, 1975.

Kilian, Rudolf. "Ps. 22 und das priesterliche Heilsorakel." BZ, n.s., XII (1968), 172-85.

Kilpatrick, G. D. "Luke XXII. 19b-20." JTS, XLVII (1946), 49-56.

_____. "The Order of Some Noun and Adjective Phrases in the New Testament." NovT, V (1962), 111-114.

_____. The Origins of the Gospel according to St. Matthew. Oxford: Clarendon Press, 1946.

_____. "Western Text and Original Text in the Gospels and Acts." JTS, XLIV (1943), 24-36.

Kingsbury, Jack Dean. Matthew: Structure, Christology, Kingdom. London: SPCK, 1975

Kittel, G. "אצטלב = σύν θῆναι = gekreuzigt werden." ZNW, XXXV (1936), 282-85.

_____. "δοκέω, δόξα, δοξάζω, et al." TDNT, II, 242-55.

Klausner, Joseph. Jesus of Nazareth. London: George Allen and Unwin, 1925.

Klein, Günter. "Die Verleugnung des Petrus: Eine traditionsgeschichtliche Untersuchung." ZTK, LVIII (1961), 285-328.

_____. "Zur Erläuterung der Evangelien aus Talmud und Midrash." ZNW, V (1904), 144-53.

Klein, Ralph W. Textual Criticism of the Old Testament: The Septuagint after Qumran. Philadelphia: Fortress, 1974.

Knox, John. The Death of Christ. The Cross in New Testament History and Faith. New York/Nashville: Abingdon Press, 1958.

Knox, W. L. The Sources of the Synoptic Gospels. Edited by H. Chadwick. 2 vols. Cambridge: University Press, 1957.

König, Eduard. Die messianischen Weissagungen des Alten Testaments. Stuttgart: Chr. Belsen, 1925.

_____. "On Mark xv. 34 in Codex D." ExpTim, XI (1899-1900), 334.

_____. "The Origin of $\Sigma\alpha\beta\theta\alpha\nu\epsilon\iota$ in Cod. D of Matt. xxvii. 45 and Mark xv. 34." ExpTim, XI (1899-1900), 237-38.

Kosmala, Hans, "'Das tut zu meinem Gedächtnis.'" NovT, IV (1960), 81-94.

Kramer, W. Christ, Lord, Son of God. Translated by Brian Hardy. SBT, L. London: SCM, 1965.

Kümmel, Werner George. Promise and Fulfillment. Translated by Dorothea M. Barton. SBT, XXIII. London: SCM, 1957.

_____. "Schriftauslegung III. Im Urchristentum." RGG, V, 1517-20.

_____. The Theology of the New Testament. According to Its Major Witnesses: Jesus - Paul - John. Translated by John Steely. Nashville/NewYork: Abingdon, 1973.

_____. "Weissagung und Erfüllung II. Im NT." RGG, VI, 1587-88.

Kuhn, Heinz-Wolfgang. Enderwartung und gegenwärtiges Heil: Untersuchungen zu den Gemeindeliedern von Qumran. SUNT, IV. Göttingen: Vandenhoeck & Ruprecht, 1966.

_____. "Das Reittier Jesu in der Einzugsgeschichte des Markusevangeliums." ZNW, L (1959), 82-91.

Kuhn, Karl Georg. "Die Abendmahlsworte." TLZ, LXXV (1950), 399-408.

_____. "The Lord's Supper and the Communal Meal at Qumran." The Scrolls and the New Testament. Edited by Krister Stendahl. London: SCM Press, Ltd., 1958.

Ladd, George Eldon. "Apocalyptic and New Testament Theology." Reconciliation and Hope: New Testament Essays on Atonement and Eschatology presented to L. L. Morris on his 60th Birthday. Edited by Robert Banks. Grand Rapids: Eerdmans, 1974.

_____. A Theology of the New Testament. Grand Rapids: Eerdmans, 1974

Lagrange, M.-J. "Notes sur le messianisme dans les psaumes." RB, II (1905), 39-57.

_____. "Notes sur les prophéties messianiques des derniers prophetes." RB, III (1906), 67-83.

Lake, Kirsopp. "The Death of Judas." The Beginnings of Christianity. Vol. V: Additional Notes to the Commentary. Edited by Kirsopp Lake and Henry J. Cadbury. London: MacMillan, 1933.

Lamarche, Paul. Zacharie IX-XIV; Structure littéraires et messianisme. EBib. Paris: Gabalda, 1961.

Lampe, G. W. H. and Woollcombe, K. J. Essays on Typology. SBT, XXII. London: SCM, 1957.

_____. The Seal of the Spirit: A Study in the Doctrine of Baptism and Confirmation in the New Testament and the Fathers. 2nd ed. London: SPCK, 1967.

_____. "Typological Exegesis." Theology, LVI (1953), 201-8.

Lane, William R. "A New Commentary Structure in 4Q Florilegium." JBL, LXXVIII (1959), 343-46.

Lang, Friedrich. "$\pi\tilde{\upsilon}\rho$." TDNT, VI, 928-952.

Lange, H. D. "The Relationship Between Psalm 22 and the Passion Narrative." CTM, XLIII (1972), 610-21.

Lapide, Pinchas. "Insights from Qumran into the Languages of Jesus." RevQ, VIII (1975), 483-501.

Larkin, William J. "Luke's Use of the Old Testament as a Key to his Soteriology." JETS, XX (1977), 325-35.

_____. "The Old Testament Background of Luke XXII. 43-44." NTS, XXV (1978-79), 250-54.

Lauterbach, Jacob Z. "Midrash and Mishnah: A Study in the Early History of the Halakah." Rabbinic Essays. New York: KTAV, 1973.

_____. "Peshat." JE, IX, 652-53.

_____. "The Pharisees and their Teachings." Rabbinic Essays. New York: KTAV, 1973.

Leaney, A. R. C. The Rule of Qumran and its Meaning: Introduction Translation and Commentary. Philadelphia: Westminster, 1966.

Le Déaut, Roger. "Apropos d'une définition du Midrash." Bib, L (1969), 395-413.

_____. "Apropos a Definition of Midrash." Int, XXV (1971), 259-82.

_____. "The Current State of Targumic Studies." BTB, IV (1974), 3-32.

_____. La nuit pascale. Essai sur la signification de la Pâque juive à partie du Targum d'Exode XIII, 42. AnBib, XXII. Rome: Pontifical Biblical Institute, 1963.

_____. "Targumic Literature and New Testament Interpretation." BTB, IV (1974), 243-89.

Leivestad, Ragnar. "Exit the Apocalyptic Son of Man." NTS, XVIII (1971-1972), 243-267.

Léon-Dufour, Xavier. The Gospels and the Jesus of History. Translated and edited by John McHugh. London: Collins, and New York: Desclee, 1968.

_____. "Mt. et Mc. dans le récit de la Passion." Bib, XL (1959), 684-96.

Lerch, David. Isaaks Opferung christlich gedeutet. Eine auslegungsgeschichtliche Untersuchung. BHT, XII. Tübingen: Mohr, 1950.

Lietzmann, Hans. "Bemerkungen zum Prozess Jesu." ZNW, XXX (1971), 211-15.

_____. Messe und Herrenmahl. Bonn: A. Marcus and E. Weber, 1926.

Lightfoot, R. H. History and Interpretation in the Gospels. The Bampton Lectures, 1934. London: Hodder and Stoughton, 1935.

_____. Locality and Doctrine in the Gospels. London: Hodder and Stoughton, 1938.

Lindars, Barnabas. New Testament Apologetic: The Doctrinal Significance of the Old Testament Quotations. London: SCM, 1961.

_____. "Re-enter the Apocalyptic Son of Man." NTS, XXII (1975-76), 52-72.

_____. "The Son of Man in the Johannine Christology." Christ and Spirit in the New Testament: in honour of Charles Francis Digby Moule. Edited by Barnabas Lindars and Stephen S. Smalley. Cambridge: University Press, 1973.

Lindars, Barnabas and Borgen, Peder. "The Place of the Old Testament in the Formation of New Testament Theology: Prolegomena and Response." NTS, XXIII (1977), 59-75.

Lindeskog, Gosta. "The Veil of the Temple." Coniectanea Neotestamentica, in honour of Anton Fridrichsen. Lund/Copenhagen: C. W. K. Gleerup & Ejnar Munksgaard, 1947.

Linnemann, Eta. Studien zur Passionsgeschichte. FRLANT, CII. Göttingen: Vandenhoeck & Ruprecht, 1970.

Linton, Olaf. "Le 'parallesmus membrorum' dans le Nouveau Testament: Simples Remarques." Mélanges Bibliques en hommage R.P. Béda Rigaux. Edited by Albert Descamps and André de Halleux. Gembloux: Duculot, 1970.

Lofthouse, W. F. "The Cry of Dereliction." ExpTim, LIII (1942) 188-92.

Lohmeyer, Ernst. Galiläa und Jerusalem. FRLANT, XXXIV. Göttingen: Vandenhoeck & Ruprecht, 1936.

_____. Gottesknecht und Davidssohn. 2nd ed. Göttingen: Vandenhoeck & Ruprecht, 1953.

Lohse, Eduard. "Die alttestamentlichen Bezüge im neutestamentlichen Zeugnis vom Tode Jesu Christi." Die Einheit des Neuen Testaments: Exegetische Studien zur Theologie des Neuen Testaments. Göttingen: Vandenhoeck & Ruprecht, 1973.

Lohse, Eduard. History of the Suffering and Death of Jesus Christ. Translated by Martin O. Dietrich. Philadelphia: Fortress Press, 1967.

_____. Märtyrer und Gottesknecht. Untersuchungen zur urchristlichen Verkündigung vom Sühnetod Jesu Christi. FRLANT, XLVI. 2nd ed. Göttingen: Vandenhoeck & Ruprecht, 1963.

Longenecker, Richard N. Biblical Exegesis in the Apostolic Period. Grand Rapids: Eerdmans, 1975.

_____. The Christology of Early Jewish Christianity. SBT, n.s. XVII. London: SCM, 1970.

Lövestam, Evald. Son and Saviour: A Study of Acts 13, 32-37. With an Appendix: 'Son of God' in the Synoptic Gospels. Translated by Michael J. Petry. Con NT, XVIII. Lund/Copenhagen: C.W.K. Gleerup & Ejnar Munksgaard. 1961.

Lyonnet, Stanislas and Sabourin, Léopold. Sin, Redemption and Sacrifice: A Biblical and Patristic Study. AnBib, XLVIII. Rome: Biblical Institute Press, 1970.

McConnell, R. S. Law & Prophecy in Matthew's Gospel: The Authority and Use of the Old Testament in the Gospel of St. Matthew. Theologische Dissertationen, II. Basel: Friedrich Reinhardt, 1969.

McNamara, Martin. The New Testament and the Palestinian Targum to the Pentateuch. AnBib, XXVII. Rome: Pontifical Biblical Institute, 1966.

_____. Targum and Testament. Aramaic Paraphrases of the Hebrew Bible: A Light on the New Testament. Shannon: Irish University Press, 1972.

McNeile, Alan Hugh. "Our Lord's Use of the Old Testament." Cambridge Biblical Essays. Edited by Henry Barclay Swete. London: MacMillan, 1909.

Maas, Fritz. "Von den Unsprüngen der rabbinischen Schriftauslegung." ZTK, LII (1955), 129-61.

Macho, A. Diez. "The Recently Discovered Palestinian Targum: Its Antiquity and Relationship with the other Targums." VTSup, III. Leiden: Brill, 1959.

Maddox, Robert. "The Function of the Son of Man According to the Synoptic Gospels." NTS, XV (1968-69), 45-74.

Magne, Jean. "Le texte du Psaume XXII et sa restitution Sur deux Colannes." Sem, XI (1961), 29-41.

Mann, Jacob. The Bible as Read and Preached in the Old Synagogue. A Study in the Cycles of the Readings from Torah and Prophets, as well as from Psalms, and in the Structure of the Midrashic Homilies. The Library of Biblical Studies. New York: KTAV, 1971. (= 1940)

Manson, T. W. "The Argument from Prophecy." JTS, XLVI (1945), 129-36.

_____. "The Old Testament in the Teaching of Jesus." BJRL, XXXIV (1951-52) 312-32.

_____. "The Son of Man in Daniel, Enoch and the Gospels." BJRL, XXXII (1949-50), 171-193.

Manson, Wm. Jesus the Messiah: The Synoptic Tradition of the Revelation of God in Christ: With Special Reference to Form-Criticism. London: Hodder and Stoughton, 1943.

Marcus, Ralph. "'Mebaqqer' and 'Rabbim' in the Manual of Discipline vi, 11-13." JBL, LXXV (1956), 298-302.

Marshall, I. Howard. "The Divine Sonship of Jesus." Int, XXI (1967) 87-103.

_____. Luke: Historian and Theologian. Exeter: The Paternoster Press, 1970.

_____. "Palestinian and Hellenistic Christianity: Some Critical Comments." NTS, XIX (1972-73), 271-87.

_____. "Son of God or Servant of Yahweh? - A Reconsideration of Mark I. 11." NTS, XV (1968-69), 326-36.

_____. "The Synoptic Son of Man Sayings in Recent Discussion." NTS, XII (1965-66), 327-51.

Martin, Ralph P. Mark: Evangelist and Theologian. Exeter: The Paternoster Press, 1972.

Martyn, J. Louis. History and Theology in the Fourth Gospel. New York & Evanston: Harper & Row, 1968.

Marxsen, Willi. Der Evangelist Markus: Studien zur Redaktionsgeschichte des Evangeliums. FRLANT, XLIX. 2nd ed. Göttingen: Vandenhoeck & Ruprecht, 1959.

_____. Introduction to the New Testament. Translated by G. Buswell. Oxford: Basil Blackwell, 1968.

Maurer, Christian. "Knecht Gottes und Sohn Gottes im Passionsbericht des Markusevangeliums." ZTK, L (1953), 1-38.

Meeks, Wayne A. The Prophet-King: Moses Traditions and the Johannine Christology. NovTSup, XIV. Leiden: Brill, 1967.

Meier, John P. Law and History in Matthew's Gospel: A Redactional Study of Mt. 5:17-18. AnBib, LXXI. Rome: Biblical Institute Press, 1976.

Ménard, Jacques E. "Pais Theou as Messianic Title in the Book of Acts." CBQ, XIX (1957), 83-92.

Metzger, B. M. "The Formulas Introducing Quotations of Scripture in the NT and the Mishnah." JBL, LXX (1951), 297-307.

_____. "Scriptural Quotations in Q Material" ExpTim, LXV (1963-64), 125.

Metzger, Bruce M. A Textual Commentary on the Greek New Testament. New York, et. al.: United Bible Societies, 1971.

Meyer, D. "ΠΟΛΛΑ ΠΑΘΕΙΝ." ZNW, LV (1964), 132.

Michaelis, Wilhelm. "Die Davidssohnschaft Jesu als historisches und kerymatisches Problem." Der historische Jesus und der kerygmatische Christus: Beiträge zum Christusverständnis in Forschung und Verkündigung. Edited by Helmut Ristow & Karl Matthiae. 2nd ed. Berlin: Evangelische Verlagsanstalt, 1961.

_____. "πάσχω, παθητός, ..." TDNT, V, 904-939.

_____. "σμύρνα, σμυρνίζω." TDNT, VII, 457-59.

Michel, Otto. "Eine philologische Frage zur Einzugsgeschichte." NTS, VI (1959-60), 81-82.

_____. "πῶλος." TDNT, VI, 959-61.

Milik, J. T. "Problèmes de la littérature Hénochique à la Lumière des Fragments Araméens de Qumrân." HTR, LXIV (1971), 333-378.

_____. Ten Years of Discovery in the Wilderness of Judaea. Translated by J. Strugnell, SBT, XXVI. London: SCM, 1959.

Miller, David L. "EMΠAIZEIN: Playing the Mock Game (Luke 22: 63-64)." JBL, XL (1971), 309-13.

Miller, Merrill P. "Targum, Midrash and the Use of the Old Testament in the New Testament." JSJ, II (1971), 29-82.

Minear, Paul S. "A Note on Luke 22:36." NovT, VII (1964-65), 128-134.

Montefiore, C. G. and Loewe, H., ed. A Rabbinic Anthology. New York: Meridian, 1938.

Moore, George Foot. Judaism in the First Centuries of the Christian Era: The Age of the Tannaim. 2 vols. Cambridge: University Press, 1927.

Morgenstern, Julian. Some Significant Antecedents of Christianity. SPB, X. Leiden: Brill, 1966.

Morris, Leon. The Apostolic Preaching of the Cross. Grand Rapids: Eerdmans, 1955.

_____. "The Biblical Use of the Term 'Blood'." JTS, n.s. III (1952), 216-27; VI (1955), 77-82.

_____. The Cross in the New Testament. Grand Rapids: Eerdmans, 1965.

Motyer, J. A. "Jonah." NIDNTT, II, 350-52.

Moule, C. F. D. "From Defendant to Judge - and Deliverer." The Phenomenon of the New Testament. London: SCM, 1967.

_____. "Fulfillment - Words in the New Testament: Use and Abuse." NTS, XIV (1967-68), 293-320.

Moule, C. F. D. "The Influence of Circumstances on the Use of Christological Terms." JTS, n.s. X (1959), 247-63.

_____. "The Intention of the Evangelists." New Testament Essays: Studies in Memory of Thomas Walter Manson. Edited by A. J. B. Higgins. Manchester: Manchester University Press, 1959.

_____. "Sanctuary and Sacrifice in the Church of the New Testament." JTS, n.s. I (1950), 29-41.

Mowinckel, S. He that Cometh. Translated by G. W. Anderson. Oxford; Basil Blackwell, 1959.

_____. Psalmenstudien. 2 vols. Amsterdam: P. Schippers, 1966.

Müller, Karlheinz. "Menschensohn und Messias: Religionsgeschichtliche Vorüberlegungen zum Menschensohnproblem in den synoptischen Evangelien." BZ, n.s. XVI (1972), 159-87; XVII (1973), 52-66.

Murphy, Roland E. "The Relationship Between the Testaments." CBQ, XXVI (1964), 349-59.

_____. "Šahat in Qumran Literature." Bib, XXXIX (1958), 61-66.

Nakagawa, H. "Typologie II. In NT." RGG, VI (1962), 1095.

Negoïtsa A. and Constantin, Daniel. "L' Agneau de Dieu et le Verbe de Dieu (Ad Jo. i 29 et 36)." NovT, XIII (1971), 24-37.

Nestle, Eb. "Mark XV. 34." ExpTim, IX (1897-98), 521-22.

_____. "The Reading of Codex D and its Allies in Matt. xxvii. 46 and Mark xv. 34." ExpTim, XI (1899-1900), 287-88.

Neugebauer, Fritz. "Die Davidssohn Frage (Mark xii, 35-37 para.) und der Menschensohn." NTS, XXI (1974-75), 81-108.

Noack, Bent. Zur johanneischen Tradition. Beiträge zur Kritik an der literarkristischen Analyse des vierten Evangeliums. Copenhagen: Rosenkilde OG Bagger, 1954.

North, C. R. "The Religious Aspects of Hebrew Kingship." ZAW, L (1932), 8-38.

_____. The Suffering Servant in Deutero-Isaiah: An Historical and Critical Study. London: Oxford University Press, 1948.

_____. "The Damascus of Qumran Geography." PEQ, LXXXVII (1955), 34-48.

North, Martin. "God, Man and Nation." The Laws in the Pentateuch and other Essays. Translated by D. R. Ap-Thomas. Edinburgh and London: Oliver and Boyd, 1966.

Oepke, Albrecht. "$\dot{\alpha}\pi\acute{o}\lambda\lambda\upsilon\mu\iota$, $\dot{\alpha}\pi\acute{\omega}\lambda\epsilon\iota\alpha$, $\dot{A}\pi o\lambda\lambda\acute{u}\omega\nu$." TDNT, I, 394-97.

_____. "$\beta\acute{\alpha}\pi\tau\omega$, $\beta\alpha\pi\tau\acute{\iota}\zeta\omega$ ...." TDNT, I, 529-546.

Oepke, Albrecht. "Der Herrnspruch über die Kirche Mt. 16, 17-19 in der neuesten Forschung." ST, II (1948), 110-65.

Oesterley, W. O. E. An Introduction to the Books of the Apocrypha. London: SPCK, 1935.

Ogg, George. "The Chronology of the Last Supper." Historicity and Chronology in the New Testament. Edited by D.E. Nineham et al. London: SPCK, 1965.

O'Neill, J. C. "The Silence of Jesus." NTS, XV (1968-69), 153-67.

Orlinsky, H. M. "Qumran and the Present State of OT Text Studies: The Septuagint Text." JBL, LXXXVIII (1959), 26-33.

O'Rourke, J. J. "The Fulfillment Texts in Matthew." CBQ, XXIV (1962), 394-403.

Osswald, Eva. "Zur Hermeneutik des Habakuk-Kommentars." ZAW, LXVIII (1956) 243-56.

Otto, Rudolf. The Kingdom of God and the Son of Man. Translated by Floyd V. Filson and Bertram Lee Woolf. London: Lutterworth Press, 1938.

Otzen, Benedikt. Studien über Deuterosacharja. Acta Theologica Danica, VI. Copenhagen: Prostant and Munksgaard, 1964.

Palmer, Richard E. Hermeneutics: Interpretation Theory in Schleiermacher, Dilthey, Heidegger and Gadamer. Evanston, Ill: Northwestern University Press, 1969.

Patsch, Hermann. Abendmahl und Historischer Jesus. Stuttgart: Calwer Verlag, 1972.

Patte, Daniel. Early Jewish Hermeneutics in Palestine. SBLDS, XII Missoula, Mont.: Scholars Press, 1975.

Pelikan, Jaroslav. The Christian Tradition: A History of the Development of Doctrine. Vol I: The Emergence of the Catholic Tradition (100-600). Chicago and London: University of Chicago Press, 1971.

Pelletier, André. "La tradition synoptique du 'roile déchiré' à la lumiére des réalites archéologiques." RSR, XLVI (1958), 161-80.

Perrin, Norman. "Mark xiv. 62: The End Product of a Christian pesher Tradition?" NTS, XII (1965-66), 150-55.

_____. Rediscovering the Teaching of Jesus. London: SCM, 1967.

_____. "The Son of Man in the Synoptic Tradition." A Modern Pilgrimage in New Testament Christology. Philadelphia: Fortress, 1974.

_____. "The Use of (Para) didonai in Connection with the Passion of Jesus in the New Testament." Der Ruf Jesu und die Antwort der Gemeinde: Festschrift für Joachim Jeremias. Edited by Edward Lohse, Christoph Burchard and Berndt Schaller. Göttingen: Vandenhoeck & Ruprecht, 1970.

Pesch, Rudolf. "Eine alttestamentliche Ausführungsformel im Matthäus-Evangelium: Redaktionsgeschichte und exegetische Beobachtungen." BZ, n.s. X (1966), 220-45.

_____. "Die Passion des Menschensohnes: Eine studie zu den Menschenworten der vormarkinischen Passionsgeschichte." Jesus und der Menschensohn (für Anton Vögtle). Edited by Rudolf Pesch and Rudolf Schnackenburg, in cooperation with Odilo Kaiser. Freiburg/Basel/Vienna: Herder, 1975.

_____. "Die Salbung Jesu in Bethanien (Mk. 14:3-9): Eine Studie zur Passionsgeschichte." Orientierung an Jesu: Zur Theologie der Synoptiker (Für Josef Schmid). Edited by Paul Hoffman in cooperation with Norbert Brox and Wilhelm Pesch. Freiburg/Basel/Vienna: Herder, 1973.

Plath, M. "Warum hat die urchristliche Gemeinde auf die Überlieferung der Judaserzählungen Wert gelegt?" ZNW, XVII (1916), 178-88.

Ploeg, J. van der. "Bijbelverklaring te Qumrân." Mededelingen der Koninklijke nederlandse Akademie van Wetenschappen, AFD Letterkunde, XXIII,n.s. (1960), 207-229.

_____. Le Rouleau de la Guerre. STDJ, II. Leiden: Brill, 1959.

Pobee, John. "The Cry of the Centurion - A Cry of Defeat." The Trial of Jesus: Studies in Honour of C. F. D. Moule. Edited by Ernst Bammel. SBT, n.s., XIII. London: SCM, 1970.

Popkes, Wiard. Christus Traditus: Eine Untersuchung zum Begriff der Dahingabe im Neuen Testament. ATANT, XLIX. Zürich/Stuttgart: Zwingli, 1967.

Prabhu, George M. Soares. The Formula Quotations in the Infancy Narrative of Matthew: An Enquiry into the Tradition History of Mt. 1-2. AnBib, LXIII. Rome: Biblical Institute Press, 1976.

Preiss, Théo. "Was the Last Supper a Paschal Meal?" Life in Christ. Translated by Harold Knight. SBT,XIII. London: SCM, 1954.

Prigent, P. "Les récits évangeliques de la Passion et l'utilisation des 'Testimonia'." RHR, CLXI (1962), 130-32.

_____. Les testimonia dans le christianisme primitif: L'Épître de Barnabé I-XVI et ses sources. Paris: Gabalda, 1961.

Rabin, C. "The Dead Sea Scrolls and the History of the Old Testament Text." JTS, n.s. VI (1955), 174-82.

_____. Qumran Studies. Scripta Judaica II. Oxford: Oxford University Press, 1957.

Rabinowitz, Isaac. "'Pēsher/Pittārōn': Its Biblical Meaning and Its Significance in the Qumran Literature." RevQ, VIII (1973), 219-232.

_____. "A Reconsideration of 'Damascus' and '390 Years' in the 'Damascus' ('Zadokite') Fragments." JBL, LXXIII (1954), 11-35.

Rad, Gerhard von. Old Testament Theology. Translated by D. M. G. Stalker. 2 vols. Edinburgh: Oliver and Boyd, 1965.

_____. "Typological Interpretation of the Old Testament." Translated by John Bright. Essays on Old Testament Interpretation. Edited by Claus Westermann. (English translated edited by James Luther Mays). London: SCM, 1963.

Rahlfs, Alfred. "Der text des Septuaginta-Psalters." Septuaginta-Studien. 2 vols. Göttingen: Vandenhoeck & Ruprecht, 1907.

_____. "Über Theodotion-Lesarten im Neuen Testament und Aquila-Lesarten bei Justin." ZNW, XX (1921), 182-99.

Rashdall, Hastings. The Idea of Atonement in Christian Theology. The Bampton Lectures, 1965. London: MacMillan, 1920.

Read, H. C. "The Cry of Dereliction." ExpTim, LXVIII (1957), 260-62.

Rehkopf, Friedrich. Die lukanische Sonderquelle. WUNT, V. Tübingen: Mohr, 1959.

Rehm, M. "Eli, Eli lama Sabacthani." BZ, n.s. II, (1958), 275-78.

Reim, Günter. Studien zum alttestamentlichen Hintergrund des Johannesevangeliums. SNTSMS, XXII. Cambridge: University Press, 1974.

Rendall, Robert. "Quotation in Scripture as an Index of Wider Reference." EvQ, XXXVI (1964), 214-21.

Rengstorf, Karl Heinrich. "κορβᾶν." TDNT, III, 860-66.

_____. "λῃστής." TDNT, IV, 257-62.

Rese, Martin. Alttestamentliche Motive in der Christologie des Lukas. SNT, I. Gütersloh: Verlagshaus Gerd Mohn, 1969.

_____. "Überprüfung einiger Thesen von Joachim Jeremias zum Thema des Gottesknechtes im Judentum." ZTK, LX (1963), 21-41.

_____. "Zur Problematik von Kurz-und Langtext in Luk. XXII. 17ff." NTS, XXII (1975), 15-31.

Reumann, John H. "Psalm 22 at the Cross." Int, XXVIII (1974), 39-58.

Richardson, Alan. Christian Apologetics. London: SCM, 1947.

_____. An Introduction to the Theology of the New Testament. New York: Harper, 1958.

Ridderbos, H. N. "The Psalms: Style Figures and Structures (Certain Considerations with Special Reference to Pss. xxii, xxv and xlv)." Studies in Psalms. OTS, XIII. Leiden: Brill, 1963.

Riesenfeld, Harold. "Bemerkungen zur Frage des Selbstbewusstseins Jesu." Der historische Jesus und der kerymatische Christus: Beiträge zum Christusverständnis in Forschung und Verkündigung. Edited by Helmut Ristow & Karl Matthiae. 2nd ed. Berlin: Evangelische Verlagsanstalt, 1961.

Riesenfeld, H. The Resurrection in Ezekiel XXXVII and the Dura-Europus Paintings. Uppsala: A. B. Londequistskan and Leipzig: Otto Harrassowitz, 1948.

Rigaux, B. "Révélation des Mystères et perfection à Qumran et dans le Nouveau Testament." NTS, IV (1957-58), 237-62.

Robert, A. "Littéraires (Genres)." DBSup, V, 405-21.

Roberts, Bleddyn J. "Bible Exegesis and Fulfillment in Qumran." Words and Meanings: Essays Presented to David Winton Thomas. Edited by Peter R. Ackroyd and Barnabas Lindars. Cambridge: University Press, 1968.

_____. "The Dead Sea Scrolls and the Old Testament Scriptures." BJRL, XXXVI (1953-54), 75-96.

_____. The Old Testament Text and Versions. Cardiff: University of Wales Press, 1951.

_____. "The Second Isaiah Scroll from Qumrân (IQIsb)." BJRL, XLII, (1959-60), 132-44.

Robinson, H. Wheeler. The Cross in the Old Testament. London: SCM, 1955.

Robinson, J. A. T. "The Baptism of John and the Qumran Community, Testing a Hypothesis." HTR, L (1957), 175-91.

_____. "The One Baptism as a Category of New Testament Soteriology." SJT, VI (1953), 257-74.

Rohde, Joachim. Rediscovering the Teaching of the Evangelists. Translated by Dorothea M. Barton. London: SCM, 1968.

Roloff, Jürgen. "Anfänge der soteriologischen Deutung des Todes Jesu (Mk. x. 45 und Lk. xxii. 27)." NTS, XIX (1972-73), 38-64.

_____. Das Kerygma und der irdische Jesus: Historische Motive in den Jesus - Erzählungen den Evangelien. Göttingen: Vandenhoeck & Ruprecht, 1970.

Romaniuk, Casimir. "Le Livre de la Sagesse dans le Nouveau Testament." NTS, XIV (1967-68), 498-514.

Rose, A. "L'influence des psaumes sur les announces et les récits de la Passion et de la Résurrection dans les Evangiles." Le Psautier: Ses Origines. Ses problèmes littéraires. Son influence. Edited by R. de Langhe. Leuven: Publications Universitaires - Institut Orientaliste, 1962.

Rosenberg, Roy A. "Jesus, Isaac and the 'Suffering Servant'." JBL, LXXXIV (1965), 381-88.

Rosenbloom, Joseph R. The Dead Sea Isaiah Scroll: A Literary Analysis. A Comparison with the Masoretic Text and the Biblica Hebraica. Grand Rapdis: Eerdmans, 1970.

Rosenthal, Judah M. "Biblical Exegesis of 4QpIs." JQR, LX (1969), 27-36.

Rost, Leonhard. Judaism Outside the Hebrew Canon: An Introduction to the Documents. Translated by David E. Green. Nashville: Abingdon, 1976.

Roth, Cecil. "The Subject Matter of Qumran Exegesis." VT, X (1960), 51-68.

Rothfuchs, Wilhelm. Die Erfüllungszitate des Matthäus-Evangeliums: eine biblisch-theologische Untersuchung. BWANT, V:8. Stuttgart: Kohlammer, 1969.

Rowley, H. H. The Relevance of Apocalyptic: A Study of Jewish and Christian Apocalypses from Daniel to the Revelation. 2nd ed. London: Lutterworth Press, 1947.

_____. "The Servant of the Lord in the Light of Three Decades of Criticism." The Servant of the Lord and other Essays on the Old Testament. 2nd ed. Oxford: Basil Blackwell, 1965.

_____. "The Suffering Servant and the Davidic Messiah." The Servant of the Lord and other Essays on the Old Testament. 2nd ed. Oxford: Basil Blackwell, 1965.

Ruckstuhl, E. Chronology of the Last Days of Jesus. Translated by Victor J. Drapela. New York: Desclee Company, 1965.

Ruppert, L. Jesus als der leidende Gerechte? Der Weg Jesu im Lichte eines alt-und zwischentestamentlichen Motivs. SBS, LIX. Stuttgart: Katholisches Bibelwerk, 1972.

Russell, D. S. The Method and Message of Jewish Apocalyptic 200 B.C.-A.D. 100. London: SCM, 1964.

Saebø, Magne. Sacharja 9-14. WMANT, XXXIV. Amsterdam: Neukirchener Verlag, 1969.

Sahlin, Harold. "Zum Verständnis von drei Stellen des Markusevangelium (Mc. 4:26-29; 7:18f; 15:34)." Bib, XXXIII (1952), 53-66.

Sand, Alexander. "'Wie geschrieben steht...': zur Auslegung der jüdischen Schriften in den urchristlichen Gemeinden." Schriftauslegung: Beiträge zur Hermeneutik des Neuen Testaments und im Neuen Testament. Edited by Joseph Ernst. Munich/Paderborn/Vienna: Ferdinand Schöningh, 1972.

Sanders, E. P. Paul and Palestinian Judaism: A Comparison of Patterns of Religion. Philadelphia: Fortress, 1977.

Sandmel, Samuel. The First Christian Century in Judaism and Christianity: Certainties and Uncertainties. New York: Oxford University Press, 1969.

Sawyer, J. F. A."Why is a Solar Eclipse mentioned in the Passion Narrative (Luke xxiii, 44-45)?" JTS, n.s. XXIII (1974), 124-28.

Schechter, Solomon. Aspects of Rabbinic Theology. New York: Schocken, 1961.

Scheifler, J. R. "El salmo 22 y la Crucifixión del señor." EstBib, XXIV (1965), 5-83.

Schenk, Wolfgang. Der Passionsbericht nach Markus: Untersuchungen zur Überlieferungsgeschichte der Passionstradition. Gütersloh: Mohn, 1974.

Schenke, Ludger. Studien zur Passionsgeschichte des Markus: Tradition und Redaktion in Markus 14:1-42. FzB, IV. Würzburg: Echter Verlag Katholisches Bibelwerk, 1971.

Schille, Gottfried. "Das Leiden des Herrn: Die evangelische Passionstradition und ihr 'Sitz im Leben'." ZTK, LII (1955), 161-205.

Schnackenburg, Rudolf. "Der Menschensohn im Johannesevangelium." NTS, XI (1964-1965), 123-37.

Schneider, Gerhard. Die Passion Jesu nach den drei älteren Evangelien. Munich: Kösel, 1973.

Schneider, Gerhard. "Das Problem einer vorkanonischen Passionserzählung." BZ, n.s. XVI (1972), 222-44.

Schoeps, Hans-Joachim. Paulus: Die Theologie des Apostels im Lichte der jüdischen Religionsgeschichte. Tübingen: Mohr, 1959.

Schreiber, Johannes. Die Markuspassion: Wege zur Erforschung der Leidensgeschichte Jesu. Hamburg: Furche-Verlag, 1969.

_____. Theologie des Vertrauens. Eine redaktionsgeschichtliche Untersuchung des Markusevangeliums. Hamburg: Furche-Verlag, 1967.

Schrenk, Gottlieb. "$\gamma\rho\acute{\alpha}\phi\omega$." TDNT, I, 742-773.

_____. "$\acute{\iota}\epsilon\rho\acute{o}\varsigma$..... " TDNT, III, 221-83.

Schubert, Paul. "The Structure and Significance of Luke 24." Neutestamentliche Studien für Rudolf Bultmann. Edited by W. Eltester. BZNW, XXI. Berlin: Töpelmann, 1957.

Schürer, Emil. The History of the Jewish People in the Age of Jesus Christ (175 B. C. - A. D. 135). Revised and edited by Geza Vermes and Fergus Millar (Lit. Ed. Pamela Vermes; organizing ed. Matthew Black) Vol. I. Edinburgh: T & T Clark, 1973.

Schürmann, Heinz. Einer quellenkritischen Untersuchung des lukanischen Abendmahlsberichtes, Lk. 22:7-38.
Vol. I: Der Paschalmahlbericht, Lk. 22:(7-14), 15-18.
Vol. II: Der Einsetzungsbericht, Lk, 22:19-20.
Vol. III: Jesu Abschiedsrede, Lk. 22:21-38.
NTAbh, XX. Münster: Aschendorffsche, 1968 (2nd ed.), 1955, 1957.

_____. "Lk. 22:19b-20 als ursprüngliche Textüberlieferung." Bib, XXXII (1951), 364-92, 522-41.

_____. "Wie hat Jesus seinen Tod bestanden und verstanden? Eine methodenkritische Besinnung," Orientierung an Jesu: Zur Theologie den Synoptiker (Josef Schmid). Edited by Paul Hoffmann, in cooperation with Norbert Brox & Wilhelm Pesch. Freiburg/Basel/Vienna: Herder, 1973.

Schulz, Siegfried. Die Mitte der Schrift: Der Frühkatholizismus im Neuen Testament als Herausforderung an den Protestantismus. Stuttgart/Berlin: Kreuz, 1976.

_____. Die Stunde der Botschaft: Einführung in die Theologie der vier Evangelien. 2nd ed. Hamburg: Furche-Verlag and Zürich: Zwingli Verlag, 1970.

_____. Untersuchungen zur Menschensohn-Christologie im Johannesevangelium. Zugleich ein Beitrag zur Methodengeschichte der Auslegung des 4. Evangeliums. Göttingen: Vandenhoeck & Ruprecht, 1957.

Schwarz, Ottilie Johann Renata. Der erste Teil der Damaskusschrift und das Alte Testament. Lichtland: Diest, 1965.

Schweizer, Eduard. Erniedrigung und Erhöhung bei Jesus und seinen Nachfolgern. ATANT, XXVIII. Zürich: Zwingli, 1962.

_____. "Das Herrenmahl im Neuen Testament." TLZ, LXXIX (1954), 577-92.

_____. Jesus. Translated by David E. Green. London: 1971.

_____. Lordship and Discipleship. SBT, XXVIII. London: SCM, 1960.

_____. "Menschensohn und eschatologischer Mensch im Frühjudentum." Jesus und der Menschensohn (für Anton Vögtle). Edited by Rudolf Pesch & Rudolf Schnackenburg in cooperation with Odilo Kaiser. Freiburg/Basel/Vienna: Herder, 1975.

_____. "πνεῦμα, πνευματικός." TDNT, VI, 332-455.

_____. "The Son of Man." JBL, LXXIX (1960), 119-129.

_____. "The Son of Man Again." NTS, IX (1962-1963), 256-261.

Scott, E. F. The Kingdom and the Messiah. Edinburgh: T & T Clark, 1911.

Scott, R. B. Y. "The Sign of Jonah. An Interpretation." Int, XIX (1965), 16-25.

Seeligmann, I. L. "Voraussetzungen der Midraschexegese." VTSup, I (1953), 150-181.

Segal, J. B. The Hebrew Passover from the Earliest Times to A. D. 70. London Oriental Series, XII. London: Oxford University Press, 1963.

Seidelin, Paul. "Das 'Ebed Jahwe und die Messiasgestalt im Jesajatargum." ZNW, XXXV (1936), 194-231.

Senior, Donald. "The Death of Jesus and the Resurrection of the Holy Ones." CBQ, XXXVIII (1976), 312-29.

_____. The Passion Narrative According to Matthew: A Redactional Study. BETL, XXXIX. Leuven: Leuven University Press, 1975.

Senior, D. "The Passion Narrative in the Gospel of Matthew." L'Évangile selon Matthieu: Rédaction et théologie. Edited by M. Didier. Gembloux: Duculot, 1972.

Sevenster, J. N. Do you Know Greek? How Much Greek Could the First Jewish Christians have Known? NovTSup, XIV. Leiden: Brill, 1968.

Sherwin-White, A. N. Roman Society and Roman Law in the New Testament. The Sarum Lectures, 1960-61. Oxford: Clarendon Press, 1963.

Shires, Henry, M. Finding the Old Testament in the New. Philadelphia: Westminster, 1974.

Sidebottom, E. M. The Christ of the Fourth Gospel in the Light of First-Century Thought. London: SPCK, 1961.

_____. "The Son of Man as Man in the Fourth Gospel." ExpTim, LXVI (1956-1957), 231-35.

Sidersky, D. "La parole suprême de Jesus." RHR, CIII (1931), 151-54.

_____. "Un Passage Hébreu dans le Nouveau Testament." JA, III (1914), 232-33.

Silberman, Lou H. "Unriddling the Riddle, A Study in the Structure and Language of the Habakkuk Pesher (IQpHab)." RevQ, III (1961-62), 323-364.

Simonis, A. J. Die Hirtenrede im JohannesEvangelium: Versuch einer Analyse von Johannes 10, 1-18 nach Entstehung, Hintergrund und Inhalt. AnBib, XXIX. Rome: Pontifical Biblical Institute, 1967.

Skehan, Patrick W. "The Biblical Scrolls from Qumran and the Text of the Old Testament." Qumran and the History of the Biblical Text. Edited by Frank Moore Cross and Shemaryahu Talmon. Cambridge, Mass. & London: Harvard University Press, 1975. (= BA XXVIII (1965) 87-100).

Slomovic, Elieser. "Toward an Understanding of the Exegesis in the Dead Sea Scrolls." RevQ, VII (1969), 3-15.

Smalley, Stephen S. "The Johannine Son of Man Sayings." NTS, XV (1968-1969), 278-301.

Smart, James D. History and Theology in Second Isaiah: A Commentary on Isaiah 35, 40-66. Philadelphia: Westminster, 1965.

Smith, David. "Crucifixion." A Dictionary of Christ and the Gospels. Edited by James Hastings. 2 vols. Edinburgh: T & T Clark, 1906.

Smith, D. Moody. "The Use of the Old Testament in the New." The Use of the Old Testament in the New and Other Essays: Studies in Honor of William Franklin Stinespring. Edited by James M. Efird. Durham, N. C.: Duke University Press, 1972.

Smith, Fred. "The Strangest Word of Jesus." ExpTim, XLIV (1932), 259-61.

Smith, George Adam. The Historical Geography of the Holy Land. The Fontana Library, Theology and Philosophy. 25th ed. London: Collins, 1966.

Smith, Robert. "Exodus Typology in the Fourth Gospel." JBL, LXXXI (1962), 329-42.

Snodgrass, Klyne. "Western non-interpolations." JBL, XCI (1972), 269-79.

Sparks, H. F. D. "St. Matthew's References to Jeremiah." JTS, n.s. I (1950), 155-156.

Sperber, Alexander. New Testament and Septuagint. New York: Jewish Publication Society, 1940.

Stählin, Gustav. "ὀργή E. The Wrath of Man and the Wrath of God in the New Testament." TDNT, V, 419-47.

Stanley, David M. "The Theme of the Servant of Yahweh in primitive Christian Soteriology and its Transposition by St. Paul." CBQ, XVI (1954), 385-425.

Stanton, G. N. Jesus of Nazareth in New Testament Preaching. SNTSMS, XXVII. Cambridge: University Press, 1974.

Stather-Hunt, P. W. Primitive Gospel Sources. London: James Clarke, 1951.

Stauffer, Ethelbert. Jesus and His Story. Translated by Richard and Clara Winston. New York: Alfred A. Knopf, 1960.

_____. "Jesus und seine Bibel." Abraham unser Vater: Juden und Christen im Gespräch über die Bibel. Festschrift für Otto Michel zum 60. Geburtstag. Edited by Otto Betz, Martin Hengel and Peter Schmidt. Arbeite zur Geschichte des spätjudentums und Urchristentums (Institutum Judaicum, Tübingen), V. Leiden/Cologne: Brill, 1963.

_____. "Messias oder Menschensohn?" NovT, I (1956), 81-102.

_____. New Testament Theology. Translated by John Marsh. London: SCM, 1955.

Stein, Robert H. "A Short Note on Mark XIV. 8 and XVI. 7." NTS, XX (1974), 445-52.

Stendahl, Krister. The School of St. Matthew and its Use of the Old Testament. Philadelphia: Fortress, 1958.

Stott, Wilfred. "'Son of Man' - A Title of Abasement." ExpTim, LXXXIII (1972), 278-281.

Strack, Hermann C. Introduction to the Talmud and Midrash. A Temple Book. New York: Atheneum, 1931.

Strecker, Georg. "Die Leidens-und Auferstehungsvoraussagen im Markusevangelium. (Mk. 8, 31; 9:31; 10:32-34)." ZTK, LXIV (1967), 16-30.

_____. Der Weg der Gerechtigkeit: Untersuchungen zur Theologie des Matthäus. FRLANT, LXXXII. Göttingen: Vandenhoeck & Ruprecht, 1962.

Streeter, Burnett Hillman. The Four Gospels: A Study of Origins. London: MacMillan, 1924.

Suggs, M. -J. "Wisdom 2:10-5: A Homily Based on the Fourth Servant Song." JBL, LXXVI (1957), 26-33.

Suhl, Alfred. Die Funktion der alttestamentlichen Zitate und Anspielungen im Markus-evangelium. Gütersloh: Mohn, 1965.

Sundberg, Albert C. The Old Testament of the Early Church. Harvard Theological Studies, XX. Cambridge, Mass.: Harvard University Press, 1964.

_____. "On Testimonies." NovT, III (1959), 268-81.

Surkau, Hans-Werner. Martyrien in jüdischer und frühchristlicher Zeit. FRLANT, XXXVI. Göttingen: Vandenhoeck & Ruprecht, 1938.

Sutcliffe, Edmund F. "Matthew 27,9." JTS, n.s., III (1952) 227-28.

Swete, Henry Barclay. An Introduction to the Old Testament in Greek. Cambridge: University Press, 1900.

Talmon, Shemaryahu. "The Textual Study of the Bible - A New Outlook." Qumran and the History of the Biblical Text. Edited by Frank Moore Cross and Shemaryahu Talmon. Cambridge, Mass.: Harvard University Press, 1975.

Taylor, Vincent. Jesus and His Sacrifice. London: MacMillan and Co., Limited, 1937.

_____. The Names of Jesus. London: MacMillan and Co., Limited, 1953.

_____. "The Origin of the Markan Passion - Sayings." NTS, I (1954-55), 159-67.

_____. The Passion Narrative of St. Luke: A Critical and Historical Investigation. Edited by Owen E. Evans. SNTSMS, XIX. Cambridge: University Press, 1972.

_____. The Person of Christ in New Testament Teaching. London: MacMillan, 1958.

Teeple, Howard M. The Mosaic Eschatological Prophet. JBL, Monograph Series, X. Philadelphia: Society of Biblical Literature, 1957.

Thackeray, H. St. John. The Septuagint and Jewish Worship. A Study in Origins. The Schweich Lectures, 1920. London: Published for The British Academy by Oxford University Press, 1921.

Theodor, J. "Midrash Haggadah." JE, VIII, 550-569.

Thomson, J. G. S. S. "The Shepherd-Ruler Concept in the O.T. and Its Application in the N.T." SJT, VIII (1955), 406-18.

Thüsing, Wilhelm. Die Erhöhung und Verherrlichung Jesu im Johannes-evangelium. NTAbh, XXI. Münster, Aschendorff, 1960.

Thyen, Hartwig. *Studien zur Sündenvergebung im Neuen Testament und seinen alttestamentlichen und jüdischen Voraussetzungen.* FRLANT, XLVI. Göttingen: Vandenhoeck & Ruprecht, 1970.

Tillesse, G. Minette de. *Le Secret Messianique dans L'Évangile de Marc.* Paris: Éditions du Cerf, 1968

Tödt, H. E. *The Son of Man in the Synoptic Tradition.* Translated by Dorothea M. Barton. London: SCM, 1965.

Tooley, Wilfred. "The Shepherd and Sheep Image in the Teaching of Jesus." NovT, VII (1964-65), 15-25.

Torrey, Charles C. "The Aramaic Period of the Nascent Christian Church." ZNW, XLIV (1952-53), 205-223.

_____. "The Foundry of the Second Temple at Jerusalem." JBL, LV (1936), 247-60.

_____. "The Influence of Second Isaiah in the Gospels and Acts." JBL, XLVIII (1929), 24-36.

_____. "The Messiah Son of Ephraim." JBL, LXVI (1947) 253-277.

_____. *Our Translated Gospels.* London: Hodder and Stoughton, n.d.

Trilling, Wolfgang. *Christusverkündigung in den synoptischen Evangelien: Beispiele gattungsgemasser Auslegung.* Biblische Handbibliothek, IV. Munich: Kösel, 1969.

_____. "Der Tod Jesu, Ende der alten Weltzeit." *Christusverkündigung in den synoptischen Evangelien.* Munich: Kösel, 1969.

_____. *Das Wahre Israel: Studien zur Theologie des Matthäusevangelium.* Erfurter Theologische Studien. VII. Leipzig: St. Beuno-Verlag, 1959.

Trocmé, Étienne. *The Formation of the Gospel according to Mark.* Translated by Pamela Gaughan. London: SPCK, 1975.

Trudinger, L. Paul. "'Eli, Eli, Lama Sabachtani'?: A Cry of Dereliction? or Victory?" JETS, XVII (1974), 235-38.

Turner, C. H. "Marcan Usage: Notes, Critical and Exegetical on the Second Gospel." JTS, XXVI (1925), 145-56.

_____. "Western Readings in the Second Half of St. Mark's Gospel." JTS, XXIX (1928), 1-16.

Turner, H. E. W. *Jesus: Master and Lord.* London: A. R. Mowbray, 1953.

Turner, N. "The Style of St. Mark's Eucharistic Words." JTS, VIII (1957), 108-11.

Unnik, W. C. van. "The Death of Judas in St. Matthew's Gospel." ATR, supp. ser. III (1974), 44-57.

Vanhoye, A. "Structure et théologie des récits de la passion dans les évangiles synoptiques." NRT, LXXXIX (1967), 135-63.

de Vaux, Roland. Ancient Israel: Its Life and Institutions. Translated by John McHugh. London: Darton, Longman & Todd, 1961.

Vermes, Geza. "Bible and Midrash: Early Old Testament Exegesis." The Cambridge History of the Bible. Vol I: From the Beginnings to Jerome. Edited by P. R. Ackroyd & C. F. Evans. Cambridge: University Press, 1970.

_____. "Le 'Commentaire d'Habacuc' et le Nouveau Testament." Cahiers Sioniens,V (1951), 337-349.

_____. Jesus the Jew: A Historian's Reading of the Gospels. London: Collins, 1973.

_____. "The Qumran Interpretation of Scripture in its Historical Setting," ALUOS, VI (1966-68), 90-97.

_____. Scripture and Tradition in Judaism: Haggadic Studies. SPB, IV. Leiden: Brill, 1961.

_____. "The Use of בר נש/בר נשא in Jewish Aramaic." Appendix E in An Aramaic Approach to the Gospels and Acts by Matthew Black. 3rd ed. Oxford: Clarendon Press, 1967.

Vielhauer, Philipp. "Jesus und der Menschensohn: Zur Diskussion mit Heinz Eduard Tödt und Eduard Schweizer." ZTK, LX (1963), 133-177.

Vis, Albert. The Messianic Psalm Quotations in the New Testament: A Critical Study on the Christian 'Testimonies' in the Old Testament. Amsterdam: von Soest, 1936.

Vischer, Wilhelm. The Witness of the Old Testament to Christ. Translated by A. B. Crabtree. 2 vols. 3rd ed. London: Lutterworth, 1949.

Waard, Jan de. A Comparative Study of the Old Testament Text in the Dead Sea Scrolls and in the New Testament. STDJ, IV. Leiden: Brill, 1965.

Walker, William O. "The Origin of the Son of Man Concept as Applied to Jesus." JBL, XLI (1972), 482-90.

Wallenstein, Meir. "The Piyyut, with Special Reference to the Textual Study of the Old Testament." BJRL, XXXIV (1951-1952), 469-76.

Walters, Peter. The Text of the Septuagint: Its Corruptions and their Emendation. Edited by D. W. Gooding. Cambridge: University Press, 1973.

Walther, James A. "The Chronology of Passion Week." JBL, LXXVII (1958), 116-22.

Weidel, K. Studien über den Einfluss des Weissagungsbeweises auf die evangelische Geschichte." TSK, LXXXIII (1910), 83-109, 163-194; LXXXV (1912), 167-286.

Weingreen, J. "The Rabbinic Approach to the Study of the Old Testament." BJRL, XXXIV (1951-52), 166-190.

Weiss, Raphael. "A Comparison between the Massoretic and the Qumran Texts of Nahum III, 1-11." RevQ, IV (1963-64), 433-439.

Wernberg-Møller, P. "Some Reflections on the Biblical Material in the Manual of Discipline." ST, IX (1955) 40-66.

Westcott, Brooke Foss and Hort, Fenton John Anthony. The New Testament in the Original Greek: Introduction and Appendix: Notes on Select Readings. Cambridge & London: MacMillan and Co., 1881.

Westermann, Claus. The Praise of God in the Psalms. Translated by Keith R. Crim. London: Epworth Press, 1965.

Wevers, J. W. "Septuaginta Forschungen seit 1954." TR, XXXIII (1968), 18-76.

White, R. E. O. The Biblical Doctrine of Initiation. London: Hodder and Stoughton, 1960.

Whiteley, D. E. H. "The Doctrine of Salvation in the Synoptic Gospels." SE, IV (1965) (= TU, CII (1968)), 116-130.

Wilcox, Max. "The Composition of John 13:21-30." Neutestamentica and Semitica: Studies in Honour of Matthew Black. Edited by E. Earle Ellis and Max Wilcox. Edinburgh: T & T Clark, 1969.

_____. "The Denial Sequence in Mark xiv. 26-31, 66-72. NTS, XVII (1970-71), 426-36.

Wilder, Amos N. "The Rhetoric of Ancient and Modern Apocalyptic." Int., XXV (1971), 436-453.

Wilkinson, J. "The Seven Words from the Cross." SJT, XVII (1964), 69-82.

Williams, C. S. C. Alterations to the Text of the Synoptic Gospels and Acts. Oxford, Basil Blackwell, 1951.

Williams, Sam K. Jesus' Death as Saving Event: The Background and Origin of a Concept. HDR, II. Missoula, Mont.: Scholar's Press, 1975.

Willi-Plein, Ina. Prophetie am Ende: Untersuchungen zu Sacharja 9-14. BBB, XLII. Cologne: Peter Hanstein, 1974.

Wilson, S. G. "Lukan Eschatology." NTS, XV (1969-70) 330-347.

Wilson, William Riley. The Execution of Jesus: A Judicial, Literary and Historical Investigation. New York: Scribner's, 1970.

Winter, Paul. On the Trial of Jesus. SJ:FWJ, I. Berlin: de Gruyter, 1961.

Winter, P. "The Treatment of His Sources by the Third Evangelist in Luke XXI-XXIV." ST, VIII (1954), 138-72.

Wolff, Hans Walter. Jesaja 53 im Urchristentum. 2nd ed. Berlin: Evangelische Verlagsanstalt, 1950.

Wolfson, H. A. Philo: Foundations of Religious Philosophy in Judaism, Christianity and Islam. 2 vols. Cambridge: Harvard University Press, 1947-1948.

Wood, J. E. "Isaac Typology in the New Testament." NTS, XIV (1967-68), 583-89.

Woude, Adam Simon van der. Die Messianischen Vorstellungen der Gemeinde von Qumran. Assen: van Gorcum, 1957.

Wright, Addison G. "The Literary Genre Midrash." CBQ, XXVIII (1966) 105-38, 417-57.

Würthwein, Ernst. Der Text des Alten Testaments: Ein Einführung in die Biblica Hebraica. 4th ed. Stuttgart: Württembergische Bibelanstalt, 1973.

Ysebart, J. Greek Baptismal Terminology: Its Origins and Early Development. Graecitas Christianorum Primaeva, I. Nijmegen: Dekkert van de vegt, 1962.

Zahn, Theodor. Introduction to the New Testament. Translated by J. M. Trout, et al. 3 vols. Edinburgh: T & T Clark, 1909.

Zehnle, Richard. "The Salvific Character of Jesus' Death in Lucan Soteriology." TS, XXX(1969), 420-44.

Zeitlin, S. "Hillel and the Hermeneutic Rules." JQR, LIV (1963), 161-73.

_____. "Midrash: A Historical Study." JQR, XLIV (1953), 21-36.

Zimmerli, Walter. "Promise and Fulfillment." Translated by James Wharton. Essays on Old Testament Interpretation. Edited by Claus Westermann. (English Translation edited by James Luther Mays). London: SCM, 1963.

Zimmerli, Walter and Jeremias, Joachim. The Servant of God. Translated by Harold Knight, et al. SBT, XX. London: SCM, 1965.

Zimmermann, Frank. "The Last Words of Jesus." JBL, LXVI (1947), 465-66.

Unpublished Material

Bampfylde, G. D. "Old Testament Quotations and Imagery in the Gospel According to St. John." Unpublished M.A. dissertation, University of Hull, 1967.

Karnetzki, Manfred. "Die alttestamentlichen Zitate in der synoptischen Tradition." Unpublished Ph.D. dissertation, University of Tübingen, 1955.

Larkin, William J. Jr. "Luke's Use of the Old Testament in Luke 22-23." Unpublished Ph.D. dissertation. University of Durham, 1974.

Snodgrass, Klyne R. "The Christological Stone Testimonia in the New Testament." Unpublished Ph.D. dissertation, University of St. Andrews, 1973.

INDEX OF ANCIENT SOURCES

Old Testament

GENESIS
-	22
6	32
22	112,115, 325-8
22:5	325
22:9	327
35:18	345n
37:26ff	348n
40-1	73
40:13	99n
40:14	348
40:16	99n
49:11	182n

EXODUS
4:22	113n
9:8	196
9:12	196-7
10:22	343
12:10	314-6
12:22	316
12:46	314-6,355, 362,386
17:12	154
20:16	247-8
21:14	348
21:32	188
23:7	48n
24:8	160,302-6, 311,329,355
28:4	255
36:8	197n
36:12	197n
36:14	197n
36:28	197n
36:33	197n
37:20	197n
39:10	197n
40:19	197n

LEVITICUS
1ff	309
5	125
6:2	175
14:23	197n
16	309
16:4	255
18:20	175
19:17	42n
23:11	320n
23:27-8	36

NUMBERS
8:3	197n
9:5	197n
9:12	314-6,355
15:23	197n
15:36	350
19:11	322n
19:14	322n
20:9	197n
20:27	197n
21:8-9	331-3,355
21:18	39
24:3	347n
24:17	37,37n
27:11	197n
30:17	42n
31:5	96n
31:16	96n
31:31	197n
31:41	197n

DEUTERONOMY
16:3	308
18	103n, 346-7
19:15	349n
27:25	199n
29:18-9	48n
32:28	33n,42n
32:33	39
33:10	61n

II SAMUEL
7	300,339-41
7:11-4	300n
7:14	156
12:17	252
17:23	190

I KINGS
2:27	385n
19:11	344
22:24	140

II KINGS
19:21	258

II CHRONICLES
5:6	134n
13:22	64n
24:27	64n
36:21	385n
36:22	385n

EZRA
6:11	99n

JOB
-	231
9:31	119n
16:4	258

PSALMS
-	225-7,356n
2	297
2:2	235,348-9, 355
2:7	112-22,156, 352
6:3	240-2,285, 354
6:4	241
11:6	119n
16	297n,299
18:4f	119n
22	227-31,232n, 258,260-1,281 288,289,297, 363
22:1-21	259
22:1	264-75,281, 285,287,288, 354,360
22:6-8	258
22:7	258,264,370
22:7a	263,285,354
22:7b	263,285,354
22:8	259,260-2, 263,285,287, 354
22:8b	156
22:11	264n
22:15	276-7
22:16	154,283-4
22:18	252-7,285, 354,362
22:20	245
22:21	272n
22:22	294n
22:24	245
22:25	346n
22:29	259-60
23	177
27	247
27:2	246-7,285, 354
27:12	242-8,354
31	227,231n,238, 297
31:5	280-2,285, 354,360
31:9	245
31:10	245
31:11	248n
31:13	234-5,248n, 285,354
31:22	245,245,248n, 346n
31:23	245-6,346n
34:20	91,314-6

35:4	246-7,248-9, 285,354	118:22	89-91,97,111, 335-7,355, 356n,357,366n	52:14	83,103n	
35:11	247-8,286, 354	118:22-7	97n	52:15	148n	
35:19	243-4,247, 286,354	118:22-8	312n	53	79-173 passim, 177n,212,232 292,303,306, 309,326,336n, 347,352,356, 364,394,395n, 396	
37:14-6	248	118:26-7	336			
38:4-5	149n	119:161	243			
38:9ff	248					
38:11	282-3,286,354	**PROVERBS**				
38:13-14	149n	5:4	251n			
38:18	149n	6:19	247	53:3	89n,90-1,94n, 141,160,163, 352	
39:12	346n	19:5	247			
41	108,231n, 238-9,297	19:9	247	53:4-5	83	
		24:22a	244	53:4	91n,162,163, 169n,177n,352	
41:9	108,235-40, 244-5,286,354	29:23	290			
		31:6-7	250n	53:5	93,95	
42	240	31:6	250n	53:6	93,95n,96, 147,153n	
42:1	276					
42:2	276	**SONG OF SOLOMON**		52:7	113,148-51, 163,171,249, 312-4,353	
42:5	240-2,286,287, 354	5:13	251n			
42:6	240-2,286,354	**ECCLESIASTES**		53:8	145-6,161	
42:9	242n	8:1	73	53:9	144-5,159 162,164,353	
42:10	242n,262,265n	**ISAIAH**		53:10-12	122-7,164,353	
42:11	240-2,286,354	-	356n	53:10	96,130,131, 309	
43	240	13:10	343			
43:1	242n	21:4	119n	53:11-12	101n,176n, 312n	
43:5	240-2,286,354	26:19	345n			
55:14	108n	27:11	33n,42n	53:11	91n,113,153, 158	
56	247	28:16	220n			
56:9	246-7	30:1-5	21	53:12	90,95n,96,97, 109n,127-38, 146,151-5, 160,162,164, 172,306,309, 353,386	
63:2	276	30:10	21			
69	231n,232n, 233n,278,281, 297	30:15-8	21			
		30:27-8	119n			
		35:4	180n			
69:1f	245	40:3	48n			
69:3	119n,245	40:9	180n	54:7	244	
69:4	243-4,286,354	42:1ff	177n	56:8	176n	
69:9	233-4,262, 286,354,362	42:1-4	79,169n	59:5	33n	
		42:1	112-22,157, 163,352	59:16	153n	
69:14	119n			61:1-2	137n	
69:21	249-52,275- 80,286,355, 377	42:6	303	62:11	179,373	
		44:2	115n	63	115n	
		47:3	95n	63:14	115n	
69:21a	286,354	49:1-6	79	63:19	115n	
69:21b	286,355	49:3	81			
75:7	177	49:4	177n	**JEREMIAH**		
78:12 (LXX)	270n	49:5-6	81	6:15	199	
78:52	177	49:8	303	13:16	343	
78:70-2	177	50-53	80	15:9	343	
80:1	177	50:3	343	16:7	252	
88:6f	119n	50:4-9	79,88n	18	194-5	
88:8	282-3	50:6	88-9,97,110, 139-44,161, 163,352	19	195-8,205-6, 208,210,355, 373,377	
88:51ff (LXX)	270n					
89:39	90					
94:21a	21	50:11	33n	19:1-13	195	
106:23	156n	51:17-23	117n	19:1	195,196	
108:2ff	247n	51:23	258n	19:4	195,199	
109:8	244n	52:13-53:12	79	19:6	195	
109:25	258	52:13	100,101n,163, 352,356	19:8	258n	
110	297			19:11	195,196,205n	

20:10	108n	5:26	38,54	12:10-14	221
22-23	176n	6:3	248n	12:10-12	232
23-25	176n	8:9	343-4,356	12:10	173-8,210-14,
23:1-5	174n	8:10	343		217,220,222,
23:4	177	9:1	343		353,362
26	341n	9:2	345n	13	223n
26:15	195n	9:11	37,38	13:1	218,220,222,
31:31-4	160,303-6				353
31:34	306	OBADIAH		13:2-14:21	174n
32	194-5,206n	7	108n	13:7-14:4	215-6
32:6	196			13:7-10	176n
32:8	196	JONAH		13:7-9	216
32:9	195	1:17	333-4,356	13:7	109,109n,147,
32:14	194	2:3 (MT)	334n		173-8,182-7,
49:12	117n	4:9	240-242		215,222,223,
51:4	176n				224,232,353
		MICAH		13:8-9	215-7,222,353
LAMENTATIONS		2:3-5	177	14:1	216
2	258n	5:1 (LXX 4:14)	141,	14:4	215-6
2:15	258,263,285,		335	14:8	218,220,220n,
	355	5:2	141		222,276,353
3	258n			14:21	340n
3:15	251n	NAHUM			
		1:5-6	344	Apocrypha and	
EZEKIEL				Pseudepigrapha	
7:10	64n	HABAKKUK			
12:6	142n	-	44	4 EZRA (II Esdras)	
12:8-16	108	1:8-9a	49	2:34	177
34-36	176n	1:14-6	49	14	66n
34	146n,174n,176n	2:16	49	14:1-18	66
34:21	185n			14:9	291
34:23	177	ZEPHANIAH		14:44-7	58n
36:16-28	176n	3:16	180n,373	14:49	291
36:23	177				
37	176n,344-5,356	HAGGAI		TOBIT	
37:6	345n	2:20-3	177n	-	16,17,22,59
37:7	344n			2:5	16n
37:12	344n	ZECHARIAH		3:10	190
37:14	345n	6:11-12	339-41		
44:15	42n	9:1-10:39	174n	JUDITH	
47:1	219n	9-14	173-224 passim,232,356n,	-	16,17,59
			357,364,378n,	5:5-19	23n
DANIEL			385,397		
2	337n	9	232n	WISDOM OF SOLOMON	
2:28	88n	9:9-10	173-8	-	15n
7	101-6	9:9	178-82,222,	2-5	290,291
7:13	105n		223,232,353,	2	260-261
11:33	101n		373	2:13-18	260-262
12:2	345n	9:10	174	16:6f	331
12:3	101n	9:11	302		
		10:3b-13:1	174n	SIRACH	
HOSEA		11:4-15	173-8,208	-	15n
4:16	21	11:10	174	3:18	290
11:4	140n	11:11	173n	13:7	258
		11:12-13	173,222,223,	37:2	240n
JOEL			353	48	82
2:10	343	11:12	187-9,209,	51:6	240n
2:31	343		222,353,377	51:23	63n,64n
3:15	343,356	11:13	189-210		
		11:15-17	173-4n	1 MACCABEES	
AMOS		12-14	217-21	-	16,17
5:26-7	36-7			2.58	291

Index of Ancient Sources

| 4:46 | 58n |
| 7:17 | 16n |

2 MACCABEES
- 16,59,290
- 7:6 16n
- 7:37f 290

3 MACCABEES
- 16
- 2:1-12 23n

4 MACCABEES
- 15n,290,293n, 326,395n
- 1:11 290
- 6:28f 290
- 17:20ff 290

LETTER OF ARISTEAS
- 16
- 155 16n

ASSUMPTION OF MOSES
- 16n
- 10:1-10 22n

I ENOCH
- 16n,82,86, 106,156,158
- 1:3-9 22n
- 37:71 104
- 49:3 115n
- 71:14 291
- 89:52 291
- 90:13-19 22n
- 90:20ff 339
- 90:31 291

JUBILEES
- 11,16n
- 4:23 291
- 5 32
- 23:23 33
- 32:21-30 66n

LIFE OF ADAM AND EVE
- 16n

PIRKE ABOT
- 1:1 58n,61n

PSALMS OF SOLOMON
- 15,59
- 7:1 243n
- 10:2 290
- 17:40 177
- 17:42 115n

SYBILLINE ORACLES III
- 16n
- 3:8-91 22n

THE TESTAMENTS OF THE TWELVE PATRIARCHS
- 16n
- Benj. 3:8 86,290
- Judah 24:2f 115n
- Levi 18:2-14 115n
- Levi 18:6 115n

Josephus

ANT.
- II, 14 330n
- II, 312 330n
- III, 161 255n

BELL.
- II, 175 203
- VI, 288-309 338n

CONTRA AP.
- I, 8 58n

Philo

FUG.
- 110-112 255n

Dead Sea Scrolls

1 QapGen
- 11

1 QH
- 15,17n,18n, 20n,21n,24, 57n
- 1:21 71n
- 2:13 71n
- 2:28 230n
- 3 84n
- 3:7-10 103n
- 3:9-10 320n
- 4:8 89n
- 4:11 250
- 4:27 71n
- 5:10-11 230n
- 5:23-4 237
- 5:23 108n
- 5:25 71n
- 7:4 230n
- 7:10 84n
- 7:26ff 84n
- 7:27 71n
- 8:26ff 84n
- 8:32 242
- 9:10 230n
- 11:10 71n
- 12:3 230n
- 12:13 71n
- 12:20 71n
- 13:2 71n
- 13:3 71n
- 15:10-11 230n

1 QIS^a
- 45n,83,126n, 140n,142,144n
- 45:33 268n
- 50:6 141
- 52:14 157n
- 53:10 177n
- 65:19 268n
- 65:22 268n

1 QIS^b
- 45n

1 QpHab
- 13,13n,18n, 29,43,46n,48, 49,50,52,53
- 3:6b-14a 49
- 4:9-11 49
- 7:1-8 69,71
- 7:5 71
- 7:8 71
- 11:9-13 49
- 11:10-15

1 QM
- 14n,18n,19n, 20n,41
- 10:1 19n
- 10:2-3 42n
- 10:2b-6 20n
- 10:3 42n,42n
- 10:6-8b 42n
- 10:6 19n
- 11:5-7 19n,37n
- 11:6 41n
- 11:11-12 20n,41n

1 QS
- 14n,18n,19n, 24,41,48
- 2:13-14 20n,48n
- 2:13 42n
- 3:23 70n,71n
- 4:18-23 103n
- 5:5ff 84n
- 5:6 290
- 5:15 19n,42n,48n
- 5:17 19n,41n,48n
- 6:24 64n
- 8:3ff 84n,121n,290
- 8:14 19n,41n,48n
- 8:15 64n
- 8:26 64n
- 9:4 84n,290
- 9:18 71n

1 QS^a
- 14n,18n,41
- 1:1 70
- 1:3 290
- 2:11ff 115n
- 5:20-23 70n

Index of Ancient Sources

1 QS^b		4:20	18n,42n	**Rabbinic Literature**	
-	14n,18n,41	4:21	20n		
		5:1-2	19n	MISHNAH	
4 Q Flor		5:2	41n	Abot 5:25-6	26
-	13n,18n,38,	5:8-9	18n	B. Qam. 3:9	19n
	41,43n,115n,	5:9	42n	Ros Has. 3:8	331n
	300n,372n	5:11b-19	33	Seqal. 6:6	19n
1:2-3	19n	5:13	33n,42n		
1:7	19n	5:13b-14	33n	TOSEPHTA	
1:10	20n,43n	5:14	42n	Sanh. 7:11	27n
1:12	19n	5:16-17	42n	Yad. 2:13	58n
1:14	20n,63n,64n	5:16	33n,41n		
1:15	19n	5:17	33n,42n,42n	BABYLONIAN TALMUD	
1:16	19n	6:2b-11a	39	Hul. 8a	204n
1:18-19	20n	6:3b-4a	41n	Meg. 31a	344n
		6:5	37n	Qidd. 49a	30n
4 QpIs^c		6:8	18n,41n	Sanh. 34a	26n
-	21	6:13	18n,42n,42n	Sanh. 43a	250n
		6:16	42n	Sanh. 98b	82
4 QpNah		6:17	42n	Sukk. 52a	175n
-	18n,42n	6:19	37n	Yom. 39b	338n
		7:6b	19n	Zebah 116b	204n
4 QPS^b		7:8	18n,42n		
-	21	7:9-8:2	36	JERUSALEM TALMUD	
		7:11	42n,42n	Yom. 43c	338n
4 QSam^a		7:11-12	19n		
-	45n	7:14-15	18n	ABOT DE R. NATHAN	
		7:15	42n	37	27n
4 QTest		7:16	18n		
-	12,18n,37n,	7:19-21	41n		
	41,372n	7:19	19n	**New Testament**	
		8:3	42n,42n		
II QMelch		8:9-10	39n,41n	MATTHEW	
-	18n,41	8:9	18n	2:6	141
1:2	19n	8:12	42n,42n	3:15	113
1:3	19n	8:13	42n	3:17	112-22,163,
1:9	19n	8:14	18n		352
1:10	19n	8:21	37n	4:5	200n
1:11	19n	9:2	18n,41n	4:6	183n
1:15	19n	9:5	19n	5:39	139
1:18	19n	9:7-8	18n,42n,42n	8:17	169n
1:19	19n	9:9	18n	9:15	145-6
1:24	19n	10:16-17	18n,41n	12:18-21	169n
		11:18	19n,36,42n	12:18	113,115n,157
CD		11:20-1	19n	12:39-41	333
-	12n,14n,15n,	11:21	42n,42n	12:40	333-4,356
	18n,19n,24,	13:9	177	12:41	334
	38,39,41	14:21	42n	16:21	87
1:13-2:1	20-21	16:6-7	18n,41n	17:22b-23	87
1:13-14	19n,42n	16:10	18n,42n	17:22	163,352,
1:20	41n	6:15	18n,42n	17:27	125n
2:14-3:12	23	19:1-2	41n	20:18-19	87
3:7	18n,41n	19:5-9	176n,177	20:18	163,352
3:13-19	23	19:5	42n,42n	20:19	163,352
3:21-4:2	18n	19:7-9	41n,173n	20:28	122-7,164,353
3:21-4:1	42n,43n	19:8	184n	21:4-5	178-82,222,
4:1	42n,42n,42n,	19:12	18n,42n		353,367n,
4:12	42n	19:15-16	42n		370n,373,
4:13-20	23n	19:15	18n		375n,377
4:13-14	18n	19:22	41n	21:5	224,254
4:14	41n,73n	19:27-8	18n	21:9	182n
4:19	42n	20:6	63n,64n	21:12	200n
		20:16	18n,41n		
		20:21	41n		

Index of Ancient Sources   459

21:14	200n	27:12	163,353	11:15ff	233
21:15	200n	27:14	148-51,163,353	12:10-11	335-7,355
21:42	335-7,355,	27:24	199	12:10	90,366n
	366n	27:30	88n,139-44,	12:35ff	300n
23:16	200n		163,352,370n	13:2	339
23:17	200n	27:34	249-52,	13:3	215n
23:21	200n		279-80,286,	14:2	319n, 322n
23:35	200n		354	14:8	159
24:1	200n	27:35a	252-7,285,	14:11	188,192
24:30	211,213		354,364n,370n	14:12	318n, 321
24:38	236n	27:38	154-5	14:13-17	318n
24:44	87n	27:39-43	163,352	14:18	108,235-40,
26:1	234	27:39	258,285,354,		286,354,364n,
26:2	92-7,109,234		355		366n,369n,
26:3-4a	234-5,285,354	27:40	259		370n,374n
26:46	348	27:42	259-60	14:20	225-40
26:15	187-9,192,	27:43	260-2,263,	14:21-5	355
	222,353		285,354,374n	14:21	86,87,92-7,
26:23	235-40	27:44	262		106-9,163,
26:24	86,163,352,	27:45	342-4,356,		188n,238,252,
	370n		370n		370n
26:25-30	355	27:46	264-75,285,	14:22	237,306-8
26:25	92,239n		354,366n	14:24	109,127-32,
26:26	306-8	27:48	252n,278-80,		164,168n,171,
26:28	127-32,164,		286,355,364n,		301-11,353,
	301-11,353,		370n		360,366n,370n,
	355,366n,370n	27:50	271,280,345-6		373,375n,396,
26:31	109,147,	27:51	338-9		397
	182-7,222,	27:51b-53	344-5,356	14:26-52	(72) 215
	223,353,366n,	27:55a	282-3,286,354	14:26	215
	374n	27:57	144-5,159,164,	14:27	109,109n,134,
26:32	215-7,222,353		353		135,147,182-7,
26:36	325				215-7,222,353,
26:38	240-2,286,354	MARK			359,366n
26:45	109,163,352	1:4	306	14:28	215-7,222,353
26:50-4	148n	1:11	112-22,163,	14:29	215
26:54	86,109,352		327,352,375n	14:34-6	293
26:55	200n	1:15	385n	14:34	240-2,286,354
26:56	86,109,352	1:44	132n	14:35	242n
26:61	339,341	2:19-20	145-6	14:36	117,241
26:63-4	261	8:3	90	14:41	92-7,109,163,
26:63	148-51,163,353	8:23	350		352
26:65	255n	8:31	87,89,133n,	14:42	92,242n
26:67-8	139-44		355	14:44	92
26:67	88n,163,352,	8:34	118	14:49	86,87,109,
	370n	9:12b	87,89-91,163,		109n,149n,
27:1-2	200n		352,369n		352,359,383
27:3-10	188,189-210	9:31	87,92-7,163,	14:50	186,216n
27:3-8	195,207		352	14:53	65-161
27:3	187n,199	10:33-4	87,88,92-7	14:54	186n,215,
27:4	200-1	10:33	163,352		216n,282
27:5	189-90,195n	10:34	88n,163,352	14:55	248-9
	202,300n	10:38	114,116-20	14:57-8	247-8,285,
27:6	192,199,202-4	10:39	117		286,354
27:7	205-6	10:40-5	118	14:58	339-41
27:8	199,205	10:45	94,122-7,	14:61	148-51,163,
27:9-10	191-8,205,		132n,164,		353
	207,209,222,		168n,171,353,	14:62	143
	224,353,355,		360,396,397	14:65	88n,89,
	368n,373,	11:7	178-9n,222,		139-44n,161,
	374-5,377,380		353		163,346-7,
27:12-14	148	11:10	182n		352,370n

Index of Ancient Sources

14:66-72	215		366n	JOHN	
15:1	92n	21:24	385n	1:1-18	312n
15:5	148-51,163,	22:15-30	159	1:29	113,171,219n,
	353	22:15-20	127,355		312-4,324,
15:15ff	143	22:15	318n		327,330,353,
15:15	92n	22:19	306-8		355,363
15:19	88n,139-44,	22:20	127-32,160,	1:34	113,156
	163,352,370n		164,301-11,	1:36	171,312-4,324
15:20b	350		353,355,361,	2:16	340n
15:23	250n,279		366n,370n	2:17	233-4,243,286,
15:24	252-7,285,	22:21-38	159-61,163,		354,368n,374n
	354,364n,370n		352	2:19-21	340
15:25	318	22:21	129n,235-40	2:19	339
15:27	154-5	22:22	86,163,352,	2:22	233n
15:28	155		370n	3:5	219
15:29-32	163,339,352	22:27	126-7	3:14-15	213n
15:29a	258,285,354,	22:29	129n,160	3:14	98,98n,163,
	355	22:37	87,96,110n,		214,331-3,
15:29b-30	259		132-8,152,		352,355
15:31	259-60		153n,154n,	3:16	220
15:32b	262		155,160,164,	4	276
15:33	342-4,356,		168n,171,172,	4:14	219
	370n		353,360,361,	6	219n,329,330n
15:34	117,264-75,		366n,383,386	6:51-8	329,355,363
	285,293,325,	22:38	133,135n,136	6:54-9	236n
	328,354,366n,	22:43-4	292n	6:55	219n
	397	22:64	142n	6:64-70	188n
15:35-6	278-80,286,	23:6-12	348-9,355	6:64	236
	355,364n,370n	23:9	148-51,163,	6:70f	245
15:35	264n,268n		353	6:71	236
15:36	252,252n	23:11	90	7:8	385n
15:37	271,280,325,	23:27	221	7:37-9	219,276
	328,345-6	23:32	136	7:38	220n
15:38	338-9	23:33	136-7,154-5	7:39	98n
15:40a	282-3,286,354	23:34a	151-4	8:28	98n,163,214,
16:7	216	23:34b	152,252-7,		352
			285,354,364n,	10:11	146-7,163,
LUKE			370n		222,352,353
2:44	282	23:35-7	163,352	10:12	183
3:22	112-22,163,	23:35	155-6,348-9	10:15	146-7,163,
	352	23:35a	259,285,354		222,352,353
4:10	183n	23:36	252n,278-80,	10:17	146-7,163,
4:16	385n		286,355,364n,		222,352,353
4:18-19	137n		370n	11:47	235
5:14	132n	23:39-43	136	12:14-15	178-82,222,
5:34-5	145-6	23:41	162		353,370n,373,
9:22	87,89-91,355	23:43	162		375n
9:31	324n	23:44-45a	342-4,356,	12:16	98n,233n
9:35	113n,156n		370n	12:23ff	98n
9:44b	87,163,352	23:45b	338-9	12:27	240-2,285,
11:29-30	333	23:46	152n,234,235,		286,354
12:49-50	166-20		280-2,285,	12:32	98n,163,352
12:49	114		354,366n,397	12:33	98,98n
12:50	133n	23:47	158	12:34	98n
16:14	259	23:48	221n	12:38	243n
17:25	87,89-91,355	23:49	282-3,286,354	13:1	319n,322n
18:31b-33	87,163,352	24	133n	13:18	188n,235-40,
18:31	107,133n	24:25	390n		244,254,286,
18:32	88n,163,352	24:39	283-4		314n,354,
19:30	178-9n	24:44	112		364n,366n,
19:35	181n,222,353				368n,370n,
20:17	335-7,355,				374n

Index of Ancient Sources   461

13:21	241n	ACTS		9:22	327
13:31	98n	-	170	11:26	269
13:34	118	1:16ff	205	13:13	269
14-16	220	1:16	87n,238n		
15:25	243-4,247,	1:18-19	188n	I PETER	
	286,354,374n	2:23	107,134n	-	170
16:32	147n,183,187,	2:30	297n	2:7	335n
	222,353	2:31	299	3:18	132n
17:11	256	2:33	99	4:13	118
17:12	188n,236,	3:13-14	158		
	238n,244-5	3:22ff	347	II PETER	
17:21-2	256	3:25-6	327	1:17	113n
18:5	92	4:11	89-90,335		
18:6	246-7,285,354	4:25-6	349	I JOHN	
18:12	325n	5:30	136	1:7	219n
18:22-3	139-44,163	5:31	99	5:6-8	218n
18:22	352,370n	7	23n		
18:28	319n,322	10:39	136	REVELATION	
18:37	347	13:29	133n	-	133n
19:1-3	143	20:28	129	1:7	211-12,213
19:1	139-44,163,	26:1	132n		
	352,370n			Early Christian	
19:3	139-44,163,	ROMANS		Literature	
	352,370n	1:3	300n		
19:6	330,355	4:25	93-94,168	BARNABAS	
19:9	148-51,163,	8:4	385n	12:5-7	332n
	353	8:32	93-4,327		
19:14	317-8,319n,	13:8	385n	DIDACHE	
	322n			-	128,129
19:17	325,328	I CORINTHIANS			
19:18	154-5	1:13	132n	JUSTIN APOL.	
19:23-37	362	10:16	128,129	1,30,2	134
19:23-4	277	11:23-5	128	60	332n
19:24	236,252-7,	11:23	93n		
	285,314n,354,	15:3	168,397	DIAL.	
	362,364n,			53	185n
	368n,370n,377			91	332n
19:28-9	243,252n,	II CORINTHIANS		94	332n
	278-80,286,	1:20	133n	112	332n
	355,370n,377				
19:28	133n,275-8,	GALATIANS		EUSEBIUS H.E. II.	
	286,355,362,	1:4	132n	23,16	152n
	364n	2:20	93n		
19:29-30	277	5:14	385n	TERTULLIAN	
19:29	316-7,355			Adv. Iud. X	325n
19:30	133n,146,218n	EPHESIANS		Adv. Iud. XIII	325n
19:31-7	213	5:2	93n		
19:31	319n,322n	6:18-19	132n		
19:34	213,214,				
	217-21,222,	PHILIPPIANS			
	223,353,363	2:5ff	127		
19:35	214,316	2:9	99		
19:36	213,218,219n,				
	254,314-6,	COLOSSIANS			
	330,355,	1:24	118		
	362-3,374n,				
	397	HEBREWS			
19:37	210-14,222,	2:12	294n		
	223,224,353,	5:1	132n		
	362,363,368n,	5:3	132n		
	374n,397	5:7	245-6		
20:22	219n	6:19-20	338		
20:25	283-4	9:20	302,304		

INDEX OF AUTHORS CITED

Aalen, S.	310,311	Behm, J.	130,303,309
Abrahams, I.	220	Bennett, W.J. Jr.	88,89
Achtemeier, P.J.	4	Benoit, P.	84,110,129,134,138,
Ackroyd, P.R.	174,176		141,142,155,164,187,
Aicher, G.	25,27,34		190,191,202,203,205,
Aland, K.	128		207,274,303,307,321,
Albright, W.F.	45,47,131,203,215,		323,349
	322,342,343,345	Bentzen, A.	228,299
Alexander, J.A.	145	Bernard, J.H.	98,119,146,152,218,
Alford, H.	151,215,256,279,314		233,236,237,241,244,
Allegro, J.M.	43		257,314,317,328
Allen, W.C.	185,194,198,201,202,	Bertram, G.	92,98,116,253,258
	205,206,258,367	Best, E.	113,116,119,122,131,
Amsler, S.	362,382,395		157,187,215,217,325,
Amussin, J.D.	6		327,358,371
Anderson, A.A.	227,228,233,239,252,	Betti, E.	30
	254,262,280	Betz, J.	176,274,307
Anderson, H.	141,142,307,342,359	Betz, O.	39,40,70,71,72,73,
Aptowitzer, W.	14		112,303,339,341,389
Argyle, A.W.	190,265,275	Beutler, J.	242,278
Audet, J.P.	191,373	Birkeland, H.	227
Aune, D.E.	177,223	Bishop, E.F.F.	238
Aytoun, R.A.	83,259	Black, M.	10,11,46,75,82,83,84,
Bacher, W.	27,30,61		94,99,100,101,103,
Bailey, J.A.	274,282		104,108,110,115,116,
Baker, D.L.	31		135,138,158,265,270,
Baldwin, J.G.	175,176,177,182,211,		320,337,347,349,366
	340	Blank, J.	100
Ball, C.J.	312	Blight, W.	273
Bampfylde, G.	219,275,276	Blinzler, J.	92,158,228,272,282,
Banks, R.	384,385		284,380
Barbour, R.S.	246,328	Bloch, R.	10,60,64,65
Barnes, W.E.	226,227,230,283	Blunt, A.W.F.	240
Barr, J.	1,31,32,265,376,386,	Boismard, M.-E.	218-332
	387	Boman, T.	246,264
Barrett, C.K.	52,86,99,100,101,112,	Bonnard, P.E.	79,81,272,274,342
	115,122,125,126,180,	Bonsirven, J.	18,25,26,27,34,35,
	214,218,219,220,233,		41,59,61,306,318
	236,241,244,247,255,	Borgen, p.	236,329,392
	256,277,278,312,313,	Borsch, F.H.	85,93,102,110,232,379
	314,316,318,322,327,	Bousset, W.	60,61,66,85,126,276,
	328,333,362,282,383,		379
	389,391	Bowker, J.W.	10,11,28,46
Barrick, W.B.	144,145	Bowman, J.	103,164,169,289,302
Barth, G.	385	Brandt, W.	265
Barth, M.	306,309,312,329	Branscomb, B.H.	187,246
Barthélemy, D.	45	Braumann, G.	118,145
Bartlett, J.R.	2	Braun, F.-M.	255,313,314,327,362,
Bartlett, J.V.	267,271		372,373
Bartnicki, R.	180	Braun, H.	44,84,156,218,250,
Bartsch, H.-W.	133,134,135,136,138,		268,274,391,392
	271,296,345	Bretscher, P.G.	113
Bauer, W.	178,181,255	Briggs, C.A.	229,280
Baumstark, A.	193,197	Bright, J.	39,383
Beare, F.W.	165,271,288	Brown, R.E.	71,84,99,100,140,
Beasley-Murray, G.R.	119,120,121,		145,146,154,179,180,
	146,218,314		182,183,210,213,214,
Begrich, J.	272		215,218,219,233,236,

Index of Authors 463

	237,238,247,255,256,	Dauer, A.	140,154,214,216,247,
	278,279,280,313,314,		254,255,257,323,328,
	315,316,318,320,321,		361,371
	322,327,328,332,336,	David, J.-E.	304
	368,371	Davies, P.R.	14
Brownlee, W.H.	6,12,36,42,48,51,70,	Davies, R.E.	125
	72,83,101,175,176	Davies, W.D.	82,101,210,305,309,
Bruce, A.B.	184,268		312,342,343,345,389,
Bruce, F.F.	70,72,83,101,102,103,		391
	135,167,174,175,176,	Deichgräber, R.	304
	177,187,202,203,207,	Deissmann, A.	123,210
	208,212,224,279,314,	Delcor, M.	176
	378,380,382,389	Delitzsch, F.	181,145,154,230,252
Bruns, J.E.	317	Delling, G.	89,116,117,119,137,
Buckler, F.W.	264,265		314
Büschel, F.	123,124,127	Derrett, J.D.M.	147
Bultmann, R.	31,118,126,146,165,	Descamp, A.	194,208,384
	218,236,239,240,243,	Dewar, L.	309
	244,262,271,292,317,	Dibelius, M.	86,135,234,246,248,
	328,361,363,371		292,346,349,371,394
Burkill, T.A.	217,246,271,273,321,	Dietrich, E.L.	13
	339,342,358,371	Dix, G.H.	175
Burkitt, F.C.	218,269,339	Dodd, C.H.	2,90,98,99,100,101,
Burney, C.F.	211,312		114,140,144,145,146,
Burrows, E.W.	314		167,179,183,187,214,
Burrows, M.	13,18,38,43,54,69,84		218,219,237,241,242,
Buse, I.	371		247,277,282,292,312,
Chary, T.	173,174,175,]11		314,315,317,323,336,
Chenderlin, F.	322		349,371,378,380,387,
Cheyne, T.K.	81		394,396
Childs, B.S.	226,384	Dodewaard, J.A.E. van	21
Christensen, J.	108,244	Döller, J.	250,251
Chwolson, D.	319	Doeve, J.W.	1,25,26,27,28,34,56,
Clines, D.J.A.	225		58,59,103,116,195,
Cohn, H.	214,379		199,341,392
Colpe, C.	103,105	Donahue, J.R.	161,248,300,338,339,
Conzelmann, H.	107,115,187,342,358,		341
	395	Dormeyer, D.	149,248,279,304,339
Cooke, B.	310	Downing, J.	117,290,291,303
Coppens, J.	81,88,138,164,306	Driver, G.R.	283
Craig, C.T.	165	Duhm, B.	79,228,283
Cranfield, C.E.B.	89,90,92,93,96,	Dunn, J.D.G.	242,246,329,379,387
	102,105,109,114,115,	Dupont-Sommer, A.	36,37,39,42
	116,123,125,145,146,	Easton, B.S.	108,221,259
	148,184,216,217,238,	Eaton, J.H.	226,228,230,231,280
	240,242,260,262,275,	Edersheim, A.	196,250
	307,336,371	Edgar, S.L.	378
Creed, J.M.	135,151,221,282,360,	Edwards, R.A.	334
	370	Eichrodt, W.	31,310
Cross, F.M.,Jr.	45,47,368	Eissfeldt, O.	45,46,47,58,79,228
Cullmann, O.	81,85,101,103,113,	Elliger, K.	13,36,40,44,50,51,52,
	114,120,157,164,169,		71,174,175,176,203
	170,312,314,386	Ellis, E.E.	1,6,11,63,72,74,129,
Dahl, G.	226,298		130,152,160,327,336,
Dahl, N.A.	327		339,349,375,388
Dahood, M.	252,283	Emerton, J.A.	265,304
Dalman, G.	151,250,265,266,270,	Essane, W.G.	345
	271,302,303,306,307,	Evans, C.F.	7,215,217,223
	311,317,325	Fascher, E.	88
Daniélou, J.	31,32,325,345	Feigel, F.K.	144,151,214,271,276
Danker, F.W.	238,260,274,342	Fenton, J.C.	144,154,215,235,262,
Daube, D.	152,324		282,306,343,344,348

464   Index of Authors

Feuillet, A.	114,115,116,117,118, 120,124,125,146,157, 158,325,330	Gottstein, M.H.	43
		Gould, E.P.	90,184,215,274
		Goulder, M.D.	203
Filson, F.V.	135,144,149,182,303, 336	Grant, F.C.	122
		Grassi, J.	344
Findlay, J.A.	192	Green, H.B.	235,274,306
Finegan, J.	135,154,192,252,260, 276,306,349	Grundmann, W.	90,91,93,112,116, 133,134,135,138,146, 152,156,157,184,242, 258,266,282,305,342, 349
Fisher, L.R.	271,272		
Fitzmyer, J.A.	5,11,12,18,19,20,40, 47,104,265,297,389, 392		
		Gryglewicz, F.	313,314
Flemington, W.F.	120	Guillaume, A.	268
Flesseman-van Leer, E.	213,231,288, 395	Gundry, R.H.	1,114,115,131,139, 140,141,142,144,145, 178,180,184,185,187, 188,191,193,194,195, 197,198,203,204,208, 233,235,240,251,258, 261,262,265,269,270, 279,302,304,306,333, 348,367,368,373,375, 378,394
Flew, R.N.	305		
Ford, J.M.	218		
Forstall, J.T.	218,314		
Fortna, R.T.	314,317		
Foulkes, F.	31		
France, R.T.	1,7,90,95,101,102, 108,113,123,125,126, 127,131,137,138,164, 171,174,175,176,184, 187,216,224,289,298, 302,305,334,340,387		
		Gunkel, H.	225,226,227,228,229, 252,258,280
Franklin, E.	154,158,170,360	Gutbrod, W.	134
Freed, E.D.	98,179,180,233,236, 240,243,244,245,253, 257,314	Güttgemanns, E.	372
		Haenchen, E.	149,188,247,254,279, 281,282,307,314,328, 342
Friedrich, G.	268	Hahn, F.	85,86,90,96,97,125, 127,131,138,165,166, 300,305,309,338,395
Fritsch, C.T.	38		
Frör, K.	31		
Frost, S.B.	67	Hamerton-Kelly, R.G.	101,103,105
Fuchs, E.	3	Hanson, A.T.	6,66,116,297,375,378, 386,389,390
Fuller, R.H.	85,89,90,91,94,103, 115,117,121,125,164, 165,303,307		
		Hanson, P.D.	68
Gadamer, H.-G.	30	Hanson, R.P.C.	38,39
Gärtner, B.	44,49,50,83,84,97, 190,204,239,244,300, 312,330,336,339,340, 389	Harnack, A. von.	152,269
		Harris, M.J.	125
		Harris, R.	12,185,372,373
		Hartman, L.	17,21,22,23,33,35, 52,54,388
Gardner-Smith, P.	371	Hay, D.M.	2
Gaster, T.	36,38,39	Hebert, A.G.	306,309
Gaston, L.	90,103	Hedley, P.L.	261
Gerhardsson, B.	151,274	Heidland, H.W.	134,279
George, A.R.	236	Heinemann, J.	66
Gese, H.	230,272,273	Hengel, M.	39,282,396
Gilmour, S.M.	221,349	Hengstenberg, E.W.	144,247
Glasson, T.F.	154,218,313,325,327, 333	Héring, J.	240
		Hewitt, J.W.	284
Gnilka, J.	255,266	Higgins, A.J.B.	108,126,128,129, 134,138,164,294,296, 303,319,322,324
Godet, F.	256,314,315,321		
Goguel, M.	187,242,274,303,371		
Goppelt, L.	1,31,32,39,85,116, 117,164,190,228,247, 299,300,302,304,308, 311,324,325,329, 371, 382,383,385,386	Hill, D.	124,125,142,146,262, 334,335
		Hindley, J.C.	16,104
		Hirsch, E.D.	7,9,30
		Hoehner, H.W.	321,349
Gordis, R.	20	Hoffman, P.	89,91
Gordon, R.P.	46	Holmes, C.	260

Index of Authors

Holm-Nielsen, S.	15,17,57,75,230
Holtz, T.	134,280,281,367,394
Holtzmann, H.J.	141,144,190,221, 247,282
Hooke, S.H.	145,226
Hooker, M.D.	79,80,83,85,89,92, 94,101,107,114,122, 124,125,131,137,138, 139,149,155,165,166, 167,303,306,312,387
Horovitz, S.	61,63
Horton, F.L.	19
Hoskyns, E.	218,232,244,257,276, 314,317,349
Howard, J.K.	313,328
Hunter, A.M.	116,164,274
Iersel, B.M.F. van.	94,165
Jackson, F.J.Foakes	165
Jansma, T.	202
Jaubert, A.	320
Jellicoe, S.	202,211
Jeremias, J.	80,82,90,92,93,95, 103,104,110,113,123, 124,128,129,131,138, 145,151,152,153,156, 158,159,164,166,174, 177,178,184,187,201, 205,215,267,268,274, 281,304,305,306,307, 310,312,316,318,320, 322,323,324,334,335, 337,369,371
Johnson, A.R.	289
Johnson, S.E.	181,194,202,272,289, 300,342,365
Jonge, M. de.	16
Juel, D.	248,338,341
Kahl, P.E.	10,211
Karabidopoulos, I.D.	154,156,162, 264,370
Karnetzki, M.	110,135,144,254,260, 282,366
Käsemann, E.	361
Katz, P.	45,95
Kee, A.	145
Kee, H.C.	360,372,388,396
Keil, C.F.	174,175,176
Kelber, W.H.	92,372
Kellermann, D.	125
Kelly, J.N.D.	129
Kenneally, W.J.	274,298
Kertelge, K.	126
Kidner, D.	226,227,228,230,275
Kilian, R.	227
Kilpatrick, G.D.	13,114,128,142, 199,202,206,266,367
Kirkpatrick, A.F.	226,227,281
Kissane, E.J.	226,227
Kittel, D.R.	228,229
Kittel, G.	99,100
Klein, G.	186,255,348
Klein, R.W.	47
Klostermann, E.	110,144,188,205, 240,242,260,271,279
Kohler, M.	204
Knox, J.	281
Knox, W.L.	250
König, E.	212,267
Kosmala, H.	310
Kramer, W.	92
Kraus, H.-J.	226,227,280,283
Kümmel, W.G.	85,117,307,339,373
Kuhn, H.-W.	70,179,181,182
Ladd, G.E.	68,85,103,116,309
Lagarde, P.	46
Lagrange, M.-J.	89,123,135,142, 146,174,187,193,206, 207,208,221,237,256, 260,263,268,270,271, 298,314,342
Lake, K.	165,190,207,215
Lamarche, P.	174,175,176,177,203, 211,212
Lampe, G.W.H.	31,113,114,115,121, 135,221,349,394
Lane, W.L.	91,115,117,120,126
Lane, W.R.	13
Lang, F.	117
Lange, H.D.	298
Lapide, P.	265,266
Larkin, W.J.	137,292,298
Lauterbach, J.Z.	30,61
Leaney, A.R.C.	72,89,135,138,152, 154,156,221,238,259, 349
Le Déaut, R.	9,10,11,46,60,63,65, 304,312,313,314,326, 345,392
Leivestad, R.	103
Léon-Dufour, X.	188,219,369,380, 389
Lerch, D.	328
Lietzmann, H.	128,246
Lightfoot, R.H.	217,234,244,271, 288,315,316,325,371
Lindars, B.	2,54,90,93,99,102, 103,105,107,108,113, 115,138,146,147,154, 157,178,180,181,182, 183,185,187,188,191, 194,196,200,202,205, 206,207,208,211,212, 213,218,219,233,234, 235,238,239,241,242, 244,252,254,255,256, 258,266,277,278,280, 281,283,287,289,292, 302,303,315,316,317, 328,340,379,389,392, 393,394
Lindeskog, G.	338
Linnemann, E.	135,186,216,240,246, 253,266,271,338,346, 372,380

Index of Authors

Linton, O. 153
Lofthouse, W.F. 274
Lohmeyer, E. 88,113,143,148,161, 162,187,189,190,191, 192,194,197,199,200, 208,216,217,251,259, 279,282,303,306,309, 338,339,348
Lohse, E. 82,84,135,137,151, 152,153,164,171,290, 295,296,303,307,308, 312,323,324,326,394
Loisy, A. 135,141,154,187,214, 218,221,254,255,259, 271,272,282,314,316, 349
Longenecker, R.N. 1,6,26,39,44,51, 57,63,64,70,72,73,75, 85,101,143,166,170, 176,346,366,392
Lövestam, E. 115
Luthardt, C.E. 247
Lyonnet, S. 311,314,316,330
McConnell, R.S. 1,194,208,380
McKenzie, J.L. 144
McNamara, M. 10,46,47,72
McNeile, A.H. 122,132,135,139,180, 190,192,194,202,205, 235,238,239,258,274, 289,306,308,309,325, 334,342,344,345
Maas, F. 26
Macgregor, G.H.C. 218,238,247,255, 277,316,325
Macho, A.D. 10,46,
Magne, J. 283
Mann, J. 62,131,215
Manson, T.W. 103,266,366,367,378
Manson, W. 106,135,162,164,295, 305,308
Marcus, R. 125
Marsh, J. 241,242
Marshall, I.H. 30,72,103,105,111, 114,115,127,138,151, 156,157,158,327,338
Marti, K. 173,212
Martin, R.P. 87,94,146,148,159, 275,308,324,338,341
Martyn, J.L. 346
Marxsen, W. 217
Maurer, C. 82,107,110,154,157, 162,164,295,359
Meeks, W.A. 315,347
Meier, J.P. 384
Menard, J.E. 102
Menzies, A. 107,184,187,267,271
Metzger, B.M. 18,19,130,152,194, 267,269,366
Meyer, D. 110
Michaelis, W. 89,90,91,250,251,300
Michel, O. 179,200
Micklem, P.A. 144,190,194,202

Milik, J.T. 16,38,104,320,321
Miller, D.L. 142
Miller, M.P. 10,46,63,72,73,359, 376,388,392
Minear, P.S. 135
Mitchell, H.G. 173,175,176,188,212
Montefiore, C.G. 26,60,107,128,138, 141,151,187,189,194, 197,202,206,221,247, 282,343,349
Moore, G.F. 26,58,59,61,63
Morgenstern, J. 144,321
Morris, L. 123,124,135,137,156, 158,171,180,219,233, 236,237,244,245,275, 309,317,322,342
Motyer, J.A. 334
Moule, C.F.D. 101,107,132,165,169, 170,213,214,224,236, 274,341,381,384
Mowinckel, S. 103,225,226,227,228, 232,283,299
Murphy, R.E. 244
Nakagawa, H. 32
Negöitsa, A. 312
Nestle, E. 267
Nineham, D.E. 112,246,247,250,262, 271,272,303,311,371,
Noack, B. 180,184,237,243,
North, C.R. 38,81,82,143,144,153, 164,226
North, M. 345
Nowack, D.W. 173
Oepke, A. 245
Oepke, A. 119,324
Oesterley, W.O.E. 228,252,260,283
Ogg, G. 319,320,321,323
Orelli, C. von 37
Orlinsky, H.M. 46
O'Rourke, J.J. 380
Osswald, E. 70,72
Otto, R. 91,108,160,164,168, 303
Otzen, B. 174,211,212
Palmer, R.E. 3
Patsch, H. 138,165
Patte, D. 7,9,10,11,15,18,21, 22,24,25,32,33,35,36, 40,54,57,59,60,61,62, 63,64,66,67,71,73,74, 365
Pelikan, J. 255
Pelletier, A. 343
Perowne, J.J.S. 229,252
Perrin, N. 92,94,103,211,294
Pesch, R. 90,91,108,111,112, 159,197,246,248,292
Plath, M. 190
Ploeg, J. van der 14,72
Plummer, A. 133,135,151,158,181, 184,221,251,258,259, 282,342

Index of Authors

Pobee, J.	135	Sandmel, S.	57,59
Popkes, W.	84,92,93,96,125,126, 227,290,342,346	Sawyer, J.F.A.	343
		Schechter, S.	26
Post, G.E.	251,317	Scheifler, J.R.	254,263,268,284,289
Prabhu, G.M.S.	179,191,378,385	Schenk, W.	221,239,247,259,260, 271,273,282,314,342, 345,346,349,350,362
Preiss, T.	321		
Prigent, P.	373		
Rabin, C.	12,14,43,50,72,176, 184	Schenke, L.	116
		Schille, G.	372
Rabinowitz, I.	73,74,75,176	Schlatter, A.	141,187,194,249,258, 262,274,277
Rad, G. von.	67,231,298,383,386		
Ragg, L.	135,305	Schmid, J.	273,279,289,308,342
Rahlfs, A.	211,261	Schmidt, H.	228,298
Rashdall, H.	126	Schnackenburg, R.	100,140,147,180, 213,218,236,237,244, 255,256,257,277,313, 315,322,328,361
Rawlinson, A.E.J.	108,240,242,274, 279,284,328,342		
Read, H.C.	268,275		
Rehkopf, F.	369	Schneider, G.	137,141,149,153,263, 271,349,361,369,371
Rehm, M.	268		
Reim, G.	2,100,140,220,233, 237,244,277,278,312, 314,316,332,357,371	Schniewind, J.	108,117,143,148,194, 196,305
		Schoeps, H.-J.	327
Rengstorf, K.H.	135,136,152,203, 204,282,333,334,342, 349	Schreiber, J.	271,342,345,370
		Schrenk, G.	339,340,384
		Schröger, F.	1
Rese, M.	1,31,82,83,128,129, 135,136,137,372,373	Schubert, P.	360
		Schürmann, H.	86,91,107,110,127, 129,131,133,135,138, 146,303,305,306,369
Reumann, J.H.	273		
Richardson, A.	105,107,113,177,218, 275,303,305,310,323, 324,327,347,386	Schulz, S.	98,273,291,332,360, 371
		Schwarz, O.J.R.	37,72,73
Ridderbos, H.N.	229	Schweizer, E.	85,103,104,110,114, 115,126,130,144,148, 157,165,194,196,205, 249,252,260,262,271, 273,279,287,290,291, 292,293,294,295,305, 312,315,323,345
Riesenfeld, H.	344		
Rigaux, B.	72		
Robert, A.	20		
Roberts, B.J.	45,46,54,211,392		
Robinson, H.W.	164		
Robinson, J.A.T.	117,121,314		
Robinson, J.M.	4		
Rohde, J.	359	Scott, E.F.	120
Roloff, J.	85,92,94,126,295, 296,307	Scott, R.B.Y.	333
		Seeligmann, I.L.	34
Romaniuk, C.	261	Segal, J.B.	321
Rose, A.	234,282,284	Seidelin, P.	83,95,339
Rosenbloom, J.R.	177	Sellin, D.E.	173
Rosenthal, J.M.	40	Senior, D.	132,142,148,183,184, 188,190,191,192,193, 194,195,197,199,200, 202,204,205,207,208, 234,235,253,260,274, 325,339,343,345,346, 360,369
Rost, L.	16		
Roth, C.	75		
Rothfuchs, W.	1,185,191,255,315,385		
Rowley, H.H.	81,82,83,84,85,102, 135		
Ruckstuhl, E.	320		
Ruppert, L.	229,272,290,291,292, 293,294	Sevenster, J.N.	265
		Sherwin-White, A.N.	253
Russell, D.S.	16,54,58,66,67,68,70, 72,103	Shires, H.M.	382,395
		Sidebottom, E.M.	100
Sahlin, H.	264,265	Sidersky, D.	265
Salmond, S.D.F.	141	Silberman, L.H.	13,40,44,49,50,72, 73,74
Sand, A.	359,383		
Sanders, E.P.	64,147,326	Simonis, A.U.	146,147
Sanders, J.N.	99,219,233,241,315, 316,321,325	Simpson, D.C.	22
		Skehan, P.W.	46

Slomovic, E.	40,51,72	Vanhoye, A.	340,341
Smalley, S.S.	97,100	Vaux, R. de	226,310,311
Smart, J.D.	106,167,382	Vermes, G.	7,10,11,26,36,40,54, 55,56,60,64,72,75,83, 103,104,105,175,313, 326,327,395
Smith, D.	228,284		
Smith, D.M.	1,359,367		
Smith, F.	271		
Smith, G.A.	342	Vielhauer, P.	104
Snodgrass, K.	128,145,336,337	Vis, A.	251,276,288
Sparks, H.F.D.	191	Waard, J. de	173,184,185,230,236, 237
Sperber, A.	47,314		
Stählin, G.	117	Wade, G.W.	144
Stanley, D.M.	135,164,303,312,314	Walker, W.O.	103
Stanton, G.N.	103	Walters, P.	46
Stauffer, E.	152,272,281,324,325, 391	Walther, J.A.	320
		Weidel, K.	149,221,235,247,282, 283,328,349
Stein, R.H.	217		
Stendahl, K.	2,43,44,46,47,49,51, 72,178,180,181,184, 185,187,191,192,193, 194,197,200,202,203, 205,206,211,260,261, 270,334,367,368,392	Weingreen, J.	30
		Weiser, A.	227,228,273,280,289, 298
		Weiss, B.	314,317
		Weiss, R.	42
		Wellhausen, J.	250,254,266,281
Stott, W.	102	Wernberg-Moller, P.	40,48
Strachan, R.H.	218,256,314	Westcott, B.F.	154,218,233,241,244, 256,278,317,325
Strack, H.L.	319		
Strack, H.C.	27,28	Westermann, C.	32,81,138,150,153, 167,226,227,232
Strathmann, H.	135		
Talbert, C.H.	9	Wevers, J.W.	45,46
Talmon, S.	47,48	White, R.E.O.	120
Tasker, R.V.G.	107,135,142,194,219, 221,252,276,280,306, 317,325	Whiteley, D.E.H.	122,165
		Wilcox, M.	6,215,216,236,237
		Wilder, A.N.	67
Taylor, V.	92,103,135,137,138, 142,145,146,151,164, 168,170,171,187,216, 217,238,242,246,258, 260,266,269,273,274, 279,281,306,307,312, 323,336,339,342,343, 369,371	Wilkinson, J.	151,250,251,275,317
		Williams, C.S.C.	130,152,267,269, 270,272
		Williams, S.K.	122,293,324,395
		Willi-Plein, I.	176,202
		Wilson, S.G.	135
		Wilson, W.R.	349
		Winter, P.	143,255,271,273,361, 370
Teeple, H.M.	346,347		
Thackeray, H. St. J.	220	Wolff, H.W.	2,81,82,85,90,91,100, 101,106,111,125,134, 138,148,151,167,169, 170,171,303,312
Theodor, J.	60		
Thiselton, A.C.	30		
Thomson, J.G.S.S.	177		
Thüsing, W.	218,219,241,277,278	Wood, J.E.	326,327
Thyen, H.	122,395	Woolcombe, K.J.	31,32
Tillesse, G.M. de.	142,157	Wright, A.G.	5,12,63,64,66,72
Tödt, H.E.	87,88,90,91,92,94, 126,127,130,132,333	Würthwein, E.	10,46
		Wrede, W.	304
Tooley, W.	187,216	Ysebart, J.	119
Torrey, C.C.	79,144,164,175,188, 191,194,195,196,203, 283,314	Zahn, T.	266,267
		Zehnle, R.	361
		Zeitlin, S.	27,61,64
Trilling, W.	281,282,338	Zimmerli, W.	80,82,90,92,93,103, 131,134,138,151,153, 156,158,159,164,166, 312
Trocmé, E.	110,371		
Trudinger, L.P.	272		
Turner, C.H.	142,266,268,269		
Turner, H.E.W.	232	Zimmermann, F.	
Turner, N.	107,125,136,188,245, 270,277,322		
Unnik, W.C. van	190,199		

www.ingramcontent.com/pod-product-compliance
Lightning Source LLC
Chambersburg PA
CBHW052048290426
44111CB00011B/1656